A JEWISH LIFE
UNDER THE TSARS

Oxford Centre for Postgraduate Hebrew Studies

A JEWISH LIFE UNDER THE TSARS

The Autobiography of Chaim Aronson, 1825–1888

*Translated from the original Hebrew
and edited by*
NORMAN MARSDEN

ALLANHELD, OSMUN   Publishers

ALLANHELD, OSMUN & CO. PUBLISHERS, INC.

Published in the United States of America in 1983
by Allanheld, Osmun & Co. Publishers, Inc.
(A Division of Littlefield, Adams & Company)
81 Adams Drive, Totowa, New Jersey 07512

Library of Congress Cataloging in Publication Data

Aronson, Chaim, 1825-1888.
  A Jewish life under the tsars.

  Includes index.
  1. Aronson, Chaim, 1825-1888. 2. Jews—Soviet Union
—Biography. 3. Inventors—Soviet Union—Biography.
I. Marsden, Norman. II. Title.
DS135.R95A683   1983   947'.004924'0924   [B]   81-10963
ISBN 0-86598-066-7

83 84 85 / 10 9 8 7 6 5 4 3 2 1

Printed in the United States of America

Dedication

◇◇◇◇◇

This book is dedicated to the memory of Albert Henry Aronson (grandson) and Arthur Aronson (great-grandson) who did so much to make this book possible.

Contents

◇◇◇◇◇

OXFORD CENTRE FOR POSTGRADUATE HEBREW STUDIES

The Oxford Centre for Postgraduate Hebrew Studies is designed to foster Hebrew and Jewish studies from the biblical period to the present time. Among its aims is the encouragement of individual and collective research projects.

The Centre is under the academic aegis of Oxford University, but it is responsible for its own finances and it is administered by its own Board of Governors.

The Centre awards Visiting Scholarships to distinguished scholars and postdoctoral students to enable them to pursue their studies in Oxford and to conduct courses and seminars on Hebrew and Jewish topics.

The books in this series were written by scholars who have been associated with the Centre and they are published under the joint auspices of the Oxford Centre for Postgraduate Hebrew Studies and Allanheld, Osmun & Co.

Publications Committee

N. S. Doniach   R. A. May   F. G. B. Millar   Dr. Patterson   G. Vermes

Acknowledgements

◇◇◇◇◇

I should like to take this opportunity of offering my thanks to the many people who showed an interest in this autobiography and to those among them who were willing to offer of their specialised knowledge to assist its translation.

Foremost amongst these must be Dr. David Patterson, Principal of the Oxford Centre for Postgraduate Hebrew Studies, who has been a source of constant encouragement and guidance. I am particularly grateful also to Professors G. Elkoshi, R. Mirkin, C. Rabin, D. Sadan, C. Shmeruk, S. Verses, the late Dr. I. Shahar and Miss S. Zfatman, of Israel, who gave me their time and scholarly knowledge, either when they visited Oxford or when I was able to see them in Jerusalem and Tel-Aviv. My sincere thanks go also to the scholars in this country who helped in the clarification of problems: Professors E.J. Simmons, N. Zernev and Mr. D.L. Howells of Oxford, and Dr. W.F. Ryan of London, for their expert advice in Russian matters; to Mr. R. May of the Bodleian Library, Oxford, for reading the manuscript and offering his expert advice and additional research information; to Dr. G. Turner for his expert knowledge of microphotography, Mr. G. Berman for his specialised advice in horology and Mr. F.R. Maddison, all of the History of Science Museum, Oxford; and to Dr. P. Beak and Dr. L. Leyton, of the Department of Forestry, Oxford, for invaluable advice.

I wish to tender my thanks also to the various people and Institutes to whom I wrote for information and who were kind enough to reply. In connection with the tobacco industry, Mr. R. Dunhill of Alfred Dunhill Ltd., London; Mr. M.F. Barford, Editor-in-Chief of *World Tobacco,* London; Mr. G.W. McKelvie of Imperial Tobacco Group Ltd., London; and Mr. H.W. Bahrenburg of American Brands Incorporated, New York, who was kind enough to send me a very useful booklet *The American Tobacco Story.* With regard to the boot and shoe industry, Miss J.M. Swann, the Assistant Curator of the Northampton Museum, and Mr. J.H. Thornton, Head of the Department of Boot and Shoe Manufacture, Northampton; and Mr. A.R. Payne, Director of the Shoe and Allied Trades Research Association, Kettering. In horology, Mr. G. Thompson, Librarian of the Clockmakers' Company, London. In the history of medicine, Mr. E.J. Freeman, Librarian of The Wellcome Institute for the History of Medicine, London, and Mr. R.J. Moore, Librarian of the National Institute for Medical Research, London. In maritime history, Mrs. P. McNulty, Reference Librarian of the Mystic Seaport Incorporated naval museum, Connecticut, and Mr. G.N. Taube, Curator of the Russian Naval Museum, New Jersey. My applications to Professor V.L. Chenakal, of the Lomonosova Museum, Leningrad, regarding any patents issued to Chaim Aronson went, unfortunately, unanswered.

My thanks must also go to the librarians and assistants of the various Oxford and London libraries for all the kind help and attention they gave me.

A special word of gratitude to Mrs. Helen Perlman and the late Albert Henry Aronson, of Washington, and to Mr. and Mrs. Milton Rosenberg of New York, who so willingly and constantly assisted me with information regarding their grandfather, Chaim Aronson.

A final word of praise and gratitude to my wife, Ruth, without whose unfailing efforts and support this work would never have been completed.

Norman Marsden
Bankstown, Australia 1982

Foreword

by
Helen Aronson Perlman

One of my delights as a child was to peer inside three small lockets, to see through their tiny peep-holes what seemed to me poster size photographs. One locket was a gold-chased hexagon, the others heart shaped, one in a silver case, one of black enamel. Only the silver one remains.

My father explained that his father had invented a process of greatly reducing pictures in size, and had called it microdiarama. Later I was to recognize this as a forerunner of microfilm.

I was partial to the silver locket through which I could clearly see the head and shoulders of a beautiful young woman, Flora, my father's niece, close to him in age.

Grandfather had been married three times. My father, Saul, was the fifth and youngest son of the third marriage and Flora of the silver locket was the second daughter of Simon, the eldest son of that marriage.

Father also showed me a leather bound volume of his father's memoirs, hand written in a beautiful script, which we could not read — Hebrew.

Some day, I hoped, it would be translated into English and I wondered what it would tell. It never occurred to us children to further question our gentle, scholarly, reticent father.

I knew all about the father of my mother, for she, far from being reticent, bubbled over with vivacity. From her vivid description I can picture him even now — his long black cape floating behind, his high black silk hat and elegant cane, as he chaperoned his daughters to balls in the university town of Dorpat in Esthonia, where they lived. I learned from her that he played the violin and sang, that he made his own musical instruments and that he would sometimes amuse his children by carrying a chair about with his teeth.

As I grew older, I often looked at the volume bound in black leather, wondering if it would ever be translated.

After Father died, a favorite nephew of his asked me to lend him the manuscript, as someone was interested in translating it. But this gentleman soon returned it in horror saying it was the work of a heretic and he would have nothing to do with it. We never learned his definition of a heretic.

Shortly after that Louis died and we lost track of the manuscript.

It was years later at a family function that Louis' son, Arthur, told my sister, Mitzi, where it was and brought it to her.

Arthur then xeroxed a few copies, one of which I took to Dr. Myron Weinstein of the Hebrew section of the Library of Congress in Washington.

After leafing through it for almost an hour, he remarked that the literary quality of the classical Hebrew was exceptional and that the content appeared to be interesting. It was disappointing that he did not have sufficient time to translate it himself.

"On the floor above," he said, "is the genealogical section of the Library of Congress. I doubt if many who go there to trace their ancestors find such a one."

Then I became even more determined. For the next few years I spoke or wrote to everyone I could think of who might be interested and capable of writing an English version.

It was discouraging. Some were too busy, some too old or ill. One distinguished scholar was interested but he was losing his eye-sight. So on it went.

Looking through some magazines, I spotted an article by a Dr. David Patterson of Oxford University, which treated of the era in which Grandfather had lived.

I wrote to him. Weeks went by, a month, two months, but there was no reply. Then I did receive an answer, explaining that the letter had been delayed because of a postal strike in England. He was interested. I was elated.

That summer I took a copy of the papers to Dr. Patterson in Oxford. Examining it, he said that it might well be worthy of publication. He arranged to have a doctoral candidate, then working in Australia, begin the translation upon his return to England.

Norman Marsden proved to be a dedicated, meticulous scholar. He spent several years working on the papers, following every slightest lead, corresponding with people in many countries, giving the task endless patience and devotion.

Few effects of Chaim Aronson are left. A cousin also had a microdiarama. There is a quaint photograph, cut out of a German newspaper which he framed. It shows Moses Mendelssohn, Lessing and Lavater in discussion. A few volumes in Russian and German are all that are left of his books. There are two business cards of clock shops that he had in St. Petersburg on Nevsky Prospect.

He notes that during a business recession he began to write the story of his life.

There are some lost clues. A cousin recalls that her father, the fourth son of Chaim, owned a box carefully wrapped and sealed, holding some of her father's things, but it had disappeared when their house was robbed. Another relative had vague recollection of having heard a second volume mentioned, but it has never been found. Perhaps it might have been in the stolen box.

In his introduction Chaim Aronson mused as to whether his children, or even his grandchildren might be interested in the story of his life.

Indeed, we have been, unto the second, third, fourth, even the fifth generation. Acknowledgements are due to the following family members for their interest and support in the publication of these memoirs: Mitzi Rosenberg, Barbara Dolgin, Josephine Bernstein, Ione Stone, Henry Aronson, Arthur Aronson, and Shepard Aronson.

Introduction

◇◇◇◇◇

"I know that I am not a person of distinction. I shall not be counted among the great, nor will the third generation after me raise up a monument to my name."

With that self-deprecating sentiment, Chaim Aronson introduced his memoirs, and then proceeded to prove that he was no ordinary person at all. His manuscript, handwritten in the flowing classical style of the nineteenth century Hebrew Haskalah writers, traces the events of his life from his humble birth in the Jewish Pale of Settlement in 1825, through the deprivations of his ghetto existence, to the failures and successes of the competitive commercial world of St. Petersburg, and his eventual emigration to the United States of America in 1888. The memoirs encompass, therefore, two-thirds of a century of Jewish life in Tsarist Russia.

The 493 pages of the autobiography are divided into three parts: an introductory philosophical treatise, an account of his early years in the repressed society of the Pale, and his adventures as an industrial technologist and privileged Jewish resident in the capital city.

The pages overflow with a host of fascinating characters and events, whose descriptions show Aronson to have been a keen and often ironic observer of his environment. People like Eliezer the kabbalistic wonder-worker, Moshe the Hasid who saved his townfolk from the Polish rebels, Joseph the all powerful Beadle, Hayyim Haikil who was Aronson's bosom friend, and the aristocratic Russian financiers Baranov and Yerakov, who helped and hindered Aronson's industrial ventures — they and many more move and live against the colorful background of the political, economic and religious events of the time: the Polish revolts, the Crimean War and its disastrous repercussions upon the Russian economy, the craftsmen's Guilds, the assassination of Alexander II, the pogroms and anti-semitic regulations.

As an epic of human endeavour, the manuscript is unique in Hebrew literature. Aronson was brought up in a traditionally orthodox family, earned his first living from the lowly calling of a *melammed,* a children's religion teacher, and studied at the famous talmudical college of Vilna. By making use of his natural technical aptitudes, he became a clockmaker and photographer. As his restless mind observed the growing technology of the time, he began to experiment with automated machinery for a variety of industrial uses — the manufacture of cigarettes and cigarette-packets, of varied-shaped bottle-corks, of wooden pegs for boots — as well as incidental instruments such as his alcohol meter for measuring the proof of alcohol, and a railway parcel cost calculator. He developed a keen interest in photographic processes, becoming one of the early entrepreneurs of microphotography in Russia and one of the pioneer Jewish photographers in the world. His "Microdiorama," a camera that produced photographic miniatures, earned him an Honourable Mention at the 1882 Moscow Exhibition. Another special award, a Gold Medal of Honour, went to his cigarette-making machine, but through the duplicity of his Russian partners, Aronson was robbed of the credit.

Aronson's technological aptitude was accompanied by a special flair for linguistic inventiveness. In common with Hebrew writers of the century, he found the classical form of the language inadequate to express the theoretical concepts and technical terms of the modern world, and like them he found it necessary to borrow from foreign languages and also to invent and improvise the terminology he required. Also like so many writers of the period, he had to teach himself the languages he needed — Russian, German, Polish.

As a family man, Aronson appears as a loyal husband and protective father. He married three times and had six sons. His marriages, arranged for him in the traditional custom of the people, brought him, in turn, the bewilderment of infidelity, the tragedy of untimely death, and the final contentment of love and compatibility. After the accession of Alexander III to the throne of Imperial Russia and the subsequent intensification of anti-semitic laws, Aronson's sons emigrated to the United States. Aronson and his wife followed them early in 1888. In New York, he continued his interest in horology and took out a patent for a special type of chiming clock.

Chaim Aronson penned his autobiography — he says — for the benefit of his children and their children, so that they might gain an understanding of the events of the life which their forebear had to endure. He wrote in the Hebrew language he loved. In the event, the autobiography has turned out to be not only a personal account of interest to one family alone but, indeed, a highly important document on Jewish life in nineteenth-century Russia and a uniquely original handwritten contribution to Hebrew literature.

Due to the fact that the autobiography portrays a profusion of incidents, aspects, and personalities in the Jewish and non-Jewish life of nineteenth-century Russia, an Appendix has been added to offer the reader an analytical summary of the special features highlighted in the work. It affords, in addition, a means of illustrating Aronson's exceptional flair for literary expression and ingenuity by providing a correlative comparison with the original Hebrew manuscript.

Although the autobiography of Chaim Aronson is here published in its English translation so that it may gain the wide readership it merits, it is hoped that the original Hebrew manuscript will be made available for the special attention of Hebrew readers.

Text
In
Translation

◇◇◇◇◇

An Autobiography[1]

◇◇◇◇◇

Introduction

THE MEMOIRS of my life, including everything that happened to me from the day I was born until this day, so that future generations may know and take note of the years which have passed with all their changing times during my brief, afflicted life, as well as my thoughts during those different periods. Let my children behold and learn and gain wisdom: ask your father and he will tell you.

I commenced on the 15th *Av,* the day on which I was born in the year 1825[2], being now forty-seven years old. In the capital city of St. Petersburg.

I have long had the desire to record in writing the history of my life and everything that happened to me, good and bad, tragedy and joy, as well as all my thoughts on the vicissitudes of my life. I have kept before me at all times the idea which the Lawgiver implied in his Song, "Ask your father and he will tell you" — meaning thereby: consider the lives of your ancestors and gain knowledge from the generations which have passed and pay heed to their instruction, as your elders have told you.

I know that I am not a person of distinction. I shall not be counted among the great, nor will the third generation after me raise up a monument to my name. I am a member of the artisan class. The vicissitudes of my life have suppressed my natural talents, allowing them no freedom to develop through higher learning, although I was able to acquire some little knowledge through necessity, which has been my constant crutch and whose tip I dipped into the flowing honey of the bees which hover between the foliage in Wisdom's pastures — where blooms and roses and sublime buds abound — yet whose fluttering wings I heard only distantly during my days of toil and sweat. Much and often did I try to soar aloft to join their company, but the heavy clouds which lowered over my burdened years did not permit my fragile wings to pass through the thick gloom which overhung the darkened skies of Lithuania.

I am truly too insignificant to be counted among the great, whose deeds are full of wisdom and whose words are replete with instruction. For this reason, I have not ventured, until now, to record in writing the history of my life, and thereby assume a mantle of pride and arrogance foreign to my nature. I was incapable of doing this until now, when half my life has passed by. In moments of repose, I have pondered upon those years and have come to realise that I earned a name for myself as an honest and upright man. Those who know me will testify that I have done my work faithfully and have sought a livelihood for my family through the labour of my hands. I have fostered these attributes all my life and shall cling to them with all my might and never loose my hold upon them, but shall stand firm as a rock against the storms which threaten to sweep me away in the torrents of events which constantly engulf me. In my troubled heart, I mused: Though the late shadows of the nineteenth century are lengthening, and the ferry is being made ready for the next generation, yet I also am bound to the boards of the ferry. If only people had the vision to foresee the future, they would understand the words and thoughts expressed by Eugene Sue[4]: Why are the murderer and robber borne through the streets in Jehoshaphat's chariot?[5] To teach the people a lesson. Why not, then, do likewise to the man who has lived a simple, righteous life, and worked industriously by the labour of his own hands? Let the people be taught a lesson through him: let him be carried, in his lifetime, in a royal coach through all the streets of the capital, whilst a herald proclaims before him, "So shall it be done————".[6]

Of this, I am proud: it is my hope that I may end my life on the upright path which I have always trodden. It is, therefore, with pleasure that I take up my pen to record the events of my life on paper, as a memorial to future generations.

If every man were to cast a stone upon his land, all the highways would be paved. If every man were to write the story of his life, including all its events and all his thoughts, then succeeding generations would find wisdom and counsel and salvation tenfold more than they can draw from the accounts and biographies left by the distinguished few. How great was the loss to Knowledge during those early days when the world was in its infancy and writing was unknown, and during later times when thought and learning were interred within cuneiform writings, and also during later periods when languages become confused. In our own day, too, the death of people entails the death of Wisdom when they leave no remembrance of their thoughts and learning for the future generations, esteeming their knowledge too little to record it. Scholars scorn to record the words of a contemporary philosopher or weigh his ideas in the scales of their understanding. Yet, man's spirit knows no bounds, though he be of great or little learning. He may soar on the wings of his spirit and pierce the heavens and split the skies and, out of the darkness which swaddles his thoughts, rise up to the highest heavens. Though his wings weary of the flight and he fall back to earth, he need never feel ashamed, for even the greatest of men and the most renowned of scholars are bound to fall once they venture to soar up to the heavens. Who can enter into the counsel of the Lord? Who has seen the Spirit of the living creatures in the wheels of Nature?[7]

I said, in the words of the Woman of Valour[8]: Had the Lord wished us to be blind and deaf, He would not have given us eyes and ears. Therefore, man should take note of all the things which draw his attention. All his theories on knowledge and the world derive from natural science, for Nature never leaps from one extreme to the other, but proceeds from one step to the next step up the ladder of knowledge: at first, the theory, and then the proof, each acting upon the other. Yet even when the proof seems decisive, we continue to grope in darkness for the truth. A later generation will come and nullify the proofs and theories of the preceding generation — and all will have been in vain. A succeeding generation will, in its turn, ridicule them. So it will go on, for ever. In their smug contempt, they cannot understand the ways of the generality of mankind, and their conceptions and perceptions concerning Nature — that she never skips over anything, but has built, from the drippings and tiny eggs of the insects of the seas, the foundations of vast islands in the oceans' depths and eternal mountains which rear their peaks towards the heavens. Gradually, Nature raises her fledglings higher and higher up on the rungs of her ladder, both by means of actions and by the spirit of knowledge. One day, there will arise a generation which will gaze upon Nature's countenance face to face, and not in riddles[9]. They will behold, and will be amazed that their forefathers could ever have thought that they had risen high on the rungs of the sublime ladder.

It was the ideas put forward by Bonnet[10] — who lived a hundred years ago — which encouraged and inspired me to account myself among those who build their chambers in the heavens[11], one of the two delicate wheels in Nature's machine, for there is a place for everything.[11a]

The world is built according to a general system. Everything in it is bound to everything else through contact, relationship and attraction. Nothing is too insignificant to be connected, for some purpose, with that which precedes or follows it.

The value to man of the vegetation on which he subsists is entirely physical, and the nature of his contact with inanimate matter is the same as with all physical bodies. However, the living creature is superior to organic matter, especially in his senses and understanding which bind him fast, with spiritual bonds, to a level higher than the material, be it for pleasure or for pain. The sense of pleasure teaches him to appreciate the value of the physical materials which are best for him; the sense of pain teaches him the value of those materials which are injurious to him. The living creature is the focus of many objects which are attracted to him: to some, he draws close, and from others retreats, in accordance with the nature of his desires and his arteries, which are the channels of the senses and run like argent cords from the brain to all the parts of the body.

Vegetation has no arteries, nor has it any property which functions like an artery. It is therefore considered to be without senses. Where, then, do the senses begin and end? The living vegetation which inhabits water (polyps) and stone (molluscs) differs only little from plants, while the plant which worships the sun differs only slightly from the mountain flax (*Amiant*) — and how, indeed, does the mountain flax differ from the limestone?[12] If it be probable that the soul of organic matter is similar to that of living creatures, then the latter might also be compared to the soul of rational man — for otherwise, we should be creating for ourselves a new world, an imaginary world, a world of illusion.

Let us consider the matter. The world is built systematically, according to a general scheme. Everything in it is bound to everything else by contact, relationship and attraction. Nothing is too insignificant to be connected, for some purpose, with that which precedes or follows it. Thought rises up to the world of vision like the thin dust which clings to solid objects. If this thought, this thin dust, were to be absent, then a new system would have to be created for those things which are related to them, and a future general scheme would also need to be changed to a different general scheme. The thought in the mind of rational man, and the dust in the mountain rock, are connected to a different thought and to other dust, which are themselves connected to other relationships as part of the general order. Thought is conceived in the soul from the movements of the vessels of the brain, its source deriving from the senses. The movements of the vessels of the brain derive from some other movement which, itself, received its stimulation from a preceding movement. The total combination of these movements is the life-chain of the living soul which bears the thought, and which exists on the level of the ladder ascribed to thinking creatures. Similarly, the fine sand on the river's bank relates with all Nature, as the river has carried it down from the mountain. The sand is related to both river and mountain. The sand, the mountain, the river in its winding course, are restricted by many thousands of preceding causes, which are themselves connected with the regulated order of the terrestrial globe — and all these form the connection between the sand and that which preceded it.

The sand breaks down into dust and changes into the material of organic matter which then changes into the material of the mountain. If a naturalist were to conceive a new theory concerning the nature of the substance of stone, and develop the theory into proof, and the proof into discovery of something new in Nature — just as the discovery of a piece of coral or of amber (*Elektron, Bernstein*) led to the first steps in the discovery of the streaks of lightning — would our distant ancestors have been able to comprehend those parts of the chain intermediate to the discovery of the streaks of lightning? There are, indeed, many parts of the chain which we ourselves do not yet know.

There can be no doubt that the Supreme Intelligence bound all parts of the scheme together with stout fetters, so that not even the least of things would be left unrelated in some way to the general scheme: even the plants of the fields, and the maggots in cheese, are bound to the general chain, just as much as the cedar tree and the elephant. The most minute of Nature's products are not simply dust which falls upon the wheels of its chariot, but are themselves small wheels caught up within larger wheels.

It is the same with everything which exists upon all worlds. Each one has its own system and is part of a greater system. These, in their turn, form part of an overall general system which contains them all together — and so on, to infinity. Nothing exists by itself. The moth is a little world related to a larger world. The motive force of their activities lies in the rungs of Nature's ladder, which extends from the centre of the coral to the centre of the sun, from the sphere which moves round the moth to the sphere which moves round the cherubs.

The elements act upon each other according to principles and rules laid down by Nature. These rules are determined by their inter-relationships, and these connect them with the organic and the living creatures, and with rational man who, superior to them all, spreads out his branches over the whole of the terrestrial globe. All the varying types and species are relative to the mass and quality of the globe. The globe has its set place in the solar system, according to its mass and quality. The sun acts through the force of gravity upon the stars, which in turn react upon the sun, and together they all act upon their own particular general system — which, in turn, affects more distant ones. The scales of all worlds stand balanced in the hand of the Eternal God.

This must surely be the chain of activity, proceeding from cause to effect — and similarly, the relation of the past and present and future with the eternal harmonies[13] of this world, and moreover all the worlds bound unbreakably to a universal harmony which is too sublime for our comprehension.

No two leaves in this world are identical, nor are two seeds, nor two insects, nor two human beings. What can we say, then, of two stars or two solar systems or two galaxies in the heavenly host? Each star must have its own individual character, its own laws and history. Why should there not be worlds which are superior to ours and which contain individual species belonging to the first and second orders of the general relationships of life, or other worlds which contain only the lowest order? There must exist worlds in which our inanimate is their organic, and our organic is their sentient life, and our living creature is their rational man, whilst our rational man would be a divine being to them.

If we could imagine (for otherwise it would be impossible) that Man's spiritual forces are arranged in accordance with the physical forces of his body, which ensheath his sentient soul — for the physical matter flows through them according to the nature of the arteries and the temperature of the blood and the flow of vitality, the soul being contained within them all — and that the physical materials are arranged in a manner related to the distance of the terrestrial globe from the centre of all the globes in the stellar system, then we should find that there are rungs of the ladder which relate in various ways with the spiritual forces, like the relation of the stars to the centre of the sun. If we say that the farther the sphere moves from its centre, its physical matter becomes increasingly refined and the physical vessel of the soul becomes more purified and is better able to accept the influences of the soul than those which draw closer to their solar centre, then the perfection of the soul will be determined by the distance of the terrestrial globe from its solar centre. Furthermore, when all the suns with all their stars revolve in perfect order around a common centre, then the perfection of the souls of their inhabitants will depend upon their distance from, or proximity to, their common solar centre. How many rungs of the ladder of the spiritual forces shall we then find between the top and bottom rungs, between the heavenly angels and the physical order? What shall we think of the Intelligences on the topmost rung — for even angels range in order among spiritual beings, from the highest to the lowest?

Nature does not skip from one species to another, or one type to another, but advances steadily, like the rungs on a ladder or the shadows cast by light. Nor is there the slightest gap between all her activities. Therefore, nothing exists which does not have a precedent or a successor, which either approaches it or withdraws from it according to their particular properties. We are able to understand their more obvious qualities, and thus separate them into species and types and individuals. However, our division of them can never be definitive, because there will always be many individual types which belong outside any particular order whilst not being compatible with any other order.

The vegetation which inhabits water connects plants with living creatures. The flying squirrel (*fliegende Eichhorn*)[14] links the bird with the quadruped, whilst the monkey links the quadruped with man.

The fact that we are unable to differentiate between the majority of species, and particularly between the individuals in each species, shows that Nature's ways are not our ways, nor are her ideas like ours. We separate them into divisions, and afford them names and terms for our own use, because of our limited capacity to distinguish between them. Beings of a superior order to ours would be able to distinguish numerous points of difference between those individuals which we, in our restricted comprehension, consider to be alike, in the same way that we are able to distinguish the differences between other types and species.

(It is manifest that all living beings, from the birds in the heavens to the insects on the ground, recognise their own mates, as well as the other individuals in their species. Each approaches, or retreats from, others according to what it sees and hears and smells, and does not err either in the light of day or the darkness of night. Nevertheless, our own zoologists would not be able to recognise them even after diligent study and search. This shows that there are many variations among all individuals of any particular species which are not perceptible to all our senses.)

The superior beings will look upon Nature's ladder and observe the rungs as numerous as the individual beings evolved by Nature. This is the case with the rungs of ladders belonging to other worlds. All of them join on to one common ladder whose lowest rung is the atom and whose topmost step is the Divine Throne.

Restrain yourself, my soul. Be not distressed. You, too, have a place in Creation. The entire earth is as a speck of dust in the aweful vastness of the whole. Your days are not more than the foam on the surface of the eternal sea. Why, then, be despondent? Why so fearful to approach the book? If you behave so foolishly, then behold and see that all things derive from vanity, for all is vanity.[15]

Part One

◇◇◇◇◇

MY BIRTHPLACE was a small town on the river Nieman called Serednik, because it lies midway[16] between Yurburg on the Prussian border and Kovno. On the left, the river Dubisa flows into the Nieman, whilst on the right a small stream[17] runs partly through the town and pours its waters into the Nieman. The exact source of the Nieman is virtually unknown since it rises from marshlands and lakes. Here, not far from the Baltic, it is almost a *verst*[18] wide. The river runs deep along its entire course, with hills and mountains flanking both banks. The towns along the banks are spread over the slopes of the hills and mountains, and where the river has over-flown its banks the people have been forced to move higher up towards the tops of the hills.

There was an incident I witnessed when I was about three years old, which was like a daydream for I did not comprehend what I saw. There was an immense cart without wheels. A fearsome-looking cartier stood on it, holding a very long pole with which he propelled the horseless carriage over the water. There were many men and women inside, including my father and my mother on whose knees I was sitting. When we reached the other side, which was to the right of the town, we stepped off the cart over some planks, and then made our way towards a ruined house where we lay down and slept.

I learned the solution to the riddle only many years later. In those days, the little town lay in a valley between the great river Nieman and the ridge of mountains which soared over it. The plain was on a level with the waters. Each year, at the beginning of Spring, when the forbidding ice which had covered the river during the Winter melted, the waters flooded over. The river Dubisa to the left of the town, also carried its ice towards it, as did the small stream on the right. The town thus lay in a state of siege.

The waters rose up to the houses on the lowland, close to the river's edge, filling them halfway up their windows, and then spread higher up towards the houses closer to the foot of the hills. The people who lived on the lowland took all their belongings and moved to the houses on the hills. Those who lived on the higher slopes of the hills brought out their household utensils and their clothing, and washed and cleaned them in preparation for the coming Passover festival, as was their invariable custom.

There had been times when, at the end of a severe winter during which the cold had been intense and the ice menacing, a sudden thaw had set in and the spring warmth had brought heavy rains. The residents of the town, perhaps deep in slumber, were not aware of this caprice of Nature. In the middle of the night, before people had time to awaken, the waters rose high in the rivers and flowed into their homes and over their beds. The strong men lifted their loved ones on to the rooftops, where they shouted for help in the darkness of the night. The people who lived up on the hills quickly bound planks of wood together to make rafts, and then rowed across the floods to rescue their neighbours. It was an awe-inspiring sight, and one which the Jews of the lowlands witnessed regularly every year.

It also sometimes happened that that dreadful ice, whose floes were hundreds of square cubits long and three hundred cubits thick, was carried by the river on its way to the sea until it met little islands at the rear of the town. The ice would stop in its course, and turn in the direction of the town. Nothing was able to stand in its way. It overturned everything, bringing houses and stout trees to the ground. For many people, their homes became their graves. Many others were left as naked as the day they were born. The waters would remain in the town as much as ten days to a fortnight, including the Passover festival. Then a quarter of the town's inhabitants would leave and go begging for alms, for the report of the terrible destruction which had overtaken them spread before them throughout the cities of the land.[19]

This, then, was the sight which I had beheld at the time — for my parents lived on the lowland. The horseless carriage was a raft; the ancient, broken-down, smoke-stained house where we had slept, was the communal bath-house situated on a hill. No other house had been found standing that night, so all who escaped the floods sought refuge in the bath-house. We lived there many a day, even celebrating the feast of Passover in it. Whenever the women had to go to perform their ritual ablutions, the rest of us climbed up on to the roof and lay down in a corner until they came out, so that we would not look upon their nakedness. Later, we moved to one of the houses on the hill. In the course of time, the survivors moved to the foothills, only a very few remaining on the plain.

It would seem that the great river Nieman has been gradually changing its course. The old people relate that, many years ago, it flowed in a different direction, so that all the trading boats and wooden ferries travelled on the other side of the town towards the Polish frontier. It had been changing direction over a long period of time, due to the silt which the waters had stirred up on one side whilst leaving deep waters on the opposite side. Little islands had also risen up in the river and, in the course of time, had formed a wide expanse of dry land on the surface of the water. I can myself recall seeing a small island rise upon the water in this manner, opposite the town.

Of that period of my life, I remember nothing beyond what my parents described to me. I can believe them implicitly for I know they never lied: both my father and my mother were honest and upright, although on occasion their words were stultified by superstitious beliefs, from which they were no freer than any other Jew who lived in the small towns and villages of those days.

It happened that when I was two years old, I developed a strong craving to eat earth. If, during winter-time, I could find none inside the house, I would tear the dry plaster off the walls and consume it with delight. My father applied many remedies prescribed by wonder-workers, but to no avail. One Summer's day, my father saw me playing under a bridge, filling my mouth with earth and devouring it as though it were honey. I did not see him. He called to me from afar. Hearing his voice, I hurriedly wiped my mouth clean so that he should see no trace of earth on my lips, and ran towards him. My father was inwardly pleased, thinking: "My son is a clever boy!"[19a]

I was his only remaining child, for seven other sons and daughters had died before me, in their childhood. When I had been born, my father had enquired of Rabbi Ḥayyim what he should do to save this child from death: Rabbi Ḥayyim had been the town Rabbi for some sixty years, and had once been a pupil of the renowned Rabbi Ḥayyim of Volozhin; although he was a scholar and learned in both algebra and nature studies, he believed in miracle-workers. He advised my father not to call me by the names of his or my mother's families, but to give me the name of Ḥayyim[20] — "and the boy will live".

It was during this time that my father gave up his petty trading, and turned to teaching Jewish children the Written Law.[21] He prospered and gained a good reputation in the town. His deep ambition, however, was to teach his only son Torah as quickly as possible, whilst still a child.

When I was two-and-a-half years old, in the year 1828,[22] a decree was issued by Tsar Nicholas that Jews would have to serve in the army. Many men were taken away to the provincial capital to be examined for their fitness for army service. They were quartered in the house in which my parents lived. Once, I was sitting in my cradle with a book of Psalms in my hands, reading aloud the songs of the Sweet Singer of Israel. The men saw me and were astonished. They sewed a small bag for me, hung it around my neck, and put silver and copper coins in it — as was the custom with regard to young children. They told the Rabbi how amazed they were to see a young child of two reading from the Book of Psalms just like an old man. The Rabbi summoned my father and told him that this was not the proper thing to do. It is written in the Bible "three years shall they be forbidden to you"[23] — and for that reason no Jewish child may be taught Torah before reaching the age of three. Nevertheless, the whole town marvelled, and declared that the son of Aaron Mendel would become a great scholar in Israel.

I remember nothing more of those early days until I became four years old, and my father sent me to study under the ritual slaughterer, who was also the town's Cantor and *melammed*. I do not know why my father sent me to another teacher when he could have taught me himself. I think, however, that the parents of his other pupils had begun to complain that he was devoting more attention to his only son than to theirs. My father stipulated with the ritual slaughterer that I was not to be whipped, because I was very young and not really in need of the lessons. I attended the slaughterer's house daily, and became friendly there with some tall, well-built youths whose little fingers were thicker than my thighs by as much as the breadth of my back. Their sole daily instruction consisted of the recitation of the prayers from a Daily Prayer Book printed in large, square characters: I myself was able to recite all the prayers by heart, with my eyes closed.

One of my fellow-pupils was a youth of fifteen. Every day we would recite the *Eighteen Benedictions* and always, when reaching the prayer "As for the slanderers", he would wrongly say "Blessed art Thou, O Lord, *shim'on u-mitvoh* of the righteous"[24]. Practically all the other boys were like him. They were grown-up and not one of them could read properly. I used to help them to correct their mistakes. They all received beatings daily from the slaughterer, whilst I was the only one spared. My friends became jealous of me, and began to pick quarrels with me, and said: "You will get yours, too". Knowing of my father's demand that I should not be whipped, I told them in all innocence that I would never be beaten since my father had so ordered. On the morrow, the slaughterer sought a pretext for complaint against me, and struck me once or twice with his whip. I was furious and, when I arrived home, I told my father, but he made no reply to me. Several days later, I fell ill and was confined to bed for a few days. Later, it was discovered that I had contracted a high fever. I suffered from it for a long time.

In those days, there was no quinine available in the small towns[25] nor were there physicians: the only healers were the quacks, every one of whom was a charlatan. There were also the old women who knew every remedy in the world, including those of the miracle-workers[26] and the Tartars and the magicians, and they offered their advice and treatment to all the sick. I did not escape their attentions.

The first remedy my father tried on me was the one prescribed by the Rabbi: he had to write over all the doors and windows of the house and to chalk upon all the walls in large letters: "The boy Hayyim is not at home".[27] The idea was that, when the demon of malaria came to visit me, he would see written everywhere that the boy he was seeking was not at home, and would therefore turn away and go back to wherever he came from. Unfortunately, the demon of malaria did not understand the Yiddish which had been written for him, and so paid me constant visits.

One day, an old woman came and shook her head at me, although I did not hear the advice she whispered into my father's ear. When, on the third day, I became very feverish, my father picked me up and placed me inside an oven which had just been emptied of bread. He told me to lie still there. My fever began to rise. A young girl came and stood in front of the oven. She was unaware that I was there, and lifted up her clothes to warm herself. I cried out that she was blocking out the light. She jumped like a startled doe, looked at me and blushed. My fever and temperature rose alarmingly. I called out: "Give me some water!" A kindly woman came forward with a brass mug, and said: "Drink, my son." I drank — and vomited up the drink and all the food I had eaten since the previous day. What, indeed, had they given me to drink? Urine mixed with crushed bugs! This was the remedy the quacks had prescribed for me. Later, I was taken out of the oven, and simpler remedies were sought for me. I was given a hen's egg, roasted, which I had to hold in my hand all day and then, later, to throw into the street: anyone who found it and ate it, would take on my illness. This did not help, either.

One day, when a gentle warmth lay over the hillside behind the house, I went out and lay down in the grass to rest, and fell asleep. Suddenly, I awoke with a start. A bucket of cold water had been thrown over me, drenching me from head to foot. My father and mother were standing nearby, observing all my movements after that fright. Truth to tell, only a few days after that treatment, I recovered from my illness — though whether by reason of the treatment or because the illness had run its course, I cannot say.

When I was five, my father began to teach me the Pentateuch with Rashi's commentary.[28] Since I was playing with other boys my own age, he made for me a fine coat of wool as red as blood. I do not know if he chose a red coat so that the evil eye should not harm me.[29] These fears were common to all the people of the town. We received daily visits from emissaries carrying, in their hands, the round head-coverings which Jews wore under their hats to soak up the sweat and also copper coins on which they scratched the name of any boy or girl afflicted with the evil eye. They recited for my father a spell which he had to learn to recite perfectly in order to remove the evil eye. Then my father had to take hold of the head-covering or the kerchief together with the coins and recite the biblical verses beginning and ending with the letter *Nun*[30]: "When the plague of leprosy is in a man, he shall be brought to the priest"[31]; "We shall go over armed before our brethren in the land of Canaan and our inheritance shall be beyond the Jordan"[32] — and similar other verses, totalling thirteen in all. He also recited further passages which I can no longer remember.

It was during that period that my mother bore a child, a brother for me. He did not remain long in this world, but died only about a month later. During those few days of his brief life, I saw some astonishing things which can never be erased from my memory. When the infant was almost a month old, he began to cry very loudly, and cried all night long. On the next night, my father called for a specialist — a first-born son to both his mother and grandmother. This man placed a cloth into his mouth and, biting tightly through it with his teeth, began to gnaw at the child's navel. My father asked him, three times: "What are you doing?" Each time the man replied: "I am gnawing" — which was an obvious reply albeit from a specialist. When that marvellous remedy proved ineffective, the man applied a different and even more obsure remedy. He told my father to fetch an axe and a short wooden peg. He placed the peg against the child's cradle and struck it with the back of the axe until it sank into the ground: residences such as ours did not boast of floor-coverings. After he had struck the peg three times, my father asked him: "Why are you striking it?" The man replied simply: "Peg!" They exchanged this question and answer three times. The little child, however, continued to scream all night long until its strength gave out, and it quietened down for a while. . .

I wore my red coat every day. People who were even at the other end of the town were able to see me and recognise me. They used to say: "The red Jew is coming!" I discovered later the reason for their calling me a "red Jew", even though I was only a young boy. The ten tribes of Israel, which had been sent into exile, dwell beyond the river Sambatyon.[33] We Jews, who live scattered throughout the world, are descended from the two-and-a-half tribes which dwelt across the Jordan. The Jews of the ten tribes who were exiled to Halah and Habor and the mountains of Gozan,[34] beyond the Sambatyon, wear red garments. No one can come close to them, for the river is in torrent all the days of the week, resting only on the Sabbath. Its waters hurl up rocks and stones, and there is no way for a boat to get through. The people are exceedingly pious, and are versed in the mysteries of Practical Kabbalah and the combinations of names that can change the face of the entire world. They have the power, also, to release us from the bitter confines of our exile. Unfortunately, they themselves cannot cross the river Sambatyon since they cannot profane the Sabbath day of rest, so they must wait for the day, at the end of time, when God will have pity upon us and will redeem us. Then will they cross the river together with the Messiah the son of David.

When I queried this, saying that, since no man had gone to them and they had not come out, how then did we know all this, I was told that, centuries ago, a Jewish voyager had miraculously forded the river, with the help of God, and found them. He had told them of all our troubles and tribulations in our exile. They had listened, and sighed and said: "The end will come for our oppressed brethren, and very soon we shall be coming to your aid". When the traveller entered their house of prayer, he saw a large golden cross hanging over the curtain of the Ark. He trembled at what he saw, thinking them to be worshippers of the cross. They were surprised at his apprehension. They told him that, many years earlier, they had gone to war against their neighbours, whose customs were unknown to them, and had found the golden crucifix among the spoils. Unaware that it was considered idolatrous by the Jews, they had hung it as a decoration over the Holy Ark. Now, they hastened to take it down and destroy it.

Once, an eastern king had decreed that all Jews were to be put to death. A time of distress came upon Jacob, for a man such as Haman had risen against them, and was purposing evil against them with the king. There was in the kingdom an old man, well versed in the secrets of the Kabbalah and in magic spells. He went to the river Sambatyon, adjured it to rest, and crossed over. He related all the troubles of the Jews to the red men. One of the red Jews, a tailor with a limp, arose and travelled back with the old man to the capital city. He called to the oppressor of the Jews, and said: "Let us see which one of us will prevail. If you overcome me, you may do with me whatever you will. But if I overcome you, then must you release my people of Israel". The oppressor mocked him in his heart, and said: "You are but a tailor, and you limp. Will you overcome me?" The red Jew said: "Bring me millstones, with the upper millstone, and I shall show you wonders". They brought him the millstones so huge that twenty men had to carry them. The lame tailor lifted up the millstones with one hand, and the upper millstone with the other, and hurled them above his head. They soared like eagles into the heavens and, joining together, began turning on each other in the manner of milling. Then the old man grasped hold of the top branches of a cedar tree and pulled down on them until they were bent over to the ground. He said to the oppressor prince: "Take hold of it with your hands". He did so. The old man then loosed his hold upon the tree which immediately straightened and hurled the oppressor into the heavens. He fell between the millstones and the upper millstone, and was ground into powder. After that, the evil decree was removed from the Jews. The lame tailor went with the congregation to the House of Prayer and sang the *Akdamot Millin*[35] in his own language on that Feast of Weeks. Thereafter, he disappeared, and no man knew where he had gone. So they included this hymn in the Festival Prayer Book, to be sung on the Feast of Weeks in memory of the miracle which had occurred during the festival.

At that time, my father's father died. I remember very little of him, for I had seen him only once. My father's mother I had never seen at all, and had heard about her only on the occasions when my parents had reminisced about their own lives. This much I remember. My father's mother had died some five years before I had been born. She was called Leah the Gracious, because all her life she had sought to perform righteous and charitable deeds, and had become a byword among the people: "as gracious as Leah, who sells a hen's egg for three *groschen,* and does a good deed at the same time"[36].

My father's father was called Mendel Ashkenazi. He had been born in Poland, on the other side of the river Nieman, in the small town of Sudarg, over against Yurburg. At that time, the Nieman was the frontier between Russia and Zamot, or Zamody, and Poland. No one was allowed to cross the border-river without a permit from the Superintendent of the frontier, who was stationed permanently in the border towns. In my home-town also were stationed a deputy Superintendent and troops who were known as 'searchers': they were the customs officers who exacted customs duty for the many goods which were brought over to us from Poland. In those days, there were numerous smugglers and contrabandists who crossed the Nieman in fishing boats, and even more in winter-time when the ice formed bridges over the deep waters. Their principal merchandise was tobacco. The searchers were stationed along the border by the river banks, to prevent anyone from crossing. Many smugglers drowned because, in their haste, they tried to cross over unfordable places where there was no ice, but only a snow covering over the waters. On those occasions, a great cry would be heard in the town, in the dead of night.

My father's father, before he had reached old age, had been a petty trader, carrying merchandise to the rural areas around the large cities, for the farmers and landowners. He kept a horse and covered wagon. He was different from his fellow Zamot Jews in that he loved cleanliness and fine and orderly appearance in everything. For that reason, he was known as the "Ashkenazi". His horse was always well-groomed, and all his equipment, including the harness, was kept neat and clean. The small wagon was also kept in good condition. Before old age overcame him, he crossed the river and moved from Poland to Zamot, and went to live in the town of Serednik. He took my father with him, leaving his two older sons in Poland.

The eldest son, Hlavna Lapidus, left home at an early age, and all trace of his whereabouts was lost. His brother remained in Poland all his life. I knew him by the name of Jacov Baredzever, after the village where he lived for many years, not far from the town of Vilkovishk in Poland. He was a righteous man, fearing the Lord with all his soul and might until the day he died. In his younger days, he had served for many years in the home of a wealthy Jew. Later, after he had left him, and had grown to an old age and the Lord had provided him with wealth and sons and daughters, he took sixty roubles and went off alone to find the man whom he had served thirty years earlier. When they met, the wealthy man, who had become reduced in circumstances, did not at first recognise him. My father's brother revealed to him who he was, and how he had served in his home when a youth. Then the man remembered him. ''Now, my benefactor, I have come to restore to you the money I stole from you, together with the required added fifth portion[37]. Take this sixty roubles, and forgive me for sinning against you''. The man was astonished: ''I was never aware that you had robbed me. I remember as if it were today that, among all the servants who were in my home, both before you came and after you left, there was no one so loyal and honest and upright as you''. My uncle replied: ''You never knew, nor did anyone else suspect at the time. When some articles of silver were stolen from you, you carried out an investigation and made enquiries but without success. I was the one who had stolen them. Now that the Lord has prospered my ways and given me abundance, I am restoring to you what I stole, and have added a fifth as the law requires. Take it from me now, and forgive me, that my soul may not bear a sin before our Heavenly Father who knows all and from whom nothing is hidden''. He urged it upon him, and he took it.

Jacob had two sons and two daughters. I knew one son well, for he turned one of the wheels of my life. He was called Ze'ev the Weaver, and lived in Vilki, about ten *verst* from Serednik. Of his two daughters, I met the elder Rachel many years later in Vilna; the other, Leah, married my father during the later years of his life. It was also there — (i.e. Vilna) — that I found my father's brother Lapidus, an old and broken man by that time. In his youth, he had forsaken his parents, family and country and had disappeared without a trace. Some years later it was reported that he had sold himself for a few coppers to a company of entertainers. Thereafter, his family despised him.

My father lived in Zamot, where he had neither close family nor relations, since all the other members of the family remained acrosss the frontier in Poland. Because of the difficulty of obtaining permits to cross the border, our families lost contact with each other and eventually became estranged. My father often tried to obtain permission to cross the border-river via the city of Yurburg, which was close to the fording point and from which the small town of Sudarg could be seen, in order to visit his relatives, Gottlieb and his sons, who were wealthy and respected people. However, he was never allowed to cross the frontier, and had to return home.

In the year 1831, the news spread through the city that the Poles had risen in revolt against their king, Nicholas. This was in the springtime. The Jewish people picked on it as their incessant topic of coversation. Some averred that the Poles would slaughter all the Jews; others declared that it presaged the coming of the Messiah, for they had discovered hidden in the mysteries of the Kabbalah and *Zohar*[38] that the Redemption was due to come at this time — as the meaning of the individual letters of the phrase *ka-afikim ba-negev*[39] was: "after the death of Alexander Pavlovich, Constantine will rule a short time, but Redemption will come in the days of Nicholas"[40].Thus, when the Poles would arise and conquer the kingdom, and bring an end to the reign of Nicholas, then would the Messiah appear. There were other people who declared, like prophets, that a written note had fallen from the heavens when the Jews had been exiled from their land and had nowhere to turn and the great multitude was encamped in the country; then this letter had fallen from the heavens before their very eyes. On it was written: *po lin*[41]. They then understood that Heaven had commanded them to live in the land of Poland, and there they would be redeemed. Then arose a Greek[42] prince who assumed the monarchy, and prolonged the exile. However, it was now predicted that the Poles would defeat the Greek prince, after which Redemption would come.

At an assembly of many scholars to discuss political affairs, other and different opinions were expressed. Some said that possibly a divine retribution would be visited upon them, similar to those in 1648 and in 1096[43] — which had seen the martyrdom of the Kabbalist Rabbi Samson of Starodub.[44] He himself had predicted, from a study of the Kabbalah, that the messianic era was approaching. Afterwards, sorely grieved, he had said that the Redemption had indeed come but had turned into a day of retribution, as had happened at the time when Israel had sinned and made the molten calf. Then the Holy One, blessed be He, had said: "On the day that I visit you, I shall remember all your sins".[45] Therefore, whenever the Lord remembers the oppression of His people, He decrees that they be redeemed — but, if they do not merit Redemption, then the Lord visits them and punishes them once again for the sin of the calf, as He had spoken. Such visitations had occurred throughout history, as in 1648 and 1096 and other occasions. The scholars trembled in their fear, although there were those who professed to believe these opinions openly while thinking otherwise in their hearts, feeling that the Poles would not harm the Jews of Serednik so long as Moshe the son of David lived among us.

There was an old man in our town, called Moshe ben David, and popularly referred to as Moshe'l David's. I knew this man. He was wealthy and owned many houses on the slopes of the mountain, as well as granaries for the produce of his fields. He owned land on which seven farmers, with their wives and children, worked for him in perpetuity: they had been left to him many years ago by the Government at that time in payment for contractual work he had carried out. Since, however, Jews were prohibited by law from having bonded Christian serfs, they served him in the name of the Polish lord of the city. These peasant farmers of his would go to his house in the town for a few days, till his fields and gardens and do the housework.[46] They knew that the Jew Moshe was their lord, and had the same power as any other lord to sell them or exchange them for the price of a dog.[47] However, they genuinely loved their Jewish master, for he never dealt harshly with them nor refused to assist them when in distress or in a year of drought. I myself observed them happily going about their master's business. Though he was a Jew, they had no contempt for him because of it. Some would chop the winter's wood for him, and others would draw the water and irrigate his gardens. This man Moshe, a truly God-fearing man, was deeply loyal to the Poles, and had only hatred for the Russians in his heart.

It so happened that, prior to this time, a Jew of the Ḥasidic sect, named Barukh the Ḥasid, had come to live in the town. He began to call upon the name of the Rabbi Baal Shem Tov of Mezhibozh,[47a] and to preach Ḥasidism in the town. The man Moshe was the first to accept his teachings: he joined him, became a Ḥasid and excelled his teacher tenfold. Nevertheless, he was not fanatical in his beliefs, nor did he scorn the Mitnaggedim[47b] or their ways. Throughout his life, he never uttered a word against the Mitnaggedim or their Rabbis. He feared God with his whole heart and in perfect belief.

That same year, the Ḥasidim, who numbered some ten men, decided to build a small House of Prayer on the hill, on land belonging to the man Moshe. The town's House of Study and Prayer also was situated on that hill, and there were some ten cubits difference between it and the small house which the Ḥasidim built as well as the residence of the man Moshe on the hillslope. Once the roof had been erected, boys and youths gathered together on the Sabbaths to talk and play. I joined them. Once, I was standing at the entrance, beside a wall, and my friends were playing on top of the roof. One of them picked up one of the bricks which were lying there for building the chimney, and threw it to the ground. It fell upon my head, and would surely have cracked my skull had the walls of the small house been taller. However, because the building was low and I was standing upon a mound of lime and earth beside the wall, I remained alive. Nevertheless, to this day there is a small, bald patch on my head, which still pains whenever I touch it.

This, then, was the man Moshe of whom it was said that, so long as he lived among us, the Poles would do no harm to the Jews in our district. His loyalty to the Poles and his love for the people was well known to the Polish leaders, who did not conceal their plans and strategies from him. Whenever Russian troops entered the town, the man Moshe would hide himself and refuse to see them.

On the eve of the Passover festival, we were sitting around our table which had been set with unleavened bread and wine and all the *seder*[48] dishes. We had just reached the part of the service in which the unleavened bread and the bitter herbs are eaten, when a loud cry arose outside, in the street. No one knew what had happened. Some people left their houses to find out, but returned hastily, in great fear, snatched up their clothes and wrapped some unleavened cakes inside them. Picking up their children in their arms, they fled as though from death itself. My father, picked me up in his arms, at the same time holding unleavened cakes and a bottle of wine in both hands. My mother took a small pillow on which to rest the head of her only son. In their trembling haste, they left the house wide open, with the candles still burning on the table, for these may not be extinguished on the holy day. They fled to the top of the mountain, where they sat down and looked back upon the town, wondering what the Poles would do. Below us, in the streets, men were running to and fro, asking each other whether the Poles had already crossed the river, and how many of them were there, and what had happened on the lowlands outside the town. One man, urging another not to delay him since his way was contrary to him[49], reported impatiently that the Poles had entered the tavern of Isaac Cossack, which was on the plain by the river, and had killed and murdered the people there. The surviving members of the family had fled for their lives. The Poles had looted the house, consumed all the liquor in the cellar, and ended up drunk and wild. We, who were lying hidden on the mountain, lost heart and moved further up the mountain, whilst others climbed even higher above us. Some men led their wives and children to the cemetery on the hill, where they lay down near their ancestors. It was said that the House of Study was filled to overflowing with men and women reciting the final Confession and preparing themselves for death.

Suddenly, a man appeared in the town on the plain. He walked through the town, calling out at the top of his voice: "Fellow Jews, have no fear. Not a hair of your heads shall be harmed. Come quickly out of your hiding places. Return to your homes and continue with the *seder* as usual. Do not close your doors, but leave them open, and when the Poles come, offer them wine and unleavened cakes. They will search your homes, but they will not harm you or destroy anything. However, any Russian man or woman who is found, will forfeit his life. No harm will befall any Jew because of them."

Thus did the man Moshe proclaim in the streets. He even pledged his life and the lives of his family, saying that if but one Jew in the entire town was harmed, they could stone him to death. All this took place in the dead of night, filled with the terror of death, our own fear making it hard for us to distinguish all the words that he was proclaiming. It sounded like the anguished cry of a man slain by the sword. The brave ones among us emerged from their concealments on the lower slopes of the mountain to listen to his words, and pass them on to the rest of us.

We descended the mountain in silence, crawling on our bellies so that the Poles would not discover that we had been hiding from them because we had believed they were murderous enemies. People whispered quietly to each other as they made their way homewards. With fearful hearts, they sat down round their tables to conduct the evening *seder*, knowing that the Poles would come, as the man Moshe said, to search every house. The *seder*, therefore, did not follow its normal course.

About a half-hour later, three Polish soldiers entered our open door. My father called them to our table. He offered each a glass of wine and unleavened cakes. They ate and drank, and then began their search. They looked under the beds and behind the stove, but found no one. They left. Then, suddenly, the wailing of a dying person arose from the vestibule at the front of the house. Our company trembled, and feared to go outside. Later, we learned that, when the Poles had looked inside the baking oven which was in the vestibule, they had found a Russian woman hiding inside it. They had pulled her out, beaten her savagely, dragged her away and killed her.

The following day, everyone in the town realised that it was only due to the man Moshe that they had been saved from the Poles who had rebelled against their king — although, in their hatred of Jews in general, they had committed outrages in many other places. Worst of all were the roving stragglers, for those large bodies of troops which passed by in military order were not permitted by their officers to loot or kill the Jews, who neither fought nor plotted against them. In truth, what did it matter to the Jews of Zamot whether it was a Pole or a Russian or a Chinese emperor who ruled over them? All treated the Jews alike. Their love for, or their hatred of, the Jews changed constantly with the changing times. The Jews, scorned and despised by all nations, could see only one of two causes for these changes in their situation: either it was to the advantage of their rulers or it was the result of miraculous intervention; (since the benefits offered did not spring from sincere motives, they had to be the result of a divine decree). These two causes are very evident wherever Jews live throughout the world. Although the external appearance differs to some small extent, as has been clearly revealed by means of the printing press, the internal condition remains the same in all particulars — even though, in some far-off land, signs of true friendship may be shown towards the Jews. However, the Jews of Zamot, at that time, were ignorant of the condition of their brethren in other lands of their exile where they had been able to find rest among the gentiles. I had heard many reports about the condition of the Jews, and their own verdict upon it: how they entreated Heaven to bring lance and sword upon their country, though it meant endangering their own lives, too. All nations live by the sword — excepting the Jewish nation, as their Father Isaac had declared.[50] The sword of the nations has not spared the Jewish people. Except for a few individuals they were not driven by the lure of the silver and gold they might loot from the confusion, but their sole intent was the destruction of the congregations of Jacob. In the words of the *paytan*:[51] "They shall be thrown into great confusion". They have been shown by the experience of their later history that, when wars break out, Israel is forgotten for a long time and is able to rest during the entire period of strife and contention between the nations. Then they dwell secure from the harsh decrees which are continually imposed upon them by all nations during times of peace and prosperity.

Such thoughts as these went through my mind in those days, though I was only a child, and my father carried me in his arms through the streets at dusk to recite the evening prayers in the House of Prayer. Before we had concluded our services, Polish soldiers entered the town, and stationed guards with drawn swords on both sides of the streets. No one was allowed to pass without first being asked: "Are you for us or for our enemies?"[52] Anyone who did not answer was thrust through with the sword. Everyone, therefore, made the same reply: "I am for us". Nevertheless, the guards we met on our way back from the House of Prayer, went beyond their orders, for after receiving my father's reply: "I am for us", they kept their swords pointing towards each other across the street and would not let us by. They asked my father: "Where do you come from and where are you going?" I had not heard their words clearly, but I was frightened by the flashing of their sharp swords, so I squeezed closer into my father's arms to hide myself. My father answered them: "We have been to the House of Prayer and are on our way to our home in this street". They asked him: "What were you doing in your House of Prayer — asking your God for our defeat?" "May the Lord have mercy upon us and you," replied my father, "but we pray together every day, morning and evening, for you, that you may conquer your enemy, who is also ours, for our only desire is to shelter under your wings as did our fathers and forefathers before us." They lowered their swords and sent us on our way in peace. It was said that some Jews who had not answered in this manner, had been beaten and even slain. Later, after our fear had abated, I asked my father about the questions and answers that had been exchanged, and he told me what had happened.

I also listened to the reports given by the teachers and the communal leaders when they assembled in the House of Study between the afternoon and evening services, and gathered around the long table alongside Rabbi Ḥayyim and the Talmud students. They reported, from the pulpit, all the news they had been able to gather. It was then that I began to understand the feelings of these people towards the Government and the police and officials. Each and every one of them dissembled in saying that he sought only love and brotherhood for those who took up arms on behalf of their flag: they spoke thus out of fear alone, for their feelings for all Governments were colder than ice. This was not due to any religious hatred, or to any differences in customs, but solely because of their continual cruelty towards the Jews throughout the whole of every year. It was the opinion of these oppressed people that the very occasional benefit which the Government bestowed upon them came from considerations of policy and economics, and could be likened to the care which a farmer showed his pig, or a shepherd his flock. They made the same comparison over the beneficent acts of all the Governments of the world — for what difference could it make to them whether this or that Government ruled over them, since none was of the royal House of David?

On this occasion, when the people assembled with the Rabbi in the House of Study, it was reported as a fact that the Government intended to expel all the Jews from Russia and settle them on the Caucasian frontier where the barbaric Circassians lived. It was related of them that they emerged from the rocky cliffs where they hid in the daytime and, in a sudden attack at night, would fall upon the settlers on the frontier, slaughtering anyone they found, and would then ride back on swift steeds to their lairs.

The people were frigtened by this report, for they believed it, knowing how the Government was continually moving Jews from the borders and villages, and constantly enacting new prohibitive regulations against them. That evil decree, then, would mean the end of this entire people (for such was the way of life of the inhabitants of the Caucasian mountains before the king of Russia subjugated them).[53]

The Rabbi spoke up calmly, whilst we all listened with great attention. "Brethren, do not be downcast or troubled by this evil report. Have no fear, the Government will not do this to us. If it were to do so, then it must also relieve us of various prohibitive regulations it has passed against us and place no further restrictions on our freedom, as it has done for all its people who have been transferred to the Circassian border. As for your fear lest the Circassians attack and slay you, they only attack those age-old enemies of theirs who are sent to settle near them and provoke them. They will not attack us Jews, for we are familiar with the quality and the merchandising of spirits.[54] Since the Government will not prevent us from carrying on this business, the Circassians will end up befuddled with wine under our tables. Indeed, they will hand over every penny they possess in order to keep us alive! They will certainly not harms or injure us". The congregation was astounded by the Rabbi's wisdom, for he had revealed to them a truth which had never before entered their minds.

At that time, work on the canal on the river Dubisa stopped. The Poles had destroyed it, and left not one stone on top of another in their hatred of the Russians. This is the affair of the canal. About three years before the outbreak of the Polish revolt in 1831, the Government began to dig a canal on the river Dubisa at the part where it flows through Serednik to the Nieman: its source lay in Courland, from which the river Aa flowed through Courland into the great river Dvina. It was the Government's intention to broaden these two rivers by digging a canal from the source of the Dubisa to the source of the Aa, a distance over dry land of some twenty *verst*. Then cargo boats would be able to sail from the hinterland to the Nieman via the Dubisa and the canal to the river Aa and the Dvina and to the Baltic Sea, without having to divert via Prussia to Memel and Tilsit. A considerable amount of work had been done along the Dubisa; it had begun here, at Serednik, and it was here that anyone wishing to cross the canal from Prussia and all the Russian regions bordering the river Nieman would have to pay customs duties. On the left of the town lay a flat plain, between the Dubisa and the mountain. A stretch of willow spread over the hill slopes along the length of the river, to a man's height. In summertime, a gentle breeze blew, so that it became a pleasant area for walking and for pleasure. However, only half a *verst* further away, a new world unrolled itself whose like did not exist in any other town in the region. It was a world of technology and labour, of man's many inventions for assisting Nature with the latest equipment and tools, and many machines to keep diligent hands busy. There were square, hewn stones, cleaned and smoothed, and bricks bleached in oil for building raised areas in the water, and iron and lead tools lacquered in a variety of colours.

My father often took me for a stroll to enjoy this marvellous sight. We wondered at the pumping machines turned by horses which stood in the river on a platform of wooden planks raised upon the water. The rotation of the pumping wheel forced the water from the lower end upwards to the higher end, into the canal which had been dug for the purpose, exposing a foundation of dry land into which iron locks could be firmly embedded. There were innumerable wooden planks there, long or square or round. Many labourers assembled there, together with assistants, police and inspectors, porters, hewers of stone, builders and cooks. The whole of creation came alive there, and turned into a little world of its own.

When, however, the Poles began their revolt, the place was abandoned and deserted, so that not a trace of life remained. The Poles vented their wrath upon the place, as they did wherever they went, and wreaked great devastation upon the trees and stones. They looted and destroyed all the workings at the canal site. The Russian Government, instead of returning later to repair the destruction, abandoned the canal project altogether, either because the damage caused by the rebels was too widespread or because it had realised that the canal would not be a successful enterprise. So all the weary labours of man remained buried there.

After the revolt had ended, and peace began to reign once more, government officials came to check the tools and equipment. They sold the iron and the lead and some of the best bricks, and left the remainder lying on the fields. The wooden planks were brought into the town and stacked in the gardens of the houses; and hewn logs and trunks were transported to the town and piled in the fields in the lowland part of the town.

When I was six years old, we were living in a house on the slope of the hill. Nearby was a field in which planks had been stored in heaps on top of each other. At first, guards had been stationed there at night, but later they were transferred and the planks were left unattended, as the officials placed their trust in the honesty of the people in the neighbourhood. When, one day, the people noticed that the planks had begun to rot, and were becoming mouldy and sprouting thorns, they began to steal the planks — at first, singly, and then in bundles — for use in extending their own houses. Other people, who did not need them for this particular purpose, argued that they could make good use of the planks for warming their rooms, and began to take as much wood as they could, using it for their baking and cooking stoves. It became an open invitation for everyone to steal, including the people on the outskirts of the town who envied them this opportunity. At first, these latter complained that the Government would levy a tax upon the whole town to pay for the stolen planks, and therefore they themselves, although innocent, would have to pay for other people's crimes. Later, however, they joined in and took whatever planks they wanted. At the end of a month, not a single plank remained. My father also took part in this plank affair. Being afraid to do it in the daytime, he went at night. Unfortunately, he struck his leg to the bone with an axe, and was laid up in bed for a long time.

Since there was neither nurse nor chemist in the town, he turned for a cure to the Babylonian Talmud, believing that the knowledge of all things lies within it, in accordance with the saying: "Turn it over, for everything is in it".[55] He prepared this prescription for himself: mixing the resin from a stout tree with an equal amount of wax and tallow, he placed the mixture inside a piece of paper, whose edges he folded inwards in the form of a crown, and then held it carefully over a flame until it melted, after which he placed it in a cool place to harden. He then smeared some of it on a cloth and bandaged it round his leg. In the early stages, he used a large quantity of the resin in order to draw the fluid from the wound, then later reduced the amount of resin whilst increasing the quantity of wax and tallow. Many days later, his leg healed completely.

Although the townspeople were surprised that no one had come enquiring after the planks, they began to construct folds for their sheep and sheds for their animals. Because Autumn was drawing close, they turned their attention to the large logs which were lying on the lowland, as these were also beginning to rot. The people who lived nearest to the plain went, during the middle of the night, to saw the large logs into smaller logs. They then wrapped pieces of cloth around them to deaden the noise as they hauled them by ropes to their homes, where they cut the logs into smaller pieces suitable for firewood. The people who lived farther away became jealous of them, and wanted to do the same. They decided to work together, to find logs for their own use and to share them amongst themselves according to their individual needs. By this time, the thinner logs had been used up, and only the very thick ones remained.

Then I witnessed a sublime sight. Each day, as the evening shadows lengthened and darkness spread over the land, work commenced on the plain of logs. All the townspeople went out, bearing axes under their clothes, and saws and hard wooden pegs to cut and hew the logs. The entire plain came to life and was transformed into a field of industry all night long. The people brought candles to light the places where they were working. The logs rustled, the saws hummed and the axes slashed with a terrifying sound. The only sound that was not heard on the plain was the voice of living creatures. The hills echoed the sound of the blows, and the wind amplified it, so that all that part of the town throbbed with subdued sound. A passer-by in the distance might just have heard it.

Suddenly, the noise sank into silence; the echoes stilled; and the silence of the grave fell over the plain. In the distance, from the highway, could be heard the faint tinkling of a bell. The trundling of approaching carriage wheels and the thudding of horses' hooves were borne upon the wind. Not one person stirred. Not even the flutter of a falling leaf could be heard. Only after the tinkling of the bell had faded into the silent distance did the field return to life and the town to activity. The scene kept changing like this all night long until the morning light. The logs gradually disappeared until not a single one was left of the thousands that had been there. The people stored up enough wood in their sheds and attics sufficient for many years to come.

To this day, I am still amazed how this matter was kept quiet from the neighbouring Christians as well as from the farmers in the nearby villages. Perhaps it was due to the fact that, as the revolt was coming to an end, and whilst there was still a great deal of confusion everywhere, they stayed away from the Jews in the hope that they would not be denounced for the many robberies, hangings, murders and other crimes they had committed. Nevertheless, the country Jews, who knew where these people had fled in hiding, testified against them to the Government officers who were investigating the actions of the rebels.

This is what happened to one Polish officer called Girkon, a fat-bellied person whose girth measured six cubits all round. He commanded a troop of farmers armed with sickles, spades and pruning-hooks. He had never before confronted an enemy in battle, but had always lived like a fattened ox on his father's estate. The sight of a naked sword made him as scared as a rabbit. Nevertheless, wherever he came across Jews, he attacked them mercilessly and commanded that they be hanged on trees. The number of widows and orphans increased considerably during the period of his command. After the revolt ended, he hid himself in the sheep pens near the forests. Troops of searchers came from Courland to aid the Government in quelling the revolt. They sought out the rebel Polish officers who had commanded the men who had terrorised the populace, and were now hiding in holes in the ground and in caves on the cliffs. The searching soldiers followed their tracks, and set their traps to take them alive. They urged the Jews to disclose the hiding-places of the Poles, but none would speak up against their Polish neighbours. However, those Jews who had lost their relatives at the hands of this cruel Polish officer, did reveal his place of concealment, and related all his crimes to the officer in command of the searchers, who went and found him. They tied him to the tails of their horses and dragged him after them. The bereaved women and orphaned children went, weeping, to look at him. They cried: "Why did you not have pity on us, instead of slaying innocent men who did you no harm? Now bear the punishment of your sins, and may your soul rot in perdition to eternity". Such scenes were commonplace in those days. This, then, is the reason why the neighbours of the Jews feared to quarrel with them, lest the Jews reveal all their crimes. The Poles began to realise that the long-suffering Jewish people would not cause their death so long as their own lives were spared. So it was that, when the second revolt broke out thirty years later, the Poles did no harm to the Jews.

As for the affair of the planks and the logs, nothing was ever heard about it, and it has been completely forgotten since.

When I was seven years old, it was the custom among the boys of my own age, and many older boys too, to gather together on the Sabbaths and festivals, on the mountain to enact the war of Poles versus Greeks.[56]. One army would take position on the top of the mountain whilst the other assembled on the slope below. We would wage battle until nightfall. The mountain peak reared over the town like a round turban, and was visible from far away. It was as high as a hundred storeys, and its base was two thousand cubits in circumference. In the centre of its peak was a crater which had been cut by men in ancient times. It was overgrown with grass and plants which were pleasant to behold, and a gentle breeze wafted its sweet scents all around. The Lithuanians gave it the nickname of *Pilnokalnis*,[57] meaning: a stuffed mountain. There was a tradition that, long ago, a Catholic church had stood there, but the ground had subsided leaving a crater in the centre; if one listened very attentively, when all was quiet, one might hear the tolling of the church bells. I tried to do this on many occasions but never heard them. I discovered later that there are many mountains like this, which have superstitious legends attached to them.

On the right of the mountain peak stretched a broad plateau. We fought our battles in this manner. The soldiers on the peak would remove their clothes, fold them, tie them into balls, and then hurl them down upon the heads of the army on the plateau below until their clothes were all gone. The soldiers on the plateau would then scramble up on their hands and knees and storm their position, shouting wildly until they had driven everyone away. Then they, in their turn, would throw their clothes at the enemy — after which, the battle came to an end.

In the summer of that year, my father sent me to the *heder* to learn Gemara. There were boys older than myself there. The *melammed* was an old man, worn out from teaching, who allowed us to play outside in the yard. It was then that I learned from my friends the difference between a man and a woman, although I remained innocent of the significance of it. Today I can appreciate how foolish are parents who permit their young children to study alongside more mature boys.

I saw the boys teaching themselves the Hebrew alphabet by writing on the table with chalk. I envied them and asked them to show me how to do it, and they did. Within two or three days, I was able to write the whole alphabet myself. When I went home, my father saw me writing on the table and asked me, in surprise: "Who taught you this?" Afterwards, I began to write the letters in ink on paper in the manner my old teacher showed me, in square letters with six corners.[58] I used this form of writing for some years, as no one showed me otherwise. Then, five years after I had first started writing, I found in the House of Study a piece of paper torn from a letter on which were words which had neither meaning nor continuity, but whose beautiful form made me feel ashamed. I realised that my own handwriting was ugly. I took the piece of paper home, and copied the letters again and again until I was able to write them perfectly. I taught myself to write that lovely script, and today I still use it. My father, however, used to write in the manner of the Jews of old.

At that time, panic spread through the cities of Lithuania and Zamot. The rumour was borne on the wings of the winds and carried by the birds of the heavens that the Government was about to issue a decree that no Jewish youth could marry before serving in the army and that only those already betrothed would be exempt from military service.[59] Thereupon the marriage-brokers, moving as swift as eagles, carried about lists of boys and girls aged from six to eleven. Using two fingers, they would point to those who, in their opinion, had been fated to marry, and indeed whose marriage had been determined in the highest heavens forty days before they were born.[60] These marriage-brokers, who multiplied like locusts in those panic-stricken days, fell particularly upon the boys of poor families but learned in Torah and upon the daughters of the profiteering rich.

One day, I went to pray with my father at the House of Study. After the service, an old man, wearing a broad fox-skin hat with ear-flaps, came up to my father and said: ''Your son is of an age to be married, and I have a rich and beautiful young bride for him. Her father will support him and look after all his needs, and will also hire learned teachers for his instruction, until both children are old enough to be married. Let him, therefore, take her now and betroth her according to our law''. My father refused to listen to him. ''Why,'' the man pursued, ''do you not wish to benefit from your son? Do you not love him? He has a reputation of a brilliant scholar, and you are a poor man. If you become related by marriage to a rich man, your own circumstances will also improve.'' But my father refused, saying that his son was still too young. The man turned away from him in anger.

I had overheard the man's words and liked what he said, although I did not understand him fully. Moreover, since it is the nature of children to oppose their elders and to compete with them, I developed a strong desire to become the son-in-law of a rich man, and have a prayer-shawl of my own embroidered in gold and silver like those worn by grown-ups. So long as my father opposed it, there was nothing I could do about it, so I kept silent.

On our arrival home, my father related to my mother what the marriage-broker had said, and added that he did not approve of the proposed match since he well knew the family concerned. As for the general panic, he would pay it no heed, for he believed that the community would offer its support to students of the Torah. When I had grown up and become a famous scholar, then a wealthy and respected father-in-law could be found for me. I listened to all this without understanding any of it. The matter ended there.

It was at that time that the cat — man's companion — came to live with us. She was one year old. She used to come into my room, and I would pick her up in my arms and play with her. My mother scolded me for it. My father heard her and came into the room. I asked them why I could not play with the cat, and what sin it had committed? They said: "Can you not see that it has not been docked?" "What do you mean?" I asked. My father then explained that a cat is considered a most impure animal, and that in the opinion of the Kabbalists it is an evil spirit, a creature of the netherworld, which defiles the hands of anyone who handles it before it has been docked. For that reason, cats which live in Jewish homes have to be docked, so that they will not defile by touch. I was astounded, and asked him what was done to the cat and who did it, and how could one tell whether a cat had been docked? My father picked the cat up, after first wrapping his hands in a cloth, and showed me that the end of its tail was whole and pointed. By cutting off the tip, in a similar manner to circumcision, it would lose its impurity. I pondered upon this, for I knew that circumcision can remove uncleanness even from the heart of man.[62] As for the evil spirits and the netherworld, I understood nothing at all.

A few days later, the skies clouded over, thunder rolled loudly above us and lightning flashed about the panes of our house. I watched my father's actions closely, for he had roused my interest in spirits and demons, which are the same thing. I noticed that, as soon as the lightning flashed, he recited the benediction "Blessed art Thou, O Lord, who has made the Creation"[63] — and then went to look for the cat. He searched for it all over the house, with the intention of throwing it out. I asked him why he wanted to do this. He replied that God had created the thunder and lightning so that people would fear Him and so that He might purify the earth of all the Devil's impurities; the evil spirits and demons were destroyed by the thunder – rocks which were hurled at their heads. Since these defiling demons always attach themselves to a cat, my father feared that lightning would flash into the house to seek out the demon-possessed cat, and at the same time strike a doorpost and burn down the house, and even injure anyone it its path. It was, therefore, right to drive cats out of the house. He opened the door, picked up a stick, drove out the cat, and closed the door behind it. He then opened up a Book of the Pentateuch at the passage concerning the Ten Commandments[64] and placed it by the window, where he left it until the fury of the storm had abated. He explained: "We do this because the Ten Commandments were given on Sinai in thunder and lightning. By showing that we are fulfilling the Ten Commandments, no harm will come to us."

The thunder and lightning, nevertheless, increased in power until the foundations of the house began to shake. My father climbed on to the table and looked in the bookcase for the book of *The Angel Raziel*.[65] He opened it at the page which gave a well-tried remedy against the terrors of thunder, and placed this also by the window. I looked, without comprehending, at the fine shapes of the amulets in it and the delicate calligraphy of the miracle-workers. When, however, I began to recite aloud the names printed in Hebrew, my father angrily stopped me. He told me that there had been instances when, through ignorance, these miraculous names had been spoken aloud, and the house had immediately filled with both good and bad spirits: had it not been for the arrival of a miracle-worker, the house would have been completely destroyed from top to bottom. The man had scattered sesame seeds in front of the house, and commanded the spirits to pick up every last one of them. In this way, the house had been saved.

A little while later, I went up on to the roof to play and talk with some of my friends. The cat joined us. We talked of all the tales we had heard from our parents about cats — stories as frightening as those I had heard. We decided that it would be only right and proper for us to dock the cat. We picked it up and held it fast. One of the boys went to fetch an axe. Whilst some of us held the cat with its tail spread across a beam, he cut off half its tail with a stroke of the axe. The cat jumped out of our hands and escaped into the eaves of the roof. We, in our folly, did not appreciate the pain it suffered, and felt no pity for it. The cat remained on the roof for two days, crying incessantly in pain. We began to regret the harm we had unwittingly done to the cat — which, in fact, we loved — for we had believed that a cat's tail was not sensitive and did not feel pain any more than the tail of a horse or cow. Such is the nature of the superstitious follies which people cling to throughout their lives and even into their old age. Like children, they feel no pity, and even compassion becomes strange and unnatural to them.

Generally, a Jew has a gentle heart, for in him is fulfilled the scriptural verse, "I shall bring faintness into your heart".[66] There is the one-in-a-thousand exception who is courageous by nature and not just when under compulsion. I myself have always been among the faint-hearted, for which I was ashamed in my adult life. I could never bear to see the sufferings of any living creature. I would always turn my eyes away from the sight of pain suffered by any creature or bird which I was unable to prevent. Had the leaders of the Society for the Protection of Animals known how utterly opposed I was to any inhumanity to animals, they would decidedly have elected me their President. The incident of the cat left an indelible scar on my mind.[67]

Incidents such as this so astounded me — their memory remaining in my mind's eye from my early childhood so that I can still see them today — that I often wonder whether they happened, in fact, when I was only five or six years old. There were simple events which, as an adult, I would ignore, but which rooted themselves deeply into my childish soul and frightened me to the very core of my being. The Jewish child, I can say with all justice, is a very sensitive creature. Particularly so are those children who were born in those dark days when every Jew who dwelt in the villages and small towns trembled even at the rustle of a driven leaf — when the sound of someone speaking Russian outside their house frightened the entire family into believing that soldiers were about to shatter the peace of their home with violence and blows. If it happened that a Jew fought with a soldier and cut his cheek and drew blood, then the police would haul the whole family before the judge. Judges took pleasure in moments such as these, for they obtained a two-fold power over these innocent people. They would, firstly, take revenge for their Faith upon the accursed Jews: they would pour out all their wrath upon them and curse their God with terrible imprecations, and then sentence them to be whipped at the judge's pleasure. A double penalty would be exacted, for the man would be sentenced to the stocks and the rest of his family thrown into jail. The leaders of the Jewish community would have to appear before the judge and plead for the lives of the wretched prisoners. If the Jew who had shed the blood of a Christian soldier was a poor man, the community would be required to pay a heavy ransom for his life, in the fulfillment of the precept of redeeming captives.[68]

I myself witnessed several such incidents which always occurred when I heard Russian being spoken. At the time, I did not know one word of a foreign tongue. I could, however, distinguish between Russian and Polish, for the sound of the latter is as smooth as oil whereas the former sounds like stones rolling about upon the seashore. When a lewd curse was vented in Russian, I realised that harsh and rough words were being hurled upon the heads of the Jews. Whenever I saw the fear of my parents and the panic of our neighbours during those awful days — which were as wretched as those desolate days in the past whose accounts have been left to us by our ancestors — I realised that not all the sinews of their soul and body could ever mould them into being as tough as brass or ever cause giants to spring from their seed. Their only heritage was a meek disposition towards all things spiritual. They were like the fig which ripens before the summer, maturing before its time.

The mind of the Jewish child is deeply sensitive and his heart easily moved. His soul is amazingly gentle — as can be seen from the numerous distinguished scholars who abounded in Poland and who, in their youth, revealed wonderful powers of the intellect but who, in later life, fell silent and became barren. They blossomed before their time; their blooms flowered and faded, without bearing fruit. They lived prematurely. I was one of those sensitive children.

Even basic natural feelings were aroused prematurely. I can remember as though it were today how young boys of my own age, my father's pupils, used to play together outside our house, in the open space on the hill. On one fine summer's day, we played a game in which one of us was the teacher and the rest were his pupils. A pupil who made a mistake would be whipped by the teacher, although without actually touching his body and causing him pain. Naturally, as the son of our teacher, I was chosen to be the teacher. One of my pupils made a mistake. Stocks were put in front of him. He agreed to lie face down. Thin, pliable whips were then handed to me. I arranged his clothes in order to uncover his buttocks, and stood over him. When I beheld the nakedness of his buttocks, a strong desire came over me, accompanied by a pleasure and satisfaction beyond my understanding. I was utterly bewildered by my elation and my desire to look upon his nakedness. My lust rose, though I did not understand what was happening. Nevertheless, despite my confusion, I gained a deep pleasure from the emotion. After that, I wanted to catch other boys in a mistake, so that I might experience that pleasure again. I did, in fact, repeat the incident two or three times until, accidentally, the tip of my whip touched a boy's flesh, whereupon he refused to lie down in front of me any more.

A friend of his went and told my father that I was beating the boys with a whip. My father called for me and scolded me for being so wicked. My friends, however, came and testified that I had not caused any actual harm and that, in fact, it had all been no more than a game. My father ordered me never to do this again. My own personal feeling was one of shame, for deep in my heart I knew that the desire I had felt was despicable, even though it was beyond my ability to understand it. Thenceforth, I drove it out of my mind. I was not to realise the import of that strange incident until much later, when those good days — the days of my innocence — had come to an end.

During my eighth year, my father began to teach me to read from his own books — from the *Sefer Ha-Yashar,* [69] on the Torah; the *She'erit Yisra'el* [70], on the distinguished Jewish leaders and their sufferings during the Middle Ages; the book of *Yosippon ben Gorion* [71]; the *Kav Ha-Hasher,* [72] in Yiddish; the *Simḥat Ha-Nefesh,* [73] which was entirely in Yiddish and contained many wonderful stories and parables. During those long winter evenings, I would read aloud to him from one of his books whilst he continued with his work of making brass and iron hooks. So I learned to read Hebrew fluently. When my father received a visit from friends who did not understand Hebrew, he would ask me to relate the story in Yiddish so that they too could hear it. I would read it silently to myself at first, and then relate it to them in Yiddish. I felt greatly flattered by their praises. One of the books I read to them was named *Marganita,* [74] which was printed in Hebrew with a Yiddish translation. Although small in size, it was great in value, for it contained a description of man's condition from his birth to his death and even after his burial. *Marganita* is the name of the Angel of Death, who has eyes all over his body and holds a drawn sword in his hand. Three demons wait upon him. The angel known as Duma [75] visits the deceased's grave, and demands of him: "Wicked man, recite your verses". There were, in addition, other books similar to this which affected my audience deeply. It seemed to me that my readings created a profound impression upon the old men who gathered in the evenings to listen to me expounding my learning. I therefore copied the little *Marganita* book on paper and took it to the House of Prayer. When the men assembled there saw the book, they took it from me, read it aloud and said: "See what the son of Aaron has written!" I was overjoyed.

Now the landlord of the house we lived in was a *melammed* who had pupils older than myself. One of them was the son of a wealthy timber merchant who lived in Prussia for half the year, returning home only for the festivals. Once, he brought his son a gift, one of the old type of 'onion' watches. [76] The boy brought this watch to the *heder*. I heard that the boy had brought something new which no one had ever seen before, so I tried my utmost to contact him and persuade him to show me the new wonder. Finally, I succeeded in getting him out of the room and into the corridor. Other boys gathered round to have a look. We were astonished that something so small and precious could make such a continuous sound when held against one's ear. I, however, was not satisfied merely with looking and listening. I urged the boy to open the case for me, and I looked inside, letting my eyes flit over the wheels to discover the cause of their perpetual movement. I saw that the wire connected to one of the wheels was constantly pulling it round. The circumference of this wheel was cut into numerous teeth which fitted into the teeth of another and smaller wheel, causing it also to rotate. So it went, from one wheel to the next, until the last wheel came up against the detainer, and thereby caused the first wheel to slow down for an entire day. I was astonished at man's ingenuity.

That evening, I took some kindling-sticks and turned them upon a lathe, which I had made for fashioning wooden rattles for the festival of *Purim*.[77] I cut a few small discs, fitted a peg through their centre, and inserted wooden teeth into holes in their circumference. I fixed them together so that the large wheel held a smaller wheel by its teeth, and this in turn a still smaller wheel, and so on. When I turned the first one with my hand, the second one revolved more quickly, and the third even more quickly. In the end, all the pegs fell apart and flew off in all directions. I was not discouraged but returned to my work afresh. When my father saw how diligently and zealously I pursued this work, he became apprehensive lest I neglect my Torah studies, and grew angry with me. He compelled me to give him the machine and broke it into pieces which he then threw into the fire.[78]

At that time, the wealthiest man of the town was an old and respected person known as Reb Joseph of the Wall: he owned the only house in the town which had a wall. It was a fine house, having three storeys built on a princely scale and standing in a spacious clearing on the plain by the banks of the Nieman. At that time, the lord of the town was a Graf Tishkewitz. Every Sabbath, this nobleman would ride in his carriage to the house of Joseph of the Wall to dine with him and partake of his special Sabbath dish (*Kugel*),[79] for that good lord had found his Sabbath over-soul[80] in Jewish food. Reb Joseph was in the habit of holding a communal assembly in his house every Sabbath to recite the day's three services and read from his own Scroll of the Law. My father was among the worshippers invited there, so he took me with him. There were large paintings on the walls of distinguished men portrayed greeting each other. I had never seen anything like this before, and was amazed. It was surprising to see how an artist could draw, in black ink on white paper, the full figure of a man so that he was immediately recognisable to the onlooker. I gazed at them, completely absorbed and utterly astonished. The old man who owned the house appreciated my feelings, and came up behind me and patted the locks of my hair. "What do you think?" he asked. "Could you paint like this?" I fled from him in embarrassment, and hid myself. The following day, I took a sheet of paper and drew pictures like those I had seen. Later, people came and bought them from me, at my price, to decorate their rooms.

My ninth and tenth years passed like a dream, leaving scarcely a memory. I can remember my father had to change my teachers several times during a period of six months. I studied with them in confined rooms.

One of those teachers, a man from Keidan, was definitely leprous and, in Temple times, would have been put into isolation by the Priest. This afflicted human being had charge of ten young children who were confined with him from morning until evening. In one corner of the room stood a woman, baking: from her I learnt the art of baking in all its details, since our table was close to her oven. The leprous *melammed* always kept a cup of cold water on the table in front of him, and he dipped his hands constantly into the cup during his teaching in order to cool them. Whenever he lost his temper with a pupil, he would strike him across the cheek with a wet hand, almost bringing the boy to the verge of nausea. The only relaxation we had was to leave the house occasionally to relieve ourselves. Another part of the house was rented by some butchers who sold their meat there, whilst at the rear of the house was a large shed where they slaughtered and skinned the animals. There was also a broad vegetable patch where we used to spend some of our time, taking a breath of fresh air and enjoying the sunlight for a few moments. A blacksmith, working with hand-bellows, occupied the garden; he was married to the landlord's sister, and had two sons.

Now this blacksmith had turned aside from the path of God, whereas his brother-in-law, the landlord, was a Hasid. Not only did the blacksmith refuse to join their congregation, but very often he did not attend the services in the House of Study. His brother-in-law hated him; his wife also had no love for him. When they began openly to spurn him, he degenerated from bad to worse, and committed greater sins than before. Hated by the orthodox, he sought friendship with his gentile neighbours, often drinking himself into a stupor with them. His brother-in-law wanted to throw him out, and even urged his sister to divorce the man. She refused. This smith became the constant subject of the town's gossip. On his part, he refused to divorce his wife at any price.

One Sabbath, when the town lay still and quiet in the silence that follows the midday rest, the leaders assembled with the community in the House of Prayer, whilst the Hasidim were reading in their own room. The men began to whisper to each other. The Beadle of the congregation was a man called Joseph, a very tall man, head and shoulders taller than anyone else: he was the custodian of the keys of all the community's affairs. The man was unable to sign his name in any language, not even in Hebrew; his sole tongue was his mother-tongue, Yiddish, although he knew enough to stammer incomprehensibly in Polish and Russian. This erudite man, this accomplished musician (a *Bassist*),[81] saw scores of Cantors come and go during his forty years in the town, and he assisted all of them with his voice during festivals and religious occasions. Wherever there was trouble or strife, he was the first to come and the last to go. Although he was able to recite the *Shema*[82] prayer, he did not understand a word of it. He mixed among the students in the yeshiva, fawned upon the mighty and lorded himself over the common people. Not a man in the community could make a move without him. He collected the poll-tax;[83] he kidnapped the children for military service;[84] he issued the travel documents;[85] he spoke with government officials; he went to the capital on the community's business; he quartered the soldiers in our homes and rooms during their stay in the town.[86]

He lived in one half of the large House of Study, a spacious building which stood like a fortress on the mountain. It was divided into quarters, one half being the House of Prayer for the people, and the other half serving as living accommodation for the Rabbi and the Beadle. Below this house, many other houses stretched along the length of the street. The floor of the house rested on a peak that jutted out of the mountain. On this peak were the two Houses of Prayer — that of the Mitnaggedim[87] on the right, and, on its own, some twenty *fut*[87a] away on the left, the House of Prayer of the Hasidim. From the top of the mountain, a spring of water flowed, summer and winter, between these two houses. On the north side, the mountain reared upwards from the base of the houses. Outside the entrance of the house, were half a dozen steps sloping down to the houses in the street. The courtyard of the house had to be widened every year, for all the filth was swept into it and left there. There were slopes on the east and west, by which the worshippers ascended and descended. In a severe winter, the spring at the top of the mountain froze, and the stream which wound its way between the Houses of Prayer and down the slopes on the left and right, became covered in snow. When the wind grew warmer and began to melt this covering, it became a skating area. There were times when, on a freezing cold morning, the townsfolk had assembled in the House of Prayer on a Sabbath and, before they had concluded their service, the overhead sun had warmed the wind and turned the hill into crystal-like glass. We had no way of dealing with this, for who would raise a pick or axe against the ice on the holy day? So the congregation had to split up. The youths flew off, racing down to the bottom of the hill; the men slid down on their backsides, using their hands and feet; the old men lay down and dragged themselves along. The women were the last to go, seven women holding on to one man[87b] and falling and stumbling seven times over before reaching the bottom. There were times when the women refused to go to the House of Prayer in the morning if they saw a south wind blowing, fearing the return home. On the other hand, the summertime was very pleasant: the hill overlooked the town with stretches of verdant grass and pretty wild flowers, whilst a gentle warmth always dwelt there.

I remember one Sabbath day in summer. People were talking amongst themselves, though I did not know what it was about. They kept coming and going to the house of Joseph, the tall Beadle, and from there to the House of Study, whispering asides to each other. In the evening, after the Sabbath was over, the town was in a turmoil. Groups of people gathered outside the Beadle's house, then marched in a body to another house from which they dragged their victim, the blacksmith, in chains. The wretched mob skipped after them. I heard people say that the blacksmith had stolen the gold and silver ornaments of the Scroll of the Law from the Holy Ark — the pointers and breastplates — and hidden them amongst his own possessions. Now the thief had been found together with his stolen goods. People came to my father's room, one after another. One of them related that the blacksmith had denied committing the desecration and refused to admit anything; he had cursed the witnesses and called them schemers of evil. However, Joseph the Beadle, who knew the law well, took hold of him and, together with the witnesses and other honest men, went to the blacksmith's house where they made a search and found all the missing sacred vessels amongst his belongings. Surely the man Joseph had worked wonders! My father, nevertheless, realised from the words of the simpleton who told him this tale, that the blacksmith had been unjustly accused. My father quietly demonstrated to him that the silver vessels had in fact not been lost, nor had they been stolen by the blacksmith, who had never before stolen anything at all. However, because the man was not observant in religious matters or God-fearing, but had even assimilated with the gentiles, therefore the leaders of the community had decided to hand him over to the authorities for military service as a ransom for the community.[88] They had demanded that he divorce his wife, but he had refused, because he had also realised what they had planned against him. So the leaders had decided to accuse him of desecration and theft, which bear the same punishment as murder,[89] and thereby force him to submit to their demands. They promised him that, if he divorced his wife, her brother would pay the full bail for his release from police custody, and he could then flee to wherever he wished. In fact, once he had divorced his wife, they had no intention of fulfilling their promise to redeem him, but would hand him over for military service as a ransom for the community.

The simpleton then said: "The silverware was found in his possession, and the vessels were shown to all the people gathered there, and I myself saw with my own eyes how Joseph the Beadle carried out an extensive search among the blacksmith's belongings and finally found the pointers and breatplates. He even held his hands aloft to show us all that the stolen vessels had been found. He also struck the blacksmith on the face two or three times." Then one of the men sitting with us said: "Cover your lips with your hand lest our words be heard outside. You are a simple man and do not understand. Nevertheless do not reveal anything to the gentiles which can be held against our community." Then he whispered into his ear that Joseph the Beadle had taken the holy vessels with him, concealing them in his sleeves, and had taken them out later. The blacksmith himself had claimed bitterly and loudly that it was the Beadle who had taken the vessels and brought them with him — but who would pay attention to him? I learned later, from the gossip-mongers, that the blacksmith had neither confessed to the theft nor divorced his wife, and that he had been released from the community's sentence after three days of suffering and severe beatings. His wife had wept and pleaded with the leaders of the community to send him away to wherever he wished to go. The blacksmith left the town and crossed the river Nieman to the Polish side of the border, where he settled in a village in which he found work. A year later, he sent for his wife and two sons. They lived there together for some six months, after which his wife suddenly returned to her brother's home, alone and without belongings, for her husband had converted to the Catholic faith and even wanted to bring their sons into it. Her family, together with the townspeople, then began to seek ways of restoring her sons to her and of obtaining a divorce for her. It took two years before they succeeded in obtaining a divorce for her and the return of one son, who was seven years old and spoke half in Yiddish and half in Lithuanian. Such is the folly of ignorance and religious fanaticism wherever it may dwell. In their haste to reform, they inflict great harm: they destroy, instead of building as they had intended.

At the time that I heard of the affair of the blacksmith and the theft of the sacred vessels of which he had been slandered, I was very frightened. I knew how grievous was the sin which lay upon any thief who stole sacred vessels belonging to the dominant religion of even the most humble of nations. Even the laws of the Jewish faith, which cannot be compared to the faith of this land, prescribe the same penalty for the theft of holy vessels as for murder. I remembered the sin I myself had committed two years earlier when, in my innocence, I had committed a sacrilegious crime, although fortunately the matter was never discovered. Had it become known, the people of that community would never have believed that I had done it entirely in ignorance and without willful intent. From my birth, it has always been foreign to my nature to take anything that did not belong to me. My parents taught me to be honest and upright, keeping far from evil. The commandments, 'Thou shalt not covet' and 'Thou shalt not steal', were deeply rooted in my heart, so that never in my life had I taken anything that was not mine. My sin was not discovered at the time, but it is inscribed in heaven for eternity, and I shall never be forgiven. The incident occurred when I was about seven. It was the custom for all the Jewish boys and girls to get together on sabbaths and festivals during the time of the afternoon rest, when we young people were not sleepy and were free of our teachers' whips. We assembled in the House of Study, for there was no other house so spacious, with open doors and windows, and with no one to order us about. We played there all day long. There were lamps of polished brass hanging from the ceiling. Each candelabrum held a number of stems in tiers above each other, with cups at their corners for holding the candles. Underneath the cups were small brass dishes for catching the wax so that it would not drip on to the heads of the worshippers. These cups and dishes were fixed into the holes in each stem but, over a period of time, had become loose. The students, during the long winter evenings, used to remove them and place them on the table near their books, for not every one could afford a candle of his own. After finishing their studies, they would extinguish the candles and return the cups to the stems. Some students would forget, and leave them on the table, from which they sometimes fell to the floor and rolled away into the darkness, never to be found again. Thus, many of the candelabra lost their cups and dishes, although no one ever noticed it since there were always sufficient left to light the House of Prayer. We children played with the cups and dishes which we found lying in the corners among the dirt. Sometimes, when we were short of dishes for our games, the taller boys would stand on the table and remove some of them for us. One day, one of my friends said to me: "No one cares about the cups and dishes because there are so many of them, whilst candles are put in only a few of them. Others lie about in the dirt and outside the house. There is a son of a German Jew living in town; he is fifteen years old, and will pay six groschen for a dish and five for a cup. He has already bought some from me and the other boys. It is a good price. Why don't you join us in the business?" I knew that, even were this disreputable act to become known, we should not be punished for it, however much we might be scolded, so I agreed and took about four dishes. The boys sent for the German who waited outside until I took my goods to him. I have no further recollection of this affair, nor do I remember why it did not continue longer — whether it was that the German became afraid or whether I came to realise that I was doing wrong. Whatever the reason, the business stopped, and I think that the other boys also stopped. In the course of time, my feeling of having committed a sin or crime faded away. However, when I heard of the affair of the blacksmith, I realised what was involved and I thanked God that my own affair had not been discovered. Nowadays, when boys who are as I was at that time, become involved in stealing or robbing, I wonder how people can condemn them as thieves, for it must have been obvious from the beginning that they were not responsible for their actions. I know that they have committed no more than an act of error, that there is no evil in them — as witness myself.

In my eleventh year, the three most outstanding students were brought together, namely: Mordecai the son of Joseph the Beadle, about ten years old; myself; and Dober the son of Rabbi Ḥayyim, also about ten — he later became the Head of the Ecclesiastical Court at Sibilen, whilst his son is the present Rabbi of Plonghien. We met in the room of Joseph the Beadle, which was at the far end of the House of Study alongside the Rabbi's quarters. A teacher, Isaac the Ḥasid, was hired for us, although we were under the supervision of the Rabbi. Every Sabbath we went to the Rabbi to recite the portion of the Talmud which we had studied that week. The Rabbi used to declare that the son of the beadle was the cleverest, that I was second, and his own son the third.

Our Ḥasid *melammed* was one of those highly accomplished Poles who could write beautifully in any language without being able to read a word. He wrote accurately in square letters of the Vilna print. He drew fine pen portraits of the great leaders in vermilion. He painted *Mizraḥim*[89a] in many colours, with flowers and roses and animals and birds: Leviathan encircling the globe of the world, its tails between its teeth, and in the middle a ship in full sail and a two-headed eagle holding a citron in one talon and a *Lulav*[90] in the other. He would take the smallest of coins, draw a circle round it on paper, and write inside it the whole of the Psalm, "A song of degrees: I shall lift up mine eyes".[91] In addition to all these, he used to make tooth-picks and ear-cleaners out of dried bone, as well as etching pens doubled or three-fold in the manner of knives. For tools, he used a small knife, a hatchet to split the bones, and a file. With these, he carried out his exceptionally beautiful work in the free hours of the day, besides the mornings and evenings. Despite all his labours, his teaching and his craftsmanship, he was desperately poor: his wife, his two young sons, and his little daughter, were all dressed in torn rags and went barefoot. Poverty reigned in their home. Yet this accomplished scholar paid no heed to their poverty, nor was he ever downhearted even when there was no food in the house all day. He always went about happy, proclaiming the glory of the heavenly worlds and spheres, his pipe in his mouth. If, however, he became exceptionally hungry, or when his wife poured torrents of imprecations upon his head — for she never appreciated the noble spirit of her lazy husband — he would take a portrait of a famous person, and some toothpicks and ear-cleaners he had made, and go to one of his Ḥasidic friends in the town who would find 20 kopeks for him by some miraculous means to buy food for his foolish wife. I learned a great deal from this teacher, although he did conceal a lot from me. I kept looking around for every item of craftsmanship; I became like a monkey that imitates men's ways. When Jews change their habits with the changing seasons of the year, especially those who live in the country towns and villages and attend to God's work — on Sabbath eve they bake; on Passover, they prepare strong drink (mead) and special clock-wheels for piercing the unleavened bread; on the 33rd day of the Omer[92] they make bows and arrows for their children; on the Feast of Weeks, they make flutes from fresh reeds; in the month of *Av*,[93] wooden swords and spears; on the Feast of Tabernacles, they build huts and collect palm branches and myrtles; for *Ḥanukkah*,[94] they bake cakes and melt tin and lead into rings with letters etched in them in commemoration of the miracle that occurred there; on *Purim*, they make Haman-rattles[95] with hand-saws and planes — then little monkeys like myself work night and day, with our parents' approval, helping them with their tasks. How bitter it is for a Jewish boy when those good days are over, especially when he takes up his precious tools and tries to improve his handiwork, only to hear his father angrily stop him: "Desist, my son, for the holy days are gone. You are not going to become a craftsman; the time for studying has arrived". Since I feared to disobey him, and could not work in the daytime, I worked at night — and in the winter by the light of wooden torches and in summer at twilight. I made a scribe's pen like the one used by my Ḥasid teacher, and practised writing in square letters, just as in print.

We three students made a life-long pact of friendship. We used to go out together on the Sabbaths and festivals for a walk through the fields. Whenever a quarrel arose between us, we did not harbour the grudge within ourselves but discussed it openly, and thereby maintained our pact of friendship. One of the games we played was a competition in which one of us said a Hebrew word of two letters and the next boy had to give another Hebrew word of two letters beginning with the last letter of the previous word. Thus, if the first word was 'mah', the next word would be 'hem' followed by 'mas' and then 'sam', 'mi, 'yam' and so on. The idea was to win by forcing the others to use the same letter so often that one of them would finally run out of words. The one who lost would be punished with one or two blows or made to do a job of work. The game used to occupy us for as much as an hour. Sometimes, when one of us was lost for an answer, he was allowed to think about it and even to look up words in a book, until he finally gave in and lost. We always tried to keep to the same letter, for example: 'har', 're'a', 'er', 'red', 'dar', 'raf', 'par', 'rats', 'tsar', 'ram', 'mar'. Particularly we tried to catch each other out with the letter *vav*[96] for there are few words beginning with this letter. The Rabbi taught his son this game so that he could play it with us.

This came to an end when the Rabbi withdrew his son in order to teach him himself, and my father sent me to a Hasid who taught in the house of the Ḥasidim under the supervision of the renowned Ḥasid Rebbe Moshe ben David, who had come to the town during the Polish revolt of 1831, according to the Christian calendar. There was a boy there, the same age as myself, who was the brother of the son-in-law of this Ḥasid Moshe: his father was the Head of the Ecclesiastical Court in Koenigsberg, Prussia. The boy's name was Shmaryahu, and his brother's Naḥman Goldberg, who was the son-in-law of the Ḥasid Moshe. Their father, desiring to bring up his sons in accordance with the Torah and commandments, as was the custom among Polish Jews so that they should not assimilate among the gentiles, the German Jews, married his elder son, Naḥman, to the daughter of Moshe the Ḥasid, and put his younger son Shmaryahu into the hands of his in-law Moshe to learn Torah and commandments. To our astonishment, although we could study Gemara with Commentaries, yet Shmaryahu was not able to read Hebrew correctly, but had to split up each word into syllables and read them slowly just like a beginner. His teacher would read the Mishna and Gemara for him, and he would recite it back by heart. Despite this, his knowledge of Gemara and the Commentaries excelled ours.

I was quite the opposite. When I arrived at the House of Study of the Ḥasidim where we were studying, I saw the yeshiva students making wagers with each other to see who could write Hebrew words correctly, although none of them could. I stood beside their table and pointed out their mistakes to them. They tested me also with Aramaic and Chaldean words, which I had not seen for a long time, but I answered correctly. They asked me to spell the word 'Artaḥshasta',[97] and I did. They were amazed, but I was more astonished than they, for I began to feel new talents which I never knew I possessed. From that time, I began to write down Hebrew and Aramaic words from sentences I remembered, without using new words, but copied them on paper and showed it to them in order to explain the etymology which had so surprised them. They continued to test me further. However, I took no great interest in the casuistries of the Talmud or in trying to find difficult problems and solutions. Therefore, when students and teachers met together in my father's house and began to test me with questions and problems, I answered no better than the dullest pupil. I remember one incident clearly. A teacher asked me: "You know that the ninth of *Av* is a fast day in commemoration of the destruction of the Temple, and therefore on that day the curtain is removed from the Holy Ark in the synagogue. Yet, in Temple times, the curtain was the covering over the Holy of Holies, which could be approached by no one during the whole year except for the High Priest on the Day of Atonement. The ninth of *Av* is not the Day of Atonement — so how could any man remove the curtain from it?" I attempted to fashion a pole which a man could hold whilst standing in the courtyard, so that by stretching it out he could remove the curtain from the Holy of Holies. It never occurred to me that my questioner was asking me a trick question, for so long as the Temple was in existence, there was neither the destruction nor the fast day of ninth of *Av*. They asked similar simple questions which, despite all my efforts, I failed to answer. Other boys, who could neither read nor understand, would put me to shame and mock me, saying: "How can your ears not hear your words, or your mind not understand?"

My father came to realise that he would be disappointed in his hope of having his son become a distinguished scholar — an ambition common to all Jewish parents in Poland — and since he found it very difficult to continue to pay my teacher eight roubles per half year plus meals for a month, therefore, when I was 12 years old, he sent me (though I do not know what reason impelled him to do so) to a primary teacher who lived in a filthy, noisome room beyond anything I had ever encountered before. He ordered me to go to his room for several hours each day to learn from this *melammed*, who was unworthy of the name of human being, alongside younger children no more than five or eight years old. The *melammed* taught no more than the Mishna. After the *melammed* had finished with the boys and girls, he would attempt to teach me Mishna, which he himself did not know, nor did he even know whether I knew it. So I was compelled to go there every day and wait until noon when all the boys and girls left, and then doze with him over the Mishna for an hour. It was the same in the evenings. I began to loathe my life. One day, when I was waiting in the *melammed's* room for the children to leave at noon, I found to my great delight a *Kol Bo*[98] Prayer Book printed in Zolkawa on quarto paper. Looking through it, I came across a remedy for the evil eye. Looking further, I came across something new which I had never seen before — a prayer for *Yom Kippur Katan*.[99] I was astonished that this minor fast had earned such reverence that it had been given the name of the most solemn day of all. I read the prayer and was attracted by it: "Lord of the universe, we can neither speak nor raise our heads . . ."[100] I determined to learn it by heart, and to add it to the *Shemone Esreh* prayer, before the benediction *Retseh*.[101] I recited it devoutly three times daily, happy with my discovery. I sought for other similar prayers, and learned them also by heart. One day my father questioned me as to how I felt about the *ḥeder* and the *melammed*. I poured out my full abhorrence of it all. I told him that, if he insisted that I continue to attend this teacher, who was unable to explain even one Mishna himself, my life would become utterly unbearable. My father put an end to that by scolding me for not wanting to learn when I had been with learned teachers, and for that reason I was now suffering. He pointed out that Dov, the Rabbi's son, who had not been as clever as I, was now acclaimed as a future distinguished scholar. In truth, the Rabbi had taken over his tuition and taught him night and day, and even slept in the same bed with him, showing him pictures from which he could learn all manner of wisdom, and sharpening his intellect with all kinds of questions and problems; he taught him arithmetic and chess, and indeed tried to give his son all he knew himself. By the end of the year, the boy went around like a sleep-walker. People even began to say that he was going insane, for whenever he was free from his father, he would walk about the House of Study, waving his arms in the air like a madman and talking to himself. Later, he suffered a hernia and had to wear, for a long time, a hernia belt which his father made for him.

After this, my father sent me to study in the House of Study by myself. When I was there outside the normal service times, I did not know what to do with myself, and simply looked through the books to find something that might be of interest. Then a young man came up to me, and said: "Look, I will teach you Gemara every day, but you, on your part, must read the portion I prescribe for you, study it carefully, ask me or any other teachers any problems you may have, and then I shall listen to you and teach you". I, however, was not used to this, having been taught only by rote, simply repeating what my *melammedim* had read, so I sat over the Gemara every day without knowing what to do. Towards the end of the day, the man came up to me, and said: "Recite". But I was waiting for him to tell me it first, so that I could repeat it after him. The man grew angry with me and wanted to strike me. He was a young man of my town, whom I knew well, and also knew his parents, so I swore at him and told him I would not allow anyone like him to beat me, and that only a teacher appointed by my father could do that. He answered me angrily that he was my teacher and had been appointed by my father. — "You are lying about my father, since he told me nothing about you", I said. He tried to hit me, but I attacked him with all my fury, biting him with my teeth and even grabbing hold of his private parts, until he let me go. The following day, he told my father all that had happened, although I had said nothing to my father, thinking the man was merely seeking a pretext against me. My father scolded me severely, and told me that, from that time on, I was to be a yeshiva student and would be taught by any learned person who felt like doing me the favour, and that I must listen to him respectfully. From that day, a period of wretched misery began for me, for I was forced to continue studying the Babylonian Talmud for the next seven years. Shortly after this incident, my father found a young man of our town, the son of a wealthy family, who was a pupil of the Rabbi and studied in the House of Study. He volunteered to teach me daily, in the early evenings between the afternoon and evening services. He would show me a portion of the Gemara which I was to learn for the next day. He was a very cruel person, who delighted in beating me ferociously, hitting me about my head and on my cheeks and pulling my hair unmercifully. I was thoroughly scared of him. I tried to study every day, from morning till evening, my fear compelling me to approach the other students with any problems I found, until I knew the Gemara portion by heart. Despite this, the man could not refrain from indulging his pleasure in beating me with all his might on every pretext. This wretched period continued throughout the summer. I knew I could not relate all this to my father for, however much he might love his only son, he would always listen to any boy who came to him complaining,"Your son, Chaim, hit me — or did this and that to me". My father would not investigate the truth of the matter but would beat and scold me. Even if I were to say to him: "If only you would try to ascertain the truth, you would find that the opposite is true, that he in fact hit me and did this and that to me. Instead, this criminal knows that you will always blame me, and because he wants to inflict further suffering upon me, he comes to you with his lies, so that you will also punish me." That, in truth, is what the boys did, threatening to tell lies about me to my father if I did not do what they wanted. However, after this had happened a number of times, I did tell my father about them and their wickedness. He replied: "In that case, they are a band of evil people; do not walk with them, my son, but turn aside from them and go not in their ways. Stay here at home, and when we go to the synagogue you will stand beside me, and they will not harm you, for I know you are innocent of wrong." After such words, how could I tell him of the cruelty of my voluntary teacher who was teaching me without payment, and of how I was studying simply out of terror of him, so that my evenings were filled with panic and fright? How could I tell my father that the man had no mercy on me, and beat me every evening without cause? I did try once to tell my mother and pour out my sorrow to her: "If only father would come and stand by the door, he will see and know the truth". My father then went to see the young man to ask him to be more merciful with me. I was not aware of this, but I noticed that the man treated me less harshly for the next three days, and then returned to his former torments. I became desperate and told my mother that, if my father insisted on my continuing to study with this murderer, I would put an end to my life. My father then decided to find another teacher for me, one Barukh the Ḥasid: he had been the first to introduce Ḥasidism to our town. He had a small house, with a small plot of ground which provided him with sufficient food for his sustenance. He consented to teach me a few hours each evening — and thus I was delivered out of the hand of my oppressor. Barukh was very pleased with me, for I learned and understood even the most difficult part once he had explained it to me; I was an attentive pupil, and he taught me as a friend. I studied with him every day for a whole year.

My oppressor and tormentor was called Jacob the son of Tsevi. This Tsevi, his father, was the only one in our town, at that time, who did business in the city of Leipzig, and was therefore called the 'Leipzig merchant'. In those days there was neither railway[102] nor telegraph,[103] so one journey each year to Leipzig at that time was like travelling to America today. He dealt in textile yarns. In his later years, he set up business in his own home, and also set aside certain periods of the day for studying Torah. He had always been a Torah Reader in the synagogue, having a very pleasant voice and being perfectly versed in all the notes. He spoke very politely, and was a respected old man. I learnt from him two things which have remained in my memory concerning the business of fine yarn and how to differentiate between similar yarns differing in price. By placing a microscope over the yarn, the number of threads observed between the sides of the round tube through the glass could be counted; the fabric showing the greatest number of threads across the diameter of the tube was the most expensive.

Tsevi related this story: "It was the eve of the Feast of Weeks.[104] We were sitting together on the balcony of the house of a Leipzig merchant, a Jew, with a samovar of hot water in front of us. There was with us also another Jewish businessman from the city of N. Now this Leipzig merchant, although completely 'Germanised' had been taught a great deal of Torah in his early youth by his father, and had not forgotten any of it. Whilst sitting there, the mood came upon him to speak of religious matters. He said to the Polish businessman from the city of N.: 'Tomorrow is the Feast of Weeks, and the Cantor will sing the liturgical hymn *Fashioned from Clay*.[105] Now, it seems to me that this hymn has reference to a Polish businessman. You are *fashioned from clay,* my ignoble Polish Jewish merchant.*What avails* — what benefit is all your business in Leipzig to you? *Whatever one has is not one's own*: the money you have brought with you to Leipzig does not belong to you for you have borrowed it on interest. *Why want that which does not belong to you*? Why do you want the goods which you seek to buy here without money? Neither borrow from there, nor buy from here, and it shall be well with you. *Take heed and understand, and rejoice, and be content with your lot and with what you have at home.'* Swiftly, before he had even finished speaking, the old merchant answered him: 'Not so. The hymn *Fashioned from Clay* refers to a German merchant. This is how. You, ignoble German, are *fashioned from clay*. *What avails* — what benefit is your way in life to you? *Whatever one has is not one's own:* even your wife is not yours, for if she should become adulterous, someone else will seduce her. *Why want that which does not belong to you?* Why should you want this adulteress? *Take heed and understand, and rejoice, and be content with your lot*, and take care that your wife belongs to you alone'. There was loud laughter from everyone at this, even the host laughing, albeit in anger, for he had to admit: 'You win.' "

Passover came round, and many of us young people got together at the House of Study to play there in the afternoon. None of the people who lived in the House was there, except for one young man from the town who also lived in the House of

Study. He was the son of a well-regarded but very poor widow, of a good family. He was called Zalman, and was about seventeen years old. He was studying Gemara. The Rabbi's son, Dober, was also with us. Whilst we were playing, the Rabbi's son forgot it was a festival day, and removed a slender bristle from the broom used for sweeping the floor, and broke it into two. We reminded him that he had committed a sin by transgressing the commandment, 'Thou shalt do no manner of work'.[106] The boy became extremely upset. We told him how great would be his punishment for this crime in the next world, and that flogging was the penalty for transgressing any prohibitive commandment. In the next world, he would receive thirty-nine strokes of a fiery lash.[107] The boy, in the innocence of his belief, begged us to flog him, here in this world, with thirty-nine strokes of a cane taken from the broom, so that he might be cleansed of his sin. We agreed to help make atonement for his sin, by striking him lightly thirty-nine times on his bare buttocks. He lay down on a long bench, and counted each stroke until the twelfth, when he could bear no more. He got up from the bench, saying he could bear the pain no longer. We pointed out that he was adding crime to sin by refusing his punishment, and that if he could not bear it now, when he was young, how would he suffer it in heaven where he would be beaten with rods of iron and fire? We asked the opinion of Zalman, who was older than the rest of us, and he agreed with us and said that now the boy's crime was indeed grievous, for he had turned against his 'good inclination' which had prompted him to accept his punishment in this world, and was following his 'evil inclination' instead. The boy wept bitterly, and begged us to bind him hand and foot to the bench with the handcuffs which were in the House of Study, and to take no heed of his cries until he had received the full 39 strokes; the first strokes which had already been given to him would not count. We did as he asked. We took two handcuffs: with one of them, we bound his hands behind his head, and with the other fastened his feet to the bench. We raised the whip and began to flay his flesh. By the twenty-fifth stroke he was screaming so loudly that his cries must have reached his father's house. However, everyone was enjoying the mid-day sleep of the holy-day, and heard nothing. We were afraid we might awaken the Rabbi, so we stopped beating the boy who was still lying tenderly along the bench, his buttocks bare. He began to plead with us to continue his penance lest it be counted invalid. Zalman mocked him with all the scorn he could muster. Then we beat him another five times, but again he screamed out loudly. We hastened to release his hands and feet, and cursed and swore at him for having twice made fools of us, and told him that his atonement was invalid. He went away dejected and fuming. We ourselves left the house to go for a walk in the fields.

On the morrow, we were told by the son of the Beadle, who also lived in the house, as did the Rabbi, that the boy had fallen ill and the Rabbi had had to send for alcohol to tend his wounds. The boy was seriously ill, and the Rabbi, unaware of the cause of his illness, permitted him to eat leavened foods on the Passover.[108] Later, when questioned about his illness, he told how his friends had whipped him, although with his consent. His father, unable to understand what had happened, refused to believe him, thinking the boy was still delirious. We became afraid lest the boy tell the whole truth of the matter, and we ourselves be punished, in our turn. We decided that one of us should go to the Rabbi and say that we had heard that our dear friend had fallen ill and we three wished to visit him. The Rabbi was delighted, hoping that our visit would relieve his son of his illness to some extent, as he would be glad to see us. He led us into the room and went out, closing the door behind him. As soon as we were alone, we reminded him of the pact of friendship we had all made together, sealed with our handclasp, for ever. Furthermore, we were not to blame and had committed no crime, since he himself had pleaded with us to do it. The boy answered: "I did begin to tell my father everything that happened, so how can I now lie to him?" We advised him to alter his words by putting the blame on Zalman for urging him to do penance by flogging. We then renewed our pact, each one holding the 'fringes of his garments'[109] in holy witness that it would never be broken. We left the room, happy and delighted. When we went to the House of Prayer for the afternoon service, we found the whole congregation in a tumult over the affair of the Rabbi's son. The boy Zalman was led before the judges. None of his excuses was accepted, for no one believed that young boys like us, friends of the Rabbi's son, would do such a thing. Once Zalman admitted that he had entered the House of Study and had seen and heard all that had happened, everyone believed that he alone, the oldest of us, was responsible for the terrible event. Since, however, the victim himself had not denounced him, which made the congregation deride the boy's folly—therefore they laid no punishment upon him other than that he be called "Angel *Duma*"[110]—for only the Angel of Death, of all the angels of destruction, comes down to earth to chastise the wicked. It is said that as soon as a man is buried, and the moment that the gravediggers turn away from him, the Angel of Death comes and smites the deceased upon the belly with his sword, and demands: "Wicked man, what is your name?" The wicked, however, forget their earthly names. Therefore, every man adds to the prayer of the *Eighteen Benedictions* a verse from the scriptures whose initial letters make up his name. I had prepared a verse for myself, at my father's command: "He asked you for life, and you gave him length of days for ever."[111] Since the deceased wicked man would remain silent, having forgotten his name, the Angel of Death would ask him again: "Wicked man, recite your verse". If he did not know his particular verse either, the Angel would pierce him in his belly with his sword, extract the excrement and scatter it over his face, in accordance with the saying: "I shall scatter dung over your faces, the dung of your festivals".[112] The Angel then says to the wicked man: "You did nothing more than eat and drink in this world. Now, therefore, behold your loathsomeness". As for the rest of the punishments for the wicked, they are all meted out to them after their trial in heaven. Therefore, since the youth Zalman had meted out punishment for a sin in this world, together with its penance, he must be an Angel of Death, and should so be called. Once the Rabbi had announced this, the leaders of the town agreed. Then all the inhabitants of the town, young and old, men and women, assembled, in two rows opposite each other, along the entire slope leading down the mountain from the House of Prayer, and waited for Zalman to come out of the House of Prayer. Everyone shouted at him: "Angel *Duma*". The youth hid inside his house, and did not come to the services during the entire seven days of the festival. Later, he thought: "People have forgotten about me". So he went there on the Sabbath after the festival — but he had not been forgotten. As soon as the people saw him from afar, crowds of them surrounded him, calling him "Angel *Duma*". The youth fled from the town and went to Vilna, where he stayed in a yeshiva a whole year. His mother urged him to come and visit her, since he was her only child. Hardly had he arrived in the town, when the people thronged about him, calling him "Angel *Duma*". He fled once again. He stayed away for five years, by which time his name was almost forgotten by everyone, although certain boorish youths still talked about him. The report of the incident spread far and wide, and was related along with the rest of the affair of the Rabbi's son.

My thirteenth year. A powerful spiritual feeling overcame me, and I was moved to become a righteous, pious and upright person. Like a monkey aping man, I began to pray with soulful devotion, confessing transgressions I knew not and had never committed. I had seen my father often distressed by his sins and transgressions, although I had never seen him commit any sin or transgression which would require him to fast and confess. Since, however, I followed my father almost as I would God, therefore it appeared to me that all men are sinners, and worthy of death, seeing that they eat and breathe and sleep at night, whereas it is man's destiny to meditate upon the Law of the Lord unceasingly.[113] On the termination of the Sabbath, when the congregation was praying in the dark, for no lights could be lit until after *Havdalah*,[114] a terrible, dark fear came over me. I began to weep copiously, and felt faint. I was put to bed, and slept as though dead. About two hours before dawn, my father awoke me to go to study with my teacher, who lived at the other end of the town. Since he could not rouse me, he carried me sleeping in his arms and wrapped in his coat. He carried me through the darkness of the night, undeterred by the rain and snow and the stormy winds. He knocked upon the teacher's door, and woke him from his sleep. The teacher seated me at the table before the Ark, and taught me from a Gemara with commentaries until the time for the morning service. This man taught me for about two years. He was the son-in-law of the old man, Tsevi, the Leipzig merchant, who conducted his business from both his home and his shop, and also reserved special times for Torah study.[115] When the month of *Ellul* came round, all those who studied at home would leave to continue in the House of Study. I did the same. With my teacher, I completed the Mishna *Seder Mo'ed*,[116] and began upon *Yevamot*[117] with commentaries. The teacher liked to engage in dialectical argumentations, and I must confess that I was unable to sympathise with the sufferings of the wife of a deceased brother. We never finished it, for we parted, for some reason I cannot remember.

At that time, my mother bore a son, whom my father named Shalom,[118] being unable to call him Chaim like me. The boy lived and was handsome of appearance. However, his intellectual ability was very limited, for he lived to the age of ten and never learned to read the prayers in Hebrew, despite all my father's efforts to teach him. In his eleventh year, he died in the city of Rasseyn, on the day after my father died, when they were both in Rasseyn together. My mother fell ill with the illness which brought her life to a close some six years after his birth, after she had been confined to bed for a long period, with intermittent periods of well-being followed by relapses. She suffered from a severe cough and spasms of pain in her chest until she died. I had never, in my life, seen her completely healthy. I remember her as a small woman, very pretty, a good housewife who never quarrelled with her neighbours nor uttered slanders or gossip, a woman as innocent as a lamb, who loved her husband and family with her whole heart, and did good wherever she could, and was honoured and respected by all women. Although she was honest and pure in public, with us, her sons, she behaved differently. She continually scolded me and my brother Shalom, during the latter part of her life. She would curse us with foul imprecations, like those heard only from market-women, if we did not carry out her wishes immediately. She sometimes became so infuriated that she would curse me with the curses of the *Tokheḥah,* [119] until I began to wonder whether she actually hated me in her heart, in contrast to the love she showed me during the days when she was well. Once, I questioned my father about this, and asked: ''Is it possible for there to be two opposites to the same subject — a true love as for an only son, and an inner hatred which comes out during moments of anger?'' My father replied: ''She is sick beyond suffering, and is therefore shrewish despite her true nature. When she is angry, she does not attack her husband or any outsider, but she shouts at her children in order to empty her chest and her kidneys of venom. She intends no harm, for her curses do not spring from her soul; they will disappear into nothing''.

I remember an astonishing thing. When people spoke together, they would utter Russian expressions which showed that they had learned them from their forebears without understanding their meaning. The surprising fact is that Russian was not spoken, in those days, throughout the entire province of Lithuania, except during the occasional visits of the army. Polish was the language used by officials and nobles. Most of the Jews, however, did not know Polish either. Only a short while before I had been born, the receipts for the payments of the poll-tax had been written in Hebrew: ''This is to certify that .... has paid the poll-tax of six Tympfs.[120] Witnessed by the minister and trustee of the community of Serednik ... and sealed with the seal of the community''. It was only after I was born that documents such as this were written in Polish. There was a certain youth in the town who was able to write them in Polish, and was highly praised for it, although, in fact, he knew no Polish at all. How then did Russian words and sayings enter into the Jewish language, for they are spoken in almost every town in Zamot as though handed down by inheritance? My mother, for example, would use Russian expressions, particularly if she called me and I answered like any other boy, ''Eh?'', she would reply with: ''May your throat be smitten!''[121] If a child shouted, she would answer: ''May the *kadik* take you'', or ''May the *kadik* snatch you''. Obviously, she was not aware of the true meaning of the word, since *kadik* means, in Russian, throat.[122] So it was with everyone else. My father told me that a *melammed* he knew used to teach the Pentateuch in Russian. He happened to be in the *melammed's* room when the weekly scriptural portion was *Re'eh* (Behold),[123] and this was how the *melammed* translated it: Behold, *smotri* (Look); I, *ya* (I); set, *dayoo* (I give); before you, *dlya vasb* (for you); this day, *segodnya;* the blessing, *blagoslavb;* and the curse, *i proklyat.*[124] The last two words prove that my father was not familiar with the printed Russian word but only with colloquial speech. Who was the *melammed* – translator? Where did he meet him? When did the Jew first decide to speak in Russian when saying *Re'eh* (behold). It is a new thing in these times, as many Jews are becoming Russianised, although the same occurred also sixty or seventy years ago. I have heard much about it from my father, and even more from my mother.

My father, in his younger days, used to travel to far-off lands where he saw many things. Once, when he was travelling in Germany, with his bag of merchandise over his shoulders, he was taken by a wicked person to the police, for a Jew was not allowed to trade in their villages. My father, realising he was in trouble, decided on a stratagem to mislead the police. On entering the yard of the police station, he picked up some chalk stones and pieces of lime and put them inside his bag, as well as any dirty old rags he could find. The policeman's wife, who was looking through a window, saw his strange behaviour, and shouted at the top of her voice to her husband: ''Get rid of that mad Jew! Have you brought him here to frighten us out of our wits?'' They quickly drove him off, and he continued his journey. He also related that, once, when walking alone through a forest by night, he saw four lights gleaming in the distance, and realised they were wolves. He looked for a refuge, and found an open barn of dry hay: in Lithuania, the farmers dry their hay all winter in an open barn which has four tall pillars and a thatched roof. My father dropped his bag to the ground, and climbed up the stack. Two wolves came and tried to climb up, but could not, so they lay down and stared up at him with venomous eyes, gnashing their teeth so furiously that sparks flew out as though between hammer and anvil. When the dawn broke, they relieved themselves upon his bag of merchandise, just like dogs, and went away. My father waited until it was fully daylight, then came down from his hiding place, picked up the goods, and fled precipitately until he reached the house of a farmer some two miles away. No sooner had he stepped on the threshold of human habitation than he fainted and fell to the ground.

He also told us of an incident concerning the bravery of a bear, which he had seen himself in Poland. There was a man who took around with him a young bear, no taller than a young kid, with which he would play in public for a few copper coins. Once, when he had a large audience around him, a young, strong Pole, about twenty years of age, came along and began to jeer at the little bear and its trainer, saying: "What kind of fearsome bear is this? Why have you brought it here? I could break it between my fingers!" The bear's owner warned him: "Sir, do not approach the bear, even though it may seem so docile, for you will surely die". The Pole laughed mockingly, and asked that he be allowed to take hold of the bear. He promised that, if he injured it or killed it, he would pay full monetary compensation, and would even give the money to any trustworthy person to hold for them. The bear's owner refused, but the Pole was so insistent that finally they called for witnesses and agreed on a wager. The Pole took a reed-cane and struck the bear a couple of times to provoke it. The little bear growled and roared. It looked around, and saw that its owner was standing well away from it. When the Pole struck it a third time, it leaped from its place and stood upright behind the Pole. Its legs encircled the Pole; its paws grasped him round his chest. Swiftly digging in its claws, it tore the Pole's heart out and threw him to the ground like a kid rent asunder.[125] It neither screamed in triumph nor went berserk, but silently and calmly went back to its place where it crouched down, waiting for its master.

My father also said that Polish noblemen were fond of keeping house-trained bears.[126] Once, a number of noblemen gathered together at a banquet. During their drinking, they boasted of their fine possessions. One of them declared that he had ten brave dogs which feared nothing, not even lions. His neighbour answered: "I have a little bear at home. Put him against all your dogs together and he will tear them to pieces". The first one laughed and derided the bear, saying that just one of his dogs alone could kill it. An argument arose, and they wagered on a fight between the bear and the dogs. The bear was brought and put into an enclosed courtyard, and then the ten dogs were sent in, and all exits closed. The dogs fell upon the bear from all sides, from the front and the rear, biting at it whilst it defended itself with all its strength. Seeing that it was attacked by so many fierce dogs, the bear began to step slowly backwards to the wall, facing the dogs all the time whilst fighting them off with its two forelegs. It reached a corner of the yard where lay a large pile of wood used for heating the house. When it was no more than twenty cubits from the wood, the bear jumped like a ram upon the pile and, standing upright on its two hind legs, it picked up a log of wood between its forelegs and hurled it with all its might at the dogs. It continued throwing the heavy logs at the dogs, wherever they fled in the yard, until it had killed every one of them. The men were too frightened to stop it, lest it throw the wood at them, too. After the bear had thrown the last log from the pile into the yard, it quietened down, and was then led to its master.

There was another Polish nobleman who kept a bear which had been house-trained from birth and lived inside the house. One day, the nobleman invited his friends to a party. He ordered that the bear be brought before them to entertain them. The bear walked around the room, sniffing at all the fine fare on the tables. In a corner of the room, a highly-polished copper stove-pot, filled with boiling water for tea, was standing on burning coals. The bear approached it and saw its reflection mirrored in the burnished pot. It nuzzled against it, and scorched its face and nose, and panicked. It stood up furiously on its two hind-legs and struck the pot a mighty blow. The pot fell over, spilling its boiling water over the bear. The bear jumped back, in fear of the terrible creature, the pot. It leaped up on to the top lintel of a door, clinging to it with the front claws whilst holding on to the doorpost with its hindfeet. Thus it hung, whilst it glared at the overturned pot, its eyes glinting like sparks of fire at the destructive monster which lay on the floor with its belly caved in by the bear's blow. The bear looked at it, wondering if it could still be alive. It did not calm down until the broken pot had been removed from the room, and an offering of honey and wine brought in to appease it.

When I was fourteen years old, I began to take stock of myself and to think of myself as an individual distinct from my parents, for hitherto my friends and I had always thought ourselves inseparable from our parents. We felt a strong desire to leave our homes, where our parents frustrated our every wish. I even felt jealous of those friends of mine who had no parents watching over them. We gave no consideration to the kindness and love shown us by our parents, deeming it no more than a duty laid upon them by the laws of Nature. Furthermore, they had by no means fulfilled all the instructions of the ancient Lawgiver, seeing that they refused far more of our desires than they granted us, and even abused us all day long for no just reason, in our opinion. Why should we be any worse than all those people who indulged their desires without hindrance? We became extremely envious of those friends of ours who had left home and gone to the yeshivot in the large cities, where they had no teacher but studied as they pleased and rested when they pleased. How good was their lot in life! Their parents still loved them, and sent them clothes and money to buy whatever they wished. If only our parents would send us also to the city of Vilna! Yet, which one of us would dare to tell his parents what we were thinking, especially when they were always observing us closely and would hardly let us out of their sight? The five of us discussed the matter constantly, wondering how we could run away considering we possessed nothing. One of our group was managing to save some copper and silver coins from his pocket-money, whilst two others also found ways of saving. A fourth had managed to steal money from his mother which both she and his father had overlooked. I was the only one unable to solve the problem. After long and careful investigation, I found that when my father had saved a number of silver and copper coins, and he had no purse available in his coat and there were no bags for the money in the house, he would hide his treasure on top of the covering over my mother's bed: this covering was made of thin boards above the bed and rested on four corner posters, and was known as a 'sky-bed'.[127] I used to keep my own handwritten manuscripts scattered about on top of that canopy. So, from time to time, I took about five kopeks from the bundle of money and hid them under the sheets of paper. I waited two or three days to see whether my father would miss the money and look for it until he found it, in which case he would not suspect me. On the other hand, if he did not miss it and did not search for it, then I would put it in my bag. In this way, I saved up a full rouble. Every Sabbath we five friends would meet and discuss our gains. Some of them had even put aside a pair of trousers and a shirt, and had prepared everything they needed for the journey. I had managed to obtain a pair of trousers, which I had hidden. One day, one of our group came and told us that there was a boy, a singer, who would be leaving in three days' time with another singer who was not of our town but who had been assisting our Cantor for some time. They would be going to Kovno. It was the month of *Ellul,* and they were trying to find a well-known Cantor whom they could assist during the High Festivals whilst, at the same time, perfecting their own knowledge of singing and music. We young lads did not know the way, for we had never been beyond the town's borders before, nor were we familiar with the language of the country farmers. We, therefore, would need to join the singers, who knew the roads and could even say a few words in foreign languages. This news came to us like a trumpet alarm, urging us to bestir ourselves for the journey. Hastily we prepared ourselves. We each ate breakfast at home, saying a silent farewell in our hearts for our parents from whom we were about to part for a long time.

It was early forenoon. The sun greeted us joyfully, shining its rays ahead of us to light our way. There was a gentle warmth in the wind. We assembled, and left the town together, the singers leading the way in full song. We were happy and contented. Hardly had we begun to take notice of our route when we came to shady wood lying between the towns of Reznik and Vilki. There were all kinds of birds singing there, and a freshwater stream flowing through it. It lies about six *verst* from the two towns. We lay down to rest and refreshed ourselves from the water. About an hour later, we arose and carried on our way, arriving at Vilki in the evening. There we parted company for the night, as two of our group went to stay with relatives who lived there, whilst a third had brought sufficient money with him to afford a hotel. My friend and I went to the House of Study where we ate a supper of bread and butter from our provisions, and lay down on a bench, our bags under our heads.

A relative of mine, Ze'ev the Weaver, the son of my father's brother Jacob, lived in a small house in the town. I did not wish to go to him, for I did not want him to know that I was running away from home. My intention, moreover, was to be independent and find my own livelihood. In any case, I did not want to desert my companion who had no relatives at all in the city. So we lay down and went to sleep. The night was bitterly cold, and we slept by a broken window, some of whose panes were missing and others splintered. I awoke, my body cold and damp, and my hips hurting from the discomfort of lying on the wooden boards of the bench. I woke up and suddenly realised that I was alone in a large room, empty of human beings. My father was not there to watch over me, nor was my mother there to attend to me. My heart grieved within me, and I trembled, thinking that I had been foolish to run away from those who loved me: "Here, no one cares about you. Would it not be better to return home — better for you and better for them, who will be happy to see you again?" Yet, how could I go back to my father, who would look upon me as a rebellious son, and no doubt punish me? Thus I tossed and turned in my doubts until daylight, when the old men came to recite the early morning prayers. I got up, my hands and feet feeling as though they were broken, and my whole body frail and weak. I looked for water and a basin to wash myself, as I had always been accustomed to do. But the only thing in the whole house was a foul barrel with filthy water, standing in the corridor for the worshippers to dip their hands in. Its surface was covered with scum and green slime; it was too loathsome to wash my face in it. My companion pointed out that the river Nieman flowed below the House of Study. I climbed down the hill and washed my hands and face in the river, and wiped them on the corner of my coat. Feeling confused and bewildered, I returned to the house.

It was the time of the morning service. All my friends had assembled there to pray. After the service they prepared to continue the journey. I was too ashamed to reveal to them my true thoughts. When I saw the singers gaily dancing about, and all my other friends in good mood, my spirits also began to lift. We left the city, intending to have our breakfast on the road. We sat down off the road, beside the hedges, sharing our food between us, and feeling content.

Vilki lies four leagues from Kovno.[128] There is neither a railway line nor a main highway between them. There were places where we walked in mud up to our ankles: only a week earlier heavy rain had fallen and left the surface of the road swamped. The singers fell silent and desisted from their skipping, walking normally and neither singing nor dancing. The sweat rolled off us like rain. Sometimes, we removed our shoes and slung them over our shoulders and walked barefoot. We kept looking back along the road for the cartiers who, the singers had promised, would soon overtake us and carry us in their carts. There was no one on the road. My friend and I were limping with weakness, for we were unaccustomed to walking, and so we fell behind the others. By four in the afternoon we had still not eaten, although we were used to having a hot meal every day. Then, in the distance, across the river, we saw a hotel. We forded the river over wooden planks, and entered the hotel. It was not, in fact, a hotel, but rather a small house in which lived an old Jew and his wife. They owned some cornfields and a vegetable plot. Their living room served as a tavern, where farmers drank brandy and bought salt herring. There, for the first time, I saw for myself the pleasant life of country dwellers, of which I had heard so much and of which city dwellers have always been envious. The house was very clean; the windows let in the clear light of the skies; the floor was flattened earth, spread over with a thin covering of white sand every day of the week, such as I had seen at home only on the Sabbath. The table was a solid piece of timber, scrubbed clean, and the benches around it were also washed and clean. The landlord was an old man with grey hair and beard, his clothes clean and made of simple, homespun yarn. He wore a tall, pointed green hat. He sat at the table intoning from a thick book which I noticed was the *Ts'ena Ur'ena,* [129] in the tune used for reading from the Scroll of the Law. His dear wife went about the house and in the dining room, attending to the affairs of the home. No sooner had we entered, utterly worn out, and sat down on a bench in a corner, than the old man closed his book, arose and came over to greet each one of us. He asked us where we had come from, and where we were going. The singers answered that we had come from Serednik and Vilki, and were on our way to Vilna to study in the yeshivot. I glanced at my friend, wondering when we would eat, and what we might eat, seeing that we had no food left in our bags. The landlord went out to confer with his wife. She came in, and laid a clean tablecloth over the table, and placed a large loaf of bread upon it. She then brought us a pot containing a red mash of gruel mixed with sour goat's milk, and said to us: "My sons, go and wash your hands. Here is water and a hand-towel. My beloved sons, you are on your way to study, and are hungry and weary. Eat, now, to your heart's content." I could hardly believe what I heard, for none of us had asked for a free meal, so possibly the woman might ask us to pay for the food. I was astonished at what I saw. When, however, the singers arose and quickly washed themselves, and in a moment were attacking the food, then my companion and I did likewise. The old man sat with us, responded amen to our blessing over the bread, and urged us to eat our fill. It was his pleasure to feed hungry students from his provisions. The bread and the seasoned vegetables were delicious, more delectable than any food I had ever tasted before. We ate and were satisfied, and recited the Grace after meals. We then left the house, for Kovno was some six miles away and we were in a hurry to arrive there before evening. The meal we had eaten sustained us on our journey until we arrived at Kovno in the early evening, and there we separated.

The singers went to look for the Cantor of the city, whilst the remaining three of us went to the House of Study. It was an enormous building, larger than any building I had ever seen. It was filled with students, old and young, sitting together at the benches, each with a candle and a book in front of him, and all of them swaying and chanting so that the sound rose like a tumultuous lament, like the noise of locusts leaping, and stormy floods. [130] A deep melancholy fell over me. The house was so large, bereft of ornament or decoration, and filled with strangers whose ways were unfamiliar to me. Outside, lay the darkness of the night and, within, flickering wax candles shed their feeble light. The stench pervaded everywhere. The students moaned and shrieked, and sometimes screamed at the top of their voices. It seemed to me that, here, I was witnessing the same scene that I would be seeing at the Vilna academies, which I had set my heart on joining.

What, or whom did I have, either here or there? I became so despondent that I almost fainted. Then one holy person approached us and enquired where we had come from, and what we were seeking, We told him. He said: "Go to the Beadle and ask him for a free 'guests' supper".[131] One of my companions went to find the Beadle, who gave him three permits, one for each of us. On each slip was written the name of a man who would offer the hospitality of an evening meal that day. We went in search of our hosts. I had to enquire for mine in three of the city's streets before I found him. I handed him my slip, and he told me to wait until the meal was ready. I found here neither the love nor the sweet fare which the old countryman had given us. The people of the family were as cold as ice. They ate in silence without asking me any questions about myself, as though to say: "Eat what is put before you, and leave". I left, returning to the House of Study by midnight. Many students were there, lying on the benches and tables, and many others were still engrossed in study. I lay down, put my hands under my head, and slept.

In the morning we went out to find cartiers travelling to Vilna, in the hope of obtaining a free ride for we always relied on the kindness of the cartiers. There were a few going to Vilna at that hour, but none of them had room for us. One cartier who had space to spare on his bench demanded seventy five kopeks from each of us, which we could not afford to pay: those of us who had any money left preferred to keep it in case of emergency in the big city. So we returned to the House of Study and, since it was the Sabbath eve, we decided to remain until the Sunday, and then continue. At midday, we were each given further meal-slips for the Sabbath. I found my Sabbath host living near the river Naviaze. On the Friday night, my Sabbath hosts, realising that I was still young and inexperienced, took pity on me and asked me to spend the night with them. On the morrow, I prayed with them in their House of Prayer, and returned to have breakfast with them. They were very kind to me. I began to have second thoughts about whether to continue my journey or return home. Our lack of funds decided the matter for all of us. On the Sunday, we turned away from Kovno and returned to our homes.

My welcome home was not what I had anticipated. My father showed none of the anger I had expected, nor, on the other hand, was he overjoyed. He said: "Why have you come back? You longed to study, so why have you returned?" I replied that I had thought I could get a free ride on a cart, but had been unsuccessful. My mother, too, neither showed joy nor made complaint. I understood that this was something they had agreed upon whilst I was away: they had expected me to return after a little while, and had decided to behave neither angrily nor joyously toward me, but to receive me coolly.

In those days, the Tsar Nicholas issued a decree forbidding the publication of books on the Kabbalah.[132] All the books in the possession of the Jews were to be censored, and the books on Kabbalah to be destroyed. Since it was unlikely that any Jew who possessed books which were precious with age and sacred to him, would willingly let himself be deprived of them, an order was made imposing the responsibility for the destruction of the books upon enlightened Jews. Men who knew about books were hired to travel round the towns in their area and examine all the Jewish books they could find. They would sign their names on the books permitted by the Government, stamp them with an official seal, and return them to their owners. Suspect books were to be confiscated and handed over to the Censor. However, who would possess books on the Kabbalah if not the Rabbis of Lithuania and other areas of Jewish residence? Now the Head of the Ecclesiastical Court of Shilel agreed to travel round the cities and examine the books. He came to our town of Serednik, whose Head of the Ecclesiastical Court possessed a large number of books. The searcher-Rabbi requested fifteen kopeks for each book he signed: it added up to a total of sixty roubles. Our Rabbi refused to pay him the price he estimated. They argued thus for several days. Then, a man who knew the intricacies of craftmanship, came to the Rabbi and said to him: "Let us call the son of Aaron and show him the seal of the searcher in one of the books he has already stamped. Let him make a similar seal for us, and we can stamp the rest of the books ourselves." I was summoned to the Rabbi, who showed me the seal on one of the books. It was black, with Hebrew letters in white. He asked me: "Can you make a seal in marble the same as this?" "I am at your service," I answered. "Then make one and bring it to me tomorrow". I, unaware that one could commit a sin by displaying the excellence of one's handiwork, took a smooth marble stone on which I engraved a true likeness of the seal. When it was stamped on paper, it produced an exact likeness of the searcher-Rabbi's seal. How utterly astounded I was when the Rabbi took my seal and smashed it to pieces. He said: "Never do this again, for you will be liable to have your thumbs cut off for such a deed". There had been stories related by people of the terrible things which had happened to those who had forged the official seal. I realised then that the Rabbi had never intended to defraud the Government, but only wanted to discover whether I was able to copy the seal as he had been told, and to teach me the severe penalty for forging the Government seal. The Rabbi finally agreed with the searcher on a fee of twenty roubles. He stamped all his books, authorising their use for study, and went on his way. The townspeople, however, complained about him, saying that, though he might be a Rabbi and Head of an Ecclesiastical Court and had never done wrong to Jews before, yet he erred now in accepting the Government's order to search for and destroy sacred books. Several days later the story spread round that the searcher-Rabbi had stopped at a hotel owned by Karaites,[133] a fact unknown to him. When he sat down to eat, he was given cow's entrails stuffed with cheese and butter.[134] He ate and was satisfied. After he had finished, a Jew who was there said to him: "Why did you eat it? Do you not know it was *treifa?*[135] These people are Karaites". The Rabbi became sick and vomited up all his food, and was ill for three days. So the people declared: "No harm can befall the righteous.[136] Now we have seen that justice is the reward of the innocent, and punishment of the guilty. Because he was dishonest, this has happened to him."

In that year,[137] the town's House of Study was in a poor condition. The roof beams on the women's quarters had fallen down, and were letting in the rain. When autumn came, and there was still no cover for them, the inhabitants of the house moved over to the little house of the Hasidim where they could be warm even on the coldest days. Many worshippers also went there and prayed. No one complained about them, because the old man Moshe — of whom I have already spoken as a man who loved Poland — was the head of that house, and was respected, modest and upright. He did not permit his Hasidim to conflict with the Mitnaggedim. I was thus able to observe the customs of the Hasidim. The man Moshe had his own place of worship in a corner on the right of the wall facing the east.[138] The floor of the house was bare earth, uncovered by boards. The man Moshe used to skip like a ram during the service: at the height of his devotion, he would leap up a cubit high, and stamp on the floor like a galloping horse. Near his place was a sunken well which, every month, was filled with earth and lime. One morning, during the first days of my attendance at the services in the house of the Hasidim, the man Moshe was dancing by the eastern wall, whilst I was standing by the table near the entrance. I began to recite the morning benedictions. Suddenly the man Moshe flew towards me as fast as lightning, and stood beside me. I was terrified, not knowing what he wanted of me. I stopped praying and looked at him in alarm. He put his ear against my mouth, and waited. One of the congregants, observing my fright, said: "Continue with your benedictions". I recited the first benediction, and Moshe the Hasid raised his head and called out loudly, "Amen". So he continued until I had concluded all the benedictions. Then he returned to his place and went on dancing. Such was his custom every day: whenever he heard a boy on the other side of the room reciting the benedictions, he would fly swiftly to him, and respond his amens until the boy had finished.

Other Hasidim would clap their hands, snap their fingers, shout, sometimes groan, though they did not dance. They used to tarry an hour, smoking their pipes, before beginning their prayers. There was one Hasid there, known as Abraham the Hasid, who was considered by the other Hasidim to have risen to one of the highest planes of Hasidic piety, for he was very forgetful and absent-minded. He would arrive on the Sabbath carrying his bag containing his prayer shawl and phylacteries. He had once even arrived at the house of the Hasidim dressed in his wife's blouse. His thoughts and spirit were raised to such lofty planes that he forgot how to behave in this lowly world. I also saw how, every day after the afternoon service, many of the men would gather round the table near the oven, and tell each other tales about their Rabbi in Lubavitch,[139] and the wonders he performed. Each day they would begin calmly and quietly telling their tales to their neighbours, until one of them would begin to speak more loudly than the rest, so that those further away could listen. Then those sitting furthest away would get up on to the table in order to hear every word he uttered. Nevertheless the narrator would not raise his voice too loudly, but would speak as though talking to his neighbours nearest to him. Such was their invariable custom. The stories were strange and utterly devoid of truth: indeed, the one who told the most improbable tales, was praised the most. In fact, those writers who have exposed the ways of the Ḥasidim and their blind belief in the powers of their saintly Rabbi, do not exaggerate at all — although this cannot be said also of the author of *Peace upon Israel*, [140] when he compared the superstitions of the Mitnaggedim with those of the Hasidim. If we ever heard, in the House of Study of the Mitnaggedim, such strange and improbable stories about our distinguished Rabbis, it would only be after they had died when it was permissible to speak in a holy manner about them. No one would relate such unnatural wonders about our great Rabbis whilst they are still alive, and who will undoubtedly become heavenly angels after their death in the stories told by the religious believers. The Ḥasidim behave otherwise, for they elevate and sanctify the living above the dead.

The Rabbi of Lubavitch was Rabbi Schneur Zalman. [141] Any Ḥasid who had not been to see his Rabbi was considered to be like the convert who has been circumcised but not yet immersed in a ritual bath. Only when, as a result of constant and great pressure, he had undertaken the journey to Lubavitch, was he accepted. On the other hand, anyone who had visited his Rabbi, was greatly esteemed, and accounted worthy of telling the wonders which had happened to him on his journey or which he had seen or heard. All the Ḥasidim would gather around him and attend upon his words devoutly. That year, a holy pilgrimage to see the Rabbi was undertaken by the Ḥasidim, both by those who had already been several times before, and by those who had not yet sheltered under his wing. Amongst the latter was the brother of Isaac Hindes the Ḥasid scholar-*melammed*, of whom I have already spoken. He was called Leib the Healer, for he treated all illnesses. He dressed in gentile clothes and shaved his beard. Because of his brother, he had joined the Ḥasidim some three years ago, but had never been to visit the Rabbi. Now he was also compelled to undertake the pilgrimage. What was he to do about his shaven beard? His style of the clothes could be changed, but how could he let his beard grow unrestrained? He would not be trusted by the gentiles whose illnesses he treated. In any case, it would not grow sufficiently in time for the journey. The Ḥasidim debated the matter and decided that he must tell the Warden: he must explain that the manner of his livelihood, to his deep regret, required that outwardly he must look like a gentile, but nevertheless, his heart and mind were faithful and true, and the salvation of his soul was dear to him. Then his Rabbi would condescend to look upon him, and shed his grace upon him, and he would become a new man.

In that year, at the time when the solemn days of the Day of Judgement were nigh, and the *shofar* began to be blown in the synagogues on the new month of *Ellul*, the Ḥasidim bestirred themselves with cries of joy. A youth, still at his father-in-law's table and dreaming of his childhood love, rises in the morning, takes his prayer shawl and phylacteries, and hurries off to bathe himself in the ritual bath and to skip and twirl in supplication of his God. Then, his prayers ended, he folds up his holy articles in his bag and goes off on a pilgrimage of a hundred leagues or more to see his *Tsaddik*,[143] without providing himself with bread or salt or even a few coppers. His faith is staunch in the wonders and miracles he had heard about the holy pilgrimages of the Ḥasidim: the merit of the *Tsaddik* protects all who seek him with a whole heart, so that the very fields grow food for them, and the forests supply their every want. The youth dare not soften his resolve and go home to tell his loved ones that he is leaving, lest they prevent him. So he sets off alone into the far distance, until he arrives at a small village where the holy sanctuary of the Rabbi stands. More than once he falls in the forest, his strength spent, for he has never before walked as much as a whole day. Nor does he meet in all the places he passes through, any other Ḥabad Ḥasidim,[144] who would sustain him from their own provisions. His staunch faith overcomes all trials, and he arrives safe and sound. He has earned the right to see his Rabbi. This sublime delight will quicken his life for evermore. It was with great astonishment that I heard of many such pilgrims. I pondered over everything I had heard concerning the *Tsaddik* and his Ḥasidim, and tried to understand the manner in which the Jewish soul could become so uplifted — for it is a soul tender by nature and easily moved, its faith deeply enshrined within it beyond all reasoning.

At that vast theatre, thousands of actors have trooped together in the immense House of Prayer, and broad enclosures have been erected all around to hold those who are unable to find space inside the house — like sheep-pens filled with human beings. Let me describe one scene for you. The House of Prayer of the Lubavitich Rabbi. It is the first day of the festival of Tabernacles, and the time of the reciting of the full *Hallel*.[145] The Rabbi, wearing silk, an expensive round hat on his head, leads the service. His face shines with angelic radiance. A girdle of pure linen is tied around his waist. His voice is melodious: he is superbly accomplished in the singing of Ḥasidic tunes, and composes delightful new melodies of his own. Swarms of the finest singers among the Ḥabad Ḥasidim have thronged to him, daily delighting in dance and song. In unison, they sing the responses, holding the *Lulav*[146] in one hand and the *Etrog* in the other. At this moment, not a sound is to be heard; the silence of this multitude fills the soul of the beholder with sublime reverence. The people are waiting for the Rabbi to recite the benediction of the *Hallel*. The fluttering of a fly's wings resounds like thunder in the silence. The Rabbi, like a general on the field of battle, raises his *Lulav* and *Etrog* and *Hadasim*, and all his troops raise their *Lulavim*, and stand ready. The Rabbi, in an astonishingly pleasant, still and small voice, recites the *Hallel*. The congregation, led by the sweetest singers, recite the benediction after him. Then, silence reigns over every part of the house, inside and outside. All eyes wait upon the Rabbi. When he holds up his green *Lulav* before shaking it, immediately the thousands of *Lulavim* will prepare to follow his every movement. The scene is like a field of battle, with swords and spears flashing in array, the army awaiting its warrior-leader. In deathly silence they wait for the Rabbi to raise his *Lulav,* and immediately all his troops will point their *Lulavim* in the same direction. Thus, as the Rabbi waves his *Lulav,* so all the others wave theirs after him, until the waving ceremony is completed. Then the Rabbi sings melodies composed by himself to uplift the souls of the Ḥabad Ḥasidim. The sweetest singers respond to him. So wondrous is it that, were army commanders to hear so sweet a choir, they would be confounded. When the Rabbi ceases, the congregation falls silent. In this manner, the *Hallel* is recited from beginning to end: the Rabbi and his singers sing each verse, in the melody of the Passover *Seder* service, and the congregation repeat the verse in the same melody. They linger over the *Hallel* almost three hours.

After all this, it can be no wonder that the sensitive soul of the Jew becomes uplifted with faith and sublime belief in things contrary to reason, for all else pales into insignificance when compared with the saintliness of the Rabbi. In this faith, the Jew lives out his days: it is his salvation in time of sorrow, it protects him from all the terrible powers of Nature, and removes his slightest doubt concerning things which are contrary to reality.

In that year, cholera broke out in the east:[147] by the end of summer it had spread along the eastern borders of Russia, and by early winter into Lithuania. Postmen came to our town bearing letters containing remedies against the cholera. One wonderful remedy was a healing lotion of Egyptian pepper and other spices soaked until soft in one-hundred-per-cent pure alcohol. Any man who fell ill with the fever had his body and limbs rubbed with woolen cloths soaked in the stinging lotion until his skin was almost rubbed off, and blood flowed. It was, however, an efficacious remedy, for, although many fell ill, and the winter cold was so intense that the rivers were covered with ice, yet not one person died. The evidence for this was attested by the men who patrolled the streets day and night, entering every house where there was fever, and treating the patient with their lotions and cloths until he revived and his body quickened to life: the men appointed for this task belonged to the Society of Grave-diggers[147a]. There was one of them, a man about forty years old, a metal-worker, who was the head of the Burial Society. He had been a happy, good-humoured person, until ten years earlier, when he had fallen ill and had been on the point of death. He had asked the people who were standing nearby: "Please take my hat and place it on my knees". They had asked why he should want such a strange thing. He had replied in a weak voice: "When the Angel of Death comes to slay me with his sword, he will see my hat on my knees and believe that my head is there. He will cut off my legs, but I will remain alive". He was now one of the men who went round attending the people sick with the fever. He was stricken by the cholera, and was laid low with fever. His friends quickly carried him home and prepared the cloths and lotion. But he refused to allow them to rub his body, and joked about them in his usual manner. At first they thought that he might have escaped the plague, for he rallied his remaining strength and kept them off him, fighting them hand and foot. He was the only one to die of the cholera.

I heard a story about him which it would be worth while to tell you. This man boasted to his friends, at their annual banquet[147b], that he was extremely brave and was not afraid of ghosts or demons. He made a wager with them that he would go alone to the cemetery, on the night after the Sabbath, at the dead of night, without fear of the numerous satyrs which would be skipping about there. He declared that he would knock a wooden peg into the ground beside a particular grave before returning home. The wager was for ten roast eggs and ten *baigels*[148] and brandy. The night was dark with cloud and mist, and a heavy rain was falling. The man went off, carrying a wooden peg and an axe. His friends waited one hour, two hours, three hours, but he did not return. They went in search of him, and found him unconscious beside the grave. It later transpired that he had gone to the grave, pushed the peg into the ground and hammered it in deep with the axe. Then fear suddenly took hold of him and he turned to hasten away. In those days, Jews wore long garments down to their heels: whilst turning away, the tail of his coat caught on the peg. He tripped over and fell to the ground. He fainted with fear. He imagined that the dead person in the grave had attacked him and would not let him go. His friends carried him home and attended to him until he revived.

One summer of that time, my father decided to send me to study in the yeshiva of Keidan, a city some seven leagues away. It was a large yeshiva, possessing some four hundred students. Keidan itself was a very large city, with a suburb across the river where a small congregation of Jews lived. My father's intentions in sending me to Keidan lay in the fact that the man who was the Cantor and ritual slaughterer of the small community across the river had formerly been the Cantor of our town for a number of years and had taught me Gemara with commentaries in the Hasidim's House of Prayer. My father hoped that he would help me. The journey would take two days, so my father found a guide for me, a young man about twenty years old, who had been born in the community across the river but had been living in our town for the past two years. By trade, he was a tanner. He was on his way home to visit his mother. We travelled together on foot, until we arrived. The Cantor was delighted to see me, for he was very fond of me. He found kind people who were prepared to offer me a daily meal. However, since he did not think he was capable of teaching me himself, he found a young man who lived with his mother-in-law, who owned a large house on the other side of the river. He had an attic room in which he studied all day. The man agreed to study with me as a friend; he tested my knowledge and found many qualities in me. He gave me an open letter to his friend to enable me to obtain my meals in the big city itself, so that I need not waste my time by having to cross the river two or three times a day for my meals. He did not know that I could read and write Hebrew better than he, and so did not seal the letter. When I had left him, I read it and found that he had recommended me as a person capable of becoming a learned Rabbi. I felt very proud. I stayed there for six months. I lived and ate across the river, but forded the river every day to study with my teacher. He even told me to come on Sabbath afternoon, to wait until he awoke from his afternoon rest, after which we would study together an hour or two until the afternoon service. After the service, I could return home in time for the third Sabbath meal.[149] He told me that, whilst waiting for him to awaken from his sleep, I could place two or three chairs against the wall and rest my head on a pillow, which he gave me, so that I could also enjoy the Sabbath rest. On one occasion, whilst lying down, I noticed above my head an old wooden shelf containing many books, large and small. I looked through them, and found a book which dealt with some sciences, astronomy and Nature and various studies. It was the well-known *Book of the Covenant*.[150] It was a treasury of knowledge for which I had sought all my life, and had never before found. I read in it that the heavens and the sun and all the stars revolve around the earth, whilst the earth remains always still. There I saw, for the first time, that there are men of profound scientific knowledge, who disbelieve the signs and wonders which Moses performed for the Israelites. They claimed that Mount Sinai had been shaken by the force of the gunpowder which Moses had used, but which had been unknown to his generation: when Moses had fled from Pharaoh, he had travelled forty years in the land of China, whose culture went back ten thousand years before the Flood, and there he had learned about the properties of gunpowder. He had kept the secret to himself, and it remained unknown until discovered in Europe thousands of years later. Now the *Book of the Covenant* refutes their opinions about miracles which depend on faith. I was greatly astonished at how men could err in matters of truth and faith. I looked for arguments against them. It occurred to me that, if it was unreasonable to think as they did, to believe that the sun did not give light, then this book would not have put forward any arguments against them, for who would be so foolish as to offer proof against a madman who declares that the sun does not give light by day? They might possibly be in the right, so I delved further into the book for fresh information. As I was studying it, my teacher awoke and angrily forbade me to read the book again. When I asked "Why?", he replied curtly: "For you, there is only the Talmud with all its commentaries, and nothing else". From that time I had to read the book secretly every Sabbath, hiding it before he awoke.

The summer came to a close. Among the three hundred students in the yeshiva were several who lived near the town where I was born, and who intended to go home for the High Holy days.[152] I joined them so that I might visit my parents in Serednik. I was walking with a group of about five youths of my own age. We had covered about five leagues when we saw a Jewish cartier coming up behind us. He asked us where we were going, and we told him. The wagon was empty, so he said: "Get in. I am on my way home to Yurburg, and can take each of you home". My father and mother were delighted to see me, and I stayed with them the entire Winter.

When I was in Keidan, I had my meals one day of each week[153] at the home of a Jew who had invented a new source of income for himself. It was something completely new. He made matchsticks which, rubbed strongly against a rough surface, suddenly and noisily flared up into flame which could be used for lighting candles. Today, of course, every child and every illiterate knows about these sulphur matches, but in those days it was an amazing discovery of great value to the people of the time: I remember well all the troubles and trials we endured in lighting our homes during the dark evenings. In my father's house there once lived a man who invented many different things for himself and his family — nor were there many men so talented as he in our town. He made iron and brass clasps for clothes. He had never been taught any kind of handicraft but had learned only from what he had observed. His sole tools were a pair of tongs and a file. Every evening, after his pupils had left, he made thousands of clasps which he smoothed and polished bright with cloths and rags and fine sand, before selling them to the shops. Whenever his shoes, and the shoes worn by his family, became torn, he would take his cobbler's tools, an awl and hammer, make tarred threads tipped with pig's bristles, buy a few pieces of leather and repair the shoes just like a cobbler. He was also able to make the plain types of clothes, trousers, prayer shawls, caps for day and night wear, and other kinds of apparel. He always repaired his own furniture, and was able to do all manner of handiwork. He kept a craftsman's pot filled with waste, burnt flax drying over the oven, and also a bar of hard iron and a piece of striking flint for use during the dark evenings: he would strike the flint against the iron until sparks flew off into the pot and kindled the bundle of flax. Then he would hold the heads of some sulpur sticks he had ready for the purpose in the burning embers until they flared up. All his neighbours in the street brought their coals to be kindled, after which they carried them back to light their homes. However, when rain fell and the air was filled with moisture which so dampened the flax that it could not be ignited by the sparks, despite their strenuous efforts all evening, then the situation of the townspeople became desperate, for they had to remain in darkness, with no light at all. This kind of misfortune occurred every Saturday night, after the termination of the Sabbath, for it was not permitted to make use of tools or axes until night had fallen. Particularly was this so on a cloudy night, when the stars were obscured, and the religiously observant feared to profane the Sabbath until after the night was well on. Then they would strike flint upon axe without raising a spark, and would have to go to their gentile neighbours to light up their coals. Every woman borrowed fire from her neighbour, and there was then light in every Jewish home.

Some six years previously, western scientists had found a very simple way of producing this precious source of light.[154] The invention came to Serednik via merchants who traded abroad. They imported glass bottles, as small as fingers, containing a special substance: when a small stick, one of whose tips had been dipped into sulphur, was inserted quickly and with sufficient force into the bottle and then swiftly pulled out, the sulphur would ignite with a small flame and set light to the stick. These kindling-bottles were sold at a price of twenty to thirty coppers. The country people called them *cinkas barabinkas*.[155] However, neither the light nor the joy they gave lasted very long, for the substance in the bottles was soon used up — and no one knew its composition.

Whilst in Keidan, my friends told me of the marvellous wonder that was to be seen there. A Jew had become friendly with a German traveller from the west. For a small payment, the latter had shown him the secret of making sulphur matches which ignited when rubbed against a rough surface. The Jew had opened a large workshop and employed twenty young men and women to produce a large number of matchsticks. These were packed into small paper boxes, each holding one hundred matches. The boxes were sold for twenty kopeks each. I dearly longed to enter the house of this wonder-man to see how the burning sticks were made. But how could I approach the man? I conceived the plan of asking my friends to introduce me to him as a worker seeking paid employment in his workshop. When, however, my friends told him how I was starving of hunger, the man said: "Let him come to me on one day of the week, and have his meals free with me, so that he may pursue his religious studies without distraction." This pleased me, for it meant I could go to his house on three occasions during the week.

I went to his house, and saw a very long table on which there were three small copper basins, each of which stood on three copper legs. On both sides of the table sat young men and women with bundles of straw cylinders in front of them. Under the table was a box containing oblong sticks of wood. The workers dipped one end of each stick separately into a basin containing a reddish doughy paste. The sticks were then positioned sloping against the straw rolls to dry. By the time the new sticks had been made ready to be placed against the second row of straw, the first ones had dried sufficiently to be picked up and put into the paper boxes, and packed ready for sale.

I found out that the man cut his own matches with an axe and hatchet. However, he kept to himself the secret of the red mixture that was in the basins: before preparing the mixture, he would lock himself into his room and close the windows, and, only when the mixture was ready, would he bring the basin to the workers' table and set it down on the three copper legs over the stove. Once, a terrible accident occurred: the mixture had flared up whilst he was preparing it; it burned his nose, and half his beard, and his face and hands. As usual, he was alone in the room, which was locked so that no one was able to come to his assistance. He escaped by a miracle, although he was ill for a long time. Later, when I realised that I would never learn his secret, I stopped going to his house for my meals.

How terrible were the circumstances of this inventor — which I witnessed myself and knew about in every detail. He undertook a new venture at a time when everyone was having the greatest difficulty in producing fire and light from flint and steel. Surely a man who could manufacture matches which could be sold for fifteen or twenty kopeks per hundred, so that every person, whether young or old or rich or poor, could have instant light a hundred times over, especially when so many wealthy people and noblemen and officials living in luxury would purchase these matches by their thousands every day — surely such a man should make a fortune in a very short period of time? What will you say after I have told you the end of this affair and this precious invention? This man, who employed about twelve young people in his factory, could find no purchasers for his goods. He packed his match-boxes in large wooden crates, and waited for the market-day held in one of the villages in his district, such as Shidlovo or Kalvariya. There, he would exchange them for shoddy articles which no one wanted to buy, such as shoes or hats, and would peddle these around the towns and villages. The man worked and toiled, but saw no reward from his labours. Yet, today, we see the match industry flourishing all over the world, and who can live without them? Although they are cheap, a lot of money is spent on them every year. Let us suppose that each household spends about three roubles per year on matches. Whereas in these days we need to use some ten matches every day, but in those days two were enough, one in the morning and one in the evening, for light and fire. For only three roubles a family could have a supply of matches for a whole year in place of all the toil and trouble which were necessary in those days.

It can be seen that new things are not welcomed by the people who live in this country, and that they are only accepted because of the need to imitate, like monkeys, the customs of foreign lands. Whether the new fashion be good or bad, it is quickly taken on. But anything, however good it may be, that does not already exist in other countries, is not favoured. Why should we, then, be astonished at the fate of our own invention, the *Microdiorama*, on which we worked six years, and which was commended by everyone who saw it? Everyone without exception, praised and lauded it. But, what can we do with it? Should we do as the matchstick maker did, and pack our products into large boxes and hawk them around the annual markets in exchange for worn goods? Even that we are not able to do. There is no counsel or stratagem that can provide the wise with food or the men of understanding with riches. Everything is folly and vanity.

At that time, since I did most of my work in the House of Study, I decided to undertake a search among the numerous books that were there to find those passages which were the most reasonable and knowledgeable. I was sick to the soul with books which tried to frighten me with demons and the fires of hell. However, I found few books which quenched my spiritual thirst — only the first five parts of Maimonides' *Yad Ha-Ḥazakah*, [156] and some Introductions written by distinguished Jewish leaders who were familiar with natural sciences and medicine. I began to write a book of my own, for which I had not yet found a title but which began with a lengthy introduction containing poems in Hebrew, Aramaic and Targum and a great deal of discussion: later, it became lost and I was unable to continue with my outpourings. [157] My Introduction finished only when I had finished with all the books and Introductions in the House of Study, for I borrowed them all to work on at home. I took two or three Gemaras each day with a volume of *Yad Ha-Ḥazakah* and other books, and Maimonides' Commentary on the Mishna,[158] and placed them on my father's table and wrote my book. My father was pleased with the work I was doing. After I had completed my Introduction, I commenced on the book. First, I divided the square sheet of paper into two: on one I wrote "The Jew", and on the other "The Adversary", an opponent I conjured up for him. I saw the Jew as a man of staunch faith and superior intellect who could contend with two opponents, whom I called the "First Adversary" and the "Second Adversary". I remember that I began in this manner. The First Adversary asked the Jew: "What is the origin of your Faith?" The Jew replied: "In the beginning came Abraham our Patriarch whose reason taught him that all the idols of the nations were folly, that there was only One God in the heavens from Whom all things derive". And so on, with questions and answers, in all of which the arguments of the Jew were justified. By the time the book had reached the discussion concerning spirits and demons, I had covered some thirty pages.

In that year, the month of *Shevat* was extremely cold. The large stove which was kept in the hall at the rear of the House of Study gave little heat and none at all in the rest of the building. Benches stood around it, on three sides, at which the students sat day and night, and on which they slept. The worshippers who came to the morning service also found places near them; on very cold mornings, however, only a few of the most devout worshippers came. The early arrivals took their places at one of the benches around the stove; those of lesser devotion remained there even during the recital of the *Eighteen Benedictions,* lest they be robbed of their places by some other person. One day, I was standing there in the midst of the congregation, putting on my phylacteries, when one of the men stumbled against the person next to him. I was standing fourth away from him. I was pushed, unwillingly, against the man behind me. He was the Cantor and ritual slaughterer of our town, a man of low moral character and no good qualities. His lies and slanders kept the town in a turmoil. His name was Hirsch Avigdor: he had come to us from another town where he had been nicknamed Hirsch the Liar. I never knew why he constantly jeered at me, for I had never done him harm; perhaps the clown needed a target for his butts. On that particular day, although he saw that I was not to blame for pushing him, he raised his voice and loudly accused me of speaking between the laying on of my hand phylacteries and the head phylacteries.[160] Everyone in the small congregation stared at me as though I were a criminal. No excuse of mine could absolve me from the Cantor's slander. I was most aggrieved and on returning home told my father and mother. My father said nothing. All day long I deliberated on what I should do to appease the Cantor's wrath. Finally, unfortunately, I found a way. I wrote Hebrew in a finer style than any other person in the town, including the Cantor. I would therefore write him a nice, pleasant letter, with my initials in large square letters at the end, in the hope of appeasing him. I would place the letter in his prayer-shawl bag, and he would find it and read it. On a sheet of paper I wrote: "To the incomparable, distinguished and renowned Cantor, Tsvi Hirsch Avigdor. Multiply not exceedingly proud talk, lest arrogance issue from thy mouth.[161] I am as God-fearing as you, and worship with no less reverence'', etc . . . At the end of the letter, I wrote Ḥayyim ben Aharon in large square letters so that they formed the initials of ten final words which would make my name apparent to anyone familiar with the Prayer Book. On Friday morning I could not find his bag, and had to keep the letter with me all day until the evening. Sabbath arrived, and I had to find a place to hide the letter, since I could not carry it on the Sabbath. No one else knew about it. There was a large notice on the wall showing the Benediction of the New Moon[162] in big square letters for everyone to read. I inserted the letter between the notice and the wall. During the evening terminating the Sabbath, I stayed at home. The students in the House of Study, having insufficient candles for reading, began to search in the various secret places they were accustomed to use. One of these places was the notice on the wall, behind which some students hid their candle bits. My letter fell out. There were about twelve people there: everyone read it, and none of them understood it. All they could gather was that it was about the Cantor, and probably referred to him disparagingly. The letter went round from hand to hand, without anyone being able to offer an explanation of it.

There was a student, a *parush*,[163] who had been praised by the leader of our community. He was an honest and upright man. It was his custom to sit alone at the Reader's dais where he studied the Law of the Lord day and night. He spoke to no one, and paid attention to no one. At night-time, he would read the books of the Kabbalah. Now, he looked up and observed that the whole congregation had stopped studying and were behaving frivolously. He said to them: ''What are you doing, brothers?'' They showed him the letter. He took it, read it and said: ''This is nonsense. Why do you waste your time over such folly instead of studying the Law?'' He held the letter over a candle and burnt it. However, the tip of the paper that remained in his hand dropped on to the floor. One of the miserable wretches there picked up the bit of paper and put it in his pocket. On the morrow, the people assembled for the morning service: it was my misfortune that I did not attend that morning. The students of the House of Study told the Cantor and the entire congregation that they had found a letter which had been sent to the Cantor from the town where he had previously lived, and where he had been nicknamed Hirsch the Liar. It contained things which would make anyone's ears ring to hear them. Although, regretfully the *parush* had destroyed it, one little corner still remained. The Cantor was furious, and declared: ''This letter did not come from anywhere else than here, in this town, and it has been written by one who is my enemy. Who is this person?'' They examined the piece of paper and recognised my handwriting. He took it and showed it to the people and the Wardens and the Rabbi, and demanded that I be given forty strokes of the lash on the Reader's dais in public, on the day of the assembly of the community, and that I be handed over to the army, and so forth. However, the Rabbi and the community's leaders knew me well enough to know that it was not in my nature to treat the Cantor in such a manner and that I had never behaved disrespectfully toward my elders and seniors. Further-more, since the letter was not available, they did not believe his accusations.

I was at home, and knew nothing of what was going on — for my father also had not attended the services that morning. Messengers, youths of my own age, came to see me, one after the other, and told me what had happened. They related that all the communal leaders had decided unanimously that I be taken on the Sabbath day and laid down the Reader's table and flogged with whips. They were lying, but I was frightened by their reports. My father asked me to tell him the truth about what I had written. He believed me, for he knew that I would not lie to him. He said: "Do not fear. I shall go before you, and hide you. I will prove your innocence to all the congregation, for I know that you are in the right." I remained shut up inside the house all day, together with my mother who was lying ill in bed. In the afternoon, I returned to my book and continued the record of my investigations into the reality of the existence of devils and demons. Although I delved into many sources in order to present the opinions of the distinguished scholars who believed in their existence, nevertheless the arguments of Maimonides against their exis-tence assumed the greatest prominence in my presentation. [164]

I had not reached the end of my investigations, when the door was suddenly opened and the tall Cantor came in, stooping under the low ceiling. He swooped upon the sheet of paper on which I was writing and snatched it from me. "It is only because I have pity upon your sick mother," he said, "that I do not make an end of you." I was alarmed. He turned and left, the sheet of paper in his hand. Swift as lightning he went to the Rabbi and showed him how my handwriting on the paper compared with the writing on the torn edge of the letter. The Rabbi read what I had written on the paper, and said: "This youth is writing about important matters concerning the beliefs of our great scholars on demons." The Cantor said: "This is enough to indicate that he will turn out bad, a heretic." The Rabbi answered: "Is it not sufficient for you that this youth attends to the words of our scholars and writes about them? In any case, we know him to be honest and God-fearing. Why should we judge him on what he might become in the future?" When the communal leaders, who were no experts on writing and disliked the Cantor intensely, heard the Rabbi's opinion, they paid no heed to the Cantor's complaints, whilst their regard for me increased tenfold. On the third day, messengers came to tell me that I could leave my house without fear of harm. However, the sheet of paper which the Cantor had snatched out of my hand was never returned to me. I stopped writing my book. I folded all the leaves together and bound them with stout thread in order to preserve them intact. The Wardens, on their part, urged me not to take home any more books from the House of Study. I therefore stopped writing my book altogether.

When I was 16, my father decided to send me to the Vilna yeshiva, for he had heard that many youths like myself had studied there and emerged eminent scholars. He had, furthermore, come across a youth who had been studying for two years and had returned home for the festivals, but was about to return and was willing to take me with him. Provisions were prepared for my journey; my mother even made long stockings for me. I departed on my journey. The youth led me to the yeshivah *Gemilut Ḥasadim*, [165] which adjoins the courtyard of the Synagogue, and handed me over to the care of the Beadle. The youth was staying at the yeshiva Remeiles[166] and promised to visit me often to advise me on the things I had to do. The Beadle took 30 kopeks per day from me. He tried to find meals for 6 days for me, but could only arrange 4 days. This is what happens to youths who go to a vast city like Vilna: no one enquires about their affairs or where they will eat, but each youth has to find a generous host who will offer him a mid-day meal and supper on one day of the week.

Breakfast, however, was taken in the yeshiva. Twice a week, on Mondays and Thursdays,[167] two yeshiva students went, with sacks over their shoulders, to the street where the grocery shops were situated. The good-hearted women gave them a handful of rye, wheat, corn, salt and butter. These were later cooked in the yeshiva kitchen in a copper pot and shared out among the students, each receiving a portion of the hot gruel in an earthenware bowl. As for bread, each student had to find his own. If he had money, he bought some; otherwise he had to beg pieces of bread from anyone generous enough to offer a slice to a beggar — and there were many beggars in the city. The youths existed on this until noon. For the noon and evening meals, the students had to seek around for charitable hosts who would feed them for one day each week. The newcomer who had not yet learned how to beg, would starve to death, and no one would come to his aid. The Beadle, therefore, took particular care of the new students and, for a payment of thirty kopeks per day, would himself seek out benevolent hosts for each day of the week. He would inform the boy of each man's name and address, and the boy would eat there on one day of the week, at noon and evening. I had paid for four days' meals, and so was left with two weekdays without food — for the Sabbath was taken care of by members of the *Gemilut Ḥasadim* Society and the Warden and the Senior Beadle (there was also a Junior Beadle); these saw to it that each boy had his Sabbath meals, and were usually able to find hosts who would take in students for all Sabbaths and festivals of the year. Students generally stayed permanently with these hosts unless they committed an offence.

During my early days in Vilna, when I had not yet found an "annual" host, I was given, each Friday, the name and address of a man to whom I had to present myself. If he liked me, he would accept the meal-slip and I would eat my Sabbath meals with him. If it happened that I was not accepted, I would return to the yeshiva, hand back the slip, and receive another name and address. On the Friday of my second week in Vilna, I was refused by the first man I went to see. I did not know at the time that I had to return to the Beadle to obtain another address, so I stayed by myself in the yeshiva that evening; everyone had left, and no one paid attention to me. When my friends returned and found me alone, and heard of my deplorable situation, that I had had to miss the Sabbath Sanctification, they all protested vociferously. Next morning, after the service, a man took me to his home for the Sabbath.

On the Friday of the third week, I was given the address of a man who would be sure to accept me: he was called Jacob Yog, a wealthy Vilna personage of the time. For the first time in my life, I saw spacious rooms with fine furniture such as even Joseph of the Wall never possessed. After the morning service, some twenty people, all members of the family, men and women and children, sat at the table with Reb Jacob at their head. He had a long beard which reached down to his waist. Opposite him sat a shaven-faced man; a youth of about fifteen sat on one side of him and a girl of about fourteen sat on his right. The girl spoke to the shaven-faced man, and asked him about the amazing story she had heard in the town: a certain woman had given birth to twenty four children, all of them well and alive, whereas another woman had also born twenty four children and yet all had died and she was left completely childless. The shaven-faced man replied that the first woman had taken the proper precautions and had been assisted by diligent nurses and so her children were still alive; the second one, however, did not know how to look after her children, so they died. Reb Jacob exclaimed at him: "Fool! That is not the true reason. God wanted to preserve the children of the first woman, therefore they lived. He wanted the others to die, so they died". The shaven-faced man fell silent and made no reply. I learned later that the shaven-faced man had once studied medicine abroad, and had now returned, at the age of forty, to study medicine at the Vilna Academy and become a physician. Jacob took him into his house to teach his son and daughter, offering him food and accommodation and a small wage.

Four weeks passed by, and then a student who had been at the *Gemilut Ḥasadim* yeshiva for two years left us. He had been having all his Sabbath and festival meals at the table of a god-fearing tailor. At this time, however, the *parush* student wanted to visit his wife for the Passover holidays, and so had left. The Beadle sent me to take his place and to eat there until after the festival of Pentecost when the *parush* would return. The tailor had an only son about fifteen years old, and it was the father's hope that he would become a Rabbi. It was a vain hope. The boy refused to study the Bible and books on ethics. On the other hand, the tailor did not want to teach him a trade, for he inwardly despised the craftsman's profession. I noticed that the tailor's books and other possessions were by no means poor. His only son refused to become friendly with me, and indeed hated me: I did not know whether it was because he despised me or because he objected to his father's constant admonitions: "Why is it that you, who are surrounded by all that is good, are not able to study, whilst this boy studies in the midst of poverty and hardship?"

The second half-year of the yeshiva studies commenced after Passover. I was told that any student who wished to be instructed by the Head of the Yeshiva would have to pay two roubles per half-year. I had only seventy-five kopeks. I gave them to my teacher on promise of payment of the remainder later, and he admitted me to the yeshiva. I wrote to my father in Hebrew, telling him all that had happened to me and saying that I had no money left and had to miss three days' meals per week. My friends were so surprised at the excellence of my handwriting that they asked me to write letters for them to their parents. Anyone who needed to send a begging letter to his relations came to me and, for the payment of a slice of bread at breakfast or for a few coppers, I wrote it for him. Thus I became the Scribe of the yeshiva; even the Beadle and the Warden came to me to write their letters — and also found hosts for my missing three days' meals.

Most of the people of the yeshiva were very friendly towards me, although towards each other they were often hostile. This may have been due to the impoverished background they came from, for they were all the poorest of the poor; possibly also, their needy circumstances had made them mean. They were not called by their proper names, but by their towns of origin — the Kovner, the Seredniker, etc. [168] If there were two or more from the same town, they were given a special designation, such as the 'big one', the 'small one', the 'white one' or the 'black one'. There was a youth from the city of Talkun in Courland, who was taller than the rest of us, but we despised him because he spoke only German. When reciting his lessons before the Head of the yeshiva, he would translate: "Said Rabbi Ḥanina — sprach Rabbi Ḥanina". All the boys, and even the Head of the yeshiva, would laugh at him. He once came to me requesting that I write a letter for him, and from that time we became friendly. In fact, he saved my life.

It happened this way. When my meals at the tailor's house ceased after the *parush* returned, a young student approached me and said: "Listen, Seredniker. You know I also spend a few Sabbaths at the tailor's house, and I found out that his only son has been stealing his possessions in order to have enough money to indulge his frivolous desires in the company of a band of loose-living young wastrels who can always lay their hands on as much money as they want, whether by stealing or as a gift from their fathers. On the period of the full moon they hold a festive gathering during which they disappear from home for a couple of days to indulge in drink and lust until their money gives out. Now, this tailor's son stole from his father some silver spoons and religious articles, and hid them. No one was able to discover who had stolen them. Later, the son sold some of the books which the father had bought for his teacher — and now he has stolen some more and brought them here, to the yeshiva, and put them in his father's box: his father is a member of the *Gemilut Ḥasadim*. The son will sell them in three days' time". It seemed to me that this student, who was telling me all this, had once been himself one of that band of wastrels, but had been thrown out by them. Wrathful and vengeful, and knowing their secret ways, he had turned to me, aware that I would not be able to restrain myself. I was so filled with fury over the son's treachery against his honest and kind father that I took a sheet of paper and wrote down all the son's crimes, in the hope that the father would search for the missing books in his box in the yeshiva. My informant took the letter and handed it to the tailor who investigated the matter and found the books. I knew nothing of this, nor did the tailor come to see me. Three days later, my friends said to me: ''Seredniker, do not go out alone in the evenings, as there are some hefty fellows watching and waiting for you. They intend to beat you to death''. My Courland friend heard this and said; ''You will come out with me in the evenings, and no harm will come to you''. He was as powerful as ten men. I agreed and thenceforth never left the house, even to perform the most essential functions, unless he went with me. Some four nights later, he went out alone, and was attacked by three men. They ripped his clothes, but he gave them such a resounding thrashing that they never returned again.

One of our students, a youth called Eliezer, was the son of the Rabbi of the small town of Doikloik,[169] not far from the city of Taurog on the Prussian border. He was outstanding in everything he did. He was about seventeen years old, and had a sickly appearance as though he had only just got up after an illness. He never studied, even for one hour of the day, yet he could recite his lessons to the Head of the yeshiva just as well as the rest of us. In his box, he kept some old and some new books which he had bought with his own money, although he never received a penny from his father. He purchased the book called *The Comet*[170] shortly after its publication. During the festivals, he preached sermons in public, at his own request. He spent the entire festival living in the homes of wealthy people, where he discoursed at the table. He was asked to deliver sermons in the House of Prayer. He could quote the place of the most obscure passages in the Babylonian Talmud, which only Bible scholars and expert Talmudists are able to do. If he were shown any Talmudic passage, he would recite it as though reciting a prayer. He studied both theoretical and practical Kabbalah.

One day, the gold spectacles of the Head of the *Gemilut Ḥasadim*, an elderly and respected man, were stolen from his box. Although a search was mounted, they were not found. Eliezer went to the man and said: ''If I were given full authority by the Head of the yeshiva, I could find the thief and the stolen property by means of the Kabbalah and the book *Works of God*.''[171] Permission was granted to him. This particular book details the preparations which must be made before using the names it contains for Kabbalistic rituals. Eliezer followed all the instructions. He fasted a whole day, immersed himself in the ritual bath, and prayed devoutly. Then he wrote the holy names on ritually fit parchment in Scroll-type letters, using ritually prepared ink. He recited his prayers with fervent devotion, and adjured the angels with fear and dread. He took his stand near the eastern window, and drew a large circle in chalk around himself on the floor: no one was permitted to enter it or approach him. These were the preparatory rules for the ritual.

Now, in order to discover the thief, it was necessary to employ a youth who knew nothing of the sin of nocturnal emission, and who could read Hebrew and was capable of understanding the visions he would see. Where could such a boy, of about ten or eleven years of age be found, and who would vouchsafe for his innocence? However, Eliezer had learned from the Gaon and the Kabbalah that, if a thread were measured round a boy's throat and then tied, and the knot were inserted between his teeth, if the thread could not then be wound round the crown of his head so that it did not overlap his ears and his forehead, then the boy was without sin — for, had he experienced even one nocturnal emission, his neck would have thickened out to such an extent the thread would be long enough to wind all round his head and face. Eliezer went to the Butchers' yeshiva, where he found a boy of about ten whom he tested and found eligible. He gave him fifteen kopeks and brought him back with him. He prepared all the rites according to the book *Works of God*. There were about fifty men standing around him, outside the circle. After going through all the preparations and prayers and adjurations and shakings, in which all the onlookers joined, he took the boy and smeared the palm of his right hand all over with black soot taken from a copper pot. Over this he smeared a little pure olive oil until it was smooth and shining as a glass mirror. It was in this mirror that the boy, and only the boy alone, would see the demon which had been raised up, as well as the thief and the stolen goods and the place in which they had been hidden. The thief's name would be seen written in black Hebrew letters on white paper.[172] Once the boy's palm had been properly prepared, Eliezer began to recite the adjurations and the names. He adjured the demon which would appear to bring with it a lamb which it must slaughter in his presence: this was a test to see whether the demon was obeying his commands to the full. He then waited some five minutes, and asked the boy: "Tell me what you see in the palm of your hand." "Nothing", answered the boy. He waited a further five minutes, and asked again: "Look well into the palm of your hand and tell me what you see". "Nothing at all", answered the boy. But on the third time, the boy said: "I see a man, a stranger, holding a lamb, and he is slaughtering it with a knife across its throat". Eliezer adjured the demon to eat the lamb. "Now," continued the boy, "he is cutting the lamb's flesh with a knife and putting it to his mouth". So he adjured it further, saying: "Bring the stolen spectacles and show the place where they are hidden". Eliezer waited five minutes and asked the boy: "What do you see?" "Nothing at all," he answered. He waited another five minutes, and asked again, and the boy replied: "There is something. I see a stove with dry wood behind it. On top of the logs is a bundle of old rags, and in them I see the gold spectacles." He then adjured the demon a further time: "Bring the thief to me." Eliezer waited about a quarter of an hour, but the boy was unable to see anything more. Eventually, the boy said: "Now I can see in my palm that the first man has returned with a second person." When questioned as to the appearance of the second man, he replied: "A Jew of medium height, wearing a round hat. He has long sidelocks, and wears a black coat". When asked about the man's nose and eyes, he said he could not distinguish these details properly since the mirror was too small and his hand was not like a burnished mirror which reflects everything in precise detail. Then Eliezer made a further adjuration: "Bring me the thief's name written in black ink on white paper." He waited about a half-hour until finally the boy saw the first man with a piece of white paper in his hand; there were Hebrew letters on the paper. "Spell out the letters you see," said Eliezer. But the boy said it was hardly possible to recognise them. With great difficulty he spelt out the letters, one by one: G d h l u y. Eliezer said: "This is the name of the thief — Gedalyahu. Obviously, the demon, unable to write God's name 'Yahu' in the correct order of the letters, has had to change their order." This entire scene took some three hours. At the end of it, Eliezer stepped out of his circle, whilst all the spectators stood in astonishment until they eventually dispersed. There were some men there, however, who did not believe anything of what had happened: they grabbed the boy and beat him with whips to force him to confess that he had simply carried out Eliezer's orders. The boy refused to make such a confession, but wept copiously, saying: "What sin have I committed? A man came to me, gave me some money, and told me to go with him and tell him everything I would see in the mirror of my palm. I did not know that you would be so angry with me." So they left him alone. Even those who believed in those wonders turned again Eliezer, declaring that it would be only right to expel him from the yeshiva, since it was wrong to make use of the angels by means of their names and spells: the wrath of the Lord could break out upon all the members of the *Gemilut Hasadim*, whilst even Eliezer himself would suffer a premature death. Nevertheless, the real wonder of it all was that nothing came of all his toil and labour: where were they to find a Gedaliah with a stove in the vast city of Vilna?

Now this young man Eliezer was constantly in trouble with people and had more enemies than friends. He came to me to write all his letters, and even foolish notes against any members of the *Gemilut Hasadim* who happened to provoke him. I wrote letters for him in Hebrew, which he could not write for himself, but which he copied out in his own handwriting. Some time later, he was expelled from the yeshiva, but found a place to live on the roof of the yeshiva. It was summertime, and no one ever went up there, for there was no attic up there nor were any goods stored there: the loft had merely tiles on the roof and earth on the floor. Daylight did not penetrate there, but there was a hole in a corner through which some dim light did seep. Some days after Eliezer had moved in there, he called me up to his loft to write letters for him to justify his behaviour and to protest his innocence against his persecutors. I found the place a very convenient one, for I could sit there and write all the letters I wanted; it was far better than the room in the yeshiva which was overcrowded with people and where there was nowhere to put a sheet of paper on which to write. Furthermore, it was not under the eyes of the heads of the *Gemilut Hasadim* yeshiva who would not approve of my engaging in any activity other than study or prayer. Eliezer had made a table for me from a wooden plank resting on two bricks. I sat on the floor, or lay down sideways against the hole in the eaves to get light for my work.

Despite all my efforts I was not able to fill the three meal-less days: my stomach was empty, and so was my purse. To add to it all, the Head of the yeshiva, Rabbi

Falk, called me to him and said: "Tell my why you came to Vilna, and who your parents are and what do they do for a living? I have been watching you, and I have observed that you are lax in your Gemara studies. Furthermore, you have not yet paid me my fees for the half-year. I want you to understand that, if you do not pay me, then you must leave. In fact, my advice to you is that you return home to your parents."

I knew my father's brother, Hlavna Lapidus, lived in Vilna. He had left home in his youth, and joined a troupe of performers and magicians. In his old age he had settled in Vilna.

Now in those days there were no Jewish jugglers, for the occupation was greatly despised. His family, therefore, hated him for what he had become. I myself had no wish to contact him. However, under the duress of hunger, I made enquiries about him in the hope that he could save me from the shame of my hunger. Because he was unique among Jews, I soon found out that he was still alive, an old and God-fearing man who had long since abandoned his former livelihood, due to the feebleness of old age and loss of income. During his act he had balanced a saucer with a glass of water on the point of a small sword which he held upright by his teeth, whilst performing acrobatics. As he became old, however, his teeth began to fall out and he was unable to hold the sword and saucer securely. In the course of time, therefore, he lost his employment and fell into dire poverty and need.

When the Head of the yeshiva threatened to dismiss me because of my inability to pay my fees, I told him that I had an uncle in Vilna who might pay the fees for me if I were able to find him. The Head of the yeshiva told me that he knew of him and would send for him. Three days later my uncle came to the yeshiva, and was delighted to see me for he had no sons of his own. He asked concerning my father's welfare, and my own circumstances. I told him. On the following day, my uncle returned and gave me sufficient money to pay for the fees, as well as food for an entire day. He promised to support me constantly on condition that I continued my studies and also, since he had no sons, that I would promise to say *Kaddish*[173] for him after his death. He also informed me that Rachel, the elder daughter of my uncle Jacob Baredzever, also lived in the city: she was a housekeeper and ran the affairs of a wealthy man's home. She had been divorced two years earlier because she was barren. He gave me her address. A couple of days later, a friend of mine told me to go into the courtyard "because a wealthy woman is waiting to see you." I went. She was there, a kind-hearted woman, for when she had heard from my uncle that her cousin was studying in the yeshiva and was a person of presentable appearance, she had been delighted; now she invited me to visit her at her masters' house in five days' time. It seemed that her employers were wicked people who suspected every stranger of wanting to rob and murder them. Therefore she needed a few days in which to present me to them in a good light as her relative studying at the yeshiva — and perhaps they themselves might even suggest that I go to visit her. I went to their house, but it was only with great reluctance that they offered me meals on one day per week. Even then I was unable to converse with her lest they suspect her of plotting against them, so I ate what she served me and left. This lasted no more than a month, for she told me that, rather than that I should go on eating food that was begrudged me, she would pay for my food herself. One day, the woman came to see me. She said to me: "I was married to a respected and learned scholar for six years. We divorced, by mutual agreement, two years ago. At the time of the divorce, he owed me nine roubles, the balance of my *Ketubbah*[174] settlement. He offered to give me a promissory note for the money, but I refused to take it because I believed him to be a God-fearing man who would be true to his word. He said he would pay me as much as he could afford." Since the divorce, he had paid her nothing, and she could not go and ask him for it, and therefore, "if you go and explain who you are and tell him that I have transferred the debt to you, he will pay you whatever he can afford each week or each month, and you can keep it for yourself, so that you need never go hungry again." She told me that he lived nearby, that he was the Beadle of the Lower Ecclesiastical Court, where he lived and slept and studied. The reason for having a Lower Court in Vilna was that any city so populous as Vilna had to have two Courts to serve its large population. In Vilna, both Courts were in the same building, and therefore the Court on the lower floor was called the Lower Court, and the Court on the upper floor was called the Upper Court.[175] I found the man studying in the House of Study of the Gaon, the same place where, fifty years earlier, the Gaon Elijah of Vilna[176] used to pray. I told the man who I was and what I wanted. He said: "Very good. I will give you one dinar every Wednesday until the debt is paid." I went to see him on the following week and he paid me the fifteen kopeks. I was delighted, for I now had a means of support which would last until the nine roubles had been paid. I made up a small accounts register in which I noted the days of payment, and which I asked him to sign so that he would know how much he had paid. He refused, however, to do so, saying: "Enter the amounts yourself. That will suffice." On the second week, he gave me only ten kopeks, saying that he could afford no more. On the third week, he gave me five kopeks, and the same amount on the fourth week — after which he stopped paying. I reproached him for it, saying that, as a God-fearing man, he knew that he was legally indebted to the woman, and that furthermore he was guilty of keeping the spoil of the poor in his own home.[177] He drove me away. I was furious with him, and told Rachel about him. She said she could do nothing as he was a poor man, and furthermore she possessed no promissory note against him.

One of my friends told me that the Community Office was not far from the yeshiva and any Jew could present his complaint there against any other member of the community. The Beadles of the Office would be sent to fetch the wrongdoer, who would be made to restore the stolen property or repay the loan: if the accused proffered his own counter-complaint, he would be sent for trial. Even a young child, who could hardly speak for himself, was listened to and given justice. I went to the Office and related all that had happened, showing them the accounts book. Immediately, they called for the Beadle, a very tall and powerful man, who carried a stout staff in his hand. "Go with this youth," he was told, "and order the man to pay his debt." The Beadle accompanied me outside, where he said: "You know that everyone who comes here for justice has to pay me a few coppers for my trouble." I answered: "That is all right. I will give you double the amount. Unfortunately, I have no money at all at the moment, but as soon as I receive my payment from this man, I shall gladly pay you." He accompanied me to the Lower Court. There, the man told this Beadle: "If it is true that I owe him money, then he must take me to Court for it. I will oppose him in this Court, but if the Court finds me guilty, I will pay him." So the Beadle left, and I was on my own. The trial began. I was astonished to see the manner in which the rabbinic judges sat on the justices' bench. One was filthy and pot-bellied, half-asleep on his chair in the heat of the day. Another kept disappearing into the next room, whilst the third sat yawning, pressing on a Gemara and occasionally mumbling something. They were all repulsive and repugnant, their appearance betraying excessive indulgence in wine and self-gratification, and their lack of humanity. None of them paid any attention to me. Nor did the debtor speak to me either good or ill. I waited until I could wait no longer, and called out to the man: "You are making a laughing-stock of me. You told the Beadle that you wanted a trial before an Ecclesiastical Court, yet now you keep silent." He answered: "These are your judges. Present your suit before them." "But who are they? I see no one." "See that old man behind the table? Tell him your case". I approached the man, who arose, bowed, and sat down again. He said to me: "This man owes you nothing. Be off with you." I began to complain against this perversion of justice which pronounced a verdict before hearing the evidence. "I even have," I said, "a register of accounts showing that the man paid me for four weeks according to our agreement, so surely this is sufficient evidence that he is in debt to me?" "How much did the man pay?" "Thirty kopeks." "Very well. Now repay the man the money you took from him — and be off." Realising that this was a court of corruption and not of justice, I left. When I related all this to my friends, they laughed at me, saying that only in the Community Office could one obtain justice, and certainly not in the Ecclesiastical Courts, for the only difference between the Lower and the Upper Ecclesiastical Courts was that the latter was worse than the former. Bribery determined judgment; corruption was common practice. Who had not heard of the injustice and perversion to be found in those Courts? Therefore, anyone who knew about them tried his best to have his case heard in the Community Office, and not the Ecclesiastical Courts.

Eliezer the Kabbalist was often engaged in preparing spells to transform his enemies into friends. One day, he showed me the sacred names written on a parchment which he had prepared for the purpose, as well as a white goose tongue which he kept in his shoes. He said: "You will see that tomorrow the Head of the yeshiva will come and ask me to return to the yeshiva — and all the people who wanted to expel me will now desire peace with me because they have become my friends." I had no wish to believe in his wonders. Three days later, I saw Eliezer sitting in state like a king in the yeshiva, as of old. I was astonished. I told my friends of the Kabbalist's wonderful power, of how he had predicted that the Head of the yeshiva would restore him to his former place. My friends replied: "The Head of the yeshiva is a very poor man, with a wife and children to care for. Eliezer is good at begging for alms, particularly as he looks as though he is wasting away. Therefore he is never short of money. He has bribed the Head of the yeshiva with three roubles to let him come back. That is why the Head of the yeshiva went round asking Eliezer's enemies to make peace with him, and that is also the reason why the Head of the yeshiva went to Eliezer's attic to tell him that he could return to the yeshiva — and receive his bribe." I believed them, for they said that this was the third time that he had been driven out of the yeshiva, and that he had been living there for years.

After that, Eliezer became my constant companion, never leaving me for even a moment. Each day he brought a variety of manuscripts mostly concerned with the spells and enchantments of miracle-workers, which I copied for him. He told me he had learned the magic use of names and spells from his father, who was a Rabbi in the small town of Doikloik and engaged in Practical Kabbalah. He also said that he was not afraid of demons and spirits, because he knew the great secret of how to subdue them. I urged him to reveal it to me. He explained that one had to form the letters of the name *Shaddai*[178] with one's fingers: the middle, third and little fingers were kept straight in the form of the letter *Shin*; the forefinger was bent into a right-angle in the form of the letter *Daleth*; and the thumb was bent over to form a *Yod*. The fingers had to be held in this position until the danger had passed. He assured me that this was a tried and tested protection against all evil. I was very surprised by his superior knowledge of Kabbalistic and supernatural teachings. I told him of the wonder which often had been related to me by reliable people who had witnessed it themselves: jesters, performing at the wedding of a rich couple, had made the house flood suddenly with water so that the men had to lift the skirts of their garments to walk through the water, whilst the women fled from the house; then, a moment later, the waters disappeared, and they were all standing on the dry floor. This was done by means of Kabbalistic names. Eliezer said: "Would you like to see this wonder? I will show you, tomorrow." I certainly wanted to see it: "If you are able to show this to me, I shall believe in you for ever." He answered: "Tomorrow I shall tell you what has to be done, but you must assist me, for it is too much work for one person to perform alone." "Good. I shall do whatever you wish." On the morrow, Eliezer brought written notes of everything that had to be done. A piece of wood, which had been split from the coffin of a man who had been dead three days, had to be shaped into a bow. A needle, which had been used for sewing the shrouds of the dead either that same day or the previous day, and also a thread which had been left over from the sewing of shrouds, were joined so that the needle formed the arrow, and the thread the string of the bow. The arrow was then to be shot into the wall, and the place where it penetrated would show the height to which the waters would rise in the room. Only after the needle had been removed would the waters recede and disappear. The description of these terrifying wonders convinced me that it was all true, so I was filled with longing to see them performed. I enquired eagerly: "Where can we obtain all these things?" He laughed: "Very easily. You know that Vilna is a populous city, and not a day passes without someone dying. The dead are taken to the mortuary yard where the coffins and shrouds are prepared. Pieces of wood from the coffins are thrown on to the ground in the yard. We shall go there and take what we need." "But what about the needle and thread, without which we shall fail?" He laughed again and said: "Tomorrow we shall both go together to the cemetery outside the city, and I shall get them." We went the next day, and saw a coffin there ready for the burial. When they passed by, Eliezer picked a sliver of wood from the coffin and handed it to me, and then said: "Wait for me here in the yard. I am going inside the house, where the shrouds are made." I waited about five minutes before Eliezer returned with all the things we required. On our way back I asked him how he had managed to obtain the articles. He replied: "I told the old women, who were making the shrouds there, that I had been sent by a distinguished and God-fearing scholar who lives in Vilna, and is a grandson of the Gaon. His gracious and modest daughter was at a critical stage in the third day of her labour, and had become so weak she could not give birth to the baby. An old miracle-worker had declared that if he could obtain a needle which had been used for sewing shrouds only yesterday, together with the thread that still remained in it, then the woman would immediately bear the child. When these old women heard that a good mother was in such extreme labour, they quickly obtained everything I asked for, and even urged me to hasten back as fast as I could." So he took hold of me and hurried me from the place as fast as we could go, so that the women would see that we were rushing away. On our return, we made the bow and the string, and fired the arrow into a corner of the wall — but there was no water. Eliezer said this was due to our ignorance of how to shoot the arrow at the wall, and that the enchantment still remained effective even though no water had come. He said he would do it by himself, alone, on another day, and then he would show me. I was deeply disappointed, and almost lost faith in his enchantment.

He continued bringing manuscripts for me to copy for him: he had to return the manuscripts to their owners after I had copied them. I found in them technical processes which I had always wanted to know, such as the materials used for making sealing-wax and pencils, and other articles: I wrote them, and all the prescriptions which seemed useful as well as the chemical processes used by dyers in a notebook, and catalogued them in the order of the Hebrew alphabet. I collected as many as 614 different items, many of them used by miracle-workers. One day Eliezer told me that he had been trying very hard to obtain a large manuscript written by a famous miracle-worker who had lived some fifty years ago and was now dead; the book was in the possession of his inheritors who were not even able to read. It told the whole story in great detail of the *Flask* with wonderful powers. What is this Flask? The miracle-workers of Practical Kabbalah can perform the most amazing wonders with a flask of water. If they only knew all its manifold powers, they could make the Messiah come that very same day! Eliezer told me astonishing tales about it. Long ago, a man had saved a city as large as Vilna from a terrible decree which had been pronounced against it by a cruel tyrant. The Kabbalist had filled a flask with water, pronounced spells over it, and suddenly the flask brought forth a man who had begun to grow in height until he stood before the Kabbalist like a flourishing tree. The Kabbalist asked him what should be done to the tyrant who had threatened to destroy the whole city unless a sum of thousands of silver talents were paid him. The genie replied: ''I shall go back into the flask, which you must then carry to the desert. When you see the water rise in the flask and spill over the brim, in that spot you will find what you seek.'' So it was. The man found a cave in which a vast store of treasure had been hidden; he removed from it the amount of the ransom demanded by the tyrant for the lives of the Jews. ''If that is true, then the Kabbalist must have become a very wealthy man.'' ''No, this is not so. Anyone who makes use of Practical Kabbalah is forbidden to take anything for himself, lest he be slain by the creature he conjures up.'' For more than a month, Eliezer tried to borrow the book, so that I could copy it for him, but without success. He did however obtain a promise from the grandson of the inheritor of the book that, for a payment of ten roubles, he could have the book on loan for three days and no longer, in case his father found out what he had done. However, little could be copied in so short a time, for it contained a vast amount of information.

We were sitting in the loft one day, when I told Eliezer that I had eaten nothing during the past two days except for the porridge served at breakfast. He said: ''You are lazy, and no man at all. If you wish, within the hour I can prepare for you a meal of any dish you desire. Order anything you like to eat, and I shall bring it here.'' I wondered how it could be possible to create any food one wished, simply by the use of holy names and without spending even a single penny. He said: ''Come, let us make a wager. Order what you want to eat.'' I began to count off all the things I would like to eat: white bread and black bread, salt herring with pepper and vinegar and onions, and a bottle of beer. Eliezer laughed at me: ''I will also bring you olive oil to pour upon it — and lots more, within the hour!'' He departed. An hour later he returned bearing dishes containing all these things, the oil and vinegar and beer. He removed a tile off the roof to serve as a tray, upon which we both ate. I asked him: ''Did you really not pay even a penny from your own pocket for all this? Tell me truly how you obtained all these things by which man does not live alone[179], such as oil and pepper and, most of all, a bottle of beer. Who would think of offering a bottle of beer to a starving man?'' He answered: ''I will now show you how beggars get all they want out of charitable fools, so that you yourself may learn and never have to suffer hunger again, for it is a shame and a disgrace that people hunger so much that some of them end in suicide. When I go out, I look for a door that opens inwards, behind an entrance gate, with a shabbily kept address over it. I know that usually that house is occupied by a Jewish baker. I open the door and go inside and tell them that I am a student at the yeshiva and have not eaten for two days. They will give me some bread. I then go to the market where the provision merchants have their shops, and go into a well-stocked shop and tell them that I have a young sister about sixteen years old who has been ill for two weeks, and that the specialists have recommended that she be fed with food made of pure oil and onions and a little pepper and pure honey, and vinegar and white bread, and she will then recover. Is there any one so hard-hearted that he will not give even a little of these things to save a Jewish life? Moreover, I tell them that I am the son of the renowned Rabbi of the holy city of Doikloik, that I study here in the yeshiva, and that my sister has been sent here for medical examination. I have no difficulty in obtaining everything I require. I bow and depart.'' ''But what do you say to obtain the bottle of beer?'' He answered: ''I know that in N. Street, in courtyard F., all kinds of broken glass containers are bought for the glassworks and melted down and made into new vessels. Now, the salesmen employed by the large stores always inspect the thousands of glass bottles brought to them. Those which show a glass thread in them are considered the same as broken glass and thrown on to the waste pile. There is a man who guards this pile, but if you ask him, he will allow you to pick a broken bottle for yourself. Look for one which is not cracked and has no more than a glass thread fault in it. As for the beer itself, you should know that my younger sister is seriously ill and has been ordered by her doctors to drink a bottle of beer each day! Thus, if you were not such a simpleton, you could do the same as I, and find enough food to keep you alive from day to day, although you will not obtain the luxuries I do.''

The next day, he pointed out youths of my age who practised his methods, and never lacked food to eat. However, I did not believe everything he told me about them, so he called them over to us, and told them how I shamefully starved on those days when I had no fixed meals. They swore at me, just as he had, and called me a suicidal fool. One of them said to me: ''Tomorrow, at ten in the morning, I shall take you with me and show you what to do. I wager that after you have done it yourself a couple of times, you will be able to go out alone as though you were going to a ball!'' I agreed to go with him. At ten o'clock next morning — it was one of his meal-less days too — we went out into the street, and he said: ''Wait here for me; I shall be back in a moment. Two people cannot knock at the same door together, for neither will get anything''. He left, went up to a door, and disappeared inside. He reappeared with a loaf of bread, which we shared between us. He said:

"Here is a door for you, which you must approach by yourself. Do not say a word, and do not ask for anything. They will give you what they want to give, and then you will leave." "But, supposing I find someone there who knows me? I would die of shame!" "You idiot! How many people in Vilna know you?" He repeated what I should do, and then left me alone, bewildered and helpless. I gathered all my strength and wits, and went up to the door he had pointed out. Placing one foot on the threshold, I lifted up my hand to knock, when suddenly the door opened and a man came out towards me. I panicked, lost heart, fell backwards, and fled as though my life depended on it. My heart was pounding with fear. I returned to the yeshiva. There, I made a decision, which I was determined to keep all my life, that I would rather apprentice myself to a cobbler for three years, and slave for him, and support myself by the toil of my own hands, than go begging for free food. It seemed to me that the man who waited upon other people's bounty was much worse than any animal on earth: the goat, ox, wolf or bear, do not beg for food when they are hungry. It is only man who humbles and abases himself until he is lower than the animals by begging for food. Though he may have strength in his limbs, he has none in his spirit. This, I determined upon, and I kept to it all my life. Later, I related to my friends what had happened to me outside the first door I had approached, and how I had run away in shame, and that I had decided to endure my hunger as long as I could, after which I would seek out any tailor or cobbler who would take me as an apprentice for three or five years, although I would prefer a watchmaker or sheet metal-worker: I would rather slave ten years for them than beg for food. My friends stared at me in disgust, jeered at me and spat upon me, and walked away.[180]

About a month after Eliezer's first eviction from the yeshiva, he was expelled a second time for writing foolish notes to one of the respected Wardens of the *Gemilut Ḥasadim*. This man kept a shop in the Street of the Germans, in which he sold expensive household goods. One day, the man set out a display of his goods in front of his shop: chairs, mattresses, large expensive mirrors and precious paintings. Eliezer passed by, and stopped to look at the expensive wares on display and the collection of mirrors and paintings. The man shouted at him angrily: "*Patron*![181] On your way!" Eliezer did not budge. The man went up to him, kicked him behind the knees and drove him away. Eliezer returned straight home, and wrote an anonymous letter in which he poured all his wrath upon the man, and cursed him with the most terrible imprecations. He handed the letter to a poor man telling him that he would receive a handsome gift when he handed it over to the recipient, for it was a precious letter. The poor man waited until the letter had been opened. Suddenly, the man attacked him. The poor man wept and pleaded that he was not to blame, that he had only now received the letter from one of the yeshiva boys, a thin youth with a lean face. It soon became known that Eliezer had written the letter. He was brought to trial before the Wardens who banished him for ever from the yeshiva. He moved out of the yeshiva and went to live in the House of

Study for lone students in the outlying Zharetsche[182] district. Some eight days later, he came to visit me. Being afraid to enter the house, he sent one of the boys to call me out. He handed me some new manuscripts to copy out for him, in order to ensure that our friendship continued and that we should never part.

Seven days later, Eliezer came again to see me in the street. He handed me a booklet for copying, about the process of dyeing and how to make honey from vegetable produce, and how to make cutting machines and other new and useful things which were beginning to be made in our land, although they were known only to one in a city and two in a family.[183] I enjoyed reading about them, and copied them for myself as well as for him, in the hope that I could use them one day to make my own fortune. Eliezer continued to visit me, and proposed that I leave the *Gemilut Ḥasadim* yeshiva and go to the House of Study for lone students in the Zharetsche district. He promised that I should never be short of food and I would be able to study much more than in the *Gemilut Ḥasadim* yeshiva, and he would even ensure that I would have a regular income. I refused. He then proposed further that I leave Vilna with him to travel through the towns of Russia, Ukraine and Podolia; he would be a miracle-worker, and I would be his collector and assistant. "How can I assist you?" I asked. He then explained: "You ought to know that the most successful miracle-workers were those who were able to put on the best performance for the ignorant men and the foolish women. They made a fortune. This is how you will help me. We shall stay together in a guest house in a small town where there are a lot of fools. I shall remain in the room so that the people do not see me, for I am a holy man engrossed all day long in the Kabbalah. You, however, will go and mix amongst them. When the guests ask you about the young man, you will tell them that I am not simply a young man but an *Avrekh*[183a]. I shall, incidentally, buy myself an embroidered prayer-shawl and large phylacteries. You will tell them that I am the son of the renowned Kabbalist and Rabbi of the holy city of Doikloik; that I have been acclaimed by all the great Rabbis of Lithuania and Zamot as a very holy person who has driven out many *Dibbuks*[184] and cured many epileptics; that I can adjure demons and spirits; that in a certain city I raised the dead who had been in their graves for ten years; and have also made barren women fertile. Indeed, who has not heard of the famous miracle-worker Rabbi Eliezer of Doikloik? You will then see that the idiots will send me their barren wives and their sick women, with gifts of money." "Can anyone guarantee this? If they do not come, as you say, then I shall starve of hunger, and will not have the means to return." "I will guarantee," he said, "that you will receive no less than three roubles each week for yourself. Whatever we get above that amount, we will share. But, certainly, you will never get less than three roubles." Nevertheless, I refused to accept the position of assistant to this new miracle-worker. In truth, I feared lest he might kill me on the way, and steal everything I possessed, for I suspected him of the worst crimes.[185]

In my haste to be rid of him, I told him that I must consider the matter, and would let him have my reply later. He urged me to go with him to his lodgings in the suburb where we could continue the discussion further. I promised to come one day, though I could not say when. "But you may come and not find me," he protested. "Tell me when I can expect you." I promised to see him on the coming Sabbath, so he turned and went away. I, however, had no intention of seeing him, for I had no wish to listen to his notions which, I believed, were utterly false. Nor was it my nature to deceive people, however gullible they might be. Furthermore, I was afraid he might trick me into agreeing to his proposition, for then I would be unable to break my promise: I had been brought up, from childhood, to tell the truth, except where there was danger of dire misfortune. All that Sabbath, Eliezer waited for me, but I did not go to see him. In the evening, he came to me, and begged and pleaded with me to visit him on the following Tuesday. I promised nothing. Whilst talking, he raised his hand and took hold of the locks of my hair, which were long at that time because of my circumstances, and pulled out two or three hairs which he hid away. "What are you doing?" I asked. "You are going to have convincing proof of the power of Practical Kabbalah, for against your will you are going to come on Tuesday to my lodgings in the Zharetsche district. I shall be waiting for you, and shall come out to meet you." "How do you know," I asked, "what time the spirits will carry me to you?". "I shall know that exactly." I laughed inwardly, not believing a word. I even mocked him: "Had you not informed me in advance, it is possible that the satyrs might have carried me off to you. Now that I have been warned, I shall not permit myself to be carried away by any ghosts and demons." "I have told you what I shall do to you on Tuesday. You will come." With that, we parted. I despised him for his delusions and, by the morrow, I had forgotten his words altogether, and thought no more about him.

On the Tuesday — (hear, now, an amazing incident, which still astonishes me to this day) — at about midday, I began to feel unwell and faint, and everything I did became a laborious effort. I did not know what was wrong with me, or whether I was beginning to fall ill, even though I felt no symptoms of illness at all. I decided to go for a walk in the fields outside the city, since it was a pleasant day and the walk would refresh me. The desire to go out became too strong for me to restrain although I had never before wanted to go for a walk alone, and only went at the invitation of my friends. I could not understand what was happening to me. I went out reluctantly, and wandered through the streets, not knowing where I was walking. It was when I came to the corner of the street in the Zharetsche district where Eliezer lived, that I suddenly remembered what he had said to me three days earlier. I began to feel frightened, for it seemed to me that this was the work of some supernatural agency. I stood bewildered for a moment, not knowing what to do. I decided that, at all costs, I must not surrender my soul to that despicable person. I turned my back upon his lodgings, and walked away to my left, but my legs could hardly carry me; my body felt as though it were weighted with lead, and my shoulders bowed down with heavy sand. Thus, I went out of the city through the recreation fields, until I came to a forest. I noticed that the evening was coming on, there was no one else about. I was afraid to go on alone, and turned back. By the time I reached the yeshiva, the clock was striking eleven. I lay down and went to sleep. In the morning, I awoke feeling fresh and completely well.

On the following Sabbath, Eliezer came once again to see me. He did not mention anything about his wonder-working, so I said to him: "What happened to that irresistible power which was to make me visit you last Tuesday? Since I was not afraid of your spells, or of any of the demons you sent to carry me off, I did not go to you." In actual fact, I was very curious to find out how such a well-tried enchantment had failed: I well knew its power, for I had had to struggle strongly against it, and only by the strength of my own will-power was I able to withstand it. I asked him to tell me about the enchantment, for I had not found it in any of the books I had copied for him. However, Eliezer would not tell me, because it had failed its purpose. I then told him what had happened to me, how I had suffered until I almost became ill, but had resisted with all the strength at my command. Then he agreed to tell me of the spell he had spun with the hairs he had pulled from my head. This is the form of the spell. He had threaded the three hairs through the eye of a needle (which had been used for sewing the shrouds of the dead, although I cannot be sure of this now), and wound them down the length of the needle; then he had thrust the needle and threads into the ground; and recited: "I want the owner of these hairs to come to me today (or in a few days' time)." That was all. I was too astonished to believe him or his enchantments. Nevertheless, since I could find no other explanation for what had happened to me three days earlier, the incident remained a mystery. From that day, he stopped seeing me and came no more to visit me. I did not know where he had gone, although I felt sure that if he had stayed in Vilna he would have come to see me. I do not know to this day whether he went off alone as a miracle-worker or found someone else to act as his assistant.

At the close of the half-year term of my stay in the yeshiva, my uncle stopped supporting me, and I heard no more from him. Even Rachel, my cousin, was unable to support me any longer. I realised that I would not be able to pay the two-rouble fee to the Head of the yeshiva for the next half-year, nor would I be able to provide food for myself. My friends advised me to go to the private-study yeshiva, where each student on his own, but where I might find someone who would be willing to help me with my studies. There, the students, who were few in number, were treated with compassion and kindness. I was advised to go to the Mendel Motskevich yeshiva. It had a small synagogue, next to which was a small room for women worshippers. The yeshiva students showed me the women's room (which was empty) where I was able to choose a box in which to keep my belongings — as all the boxes in the men's room had been taken. So I began my studies in the large room, whilst my belongings were in my box in the women's room. After several days I realised that here, too, there was no supervision over the students and no one cared whether they ate or starved.

One day, a former student of the yeshiva approached me and walked outside with me into the street. He questioned me about my circumstances and my meal-days. Bitterly, I told him everything. He said: "I shall see to it that you can take my place as treasurer of the *White Society*.[186] I am leaving it because I want to visit my uncle in the city of P., so the Society is left without a treasurer." I was completely nonplussed, for I hardly understood a word he was saying: "Tell me, my brother, what is all this about? I have not been here long and know nothing about this Society. Who are they? What do they do? Why do they need a treasurer and what are his duties? How can all this help me?" He replied: "The Society consists of a number of youths like us, about our own age, but who live at home. Each one saves up the monthly or weekly allowance he receives from his father: any member who does not receive an allowance, either steals the money or sells any small item he is able to steal. The money is kept by the treasurer who is chosen by one of the members. Every two or three weeks or every month, on a particular day chosen unanimously by them, they arrange a celebration: they leave home for a few days, or for as long as they are able to be absent without their families worrying over them, and indulge in wild celebrations outside the city." "Yes, but what do they do there, and what do they eat, and how do they live?" "You ask questions like a simpleton! Look, they have saved money, so they go to houses where they can eat the best foods and drink the best wines and spirits and also have beautiful girls for their amusement. They enjoy themselves for a few days, and then return home." I could not imagine why they did this, nor could I understand why rich youths, who enjoyed the best that their loving parents could give them, should behave so madly and hoard their money for a month in order to hide away for a few days and drink and eat in a storage place. As for the pretty girls, I imagined they were the landlord's daughters, who therefore could be of no service to them. I was so far from comprehending the kind of pleasures they could find there, seeing that they came from wealthy families who indulged their every desire, that I became too ashamed to question my friend further. I realised that, because of my restricted upbringing at home, there were many things I would not understand or know anything about. Instead, I asked him about the treasurer's duties. He said that, since it was impossible for them to carry their money about with them lest their parents or sisters find out and take it from them or lest it be lost, therefore one of them would seek an honest youth from a poor family, or an orphan living on the charity of his relatives, who would be responsible for the money handed to him from time to time. He also had to keep a book in which each member recorded the money he gave them. For this he was rewarded by being permitted to join in their festivities in the Povelanka[187] district at their expense. I asked: "How am I expected to live for a month whilst waiting for a couple of days' merriment?" He replied: "You should understand that, however honest you may be and though you may never take a penny of their money, nevertheless they will allow you to buy your food with their money; or alternatively, they may offer you a wage of some kind, since they will see that you are an honest person, and that moreover I am recommending you. I will give you my accounts book, and then they will accept my recommendation.'' However, I did not fully understand the situation, and therefore did not give him a definite reply, being afraid of falling into a evil and corrupt trap. He turned and went away and I saw him no more. Later, I remembered an incident concerning a tailor's son who stole his father's books. I was never able to understand why that youth, who was the only son of a wealthy man, and never lacked anything, should want to steal from him, and furthermore break open the Rabbi Meir Ba'al Ha-Nes[188] collection box for the few coppers that were in it: indeed, what could he wish to buy seeing that he was not short of anything? I realised then that he must also have been a member of the White Society. This later transpired to be the case.

During this period, a youth came to our yeshiva who, according to his account, had previously studied at another yeshiva in Vilna, but now wanted to return home. He had no money for the journey, and so he offered to show me three secrets which he had kept to himself and for which he had paid a lot of money. Necessity compelled him to reveal the secrets at the present time, for he had to leave but was without funds. He was therefore willing to reveal a secret which he said would one day earn me a fortune. I had no money at that time to pay him, so he said: ''Bring four youths, each willing to pay a quarter of a rouble, and I shall show you in one night all three secrets. The first secret is how to peel off a layer as thin as skin from each side of a coin without altering its appearance, except that the letters and inscription will be less prominent and it will look like an old coin. These clippings from both sides of a rouble coin can be sold for twenty kopeks. If you could obtain a hundred roubles and splice off the clippings, you could still sell the coins at their normal value, since they will not have devalued in appearance, and you could keep the twenty kopeks from each. The second secret will cost you very little money to make, and even though it is of little practical use, it is exceedingly lovely to behold. It is a method of cultivating beautiful flowers inside a glass bottle: these flowers glitter like purest silver even though they are not made of silver. If, however, the bottle is shaken, the flowers will fall and wither away. Therefore, they are best kept in a sturdy, immovable container where they cannot be shaken, and then the flowers and blossoms will last for a long time and will be a delight to behold. The third secret is how to prepare sealing wax of superior quality.'' It was the first secret which attracted me most: I had always been interested in fine craftwork, and this promised in addition a good reward. I found two other youths willing to learn the secrets; the fourth was brought along by the young man himself. That evening, we gave him our quarter-roubles. He then said: ''Now give me brand-new silver coins of twenty or thirty kopeks value and, later when everyone is asleep in the house, I shall show you what to do, and you can then do it for yourselves in my presence. As for the other two secrets, I shall write them down for you.'' However, there was not silver coin[189] among us. It was ten o'clock at night, and people were going to bed. I went with one of my friends into town to find a money-changer. They were all closed, but we found one still open in the fifth street we went to. He charged us ten kopeks for exchanging twenty copper kopeks for silver. Our teacher heaped fine sulphur on the coin, which he then secured to a metal wire and held over a candle. When the coin became heated by the flame below it, the sulphur began to burn. With a knife, he peeled a thin layer, together with the burning sulphur, off the coin. It was as black as coal, and crumbled into pieces between our fingers. Nevertheless, it was a piece of silver from the coin, except that it was black in colour. He peeled off another layer from the other side of the coin in the same way. The coin itself appeared normal, and no one would have refused to accept it at its face value. If, however, several clipped coins were tendered together, it would be noticeable that something had been done to them to reduce their value, and that they were not simply old coins. As for the blackened peelings, he said he would immerse them in an acid to purify them (probably hydrochloric or sulphuric acid). Each piece taken from a silver rouble was worth a clear twenty kopeks. We understood full well that, despite his assurances, we would not gain any great benefit from all this, for in order to make a hundred roubles profit, we should need to buy a thousand roubles,[190] which we could not. Indeed, if we had possessed a thousand roubles, we would have been able to live comfortably without resorting to fraud. Nevertheless, the method was worth knowing for its own sake, so we did not regret the small price we paid for it.

A very astonishing incident, which I shall never forget, occurred at that time. One of the yeshiva students brought a small, very old book called ''The Science of the Hand''.[191] All the boys gathered round, and held out their hands in order to learn from the book how the lines of their palms foretold their future. I joined them. I saw from what the book told of the lines of my hands that I would succeed best in craftmanship which would assure me a successful living. Other boys had different lines, which foretold their success in business or good luck and such-like things. In truth, for many years thereafter I had to earn my living from teaching writing and arithmetic, until in the course of time I learned the craft of the clockmaker, when I had married for the third time and had two sons, one from the first and the other from the last marriage: from that craft I was able to invent new machines for practical applications which put me on the road to success. My friends and contemporaries, on the other hand, remained dissatisfied teachers and *melammedim*. It is a puzzle which I cannot dismiss, for the book is still in existence: it has a large illustration of a palm complete with all its lines which reveal the future. There was another remarkable thing shown in the book: when the hand is doubled up into a fist, if one examines the folds of skin between the little finger and the thumb, one can discern among the long and deep lines traversing the width of the palm, other lines which are shallow and short and which are different with each person. One particular person, for example, might have only one deep line, whereas another might have two or three lines, and someone else one deep line and one shallow line. The book foretells, in accordance with these lines, the number of wives a man will marry in his life; the smallest lines denote the betrothals which are later broken. Thus the lines of my right hand foretold that I should marry three times, and be engaged once. I was greatly troubled by what I read, although I did not put much credence in it. My friends, however, had a good laugh at my expense. Today, when I recall how correct the book had been and that not one of its predictions had failed, I can understand how even the most learned of scholars can come to believe in the most foolish superstitions, such as cartomancy, etc. Furthermore, if I had the book in my possession today (although I am not looking for it) and saw that, according to the lines on the palm of my son's hand, he would succeed best in commerce, I should not specifically advise him to learn a trade — or vice versa. If it indicated that he would marry twice or three times, I would not advise him to build a house with a wall which might be taken over by this father-in-law in the event that he divorce his wife or that she died. There are other similar things which I cannot reasonably explain despite all my efforts to rationalise them, and therefore, I have to believe in them. I must accept factual reality which demands: Do you have proof to the contrary? What if it is all no more than coincidence? How can the same coincidence occur in so many different ways? What sensible man believes in dreams? Yet what man is there so wise that he will not believe in a dream which is frequently repeated and predicts as truly as did the breastplate vestment of the High Priest? He must surely concede, to some extent, that man's spirit conceals many powers and qualities which are still unknown to us. Take particularly all the discoveries made in recent times, which are so simple and clear today that they cannot be disputed, but which were considered contrary to reality, until they were brought out of Nature's repository. Did scientists believe there was a force of electricity until it was discovered? Are today's scientists prepared to guarantee unconditionally that there is no ethereal force in Nature which can be given material form — any more than they could solemnly avow that the sounds emitted during the operation of a talking machine, when it acts upon an iron spring and reproduces sounds on a thin sheet of lead, would not be reproduced in a hundred years' time to act upon the eardrums of their grandchildren and relay their words to them, in the manner of the Phonograph? Even those believers in spirits, the Spiritualists, have a firm basis for their beliefs: it is only because they are ahead of their time that they are derided. Nevertheless, the physical scientists, the materialists, would not be wise to rush into total opposition to them and reject all they stand for, since it is highly probable that the Spirit itself is an undiscovered physical force which manifests on rare occasions, and which may well be revealed at some future time. Eventually, the Spirit may also be revealed as a form of matter more delicate than light and electricity and magnetism, and to whose sensitive action only the spirit of man and the soul of the animal respond. We do not understand how it works, nor can we explain how it etches lines in the skin to coincide with events which occur to a person over a long period of time — or how the dream can foretell to the sleeping soul events that are happening, and will happen, in some distant place and time. We have not the least understanding of these things. Since the force does exist in reality, we may confidently assert that even this undiscovered force acts in a very fine physical form, and behaves in the same manner as all other natural forces, and is not supernatural. Once its qualities become known to us, then probably it too may be made to operate, by means of simple material objects, and perform the tasks we devise for it so that it will serve us as do light and electricity and magnetism.

That winter, prices rose steeply in Vilna — not because of drought or an abundance of rain, but because the roads around the city became impassable and the farmers were unable to bring their produce into the city. I was studying in a part of the Great House of Study, and kept my belongings, together with the occasional morsels of food which my uncle brought me, in my box in the women's room. About a month later a new student arrived at the House of Study. He was the son of a wealthy man of the village of Dolina, about an hour's journey from Vilna. This new student was about twenty-four years old. In his youth, he had been a devout student at the yeshiva of Eishishok[192]. On his return home, he had married, and later divorced. His parents had compelled him to resume his studies, much against his will. He chose this private-study yeshiva, and had his own room in the women's house. Because I had to keep coming and going into his room as my box was there, he grew angry with me and ordered me to stay away. I told him that my box with all my belongings was in the room. He said haughtily, in the manner of a rich person: "Take your things and leave." Since, however, no other box was available for me at the time, he allowed me to use my box a few more days until I could find another. Now, amongst my belongings which I kept in my box was also the book I had written when I was still at my father's home, and which the Cantor had prevented me from finishing when he had snatched the last page from me. One day, the man who was known as the Doliner, watched me as I was opening my box, and looked inside. He noticed the sheets of paper written in the form of a book, a rare and uncommon thing for any yeshiva student to have. He took the manuscript out, loosened the binding and read it. I stood by, full of joy. He asked me who had written it. I told him I had written it when I was at home, in Serednik. "From which book did you copy it?" he enquired. "I composed it myself," I answered. "Do not lie to me, for I might put a pen in your hand and ask you to continue it." "Give me a pen this moment, and I shall write seven times as much!" The man realised I was telling the truth, and asked me to lend him the manuscript for that day. He took it and went out. It was his custom to study no more than two or three hours per day: what he did the rest of the day or night, I did not know. On the following day, he returned the manuscript without saying a word, although he did permit me to continue to use my box in his room without further provocation. Some days later, Yudel came and spoke to me: "Tell me, why did you come to Vilna, and what were you seeking here? If you want to study by yourself, as you do here, you could do so in the House of Study in your own home-town, without all the suffering you endure here." I replied: "I came here for three reasons. Firstly, I had heard that young people like myself could gain entry into the Gymnasium, from which they could go on to the University and qualify as physicians, which is what I wanted. If that failed me, then I should have the opportunity of studying at a great yeshiva and becoming a Rabbi. If that also failed, then there was still the possibility that I might become apprenticed to a craftsman, a watchmaker or a sheet-metal worker, with whom I could gain the skill to devise and invent new tools and machines of all kinds." He asked: "Did you pursue any of these aims?" "I made many enquiries but without any success. I cannot even settle down to study in the yeshiva because I cannot afford the annual fee of four roubles. I cannot afford even to buy food, so how can I sit down to study on an empty stomach?" "Look, I shall take care of you, for I believe that I can help you to fulfil one of your ambitions. I shall begin with your present studies. I shall let you know in another couple of days." Three days later, Yudel informed me: "I have been speaking with a young man who lives with his parents-in-law and studies in an attic in the house. This evening, I shall take you to him, and if he likes you, he will work with you as a friend and teacher." So it was. The man questioned me a while on my knowledge of Talmudic disputation, and was sufficiently satisfied to offer to teach me every day. On my return to the yeshiva, I told my friends that I had found myself a teacher. They declared unanimously that I must leave the yeshiva, for only students who studied there all day were allowed to sleep there. "Why?" I asked. "Because the members of the Society who support the yeshiva will not believe that you are telling the truth." "Why should I lie? Can they not find out the truth by enquiring of the man who teaches me?" "They will not do so. In any case, they have an old rule that any student, young or old, who does not study in the yeshiva in the daytime is not permitted to sleep there at night." There was a possibility that Yudel might be accepted as a guarantor for me, in which case I might be allowed to sleep there. I asked him. He said: "This is possible. However, the young man informed me yesterday that he does not want to study with you unless you have your own Gemara. He wants you to bring one." "Where can I obtain one for myself?" "Well, if you cannot borrow one from your friends, you will have to buy one for sixty kopeks." I did not have a penny even for food, but I felt too ashamed to tell him. The matter ended there, and Yudel pursued it no further.

A few days later, Yudel said to me: "I have found a craftsman for you, a clockmaker who recently settled here in F. Street, after his wedding. He is a good friend of mine. I told him about you, and also stood surety that you would work for him for a period to be agreed on by both of you. He is willing to teach you, so I will take you to meet him in five days' time." The days passed. Later he said: "You will have to wait until after Passover, for during the winter trade becomes very slack. He is not a rich man, and cannot afford to support an apprentice before the festival. After Passover he will take you." It was then just after *Ḥanukkah:* how was I to live until the summer[193]? I said to him that I could not wait that long, and it would be better if he could find another craftsman for me, perhaps a metal-worker or goldsmith. He answered: ''I have looked and tried everywhere, but the people who do not know me, will not accept my guarantee on your behalf and therefore will not take you in.'' Thus the second plan came to nought.

Several days later, my friend Yudel informed me that he had been making enquiries about my entering the Gymnasium. This was a very difficult matter. For one thing, a uniform had to be bought. Furthermore, no pupil could gain entry without a knowledge of Russian and German and mathematics. Yudel said he would find teachers to instruct me in those subjects without payment and, when summer arrived, they would also help to find the necessary uniform for me as well as the text books. In the meantime, they would try to persuade their in-laws to invite me to have my meals with them each day: they themselves were being supported by their in-laws. Better still was the news that, for the past three years, the city's wealthy patrons had been petitioning the Government to open a Rabbinic Seminary in the city, similar to those which had already been established abroad. Their applications had finally succeeded, and the school would be opened that same year [194]. Since orthodox Jews were not willing to be the first to send their sons to the new Seminary, the first intake of students would come from the poorest homes: ''You will be the first of these students — a pillar of the establishment. You will be more privileged than anyone else, and if you excel in your studies, the orthodox Jews will learn from your example.'' My ears rang with this wonderful news, for it seemed that at last I would find relief from my sufferings: it should be no problem for those rich young men to find food and clothing for me as well as to teach me, and so enable me to live until the summer when I could join the new school, which had been my main ambition. Moreover, Yudel described for me the wonderful future that lay ahead of me. He said that, although in my present humble circumstances I might look up to him because of his superiority in Torah and learning, and for his wealth, yet in ten years' time he would come to me when I would be a fully qualified physician, and would doff his hat to me in respect etc. etc. He told me that he had once learned the art of tanning in case of need. I was very surprised and asked him: ''Why should you need a trade? You are wealthy, as are your parents and your sister who comes to visit you here. So why should you not continue to live in the manner of your forbears without a trade, especially one that is neither clean nor simple?'' He replied: ''In my young days, I thought the same as you. My one ambition was to spend my life studying at the yeshivas of Eishishok and Volozhin. However, since my return to Vilna, I have come to realise how foolishly I wasted those youthful years. The students of Gemara and all its commentaries have no contact with the realities of this world; they will not be able to survive the hard times to come when they become burdened with a wife and family. They will deplore these wasted years when they suffer the shame of starvation and poverty — but it will be too late by then. If they had only learnt a trade by which to support themselves during times of hardship, they would not need to fear anything." His words worried me, for he spoke derisively of those who studied the Talmud. Though somewhat abashed, I could not refrain from retorting: "Sir, you speak presumptuously against the Talmud, which is the repository of all wisdom. Its scholars are honoured by all people and they live by it." He laughed at me, and said: "You are a foolish and simple lad. Hand me the Gemara in which you meditate day and night, and show me what wisdom you have found in it. From the first page to the last, it is nothing but folly and phantasy. See how these *Tannaim* and *Amoraim* spend their time delving into the problem of whether it is permitted to eat an egg laid on a festival [195]. What difference can it make to us whether it was laid on that day or any other? This is how they spend their time to the detriment of more important matters. Take any Gemara, or even the entire *Shass* [196], and if you read it with an open mind, you will see that, from beginning to end, it is all folly." I refrained from replying to him for, when I was a child, I had been told that there are Jews who are learned in the Talmud but are nevertheless heretics. I had never met one before; now that God had brought me into their company, I was in great danger of being enveigled into heresy myself. I decided to let him say what he pleased without answering him. I would remain steadfast in my faith, and would accept only the good and reject the evil.

Some days later, Yudel handed me an address where I could find a teacher who would also take care of all the things I needed for admission into the new school, which was due to open shortly. I saw the address was the courtyard of Reb Eliezers in F. Street. I was surprised, and I looked forward to seeing the basement which had once been claimed by the ghosts of the owner's relatives as their inheritance [197]. It was an account I had read in the book *Kav Ha-Yashar* [198]. One hundred years ago, a wealthy man of Vilna, Reb Leib Lezers, had died and left his house to his sons. Some days after his death, ghosts began to haunt the house and wreck the courtyard. The tenants of the house fled. The sons brought in miracle-workers to exorcise the ghosts, but without success. The city was in a turmoil. The pious and righteous men of the town held services in the house, and took their Scrolls of the Law with them in order to study there all night. Just after midnight, they heard a voice speaking from under the ground. It said: "Leave this place. It is not right that you drive us from our inheritance. The owner of this court was our father, and therefore we, his inheritors, have come to take possession of our share of the inheritance together with his living sons." On the second night, ten learned and pious men stayed the night in the house. They prayed and blew the *shofar*. Suddenly, a different voice was heard speaking from beneath the ground: "We will not leave this house, for it is our inheritance. If the living people are willing to share it with us according to law, let them occupy the upper floors. We shall take the lower rooms, and shall do them no harm." Then the men blew again on the *shofar*, and adjured the ghosts to abandon the house or suffer excommunication by the Ecclesiastical Court. The voice replied: "We refuse to leave until the living inheritors agree to judge this matter in court." A date was fixed for the day when the Supreme Court would convene in the city's courthouse, and listen to the plea of the ghosts. The day came. As the people looked on, they saw a whirlwind emerge from the basement of the house and storm through the streets, tumbling burning brands down the streets towards the courthouse. The courtroom had been divided by a cloth into two sections so that the ghosts could make their plea on one side of the cloth without being seen by the judges. The Rabbis commanded them to present their suit and prove their entitlement to the inheritance. A voice, deep and low, spoke from behind the curtain: "The deceased was our father, and we were born to him out of the act of onanism[199]. We have therefore taken our rightful share of the inheritance, for we are more numerous than they. If however, you allot us our part in the downstairs rooms and the basement of the house, we shall do no harm or injury to any man." The living sons heard the voice and quaked with fear. The Rabbis declared: "It is the opinion of this court that only human sons can inherit the effects of a human father. On the other hand, human sons cannot inherit the possessions of a ghostly father, nor can ghosts inherit or be called the sons of any human being. Therefore, it is the sentence of this court that the ghosts shall leave this house and go to dwell in the wilderness, never to return again to disturb the rightful inheritors of the house." Then the storm came out from behind the partition and returned to the basement. On the morrow, people saw a tremendous dust-storm sweep out of the windows of the basement. Thereafter the house was still.

I arrived at the courtyard of the house of Reb Lezers, and asked where the basement was. I was shown the windows by which the ghosts had departed: they were broken and in ruins, for no man had set foot in the basement since that time.

I climbed up six steep flights of stairs until I arrived at a small room cluttered with filth and refuse. The man I sought lived there. We spoke together for a while, after which he handed me a Russian book to read, and asked me if I understood the words. I did not. He gave me a German book to read. He then gave me pen and paper to write down in Hebrew anything I wished to write. He said: "Come here every day at three o'clock in the afternoon. I will let you have a Russian book which you can read to me, and you can write down the words which are unknown to you and I will tell you their meaning. On your return to the yeshiva, you must revise those words until you know them. Then, when you see me the following day, you can tell me the contents of the passage we studied. This, we shall do every day. Later, I shall introduce you to a man who will do the same for you in German, and also to another teacher in mathematics." I picked up the sheet on which I had written the words I had to learn, and went back to the yeshiva. I met Yudel, who said: "Be careful not to let any of your friends know that you are learning a foreign language, for they will certainly drive you away." I asked: "In that case where can I study my lessons?" "Do as I do," he said. "See this Gemara open before me? I have a little Russian book hidden inside it. If anyone happens to come into my room, I put the book away under the Gemara so that it cannot be seen." [200] I went to my teacher in the afternoons for three days. On the fourth day, Yudel told me that the man wanted me to see him at nine in the morning. However, this was also the time of the morning service in the synagogue, and I felt sure that there would be no place for me to pray in the man's room. Therefore, I arose at eight o'clock, took my phylacteries with me, and went to the new-old yeshiva adjoining the old-new [201] yeshiva not far from Reb Lezer's house. I entered, put on my phylacteries and prayed alone. I hastened to remove the phylacteries in order to be ready to see the man at nine o'clock as he had requested. When I entered his attic room, I saw three or four young men there, with their phylacteries and prayer-shawls lying unused and unwrapped on the table. Beside a wooden bed in a corner stood a tall, dark skinned young girl about twenty years old: she was dressing herself in front of them, whilst they watched and joked. I was stunned. I realised that these young men had left their homes ostensibly to go to pray, but had come here instead to amuse themselves. I told myself: "Let them do whatever they please, so long as they are willing to help me do what I want to do." I stood there uncertain of what to do or say. I looked about, and saw a large picture on a wall, and began studying it. The men gathered around me and asked if I recognised the painting. I said: "I know the picture, for the man's name is written at the bottom, *"Alerander Pavlovich"*. They laughed and said: "Are you sure that is the man's name?" "Yes," I replied. "Here is his name, *Alerander Pavlovich,* in German letters." The men were surprised, and asked: "Do you read German?" "I do." "But how can you read without knowing the letters?" I read the letters again — A l e r a — "That letter is not r but x," they pointed out. I was surprised to find a new German letter composed of two letters *"ks"* joined together. The men asked me again how I could read a book without having first learned the alphabet. I told them that I had always longed to be able to read German books, for I thought that German books contained interesting stories: since the German people do not have the Talmud with its Commentaries, what else is left for them to write besides stories and yarns? I had searched all over my home-town for a German abc book but without success. My father had taught me to read Polish from the inscriptions printed on the front of Hebrew books, where the name of the book and the Censor's permit were written in Polish. These did not have the letter 'x'. One day, when I was making my way through the vegetable plots which lie like a broad sward in front of every house I came across a number of Hebrew-printed sheets of paper strewn upon the ground. I examined them and found that, on one side, were passages from the Prophets and Holy Writings in Hebrew, whilst on the other side they were in German. I picked up some of the sheets and took them home, and showed them to my father. He said: "These come from the Bibles which are distributed in Prussia to the Jews who come over from Russia by ferry-boat. They are given to them free. The Bibles are well-bound and printed. However, a few Scriptural passages have been appended to the last pages which refer, according to the missionaries, to their Messiah. These are the passages which are translated into German on the reverse side of the sheets. These Bibles are given free to anyone, even to those who cannot read Hebrew, so that they might see that the Prophets had prophesied about their Messiah. The Jews, when they saw that the Bibles were printed properly and correctly, accepted them but, on their return home, tore out the pages at the back containing the Hebrew and German passages and threw them away. These are the pages you found.'' I realised that, if I could only learn to read German, I had before me passages in both Hebrew and German. Nevertheless, how was I to read without knowing the alphabet? This upset me considerably. Some days later, I noticed that the forms of the German letters bore a resemblance to Polish letters. On a sheet of paper I copied the outline of the letter resembling a German letter 'a', and followed this with 'b' and 'c'. One letter I found confusing, because I could not tell whether it was 'f' or 's', so I wrote both letters over it in the hope that, by reading words which contained it, I would be able to discover how to pronounce it. Thus, if I read *fagte* I would realise that it was actually *sagte*, a word I knew, especially since its position in the sentence referred to the Hebrew word *vayyomer*[202]. I then erased the doubtful 'f' and wrote 's' in its place. In this manner, I wrote the whole alphabet. I read through all the sheets, and was able to understand the translation from the Hebrew original. Thus I learned to read German. However, the letter 'x' differs from the letter 'r' only by a short stroke, and has no equivalent in Polish. Nor did it appear on any of the sheets of paper. Therefore, I was not aware that it existed in German, and that is why I read the name as Alerander Pavlovitch.''

The men were surprised by what I told them. One of them gave me his address and told me to call upon him every day at eleven o'clock, and he would teach me to read German. The next morning, I called at his house. It was the house of a wealthy person, with spacious rooms and fine furniture. His wife came in and looked at me with disgust, for my clothes were ragged and torn. I wore a fox-skin hat which had two straw-lined side-pieces to cover my cheeks; I had bought it with a rouble coin I had found when I was at the *Gemilut Ḥasadim* yeshiva and was studying in the attic. I used to rest my feet in the dirt on the floor, and one day I had found a coin there. It was rusty, but I cleaned it and it turned out to be a silver rouble. However, the young man's wife and his father-in-law treated me uncivilly, and stayed at a distance from me. The man showed me a small German book which had also a Polish vocabulary, and told me to read it exactly as he would teach me. He also told me that I should obtain a copy for myself, or if I wished I could buy his copy for fifteen kopeks. His words troubled me for Yudel, my friend and benefactor, had assured me that these people were wealthy and would support me with food and clothes and tuition, and prepare me for admission to the new school. Now it seemed that all these promises might be false. He himself lived in regal manner, eating and drinking as he pleased, whilst fully aware that I was starving. In fact, on one occasion, during his lunchtime meal, he cut off the top of a radish and threw it to the floor under the table; I waited until he had left, picked up the pieces and devoured them. He was well aware of my constant hunger, and on one day in every three days, he would give me money to go and buy for him apples or nuts, and if there was a kopek change, but no more, he would let me keep it. I began to think that people like these promised a great deal and gave nothing. I looked at my teacher of German, living in this sumptuous house, with piles of books lying in a corner, all probably foreign books — as he had taken from them the precious book entitled *Ogedik* [203], for which he had requested the price of 15 kopeks from me — and I despaired of understanding their motives. I tried to see him on the following day, without bringing the money in the hope that he had not been serious, but he ordered me to bring the money or else he would take the book back. He did offer me one concession, that I could pay him ten kopeks now and the balance later. I told my friend Yudel about this, and he said that the man was only testing me. So I sold a small pair of scissors and a pocket knife, and paid the man his ten kopeks. He took them and then wanted to know when I would pay the other five. I realised then that the man was quite serious. In any case, I had not found the *Ogedik* particularly helpful, for I could understand almost all of it without his assistance. Therefore, I stopped going to him. It was clear to me that I must not pin my hopes of salvation on this kind of person, nor even wait for the new school to open, that is if ever it did open and if I were accepted. Some three weeks later, I told Yudel that I was almost in despair, that I wanted to return home and wait there until the school opened, and then return to Vilna. Yudel urged me to reconsider, to stay on and suffer rather than leave, because things would be bound to improve, and once the men understood me better, they would endeavour to obtain for me all that I required. However, I could not believe him, nor could I see him as the type of man whose kindness lay in deeds rather than words. He went on to paint a picture of the future that awaited me at home, of how I would have to become a *melammed* teaching little children; he painted it in the blackest colours that pierced deep into my soul. Nevertheless, I had lost faith in him, for I saw that all these people had forsaken their religion and faith, and neither feared the Lord nor loved their fellowmen. What could I hope for from them? It is possible that the fault lay in me. I had always been extremely shy, and always lived in poverty, and never had shown sufficient temerity to prove that I would ever amount to anything. I decided to return home, come what may.

One day, the wife of my former teacher Reb Berl of Serednik came to Vilna to buy goods for her shop. She brought me four zlotys [204] from my father. I told her I would not accept the money, but would give it to her if she agreed to take me back home with her, for I had no wish to stay in Vilna any longer. She agreed, and took me back with her to my father, in Serednik.

My father and mother were still living in the same house and in the same room they had occupied for the past six years. The house was situated half-way down the street and near the foot of the hill. It was ten cubits [205] long and six wide, with a door leading from the street into a hall which ran along the width of the house. At night, the door was barred like an impenetrable fortress by a stout beam propped against it and slanted into the floor. There were two large rooms at the right of the hall, whilst the apartments of the residents were on the left. One room, four cubits square, was inhabited by the landlord; a second room, three cubits square, was inhabited by a man and his wife with their three children, who rented half the room to another man and a school for seven pupils who studied Torah and Gemara all day-and they still had space left for preparing the oats which they sustained themselves. In the hall, they kept a millstone for grinding corn, and in a corner of the room they had an oven going summer and winter to dry the grain, with tables near the oven on which they sieved the oat grains. These people had combined with the teacher to rent jointly the half of the house on the right of the hall. It had two windows set in the wall overlooking the street: one window served the part of the room used as the *Talmud Torah*, and the other, set in the wall near the door, the part used for drying the grain. The landlord had built a small hut behind the house at the foot of the hill, using the side of the hall as one wall and hewing the other three walls out of the hill: it was three cubits wide, the same as the hall. A door led from the hall into the hut. There was a small window in the wall opposite the hill. The hut was four cubits long, the ceiling about three cubits above the floor, whilst the roof reached the hill above it. Originally, it had been intended for use solely during the festival of Tabernacles, but later, when the landlord fell on hard times, an oven had been put inside it and it was rented out for six roubles a year. It was in that room that my father lived for six years. There I spent my early years, and there my soul budded and blossomed and flourished. In that hut, twelve boys and girls crowded together around the table by the window all day long, learning to read their prayers. At the side of the wooden plank which served as a table, my father kept a barrel filled with potatoes and vegetables. At noontime, when the children went to have their meal, the plank was covered with a white cloth and bowls and spoons for our own meal. There, at that table, facing my father, I used to sit when I was writing my book *Studies in Religion*. On the window ledge I kept all the books and volumes of the Talmud which were the source of my studies, together with my writing materials. One thing, however, was a constant source of annoyance to me. Between the wall and the side of the hill was a gap about a cubit wide, which was used as a path by people going to and fro. Anyone passing the window blocked the light from outside so that the room was plunged into darkness. Worse still was the disturbance created by the pigs which wandered about the rear of the house, and found the corners of the walls a suitable place for scratching themselves. Whenever one of these enormous swine stopped to rub himself against the wall, the whole house shook from floor to ceiling, until it seemed that our home would become our grave. Then we would all go rushing outside with sticks in our hands, to drive off the monstrous beasts which were threatening to pull down our peaceful abode and raze it to its foundations. Added to this anxiety was the gloomy belief my father held that pigs only rubbed themselves against houses which were threatened with misfortune. He would sigh deeply and despairingly, and my mother and I would sigh with him, for we had boundless faith in his wisdom.

The hall, in its entirety, was shared by the residents. A large stove had been built into the wall of the hall which formed part of the landlord's room, to provide heat during the winter; he also had a big oven on which he and his family prepared their meals and baked their bread. He kept one corner of the hall covered with straw and hay for the goat which was kept there. The other corner of the hall belonged to my father who built a pen there, strewn with straw and fodder for his own goat. Our other neighbour, however, could not keep a goat in the hall since he had already filled his share of the hall with his millstones. There was always a pool of foul, brackish water near the entrance of the hall which was formed from the two rivulets of water which trickled down the wall, through the goat's pens, and along the slope of the hall. During the cold days of winter, this water froze into thick ice. Nevertheless, no one would shame us by asking why we lived like this, for everyone knew the value to human beings of an animal which was pure (in the religious sense): its milk supplied blessed sustenance to the family every day, and often there was sufficient left over for the next day's breakfast which the children could enjoy with a slice of bread. However, in the autumn and winter the goats looked wretched. Because they were unable to withstand the severe cold in the hall, they would emerge from their pens and climb on to the stove which was kept hot all day long for cooking and heating the room, and would lie there all night. Sometimes, if glowing coals and brands had been left in the stove, the goats' hair and skin would be singed, so that by morning they appeared spotted and speckled all over. They were such a sorry sight that they became a byword in the town: "singed like the *melammed's* goats". This is how these inhabitants of small towns and villages lived and carried on their lives — and so they will go on living for ever, like the primitive dwellers of Kamchatka and Samoyed. When, therefore, I returned from the big city of Vilna I realised how poorly we had lived — although before I had ever left my father's home I had always considered it a veritable paradise.[206]

My parents welcomed me happily, and my father asked me what my plans were for the future. I was feeling despondent and had no answer for him. He said: "My advice is that you return to the House of Study and continue with your studies, and God will help you." I replied: "That is all very well, but may I ask where my food is to come from? No doubt, the Law of the Lord is perfect, reviving the soul, [207] but where there is no bread there can be no learning.[208] You are much too poor to support me." "Put your trust in the Lord and He will sustain you[209]. Continue with your studies in the House of Study, and I will bring you food every day." "Very well. I shall try it. However, when you bring me each day my single portion of potatoes baked in their skins, and without bread, you will realise that I shall soon be living on the Gemara alone — and then you will have to change your ideas." "I will never change. God will help me, and you will have plenty to eat." It was the month of *Adar*. I sat in the House of Study, studying the tractate *Megillah* [210] day and night, and sleeping all alone in the frighteningly large House of Study. I was not influenced by fear of the dead or ghosts, for I had left all that behind me in Vilna. I was impressed by my German book, the *Ogedik*, which I had bought in Vilna and brought home with me. In it I read that the lights of the will-o'-the-wisp, which I had always believed to be mischievous spirits — when ever I saw a light at night in the distance I was certain the spirits were making fun of me — were in fact no more than vapours which issued from swamps and ponds, and glowed like phosphorus. As a wayfarer draws near to them, he is repelled by the obnoxious atmosphere, and flees from the place in panic, imagining that mischievous spirits had led him astray. Since I knew that Maimonides did not believe in the reality of ghosts, I concluded that all men are liars and there are no ghosts or mischievous spirits, and that the dead will never call upon me to take part in a nocturnal Reading of the Law, as superstitious people believe.

Word went around the town that Aaron's son, a distinguished scholar, had returned from Vilna. By noon of the third day I had consumed nothing but my problems. My father brought me potatoes baked in their jackets, with some cooked groats. This sustained me all day, albeit with a certain degree of discomfort. Afterwards my father brought me food twice or three times each day. Finally I said to him: "Forgive me this time father, if I say that it must be plain to you that the Lord does not wish us to kill ourselves over His Torah, seeing that He does not provide you with sufficient means to support me. What good will it be for us if I go on like this? Far better that I learn some trade from which I can gain a living." "The Lord will help us," he replied, and left. About two weeks later, Jeremiah, a wealthy young man of my own age who had recently married the daughter of Rabbi Ḥayyim, came up to me and said: "My father-in-law, who is very fond of you, has spoken to me about you, and believes that it is not good for you to sit in constant study like this and live off the meagre bread of your father. He suggests that you become a teacher of young boys and girls, teaching Hebrew language and reading together with some arithmetic, and you will be able to find a living here." I pricked up my ears at hearing this suggestion which I had never before considered as a means of income. I asked how I could be certain that pupils would come to me. He said: "My father-in-law, the Rabbi, says that since you cannot expect them to go to you, you will have to go to them, to their homes, where you will teach them an hour or two, according to your agreed fee and time. You will go from one house to the next during the day, giving lessons." "In that case, my dear Jeremiah, will you explain to me how I can be so bold as to approach the rich and ask that they entrust their daughters to my tuition? I cannot do this. If they send for me, I will go." "Good. First, my father will send for you to teach my sister, and you will ask him for a fee of two roubles per month for one hour's tuition per day. Once you have begun to teach at my father's house, then the neighbours will also send for you. For teaching ten hours per day, you can earn twenty roubles per month, which you would not earn if you were teaching boys alone. Furthermore, your pupils will be from wealthy families and so your payments will be assured." I related the Rabbi's proposal to my father, but he remained silent, for he would never speak against the Rabbi, whose words were always holy to him.

The following day, Jeremiah told me that his father wanted to see me about his sister. I was sceptical, thinking that he was using this excuse as a means of getting me to see his father and asking him for lessons. He then said: "Look, I will take you to my father myself, and I will do the talking about your fee, and all you need do is listen." We went, and it was as he had said. On the following day, I was called to see a wealthy neighbour of theirs, to arrange tuition for his daughter also. On the third and fourth days I was invited by their other neighbours to teach their daughters. I also had a group of two or three girls whom I taught together for one hour at a fee of three roubles per month. The parents were delighted at having found someone who could teach their daughters writing and arithmetic, which their own forbears had never learned. I made the staggering sum of twenty roubles per month. It was, however, sufficient to arouse the jealousy of the older *melammedim* — and especially so on the Sabbath when fathers tested their sons on the week's lessons and found they understood nothing, whereas the parents of my pupils were full of praise for me. I was very pleased, and said to my father: "For sixteen years [211] I toiled night and day over the Gemara without earning one penny from it. Yet this writing and arithmetic, which you so begrudgingly permitted me to study for an hour or two in the evenings, is now bringing me in an income higher than that of all the learned *melammedim* here." He made no reply, and indeed had no reply to give. From that day, I assumed the liberty of reading any banned secular book I wished, without any protest from my father who saw that I was now able to support myself. Nevertheless, licence to read freely is useless without books to read, and all I had with me was the little reading book which I had brought from Vilna and which I had read a hundred and one times already. A few days later, I found another German book, a novel, but could not understand it, and was deeply grieved. Now, I was teaching the daughter of a rich woman, whose husband had left her and gone to France and become a missionary. She possessed a large Prayer Book for use during the whole year, with the prayers translated into German and printed in Hebrew letters. I was very interested in the book, and asked the girl if her mother would allow me to borrow the book for a few days. After some difficulty, I was given permission to borrow it, and so began to learn German from Hebrew prayers. I copied out all the words together with their meanings, and found, after a month's study, that I was able to understand the German very well.

It was at this time that I came across the amulet which my mother had worn over her heart since I was born, and which had been given to her by a holy miracle-worker named Elkanah of Regiole. It was triangular in shape and was encased in leather. I said to my father: "My mother will not bear any more children, and I am too old to suffer the ailments of little children. Let me open this amulet and copy its contents into my own book of the Kabbalah." He agreed, but warned: "Take great heed of your safety, and never engage in Practical Kabbalah and the use of Names. My grandfather, whom I never saw or knew, used to practice Kabbalah and conjured Names, although it is a well-known thing that whoever does so will not see his children live. [212] I am now the third generation of my family who have suffered this punishment. You are the fourth and, please God, your children will live if you do not engage in this practice.'' I promised him faithfully that I would not do so, but would only copy the inscription. I took a knife and cut through the outer leather cover. Under it was a cloth covering, which I tore open, and found a case made of tin and iron. I broke this open and found inside a folded piece of paper on which strange letters such as ⟨symbols⟩ had been drawn in ink. [213] I copied them into my book. The word spread around that I kept a book for working miracles.

One day a woman came to speak with my father. She was very poor, depressed, the wife of a ferry pilot on the river crossing to Prussia, whom she never saw for periods of six to eight weeks at a time. After she had gone, my father came and told me her secret. This woman had lost her first six sons, and now the seventh son was not expected to live more than a month. She suffered from hallucinations. ''What,'' I asked, ''is this sickness?'' ''It is a form of illness common to women, which results in their children dying early.'' ''But what kind of illness is it? What are its symptoms?'' ''She does not suffer any pains, but at night she dreams of being raped by Germans. [214]'' ''What does she want of me, father?'' ''Well, a certain miracle-worker has been giving her enchantments to perform during her pregnancy. One of them is a spell she has to say when she goes to the ritual ablutions. However, she cannot read Hebrew, so she had to find a man who would agree to read the prescription for her whilst standing behind the wall, and she would repeat his words. This man is also unable to read the writing, so she wants you to copy the spell in square block letters so that the man will be able to read them aloud to her from behind the wall.'' I agreed to help her. She brought me all her enchantments, and I read them. They were full of incredible remedies, such as tearing a black cockerel into halves which she then had to bury in an earthenware jar in the ground whilst reciting meaningless spells, etc. I therefore told her to recite her prayers in the evening when in the water, and these would be beneficial for her, for I considered that her recitation of prayers in Yiddish would strengthen her spirit and enable her to resist the visions she suffered in her sleep. I also told her to stop using the strange enchantments as they would harm her but, instead, to use one which I would write for her which was that she was to sit on the edge of her bed, before retiring, squeeze her fingers as tightly as she could into her palms, and say: *''Ich vil nit as es zolen mir holmen, ich vil nit, vil nit, nit''*. [215] She was to repeat this three times, quietly and with absolute confidence in its efficacy. She should then lie down to sleep, and she would be troubled by visions no more. As soon as the woman understood that she need not continue with the previous strange spells, she put complete faith in me and followed all my instructions. In the following year, the woman came to see my father again and to express her heartfelt thanks for my advice and remedies, for her son was now about ten months old and healthy and well, and he was the first of her sons to live even to this young age. She brought me a gift, a pen which cost at least two roubles. My father handed it to me. We were both amazed at the outcome of my advice.

A year had passed since I had begun teaching. I had bought myself new clothes, particularly for Sabbath and festivals. At that time, my mother fell ill with a fatal sickness although she lingered some seven months. My father became poorer as time passed by, losing even the poorest of his pupils to the new *melammedim* who were able and willing to teach in their pupils' homes. I therefore found it necessary to give part of my income to support my parents. My father still deplored the secular books which I read every evening, for he could not bear to see that I, his only son for whom he had had high hopes of becoming a leading Rabbi, had stopped studying the Gemara. One day, on my return from a walk in the town, my mother said to me: "Take the German book you brought from Vilna, and hide it. Your father threw it into the toilet bowl but I have retrieved it and hidden it." I understood what had caused my father's annoyance with the book. A day or two previously, I had read to him from it about the causes of rain, snow and clouds, of thunder and lightning, the rainbow and the lights of the will-o'-the-wisp. He had listened attentively, and, it seemed, with some satisfaction, to my descriptions of Nature. However, he must in fact have been filled with despondency, believing all this to be heresy. Although he had not cared to tell me how he felt, knowing that I would have answers for all his arguments, he had revealed his hostility to this accursed book to my mother.

About a month later, my mother passed away. She put her hands in my palms, and I felt her fingers were cold as ice. Her feet also were cold: only her bosom burned hot as an oven. She said: "My son, why are your hands as cold as ice?" I realised then that she was near the end. An hour later, she closed her eyes, and fell into everlasting sleep. It was Friday, the sixth of *Tammuz*.[216] She was buried the same day.[217] On the Sabbath, *melammedim* and scholars came to visit my father, and discussed death and the soul. They said that the soul returns to the room where the corpse is lying in order to see its body again — in accordance with the scriptural verse, "But his flesh grieves for him, and his soul mourns over him."[218] Therefore, we keep a lighted candle in the room, as well as a bowl of water in which the soul can dip itself when it enters.[219] I was unable to tolerate their misconceived ideas about the soul and their native belief that it actually dips itself into the bowl of water. I therefore began to discuss with them the nature of the soul. If we assume that the soul is a burning flame of a candle, then it will not dip itself into water, for fire will only combine with fire. In fact, the soul is not a flame, for fire is matter, however fine its composition, whereas the soul is divine and ethereal, and cannot be immersed in water. Our reason for performing all these rituals is only in order to direct our thoughts to the nature of the soul that lies within us. The body defiles the soul; the moment it leaves the body, it becomes pure again. If, however, it returns to look again upon the body, it becomes impure again, and requires ritual immersion. Similarly, the candle is kept lit in the room in order to remind us that "the soul of man is the light of the Lord",[220] and we should keep it pure. The people sat and listened to me without saying a word. Finally, my father arose, his eyes flashing fury: "You wicked and evil person! By right, I ought to take you and beat you until you die. It is only my reverence for God and this Sabbath day that restrains me!" The men, afraid of his towering rage, held him back. I kept silent, realising how wrong I had been to try to teach wisdom to the ignorant. From that moment I decided to keep a firm rein on my tongue, and never to speak with ignorant people.

Some time later, people began to urge me to open my own school. They said that, since I was a successful teacher, my pupils should come to me and that I should not have to call upon them in their homes. It was then springtime. They told me about the hut that belonged to Moshe ben David the Ḥasid. It stood apart like a small private house and was kept closed all year round except for the festival of *Sukkot*. It had been nicely decorated inside with pictures of diverse animals on the walls, and the great Leviathan crouching in a ring with its tail between its teeth, and also the wild ox, and paintings of the Patriarchs. Moshe ben David the Ḥasid let me use his hut free of charge for teaching during the summer. I realised that my success was due to my desire to learn writing and grammer. I felt pity for those young men of my own age who were too poor to pay for their lessons, so asked them to come to my school for one hour each day and learn writing and language, which they could then continue to study at home on their own. However, I soon came to realise that not all were like myself, for although many came to the school, hardly one of them was really interested in learning. I wearied of them, and finally sent them away.

In the month of *Av*[221] I was told to vacate the hut, because the circuit-preacher was coming to the town. I asked about him, who he was, and what was his function. I was told that the Rabbi of the Ḥasidim made a circuit of the towns where his Ḥasidim lived and expounded on his new teachings. Since, however, the distances were so great and there were so many towns to visit, he normally sent a learned Ḥasid in his place to relay his instruction to his people. The man who came to us this time was the representative of the Lubavitch Rebbe. The Ḥasidim congregated in the hut for two or three days and allowed no outsider to enter, except for myself seeing that I had been given permission to use the hut during the Summer. I was very keen to hear the preacher speaking to the Ḥasidim in Yiddish. All that I was able to hear however were the fables and aphorisms which he related in a loud voice, such as "like a solid mirror which looks like plain glass but reflects all images". The rest of his discourse was delivered in an inaudible tone and indistinguishable words. Thus the Ḥasidim sat before him for five or six hours at a stretch without moving a hand or foot. When they eventually left, even those too ignorant to recite their daily prayers declared his praises, and said that this time the preacher had uttered teachings so sublime that they were beyond the comprehension of mere mortals, or even of the angels in heaven.

One Saturday night, my father stole quietly away from home. When I arose in the morning I found on my table a large three-branched candelabrum. I understood from this that my father had remarried. She was a young girl from a very poor family. They had been married only two months when he divorced her. He married again; this time it was his niece, a divorcee, about forty years old. She was a bad-tempered shrew whom I could not endure. She treated me as though I were her close blood-relative, making me toil for her for nothing, and taking all my wages from me. So I left my father's home and went to lodge in the house of a rich man, whose two sons and a daughter I was teaching.

I was eighteen years old[222] when my cousin Ze'ev the Weaver came to visit us: he was the son of my uncle Jacob Baredzever, and the brother of my stepmother. He lived in Vilki, about one hour and a half-hour journey from Serednik. He had a small house with a vegetable-plot. Weaving was a poor trade but he had earned his living from it for thirty years. Three times every year he would come to Serednik to obtain yarn for weaving: there was no weaver in Serednik. He had often spoken to my father about a neighbour of his in Vilki, a very wealthy though miserly man, who owned a large orchard and vegetable-plot and horses and cows. He was a tanner. He had two young sons and a daughter, who was the eldest of the three. He had mentioned to his neighbour that he would like me for his son-in-law. My cousin spoke to me at length about it, now that he saw me dressed in good clothes and with a regular income. I told him: "My dear cousin, I see no way of getting married, since my income is insufficient to support even myself alone. Even though my father-in-law might maintain me for the first few years, how will I be able to support a wife and children afterwards? That is the reason why I do not consider marrying at present, and will not do so until I am able to obtain a good livelihood from a trade or a business." My relative, the weaver, answered: "You know very well that I am not a marriage-broker and that I expect no payment from you or your father, so you can trust me to understand your feelings. Now listen to what I have to tell you. Your father-in-law will support you at his table for three years, and at the end of that time you will be able to leave him with at least one thousand roubles of your own. I have seen this actually happen in Vilki: a certain tanner took in a son-in-law, gave him a dowry of one hundred roubles, which the son-in-law turned into several thousands during the three years he was living with his father-in-law." I could not comprehend this, so he explained: "Listen and understand. A tanner buys skins, which he then treats for three or four months until they are thoroughly tanned, and sells them for a third profit. This is what he does with the skins he stores in his tannery four or five times each year. Now, you will receive a dowry of a hundred roubles from this tanner, who is very fond of his only daughter and will take good care of her, and you can invest that money in his business. From the very first sale, you will have gained a third profit, and you will then have one hundred and thirty-three roubles; on this you will gain another one-third profit from the second sale, namely one hundred and forty-one roubles; and so on.[223] Think how much you could have by the end of the first year!" The calculation was very attractive. Furthermore, whatever my cousin related about these people must be correct, for he lived next door to them and could observe and hear everything for himself. Although the tanner was not highly esteemed, because of the lowly trade he followed, yet he would surely not object to his only daughter investing the dowry in his own business? That being so, I should not object to take a wife who could help me to succeed in life. A thousand roubles seemed to me to be a fortune beyond the reach of even the richest men in my town. Our discussions lingered on until the month of *Nisan,* [224] 1844, when my father decided: ''Come, let us go and see this Hillel the tanner and his house and his daughter. If it is God's will, we will enter into a marriage contract.'' We were relying entirely upon the reports given us by our relative, the weaver. When, therefore, we entered Hillel's house, we did not make detailed enquiries. Hillel sent for his friends and relatives, who liked me, and urged Hillel to take me for his son-in-law. He was reluctant, saying that his own poor straits would not permit him to take a young man who was unable to earn a penny for himself. However, they did not believe him, for the whole city knew that he had hidden in his garden a jar full of gold and silver which he was too mean to unearth and spend. His relatives, knowing that the miser was thinking of the expenses involved, boldly urged that the normal contractual period be revoked, and that the wedding be held on the very next day in order to reduce expenses to a minimum. He agreed to this. When I was asked for my opinion, I turned and asked my father for his, and he then asked my cousin the weaver. The decision was taken to go ahead. On the following evening, therefore, I stood under the wedding canopy, whilst all around me people were laughing and joking, although I could not understand why they needed to be so merry. On the third day, which was a Sabbath, I was led to the synagogue and clad in a prayer shawl. The women in the women's gallery gazed at me in astonishment and said: ''How handsome he is! How is it possible that such a handsome and learned young man could become the son-in-law of the contemptible miser, Hillel?'' When the Sabbath was over, I returned home with my father in order to say farewell to my friends and collect the remainder of the fees still due to me and also any gifts that people customarily give on these occasions. I bought my wife a fine shawl as I had promised her. From the father of one of my pupils, the only one in our town who possessed any German books, I received a wedding present of a small German book called *Die Lyrisch Poesie*[225] which contained selections of poems by the great German poets: I treasured the book more than money. When I returned to live with my father-in-law, I made it my first task to copy all the German poems on to paper in Hebrew characters. I bought a pen and ink and began to do the copying. It took me all day to do it. My father-in-law's house consisted of only one room. My father-in-law slept in one corner on a large, covered bed; I was given the corner opposite to him; in a third corner stood a table used for both eating and working; whilst in the fourth corner was a large stove. The sons slept on benches beside the table. After my wedding, a curtain was hung over my small bed. The skins were treated in this house: they were brought out, stinking, from the verminous pit or the plastered cistern where they were kept, and their hair removed with iron and wooden tools over the table which became covered with filth. I thought I would please my in-laws by showing them how well I could copy from a German book. This, however, caused my father-in-law to shed copious tears. That very day he told his gentile neighbour how grieved he was to see that his new son-in-law had fingers as thin as straw, totally unsuited for manual work. He wept so bitterly at his misfortune that the neighbour misunderstood him and later asked the weaver, who also lived nearby, how it was that Hillel was weeping so bitterly over his son-in-law who had no fingers, for he should have known this long before the wedding! The festival of Passover was approaching, and I began to appreciate my situation, for never in my poverty-stricken father's home had I seen, at a festival time, the scarcity that reigned in this house. As for the dowry and investment in the skins, not a word had been said. When the festival ended, my in-laws began to urge me to return to Serednik and resume teaching as before in order to save some money. Believing this to be their only reason, I agreed. I went back home, and found that a teacher from Rasseyn had come to Serednik on hearing that I had left. I remained until Pentecost and managed to save six roubles. I returned to my in-laws, who were delighted with my success. I did not, however, wish to go back to Serednik since there was no room for two teachers, so I remained in my in-laws' home.

There was a man from Vilki who spent most of the year in Memel on business for his German employer, but returned home for a couple of months during the festivals and continued to attend to his business affairs whilst at home. He was looking for someone in the town to write letters in German for him. He heard that I could write in foreign languages, and approached Hillel for permission to dictate business letters to me for which he would pay normal business rates. He dictated his letters word by word in German, and I wrote them down on paper. How delighted he was when he received replies to his letters! He knew then that I could truly write in German. He requested me to continue to write his letters, and closed the door so that no one should hear his business affairs. One day, whilst I was writing a letter for this businessman, a young man entered and looked at the letter as I was writing it: he was from a wealthy Kovno family, was also being supported by in-laws as I was, and also knew German. At the time, he said nothing, but on the morrow, when I entered the House of Study where he spent a lot of his time, as I did, he called me aside and said: "Tell me, brother, how do you manage to write German without knowing the alphabet?" I was astonished, and said: "What are you talking about? My letters are read in Prussia, and even answered!" "That is so. I also know that you write correctly, even better than I, but there are certain letters which occur only at the end of a word but which you are writing in the middle and beginning, and vice versa. I wonder, therefore, how you came to write German without having first learned the essentials of the abc which every child knows?" "Well, what mistakes have you found?" "There are three letters in the

German alphabet whose pronunciation is *samakh*. One of them is like a *samakh* and a *zayin,* but is written at the beginning or middle of a word. The second occurs only at the end of a word. The third is 'sz' like two *samakhs*. Now, the *samakh* which should occur only at the end of a word, you are writing at the beginning, whilst the second one you write sometimes at the beginning and sometimes at the end. Similarly, you do not put the double 'ff' letters in their correct place.'' I then told him how I had come to learn the German language. In Vilna, I had been shown the letter 'x' but not the alphabet. I had also read many books, but had never learned to write letters until a man from Keidan had come to our town; in his younger days he had been a teacher. After much persuasion, I got him to do me the favour of writing out the German alphabet for me. I copied down exactly what he wrote, but there was no one to tell me of any mistakes I may have made. ''Now, therefore, I must thank you for what you have told me, and ask you to teach me what I still need to know.'' He did so. Because of his interest in me, he also asked me how I had come to understand the meanings of the words I read in German and Russian. I told him: ''Most of the words I understood from the Daily Prayer Book, the German from the translation and the Russian from the context. Many words I learnt from the *'Me'ir Nativ'* [226], in which the Hebrew roots are translated into Russian.'' ''Oh,'' the man exclaimed. ''Did you not know that there exists a dictionary which gives both German and Russian words together, side by side?'' ''Is this possible? Why, all the words in the German language alone will fill a volume as thick as the Talmud itself! It is the same with the Russian language. How would I ever find the word I wanted? Or do I have to learn the language by heart from beginning to end?'' ''You are mistaken, my friend. The book which contains all the German and Russian words is no thicker than a man's palm, and no bigger than a small prayer book. Furthermore, it is simple to find any word you want, because the book is arranged in alphabetic order. It costs no more than one and a half roubles. I do not have one with me here, but in a few days time I shall be going to Kovno, and shall get the book from my brother who will be able to buy another copy for himself. If you give me the one and a half roubles, you can have the book in a couple of weeks.'' I had the required amount left over from my fees which I had collected in Serednik, so I gave it to him. Two weeks later, the book was in my hands. I opened it and my eyes lit up. I was now able to read a Russian book and look up the words I did not know, in a language which I had never thought I would learn. Understandably, I came to love this 'heretical' book with a love surpassing that of women — even of my wife, whom I did not love, and had not married for love, but only out of consideration of the material benefit she could bring me. It was summertime. I lay down in bed beside my wife, and read the book until it became dark. I awoke early before daybreak, placed the book in front of me together with a German and a Russian book, and enjoyed myself looking up the words I needed. Apart from all this, my wife gave birth to my firstborn son, Judah Leib.

Her parents conceived the notion that I did not love their daughter; they blamed the 'heretical' book I had brought into their pure home. When they reproached me about this, I told them openly what I felt, for I had never in my life been able to lie: only out of compulsive necessity had I ever veered from the truth, and even then I had merely concealed the truth without actually lying. I said: "I did not marry your daughter out of love, for I knew I was in no position to support a wife and family on my income as a teacher. When my relative, the weaver, promised me, in your name, that you would give a dowry of one hundred roubles to your daughter, and you would invest it in your tannery business so that during the three years I lived with you the money would increase to two thousand roubles, and knowing further that I could earn some income from my knowledge of languages, I agreed to marry your daughter. I do not hate her, nor do I have the slightest thought of not loving her, for she is my first wife and I want to remain with her for ever. Nevertheless, if you persist in refusing to fulfil your promise, and you imagine that I shall always be a *melammed* and will support your daughter on love alone, I must warn you that you are greatly in error. The bread and food which you offer me will be in vain, for I shall never be yours, nor will your daughter be my wife, though she bear me ten children." They stood amazed at my words, uncomprehending, but believing that I was only attempting to frighten them in order to obtain the dowry. Later, I heard from others that my wife's clever relatives approached her and asked her about her relationships with me. When she replied that these were 'normal', then they concluded that I had been only threatening to leave my wife if they did not fulfil their promise. After I heard of this, I continued to live with my wife, whose name was Bathsheba, for seven months, sleeping in the same bed, without touching her: nor did she attempt to arouse me, for she had been brought up in a small town. When her parents and relatives learned of this, they took me to court before the Vilki Rabbi, and a divorce was arranged and written out. However, the affair was delayed until the evening, and so the matter became invalid.[227] That night, I returned to their house, took my pillow from the bed and lay down to sleep beside the stove. The next day, they decided to come to terms with me. My father-in-law promised to invest, at first, twenty-five roubles in the tannery, and then a further twenty-five in another six months time. I accepted this compromise, and returned to my wife as before. Assuming that, if my wife bore a child, I would not want to divorce her, they delayed giving me anything, although I was not certain whether they really did not have the money or were actually refusing to pay. When, therefore, my wife gave birth to our son, and her relatives saw that I had great compassion both on her and the child, for it is not my nature to hate without cause, any more than I love without cause, they believed that I would now shoulder the burden of supporting them myself from my teaching. In fact, I did make preparations for setting up a school in Vilki, but at the same time I reminded them of my earlier warning, that I would leave them if they did not fulfil their promise. I began taking some of my meals in my school and only returning home to sleep, until it became clear to them that I was quite determined on my course. They also feared lest I sue them in the district *(Stanovoi)*[228] civil court, for an incident had once occurred which so panicked them that they almost died from fear. I was in my school when a gentile was sent to find me by the *Pristav*. My in-laws knew that I could write but not speak German or Russian. They believed that I was in some kind of trouble and were delighted, for their hatred was greater than their fear. They therefore told the man that I was at the school. I asked the policeman what he wanted of me, and he said that a case had arisen requiring a knowledge of German language, and so I had been sent for. I put my *Schmidt Dictionary*[229] in my bag and went off with him. In the Court I translated, with the aid of the dictionary, that a legitimate son had been born to a German potter in a village some distance from the city, and that his name was so-and-so. This was done so that the child might be properly registered at the *Pristav* offices. When I returned to my in-laws' home safe and sound, they feared me as much as they feared the District Judge.

In the month of *Ellul,* I announced that I wished to go to see my father in Serednik and to visit my mother's grave, as is the custom at this season. I had saved a little money for my expenses, and intended to stay there until after the *New Year*. I knew that my relatives would suspect me of wanting to run off to America, and would not let me have my prayer shawl and phylacteries. I therefore kept them in the school. When I told them I was going home to Serednik to visit my mother's grave, they asked where I had put my prayer shawl and phylacteries, and I told them I had them in the school. ''You are running off to America!'' they cried, and grabbed hold of my coat, and held on tight to me until we reached the Rabbi's house. There, a divorce was speedily written out. They took all my possessions, including the prayer shawl which they had bought for me, whilst I even had to pay the expenses of the divorce. It was not until the evening that I was able to leave the Rabbi's house and go off alone. On the morrow, the Rabbi gave me an old prayer shawl in payment for teaching his daughter during the summer. I was forced to remain in that town over the period of the Day of Atonement and the festival of Tabernacles in order to collect the money my pupils owed me.

I am never surprised when I hear that a man who had divorced his wife, later remarried her. I myself had waited such a long time for my wife's parents to agree to our divorce, for there seemed to be no other course for me to pursue, yet when I finally succeeded and became free, I was struck with remorse, and felt as though I had lost a hand or leg. It is even possible that, if any one had approached me at the time to take her back, I might have given in to that error, however reluctantly. It is all very astonishing. I was now in a position where I was obliged to remain in the town the whole winter, much against my will, for it was too late in the year to set up a new school in some other town. I was very distressed.

During the intermediate days of Tabernacles, I was informed that the owner of the Barak Hotel near Yurburg was looking for a teacher for his two sons and a daughter. My name had been mentioned to him. On the morrow, I took the wooden raft on the river Nieman as far as Tilsit, in Prussia. Barak was near the bank of the river. I paid the fare and left. I arrived at the hotel the following morning. When I entered, I found some forty men praying the morning service. I put on my prayer shawl to worship with them. When it became known that I was a teacher, the landlord told me that I must go up on to the Cantor's forum and recite the *Hallel* for them: it was apparently the custom in rural hotels for *melammedim* and teachers to perform the duties of Cantor and Reader of the *Megillah*,[230] etc.. I protested that I had never performed these duties for any congregation at all, that I was not sure of how to perform them, that I had a voice like an ostrich totally unsuitable for their purpose. They knew, however, that I could write in several languages, and had also written posters for synagogues — for I had once covered the walls of my town's synagogue, which had been built in 1842, with large Hebrew notices — so they refused to believe that so accomplished a person did not know how to perform the duties of a Cantor. Five of the men took hold of me and led me to the pulpit, ignoring my protests. I was so panic-stricken before this congregation that I forgot that the Cantor has to wave the *Lulav* and *Etrog*[231] during the intermediate days of Tabernacles as though he were a soldier in battle. Now, I had never possessed any of these articles and had always made the benedictions over a borrowed *Lulav* and returned it, without actually knowing the correct manner of waving it. Had I remembered, at that moment, that I should have to wave the *Lulav,* then not even the entire congregation could have forced me on to the pulpit. I decided I would simply pray the *Hallel* as well as I could, seeing that I had not come to this place in order to seek a position as a Cantor. However, no sooner had I opened my mouth to say the benediction over the *Hallel*, than the whole congregation called out: "First you have to make the benediction over the *Lulav,* and then over the *Hallel!*" Then it all came back to me, and my legs began to shake with fear. However, there was no escape. One of the congregants came and stood by me and showed me how to perform the wavings. In this manner, I completed the *Hallel*. I was not asked to read the Additional Service as well.

Among the congregation was the son-in-law of the landlord, a Ḥasid, son of Moshe ben David of Serednik: he had known me since childhood. He rebuked me: "I know that you did learn a great deal of Gemara with Commentaries, so how is it that you never bothered to learn the order of the wavings from the Gemara or the *Shulḥan Arukh*?" It was a difficult question for me to answer. I had once studied, in the tractate *Yoma*,[232] the order of the High Priest's services during the Day of Atonement, and it had seemed quite unnecessary for me to know all the details of it. Similarly, I had felt there was no need for me to know the details of the waving of the *Lulav*, for it had not occurred to me that I should ever be required to lead a congregation[233]. In the event, I was forgiven, and I remained there as teacher to the children at a salary of twenty-four roubles per half-year. I then found myself with time to read my books without interference. My book, *Me'ir Nativ*, was a Hebrew dictionary which gave the translation of each root in Russian and German, and its source in the Bible. I also made a Hebrew translation of my book *Die Lyrische Poesie*. I also began to compose a book of poems of my own, which I called *Eshet Ne'urim*.[234] I had brought from Vilki a book by the Gaon of Vilna on geometry called 'The Three-year-old Ram':[235] although I had only borrowed the book, I had not yet returned it since I valued it highly. I had also brought a German book, 'The Seven-Years' War of Frederick the Great'.[236] I also had a very thick book which contained all my own writings, including the *Lyrische Poesie* in Hebrew, which I had written in Vilki, as well as many letters in German and Russian. The book I used most was the Schmidt Dictionary. With these books I spent my winter days. During *Purim*, the hotel landlord suggested that I read the *Megillah*, as the worshippers would be paying three or four roubles to hear it read. I accepted, and prepared myself to read it in the required intonation.

The end of winter brought an end to my teaching. I decided to return to Serednik and celebrate the Passover with my father. The hotel landlord did not ask me to come back in the following summer to continue to teach his children. With about eighteen roubles in my possession, I packed my belongings and left. I found my father in extreme poverty, so I paid the expenses of the Passover celebrations. During the intermediate days of the festival, I made a trip to Vilki to see my relative, the weaver, as well as my first-born son. I arrived in Vilki on Friday, and next day went to pray in the synagogue. During the service, I was asked by Gedaliah, the merchant for whom I had written letters in German, to see him outside. We were both still wrapped in our prayer-shawls, but we went outside and strolled through the street and the garden. He tried to persuade me to marry a local girl and settle down in the town — his interest being that I should always be at hand to help him with his letters. The proposition seemed very attractive. The father was called Tsevi Subbotnik.[237] I knew him only distantly, and also his young daughter whom I had often seen sitting barefoot with her friends on the balcony outside the window. I said to the man: ''She is only a young girl, no more than twelve years old.'' ''Not so, my brother. She is now sixteen years old, and very pretty, clever and diligent. Furthermore, her father will give you two hundred roubles as your dowry, and will maintain you in his home for three years or even more, for he is a wealthy man. It was he who asked me to speak to you about this.'' I answered: ''I shall ask my relative, the weaver, for he must know this family.'' Now this man Tsevi Subbotnik was so called because he used to supply the Russian troops with food during the Polish Revolt of 1831, when he profaned the Sabbath by following the soldiers from camp to camp: because of this, he gained the nickname of Subbotnik. In Vilki, the custom was to call a man, not by his proper name, but by a nickname which, whether a true or false description, was inherited by his descendants. Most of these names were derogatory, for the people were generally quarrelsome. Not a month passed in that town without a quarrel breaking out in the synagogue on the Sabbath between two families, with heavy blows struck and hats flying from one corner to another, and sometimes ending in a scuffle outside. The women came to the help of their menfolk. The following day they would send messengers to Kovno, the capital city, bearing slanderous accusations and libellous letters in order to sue each other. Moreover, the Lord had provided them with a Rabbi who enjoyed these disputes: he used to relate how, when he was a Rabbi in the city of F., the people used to smash the stoves and hurl bricks at each other.

I went to visit my relative the weaver, and told him of Gedaliah's proposal. He said he had already heard about it from the girl's mother, but had not wanted to say anything himself because of the earlier mistake he had made over the first marriage. "Nevertheless," I pursued, "How true is it? Is the man really rich? Can it be true that the girl I saw only a year ago walking about barefoot is now grown into a beautiful woman ready for marriage?" "It is quite true," he replied. "If you wish to see her, come with me tomorrow." Whilst we were talking, a younger brother of the girl arrived with an invitation for me from the father to dine with them. I refused, saying I was dining with my cousin. A second messenger came, urging me to accept the invitation. I told him I would go next day: I intended first to make enquiries about them. After the Sabbath, I asked one of my acquaintances, who said that it was true that the girl was a very good girl, and though her father was not wealthy he would be able to afford a small dowry plus subsistence. On the following day, after the service in the synagogue, the man came to take me home with him. When I entered, the girl hid herself in embarrassment. Her parents insisted that I stay with them all day, and even spend the night there. So I spent the last two days of the Passover with them, without a word being said concerning the marriage or the dowry. In the evening, after the service, I went to the man's house, but he had not yet arrived. I waited some two hours for him to come and say the *Havdalah*[238] service, according to Jewish custom. Then some of his relatives and friends came storming in, like drunkards, calling out *Mazel Tov!*[239] They wanted to know why the Beadle and the Cantor had not yet arrived, and others said that Tsevi would bring them along very soon. When I asked why a Beadle and Cantor were required, since one could say the *Havdalah* without their services, they replied: "We are here for the marriage contract![240]" This frightened me, for I now realised that Tsevi was deceiving me, and had already decided on the marriage even before asking me if I wished to be his son-in-law or discussing the terms of the contract. I told them I wanted my relative, the weaver, to be present. They sent for him. He came, followed by the Beadle and Tsevi: the Cantor was not with them.

They drank one glass after another, and invited me to join them, but I refused on the excuse that I did not drink. I urged my relative to begin to discuss the terms of the contract, since no one else was bothering about it. Everyone was busy drinking and shouting, and then the host himself was fully occupied serving drinks and food. He did say, however, everything had been arranged in advance by Gedaliah the merchant. My heart beat with trepidation. I said: "I can write in all languages, so why should I not write the terms of my own contract?" They said that it was the custom for the Beadle to write it. I replied: "Let two copies of the contract be written, one by the Beadle and one by me.'' It was in my mind that, when we came to writing the terms, if I found them unacceptable, I would stop writing. They agreed. For the terms, Tsevi proposed fifty roubles before the wedding, and fifty a year later. I stopped writing, and left the table in order to speak with my relative, leaving the guests to continue their noisy merriment. One of them approached my relative, took him aside, and told him that he had heard one of the drunkards promising Tsevi to take me outside and beat me up if I persisted in being obstinate. I then returned, sat down again at the table and completed the contract according to their wishes. I said to myself: ''Tomorrow, I shall be on my way, and you can marry the contract!'' Once the contract was completed, all the drunkards shouted *Mazel Tov*, and smashed the earthenware jars, and raised a noise that shook the house, and then drank one more round before departing. I remained in order not to give the impression that I intended to run away.

When everyone had gone to rest, and only Tsevi and I were still up, he said to me: ''No doubt you are astonished at me for deceiving you like this. I will tell you why I wanted only fifty roubles to be written in the contract. You have already been married, to the daughter of Hillel the tanner. He promised you fifty roubles before the wedding, and did not even give it to you. Now, you are a divorced man, and a father. If, therefore, I agreed publicly to give you two hundred roubles, I would lose the esteem of my friends and give satisfaction to my enemies, of whom I have more than enough in this town. However, in actual fact, I shall give you everything I promised Gedaliah the merchant that I would give you — and even more, for I am fond of you, as I am of my daughter. It may be that you do not believe that I possess the means to do this, then come with me into the next room and see for yourself.'' He brought out a leather bag containing about one hundred and fifty roubles. He said: ''Do not imagine that I lie to you. This, and more, is all mine. Unfortunately, I am not able to give you even one penny at this moment. You see, I own inns and mills which are some four hours journey from the city, with large gardens and wheat fields. It is at present the sowing season, and all this money is needed for sowing. I cannot, therefore, give you anything until after the harvest is over. Then, on the day of the wedding, I shall give you one hundred roubles, as promised and a further hundred one year later. You can live with me at my expense for three years or more.'' I was swayed by the apparent honesty of the man, yet the hatred that had been aroused in me during the signing of the contract did not allow me to veer from my decision to leave him and his daughter. I thought: ''The Devil take you together with your money and your daughter, for tomorrow I will be on my way and will never see you again!'' I stayed there the night. In the morning, Tsevi told me: ''Look, my son, I and my wife and our oldest son have to go out to the fields, and we shall not be back until the Sabbath. This happens during every sowing season. The house is left in the care of our oldest daughter, together with the two younger girls. You stay here, and do not leave us or the house. Eat and drink here, and sleep in this room: the girls will sleep in the other room.'' I promised him I would do as he wished. They left.

The girl who, hitherto, had been too embarrassed even to look at me, was now left alone to look after me. I began to notice that she was indeed a diligent girl, and furthermore that, since necessity compelled her to look at me and speak to me, she spoke as a mature woman should. I began to reproach myself for having unjustly despised her. In any case, I had nowhere else to live, and there was no opening anywhere for a teacher at the time, whilst here I had everything I needed. My fiancée began to speak more often with me, and sometimes in the evenings, after her sisters had retired to bed, she remained with me in my bedroom. She was clever and beautiful, and made me feel as though I were the man of the house. I bought paper and ink, and spent my days translating, according to my regular habit. On the Sabbath, Tsevi returned with his wife; his son had remained behind in the fields. They were pleased to see me. After the Sabbath was over, they left again. They gave me complete authority over the house, to look after it and the family as I thought best. During that second week, I began to fall in love with my bride, and she returned my affection. Every night we delighted in our love for each other, although she would not permit intercourse, saying wisely: "If I let you take my virginity, you might cease to love me and suspect me of behaving wantonly with other men. Far better to wait for the proper time, and I shall give my love to you." She was right, and her words etched a deep love for her in my heart. She, of course, had no way of knowing that it is my nature to be constant, and that if she had given herself to me, I would have been faithful to her for ever, for I had never been a promiscuous person. I remained silent, and felt ashamed that so simple a girl should have to rebuke me on a matter that was so clearly right, yet which I, because I was overcome by emotion, had not realised.

At that time, I obtained a small book called *The Path of Learning*[241] by Ben Ze'ev, which contained many learned essays on the Greek philosophers. I was profoundly impressed by the wisdom of the Athenian philosophers and their method of extracting the core of truth out of every act and event. Their unswerving loyalty to truth influenced me so strongly that, from that day to this, I have followed in their ways. Truth became more precious to me than anything else in this world. I shunned falsehood completely; even on those occasions when necessity demanded that I lie, I would neither lie nor tell the actual truth. This is the lesson I learned from my reading of the lives of those wise men. Especially Socrates, and his method of always replying to every question with another question; the questioner then became the responder, and from his own replies he learned the truth for himself. I have abided by these principles all my life: these have strengthened my temperament and enabled me to bear the vicissitudes of life with fortitude.

It was at this time that a number of enemies rose up against me and my father-in-law Tsevi, spreading slander through the town that I was living alone in the house with Tsevi's daughter, in sin. I also heard another rumour, that the girl had already lost her virginity to one of the young men of the town. I knew the man, so I asked my relative whether he had heard anything to confirm the rumour, but he had not. There was a further rumour. On those days when the shepherd did not arrive early enough in the morning to lead the cow to pasture in the meadow, my virgin bride would take the cow herself, and meet the young man in the field, where he was also tending his cow, and there they made love without being observed. I made enquiries, but was not able to discover the truth of the matter. It was true that they owned cattle. It was also true that the herdsman who came to tend the cows belonging to the townspeople, sometimes arrived early and sometimes late. In the latter case, the fathers or sons or daughters would themselves lead their cows to the pasture. Whether or not the couple met later on in the field, I was unable to determine. On the other hand, I had ample evidence of something else: the girl did not submit to intercourse with me when we were together. Gradually, I began to be influenced by the rumours spread by her enemies through the town, and I began to wonder whether her reason for not giving her love to me before the wedding might be, in fact, that she was not a virgin, and was afraid I might jilt her. Whilst I was thus torn by doubts, a man from Barak came to see me, with an invitation to teach the children there during the summer. I welcomed the opportunity. I told my bride that I was going back to the Barak hotel, but would not forget her and would return at the end of the summer, which would be also the harvest season, and would marry her then. She believed me, and I left. Each week I wrote her a love letter in German: as she could not read even Yiddish we had agreed that I write to her in German, and her neighbours, who were painters from Germany, would read the letters for her. Unfortunately, the daughters of the painter relayed the contents of my letters to the whole town. I wrote in a literary style, in words culled from German books, in the same way as Hebrew writers borrow verses from the Scriptures for their own laboured, florid style. Now, these German painters of Vilki were not very familiar with their own literature, and so were greatly surprised that the son-in-law of Tsevi should write German so well that he was able to declare his love so strongly. The gossip spread so wide that Tsevi wrote asking that I stop expressing my love in this manner. Throughout the Summer I continued to be disturbed by the rumours that had been bruited about against my bride, and I was unable to come to any decision as to whether or not I should marry her. Nor could I decide whether my friends had spoken the truth when they had stated that her father was a poor man and a swindler.

Then came *Shabbat Naḥamu*[242], a period when teachers and *melammedim* enjoy a few days' rest. I asked for leave to go to Vilki. I left in the morning and walked the four miles alone, very discontented. I stayed overnight at Vilon, arriving at Serednik the following day to see my father. I reached Vilki before the Sabbath. I had brought some small presents for my bride. First, however, I called upon my relative to ask for news about her. He told me there was nothing new, that everything was the same as it had always been except for the additional gossip concerning my love-letters. I stayed the night with him. On the morrow, my bride's parents called and asked me to spend the Sabbath with them. I did so. On the following day, they left, and I was once again alone with my bride. This grieved me, for it would only lead to further gossip and slanders. I stayed there two days, without leaving the house at all except to go to visit my relative for one hour each day.

On the afternoon of the third day, I went out to buy some paper, and returned half an hour later. As I approached the door, I heard a noise inside the house, and this surprised me, for only my bride and her two sisters were in the house, and they were always peaceful and quiet together. I stopped a moment to identify the noise. It seemed a kind of subdued sound, like a man makes when moving furniture as quietly as he can: it was neither the sound of dispute nor of exultation[243], but rather a sound of gaiety. I opened the door, which had been left unlocked, and stepped across the threshold. The door of the other room was closed, but from behind it came the sound of whispering voices. I saw my bride stretched on the bed, from which she now rose hastily, her hair in disarray and her cheeks scarlet. Beside her stood the young man, the one who, according to the rumours, made love to her in the fields. He stood, trembling with fear. However, being a man, he quelled his fear, and extended his hand to me in greeting. I would not return his greeting, but turned away in sorrow to the table where I kept my writing materials. I sat down to write, I know not what, for my whole body was quivering with fury. The man asked my bride when she would be able to send him the seed he had bought, and she said she would sent it the next day. He then turned and left the house. I had no wish to question her about what happened, nor was she bold enough to try to explain it, for she was exceedingly ashamed. I stayed until the evening, then went out to my relative, to whom I related all that had happened. I spent the night with him, and did not return to her house.

When her parents returned home three days later, they enquired about me. They quickly sent for me and, seeing me looking downcast, asked me to tell them what had happened. I did not know whether or not she had already told them about it, but I, in my hatred of falsehood, could not refrain from telling them of the rumours I had heard in the past, and of how she had given her love to the young man called F., although I found it hard to believe. I told how I arrived at the house to hear the sounds of merriment and found her arising dishevelled from the bed, with the young man beside her. There was no one else in the house, not even her younger sisters. Nevertheless, she had not kept him outside the house but had allowed him to remain as long as he wished. Whilst I spoke, my bride sat to one side, listening to everything. I asked Tsevi what explanation he could give for this incident. The man became furious with his daughter and wanted to strike her. After he had calmed down, he told me: "The young man came to my mill three days ago, and I gave him twenty roubles to take to my daughter so that she could buy seed for sowing this season (in the month of *Av*[244]?) and it is probable that he came here whilst she was having a noontime rest. Since there was no one else in the house, he awakened her to give her the money and my message. You came and found them like that, although nothing wrong had actually occurred. In fact, that young man has been chasing my daughter for more than a year, but she is not for him.'' The girl, who was weeping copiously, said nothing. A great compassion for her came over me. I realised her father's words had opened a way for me to make peace with them, whilst leaving me free to be guided by future events. I therefore made a reconciliation with them, for it was possible that my deep love for her had made me unreasonably jealous. I took out the presents I had brought, handed them over to my bride, and asked her to forgive me for having misjudged her. We all rejoiced, and my bride stopped crying although her embarrassment still showed on her face. The following day, I said farewell to them, and returned to Barak. My heart was still full of misgivings and I was uncertain whether to leave them finally or return to them. I knew, on the other hand, that when my lessons at Barak ended with the close of the Summer, I would have nowhere to go, and necessity could compel me to go back to my in-laws.

One day, the wealthy owner of a distillery came to see me at Barak, as my name had been suggested to him as a possible tutor for his sons. During that Summer, a German who owned a cargo boat plying the river Nieman had stayed at the hotel. Now, the hotel proprietor had owed this man about three hundred roubles for the past five years, and had made no effort to repay the debt. The man had come to claim his debt, leaving his boat moored by the shore. The hotel proprietor was very worried, because he was in the middle of preparations for his daughter's wedding, and did not know what to say to the German. His family suggested that he write to the man in German, inviting him to attend the daughter's wedding. So they sent for me to write the letter, as I had letters for all occasions, weddings as well as deaths, which I had copied from German books. I now drew on them and wrote an appropriate invitation. The proprietor was concerned lest the German would not be able to read my letter, and therefore his joy was all the greater, and his esteem of me rose higher, when the German read the letter and asked: ''Who is the person in this village who can write such fine German?'' They made their peace; and I became known as an accomplished linguist. It was because of this incident that I had been referred to the Courland merchant as a tutor for his sons. We travelled in his carriage to Rasseyn where his friends lived, for there I was to be tested to see whether I was suitable for the position: he offered to pay all the expenses of the journey. The man took me into his home in Rasseyn. Two young men came in and asked me to prove my knowledge. I showed them the book I had written, *Wife of My Youth*[245]. It led to an unfortunate incident. When I had first begun the book in Serednik, I had a good friend, a teacher like myself, who used to compose poetry with sublime expressions in finer language than I knew. I was not aware that the city of Rasseyn was far different from Serednik, and that many writers in all languages lived there. At that time, Abraham Mapu had lived in Rasseyn and had written his novel *The Love of Zion*[246]. I knew nothing of all this. My friend used to write down from memory poems and verses which were, however, full of errors, even though the sentiments they expressed were sublime. One of the poems he had written so impressed me that I included it in my book. It went like this: "If I could but grasp the pillars of the world, and with all my might crush them to destruction, then would I return to oblivion and find rest[247]." To this, I added a seasoning of my own. I was not aware that this poem had been composed by a famous poet and had appeared in print. When, therefore, the men found the beginning of this poem with its errors in my book, they accused me of stealing all my compositions from different books: the mistakes, of course, were ascribed to me. Even though I explained the truth of the matter, the Courland merchant sent me away and paid for my return to Barak.

One day, a man arrived from the city of Kelm. He was employed in the large business owned by Meir Kelmer, who lived in Prussia but had his business in Kelm. This man, Lebel Kelmer, was the agent for the export and import of goods for the business. He made periodic visits to Shavel to purchase flax and seeds which he then transported overland to Barak where he loaded them on to ships going to Prussia. He remained at Barak about one month each year, staying at this hotel. He would eat with us at the landlord's table. One Sabbath, we were all sitting together at the table, when a conversation arose on demons and devils, on the dead and the living. I offered my opinion, also. The man tuned towards me and entered into deep discussion with me, only to discover that I knew more about the subject than he did. After I had left, he asked the others who I was. He became a good friend to me, and even tried to find means to enable me to give up teaching. He wanted me to take employment in the business in Kelm. Because of his own inadequate knowledge of Russian and German he tended to over-rate me. However, nothing came of it all. Some time later, he went to the city of Shadova, where he discovered that there was no teacher for the children of the town. He proposed to the most distinguished families of the town, including one Isaac who had a favourite son, that I be brought to Shadova to teach their children. On his return, he told me about it, and gave me a letter to Isaac. It was now the middle of *Ellul*, so I thought of going first to Serednik and later to Shadova. I was paid the money remaining due to me, and had a total of sixteen roubles. In Serednik, I was told that a young man who lived in the post-house, had recently died, leaving a number of non-Jewish books which his widow was trying to sell. I went to have a look at them, and found a German Dictionary by Weber[248] which explained in very simple German even the most unusual German words. It was very useful, since my Schmidt Dictionary only gave the translation without explaining the meaning. I bought the book for 1.50 kopeks. I was then able to understand many frequently used words whose proper meaning I had not been able to ascertain from the Schmidt Dictionary. I arrived in Shadova in time for the New Year.

When I recall those days, I feel overcome with despondency. I was in my twenties, neither an ignoramus nor a fool, yet I was ignorant of the ways of the world, of the way of life of wealthy Jews or their gentile neighbours. Indeed, their way of life had assumed an idealised image in my mind. Whenever I saw people dressed differently from me, and their hair styled differently, I immediately believed that they were rich people from the New World whose ways were foreign to my father and to everything he held dear. There was no purpose in thinking about them, for they were not for me. So I went to the city of Shadova.

It was the year when Tsar Nicholas 1 had decreed that all the Jews must cut off their sidelocks, wear short coats and gentile hats[249]. That decree had come into force when I was still at Barak. I had bought myself a short, knee-length coat and a pair of long trousers, and made for myself a cotton top-coat, known as a morning-coat or Turkish coat, patterned in flowers and bright colours. I wore these clothes when I went to pray in the synagogue of Shadova. My phylacteries were as big as a bucket: I had left my other phylacteries behind in Vilki, for I had been in such a haste to leave that I had bought this pair from the effects of an old man who had died at the age of eighty; I wore them until I was thirty years old. Today, I can well imagine how strange a creature I must have appeared to the worshippers in the synagogue, especially when they heard that I was a teacher of both Hebrew and foreign languages and had come to teach the children of Isaac. In those days, I wore a skullcap upon my dented head at all times, night and day: if ever it came off whilst I slept, I would awaken in a panic and search for it. Bathing was something I abhorred; I never went to bathe in the public baths although I did bathe in the river during the warm summer days. When, therefore, I arrived in Shadova and presented myself to my employer, he urged me to accompany him to the public baths. I was afraid to refuse lest people thought that a heretic had come to defile the city. I suffered severely all over my body from that bath. It was my custom, when arising in the morning, to ensure first of all that my skullcap was securely fastened to my head, and then rinse my hands and face according to the prescribed ritual[250], but without wetting or combing my hair which, as a consequence, was filthy. On the night of the New Year, Reb Isaac took me home to dine with him, for the man Lebel Kelmer had been generous in his praise of me. We sat at the table which was laid in the manner of rich people familiar with gentile customs. I observed that, at my place, were two plates, one on top of the other. I thought that the mistress of the house had erred: I did not think to look around to see wheher there were also two plates at all the other places. I held up my top plate and showed it to the mistress of the house. She was going round serving the fish and, seeing my raised plate, placed a portion of fish on it. I was astonished and, not knowing what else to do, put the plate on the table in front of me. I then noticed that everyone else had two plates, though I could not understand why. To my relief, the family did not linger over the meal. The father took me and his son aside to listen whilst I taught the boy. No sooner had the son begun to translate into Hebrew ''And the Lord said to Moses'' than I realised that he was confusing the future and past and present tenses, and misusing the Consecutive Vav as in ''And he said'' — and so on. The father listened whilst I explained to the boy what other teachers had omitted to tell him.

He was very pleased with me, and was satisfied that Lebel Kelmer had been telling the truth about me. After the New Year, I entered into agreement with Reb Isaac to teach his son and three other boys the Pentateuch with Rashi's commentary, and also how to write Hebrew, German and Russian, at a fee of 24 roubles per half-year. A number of young girls would also come to me to learn language and writing, but they would pay me monthly. I then returned home to my father, after promising to come back when the festival of Tabernacles was over. I had no wish to visit my bride and in-laws during the festival, for I could not forget what had happened during *Shabbat Naḥamu*; I felt that I would return to them only if it was absolutely necessary to do so. Here in Shadova, my circumstances had improved, for I was now a teacher in a city and not in a village. No doubt, God would make it possible for me to marry a suitable woman of my own choice who would enable me to cast off the burden to teaching and achieve my ambition to learn an art or craft — for this was something I was too poor to do for myself. I did not, therefore, write to my bride, and she did not know where I was. After the festival had ended, I walked on foot towards Shadova, accompanied by a man whom I had hired to carry my bag of belongings and my books as far as Keidan: I could not find a cartier to take me; the roads had become so impassable that there was no transport between cities which had no interconnecting highway. I stayed overnight in Keidan, partly to rest from my fatigue and also to find a cartier to take me to Shadova. During the day that I was there, I went to the Gymnasium to buy Russian books, and bought a two-volume chrestomathy. On the fourth day I climbed in to a wagon laden with sacks of corn and set off for Shadova, a distance of four leagues. We stopped for the Sabbath at a delapidated inn, where the pigs entered through the gaps in the walls and clambered over our heads. The inn was owned by a gentile farmer who had no other provisions than salt herrings and brandy. The three cartiers and I recited the Sabbath sanctification over a glass of brandy and said the benediction over the bread which the cartiers had brought with them from their homes. We had not expected to spend the Sabbath on the journey. I finally arrived at Shadova two days later than I had promised.

I found the place seething with news. A young man, Ḥayyim Ḥaikil, who had taught in Shadova some years earlier, had now returned. He was a brilliant scholar, and grandson of the former Rabbi of the city, Rabbi Gershon, a nephew of the Vilna Gaon and himself a pious and humble Kabbalist who had ministered to the congregation until his death. The young man had been brought up by his grand-mother because his father, Samuel the son of Rabbi Gershon, had not been a good person. After studying to be a clockmaker he had divorced Ḥayyim Ḥaikil's mother and married a Courland woman; and no one knew of his whereabouts until eventually he emigrated to America. For the past two years Ḥayyim Ḥaikil had been wandering through Russia, far from his family and home, because of a dispute which had arisen between the people of the city and a "bereaved bear"[251] called Berke Shadover. He was well-known in Shadova, his native city, where his father owned an imposing house by the street. As the boy grew up, he had learned to write in Russian in fine literary style. He had also learned the Russian Code of Laws by heart. Seeking to rule over the city, he appointed his father in charge of communal administration. He oppressed the poor, and controlled the community's finances. When the people rose up against him, he was able to confirm his authority by the simple fact that not one of the people could even sign his own name. He brought slanderous tales about them to the Governor in Vilna. They were forced to empty their coffers in order to raise a sum of money equal to twice the physical weight of the ''bear'' — who was a tall man, taller than any of them, of imposing appearance, and able to speak Russian well. Once it became known that he was an informer, the people devised a plot to hand him over for military service. After a certain amount of bribery, he was put into chains and taken to the army recruitment centre. However he had cunningly purloined the register of the Burial Society, on the pretext of demonstrating the loyalty of one of the Wardens to the Governor, but in fact in order to prove that all the dead people had not been entered in this book of fiction and that many of the living also could not be accounted for. The people were so distressed by this that they secured his release from military service at great financial cost. They were still suffering from his rule when I arrived in the city.

The young man Hayyim Haikil, whose father had fled on the day Hayyim was born, had been in the list submitted by the ''bear'', and had been forced to leave his wife and family in the care of the community whilst he fled and became a wandering preacher. His learning and his gift of speech soon made him famous. When, therefore, in this particular year, the people and the ''bear'' made peace so that the latter's father was reinstated in his position in the community, Hayyim Haikil decided to return home to celebrate the feast of Tabernacles. His sermons in the House of Study earned him great esteem. However, there was no position available for him, since I had taken his place as the community's teacher. When, therefore, I was two days overdue, Mordecai, a relative of Reb Isaac[252], sent his son to Hayyim Haikil rather than wait for me. After I arrived, he promised that instead, he would send me his daughter and another son. Hayyim Haikil thus became the only antagonist I had in the city. On the second day, he came to my class room to speak with me. I was wary of him, but he said: ''Do not imagine that I am your enemy, and do not be afraid of me. Though I lack an adequate income, it is no fault of yours. In any case you are not rich yourself.'' He questioned me about everything that had happened to me and, noting that I was not married, took compassion on my poor circumstances. He said: ''Far from being your enemy, I shall be your good friend. You are a stranger here, and do not know your way about. Let me help you in any way you wish.''

It was not long before I discovered that he was a skilled chess player, a game I had longed for years to learn. We arranged that he should come to see me the following evening, and teach me the game. During the first two days, my heart stirred with love for the man. By the third day, I knew that by his nature he was genuine and honest, a lover of mankind and particularly of the upright. He understood and loved me. With his guidance, he protected me from all woes. Such was the Ḥayyim Ḥaikil to whom I became joined by a bond of true and unselfish love until the day he died.

He introduced me to the Rabbi, who warmly welcomed me. On the *Shabbat Teshuva*,[253] the Rabbi gave his customary sermon in the synagogue. I went to hear him. His subject was Maimonides' conception of Man's freedom of choice and God's foreknowledge of events. These are, of course, two irreconcilable opposites. Obviously, God must know in advance whether a man is going to be righteous or wicked. If He knows that a certain man will be wicked, then that man cannot be other than wicked, for if he had the freedom of choice and chose to be righteous, it would follow that God had no foreknowledge of the true situation. The Rabbi propounded this problem in all its complexity, then answered it by means of an illustrative comparison. A shepherd is leading his flock through a forest. Ahead of them lies a road junction. The road to the right leads to dangerous hazards and pitfalls, whereas the road to the left is straight and safe. The shepherd knows this but the flock does not, and therefore makes its own choice of direction. I listened to this with astonishment. How could the Rabbi, in front of a large congregation comprising many men learned in the Torah, make so illogical a statement? Certainly the shepherd knows that a road junction lies ahead, but God knows the direction they will choose, whether they will go right and come to harm or go left and be safe. The question, therefore, had not been answered. Some time later I visited the Rabbi at his home. I waited until we were alone in order not to embarrass him, and then said to him: "My Rabbi and teacher, I heard your sermon on *Shabbat Teshuva* but I was not able to understand it." He said: "Please tell me your problem." "Well, you offered an explanation of the problem of freewill with the illustration of the shepherd and his flock. The shepherd knew about the two roads that lay ahead, yet he allowed his flock a free choice of direction." The Rabbi answered: "That is so," and then repeated his explanation so that I might understand it more clearly. I then said: "But God's knowledge of man's future is quite different from the Shepherd's realisation that a road junction lies before him. The latter does not know which road the sheep will choose, whereas God does know which choice man will make. Since He knows whether man will be good or evil, how can man choose the opposite of what God knows?" The Rabbi began to rock in his chair as he propounded his explanations in the casuistic manner common to all Rabbis. I continued: "Maimonides dealt with this problem in his *Yad Ha-Ḥazakah*, but was severely taken to task by the *Kesef Mishneh*[254] for raising a problem which could have no true solution — after which the *Kesef Mishneh* then offered his own solution which was worse than Maimonides'. The Rabbi of Bertinoro,[255] commenting on the Mishna verse 'Everything is foreseen but permission is granted',[256] which concerns man's free will and God's foreknowledge, rejected the explanation made by the *Kesef Mishneh* and instead preferred his own solution which was even worse! Now you wish to deal with this complex problem in public, even though your explanation is the worst of all!'' The Rabbi flushed and said: ''This was not something I myself thought of. I saw it in an ancient book that was lying on the bench in front of me, although I did not entirely understand its meaning.''

Later, I related to another Rabbi what the Shadova Rabbi had said, and he replied: ''Maimonides' opinion stems from a verse in the Scriptures, from the prophet Isaiah xl.27: 'Why do you say, O Jacob, and you, O Israel, declare, My way is hid from the Lord, and my right is passed over from my God?' In this, the prophet is making an either-or statement: Why do you imagine, O Israel, that God cannot work in one of two ways, that *either* 'my way is hid from the Lord' and therefore he has no foreknowledge, *or* if He has foreknowledge, then He knows in advance that I am to be wicked and therefore 'my right is passed over from my God' and I shall be wicked because I am compelled to be. In such case, I cannot be condemned. The prophet supplies his own answer in the next verse: 'Have you not known or heard that the everlasting God, the Lord, etcetera, and His discernment is past searching out.' Now, this is really the reply given by Maimonides. Human intelligence considers the present and the future as occurring together at the same time. Just as ''place'' is an abstract term denoting a finite reality, where one end marks both its beginning and its end, so if it were not finite there would be no ''place'', for then it would not have an end, and there would be no beginning or end. Time, similarly, is finite, with an end and a beginning: if it were not, then there would be no time, or beginning or end, or past, present or future. We cannot comprehend this by common reason, since we have no non-finite yardstick by which to measure it. In order, therefore, to obtain some conception of it, I shall approach the problem gently by means of an illustration. Let us consider the speed of light rays. When light is reflected from a polished mirror, which is a solid object, whether it be to the degree of light which pours upon all physical matter or of that light which stirs the particles of primeval matter and the ether in infinite space, it is in both cases a material substance. We therefore find it almost impossible to comprehend how this physical substance can be unaffected by time. If we take a small piece of polished glass and turn it at an angle of forty-five degrees to the sun so that it reflects the light on to the wall or ceiling of a house, the light will reflect just as brightly even if the wall were as high and as distant as the heavens. If we pivot the glass so that the light reflects upon the concave surface of the ceiling, from one end to the other, and if we turn it swiftly at a speed of one-thousandth of a minute, then the rays will also turn across that sky-high ceiling at the speed of one-thousandth of a minute — and so on at increasing speeds, even to the most minute fraction of time. Where, then, is either the Time or the Place in this material substance? Surely, from this we should understand that the spiritual is just as far removed from the material as is the Thought, which can reach to the highest heavens in a fraction of a moment, from solid objects like a hand or leg or anything capable of movement. If we can imagine these rays of reflected light striking against an object and making a photographic imprint, so that they register an action in a fraction of a second and imprint the movement of each part of that moment upon the object, then we shall see clearly every part of that moment, from the beginning through the middle to the end. Where, then, is the Time and Place which human intelligence can comprehend? We should also bear in mind that there are rays of light which have emanated from distant, solid stars many years ago but which we see only now, even though those stars may no longer exist, because of the vast distances the light has to travel. If it were possible for the terrestrial globe to preserve a record, like a photographic imprint, of every ray of light which has travelled to it from the beginning of time, we should find on its surface a record of all the rays which reached it from the moon and Uranus and Neptune. We would see them all in one moment, the past and the present together. Yet they are no more than rays of light, physical matter dependent upon time and space. Surely, then, we should realise that the Spirit exists; though we may not distinguish it, we can acknowledge it. We should understand that it has neither time nor place, and has no past or present or even future. Similarly, Thought, which acts on the physical matter of our brain and whose impulses vibrate on our membranes at a speed of a minute fraction of a moment, is also almost independent of time or place, and yet it puts before us the past and the present with their myriad transformations, so that we may sense them with our sight and hearing, our taste and smell and feeling, and remember and observe them all together in a space of time that is almost timeless and endless. This is the burden of Maimonides' reply on the subject of free will and foreknowledge."[257]

The preacher Ḥaikil acted like a father and counsellor to me, and had a sincere and genuine love for me. He was a loyal friend, and I did nothing without first seeking his advice. When I opened the school to teach the boys and girls of Shadova arithmetic, Hebrew and German, one of my first pupils was the daughter of a wealthy man, Reb Mordecai, the father-in-law of Reb Isaac. She was an exceedingly beautiful girl, and it was not long before she had captured my heart. About a year before, she had been married to Isaiah, the son of the Gaon Rabbi Joseph Slutzker who had recently come to the city, and had so impressed the people with his sermons and personality as well as the merits of his ancestors that he had been offered the position of Rabbi in place of the Rabbi who had already been ministering to them for the past two years — the same Rabbi who had given the sermon on free will, as I have related, and who, though unfamiliar with methods of research and investigation, was nevertheless a pious Rabbi distinguished for his learning. The Gaon's son Isaiah, was foolish and ignorant. However, by virtue of his father's name he was able to obtain the favour of the people with fine words, although his heart was filled with falsehood. The rich man, Mordecai, decided to have him as a son-in-law, the husband of his daughter Moska: he was prepared to offer him a large sum of money, and to maintain him for ever.

During the early part of my stay at Reb Isaac's, the son-in-law of Mordecai, I learned that this son of the Gaon had begun to lose the favour of the people, for much of his true nature had been discovered. Whilst I was at Isaac's house, this son of the Gaon came to visit his brother-in-law Isaac, the husband of his wife's sister. By design or cunning, the rich man Isaac got me into conversation with Isaiah. I showed him my book, *Wife of My Youth,* which I had written in Barak and always carried in my bag. He, on his part, showed me a letter he had written in highly ornate style. I read it and found it full of errors. When I began to point these out to him, he took the scroll from my hands and replaced it in his bag. Then he recited it by heart, from beginning to end, in a refined scholarly voice astonishing to hear. It was in this fashion, and by similar means, that he had been able to attract the people of the city. When he had finished, he drew a sheaf of papers from his pocket, held them up and said: "With this shall the whole world be filled." "And what is it?" "It is an explanatory commentary on every difficult passage in the Scriptures. I have composed it myself, and shall soon have it finished and published." We parted after that, and never saw each other again, for three days later he deserted his wife and fled from the city, realising that the people had seen through his subterfuges so there was no longer any place for him there. By the time I returned to Shadova after the feast of Tabernacles he had gone, leaving the girl Moska an *agunah*.[258] Although enquiries were made after him, in order to obtain a divorce, it took three years to find him.

On the fifth day of her attendance at my school, the girl Moska lingered behind to talk with me. She asked about my circumstances and where I lodged and had my meals. She shook her head over my poverty. She said she would ask her parents to let me have my meals with them for the same charge which I paid the poor baker, and to permit me to lodge with them in their house, which was a high-class hotel catering for aristocratic guests — and she would even give me . . .[259] the bed which had been empty ever since her husband had left her. On saying this, her cheeks blushed like a rose, so that she looked very desirable and beautiful. I told her that I would be able to give my reply on the following day. In my heart, however, I was undecided whether I should allow myself to fall into this trap. I sought the advice of my loyal friend, Ḥayyim Ḥaikil. I had hardly finished relating all that she had told me, when he stopped me and exhorted me not to accede to her at any cost, for I would surely come to harm. His advice lay like a burden upon me, for . . .[260] However, I listened to him, and on the morrow, when she asked me for my reply, I turned her offer down. She stopped coming to my school to learn Hebrew. So my friend guided me, wisely and prudently, all the time I was in Shadova, and even later after I left. Never have I come across a man so true and honest, so learned and wise and scholarly: may his soul rest in peace.

Winter was ending, and *Purim* was approaching. My father paid me a surprise visit. His financial circumstances had worsened, and he was now destitute. He had journeyed on foot from one town to the next, enquiring about his son in Shadova, and was pleased to hear that I was living the life of an observant Jew: this had been one of his fears about me — what would I do when I became independent of him? I was teaching foreign languages to children, and would I not therefore turn to corrupt ways as did all the young men of my generation who tasted Haskalah? He stayed with me for three days. He told me that, in Serednik, there was a large garden which could be rented for six roubles; and if he had the money he could develop it so that he would be able to live off its produce all year round. I possessed three roubles which I had been saving in order to buy myself an overcoat, which cost six roubles, as my present coat was very shabby. I said to my father: "Take these three roubles now, and tomorrow I shall ask Reb Isaac to let me have another three, and you can have those, too." My father thanked me, took the six roubles and showed me another two roubles he had in his pocket. He departed to return home.

On the third day after Passover, a messenger came from Rasseyn with a letter. It stated that my father had died two days after the conclusion of the festival, in the city of Rasseyn, in the house of a relative of my mother. He had stayed there to celebrate the festival and had fallen ill. Some time later I learned that my younger brother, Shalom, had been with him at the time, and he also had died, immediately after my father. I was now an orphan and alone. In the customary manner of mourners, I tore my garments, and sat on the ground. I went every morning to pray and to study a portion of Mishna and recite the *Rabbanan Kaddish*. [261] I did this for the whole year. When the first month of my mourning had ended, my cousin, the weaver Ze'ev, the son of my father's brother came to see me. He was now in reduced circumstances and needed financial assistance. He had to sell his humble house in Vilki in order to obtain his son's release from military service, [262] and was now without a roof over his head or food or clothing. I told him that my father had taken the money which I had been saving for my own clothes, and had left for Rasseyn where he had died. He begged me to write a letter to my mother's relative in Rasseyn, asking him to let him have any money that might have been left over by my father. I wrote the letter, and he went off to Rasseyn. Then, towards the close of the summer, my stepmother, the sister of Ze'ev the weaver came to see me. I had always hated her. Now she came to demand the effects left by her husband, my father. She had already been to Rasseyn and demanded my father's effects from my relative there. He had given her nothing and told her that I had authorised him to hand everything over to the weaver from Vilki, which he had done. Now she was demanding everything from me, seeing that I was not legally permitted to transfer my father's effects to any other person so long as the conditions in her marriage contract had not been fulfilled: she was now seeking the inheritance to redeem that contract. Because I refused to give her money I did not have, even though I had not taken anything for myself from my father's effects, she threatened to take me to court before the Rabbi of Shadova. I knew the Rabbi, so I went to see him early next day and related the whole affair. I also mentioned that I knew that the Rabbi could not give a reply on the spot to a petition such as mine, and therefore requested that he show me the section in the *Magen David*[263] relating to my circumstance. He pointed it out, and I saw that the widow actually had no case against me. I then left. The widow came to see me again, and I told her: "I want you to understand that if you take me to trial, you will gain nothing at all. But if you do not compel me to go to court, then I shall help you to defray the expenses of your journey. If you insist on going to trial, you will not get even that little." Knowing that I would not lie over such a matter she believed me. She began to weep, and begged me to give her also a letter to my relative in Rasseyn, in case there had been anything left over from my father's effects which he had not given to Ze'ev and which he could give her. I thought that, in fact, there must be something left over, since I could not believe that he would hand everything over to Ze'ev especially since I had mentioned in my letter that I was assisting Ze'ev out of kindness, and not because of any legal claim.

When the year of mourning came to an end, in the following summer, a strong urge came over me to see my father's grave, and to hear about his death and how my younger brother had died at the same time with him. It was the period when farmers were preparing for the market in Rasseyn, so I had no difficulty hiring a cart to take me there at a cheap fare. I arrived at the home of my relative, whom I had known for many years, to find him very annoyed with me and unwilling to discuss the deaths of my father and brother. I was greatly surprised. The reason was this. During the year I had been teaching at Shadova, I had made for myself short coats in the German style, as well as an overcoat with a wide cape. He, however, was a simple Jew, a shoe-repairer from youth, who could not even pray in Hebrew. When he grew up and became rich and had established a tannery in addition to his shoemaking business, he took a *melammed* into his house and studied with zealous devotion until he was able to understand the Mishna. He became twice as religious as before. At that time, Rasseyn was full of *maskilim* under the leadership of Abraham Mapu.[264] The hatred between the two factions was intense. When, therefore, my relative observed that I not only dressed like a German but also taught languages, he developed a hatred for me. He said: "I spent a lot of money on your father when he became ill, and on your brother as well. Then after his death, you took more money from me when you told me to give it to Ze'ev. Then came the widow, who forced me to give her money by law. Furthermore, in order to pay for your father's burial, I was forced to give my set of six volumes of the Mishna in pledge to the Rabbi and they are still there to this day. I am glad you have come, for now you will certainly pay me for all my losses on your behalf." I replied: "Regarding Ze'ev, I wrote to you that 'if there is anything left over, give it to him'. Yet you tell me that my father had not sufficient money to pay for his own funeral. Where, then, are the six roubles I gave him before he left me to visit you? If, furthermore, you gave Ze'ev everything so that there was nothing left, how could you give the widow anything out of your own pocket?" He answered me: "She took me to court on the grounds that I was wrong to give Ze'ev anything according to your instructions, and that she should be the beneficiary in accordance with her marriage contract. So now I shall sue you in the Ecclesiastical Court here, and you will have to repay me everything.'' The next day, he took me to the Rabbi, who looked upon me with disfavour and was not prepared to greet me. After my relative had told him that I was the son of the deceased in the matter of the widow's claim, the Rabbi became angry with me and, without hearing my side of the matter, declared that I must pay everything. I said to him: ''I did ask the opinion of the Rabbi of Shadova, and he informed me that the widow had no claim whatsoever against me.'' No sooner had I said these words than he rounded on me furiously and said: ''The Rabbi of Shadova gave his verdict without a trial and without hearing the evidence of the widow. Who is this Rabbi of Shadova? I shall write to him immediately and, if what you say is true, I will have him excommunicated.'' I became terribly upset, for I had unwittingly brought trouble upon the Rabbi of Shadova. I left. On the morrow, I returned alone to the Rabbi and related to him the entire sequence of events. I told him that I was a teacher of Jewish children, and taught Bible and Rashi and Gemara, and that I was also exceedingly poor. My impoverished father had come to me with the proposition that, if he had six roubles, he could support himself with food for the whole year, so I had given him my last penny. Then my relative Ze'ev had come begging for aid, and I had supplied him with a letter that authorised him to receive anything that was left over from my father's effects. I had not committed any sin at all. Then had come the widow, who had wanted to take me to law. I spent much of my time in my Rabbi's house, and lived an honest life, and he was very fond of me. I had asked him to show me the law according to the *Yoreh De' ah*,[265] for if she were in the right then I would sell my last bit of clothing to pay her claim. He had proved to me that, by law, I was not compelled to pay her anything. When I had finished, the Rabbi extended his hand towards me in a gesture of peace. My face crimsoned with embarrassment and joy. I went on to tell him that I had given the money to my father and to Ze'ev only as a voluntary gift. The widow, on her part, never knew of the money I had given to my father, since he had not reached home. Now I had come to this city solely in order to visit my father's grave, for the year's mourning had ended. I possessed nothing, yet this man was demanding that I pay him for my father and my cousin and my father's widow, and I had not a rouble to my name! He took pity on me, and said: ''No, this man has no claim on you whatsoever.'' Swiftly I rejoined: ''That is exactly what the Rabbi of Shadova told me.'' The Rabbi looked at me piercingly, but said not a word. I bade him farewell and left. My relative did not pursue his claim, and did not take me to court. Thus ended the affair of my father's effects.

I gained little pleasure from the one and half years I spent in Shadova. Every six months my pupils dwindled in number. The profession of a Jewish teacher is very poorly paid anywhere, at any time, but particularly so in a small town in a year of drought.

At that time, the new Candle Tax[266] was imposed upon the Jews. It was also said that *melammdim* would have to have a certificate in order to teach, and would not be given one unless they knew the Russian language.[267] I was worried lest I be deprived of even the small livelihood I was then receiving. Now, a clockmaker with whom I had become very friendly had been living in the city for the past two years. During my second Summer there, I once again developed a strong desire to learn a craft of some kind, for I had begun to loathe teaching more than ever. I made an arrangement with the clockmaker to see him every day after my lessons had finished; he would instruct me in clock-repairing for three hours each day at a very low fee, because of our friendship. We held a small celebration to cement our arrangement. On the first day he showed me how to repair a broken clock-chain, and on the next day a broken spring. By the third day, the whole city was gossiping about the Hebrew teacher who had gone out of his mind and was learning the craft of clock-repairing from the feckless and reckless Yeḥiel, who was not an observant Jew and even frequented the taverns and brothels. On the fourth day, my friend Ḥayyim Ḥaikil advised me to stop seeing Yeḥiel as the parents of my pupils would withdraw their children from me because of all the gossip. After this, I decided to assemble a clock by myself. I bought some small wheels and broken clock-mechanisms from Yeḥiel, and repaired them as well as I could. I even put together clock-faces from broken pieces of white plates. In this manner I managed to satisfy my desire to learn this craft without, at the same time, incurring the scorn of the people.

At that time, it was one of the duties of my good friend Ḥayyim Ḥaikil to accompany the Rabbis of the province, with all of whom he was on very good terms, from one city to another, and to assist any Rabbi who wished to take up a new post in any city. It was summertime. Ḥayyim was accompanying Rabbi V. of Ponevezh to the city of Pumpian. At the crossroads in a forest there was an inn, owned by a miracle-worker. This man had gained the reputation of being able to heal all manner of illnesses which the physicians were unable to cure, and especially mental illnesses. This miracle-worker was comfortably off, having purchased the inn out of his own means. He was also very learned in Torah, and a God-fearing man. He had divided his inn into two sections: in one part, he lived with his family, and this part contained four rooms which he used for treating his patients; in the other part were the accommodation for the guests and the bars for the farmers. The miracle-worker and Ḥayyim Ḥaikil had known each other for a long time. It happened, therefore, that when the cartier stopped at the inn for a short rest, the Rabbi suggested that they go inside "so that I may light up a pipe". They went inside. There was a distinguished looking Jew there, dressed in the manner of the old Jews, his clothes clean, this beard trimmed and a silk girdle around his waist. He greeted Rabbi V. and shook hands with Ḥayyim Ḥaikil. He then began to walk up and down the room like a man lost in thought. They believed him to be a merchant who had stopped on his way to do business. Some minutes later, the man turned again to the Rabbi and enquired respectfully whither he was bound. The Rabbi told him he was going to Pumpian. "Where have you come from?" the man asked. "From Ponevezh." "Where do you live?" "In Ponevezh." "What are you going to do in the city?" The Rabbi was too embarrassed to answer, not wishing to tell him he was the local Rabbi. The merchant, however, kept urging him, with all respect, until finally the Rabbi told him what he was. The man then began to treat him with the honour due to a Rabbi, and further asked him humbly: "May I know your name?" "My name is V." "And your father's name?" The Rabbi asked him: "Why do you wish to know my father's name when you do not know even me?" The man nevertheless insisted, begging to be told his name since he had always respected Rabbis and always wanted to know the names of the Rabbis he met and conversed with. In the end, the Rabbi gave in to his pleas, and told him that his father had been called "Z". No sooner had the man heard the name, than he placed his hand over his throat and began to sing "O God who art full of compassion", [268] at the top of his voice in the manner of the synagogue Cantors. The Rabbi became nervous of him, and drew away from him. He grabbed hold of Ḥayyim Ḥaikil and hastened to leave the inn. They both ran outside and climbed on to their seats in the cart, and ordered the cartier to whip up his horse so that they could flee from the place. Even after they had entered the forest and were some distance away from the inn, they could still hear the voice of the merchant reciting "the soul of our teacher, Rabbi V., the son of our teacher Rabbi Z., who passed away". . . . . It transpired that the merchant was one of those mad patients who were being treated by the miracle-worker. He had one peculiar form of behaviour: whenever he saw a stranger he would go up to him and urge him to tell him his name and the name of his father, and then would immediately put his fingers around his throat and recite "O God who art full of compassion . . . the souls of . . ." Such was the nature of his madness.

At that time, the Candle Tax decreed by the Tsar Nicholas came into force: it is still in force today, in this year 1886,[269] even though originally it was declared to be only a temporary imposition. The purpose of the tax was to promote modern learning among the Jews. The money would be used to build schools throughout all the areas of Jewish residence, including rabbinic seminars where future Rabbis would be given a combined religious and secular education. Today, forty years later, the schools no longer exist, [270] and the tax fund has grown to a colossal amount, the interest on which would itself be more than enough to pay for all the modern schools in existence. This tax impoverished the already overburdened Jews. Yet it is still in force, and nobody knows what happens to the money. This much, however, we do know: those highly-placed ministers who are pleased to be known as people who "care for the Jews", receive tens of thousands of roubles annually from this tax, both as salary and gift - and not a word is heard about it.

Immediately after the proclamation of this tax, a further announcement was made to the effect that every Jewish *melammed* would be required to pass an examination in the Russian language[271] before the officials and Goverment Rabbis: those who passed successfully would be given a teacher's certificate. A number of *melammedim* of Shadova came to me with the request that we travel together to the provincial capital Shavel, where I would be awarded the certificate and they would be recognised as my assistants and would teach under my supervision. We went to Shavel. However, the Rabbis themselves had no idea of what they were supposed to do, for they had not yet received the actual order from the Government. They, therefore, ridiculed the matter, asking the *melammedim* questions concerning the number of knots on the fringes,[272] and similar religious matters, and then sent them away with the promise to send them the certificate in due course. In my case, however, they neither ridiculed nor asked questions, saying that they did not know what to do about me. I returned home. Now I began to wonder whether my knowledge of Russian would be adequate, seeing that I had acquired it only by my own learning and without the help of a teacher, in the same way that I had learned Hebrew, without studying the grammar and correct pronunciation. I had never heard the language spoken by a person who knew it well: my sole interest had been to understand what I read. There was a school in the city, with two classes for beginners, although no Jewish boy had ever attended them. I went there to ask the teacher to teach me the Russian language, one hour per day, at his own fee. The teacher answered: ''I cannot do this, since I do not have the time to spare. But if you will come and join the class in the school, I will teach you.'' I agreed to do so. He then said: ''In that case, you will of course remove your beard and sidelocks.'' ''I cannot possibly do this. My people will stone me to death!'' Thus my hopes were left hanging in the air.

There was a young man, an acquaintance of Ḥayyim Ḥaikil, who lived in an inn not far from the town. He often came to visit me. We had become close friends. I told him of my lack of Russian. He himself had once begun to study the language, and learned a little with the help of a teacher, and therefore what he did know was correct. He was familiar with methods of study, and pointed out that all foreign languages were taught by a different method from Hebrew: first and foremost, it was the grammar that was studied, and only afterwards did the students go on to reading books. This was something new to me. I asked him where I might find books on grammar, and how I could learn grammar before knowing the language. He said: ''Look, I can buy you a Russian Grammar by Vostokov[273] for forty kopeks, and I will also show you how to study it.'' He told me that the grammar book had to be learned by heart, but that there were certain rules of grammar which need not be learned by heart but had to be known, whilst certain others had to be known word perfect and by heart. He marked on the pages of the book the rules which I needed to learn by heart. I began to study them according to his instructions, and found the task very laborious. I had never in my life been able to learn anything by heart, but contented myself with reading and understanding. Later, the young man left the city, and I never saw him again. I pored over the first part of the book, and learned it. The second part was a selection of articles and, since my friend had departed, I had no way of knowing whether it was important for me to learn the second part by heart, too. Nor could I tell which were the essential rules in this part. I therefore ended up knowing only the first part of the book, even to this day.

At that time, it became necessary to have a travel permit.[274] Rumour spread in Shadova that no one was exempt from the order, and that anyone who did not possess a valid document would be clapped in irons and returned to his home-town. I had never been officially registered — nor, for that matter, had my father or his parents. Now, I was compelled to request a certificate from the community in Serednik. I knew that no one by the name of Ḥayyim and aged twenty would appear in the records — except for one name, Ḥayyim Isaac ben Joseph Stinker,[275] which was the name I had been called when I had gone to Keidan. It worried me for I was uncertain of whether I might be caught. Serednik was some distance from Shadova, and I could not forsake my pupils in order to go there. I was left with no other course than to send a messenger to Serednik with a written request to the heads of the community, and particularly Joseph the Beadle, who ruled the lives of all the Jews in Serednik and had been my enemy every since I can remember, from the time that I had quarrelled with his son Mordecai. There was, unfortunately, no other course available to me. My friend, Ḥayyim Ḥaikil, brought along a poor man who, for three roubles, agreed to travel on foot to Serednik and present my petition to the communal leaders. Furthermore, my friend advised me to send the man by way of the city of Vilki, which was not far out of the way, to visit my bride and her parents, although without disclosing that I had sent him: he would enquire as to the financial condition of her father, and how she felt towards me now that I had been absent two years. My friend, Ḥayyim Ḥaikil, had explained to me the nature of the hatred which had filled my heart, in place of the love I had formerly borne for her, because of that particular incident. According to what I had told him, he had come out in favour of the girl. In any case, he said, since I had found no peace or contentment, as I had hoped, in Shadova, nor had I been approached concerning a suitable marriage alignment, I might as well endeavour to find out, through the services of the messenger, the situation in my in-laws' family. If it were favourable, then the messenger could disclose to them that I was still waiting to complete the marital arrangements. If it were not, then he would say nothing. I prepared letters to all the communal leaders, and to Joseph the Beadle, asking that they rescue me by sending me a certificate forthwith, and promising to pay henceforth annually whatever fee was required from me, seeing that I was a Jewish teacher and would be their slave for ever. I also asked the messenger to enquire of Joseph the Beadle whether he would let me have a certificate even without consulting the communal leaders, for which I would pay him personally and in secret a fee of five roubles: if he could not, then he should present my petition to the community. The messenger left, returning two weeks later empty-handed. He had not found Joseph the Beadle, who had gone away to the district capital, Kovno. When the messenger had presented my letters to the communal leaders, they had said nothing, merely referring him to the Beadle, without whom nothing could be done. The messenger had then left for Kovno, passing through Vilki on the way. He visited my father-in-law, and found that he was indeed poor, but that my bride was waiting for me impatiently and refused to listen to any marriage-brokers because, she said, she knew how much I loved her and that I would never deceive her, and therefore she would wait for me until she heard that I had fallen in love with someone else. The messenger went on to Kovno and learned that Joseph the Beadle had left the city two days earlier to return to Serednik. He therefore also returned and met Joseph on the way. Joseph told him that he could do nothing about my request at present because he was obliged to make another trip to Kovno. However, on his final return to Serednik, he would attend to my matter, and might obtain a certificate for me, which he would then bring to Shadova himself. I began to despair of ever obtaining a certificate from my home-town. My friend, Ḥayyim Ḥaikil, advised me to abandon the hope of a certificate from Serednik, for it was obvious that they did not count me as one of them, and there was no one of influence in my family to speak on my behalf. He suggested that I apply for a certificate from a small town, Loigzoim, not far from Shavel, whose Beadle was also the communal head and tax-collector. He was a good friend of Ḥayyim, and would assuredly grant me a certificate for a fee of five roubles, and would renew it annually for a prescribed fee. So it was. He brought me a certificate authorised by the provincial officials in Shavel, made out in the name of Ḥayyim David ben Simḥa Ratskovski, a resident of the town of Loigzoim — although I had never been to the town or met the communal head. I remained a member of the Loigzoim community for three years, until I finally transferred to the city of Laukave, in Vorne, to which I still belong today.

At that time a new marriage-broker came to speak to Ḥayyim Ḥaikil about me. My friend approved, so I agreed to pay a visit to the hotel Vobelitsk, which stood at the crossroads on the main highway between Shavel and Kelm. The owner of the inn, Menaḥem Monesh, had built the place long before the stone highway had been laid there; it was on private land belonging to a landowner to whom he paid a small annual rent for the site of the house and the surrounding garden. The place was called Vobelitsk, and its owner Manaḥem Monesh was a God-fearing and learned man descended from the family of the five Geonim who once lived in the Telz district. It was his daily custom to rise early and study the Torah in a small room reserved for study until ten o'clock, after which he would attend to the business of the inn. His wife — she was his second wife — was a shrewish and hard-hearted woman. She cooked the meals on the oven and stove. The practical management of the hotel was run by their elder daughter, Ḥannah Rivkah, who received the guests, and attended to the daily affairs of the establishment. Their younger daughter was only twelve years old and not yet capable of attending to anything: she followed her father's ways in every detail, like a monkey imitating a man, even in prayer and religious devotion. They had no son, although Menaḥem Monesh did have a son by his first wife. I never met him, for his father had sent him away, at the request of his second wife, because he did not conform to the father's religious orthodoxy; he had been away ten years, and no one knew where he was. The daughter, Ḥannah Rivkah, was both an excellent housekeeper and a woman of valour who was held in such high repute in the whole district that people came to stay at the hotel simply because of her. She was not especially good-looking, but she had a graceful figure and spoke well, whilst her intelligence shone through her eyes. Three years earlier, she had entered into a marriage which had lasted only three days, and then had obtained a divorce. It happened this way. Two conflicting interests had opposed each other in the house. The father, who was as fanatically devout as anyone could be at that time, was looking for a son-in-law among the yeshiva students: he would help him to become a Rabbi, and the student would take the place of his lost son. The daughter, this girl of virtue and worth, had met many learned and devout men who were also accustomed to the ways of the world, and therefore had little respect for the yeshiva students who had no modern learning. Nevertheless, she could not disobey her father's wish. With much weeping and sobbing, she let herself be married to a husband she hated. Two days later, she was stricken with an illness which lasted for two months. The father paid the husband a considerable sum to divorce his daughter by proxy, for it was feared that if she had to appear in person she would die on the spot. After a while, she began to recover, and soon became well, although she never fully recovered. The marriage-brokers scoured everywhere but none had so far found a son-in-law to suit the father or a husband to please the daughter. Such had been the situation for the past three years. Now, the Shadova marriage-broker considered me a suitable suitor. It happened that there was a Jewish tailor from Shadova staying at the hotel, making clothes for the landlord's family. They asked him about the teacher in his city. He spoke well of me, although I was not acquainted with him. He said I was generally highly esteemed by the community, for during my year's mourning for my father I had prayed at the synagogue three times each day and studied Mishna in order to be able to recite the *Rabbanan Kaddish*, and lived an honest and upright life. The father was willing to take for a son-in-law the teacher of gentile children and religiously forbidden books. Thereupon the marriage-broker repaired to Ḥayyim Ḥaikil and persuaded him to accompany us to arrange the marriage contract. However, he insisted that I must not wear my short coat, and should cut my hair shorter, and should wear a white blouse and other items of their choosing in order to please both the father and the girl. I did not possess any clothes suitable for wearing at the hotel, as my upper garment was too short and the lower too long. Fortunately for me, it was winter-time and Purim was at hand.

I had a long, loose-fitting fur coat, like those worn by the rich — but nothing else. My friend Ḥayyim Ḥaikil borrowed a long, woollen coat of good quality from a blacksmith who had ordered it for his own wedding: he promised to give the coat back in three days' time, since all we needed to do at the hotel was to agree upon a marriage contract, and then return forthwith. From a clockmaker he borrowed a white lace collar to sew on to the neck of my shirt — and from one of the sons-in-law he borrowed a scarf of fine silk to go over the shirt-collar. He promised them all that he would return this clothing in three days' time. I hired a covered wagon drawn by two horses, and the four of us rode off on the wagon — Ḥayyim Ḥaikil, the marriage-broker, myself and the cartier. Before we left, however, the marriage-broker told me to ask Reb Isaac, whose children I taught, to give me a note stating that he held a hundred roubles which I had given him to keep me. The reason for this was that the parents might wonder why this Shadova teacher was a poor man and whether he was a profligate person. When I requested Reb Isaac for the note, he said: "I know the hotel owner of Vobelitsk and his whole family very well, and they have known me for a long time. I am going to Kelm on business tomorrow. After I have finished, I will go to the hotel and confirm your story about the hundred roubles. They will believe me." We left for Vobelitsk.

There was one room for guests, and another room which served as a dining room, whilst the remaining rooms were used by the landlord and his family. I stayed in the first room whilst Ḥayyim Ḥaikil and the marriage-broker remained in the other room talking with Reb Monesh and his wife and daughters, without my knowing what they were saying. At times, the father would come into my room to greet me, and the wife and the girl came to look at me but without speaking to me. I looked at them, also without speaking. Whenever I was able to ask the marriage-broker how things were, he replied everything was all right. Even Ḥaikil my friend would not give me a definite answer. So it went on until the evening, when a meal was set for the four of us, and we ate and drank whilst the family served us as though we were normal guests. They also prepared beds for us in the other room; my bed was, however, made in the first room, where I was to sleep alone. We arose early next morning, prayed and ate: they saw the phylacteries I wore, as large as a small barrel. Later, Ḥaikil told me that, since Menaḥem Monesh did not know my family, nor was he impressed by my short coat, he felt I might not be a suitable suitor, and therefore had sent for his relatives to come over immediately to give their opinion: they lived in another inn, some two miles away. Later, the man came into my room, and stood by the oven to warm himself, but he did not speak. I decided to open the conversation: "I am rather astonished at the passage in the Gemara[276] which says that if a man is unknown in a place, he should be addressed as Rabbi, meaning thereby that because he is unknown, he should be honoured as a Rabbi and considered an important person. Yet, another passage states that such a person should be respected but suspected, meaning that he should not be honoured as a Rabbi or an important person." The man asked me: "So what?" I continued: "Both passages are true. The unknown person should be addressed with the respect due to a Rabbi, but should be at the same time suspected, though not openly.'' The man turned from me and left the room. He had hardly closed the door behind him, when he began to clap his hands together like a man who is happy. This surprised me. I asked my friend about it, but he did not know, so he went to listen in the other room. He returned to say that it was nothing important, but that the girl would be coming to enquire why I had not spoken to her. I said: "How could I possibly speak with her and meet her near the stove or in her room? I am no more than a guest here, like any other person who stays here. In any case, why does she not come to me, here, in this room?'' My friend went out to report what I had said. About an hour later she entered and stood by the stove to warm herself. I began to ask her about the hotel, and whether her father owned it himself, how old it was, and similar questions. She answered these and other questions fully, and stayed about a half-hour before leaving. I was left alone for an hour, then the girl returned, resumed her place beside the stove and continued our conversation. She asked me about the discussions that were taking place concerning a bride and groom. I told her I knew nothing about them. She said that she had always heard that a groom brought fine presents for his bride, such as gold and pearls and ornaments. Swiftly I rejoined: "Gentle maiden, your own words testify to the truth of what you say. You said that 'the women' have told you about the gold and jewel ornaments. Why only women, and not men? It is because Jewish women are not learned and therefore judge only by externals; they value the groom according to his gold and jewels. But men who, in the main, are learned and wise do not judge like women, for they know that there are grooms who do not possess gold or silver or pearls, yet are themselves more precious than these, so that their learning will provide the bride with adornment finer than gold and pearls.'' I watched as her face flushed a little, and she turned and went away.

I was still ignorant of what was going on, for even my friend Ḥayyim Ḥaikil had said nothing, nor had the marriage-broker. The relatives arrived, greeted me without saying anything more but spent the day in the other room, whispering together with Ḥayyim Ḥaikil and the marriage-broker. Meanwhile, the cartier passed the time with tending to his horse, and eating and drinking at my expense. Beyond that, nothing else happened. Then a merchant arrived from the nearby town of Kurtovian. He left his horse and carriage in the care of the inn's Jewish servant, and went inside. I saw him conversing with Ḥaikil and Menaḥem Monesh, but I was not able to hear anything. Suddenly, Ḥayyim Ḥaikil came running into my room, and asked me what my father's name was. "Aaron Mendels,'' I told him. "What is your uncle's name?'' "Jacob Baredzever.'' Immediately he returned with the new guest, a wealthy and important contractor who owned walled houses in Shavel although he himself lived in Kurtovian. He was called Isaiah Goldberg. Later, he climbed into his carriage and continued on his way. Menaḥem Monesh came back into the house, clapping his hands once more, rejoined his relatives and continued his whispering. I could find no explanation for his behaviour, nor did my friends offer a clear reply to any of my questions.

I was repelled by all the secrecy that was going on, and considered to myself: "I have now been in this room, alone, for the past two days. No one speaks to me, nor is marriage even mentioned. Why should I wait any longer?" The cartier was sitting by the big stove in the tavern, facing the door to the second room. Angrily, I turned to him and, in an authoritative tone called out to him: "Why are we staying here? Are there no other inns on the road? Hurry and harness the horses, and let us be on our way!" Inside the room of the whisperers, a sudden silence fell. The marriage-broker emerged and said: "What makes you so angry? There is plenty of time, and it matters little to us whether we leave tonight or tomorrow." I answered: "To you it will not matter, for you will not have to pay the bill. For my part, the sooner we leave the better." Two people came out of the room, and asked me not to leave so hastily. They said it would be better if I joined the group and listened to their discussions. I went into the room with them. They were discussing the marital contract and the dowry and the period of maintenance. Evening came, and with it came Reb Isaac of Shadova on his way back from Kelm. I greeted him, and he went to speak with the.family. He urged them to arrange the wedding immediately in place of the contract, saying he would not be willing to let me stay there all the time since he would want me to go to Shadova to teach his children after Passover for the whole of the summer, after which I could return to the hotel. He made this proposal on the advice of Hayyim Haikil who was worried lest I return to Shadova immediately after the contract and, in the course of time, it became known to them that I was really very poor and that even the hundred roubles I was supposed to have entrusted to Reb Isaac was only a figment of the imagination, that in fact I did not possess enough to pay for the expenses of the wedding. There was a further consideration that, during the next summer, I would be losing some of my pupils, and would hardly be able to earn a livelihood for myself. For these reasons, he had advised the rich man to urge a speedy settlement and obtain from the father a promise to let me go to him for the summer. After this had been done, he left and continued on his journey.

That night, Hayyim Haikil revealed the mystery of all that had happened. I had always been shy and reserved, to such an extent that people who did not know me considered me an inferior and spiritless person. It was only after they had begun to speak to me and aroused my interest that they discovered my true qualities. Although, therefore, this family had believed all that they had previously heard about me, when they laid eyes on me in person they began to look askance at me. The father was also dissatisfied with my clothes which were too short, and with my vocation as teacher of languages, which seemed to him heretical. The girl also complained to the marriage-broker: "Why have you brought me this teacher whose only income is three roubles per year?" My poverty was plainly obvious to her from my clothes and the white, lace collar I had sewn on to my shirt. Yet, after I had spoken with her father concerning the passages in the Gemara, he relented, and said to his daughter: "I am not certain what to do, but if you are satisfied I shall agree.'' She took this to mean that her father no longer opposed the union. Then Haikil and the marriage-broker urged her to go into the room and have a word with me: if, after that, she still refused, then they would agree to drop the matter. They eventually persuaded her to see me. She came and listened to me, especially on the matter of the 'women' and the gifts. From that moment, her whole attitude changed, and her former antagonism turned to deep love. When her father asked for her decision she replied: "If this son-in-law pleases you, I shall heed your advice." He understood that his daughter would agree to the marriage. He then began to wonder about my family, whom nobody seemed to know, so perhaps my father may even have been a horse-thief of some kind? In the midst of all this, the merchant Reb Isaiah Goldberg entered. He was acquainted with Hayyim Haikil, and asked him what he was doing there and who was the young man with him. Hayyim told him all about the marriage negotiations and the final obstacle of my unknown family, for he was related to one of the prominent families in the land. Goldberg asked them to enquire of me the name of my father and my uncle in Serednik. On hearing the replies, he said he knew the groom's entire family, that his father was a very learned teacher called Aaron Mendels, and the uncle Jacob Baredzever was also a pious and honoured man. Then the father clapped his hands joyfully, since now even my family was known. It was at that very time, when they had been discussing the terms of the contract, that I had called out angrily to the cartier to harness the horses and prepare to leave.

Reb Isaac came in the evening and completed the marriage formalities. It was arranged that, since both the bride and groom had been married before, the relatives and a quorum of men would assemble the next day. The wedding ceremony would be held beside the stove. The next morning, Menahem Monesh drove off to Shavel to fetch the officiants of the ceremony and also his relatives and friends. The marriage-broker and Hayyim Haikil came and told me to get ready to bathe in the ritual bath attached to the hotel, together with the other guests. The innkeeper, being a religious man, had built a ritual bath for the hotel. He used this himself as often as he thought necessary, in addition to the ordained Fridays and holy days. Hayyim Haikil, who knew of my aversion to bathing in public, and of how I had been ill for a long time after bathing in public during my first few days in Shadova when I had been compelled to bathe for the New Year festival lest I be considered a heretic, nevertheless urged me to attend the bath with the others. I pleaded that this was utterly foreign to my nature, because I was repelled by the sweaty smell and the steam which exuded from the flesh of the bathers and the walls of the bath. It was to no avail. He said: "You must at least come into the vestibule next to the bath, remove your clothes there, then come into the bathroom itself and stay for a few moments. If you wish, bathe in the hot water, but if you do not, we can say that you have already bathed. Then you can leave." I asked him why, in that case, I was being forced to do all this seeing that it was in fact unnecessary. He replied: "The truth is that it is essential that you come with us. You will be told the reason later." So I went along with them. I removed my clothes and went into the bathroom. The place was full. I had hardly entered the room when Ḥaikil said to me: "Now go and put on your clothes, and leave." I thanked him profusely for his kindness. It was not until three days after the wedding ceremony that Ḥayyim Ḥaikil explained the affair of the bath. Apparently, because the clothes I had borrowed did not fit me, nor did my trousers hang properly upon me — for never in my life had I had a suit made to measure but had always bought second-hand clothes made for others — therefore, when the family saw me walking with measured and faltering steps, they thought I was suffering from hernia. They had arranged that I attend the bath so that they could inspect my naked body. When my friend protested that I could not endure the bath, they concluded that I did indeed suffer from hernia, and they told him of their fears. He laughed and ridiculed them, but they would not believe him. Finally he promised that I would be there, even if he had to use force upon me. After they had seen me completely naked, they were satisfied, and left me alone.

Menaḥem Monesh returned from Shavel prepared for the wedding ceremony. He promised to give his daughter a dowry of three hundred roubles plus three years' maintenance and to pay the cost of our food thereafter. The canopy was put up, a feast of wine and meat laid out, and everyone ate and drank — but without the services of musicians and Cantors and singers, for such is the custom where bride and groom have been already divorced. That evening, they all went off to their homes, whilst my wife and I remained in the second room. Because of the hastiness of the arrangements, she had not had time to purify herself in the ritual bath.

Next morning, we went to have breakfast in the first room with the rest of the family. My father-in-law, Menaḥem Monesh, began to discuss Torah with me, to ascertain whether his new acquisition was indeed learned in the Law, for this was his one desire, and he could not wait another day. Both Ḥayyim Ḥaikil and the marriage-broker were there, and they decided to do my job for me. Without allowing me to utter a word they engaged him in discussion, but he addressed himself only to me. Later that day, they left and returned to Shadova. On the following day, my father-in-law opened a copy of the tractate *Bava Batra*[277] and said: "I find this page particularly difficult to understand. Can I ask you to study this with me?" He showed me the page. The text of the Gemara was very short, but the margins on both sides were filled with the commentaries of Rashi and Tosefot.[278] We began to read. I had not looked at a Gemara for years, nor had I ever studied *Bava Batra*. Therefore I slyly let my eyes flit over Rashi and the commentaries very quickly whilst he, like all religious men who can read without being particularly learned, pursued his measured way through the text. When he heard me relaying the comments of Rashi and Tosefot together, he obtained the impression that I was profoundly learned in the Law. He put aside his Gemara, arose and went out. He told his wife, my mother-in-law, that their son-in-law was a brilliant Talmudist, who was ten times more worthy than he. She thought I must be an outstanding genius. He, on his part, never tried to test me again.

He fixed a room for me away from the noise of the hotel, at the other end of the house, and placed in it two beds and mattresses and a table and a chair. He urged me to stay there all day and study the Law of the Lord so long as I lived with them. Reluctant as I was, I could not refuse, although I told him that I would also be writing my Hebrew book which I had begun some time before — my autobiography whose title *Wife of My Youth* I had written in large square letters on the first page: it included some poems I had written and was the same one I had in Rasseyn, as I have mentioned above. I was also translating a very good German story about the black slave trade, *Loango,* [279] which I intended to include in the first part of my book. My father-in-law could not understand a word of Hebrew written in ornate literary style, and therefore allowed me to do as I pleased. That day, my father-in-law went to Shavel to buy for me some cloth patterned in a flowery design, which he gave to the tailor in the hotel to make into a summer coat for me. It was a gift to show his love for me. I wore the coat every day: at that time, I was still wearing the coat I had borrowed from the Shadova blacksmith, for I had left my own short coat behind as I had thought that I would be staying here three days only.

It was the fifth day after my good friend had gone away. My wife had never left my side for a moment, either because she wanted to find out the truth concerning my financial circumstances or because her heart told her that things were not quite what they seemed. A Jew arrived at the inn, and sat at the large table opposite the room where I was. Whenever I passed by he stared at me, and kept his eyes on me until I had gone. It seemed to me that I had met him before in Shadova. The man remained silent until eventually my wife left me to go into another room. He then turned towards me and put a letter into my hand. I took the letter outside the house and read it. How great was my distress! My friend Hayyim Haikil had sent this messenger to tell me to hurry and give the man the coat I had borrowed from the blacksmith. The Passover was approaching and the blacksmith was anxious to wear it on the festival. Furthermore, I was to return the silk collar I had borrowed to sew on my shirt: I had borrowed it from a bridegroom who had received it as a gift from his bride, who would be visiting him during the Passover and would expect to see him wearing it. Despite all that my friend could do, the blacksmith was adamant that I return his coat, otherwise he would inform the local judge that I had fled from Shadova and stolen his coat. In those days judges welcomed any excuse to arrest Jewish innkeepers, whom they would keep in the stocks until a ransom had been paid for their release. For me, a newly-wedded groom, this boded no good. I had no recourse but to take the messenger outside to the woods where I asked him to wait for me. I changed my coat, handed him the blacksmith's coat, and also paid him one rouble and fifty kopeks for his errand. However, I did not give him the silk collar: its owner, the groom, was from an important family and would to able to obtain another one from the wealthy Reb Isaac on my account; in any case he had once been a pupil of mine, and I thought there would be no harm if I kept it. My wife observed my anxiety and began to question the messenger, asking him where he was from and what he was doing. She also glanced at the peg on the wall where my coat usually hung, and noticed that it was missing. She then grasped the situation. She came to me and said "Listen, my beloved. Tell me the whole truth now, for I shall not think any the worse of you for it. If it is true that you are poor, I shall know how to conceal it from my parents. If, on the other hand, you do not tell me the truth, then I cannot guarantee what my mother will say, and you know she is a very shrewish woman. So tell me the truth. I know that the hundred roubles are not yours, any more than are the clothes you wear. But did you borrow the fur-coat too?" I then told her: "The truth is that I have a better coat than this, but it is too short; and I also have a very fine summer coat, but it is made in the style of the gentiles. When I heard that your parents would not receive me if I came looking like a German and a heretic, I left my clothes in Shadova, and borrowed this coat for three days, thinking that I would be able to return within that time. However, the fur-coat is mine, and I paid twenty-five roubles for it. Now, the blacksmith wants his coat back in time for the festival. This is why Hayyim Haikil has sent this messenger to me. What am I to do?" "I believe you, and I shall never stop loving you for one moment," she said. Tears began to shed down her cheeks. She turned away, and left the room. A few moments later she returned, fully composed. She told me the explanation I should give her father if he discovered the truth, although she would try to ensure that he did not. There was no one in the hotel who took any notice of my flowered coat, but it would be noticeable during the Sabbaths and festivals when people came to hold the services here. Time was too short for me to do anything about it. Passover arrived, and I was in despair over my coat and my torn prayer-shawl and my large phylacteries which were as large as my head. Despite everything, my wife's love for me increased day by day, and her parents esteemed me more and more. My wife, who was a wise woman, appreciated my personal qualities which she often compared with those of the guests she received at the hotel, whose sole wit was to pass crude remarks about her. When, on the occasions we made love, she began to tell me what she had heard them say, I would quickly stop her saying that I did not wish to hear such language from so beautiful a soul, that it was unbecoming to her and suitable only for cartiers and drunkards. Thenceforth, she guarded her lips and never strayed beyond the bounds of modesty. She took my words to heart, knowing that I was no simple yeshiva student, nor was I a dissembling hypocrite. The festival came to a close, and I began to make preparations to go back to Shadova. She gave me ten roubles for the journey, without her parents' knowledge, and told me to make new clothes to satisfy her parents and herself. She would give me a further sum of money when I returned for the festival of Pentecost. I then left.

I returned home for the festival, dressed in a manner to please my father-in-law.

After the festival, I went back to Shadova. My wife gave me another ten roubles and fifty kopeks to purchase a new prayer shawl. I came home again for *Shabbat Naḥamu,* when she gave me more money. Finally, I returned at the end of the summer, towards the month of *Ellul,* to rest from all my toil. I had high hopes that my father-in-law would find a worthwhile means of livelihood for me, and would also pay me the promised dowry. The High Holy Days and festival of Tabernacles passed by. One day, my wife and I went for a stroll in the fields and the wood. Guests arrived at the inn, and my wife was not there to receive them; my mother-in-law cursed us, that our legs should be broken. However, when we returned, she spoke no evil but kept her peace. On the morrow, she said to me: "Look, my son. Your father-in-law promised you a dowry, but I know he cannot give you it as he has no ready cash. Nor will he try to pay you in instalments, for he trusts the Lord and believes that, if ever the need arises, he will be able to find the money for you. Nevertheless, I will pay you on his behalf, in instalments, without anyone else's knowledge." She put ten roubles into my hand, saying: "Keep an account of everything I pay towards the dowry."

At that time, all the silverware was stolen from the house. My wife had removed all the silver, which was worth about seventy roubles, from the room after dinner. In her haste to receive new guests, she had put the silverware under the pillows of the bed in the adjoining room. When she went back for them, they had disappeared. She fell into a profound melancholy over the incident, and this led to the onset of her illness. At the time, she was several months pregnant: her parents were delighted that she had conceived and still remained healthy and vigorous. This affair, however, began to eat into her soul. Suspicion fell upon a certain Jew who lived in a village not far from the hotel. He had been in the hotel on the day of the theft; even though he paid frequent visits to the hotel, because he was a close neighbour and was considered an honest person, he seemed the obvious suspect. My father-in-law said to me: "Let us go together to this man. Perhaps we may learn the truth from him."

My father-in-law was continually asking me concerning my religious beliefs, for he was unable to accept that a person like myself, who was familiar with Russian and German and Hebrew belles-lettres and scientific works, could not have been singed with the flames of heresy. It became a habit with him to broach the subject of my religious studies and beliefs. On our journey, therefore, he related an incident which had happened that very day. A guest had come to the hotel, a wealthy and respected man whom they had known for some time. In reply to their greeting, he had said that everything was fine, thank God, that business was well and his family well. Unfortunately, there was a plague in his home — his mother, who continuously embittered his life, though without provocation, for he always treated her respectfully and tended to all her needs. She had always been a very shrewish woman who looked for trouble and sought any pretext to belabour him with her tongue. He had scornfully — and wrongly — described the great favour his mother had done for him by bearing him and rearing him in a world in which he would find seventy-seven times more trouble than pleasure — although, so far as she was concerned, she had not considered she was doing him any favour. To this day, he still curses the day he was born. Despite the endless bitterness of his burden, justice demanded of him that he repay the debt he owed her for the harm she did him by bringing him into this world: it was a crime greater than murder. He knew no way of doing this. Should he repay the milk with which she suckled him by giving her a large barrel of cow's milk — or was there some other way in which he could discharge his debt? My father-in-law gazed into my eyes, awaiting my answer, for he had become involved with the problem and wondered whether the man's question was not indeed true? I thought of a reply which might satisfy him, and said: ''This situation has been discussed in the Gemara where it was stated that 'in the final conclusion, it were better for a man not to be born than to be born, but since has has been born then let him examine his own deeds and actions', to which they added 'let him search his deeds'.[280] Let us consider their words. What did the Sages mean by saying that a man should examine his deeds: what will he find, and what will he do? Furthermore, why this difference of opinion between them, with some saying 'examine' and others 'search'? Actually, they mean the same thing. Our Sages would not give senseless advice to a man born into this world. They meant, therefore, that any man who is imprisoned, bound hand and foot, with iron chains and confined in a small, dark cell, and has to live off nauseating scraps of food, should dance and sing and rattle his chains with glee inside his cell, and enjoy every last pleasure he can wring out of life with all his senses — unless he has already lost them. This sort of behaviour will naturally give the impression that he is happy with his lot, and enjoys his chains and his confinement. That is what our Sages meant. Truly, the world is more full of sorrows than joys, and therefore it were better for a man not to be born. But once he is born, then let him examine the deeds he performed in his prison, and he will discover that there were times when he was happy and rejoiced and rattled his chains and enjoyed everything he could, however senseless it was. Since the Sages did not wish to slander men by declaring that their deeds defile their souls, therefore they stated 'let him examine', namely let him search diligently for any deed, however small, which appears contrary to reason but which can afford him some pleasure in his confinement. The word 'search' really applies to externals, to clothes and utensils, as when a man searches occasionally in his pockets to ensure that nothing is missing. Thus, the Sages who added this second phrase meant that a man does not need to examine his corrupt ways — for they are generally a form of protest against being born — but that he should 'search his deeds' objectively and he will find that, in fact, it is good to be born, since one is able to enjoy the pleasures of life. Now, this man who complains against his shrewish mother for having brought him into this world, and declares that he detests his life, is in fact seeking a pretext to punish himself.'' My father-in-law listened in astonished silence, realising that these thoughts had come spontaneously into my mind in answer to his question. He marvelled, and was silent.

The stolen silverware was never found.

At that time, there came to the inn the man Aaron of Kurtovian; he had been in Shadova and was a good friend of Ḥayyim Ḥaikil. He urged my father-in-law to let me return to Kurtovian for another half-year. I would have no more than three pupils who would study writing and grammar and Hebrew and Gemara. One of the pupils would be the son of the wealthy Isaiah Goldberg and the others his daughters who wished to study Yiddish and German. My fee for the half-year would be 60 roubles. Since the city was not far from the hotel, I would be able to return to my wife every week-end for the Sabbath, and return on the Sunday morning. My father-in-law said he would provide me with sufficient food to last the whole week. I would have a room in the man's house where I would live and teach. His wife would prepare all my meals. The sixty roubles could remain unspent in my pocket. My father-in-law was willing, so they asked my wife, who also agreed, but only because of her fear of her mother who would surely come to hate me if I remained all winter in the hotel without work and without helping to manage the hotel. It was better, therefore, that I should be out of her sight. I listened to my wife's advice, and agreed to go. I arrived at Kurtovian, and examined Isaiah's son. He was a lad of sixteen, who had been previously a pupil of the Rabbi of the city. He was a wild youth and very sharp. Two years earlier, he had stolen some expensive wool cloth from a Jewish merchant, forged a false passport, and run away from home. After a concentrated search he had been found. When, therefore, I met the lad, I told his father: "I agree to teach him but on one condition, that you will immediately, without question or enquiry, upon receipt of a note from me, punish him for any transgression he commits. If you have to be out of town, then let me know which of the city's police can perform the punishment at my request. In this way I shall have a chance to teach him. He had good capabilities and should do well." Goldberg promised to do all I requested, and to punish the lad with all his might if required, and he hoped there would be no need for him to be away from home that winter. My father-in-law gave me a pillow and a Gemara and food and other items I would need, and I began my term as teacher in the small town of Kurtovian.

Every Friday afternoon my father-in-law called for me and took me back home in his carriage for the Sabbath. My wife asked me to write to her during weekdays and send the letter with anyone travelling that way, for she could not bear the six long days without me. I did so, and my father-in-law later told me how he himself had seen her take a letter from under the pillow of her bed and read it, and kiss it before replacing it under the pillow. Later, my mother-in-law paid me another ten roubles toward the dowry, and I put the money inside my box in my room.

These days of peace and contentment did not last long. My wife had been ill ever since the theft at the hotel, and furthermore she had never fully recovered from the illness which her first marriage had brought upon her, because of the husband she had loathed, It was just after *Ḥanukkah* that she had a miscarriage; it was a male child. She lay confined to bed for a long time. I returned home one Sabbath, during the *Purim* period, and stayed with her and did not leave her for a moment, until she finally passed away and died in my arms. Right up to the end, she spoke words of solace to me, urging me not to be distressed, and saying that she had asked her parents not to deal unkindly with me in the event of her death. I, on my part, did all I could to comfort her. I told her she would certainly recover from her illness and that we would enjoy many more happy days and good times together. Then I saw the cold sweat that streamed over her body, and the flies of death[281] that appeared on her in that cold winter. I could restrain myself no longer, and against my will I wept. I turned my face away, and took my eyes off her. She saw my tears, and immediately became faint and said: ''What frightens you so much that it brings tears to your eyes? It must be that my end is near.'' She turned her face to the wall, and continued speaking but I could not make out her words. So she passed away. Her parents approached — and the wailing began. I too wept sorely until I felt I should die from weeping. What was to become of me? I could not bring her back to life. I would surely die. Yet, if I stopped lamenting and weeping over her, her parents would think I had not truly loved her. I went outside to the rear of the house to seek some relief, but even there I found little rest. A cold wind was blowing; snow was falling; my bones felt racked with pain. I returned indoors and lay down to rest on a hard bench. I covered my eyes so that I should not look upon her. I sighed deeply, and rested awhile.

I have often heard people say that trouble never comes alone, nor pain singly. We had completed three days of the required seven days' mourning, and the fourth day was a Sabbath. On that day, a policeman came to the hotel. He had been sent by the district official in Kurtovian to find the person called Ḥayyim who had been born in Serednik and who was the son-in-law of Monesh. Apparently, Joseph the Beadle of Serednik, after he had sent my messenger away empty-handed without a certificate, had later obtained one for me from the clerk of the Kovno province for a fee of two roubles. Six months later, when his own messenger was about to go round collecting the impost, he had handed him my certificate to give me in Shadova. The messenger had not been able to find me, so he had made enquiries and discovered that I had become the son-in-law of the owner of the Vobelitsk hotel. He had therefore written to the district officer requesting that I be contacted and sent back to Serednik to collect the certificate. My father-in-law knew all about my registration with the town of Loigzoim, so he told the policeman that there was no one from Serednik staying at the hotel, nor did he know of anyone from there. He offered the policeman wine and strong drink in liberal measure, and then went out. However, the policeman did not believe his account, and he walked round to the back of the hotel where he questioned the Jewish servant, who knew nothing about the certificate but did know that the son-in-law of the hotel proprietor was called Ḥayyim and came from Serednik. The policeman became very angry, and demanded to know why my father-in-law had deceived him. I was sent for, and came in feeling frightened. I said: "No, sir, I am not from Serednik, nor have I ever been there. My parents, however, did say that they once lived there before I was born." "Which town are you from, then?" "From Loigzoim." "Show me your certificate." I did so, and also showed him the tax receipt for the year stamped with the seal of the community. The policeman read it and said: "The district officer is looking for a person called Hayyim from Serednik. It is said that he is the son-in-law of the Vobelitsk innkeeper. I can see now that this is not so." He then recorded all the details, noting that that particular person did not live here. He sat down to write to his district officer, so paper and ink were set before him, and he was also plied once more with large quantities of drink. After he had finished, he left. We remained panic-stricken. Obviously, the officer had not yet heard that I was staying in this town, Kurtovian. If this became known, then even Joseph the Beadle would not keep silent, and another search would be made for me. Where would I then go? My father-in-law had not previously known that my Loigzoim certificate had been obtained secretly from the community by its officials, so now he also began to be afraid, especially since now I was virtually no longer his son-in-law. He even said openly that he could not understand why he had made no enquiries before the marriage concerning my Loigzoim certificate. I, on my part, had been wondering, for the past two days, how I could leave this house of mourning which was so depressing me. This incident, therefore, gave me the excuse to leave hurriedly the very next morning, which was a Sunday, even though it was still in the middle of the prescribed period of mourning. I would flee to Shadova, and wait there until the district officer had abandoned my case and was no longer searching for me, and then I would return to my room. My father-in-law agreed that this was the best thing to do, even though it meant breaking the laws of the mourning period.[282] I left in great haste for Shadova.

My friend, Hayyim Haikil, was concerned to see me wan with worry and sorrow. He comforted me, saying: "When we left the marriage-broker to go to Vobelitsk, we stopped on the way at a big hotel in Shavel, whose proprietor I knew." The man had asked him where we were going, and who I was, and Hayyim had told him I was on my way to complete the marital contract to become the son-in-law of Monesh of Vobelitsk. Now, that man had a daughter, too, very pretty and diligent, and he offered us better terms if I married his daughter than I would be getting at Vobelitsk. However, neither Hayyim nor the marriage-broker wanted to stop the journey half-way, so we continued on our way. Now, I ought to return to Kurtovian, and my friend would accompany me to Shavel where we would stop at the same hotel and he would try to re-open the subject of the marriage with the girl. We left on the third day and lodged at the hotel. We tried to broach the matter, but without success. He then went back to his own town, whilst I carried on to Kurtovian — for Hayyim Haikil had dispelled my fears concerning my cer-tificate, assuring me that the official of the Loigzoim community was not afraid of anyone and would stand by his promise to acknowledge me as a native of the town, even though I had never been to the place in my life. So the matter ended, and no harm came out of it, for even in Serednik itself there was no record at all that I had belonged to their community. I went back to Kurtovian and resumed my teaching as before, without a word being said.

After the Passover, I decided to remain in the town for a further period, as my pupils' parents were satisfied with me. It was my custom to take my pupils with me to the daily afternoon and evening services, and to recite the prayers aloud in the traditional melodies and chants so that they would become accustomed to public worship. I also prepared daily lessons for them in Russian and German, and gave them homework which they had to learn by heart. Even my wild pupil obeyed me: he had once tried to test me by disobeying me, so I had written a note to his father who had broken a stick over his back, and since then had he behaved himself, although he kept looking for all manner of ways of bribing me which I firmly declined. The two daughters of the wealthy man, that is the youth's older and younger sisters, also studied with me: I taught them grammar and literature, and on Thursday the Bible with Rashi, and had even begun to teach them Gemara but abandoned this on the advice of their father who said it was not for them.

At that time, the marriage-brokers began to approach me once more. Now, I had not been back to see my in-laws since the day I had so hastily left them. When they heard that I was willing to seek another wife, they became angry because the year's mourning was not yet over. The mother-in-law revealed that she had given me twenty roubles on account of the dowry, and the Jewish servant also mentioned that he had seen my wife give me money on my return from Shadova. They thought that she must have given me several hundred roubles, because of her deep love for me. My father-in-law came to me and demanded that I give back everything I had that belonged to him — the Gemara *Berakhot,* [283] the pillows and chair, the money my mother-in-law had given me, and whatever else I had. I told him: "Take the Gemara, but the pillows and chair you cannot have since they were given by your daughter, my wife. As for the money, you will have to take me to court, here or in Shavel." He protested and said: "Is it not enough that your wife stole money to give you, and who knows how much? At least return the money your mother-in-law gave you, and the pillows and chair which do not belong to you." I replied: "My beloved father-in-law, when your daughter was alive, you loved me. Why do you hate me now? I have not forgotten your daughter's death. What wrong have I done that you should wish to do me harm?" He replied: "So long as you were my son-in-law I glossed over your faults, which I knew too well. Now that you are no longer my son-in-law, and you have even forgotten the love my daughter bore for you, since you cannot wait even for the full year of mourning to end, why should I still love you?" "If you will not pursue this matter in love and peace, then be assured that you will get nothing from me by hatred and dispute. You may have the Gemara, as I said, but not the pillows and chair. As for the money, if the law awards it to you, I shall give it to you." Some weeks later my father-in-law took me to the Ecclesiastical Court in Kurtovian. In order not to have to dispute in person against each other, we arranged for our cases to be heard by proxy. The Rabbi of the Court, after a great deal of investigation, pronounced the verdict that, according to law, the husband is entitled to everything he has received once a complete year has passed since his wife's death. Until the complete year is over the husband cannot retain anything. Now that year was a leap year, and had an additional month.[284] Therefore, if the term 'year' meant the normal twelve months, then the year had been completed since my wife's death. If, on the other hand, the term included leap year too, then the legally prescribed year was not yet over. So the Rabbi made a diligent search until he came across the opinion of one of the Geonim which satisfied him, namely that the year included leap years also. I therefore gave my father-in-law his twenty roubles, but kept the pillows and chair for myself.

In the month of *Tammuz,*[285] in the year 1848, an epidemic of cholera swept through Lithuania and Zamot. It spread through the city of Shavel on one side of us, and the city of Kelm on the other side, but by-passed my town of Kurtovian. Many people died, and fear spread through my small town, since it lay between the two larger cities. We began to take precautions against the epidemic. Reb Isaiah Goldberg and his brother, as well as my landlord Aaron who was popularly called Artsik Kurtovianer, went to the forest outside the town, cut down trees and built a hut which they covered over with leaves. They also fashioned a table and chairs out of earth and plants and greenery for the use of my pupils and myself, so that we could study there all day and only return home for meals and sleep. So we lived through the whole summer, and the black cockerel[286] did not visit our town during that summer.

At the beginning of the summer, an old marriage-broker, Tsevi Hirsh of Kurtovian, approached me. He spoke to me about a girl, the daugher of Reb Shemaiah Vishevianer — my children, he is Shemaiah, your grandfather, and the girl is your mother Chinah[286], may the Lord grant her long life. Tsevi and I travelled together to the hotel in Vishevian, not far from Telz. I liked the girl, and her parents liked me, so we bound the agreement with a holy oath. I was promised a dowry of 200 roubles plus maintenance for three years. Shemaiah rented the hotel from the lord Boinitsky: he had lived there for a long time but was not a wealthy man. Nevertheless, his house was full of good things, and he possessed horses and cattle and wheat fields. The girl, herself, was very pretty. However, she did not speak to me for the two days I was there — whether from shyness or because I did not appeal to her or for any other reason, I could not tell. I returned to Kurtovian. I hoped to receive a letter from her so that I might get to know her better, but none came: she was unable to read or write in any language. I could not tolerate the idea of marrying without knowing the woman's mind and heart. The wedding had been arranged for the period between New Year and the Day of Atonement, when my work in Kurtovian would come to an end. If, therefore, I went to my in-laws' home at the end of the summer, it would be too late to cancel the arrangements. I wrote to her father asking if I could visit them for *Shabbat Naḥamu,* in order to make closer acquaintance with the girl. He agreed. I spoke with her but did not succeed in obtaining from her more than a yea or nay. I wanted to hear her speaking with someone else, but there was no one for her to speak with in Vishevian. The hotel and the seven farms around it were classed as a town even though there were only a Jewish tailor and two other people living in it. During the period of Polish hegemony over Zamot, all villages were classed cities, whilst the residences of the noblemen became castles and cities. When the province of Zamot later came into Russian possession, the designations remained unchanged.

My father-in-law rented a mill about a half-mile from Vishevian; it was situated at the foot of a hill, and it was there that his oldest son, Moshe, lived with his wife and daughters. I was unable, therefore, to find anyone who could talk to the girl, so that I might hear her speaking. I stayed another two days, but she said nothing more. Now, my mother-in-law's sister was staying there for a few days on a visit from her city of Rasseyn. I told her I wanted to take my bride for a walk in the fields in order to engage her in conversation, since I was not sure whether she was even able to talk. We went out to the woods, the three of us together. She did the talking, but the girl said nothing. I then took the girl by the arm and drew her aside from her aunt, and took her into a shady part of the wood where the aunt would not see us. It was a warm day, and we sat down on a carpet of leafy grass. I spoke and the girl gave merely brief replies. I asked her to tell me whether she was pleased with me, and she answered: "It is not that." "Then why will you not speak with me?" "What shall I say?" I realised that she was neither stupid nor simple, but neither did she appear wise. I considered further that where love is concerned, there is no reason, for how could I love her when she could not talk, or yet hate her without cause? So the three days passed by, and I returned to Kurtovian feeling dissatisfied.

At that time, the wealthy Madame Goldberg was visited by her brother, a poor man from Neustadt. They had another sister who lived in a hotel near Vilkomir: she managed the hotel and a mill and the posthouse. She had a daughter who was very pretty, intelligent and diligent. Mrs. Goldberg mentioned to her brother about the teacher who tutored their children, and also mentioned that she had heard that I was not too happy concerning the marriage I had recently agreed to. It seemed to her that it would be better if this teacher became the son-in-law of their sister in Vilkomir. She told her brother to ask my opinion, and if I agreed, he would then go and act as the marriage-broker on my behalf. The man put the proposition before me, saying that the father, his brother-in-law, was a wealthy man and would provide his daughter with 500 roubles dowry, and the girl herself was diligent and pretty, and that both he and the whole Goldberg family would urge my suit favourably and I would be accepted as the son-in-law. "Very well," I replied, "but how shall we conduct the arrangements seeing that there is such a great distance between us?'' He said; ''If you will give me four roubles, I shall go on foot to my sister and put the proposition to them. I know she will welcome me as she always does, for she is a good-hearted woman. Afterwards, they will come here on a visit to her sister, and will meet you then.'' I agreed, and gave him the four roubles, and he left. Ten days later, he returned with the answer that the people were willing to make the marital arrangements, but wanted me to go to them and see the girl and her family, and finalise everything there. ''How can I possibly do so?'' I cried. ''I have no money for such a long journey, nor do I have the right kind of clothes. In any case, how can I desert my pupils — especially since I do not know whether the people will even like me?'' The man said: ''You should have realised in advance that it is the groom who must seek the bride, and not *vice versa.*'' ''That is true. But you should have told me in advance that I would have to go to the girl, and then I would not have agreed to this matter.'' The man became angry, and said: ''Why did you put me to all this trouble, making me go there on foot and speaking on your behalf, whilst in fact you had no intention of going through with it?'' He departed. Later, I discovered that it was true that the people were wealthy, and their daughter was pretty and diligent — but she was immodest and wanton. I drove the matter from my mind.

A little while later, I had a visit from my friend Ḥayyim Ḥaikil, who had nothing to do at home at the time but had some business in the neighbourhood. He spent a few days with me. I related to him the whole story of my bride, and the fact that I had nothing against her except her silence. I was merely anxious lest she be a country girl unable to speak properly, and that was the reason for her silence. ''Get me a horse and saddle,'' he said, ''and I shall be on my way. If she is not dumb, and does speak to me, I will return forthwith to explain everything to you.'' I knew I could rely on him, so I hired a horse for him and gave him bread and salt herrings, and he set forth for Vishevian. Four days later my good friend returned, with his bag filled with cheeses and white bread. I realised that everything was all right. He told me that not only did she speak with him for hours on end, but she was a diligent woman too. On one occasion, he hid himself and listened unobserved when a friend of hers came to the hotel and asked about her brother Moshe, and she told him in full detail all that had been happening to Moshe during the past few days. Ḥayyim knew then that she was an intelligent girl who spoke well. He was willing to bet with me that, if she became my wife, we would live together happily for ever. My faith in his knowledge, wisdom and love was so strong, that I believed him implicitly. He had also arranged with her parents that he and I would visit the hotel during *Ellul,* and stay there for the New Year. It had been the custom for many years past for all the Jews who lived in the region to meet during the High Holy Days and hold the services together in the mill. In this instance, Ḥayyim Ḥaikil undertook to perform the duties of Cantor, Torah Reader and *shofar* blower, for which he would be paid a fee. Our wedding would be celebrated between New Year and the Day of Atonement. Since no mention had been made of a dowry,

Ḥayyim had told them that there would be no wedding without a dowry, and they had said that money would be available when it was required.

We left, and in due course arrived there. The New Year passed, and preparations were made for the wedding. My friend reminded them of the dowry. They hastened to Telz, but did not obtain what they wanted. The Day of Atonement came and went. Then they hit upon a solution. In Telz, at that time, lived a very wealthy man named Todros — who was familiarly known throughout the province as Todi. He owned many large houses, and was the official contractor to all government hospitals. He was known far and wide for his wealth and his philanthropy, and also as an eccentric: he was exceptional in everything. Now, my father-in-law had a good friend, Samuel Ḥayyim, who was highly esteemed by the wealthy Todi. If he gave Todi a promissory note for 100 roubles, the wealthy Todi would give me a third note[287] stating that he held 100 roubles as dowry which my wife and I could redeem any time we wished. I agreed to this arrangement. Preparations were made for the wedding to be held on the day before the eve of the feast of Tabernacles. On that day, the musicians and the relatives and guests and acquaintances arrived in a large crowd. Since no further allusion had been made concerning the third note, Ḥayyim Ḥaikil asked about it, and was told that Samuel Ḥayyim would shortly arrive with it. Evening came. Everyone was drinking and eating and making merry. I sat at the head of the table. Samuel Ḥayyim did not arrive until midnight. I read the note he handed me: it said that the husband and wife held a note each, and if these notes were handed to the undersigned, he would be legally obliged to pay 100 roubles. I asked: "Where is the other promissory note?" "I left it at home in my weekday coat, when I changed my clothes. It does not matter. Take this note now, and tomorrow I shall give you the second one." "Do not imagine, my friends, that you can obtain your desires so easily. No, my friends, if you do not give me both the notes, I will call the marriage off." "But the night is already well advanced, and if we send a messenger to Telz for the note, the night will have gone before he returns." "It will not matter if the wedding takes place tomorrow." All the guests left the house, leaving me alone. My friend went out with them, and they all urged him to persuade me to wait till the note arrived next day. I went out and mingled among them. It was not a dark night, nor was the wind cold. The guests were standing in groups of fives and tens all over the place, discussing the groom and his friend. Some complained and condemned whilst others justified; some praised and others vilified. When they realised that I was among them, they took my friend and me back into the room. They sat me down at the table again, leaving some men to guard me. Then they urged my father-in-law to beg me to go on with the wedding on his solemn promise to give me the note the next day. He himself added to this that he felt great pity for his daughter who had not eaten all day, as she was fasting in accordance with the Law.[288] His words cast a deep gloom over my spirit: after all, this man was to be my father-in-law for the rest of my life. I arose, went up to him and embraced him, and said: "It hurts me

deeply, my father, to go against your wishes. This man Samuel Ḥayyim sought
to make a fool of me, for otherwise he would have put the note into his bag and left
it there until such time as I asked for it. The fact that he actually left the note behind
in Telz proves that he has no intention of guaranteeing the money on your behalf.
He was either deceiving you, or he thought me a simple youth who would believe
him and accept only one note. Now therefore, the only thing for him to do is either
to go himself or send a messenger for the note. When I receive it, we shall celebrate
the wedding. As for your daughter, my bride, tell her to eat, for the Law is that one
should fast during the day and not until the wedding itself.[289] Everything will be all
right.'' Shemaiah was a good man. Knowing that I was right, he said no more but
harnessed his horse and went off with the man to Telz. At five o'clock in the
morning, before the dawn had broken, the note was put into my hand. Then did the
Cantor sing and the musicians play, and everyone rejoiced.

On the following morning, I arose early and went to find my mother-in-law
whom I had not seen the previous day. She was in the kitchen. I called out to her:
''*Mazel tov,*[290] mother-in-law!'' She replied: ''May you also have good luck, but
you will not be eating a full barrel of salt in this house!''[291] My father-in-law had
not yet arisen from his bed, but he heard her words, and called out: ''Be assured of
this, that he will eat even three barrels of salt with us.'' In the course of time,
however, she became very fond of me, and loved me more than her own sons. She
was a wise woman, modest, pious and charitable.

We celebrated the festival of Tabernacles, during which Ḥayyim Ḥaikil
preached the sermons. The congregation esteemed him highly, for he was a
descendant of the Gaon's brother, and fulfilled his official duties worthily. He was
paid well for his services. The days of *Ha-Simḥah Bet Ha-Sho'evah*[292] came,
everyone assembled to rejoice on the Rejoicing of the Law.[293] They brought
alcoholic drinks, and drank in their usual way. Even my good friend imbibed more
than he should, and began to discourse foolishly about the righteous and the pious,
until his provincial listeners turned away from him impatiently. As much as I
begged him, he would not listen to me. Finally, I gave him some money, and he
went away.

Now I wanted to rest from all the toil and trouble of the past years. Although my
in-laws were not rich, they had a comfortable income, and loved me very much and
were willing to let me do whatever I wanted during the three years I was to be
maintained by them. I bought ink and paper and began to translate the German
books I had. I copied the ancient book on astronomy, which was bound in
parchment and wooden board covers.[294] In order to fill in my time, I went often to
Telz to buy the mechanisms of watches from which I constructed a seven-day wall
clock with weights. In addition to the usual hour and minute hands, I made a longer
third hand for indicating the whole calendar of the year. It was constructed in this
manner. On to a sieve, of the type used for winnowing wheat, I fixed a round piece
of wood. To this I nailed the mechanisms of the clock movement with all its

wheels, and fitted them together so that they would rotate the third hand for the three hundred and sixty-five days of the year. This hand moved over the face of a dial which I had made from the base of a white, earthenware pot. Around the clock dial, I fixed a broad ring, about two inches wide and made of stiff paper, which I had divided into four circles to show both Hebrew and Christian dates and all the festivals and holidays of the year. The days were cut individually into each ring, and were alternately open and closed. The numbers were written upon strips of paper according to the sequence of the incisions in the dial, and these were then folded between the incisions so that the upper part showed the number and the lower part concealed it. I did the same with all the festivals and holy days in the broad ring, arranging them so that they moved from one division to the next. At the close of the year, a new annual dial could be used by transferring the strips and their ring-frames so that they showed the divisions of the new year. All these I affixed to the round piece of wood with screws and nails. I fixed the iron springs to the wood with liquid adhesive and sealing wax, for I had not yet learned how to solder metals together. Now, I had bought the wheels and movements from broken watches supplied by a craftsman clockmaker in Telz called Joseph Kaplanski. Once he was satisfied that I had no intention of setting up in competition with him, he agreed to show me how to solder metals together with tin and lead. From that time, my work improved considerably and I was able to carry out whatever I desired. I also made a round, glass cover to fit upon the ring, and also a chime to tell the hours from parts of a third mechanism which I had altered for the purpose. All these were activated by small weights suspended from brass chains. I covered the sieve with gold leaf. I fixed the clock to the wall, and found it to my complete satisfaction. It showed the minutes and hours, the days and months, and all the festivals and holy days. Each hour it rang out the time, both day and night. However, my work on it never ended, for though it went all right on one day, thereby allowing me to rest, it would break down the next day and come to a stop, giving me more work to do — and so it went on. Nevertheless, I was content, for I was fulfilling my lifelong ambition. I enjoyed peace and quiet during all that period.

Then came a new storm to vex my life. My mother-in-law's sister, the widow Big Reche, came to live with us. She was quarrelsome and cantankerous. She developed a hostility towards me, being displeased with my way of life and the fact that I was living in her brother-in-law's house in comfort without doing anything for it except to study foreign books. She disapproved of everything. Furthermore, her oldest son, who lived in Loigzoim, was one of those ''dogs of heaven''.[295] She had been acquainted with my former wife and the Vobelitsk family, and spoke slanderously against her to her brother-in-law. When I heard about it, I quarrelled with her over it. She, in the typical manner of witches, became more venomous against me, and constantly inveighed against me and my daily life. Although my in-laws refused to listen to her, nevertheless she was a cause of unceasing distress. My father-in-law's invariable reply to her was: ''My son-in-law is doing no harm by wishing to relax after all his troubles. Let him rest, and when the time comes that he will want to find a livelihood for himself and his family, he will go and find it.''

During *Ḥanukkah*, we had a visit from Abraham the Cantor of Telz: he had lived there for the past thirty years. It was the custom of these clerics to make a circuit every *Ḥanukkah* of the Jewish habitations in the country areas outside the towns, to collect charitable donations of money and food and anything else which the people felt like giving. He lodged with us, and we became acquainted. He was a craftsman watchmaker — in his opinion, the best in the trade. He looked at my clock and annual calendar with astonishment. He asked me about the movement of watches and their internal mechanism, but I could not tell him. He had pity on me, and showed me how the hairspring in the old, small watches operated to keep the correct time. He praised me to my father-in-law, who asked him to stay on at the hotel for another day. He became a good friend to me. He urged me to study the craft of clockmaking. He said: `` Telz is a large city, and there is not one good clockmaker in it or near it. Even Joseph Kaplanski did not really learn the craft properly. He simply watched his father-in-law working, although he was never more than a builder of brick and earthenware stoves who laid down his tongs and hammer to become a clockmaker. A man with your ability could perform outstanding work, so that your fame will spread far and wide.'' I had always loved this kind of work, although I had almost forgotten about it during the time when I had been prevented from engaging in it. Now the Cantor's glittering description of the work I could do in Telz gave me a new life. I wanted to know where I could learn the craft properly, and what my father-in-law would say to his son-in-law becoming a craftsman. The Cantor, however, advised me that I need not go seeking how to learn, but that I should move to Telz, and put a few clocks in my window. Then people would bring me their clocks for repair. He would carry out the different repairs for me every day, at a small charge, seeing that he was free of work during weekdays. In this way he would be able to teach me all the work involved in the craft. Since it seemed to me no great task to learn, in a short time, more than he knew, I kept his suggestion in mind, whilst agreeing that it was necessary to learn the craft proficiently, but not that I should wait like a simpleton until he came to do the repairs for me. Later, I paid frequent visits to his home, and noticed that he did not have even pliers and hammer for the work. I learned that there was another clockmaker in the city, a German by the name of Schaeffer, who owned his own home on the outskirts of the city. It was said of him that he was an excellent craftsman, but that he did not gain his livelihood from this alone as he had other business interests too. I went to see him, and asked whether he would be willing to teach me the craft and what his fee might be. He refused, without proferring any reason. He showed me the tools he used, and the machines for making cogged wheels, and coiled springs which pulled the chains of the old watches, and also many other things which astonished me. I was not to know that they were all worn with age and that he had discarded them. I was able to purchase them, therefore, for the price of the metal alone. I bought a table-vice and a few other small tools, and returned to my work.

At this time, Naḥum Meir, a neighbour of my father-in-law, who was employed by flax merchants in Telz, made me the following proposition: "What are you going to do, seeing that you have no trade, and you will not derive any benefit from simply being able to read and write? Let us set up in business, in flax and seeds, and the Lord will prosper us. You will become a rich man, and I will also prosper through you by assisting you. I am known as a trustworthy person, for I have assisted all the merchants of Telz in their business dealings. I have bought and sold for them, and they have trusted me with their money." "Where will I get the money from? It will require a lot of money, and I have none at all." "Not so, sir. Certainly, some money will be needed, but no more than fifty or a hundred roubles to start with. Within a month or two, the goods will be all sold, and then new goods can be bought, and the profits can be added to the capital. With God's help, you can amass a fortune. If you are willing, and want to go into business, come round the villages with me and you will learn how to assess the value of things and buy shrewdly and knowledgeably. Then you will be able to buy and sell without my help." "But what will my father-in-law say? Will he be willing to give the money?" "If you agree, I will speak with your father-in-law. He will listen to me, for he knows I am to be trusted." "In that case, speak to my father-in-law, and let us hear what he has to say." On the following day, my father-in-law said: "It is true that he is trustworthy and understands business. We will try him. Here are thirty roubles on account of the dowry. Let the man begin his negotiations, and later I shall add more money." I gave the man ten roubles, and he bought flax which he brought to us and stored in my father-in-law's granary. I opened a small account book in which I recorded the expenses and purchases. The man, it seemed to me, stored up a large amount of flax in our granary. I had, by now, invested some seventy roubles in the business. It was time to sell the invested goods and buy new merchandise. Flax, however, cannot be sold in the condition in which it is bought. First, it has to be sorted and graded, and then bound into bundles according to quality. For this, three flax-workers were hired for a period of five days for a wage of five roubles. Then, the flax was in the proper condition to be sold. Alas! The market rate fell, and nobody wanted to buy. We waited a further fortnight, by which time we had no money left to continue in business. My partner came and said that the rate had risen slightly so it would be wise to sell now. The flax was loaded on to carts and sent off to Telz, where it was sold. According to our calculations we had made a total profit of three roubles. We divided the profit between us, so that the man received one and a half roubles for his two months' labour and industry. It was not worth continuing in the business as the price of flax had fallen in the commercial exchanges of Libau and Riga and it was doubtful if it would rise any further that winter. It seemed to me that a business of this nature was not worthwhile, considering how unpredictable it was and the hard work involved and the small profits gained. Instead, my father-in-law set up for me and my wife a small business in the house, selling salt herrings to the customers. This business was not particularly successful, either, for the farmers of the surrounding villages used to attend the market in Telz twice a week, and buy all their requirements there, leaving very little to be bought from my wife.

At that time, the owner of the hotel and mill, in which my father-in-law had lived for many years, was an elderly, wise Polish aristocrat, Boinitsky. He was a kind man and friendly towards the Jews. He heard about me and asked to see me. My father-in-law took me to his house and left me there. The nobleman greeted me warmly. However, I did not speak either Russian or Polish properly, nor did he know German. He began to speak lightly about Jewish customs. "Your leader Moses lived in a hot, eastern country, where he saw that pig's meat was not good for man, and therefore he prohibited it. In our own land, on the other hand, it is not harmful. The Jews are merely being obstinate and foolish in not considering this point." I replied to him in half-Russian and half-Polish: "Would you answer me honestly on a matter of your own faith? If you had the freedom to judge, with your own mind, every commandment of the Lord as spoken by His prophet, whether the reasons for them were for one purpose or another according to the time and place, and you found that one of them was only to suit the particular time, would you refuse to obey it? If you would, then I would be prepared to prove to you that there is no God that rules the world, and you would not be able to disprove my contention. I would prove to you by sheer logic that prophets spoke in the name of a non-existent God only in order to teach their contemporaries the way of goodness and righteousness, and that they frightened the people with gods who ruled the earth but in whom they themselves did not believe. If I were to do this, then it would put all our knowledge and wisdom to nought. Therefore you must admit, if you believe in your God and the prophets who spoke in His name and whose commandments cannot be judged by human intelligence, that we must believe implicitly in the traditions handed down to us by our fathers. This being so, you must also believe in Moses the man of God, who commanded us in God's name not to eat the flesh of the pig, even though he did not tell us the reason for it,[296] or to which country and in which time it applies. How are we to determine, through our own intelligence, that the prohibition applies only to warm countries and certain times?" The nobleman remained silent, and then turned to another topic. He said: "What you have said is true, for even the beasts of the field believe in God and praise and worship Him, although they can neither speak nor think. When I have gone out in the early morning to the fields, when the sun is beginning to shed its rays over the earth and warm the land, I have seen cattle lying on the grass and opening their mouths and yawning. This is their way of blessing and worshipping the Almighty." From that day, the nobleman became my good friend to the end of his life. He extolled me to my father-in-law, saying he had never before met a Jew so understanding and wise, even though handicapped by having to express himself in a foreign tongue.

It was at that time that there came to the hotel a group of students from the Christian theological seminary at Vorne. They ate and drank, and then engaged me in discussion concerning the Christian religion, and why the Jews refused to believe in the wonders and miracles performed by their Messiah in public. I pointed out: "Did not Pinette[296a] also perform many great wonders?" They replied: "Our friend, miracles may be divided into two classes: good ones which confer benefit upon humanity, and bad ones which result only in evil. All the wonders performed by the messengers of God, by Moses and all the prophets who followed him, including our own Lawgiver, were beneficial to people, whereas the wonders performed by Pinette and his like never brought benefit to human kind." I remained silent and had no reply for them. These students were truly well-informed.

The festival of Passover was approaching. On the Sabbath before the festival, at dinner, I was sorely provoked by the shrewish sister of my father-in-law. In my anger, I swore that the two of us would not celebrate the festival together in the same house. After the meal, my wife went out to see her brother at the mill, and I was alone in my room. The rest of the residents and family had retired to sleep: that day was also a Christian festival[297] which was being celebrated in Telz, so there was no one to disturb our sleep. I, however, was pacing backwards and forwards in my room, still feeling upset from the dinnertime provocation, when I heard the sound of hushed voices coming from the tavern. I stopped and listened. The subdued sound continued. I opened my door and saw that the door opposite was open. Suddenly, someone came in from outside, shouting: "The whole roof is on fire!" I ran through the house to the stables and found them also covered in flames. There was no one inside the house: my father-in-law had hastened to drive away the cattle, and then gone for the horses which were too frightened to come out and away from the fire; and my mother-in-law had fled to the basement. There was no one else nearby. I returned to my room to see what I could save, although in my panic I could not decide what to take. I took my 'Turkish drum',[298] that is the clock with the annual dial and the weights and chains, and carried it outside. I forgot my clothes and all the bedclothes and my prayer-shawl and all my other belongings in the room. It so happened that the Clerk of the village, a brave man, was on his way to Telz. When he was about half a mile from the hotel, he turned to look back behind him and saw the roof in flames. He hastened over. He came into my room, smashed all the windows and threw my belongings outside. He then hurried through the house and salvaged whatever he could. He did not know about the barrel of salt fish. There was a sheep-pen outside in which were some fifteen sheep and some calves: no one thought of them, and they were later found burned to death.

I remembered that my wife was pregnant with her first child — our son Simon Aaron — and that she was at the mill, so the news of the fire would not yet have reached them. Worried in case someone might take the news to her and frighten her, I went myself. I found her brother asleep in bed, and his wife and children in the other bed. My wife was lying on another bed. I said to them: ''The Vishevian hotel no longer exists.'' They thought that I meant that someone had come to offer a higher rent to the nobleman who owned the hotel, and that we were to be driven out: this was a common occurrence. They began to enquire what had happened, and I repeated what I had first said, that the hotel no longer existed. My brother-in-law, who understood what I meant, arose and dressed and ran outside, but the women continued to question me. I told them that we had saved almost everything although the building itself was completely destroyed. Later, all our salvaged belongings were brought to the mill, and we crowded in upon each other. The shrewish sister left us and went her way. My father-in-law rented a farmer's cottage from his neighbour, in which he put his drinks and merchandise. We kept the Passover in the mill. The people of the district sympathised with my father-in-law and helped him in every way, even assisting him to build a new house which he could purchase for himself: the ruined hotel had belonged to the Government which had leased it and all the land to the nobleman Boinitsky.

During the following years, my father-in-law prospered and built a large hotel on his grounds, with additional living accommodation for himself and his family, and became a wealthy man — whereas, before the fire, he had been a poor man, constantly harassed by people seeking to offer a higher rent for the hotel. However, at this particular time, after the festival had ended, we sat down to discuss our future plans. There were too many of us to remain in the mill together. My father-in-law was not sure what was going to happen to him, so he could not promise me anything from the dowry. It was decided that I should open a school in Telz — for there was none there at that time[299] — whilst my food and anything else I needed would be brought to me daily. I would be able to save up my wages, little by little. In the course of time, we would see what else could be done. I went to Telz, and rented a room as a schoolroom in the house of Reb Joseph Nehama's. I wrote out notices which I sent to every family with a boy or a girl, inviting anyone who wished to learn to come to me: my fee, sixty kopeks per month. I obtained a long table and a chair. In a few days, boys and girls from all over the town had gathered to my room; I became once again a teacher of Jewish children.

At the end of the first month, when I asked my pupils for my fee, half of them did not pay me. Furthermore, the children, especially the girls, were wild and disobedient and utterly devoid of manners. I began to loathe my means of livelihood. I remembered that, in Shadova I had been the first to teach reading and writing, and had been respected as a teacher by parents and young people alike, and had been feared by my pupils; anyone who did not pay my fees was condemned by the whole town. Here, however, where many teachers had preceded me, the reverse was true. I determined to abandon this despised profession for ever. I would take up a craft of some kind. When I had first opened my school, the fathers had said I was really a craftsman clockmaker; when, later, I became a craftsman clockmaker, they declared unanimously that I was the best teacher who had ever taught Jewish children. They were contrary people, indeed!

I stayed on another month in order to collect the fees due to me for the first month. There was one girl among my pupils whom I had occasion to rebuke; she thereupon arose and left, and never returned. I waited until the end of the second month, and then went to ask her father for my fee. During our discussion about her, he said that I had refused to teach the subjects which my pupils had requested and that I also refused his daughter's request. I spoke up at that, having no fear of anyone since I had already decided to cast off their burden for ever: ''You should be ashamed to say such things! Do you not know that these maturing girls are all wayward, to lesser or greater extent? I, however, am a man and not a boy. Why has it never entered your mind that perhaps she is not telling the truth. You should have told her: 'Daughter, continue to attend the school', and then consulted me on the matter. You would then have found who was in the right. The other girls would also have told you the whole truth of the matter. You have not behaved properly with me, you Jewish people. You despise and belittle your children's teacher and are unwilling to bestir yourselves even to speak with him. Far better that I become a cobbler than a teacher to Jewish children!'' I picked up my fee and left.

At that time, Shemaiah Perl, the son of my father-in-law's second sister, came to visit us. He saw my annual-calendar clock, and I told him of my desire to learn the craft properly. He advised me to go to the city of Mitau where lived his relative, a well-known clockmaker called Zimson, with his brother: they both carried on a flourishing business making expensive wall and table clocks. He would ask them to accept me as an apprentice. The old longing to learn the craft came strongly over me once more. However, I had no expectation of earning my living from it, but wanted to learn it for its own sake, so that I would be able to design new and different types of mechanisms. First, I needed a travel permit. Courland, where Mitau was situated, strictly forbade any Jew from staying in its borders for even one night unless he had a permit and paid fifteen kopeks daily up to a maximum of three days. Police were constantly conducting searches in the city, both day and night, entering hotels and other places in search of Jews whom they despatched in chains to the frontier. These police were known as the kidnappers of the Jews [*Judenhäscher*]. However, it is always the case with all unjust laws that the police will find a way of bypassing them by means of bribery and ransom. It was so in that city, too. The Jew who slipped two or three roubles into the hand of a policeman could live there unmolested for a month or more, so long as he had a permit and declared that he had arrived only the day before. I, therefore, wrote to the town of Loigzoim to send me a permit for one year. I received no reply. I wrote again, and then sent a third request with a messenger who was to speak on my behalf before the community's leaders. He brought me the reply that the head of the community would be coming to Telz in the near future and would give me the permit personally. I waited another month, and received no word. I then journeyed to Shavel to find him. He was not there. I was told that I would not find him at his home in Loigzoim, either. I returned home, cursing my fate and him. At the time I did not know that my father-in-law's shrewish sister had warned him that I wanted a permit in order to desert my wife: she had come to visit us during the feast of Pentecost, and had learned of my desire to go to Mitau. When my in-laws refused to take any notice of her, she secretly wrote to her son, that dog of heaven,[300] who lived in Loigzoim, telling him to prevent the communal head from granting me a permit. I decided that, come what may, I would go to Mitau by way of Shavel and Loigzoim and obtain my permit from the man.

My wife was near to giving birth to our first born, Simon Aaron, so I stayed on longer. I then set about cutting teeth for the wheels of wall-clocks, ten at a time, in the belief that the basic movement of a clock derives from its cogged wheels and pinions. I roped one end of a saw to a wooden beam in the ceiling, and the other end to a wooden plank above my feet. I fixed the ten wheels to the table, and beneath them another toothed wheel containing the number of teeth I wished to cut, on the end of an iron tube running through the centres of all the wheels. In this manner I spent my hours in the mill until my wife bore our son. By the month of *Ellul*, I had saved about twenty-five roubles. I obtained a letter of recommendation from Shemaiah Perl to Zimson in Mitau. I left to get my travel permit and finally arrived in Mitau.

I lodged in the Jewish Guest House. I bought some salt herring and dry bread, because I could not afford the meals at the Guest House. I booked a bed with a mattress for the night, for otherwise the proprietor would not have permitted me to stay there: I paid fifteen kopeks per night. Next day, I went through the city until I came to Zimson's house. I showed him Perl's letter and told him what I wanted. He said: "I hardly know this man Perl at all. As for your desire to learn the trade, I am willing to teach you, providing you pay me 100 roubles in advance." I told him I would give him 25 roubles down, and my father-in-law would send me 25 roubles on account of the dowry next month, and so on each month. The man refused, saying: "I know you Poles. You work for two or three days, learn a little of the craft, and then run off and set up in business on your own!"

I called upon the man during the following three days, but he would not change his mind. I then asked his brother, who also was a craftsman clockmaker, but he too refused to teach me. On the fourth day, towards evening, I was sitting despondent and hopeless in the hotel, when the proprietor called me over and asked me about myself, saying that for three days he had seen me coming and going, without eating or drinking, and apparently without doing anything. I told him the whole story: that I had been hitherto a teacher of Jewish children but had always wanted to learn a craft, although circumstances had never favoured my desire; that I had now left my wife in the care of her father and brought a little of my dowry money here with a letter of introduction to the clockmaker Zimson, who, however, would only help me if I paid him 100 roubles in advance, or at least 75; that I did not have this amount of money because my father-in-law's hotel had been destroyed by fire and he was now in the process of building another house and could only let me have monthly payments in small amounts. So now I was at a loss what to do. "Have you not tried asking other craftsmen, for there are many Jewish clockmakers here?" I told him I had also asked Zimson's brother, and he had refused. These people knew me because I had a letter of introduction, so why should others, who did not know me, grant my desire? Now, this hotel proprietor was a God-fearing and learned man, who had formerly served the community for many years as the ritual slaughterer. He had forsaken the slaughtering trade two years ago, and bought the guest house, where he lived with his wife: his sons were Germans,³⁰¹ who lived in the modern fashion of the time. He then began to discourse on the Torah and Prophets and Mishna with me, and after hearing my replies to his questions, he said: "I feel a great compassion for you, for I have always esteemed people who want to learn a craft or trade, and not spend their life in useless frivolities. You now wish to abandon all your knowledge in order to learn a craft. I consider you a very worthy person. Wait until tomorrow evening, when I hope to have found something for you." Next day, he told me: "I have spoken about you to another ritual slaughterer, my friend Israel. He has a son, Sholem Vildoyer, who is also a clockmaker. We shall have an answer from him by tomorrow." The next day I went with the proprietor to meet his friend Israel, who also examined me on my knowledge of Torah and Gemara, and asked me about the fee I could pay in advance and the amount I could pay later. Then we returned to the Guest House. The proprietor explained what this was all about. "This ritual slaughterer is an honest, simple and God-fearing man, of whom there are too few in our Courland cities. His son, Sholem the clockmaker, is also God-fearing but not the same as his father, for his home is half-Jewish and half-German. Now, I presented you to him as a learned scholar and observant Jew, even though you are familiar with the German language and modern customs. I aroused his desire to take you into his son's home and show him and his family the true way of life and the customs of the Polish Jews. At his request, his son will take you in and teach you the craft, and not for a high fee. Go to the son tomorrow, and you will find everything ready for you." I went to see him, and he asked for twenty-five roubles in advance, to be followed by a further payment of twenty-five roubles in three months' time. He would provide all my meals, and would teach me everything I wished to know, and without treating me as an employee. Thus, if he should begin to show me how to do a certain thing, and I told him that I already knew how to do it, he would not require me to do it once again but would teach me a different task. Once I was satisfied that I had learned all that I needed to know, I could leave whenever I pleased, providing I had paid him everything I owed him. I was, however, doubtful whether I would be able to pay him the second sum of twenty-five roubles, seeing that my father-in-law was so occupied with building his new house and had no capital to spare. Reluctantly, therefore, I had to resort to deceit. I mentioned the possibility of my being detained by the Jew-catchers who might not permit me to remain in the city, and then what would become of our agreement? He replied: "It is well-known that any Jew who pays the policeman sixty kopeks per month will not be searched for or detained." "That is true. But supposing the catcher becomes angry with either you or me, and does expel me? We ought to consider this and reckon how your fees may be paid." He answered: "If you are expelled, then you will pay me one rouble for every week's board at my table, plus a further thirty kopeks for the training you receive." I agreed, thinking that if, at the end of the three months, my father-in-law could not send me the money, then I would bribe the catcher to expel me from the city. As for my training, I would by then have acquired sufficient knowledge of how to use the various tools and how to file metals, and so on, so that I would be able, through my own ability, to pick up whatever else I needed, and become even better than my teacher who had no special talent for the craft but had seven years' practical experience. We agreed on the terms, and went to the city's Rabbi, who was also the Government Rabbi[302] and had the authority to register all agreements made by Jews and stamp them with his seal so that they were as valid as though done by any Notary or Court of Law, except that they were written in German. We paid him his fee of two roubles, and he entered all the terms of the agreement in a book.

I had now achieved my heart's desire. I sat at the work-bench whilst the craftsman taught me. I began to construct a new table-clock. There was a youth of seventeen there, who had been apprenticed there for the past two years. His name was David, and he was the son of the Beadle of Boisk, in Courland. We became firm friends, and he also helped me with my training. By the third day, a Sabbath, it became evident to me that the family was not as wealthy as it appeared to be, and David confirmed this. A woman came to the house daily to teach the eldest daughter to play the piano: the daughter also attended the local school every day to learn language and literature. The house was kept tidy and clean, in the usual German manner. Sholem, however, was poor and his income small, so that at times there was no food in the house, not even dry bread. His sons were devoid of manners, far worse than even the poorest and most ignorant of Polish Jews. These things could only be seen from inside, for externally all seemed well, at it does in every well-to-do German home. The High Holy Days were approaching, and the period of the penitential prayers. The man was God-fearing and observant of every Jewish custom, although this was also no more than superficial and to satisfy appearances. At the end of the first week, I still had some money left which I had been keeping for additional expenses. The man asked me to lend him some money right away, and promised to repay it. When I finally spent all I had, and was left without a penny in my pocket, I asked him for the money, but he made no reply.

During the second week, my meals were inadequate, although my daily work had increased my appetite. My friend had to buy bread each day to overcome his hunger: he understood the situation, and was careful not to let the others know that his father sent him money from time to time. I, however, had not a penny to buy even bread, so I starved all day. Now, in my bag I kept a small music box. A man came by wanting to buy musical instruments for his children. Sholem had none, so I asked him if he would permit me to sell the man my instrument. He agreed. I sold it for two roubles. The following day, Sholem demanded the money from me, saying that he had permitted me to sell in his house on condition that he received half the proceeds. I answered him: "You have already borrowed three roubles from me, which I let you have out of kindness. You have not repaid me, nor will I ask you again to repay me the loan. I have no more money to lend out of kindness, nor will I be able to give you anything until the time for the next payment of your fee, seeing that I have to starve every day." He made no reply.

During the period of the penitential prayers, he asked me to teach him a portion of Mishna in the evenings. It became intolerable to me, for he was an untutored person who had never learnt to read Mishna. After the festival of Tabernacles, he asked me to write a letter for him in German to his brother-in-law who lived in Prussia, requesting a small loan. That particular person had converted to Christianity some time ago. I wrote the letter, and they were pleased with it. These people knew that I was superior to them in all ways, and treated me with respect. Nevertheless, their hatred of their fellow-Jews of Poland exceeded the hatred of Christians, so that they despised Polish and Lithuanian Jews and considered them contemptible even though those Jews might tower like giants over them. They treated me in the same manner. By the end of the first month, I had come to realise how they felt about me. My last pennies were spent and I began to suffer the pangs of starvation once more. Because of their contempt, they slept in the second room, where they kept the wash-bowl and water-bucket and drinking vessels. I and the other apprentice slept in the first room. It was the man's custom, when he arose every morning before daybreak, to arouse me by pulling the plank out from under me so that I fell on the floor. This infuriated me, but I never said a word, knowing that this was his normal way of awakening people. After arising, I asked for water to wash my hands, and he showed me a hand-pump outside in the yard. By pulling the handle five times or so, I could draw a flow of water for washing my hands. With further pulling, I could draw more water to wash my face. However, in the cold autumn, when my flesh prickled with cold and frost covered my hair, no water came from the pump.

During all that period, I was like a man bereft of his senses, but my ambition to learn the craft did not permit me to run away. I became desperate. My young companion in distress was too frightened to say a word against his master. The reason for his fear lay in the fact that he wet his bed every night, and he thought I did not know about it and was afraid lest I be told, to his utter shame. I learned this secret of his on the second day I was there, for they told me of it. Now, however, I wanted everything to be open between us, with no secret thoughts, and I wanted him to help me with my training and show me how to use all the many, various tools. I had realised by now that the man was not going to teach me as we had agreed. When, for example, an instrument for letting blood was handed in to him for repair, he gave it to me saying that I ought to know about this, too. The instrument contained four toothed bars and about twenty small knives which turned and cut into skin and flesh to draw blood.[303] I worked on it for eight days. Yet, when a clock was handed in for repair, he would not let me watch him working, but turned away from me and held his hands over his work to cover it. I protested that this was contrary to our agreement, but he paid no attention to me. When I brought my complaint to the Rabbi who had registered our agreement, he said to me: ''If you had come to me before concluding your deal with him, I would have advised you to keep away from him. He is well-known to me as a scoundrel and swindler. There is no other recourse for you but to avoid any dispute with him, and to leave his house without exchanging a word with him, either good or bad. He is capable of any robbery, murder and falsehood.'' Since the people of the city honoured their Rabbi and spoke well of him, I was astonished at his words. Later, I took the young man, David, aside and said: ''Do not imagine that I am not aware of your weakness, that you wet the bed. I was told about it on my second day here. What of it? The pillow and quilt belong to you, and you yourself hang them up to dry — so what harm is there in it to them? Why, then, are you so frightened of them? If you leave him and go to another craftsman, you will certainly learn a lot more, without having to go hungry, and you will be treated as a man and paid a wage. Because you are so timid and humble, these wicked people are able to torture and starve you.'' This encouraged him and raised his spirits, and he began to think of himself as a man. He realized how the people despised him. Some days later, he asked me what we should do to the man for starving us. I told him that, on the morrow, after we had been served with bread, the size of two olives,[304] and a small piece of radish with salt, we should eat it and then send their youngest son to the other room where they were all dining to announce: ''The man Ḥayyim asks for a little more bread.'' If we were given it, we should eat it — and then do the same on the following day. If, however, the man refused to give us more, then ''you must go and buy a whole loaf of bread and some butter, and we will give them to the little boy to hand to his parents, and to say: 'The man Ḥayyim has seen that you have no food of your own, and therefore sends you this bread and butter that you may eat and be satisfied.'''

On the first day we sent the boy with our request, he brought a morsel of bread for me alone. I sent him again on the next day, but he did not come back. On the third day, the young man went out and bought a small loaf and some butter. We gave them to the boy to hand to his parents. Now, they had spent the whole day together, as though they were afraid to come out and confront me. After this, however, they came out and sat at the work-bench, their faces fuming. The wife was a very wicked woman, and she began to curse me. I said to them: ''If I had asked you for the finest dishes, you would have been right to refuse. But we have asked you only for dry bread to stave off our hunger. Are you not ashamed? I would give bread even to a starving dog. And I do pay you for my food.'' Nevertheless, she continued to argue with me, shouting and giving me no peace. She became so overwrought that she shouted: ''You even attempted to force me when I lay in bed!'' I was so amazed that I laughed. In truth, she was an old woman past her prime, and quite ugly. Yet she spoke in this manner in the presence of her husband. I thought she had gone out of her mind, but she repeated it and added that, not long ago, her husband had arisen early as normal, and left the room. The window was shut, so the room was in complete darkness. She was still lying in the bed when I opened the door quietly and entered the room and felt with my hands over the wall and her bed, and then went out. I remembered the incident. It had happened one cold and icy morning. I had got up out of bed, and was reluctant to go outside to the pump because of the extreme cold. David had once shown me how to enter their bedroom in order to get the bucket of water and the wash-basin which were kept behind the door. I decided to wash myself in the corridor. I had not known that the window was closed, and the room was in deep darkness. I opened the door and felt behind it along the wall, without finding anything. I then went out. It was possible that her bed was there, and that fornication-faded hag had thought I was a procurer of harlots, for what other reason could I have for being there? I decided to remain until the three months were over, and then return home. I stayed on, filled with anger. The members of the family continued to hate me.

One evening, when we were sitting idle, having nothing to do, I took a German book and sat in a corner of the room and began to read it. It so happened that in the other half of the house lived a Germanised Jew, a cap-maker; he had a brother, an old man, who considered himself completely German and who assisted him in the work. Sometimes, when he was free, he would visit this craftsman and his family. On this particular evening when I was sitting reading in the corner, the old man was talking and playing with the daughters and the wife of the craftsman, in their usual hilarious manner. He looked over at me and made a jeering remark, but I gave no reply, for I thought that the woman had encouraged him to do this. When, however, he approached me and mockingly asked me to explain the foolish beliefs of Ḥasidism which the Polish Jews had accepted, I said: ''Tell me, Sir what is this *Disput* in which you wish to engage me?'' He laughed and said: ''What word is that — *Disput?*'' I said: ''It is a verbal disputation, and you are trying to engage me in one.'' He said: ''Indeed? What language is it — Turkish or Chinese?'' I then realised that he was an ignorant person, who had become Germanised but did not know the language. I arose and took my Weber's Dictionary, opened it to the word and showed it to him: ''This is the word. It is neither Turkish nor Chinese, but German, and used even by peasants.'' He became highly embarrassed and said: ''This is the second time, to my great shame, that I have tried to make fun of a Polish Jew, and the tables have been turned on me. Some years ago, I met a Jew who appeared by his dress and all his ways to be a contemptible Polish Jew. When I began to ridicule him, the man replied to me in perfect German and French, and talked about all the latest advances in science and knowledge. I was completely overcome, and begged him to forgive me my sins. We became firm friends after that, and still are to this day. Now today, too, I forgot myself again. But this will be the last time, for I will never again belittle any Polish Jew, no matter what.'' We became good friends until the day I left them. In fact, he helped me when I left, for I had no money, and he bought from me a few German books and some articles which were of no value to me.

The three months of toil came to an end. I prepared myself for my journey home. The craftsman did not oppose my departure, knowing full well that, if we went to trial before the Rabbi, he would be found guilty. I bought some burnished brass plates for making wall-clocks, as I had learned to do, and a few tools as well as a toothed axle for the pinions: these were unobtainable in Telz. The toothed axle used in Mitau for wall-clocks had only eight teeth.[305] When I went in search of an axle, I was unable to find one at all, because a certain clockmaker in that city had bought up all the eight-leaved axles in the shops to prevent the other craftsmen from buying them, for there were many clockmakers there. I therefore bought axles with ten teeth, from which I made wheels with the amount of teeth I wanted. I left, and went on to Vishevian to my wife and son. I found that my father-in-law had built a new house on his own land. Although it was only half-completed, they were able to live in the part set aside as the tavern for guests. A small room with a table and chair was prepared for me, and there I set to work on a new clock. I worked day and night.

During the festival of *Purim,* Shemaiah Perl, my father-in-law's nephew, came to stay with us for a few days. He saw my work and said to my father-in-law: ''You know that I conduct my business in the city of Shvekshne, on the Prussian frontier. Once, I was doing business with a wealthy man, Raphael Manushevitz, who had three sons attending the local *ḥeder.* He complained: 'My boys are growing up without knowing anything about modern studies, for there is no teacher in this small town other than an ignorant *melammed.* I had thought of sending them to one of the big cities, either in Prussia or in this country, but they are too far away. In any case, their mother protested that no one will bother to look after them in a strange home. If I could find an enlightened teacher who is learned also in Torah, I would take him into my home and look after all his needs, and pay him ninety roubles per half-year to teach my sons Torah and modern studies.' '' Perl had then told him that his uncle's son-in-law in Vishevian was just the teacher he was looking for. The rich man thanked him profusely, and made him promise to go to Vishevian to ask my father-in-law to release me. Now he had come with this proposal — and I had hardly had time to set up in my craft; in any case, I did not have the necessary tools, nor could my father-in-law afford to pay for my journey to Memel, in Prussia, where these could be bought. I was really idling my time away here. Far better that I teach in Shvekshne and live comfortably in the rich man's house. They would certainly treat me with respect, and my salary for the year would be almost two hundred roubles. With that, I could set my trade on a proper footing. My father-in-law asked me, and I agreed. So he harnessed his horse, and sent his servant who was in charge of the horses with me: at that time my father-in-law held the contract for delivering the post to the district's villages. We seated ourselves in the cart, and left. I arrived at the rich man's house, examined the boys, and agreed on terms with their father for my board and all my needs at their expense plus a salary of ninety roubles. We shook hands in agreement, and I promised to start after Passover, on the new moon of *Iyyar*. [306] I returned home to celebrate the festival.

My father-in-law ordered a new coat for me to wear at the Manushevitz house, but the tailor was a day or two late so I was not able to leave until the eve of the New Moon. The horse was harnessed to the cart, and the servant took the place of the driver: he would take me to Shvekshne and then return. During the past few days, the snow had melted, and rain had begun to fall. The road was in very poor condition and in places it was impassable for either sleighs or wheeled carts. Sometimes we sank into mud and sludge, and it was difficult for the horse to drag us out, whilst in other places the winter's snow still lay upon the ground. We spent the New Moon on this awful road. We were not far from the city of Ritave, [307] when evening came on. The town seemed to lie directly ahead of us, judging by the many lights in the windows. Furthermore, by the tracks in the mud and slush, it seemed that we were on a main road leading to the city. To our left we saw another path with the tracks of many travellers in it, but it led away from the city. We stayed on our own road until we came to the foothills descending down to the valley. I heard the sound of water falling, like a river in torrent. The ice cracked under the horse's hoofs. I called out quickly to the driver, and he stopped the horse. I jumped down and stood beside the cart, and told him to do the same. He walked a little ahead of us, testing the ground, for a deep river was flowing there, half covered in thin ice and snow. If it cracked under the cart, we should all sink into the depths. In those places where the ice was swept along by the swift current of the river, the waters could be plainly seen. At the sides, the banks were hidden under snow and ice. We were travelling on the winter road which led over thick ice directly towards the city. The other road, which we had seen, led away from the city: it was the summer road and had only become passable during the past few days. Thanking God for saving us, we carefully pulled the cart backwards until we were standing once more on firm ground. We turned in to the side road, without knowing where it led, although it seemed to be going farther away from the city.

Darkness came on, and we were lost. We came to a village. The people were preparing for bed, and there was no one about. The village belonged to the lord of Ritave, the Graf Oginsky. He had issued a command to all the people in all his villages forbidding them to take any Jew into their homes; both the villager and the Jew who disobeyed the command would be flogged together. His reason was that the Jews who travelled the villages brought whisky and other evil things to these villagers, who were his bondsmen in perpetuity. We were afraid to approach the first house but, having no alternative, the driver knocked upon the door. The peasant came out, cursing "Why do you disturb my sleep? Do you not know my lord's decree?" The driver told him we had lost our way, and almost drowned in the river. He said: "Many people lose their way when they come here, because that road is the winter road that leads directly to the city, whereas the summer road makes a detour. Take this road here through the village. You will have to cross over a bridge before you enter the city." We left next morning, and went on our way to Shvekshne.

When the rich man saw us, his face fell. He said angrily: "I cannot accept you now. You are two days late. I thought you would not come at all, so I sent the boys back to their previous *melammed*". I told him that the roads were so bad at this season that he should have realised that I might be late in arriving, so why had he been in such a haste to send the boys back to their *melammed?* He replied: "Circumstances have changed a great deal since we met, in both my personal and my business affairs. I am sorry we made an arrangement for you to stay in my house. It cannot be helped now. I will pay your expenses for the journey." I accepted. He gave me five roubles, and I departed. I went to the inn where the cartier and some old friends of my father-in-law were staying. They told me the reason for the rich man's change of mind. As soon as the word had spread in the city that the wealthy Raphael was bringing a new teacher into his house, the people led by the *melammedim* and the Rabbi had united against him, saying: "Our city has been a *kosher* city from time immemorial. Our children are God-fearing and have never been tainted by the accursed *Haskalah*. Now you, of your own accord, seek to transgress, and to open our gates to defilement with all manner of heresy." There were even witnesses who testified before the Rabbi that the son-in-law of Shemaiah ate forbidden food and did not put on phlylacteries, etc. They told the rich man that he was standing alone in opposition to the whole city and was endangering his own life. In addition to all this, his business suffered a recession at that time, for a great deal of illegal merchandise had been confiscated on the frontier, causing him extensive loss. When, therefore, I had been delayed, he had done what he had to do. So I returned home, with the clock I had made and which I had packed in my bag along with my books. I was not upset by what had happened, for I was assured of my regular meals and had a comfortable income at my father-in-law's. I settled down to finishing my clock which I had begun to remake. It was springtime. The weather was delightful, and the countryside enjoyed peace and quiet all that summer.

My fame spread throughout the entire district of Telz. People said that there was a craftsman clockmaker living in the Vishevian hotel who was without peer, since there was no other artisan in all Lithuania and Zamot able to produce innovations in the craft of clockmaking. One market day in Vishevian, when the city and the hotel were crowded with people, the District Governor, who resided in Vorne, came and enquired for the famous clockmaker who made new clocks. He had a pocket watch whose cylinder had broken: no one in the whole district had been able to mend it, for all the craftsmen had declared that this kind of repair could only be carried out abroad, in Prussia. He came up to me and said: ''Are you the famous craftsman who can mend this for me?'' ''Yes. I shall get it to go again so that it keeps the time as accurately as it did before.'' He said: ''If you do so, I will pay you five roubles. I want you to bring it to me at my house in Vorne.'' In actual fact I knew nothing at all about this cylinder: my teacher, Vildoyer, had concealed its operation from me, nor had I known enough at the time to ask the young man from Boisk about it. Now that I had been given one to repair, and had plenty of time in which to do it, I tried different methods of repairing it until finally I suceeded. The watch came to life and kept correct time, to my unbounded joy and the astonishment of all who saw it. I travelled to Vorne to return the watch to the Governor. Before calling upon him, I went to see the clockmaker who had been in business in Vorne for many years; his father, who was eighty years old, had also lived there but had since moved to Plungian. He had heard about me, and also knew about the watch as the Governor had offered it to him but he had refused it. Now he was amazed to see that it was going perfectly. He said: ''My old father always said that the cylinder cannot be made by human hands. [308] How foolishly he erred!'' He begged me to explain how the shaft operated and moved together with its wheel. I took some paper, and cut out the shape of the teeth of the wheel, and made a paper cylinder. I showed him how they moved the balance backwards and forwards. He understood and cried: ''This is utterly amazing!'' Some time after this, the lord who owned the village land neighbouring ours sent for me. His wife possessed a lady's watch which she kept in her bag. The tiny wheel which regulated the minute hand had been lost. She had also sought someone to repair it, but no one in the district had been willing to undertake it. I accepted it and did it. However, it was not easy to make this tiny wheel which had a toothed axle with a hollow centre running lengthwise through it. Nor did I have a machine for making cogs. I therefore constructed a machine for cutting teeth out of wood and sheets of polished brass, and transferred to it the thirty teeth required from an old wheel of a wall-clock which had sixty teeth. It was with great toil and labour that I finally made this small wheel. I earned my fee of three roubles. My fame spread throughout the province, and I was highly esteemed.

That year, the Lord blessed my father-in-law's house. The mill produced profits seven-fold more than all previous years, and the cornfields raised corn and wheat in abundance. He became a wealthy man, whereas hitherto he had been always on the verge of poverty. At the end of that summer, he gave me 100 roubles, so I travelled to Memel, in Prussia, to buy tools similar to those I had seen in Mitau.

One day, I was out taking a walk through the field with my friend, who lived near the hotel of Gorgzdine near Vishevian. He told me that he had seen in his own home-town of Luknik a maiden, daughter of a wealthy man there, who had been ill for many years with epilepsy. Many distinguished physicians had attempted to cure her, but had failed. Her father took her to all the large hospitals in every large city, but she finally returned home without showing any improvement. People wearied of seeking a cure for her. Finally, her hands and feet contracted and she lay as still as a stone. Then people came and spoke about a Turk[309] who lived in a village near Vilna, and who could heal all illnesses and drive out demons and spirits, and even restore a person to life. The people, who felt very sorry for the girl, urged her parents to seek out this Turk and try one final cure. The girl's mother took her daughter to the Turk's house, where they stayed three days, and then returned home. The girl began to get up; her condition improved so that, to this day, she is still well and healthy. She walks, and is capable of doing all kinds of work with her hands. She lives a full life. My friend had heard the mother relating how the Turk had healed her daughter. He had repeated the same procedure two or three times. He had put wood into his stove and lit it. He then told the mother to stand in a corner of the room, and not to move. He picked the girl up on his shoulders and carried her all around the room, walking from wall to wall. He had then gone over to the stove, and sprinkled salt and dried herbs upon the fire. He placed the girl upon the bed, and began to move her limbs with his hands. Each time he carried her around the room on his shoulders, he muttered to himself, although not a word could be heard clearly. Afterwards, he gave her a bottle of herbal mixture to take regularly at home, and also gave her a draught of the mixture to drink. When the period of the treatment had ended, he sent them home telling them that she would assuredly be healed and be well again. So it turned out.

My friend was watching me to observe my reaction, knowing that I did not believe in magic spells and supernatural effects. I said to him: "I shall tell you a fundamental principle which you must always bear in mind when you hear tales of wonders performed by people such as these Turks and miracle-workers and magicians. Whenever you hear of any wonderful and apparently unnatural event, separate it into three parts. The first part you must consider as coming from the eye to the mouth: every man embellishes everything he sees in order to make it seem wonderful to his listener, so that he will imagine its every detail in the hues he portrays; in this way, the listener hears a report that is above the truth. This is the third part that is added on to the actual incident, although it does not detract from it in the least, since it is neither truth nor falsehood — and you can find an example of this if you watch a man looking at himself in a glass mirror: observe his reflection in the mirror, and you will notice that the mirror alters his appearance by almost a third. Then consider the other two thirds of the report, and divide them into two parts, one half the truth, and the other false. You will then have the solution to all phenomena. Let us take the miracle you have just related to me. I hope you will not be angry with me if I suggest that the girl's illness was not by any means as severe as you described: you did not observe her all day long, nor are you a physician able to determine the severity of an illness. You may also have over-rated the extent of her cure after she had returned home. This is the third part of the wonder, the part that is neither truth nor falsehood. You must also take into consideration the story told by the girl's mother, and of the way she transferred her eye-witness account into your ears. Even though she may not be familiar with the art of rhetoric and persuasive speech, nevertheless it is natural for any teller of a tale to embellish his story for his listeners. So it is in the case of the Turk who seems to his followers to be so completely wonderful and supernatural that they have the utmost faith in him. We could take this third part and analyse it in detail and find it to be neither true nor false. In the remaining two parts, we find half is true and half is false, with the truth serving merely to embellish the false. We now come to the final part, the one-third that is true. The truth is that the Turk was familiar with the properties of roots and flowers and herbs whose healing qualities have been overlooked by the physicians. Not every patient can be cured by him, nor can he heal many sick patients every day. Should any one of his patients die, no one will mention it or speak of it, since even the most reputed physicians also lose some of their patients. Furthermore, physicians kill more people with drugs than does the Turk with his roots and leaves. Therefore, you will never hear that a particular patient did not recover after being treated by a Turk. It is nothing unusual, and need not be mentioned. On the other hand, when a patient is given new life by virtue of the treatment, then that is a wonder which can be related from one generation to another, and everyone will believe it.''

At that time, Hypnosis, the domination of one spirit over another or one soul over another, was still unknown, for it has only recently achieved popularity and come into practice.[310] Rambam — that is, Maimonides who spoke wisely and truly, like a prophet of God — declared that all the deeds of miracle-workers and sorcerers who make use of demons and spirits can serve to help those who believe in them. He said this also about amulets. It appears from this that he, in his generation, knew of the domination of one soul over another, and how the spirit of the giver of the amulet can influence the recipient who wears it. Who, however, took notice of him? The orthodox and Hasidim were afraid to refer to him, much less to accept his opinion. The *maskilim* refused to accept his statements regarding the influence of one soul over another soul — for no matter how deeply a sick person may believe in an amulet, it will not cure his illness. I, on my part, have not been able, in my poor command of words, to put forward one small amount of the true third part I have described — the operation of Hypnosis, of one soul over another, although I believe Maimonides to be right. I have already related above about the woman whose children had died, and whom I had advised to recite with the utmost belief: ''I do not want the Germans to come to me,''[311] and she had been healed and her children lived. In truth, during the past few years, from the year 1780 to 1785[312] in which we live, new wonders are being daily revealed concerning the action of one soul over another, and even upon one's own soul — as happened in the case of the man bitten by a mad dog: he had never believed in the existence of this sickness, but when it began to take a hold upon him, he gathered all his strength and power of mind and spirit so that he was able to overcome it and was healed. A hypnotist also can save a man by strengthening his mind and soul so that he will be able to conquer the weakness of his body and be made well again. The subject is still new and has only recently come to the fore. We do not yet know how Hypnosis works — but Time will provide the knowledge.

The first part of the history of my life is hereby completed.

The Second Part of the History of My Life
The Period of the Craftsman-Technologist.

◇◇◇◇◇

I NOW STOOD on the line bordering the periods of my life. Hitherto, I had been bonded like a slave to teaching — a teacher of Jewish children and a servant of boors whom I feared because they had the power to cut off my staff of life. I was not trained in a manual trade which would enable me to stand free and firm. Thus, from the time that I was competent enough to earn a living from my craft, I entertained the hope that I might be liberated from the bondage I endured during the first part of my life, so that I could walk firmly and freely into the second part, and earn my living by the labour of my own hands wherever I wished, be it in city or village or any human habitation. Deciding to work wholly in my craft, I turned to the nearest city, Telz, where it was possible I might settle and work. I asked my father-in-law for a further hundred roubles to buy tools, and he gave me the money.

I travelled to Memel, in Prussia. I had never before been to large cities, except for Vilna. Therefore, the journey over the frontier from Russia to Prussia seemed as far as from east to west. When I arrived at the customs post on the frontier, I looked at the policeman and the guards, and listened to the harsh words they directed against every traveller, especially the Jews, and it seemed to me that I saw fear and panic on every face. Suddenly, we were over the frontier, and at the Prussian customs post on the opposite side. It was a small house, like a lodge in a vegetable garden,[313] with flowers and roses growing around three sides of it. We entered the house. In the hallway stood a customs officer holding an iron staff which he poked into the carts several times. Then, the cartier was asked, respectfully, if he had anything to declare. The officer neither raised his voice nor showed anger even when he found something that was dutiable although the owner had stated that he had nothing to declare: the officer simply carried it to the scales in the hallway and estimated the duty to be paid according to the weight, whilst muttering under his breath about people who tried to lie to him. Inside the house was a small room furnished with only a table in one corner, at which sat the

175

Inspector in charge of the customs post. There were about twenty men milling around him, all speaking at the same time, and all of them were Jews. The officer calmly silenced them. He then began to question each one in turn, in the order they had entered the room. ''What is your name, sir?'' ''Shemaiahu.'' ''Your father's name?'' ''Potiphar.'' He wrote these down on a sheet of paper: Shemai Potifar[314] from Russia. ''What goods are you carrying?'' ''Old iron nails.'' He wrote down: ''merchant in old iron nails.'' He then handed the paper to the traveller: it was a stamped certificate permitting the traveller to journey throughout the length and breadth of Prussia. The Inspector did not ask the travellers for proof of the truth of their declarations, but accepted their replies in good faith, as though they were as valid to him as the testimony of a hundred reliable witnesses.

We journeyed on. On both sides of the highway were fields of all kinds of produce, and cornfields and fruit orchards. The faces and garments of the farmers themselves expressed the freedom they enjoyed. My heart rejoiced and my spirits rose, for it seemed to me that I had emerged from the darkness of prison into the light of freedom, into a land which seemed like the Garden of Eden in olden times. About a league from the frontier we came to a gate across the road. At the side stood a hut encircled by a garden of herbs and pretty flowers. Our cart stopped. From the window above, a long pole was lowered down to us. It had a wooden cup attached to the end into which the cartier placed the required coins. I wondered about this, and then saw a plaque on the wall of the hut, inscribed in German, in the dialect of the farmers of Zamot: ''Pay here the road toll of one penny per horse's foot.'' I realised that the toll-collector was cleverly sparing himself the necessity of going out to meet every cart that passed, especially during times of wind or rain or snow. He had, therefore, made the long pole with a cup attachment which he held out through the window to the cartier who remained seated on his cart; the cartier placed the required toll-charge into the cup which the collector then drew up into the house. The German had introduced a new and clever method, small though it was, whose like I had never seen or heard before.

In Memel I bought all the tools I needed, new and old, for eighty roubles. I returned home and began to make clocks with the aid of my new tools. A whole year I lived in my father-in-law's home. He built a large hotel adjacent to the little house which he had built earlier after the fire. The desire came over me to earn my living from clockmaking, for hitherto I had been interested only in learning the craft, but without making use of it for my livelihood. At that time, I withdrew my name from the register of Loigzoim, and instead registered with the small town of Loikave,[315] which at that time came under the jurisdiction of the city of Vorna. I am still registered there to this day. Since, however, they did not know how to read or write Russian correctly, they registered me as Aranzon — and this is the spelling I use for my family name to this day.

On the way to Loikave, I was joined by a man who came from the town of Kroz, a teacher of Bible and Gemara to the wealthy Jewish children of the town of

Zhager.[316] His route to Loikave lay via Kroz. We sat together and marvelled at each other, for I could hardly restrain myself over the follies uttered by this ignorant man, who was devoid of all knowledge and learning, as are most Jewish *melammedim*. I spoke to him in a simple manner in order to give him a little knowledge. He told me: "Today, even the scholars of Zhager have begun to repent wholly of their former methods of critical research because of an incident which recently occurred in their city. In the house of one of the *maskilim* were demons and spirits which turned the house into a shambles every night before midnight. Searches and investigations were undertaken, without result." I had never heard of such an incident at all in Zhager, although it was not far from my own town. I thought: it is nothing new for old women, who have been alarmed by a stone falling from a roof, to say that an army of demons and poltergeists have invaded the house. Even the *melammedim* have testified in the Houses of Study that they have themselves witnessed the same thing — for fear creates panic-distended eyes. So they talk about it all day long, and their words pass through the town, from mouth to mouth, until they finally cease.

My companion, seeking to persuade me of the truth of his fantasies, continued: "I myself read, in a book written by a distinguished scholar of old, a most astonishing thing. He stated that all enlightened scholars and men of science should endeavour to solve an amazing wonder of our everyday lives. It is this: a cart has both a large wheel and a small wheel which are fixed to each other. How is it that these two wheels arrive at the same point at the same time? If we rolled the large wheel by itself along the ground, it would quickly come to a stop. But if we rolled the small one along with it, it would stop a long time after it." The man, even more astonishingly, added: "Truly, only a distinguished scholar such as he could propound so difficult a problem, for no man can understand this thing which can be seen every day." I flushed, and made no reply, although I felt amazed. I realised that this man was not lying, but was speaking only out of his own folly. Was it possible, however, that the Gaon of old who wrote that book could have been as foolish and ignorant as my companion? Did he not know what any child knows, that the little wheel at the front of the carriage turns more quickly on its axis than the large rear wheel, which turns slowly upon its axis, and for this reason, they arrive together at the same point at the same time? For the rest of that journey, and the whole of the following night, I could not overcome my astonishment at the words of the Gaon of old. Much as I loved truth and my people, I could not bring myself to believe that a Gaon or Rabbi capable of writing a whole book in days of old should be so stupid and ignorant. On the third day, a light suddenly shone into my mind, and revealed the solution. This man had read the book by the Gaon, but had not understood him. The Gaon had spoken of the large wheel of the carriage, and the small wheel which turns with it on its axis: the two are alike except that the large wheel rolls over the ground, whilst the small wheel fitted to the hub revolves with it during every revolution. Here we have a simple problem which, however, can not be comprehended at first glance by anyone who has not studied modern science and technology. If we were to place a plank above the ground in such a position that the small wheel rested upon it whilst the large wheel did not touch the ground, and if we then turned the axle we should find that both the large and small wheels together will make many more revolutions than the number performed by the large wheel when it is resting normally on the ground or on a plank whilst the small wheel is not on the ground or on a plank, but simply turning freely on itself. When the two wheels reach the same point at the same moment, then the small wheel cannot revolve faster than the larger wheel, since they have become one, and the number of its revolutions then equals that of the larger wheel. It has not changed its position, but has turned together with the larger hub. The explanation is straightforward to anyone who has had even a little modern education but is difficult for someone who has devoted his entire life to Talmudic casuistry and Kabbalah, for he will not know how to reduce the minute fractions of minutes to infinity, or to visualise how each infinite particle of the large wheel's revolution can be split into halves, so that during one half the small wheel is revolved whilst, during the other half, it is raised and moved from one point of infinity to another. The procedure is the same with all its parts during its revolution.

Many years later, when I was living in the capital, Petersburg, an engraver, Asher Ber, showed me a discovery of his which had astounded the scholars and academics: when three wheels, bearing an equal number of teeth, are aligned so that their teeth engage, the first with the second and the second with the third, then when the first wheel turns one revolution on its axis, the third will turn one-half of a revolution — and vice versa, when the third wheel makes one full turn on its axis, the first wheel will make two turns. It is a strange and wonderful law of mechanical movement. The engraver, Asher Ber, arrogantly informed me that, even were he to demonstrate the three wheels in motion, I would still not understand the reason for it. When, later, Asher Ber came and handed me his small machine, I turned the first wheel twice: above its axis was an arrow pointer which indicated its rate of motion. The third wheel had a similar pointer, and this showed only one revolution. The machine was small, made from the wheels of a pocket watch. I examined it for a few minutes and found that the solution to this phenomenon was the same as for the two wheels, the large and small wheels. The middle wheel, which revolved between the first and the third wheels, actually performed only a half-revolution on its axis whilst its other half was pulled round by the revolving axle; the act of separating the two half-movements is spread amongst all the infinite fractions of each moment of each revolution. The small machine was made in the form of a closed lantern, built on a base of a square piece of wood with four pillars supporting another square piece of wood. The first wheel was fixed to the wooden base and held so that it could neither turn nor move. A bar, inserted through the hole in the middle of the wood-base holding the fixed wheel, fitted into another hole in the middle of the upper piece of wood. Resting on the top of this bar was an arrow which pointed to numbers on an indicator table. The third wheel, located below the upper piece of wood, rested freely on the bar. A thin, short bar slotted through the centre of the hole in this wheel and emerged through the piece of wood and the indicator table above it. Another pointer turned together with the bar of the wheel — in the manner of the hands of a clock. If this central bar is turned from below with a key, then the first wheel will not turn with it, because it is fixed to the piece of wood, nor will the third which has the pointer, since it is not fixed to the bar. Only the pointer, which is fixed to the bar will move. In order to turn the third wheel and its pointer, the second wheel is placed so that its teeth engage with those on the first wheel below it and on the third wheel above it. From its centre, a small peg is inserted into the centre bar, and the second wheel rests freely upon it. When the long bar is turned by a key, the peg fixed to it will also revolve and will turn the second wheel. If the teeth of this second wheel did not engage with the teeth of the wheel fixed to the base, then it would make one turn together with the bar but not on its axis, and its teeth would not turn round. However, by engaging the teeth with those of the fixed wheel below it, it moves its axis as it revolves around the bar. In truth, only half the number of its teeth change with the total number of the teeth of the fixed wheel, for the other half is raised up by the bar which pulls it, as though they are not engaged with the teeth of the fixed wheel. The movement of each tooth is not divided into halves, either for the purpose of turning or being raised, but in each infinite part, one half revolves and the other half lifts up. The changeover from the circular movement to the lifting movement is not visually obvious: what can be seen is that the second wheel makes one complete revolution on its axis during the time that it has engaged half its teeth with those on the fixed wheel. If the bar is turned by a key one more complete revolution, it will engage with the other half of the fixed wheel, for now, also, half will revolve and half will be lifted up. Therefore, when the teeth of the second wheel engage with those of the upper third wheel, they turn them with them, so that the third wheel and its pointer revolve in the same manner as the second wheel, making one revolution during the time that the bar with its pointer performs two revolutions. Since the teeth of the standing wheel, namely the second wheel, are beneath a vertical diagonal, then if the centre of that tooth which fits perpendicularly between two teeth of the fixed wheel is pulled forward by means of its bar, the tooth will also move forward beyond the tooth blocking its path in the part of a fraction of a moment; the obstructing tooth, however, will compel it to alter its forward movement to a circular movement — and that movement is also fractional with regard to time and position. Thus, that tooth of the second wheel will have two movements divided into half-forward and half-rotating in its position. It will transfer these movements on to the third wheel and its pointer. These two halves of its movement cannot be discerned by human eyes or sense, for they are two fractional parts of infinite time and place and are too infinitesimal for our senses. This is why all infinitesimal parts of substances and solids are known to chemistry only by numbers, or by the movement of parts of metals during the flow of electricity or magnetism, and when agitated with heat or light.

I went alone to live in Telz, for I had decided to try to earn my living from my craft. I rented a small room in a house in the centre of the city, with a window overlooking the rear of the house and a door to the street. My father-in-law asked me to return home for every Sabbath and festival and be with my wife and son, for in any case my workshop would be closed at those times; since, moreover, there was no great distance to travel, I would be able to use his horses which made a daily journey from his hotel to the city. I was in Telz a whole year, and earned very little. I spent most of my time making wall and table clocks, but I was not content. Then my father-in-law sent Nehemiah, my wife's brother, to be my assistant and apprentice. He also sent us food two or three times per week, which was sufficient to last the two of us the whole week. Although my expenses were few, yet I made hardly a penny profit from my labours. I was not familiar with the business side of the trade, nor did I have sufficient money to engage in business. I confined myself to doing only repairs in my backroom workshop (I thought that it would not matter if I did not have a room overlooking the front street, for there was no other craftsman in the city as capable as I was, and therefore people would naturally bring their clocks to me for repair). My work did not prosper, nor was I able to sell any of the new clocks I made, as more and better clocks were being imported from abroad at a cheaper price.

My neighbours gradually became very friendly with me, and even praised me as an excellent teacher. They used to visit me in the evenings to discuss world affairs and the latest news. However, during the idle days, namely the Sabbaths and festivals, when my shop was closed and I was away, we had to forgo this pleasure. Towards the end of the year, a neighbour of mine, Ze'ev Schulman, offered to take me into his house and let me have at a small rental the window overlooking the street, where I could do my work, and also a small room for my living quarters. Being wealthy, he would not press me for the rent. Normally, he would not have thought of letting any room in his house at any price, but his friends had urged him to do this, not only for my sake, but also to provide a place where we could converse together during our idle periods. My income did increase a little whilst I was there, but it was very little. I stayed there about a year.

One lovely evening in the month of *Av*, fire broke out in a house in another street and destroyed the whole of the city centre. My lodgings also went up in flames. I snatched a few hasty belongings and fled out of town to the canal. The cries of the wailing victims, and the sight of the terrible conflagration, frightened me and I refused to return home where the roof had been destroyed by the fire. However, Nehemiah, my wife's brother, against my protests, went to the house, collected whatever things he could find and brought them back to the field. My book, *Wife of My Youth*, had been consumed in the flames, together with the letters I had been collecting and the large, heavy, monthly-clocks which I had been repairing for a fee of ten roubles. The conflagration had been seen from the hotel in Vishevian, so my father-in-law sent horses and cart to fetch me and my goods. I remained with them until after the festival of Tabernacles.

It was whilst I was in Telz that the brother of my former wife, whom I had divorced in Vilki, paid me a visit. He told me that I had a son there, who was named Judah Leib, and whom he had undertaken to look after until he was two or three years old. He was now nine years of age. The mother's parents had died, and she herself had been married to a cap-maker. They were in dire poverty. He had, therefore, been searching for me, and had now found me. My in-laws assured him that they would take the boy into their home and look after him, so the man went on his way. My in-laws had not known about the boy until the day that that man came, for I had never mentioned it to them. Nevertheless, they did not rebuke me at all whenever they spoke about the man's visit. On my part, I acknowledged the facts of the situation. When, later, one of my acquaintances left Telz to go to Vilki, I asked him to bring the boy, and offered to pay him for his trouble. Eight days later, he returned with the boy, whom I took into the house of my father-in-law, where he was generously welcomed and accepted as their son.

Then followed a period of several years which seemed to pass by without any incident of note. Three years after my wedding, I took stock of my affairs and realised that if I continued living partly in Telz and partly in Vishevian, I should not prosper or be content. I thought: "The man who prepares for battle should not fear the gunpowder. I have a family, and the time has come to fend for them. Although I do not earn enough even for myself, I shall settle in Telz with my wife and sons." My father-in-law had never asked this of me, for, in his love for us, he would have maintained us at his own expense: never had he even hinted that we should leave his house.

I moved into a new house in Telz that had been built after the fire. My earnings began to increase — and so did my cares. It was as though I had been predestined to live in want. Yet, as the number of my children increased, providing me with more mouths to feed, so did my income grow. I have often heard other people say the same thing, although they were mostly men who believed in all kinds of superstitions, having been taught to do so from childhood, without thought or reason. If, however, these circumstances had not happened to me personally, I should never have put any credence in their words. But I experienced them myself. How wondrous is Divine providence over all Creation! Its ways cannot be measured, nor can man predict the beginning or end of all his acts.

At that time, a decree was issued by Tsar Nicholas which divided all the Jews in the land into five classes: Guild merchants, petty traders, artisans, labourers and unemployed idlers.[317] Rumour spread that the fifth class would be conscripted into the King's service in the army, whilst the fourth class would be exiled to work on untilled soil in a barren land. So the Jews got together in all their towns and set up Societies of Artisans similar to those of the non-Jews. Where, however, there were less than five craftsmen in one particular place, a Society could not be legally formed: they therefore combined two or more, and even ten, different kinds of crafts together to form one Society. They appointed a common Head, and registered the Society. We, in Telz, did the same. We formed a group of all metalworkers, watchmakers, sheet metal workers and tin workers, and set up a Society under the name of the Society of Sheet Metalworkers *(Blecharbeiter)*. We appointed a goldsmith as our Head, and two sheet metal workers as his assistants. Any one who joined later had to pay a fine according to the amount stipulated by the Head, whom we called the Elder of the Society. The Elder and his assistants served us for one year, during which time they fleeced the late-comers and kept all the monies and dues for themselves, spending it all on food and drink as soon as they received it. When the members of the Society discovered this, for no monies had been disbursed among them, disputes and quarrels arose. At the end of the first year, they held a meeting to discuss the matter. The honest and intelligent ones among them said: "Our leaders cannot read or write or speak the language of the land, and therefore they employ Christians to do this for them — but these also teach them their corrupt ways. Let us appoint a new leader, a Jew who knows the Russian language, and who will lead us honestly and justly." They all looked at me, for there was no one else among them with my qualifications. I accepted the position on condition that the new assistants appointed to help me would carry out all my instructions. It was agreed. I took the Society's cash box into my charge, but gave the key to one of my assistants. Any new member had to pay three roubles to the Society's funds plus an additional rouble for expenses. Any member who fell ill or became incapable of work was able to pledge with the Society any article whose value was equivalent to the amount of the loan he sought; the loan was given free of interest. When he had repaid the loan, either by monthly instalments or by one single payment, the pledged article was returned to him. The dismissed former leaders were hostile towards me but there was nothing they could do or say. I was elected for a period of three years; after that, I was re-elected a second and a third time, so that I held the position of Elder for twelve years.[318]

It was after my election for a second term as Elder of the Society that the City Mayor's term of office came to an end: he was the Supreme Elder of all the Societies in the city, most of which were composed of Christian tailors and cobblers who had formed Societies many years ago. After the Tsar's edict, the Jews had joined them. Now all the craftsmen in the city — about two hundred men — assembled to appoint a new leader for the next three years. The voting was done by means of balls. Most of the city's craftsmen were Jews and, because of their majority vote, could elect a Jew to the office. There was, however, an old law dating from the Empress Catherine, which prohibited the election of a Jew to the post of City Mayor.[319] On this day, when the Christian craftsmen met to elect a new leader, they could not find a single member able to read and write Russian — and the Book of Statutes stated explicitly that no man could be appointed to this position unless he knew the Russian language. A dispute broke out among the voters. Some said that, even though no one present knew Russian, nevertheless someone had to be appointed. Others replied: ''In that case, if we are going to elect a Mayor in contravention of the Book of Statutes, we could properly elect a Jew who knows Russian.'' There was no other person there besides myself who fulfilled that qualification. They began to count the white balls, and found that they outnumbered the black ones — for the Jews were in the majority. The officials of the City Hall also agreed to my appointment as the City Mayor in place of one of their drunkards. Reluctantly, I became the Mayor of the city. I had always preferred to be able to weigh all my actions in advance, with a clear mind, yet here was something I knew nothing about and had certainly never contemplated. It had all happened at that one meeting. After the hubbub and noise had subsided, I fled from the place and went home. It was the rule for the newly-elected official to make a feast of wine and strong drink and food for all the voters before they left the City Hall. They looked for me but I was not there. On my way home, I met some policemen who had heard of my election. They greeted me mockingly: ''On your head.'' I was furious with them but made no response. When I arrived home, I found that the news had preceded me. My wife upbraided me and stormed at me for permitting myself to be elected. However, my appointment had been signed and sealed and registered at the City Hall, and it could not be revoked. The Christians, much as they did not want me, did not speak badly of me, although they realised that I had run away from them and did not wish to help them. About nine days later, an official of the Council came to question me about the affair, and to promise their support and guidance in all my functions. I refused. A month later, an emergency meeting of all the city's artisans was called, and a new election was held. A cobbler was elected who could not even sign his own name: he is their Head to this day.

In the year 1854, war broke out between Russia and France and England, who were the allies of the Turks. This was the Crimean War; it ended, after the death of Nicholas the First, with a Peace Treaty made with his son, Alexander II.[320] As the conflict increased, England blocked all the seaways to Russia. Goods then had to be exported by way of the Baltic Sea: at the time, Russia and Prussia were at peace, so all goods from the Russian interior were brought to the Prussian frontier. There were, as yet, no railways or locomotives in our land, for whenever Russian officials had recommended the new inventions which steam power was producing across the frontier, Tsar Nicholas' reply was always: ''The Germans are fools!''Now that the country was under siege, and the sea-routes blocked, our merchants had to send their wares by horse and cart a distance of thousands of *verst* to the Prussian border. It took them about half a year to make the journey. It was also difficult for them to find sufficient horses in Russia to carry their goods. The country suffered considerably. During the summertime, goods were transported by river to points close to the frontier, where they were then loaded on to carts and horses for the journey into Prussia. Since the Russian merchants were not familiar with the route or the language, they found it more convenient to place their wares in the hands of middle-men: these transported the goods to Prussia and also purchased new goods which were not made in Russia and which could not be imported by sea because of the blockade.

Many ordinary people, therefore, set themselves up as contractors to haul the goods from the Russian hinterland to the border. Many of them were Jews, ever alert to act as middlemen in any kind of business. Many Jews of the provinces of Vilna, Kovno and other areas, forsook their taverns and shops, and even the Houses of Study and the schools and became contractors and middlemen and hauliers. Some were successful, and within a month amassed a fortune, either by honest means or otherwise. There were some who, only yesterday, had been on the point of starvation, yet became millionaires within a few days. There were those who attained distinction and great wealth, and forgot their earlier way of life; they became arrogant, and convinced they would always be wealthy and would never again endure poverty or want. Daughters of marriageable age were forced to wait, because their fathers hoped to amass greater riches so that they could marry the finest suitors. When the war came to an end, and there was peace again in the land, the sea-routes were opened. Then all the riches that those people had amassed were swept away on the waves of our waterways. They looked behind them — and there was distress and darkness. There was not enough left of all their riches and wealth even to dress their daughters in rags; so their daughters remained maidens for ever.

At that time, the value of Russian currency fell considerably.[321] Rouble notes were carried across the border and sold for fifty-five kopeks. Gold coins were smuggled out; later silver coins were exported, and finally even copper coins. A decree was passed forbidding the export of all prohibited goods including coins. Nevertheless, these were still exported secretly, so that eventually, throughout the country, from the frontier to Kovno and Vilna, no coins were available for normal trading. If someone wanted to buy something which cost half a rouble, and had no less than a rouble on him, he would not be able to obtain any change. Similarly, if a worker had done a job which was estimated at thirty or forty kopeks, and his employer had only one rouble, he would have to search the whole city for small change. This created extensive confusion throughout the country. All coins, copper and silver and gold, were declared prohibited goods at the frontier, and so were the metals themselves. Smugglers flourished, and many of them were Jews. Then the Government brought out new coins containing less silver or copper so that their weight was not equal to their face value. This stratagem, however, failed, for these were also smuggled across the border since the value of their weight in metal was still greater than the value of the paper notes, which had become suspect: notes could lose their value overnight, whereas metals would always retain their value.

The merchants themselves tried to find a solution to the problem by issuing paper notes of their own, in all denominations. These served as promissory notes which the vendor collected and sent to the issuer of the notes who redeemed them for Government rouble notes, in tens and hundreds. The first ones to issue these paper-notes were wealthy, distinguished and respected people. Their notes were made from thick, gummed paper covered with a thin sheet of white paper, on which were printed the issuer's name and patronymic, together with the denominational value of the note, and his signature. They were welcomed by the people in general who found in them a way to overcome their difficulties. The landowners and the country farmers accepted them as common currency. However, as these notes became more widely used in the country, and more and more people began to issue them, then poor people, who did not have adequate means began to spend far more than they could afford to repay, and so became bankrupt and had to flee. Confusion abounded as people lost faith in each other.

A troop of Hussars was stationed in Telz, and their Commander over a Thousand had his residence in the city.[322] I had to go to his house to repair a clock. He handed me a paper note for three roubles, and I did not have sixty kopeks in change, nor could he help with the forty kopeks required. He said: "This is the result of the wickedness of your brethren who have smuggled all the money out of the country." I replied: "I am the only one in my family, and have no brothers." "All the Jews are your brethren." "Permit me to enquire, Sir, whether all Russians are your brethren?" "That is so. All Russians are my brethren, and all Jews are yours." "In that case, forgive me for saying so, all the Russians who are imprisoned in chains for robbery and murder, are also your brethren!" He answered: "It is true, they are also my brethren." I then said: "In that case, why do you not despise yourself for the violence and murder which your brethren commit? Yet you curse and despise me for the smuggling committed by my brethren." He said: "It is because so many of your brethren commit this crime." I replied: "You see, Sir, how all crimes are blamed on Jews. Several years ago, some violent Russian brethren of yours set fire to the Tsar's winter palace in Petersburg[323] and looted many valuable articles which they sold to the Jews. Tsar Nicholas announced that the blame lay not on the thief but on the receiver of the stolen property, since thieves cannot exist without a receiver. Now in this case which we are discussing — smuggling through the customs — the thief is the Jewish smuggler. The receivers, however, are mostly native Russians, the kind who own all the businesses in Nevsky Street, in the capital. The Tsar issued a decree that, firstly, all Jews shall be expelled from the capital, and secondly, that all Jews, good and bad alike, shall be prohibited from residing within a distance of forty *verst* from the frontier.[324] The reason given for this is that, if the Jew did not smuggle his stolen wares across the border, then the Russian would not buy the prohibited goods. This, Commander, is your kind of justice — but who can complain against people more powerful than himself?" He said: "How do you know that the merchants of Nevsky deal in smuggled goods? Have you ever been to the capital and seen it for yourself?" "No, Sir, I have never been to the capital. Nevertheless, I have often heard my brethren say that most of the smuggled articles are sold in St. Petersburg.'' He looked at me haughtily, but made no reply.

My enthusiasm for technology increased with every day that passed. I worked night and day to invent new things, new mechanisms for clocks, even perpetual motion, and silver cases for watches engraved in the same manner as those made abroad. I copied everything like a monkey, not knowing which were the best tools to use; my own tools were not the most suitable. So I spent my time and labour, without looking for material gain: I was in no hurry to make a fortune, for I was content to earn enough for my needs. However, as my family increased and my children grew up, I began to make things of practical use to people and of benefit to myself. One day, I was given a table clock to repair. It had a garland made of polished brass around the numbers on the clock face, and very pretty flower-stalks over which were three cherubs holding trumpets to their lips. I wanted to make a plaster mould of it, into which I could pour molten tin so that I could make many copies of it. I therefore made enquiries about tin-smelters who would show me how to prepare the moulds. I called upon one of them, but he was not at home.

There was a cobbler in the house, sitting on a three-legged stool. I watched him working, and saw something that was new to me, for although I had heard about it before, I had never seen it. He was not sewing with waxed threads, but was using wooden pegs which were lying in a bowl in front of him.[325] With an awl he pierced a small hole in the leather, and inserted a small wooden peg in the hole. He then hammered it in hard until it sank deep into the leather. Finally, he sewed it all together. I asked him whether this was a new procedure, and he said that this had been the practice for many years. ''Where do you get these pegs?'' ''They can be bought in the shops.'' ''Do the shopkeepers make them for you?'' ''No. The shopkeepers import sacks of them from Prussia, in all sizes, by length and breadth according to order, thick and thin, long and short. I have also heard it said that they are not actually manufactured in neighbouring countries, but are imported from America.'' After this, my thoughts gave me no peace. The idea became fixed in my mind: 'If I could make a machine which could produce these pegs in quantity, I could make a fortune'. I had made enquiries about the price of the pegs and had been told that they cost five kopeks per quarter *funt*. The wood itself would not cost more than one kopek. I therefore stopped working on the table-clock face with all its ornamentation, and began instead to investigate the production of pegs. I confirmed that the shopkeepers did purchase them from Prussia which imported them from America. All the cobblers in our country used these wooden pegs. I was shown the different types of pegs that were used. They were made of a white wood, four-sided, with rectangular pointed tips. The wood was Birch *(Berze)*.[326] I swiftly set to work on a machine which would produce sharp pegs from long, rectangular stems. As the stem rotated in the machine, a heavy, iron axe cut one end to a pointed tip. At the other end, a small saw, almost semi-circular in shape, and having narrow teeth, pulled the finished peg away and pushed it forward to make room for the next peg — and so on. I needed, therefore, to construct a machine for cutting the rectangular pieces of wood to a length of about one cubit. I found it exceedingly difficult to build a machine which would cut a number of pieces of wood in one operation to the length of one cubit. It was beyond my capacity — nor was there anyone to do the job for me.

Now, there was a German locksmith who was very fond of the bottle. He promised to make a machine of this type in the form of a joiner's plane. He charged a fee of two roubles, which was to be paid after the plane was seen to be working properly. I agreed. He told me that he did not have a penny to buy the iron and copper. I was hesitant to give him any money, for he was a habitual drunkard. He then said: "Let us do it this way. You will entrust the two roubles to the apothecary, who is also a German, and he will trust me to deliver in advance. My hand upon it." I gave the money to the apothecary on condition that he should pay the locksmith only if the plane worked properly. A month later, the locksmith brought me ten four-sided stems of wood, and said that they had been produced by the plane he had made, thus proving that it worked properly. "Where is the plane? After I have seen it in operation, then I shall pay you." "Not so. First, you must pay me my fee, and afterwards I shall demonstrate it and give it to you." I had no wish to argue with this drunkard, so I went to the apothecary to ask for my money. He stormed at me angrily, and swore: "So this is what the accursed Jews do. What you want is to see how the machine works, and then to find an excuse for not taking it. You will take your money back, and make another plane like it yourself. And this poor man will lose the money he earned by his labours." He raised his hand to strike me. In those days, no judge or Governor in any provincial city would have given a decision in favour of a Jew, so I lost both my money and my machine. I therefore abandoned the idea of a peg-machine for a later date.

I went around the shops in search of an article which was in common use but was not yet made by machine. I found nothing, for we were behind the times, both Russia and I. There was nothing which could be made by human hands for human use which was not already being manufactured by a machine propelled by some kind of power — for, long ago, people in the west and the New World had explored the properties of Nature in order to find things that would benefit mankind to greater or lesser extent. Worst of all was the fact that no one in our country took any notice of new discoveries, and therefore they were unaware of the things they lacked. Who told me about the wooden pegs, and that no machine existed for producing them? Was it not the chance accident which led me to the cobbler?

At that time, the clockmaker Joseph Kaplanski had a trainee apprentice who was a relative of his wife. His name was Marcus Beniaminovich. After he had concluded his apprenticeship, he left, on my advice, to finish his studies in Prussia. Now, in Memel, near the Russian border, lived an assistant to a craftsman clockmaker who was also a photographer; he was a German named Kenklies. He heard that the craftsman was willing to teach photography for a fee of fifty roubles, so he wrote to me asking whether I should like to learn it. We exchanged correspondence until we finally settled on a fee. I bought the apparatus and went to Memel. I stayed there about a month. One of my conditions was that he teach me the galvanoplastic method of plating metals, for he had claimed to be a craftsman in this work, also. Three weeks passed by during which he made no attempt to show me this method of plating metals, so I urged him to do so. He told me to buy some copper, zinc and earthenware pots. He then began to work by following the instructions in a handbook manual for clockmakers, which described how to plate parts of a clock with silver and gold. I realised that the man had lied to me when he said that he knew this craft. When he had finished without having made any effect on the metal parts, he said he would send for a friend of his, a German goldsmith, who was a first-rate craftsman. He came and showed him how to prepare the apparatus for the work. After his friend had left, he tried to carry out the work in the way he had been shown, but again without success. I then went myself to the goldsmith and offered to pay him five Reichsthaler to show me how to perform this work: I intended to deduct the five Reichsthaler from the fee I was due to pay Kenklies, despite any protests he would make, for he had deceived me in the matter. So it was. I then bought all my photographic apparatus from him, and the metal platings, and returned home. I added the art of photography to my clockmaking.[327] My circumstances began to improve a little, for both trades together afforded me a comfortable livelihood. However, my third craft, metal-plating, brought me no income at all in the little city of Telz. Later, I sold my galvanic apparatus[328] to a goldsmith, and abandoned the craft altogether.

One day, I was in a large department store and noticed that scores, even hundreds, of ladies' hose were being sold. I had not known, until that day, that stockings were being made in any other way than by women who wove them by hand at night. I enquired about the goods and the price. They were sewn with thread like all garments, but the yarn was not woven in the same manner as cloth fabric. The weaving was similar to that done by women, but instead of having a single thread twisted in a complete winding, its two ends were joined together lengthwise. I sat down to devise a machine which would weave like the women, and use one continuous thread. Unfortunately, I was not successful, for the machine produced network suitable for nets but not for hosiery. Later, I found out that there were already in existence large and successful machines which manufactured hose without seams like those made by women.[329] It seemed that nothing had been overlooked by foreign inventors who devised means of producing goods without the use of hands and feet.

I was told by people in the trade, by merchants and cobblers, that wooden pegs were being manufactured only in America, and from there they were exported to every country in Europe, including Russia. It made me wonder why the technologists of France and England had not devised a machine for producing these wooden pegs. There were, in fact, machines in Europe for producing pegs in quantity, but they did not make the pointed, square pegs but only those with broad tips like a woodcutter's peg. These were bought only in small quantities and used in only a few places abroad. The square-pointed pegs were widely used everywhere, including our own country. These were the ones which were imported from America. I turned again to the problem of making these pegs and tried a different method. Instead of using rectangular pieces of wood, I obtained blocks of wood from which I could cut pegs according to the required length by means of four or six saws attached lengthwise by a thick iron bar to the four sides of a beam. The teeth of the saws were shaped like the points of the pegs. As the bar revolved swiftly, the teeth acted like a chisel cutting deep grooves the length of the pointed pegs. The beam containing the saws, also rotated quickly. Underneath it was a trolley covered with a board on which the blocks of wood lay: this board was able to turn over so that the wood dropped into the trolley. As the blocks moved slowly along, the saws cut into them crosswise, like grooves, and split them into individual pegs. Finally, a quantity of four-sided pegs was produced in one operation. My father-in-law suggested that I take Tsevi Beniaminovich as my assistant, as he was a craftsman joiner. I explained the machine to him, describing it as though it were a wooden table on which moved an iron container with iron trays. My father-in-law let me have the use of his house in Vishevian, which he had built immediately after the fire, and before he had built the hotel. I offered Tsevi three roubles per week to assist me, and brought him to live in the house. I showed him the whole operation of the machine, and provided him with all the parts required, and put him in charge of the work. Meanwhile, I stayed in Telz continuing with my clockmaking, although once or twice every week I went to Vishevian to see how he was getting on. I expected the work to be completed within three or four months. I was not familiar with the various types of tools used by mechanics, for my only training consisted of the clockmaking I had learnt in Mitau. Tsevi himself was only familiar with his own carpentry tools. A whole year passed by and the machine was not completed. By that time, I had spent my last penny; I was in desperate straits and did not know which way to turn. Then Saul, my wife's brother, came with three hundred roubles he had made from his own business. He agreed to become a partner in my machine. This gave us renewed strength and we continued the work together. Finally the machine was finished. I bought the maple wood *(Klon)*[330] and then went to fetch five workers from Telz to operate the machine and produce the pegs in quantity. We began to manufacture the pegs, and the first day was very successful. It was the Sabbath eve, so I left my brother-in-law to carry on with the work whilst I returned to spend the Sabbath with my family in Telz. On the Sunday morning, Saul came and told me that the machine had become erratic and unstable and it was impossible to operate it. I hurried back to Vishevian with him, and found that it had to be nailed firmly down to the floor. I told the workers to carry on with their work for one more day. The machine became loose again, so we again fastened it down to its base. On the following day, I fell into great distress and despair as I saw the results of my own error. Although the teeth of the saws were sharp and as hard as glass, yet after five minutes of cutting into the damp maple wood they became blunted and were unable to provide a clear cutting action. They would have to be sharpened again and this involved removing each saw separately from the iron beam and sharpening each tooth individually with a whetstone. Thus, for every five minutes in operation, they would be idle ten-fold the amount of time. This particular machine could not be successful. I realised, at that moment, that all my labour had been in vain, and all my brother-in-law's money and toil had also been for nothing. I wept, despite myself. My brother-in-law was heart-broken and returned home. Tsevi and I sat in a corner of the room and wept inconsolably.

It was a fine day with clear skies, and I told Tsevi that we should go for a stroll in the fields and the woods, and throw off our despair. We went out, and lay down in a shady patch of grass. Tsevi said that we had already, once before, tried to make the pegs in a different manner, so why should we not try another new method? We cut off some reeds and thin stalks, and made a design in the grass of the kind of machine we thought we should build. It seemed feasible, so we resolved to return to our work with renewed vigour. However, I had no money left. On our way back from the fields, we met my father-in-law who wanted to know what we intended to do now. We told him of our decision, and that now we knew the source of all the troubles, we could finish the work in two to three months — but we lacked the capital for the purpose. Tsevi, on his part, was willing to work for only a slice of dry bread and salt, so long as he could finish the machine. My father-in-law said: "I can always provide food, not only bread but also meat and milk from my own provisions. But you yourselves must provide whatever money you need." We agreed, and returned to our work.

The machine had to be built in three stages. Firstly, we already had the parts we had made, namely, the blocks of wood we had cut; secondly, those blocks would have to be cut into small pieces and into the correct length and breadth measurements for the size on the pegs; thirdly, we would have to make a new machine, like a knife, for sharpening each peg on one side. We made two iron rings which rotated on axles so that the small pieces of split wood could be forcibly pushed between them. As they emerged under the pressure of the rings, they came under two hard iron cutters with points which slanted towards each other. These cut two splinters down one side of each piece of wood, leaving it as sharp as a knife. The pieces were then passed on to the new machine to be made into pegs by sharpening them on their other two sides, thus forming a four-sided point. It also separated the pegs from each other. Then, two other rings, like the first ones, pushed the small pieces of wood further along between them until the original block was finally reduced to the size of a peg, whereupon the rings stopped still, and the wood also came to a standstill. An iron triangle, suspended over the block of wood, then approached the sharp side: under the block was a triangular hole. The upper triangle descended into the triangular hole, cutting a triangular piece of wood out of the block. Thus each part of the machine moved together with the two triangles we had constructed in a manner similar to that of those small machines which are used for cutting quills for writing. As the operation continued the block of wood was cut breadthwise, and each finished peg with its four-sided point was separated from it. And so on. If we should want to make pegs which were not four-sided but were as broad as a woodcutters's peg, then the beams of wood would not be brought to the final operation of the machine, but would be cut up after they had passed between the first two rings. They were then ready for sale. We worked as quickly as we could to complete the machine which had only two triangles for cutting at the two ends of the revolving lower beam; one ring had been made for each of its ends. Above the lower revolving beam was another one with two rings on its ends, which could press lightly or heavily upon the lower rings to hold the wooden beam between them and push it forwards and onwards. When these stopped, the beam also stopped, and then the triangle would cut deeply into the beam, splitting it along its breadth. We did this primarily in order to be able to demonstrate the method of our operation of making the pegs — for, if we found a partner willing to invest money to develop the machine, then we should make one which, instead of having only two rings on the lower beam, would have twelve on both the lower and upper beams in addition to twelve triangles, so that in a single operation twelve pegs with sharp, four-sided points could be produced. We finally completed our work.

I bought logs of fresh birch wood, and told Tsevi to prepare pegs suitable for sale in Telz. Tsevi brought in his brother David, to help him to manufacture a large quantity: from the sale of the pegs, I would be able to pay them their wages. In the meantime, we would look for a wealthy investor to finance our operations. However, instead of it taking only three months to complete the machine, as we had hoped, it took us a whole year. Pegs of all sizes piled up in sacks in my house, and there was no buyer for them. I separated the pegs into their various sizes, parcelled them in paper, wrote the prices on the bags, and then sent a representative to show them to the shopkeepers. I lowered the price in order to compete with the pegs imported from abroad. A certain merchant, Bendet, came and asked me to produce the pegs for him alone: he offered to take as much as I could produce, on condition that I did not sell to anyone else. He would pay me in advance so that I could manufacture them in increasingly larger quantities. I agreed. The time had now come to take out a patent for the machine, because it was not yet legally mine. I had had to work secretly behind closed doors and draped windows, for many people had come from Telz and other places to view the machine and make one like it for themselves. I knew nothing of the procedure for taking out a patent. I remembered I had once come across it in a book of laws and regulations, but could not recall where: there were many lawbooks in our country, but at the time I had not paid any attention to this particular matter. I asked the legal advisers in the city, but they did not know. All they could say was that a book of statutes, which included the regulations for patents, could be found in any Courthouse; they did not, however, know where the book was. Eventually, the District Officer came to my house, looked at the pegs and understood the kind of machine I had invented. He asked: "Have you taken out a patent?" When I told him that I could not ascertain how to do this, he said: "Come to see me at the Courthouse, and I shall make one out for you." I learned later that the regulations exist in Part eleven of the Book of Statutes, which can be found in every society of craftsmen, since it contains all the regulations pertaining to them. During my term of office as the Elder of my Society, I had had Part 101 in my possession, and had frequently referred to it in connection with Society regulations. I had never, however, needed to look at the patent laws, for I had not invented anything at the time. I now prepared on paper diagrams of the different parts of the machine, with a precise description of the operation of each part; I had to make the diagrams according to my own idea of what was required, for I had never before seen diagrams of machines or even of draughtmen's tools. Since I did not know the technical terms for the different parts of the machine, I had to provide names according to my own judgment. No one else beside myself knew of this matter.

One day, I was visited by Ephraim Finkelstein, who originally came from the city of Shad but now lived in the capital Petersburg. He said to me: "Give me the diagrams and descriptions you have made, and I will hand them in to the Patents Department on your behalf. I will also seek a wealthy partner for you, who will take you into his care and provide for all your needs, in return for a share of the profits." He himself would also receive a small share out of the profits for his services. Gladly and gratefully, I handed him everything he required, and he left. Three months passed before he wrote saying that I had to send a letter of application, together with a fee of one rouble, to the Patents Department for a patent in my name for a period of ten years; he also said that a receipt for payment of 450 roubles would be sent to a certain Hartung, a German who lived in Petersburg. Five more months passed by without a word from him, although he had assured me that Hartung would soon send for me and open a factory for me, and finance the construction of a number of machines. In the meantime, the man Bendet stopped purchasing any more pegs from me, because he had not been able to sell many of them, and had nowhere to store the remainder. He had no money left, but did have about twenty-five roubles' worth of goods on order with me, so I sent him my last lot of pegs, about ten roubles' worth, and then sent no more.

Tsevi and his brother had been working on the machine when the belt broke, and the work came to a standstill. Tsevi had about eight sacks of pegs left. My brother-in-law, Saul, took them to the city of Shavel, where he had relatives, Simon Arenstam and his wife Frumah, the aunt of my wife and Saul: they are all today living in New York, America. Simon traded in wooden pegs, so he bought all the sacks from Saul at two roubles per *pud*[331] promising to buy more in a month's time. We filled more sacks, and Saul went to see him a second time in Shavel. He refused to take them, however, explaining that the cobblers would not buy the pegs because they were made from wood which was too soft to ensure a firm repair. Now I had known that the wood from the birch *(Berze)* tree which grew in our country was soft, and that the wood used in America came from a different kind of birch, which was harder and better in quality. The only Russian tree that gave wood suitable for the pegs was the maple *(Klon)* tree, but it was too expensive for us. The manufacture of the pegs came to a stop. Poverty and want abounded in our homes. Tsevi went off to find whatever means of livelihood he could, and I sat down to write to Ephraim and Hartung in Petersburg. Several months later, I received an encouraging letter from Petersburg, stating that shortly the sun would shine again through my windows for Hartung would soon transport me in a covered wagon to Petersburg. Meanwhile my final means of support, my one and only cow, a fine beast which I had thought of selling in order to raise the fare to Petersburg in the coming Spring, died.

There was a famine that year in Lithuania and Zamot, which claimed many victims. Collections were held in many countries for our relief, but brought little benefit to us. The winter plus severely cold weather added to the sufferings of the starving. My father-in-law supported us with food and kept us alive. I had never experienced such bad times before, for even during the Polish Revolt of 1861 – 2, when the Poles "fled to the forests",[333] I was able to subsist on my photography. Previous to that, the proud Polish noblemen had considered it beneath their dignity to have their photographs taken by me — and, truth to tell, at the time I had neither a proper knowledge of the art nor the right apparatus, for I had been taught by a man who was himself untrained in the craft. When, however, the revolt broke out, many of the Polish officers believed they would either have to remain in the forests without a leader or would be sentenced to hard labour in Siberia.[334] They wanted to leave a picture of themselves for their relatives and loved ones, so they came to me. They dressed themselves in the fine fashions of Polish nobles eight centuries earlier when Poland was a great country. I thought they looked ridiculous in their splendid apparel. For them, however, it was a remembrance of their ancient past glory.[335] My family benefited from it.

When Muraviev,[336] the Governor of Kovno, heard of it he issued an order closing down all photographic establishments which did not pay the sum of two hundred roubles by way of a pledge not to photograph the Polish rebels in their rebel raiment. With great difficulty, I collected about one hundred roubles, and borrowed another hundred from Moshe, my wife's brother, who went to Kovno and obtained a licence for me to reopen my business, which had been closed down. My money had been lodged with the Governor's office about two years, when two photographers came to Telz, a Jew and his friend, a German. They set up in business, thinking that the revolt would go on for ever and they would find a lot of trade in Telz. The result was that my clients stopped coming to me and my own business began to fail. I knew that these men had come from the city of Liboia[337] in Courland, and were therefore exempt from the financial pledge to the Governor, since there had been no Polish revolt there. I also knew that if I lodged a protest with the District or City officials, I should receive no satisfaction, for they enjoyed the protection of the army officers and the Commander of the Thousand. I therefore adopted a devious method in order to avoid arousing the hostility of these officers. I wrote to the Governor Muraviev, saying: "Certain men have come here and opened in business as photographers. I believe they have not sent you a monetary pledge in accordance with your decree. I assume, therefore, that the period of the decree has now elapsed, and there is no longer any need for a pledge, seeing that the revolt is over I am a poor man, and shall be most grateful if the Governor would graciously return my two hundred roubles to me." Four days later, I was summoned before the District Officer, who was attended also by the City Officer. They attacked me furiously: "Why did you take your complaint direct to the Governor without approaching us first?" I replied: "Sirs, I was not making any complaint against you. It simply seemed to me that the pledge was no longer necessary, so I asked the Governor to return my money as I am in need of it." Then they brought out my letter which, much to my surprise, had been passed on to them by the Governor. This was his idea of justice, to deliver me into the hands of those whom I had indicted so that they could wreak their vengeance upon me. They read the letter to me. Once my shrewdness became apparent to them, their anger began to subside. They looked for various pretexts not to close down the photographic business, but without success, for when a further order came from the Governor to close it forthwith, they had to do so. It remained closed for some months — and the men starved along with me. By the time their business reopened later, the revolt had ended and most of the Polish officers were either in prison or in Siberia. They stayed in Telz until they ran out of funds and then sold their apparatus and left. I remained alone there until the year 1868, the year of the famine, but I had no customers either for photographs or for clock repairs. I had no means of livelihood, for I had sunk everything I possessed into the peg-machine. We therefore waited impatiently for Hartung and Finkelstein to come and save us. To add to our troubles, I had become indebted to a poor tailor for the sum of sixty roubles, and there were other loans which I had borrowed from some merchants at the time when hope in the future of the machine had been high. We were now left with Petersburg as our sole hope. Autumn came, and brought the cold and the ice to complete our distress. I abandoned photography, for there were no customers for it.

There came to Telz a photographer, Shraga Lunz, a native of Shavel: he had three brothers, two of whom were chemists and the other a doctor. He was on his way from southern Russia, and was looking for a place where he could settle down in his profession. I asked him to come to see me, and told him: "My workshop has all the apparatus you need, and I have a large house. Live here with me whilst you carry on your business. I will not pursue the same business, and I will even send to you anyone who comes to me for a photograph. You will pay me three roubles per week for as long as you stay in my house.'' The man agreed, and came to stay with us. He ate his meals at the house of a relative of his. I was delighted, because the man paid his rent regularly each week as promised.

My son, Simon Aaron, went to the town of Liboia where he stayed with a craftsman clockmaker. My younger sons, Shraga and Abraham, went to stay with my father-in-law. To my deep regret, the photographer Lunz, who was an honest man, was unsuccessful in his work, so that not one picture developed properly. It was as though some evil demon had got into his apparatus. I tried everything I knew to help him. Each day we renewed the liquids and renewed the utensils, but nothing helped. Even had he been able to provide the best of work, he would still have had no customers. The man stayed with me for about three months until he had spent all his money. Necessity compelled him to leave the city, although reluctantly, for we had become good friends. He realised that he would never be successful at his trade, for he had already tried it in Rasseyn without success, and therefore decided to take the advice of his brothers and study to be a chemist. They assured him that they could help him to qualify within two years of study, and that in the third year they would obtain a chemist's diploma for him. However, he could not write either Russian or German properly; he wrote ungrammatically and with many mistakes. I undertook to teach him Russian grammar, but even with all his willingness to learn, he was unable to do so. He was twenty-five years old, and had never been accustomed to learning grammatical rules by rote. In his youth, he had run away from home and had wasted his time in southern Russia, before returning. He left us, went to Rasseyn, and studied to be a chemist. Five years later, he became a chemist in some city — since when I have heard nothing further of him.

Toward the end of winter, I began to make preparations for my journey to Petersburg. Some four years earlier, a decree had been promulgated permitting Jewish craftsmen to reside in the hinterland of Russia.[338] Here, in Telz, there was no hope left for me, for I now had competition in my clockmaking from Mordecai Beniaminovitz who had settled down near me and opened up in business: he was a very talented craftsman indeed. I was left with no other alternative but to go to Petersburg. On the eve of the festival of *Purim* , I went with my brother-in-law, Meir Groslavski, to Riga, where Hina Leah, the daughter of Moshe my brother-in-law, lived with her husband, whom I had never before met. I stayed with them over the Sabbath. The man heard about my machine, and saw the document concerning the patent published by the Department. He took it to show a wealthy German merchant in Riga who dealt mainly in these wooden pegs. He told him about the machine I had invented and proposed that he should take a share in it. The merchant replied: ''We do not use pegs with four-sided pointed ends, but only pegs with broad points. What use is this machine to me?'' The man returned to me and asked: ''What kind of an invention is this? Nobody needs it.'' I answered: ''The

German is making a fool of you. I have been making pegs for the past eight years, and no one has ever asked me for broad pointed pegs.'' He said: ''Come with me to the merchant and you will hear for yourself what he has to say. He is a good friend of mine, and would not make a fool of me.'' We went to see the merchant at his business. I listened to him, but did not believe him. He then showed me a printed price list with two tables of prices, one for four-sided pointed pegs made from birch wood, and the other for the broad-pointed ones of maple wood. At the head of each list was a description of the pegs and their prices, in both Reichsthaler and zloty per litre. I was amazed to see that the price of the broad ones was more than twice that of the pointed ones, for wheras the latter cost two roubles, the price of the former was five roubles. The merchant declared that he sold the broad ones throughout the country, whereas the four-sided ones sold only in Lithuania and Zamot. I became deeply upset, because it now seemed that I had laboured in vain for the past eight years, without knowing I was making something which was not needed anywhere except in the district where I was living, since it was close to the Prussian border across which the four-sided pegs were imported; furthermore, our cobblers were not concerned to improve their work, and so bought the cheapest they could obtain, namely the four-sided pegs. I tried to explain to the merchant that the four-sided pegs could be fixed firmly into the leather through a small hole, since they were pointed like an awl, whereas the broad ones would not hold firmly and would slow the cobbler's work. He merely replied that the cobbler was trained for his job and would not work slowly.

I left Riga and went to Petersburg, to Ephraim Finkelstein. He took me to a merchant shoe-maker who had his business in the glass arcade in Nevsky Street.[339] He confirmed that the broad pegs were in general use, and only few requests were made for the four-sided ones, as the former were made from hard maple wood which, although expensive, gave a stronger join, whereas the latter were made from soft birch wood which was cheap and therefore bought by cobblers who made a cheap job, like the cobblers in the village of Kimri, in the province of Tver in the district of Kasina, where all the inhabitants were cobblers. When I pointed out to him that the four-sided pegs could offer speedier work as they could be inserted into the hole quickly with an awl, he replied: ''That is true, but there is little profit from quick work, nor does it compare with the loss caused by the insecure fastenings of the four-side pegs. If the peg does not penetrate deeply enough into the shoe-leather, then only part of the point will sink into it. The broad peg will adhere tightly inside the hole since it is of equal thickness throughout its length. The four-sided peg, however, has a point which is thinner than the hole, and if it does not sink deeply into the leather, it will be left with only half its point in the leather, and will soon loosen and fall out under one's foot. That is why the best cobblers use only the broad ones.'' Had I known all this eight years ago before embarking upon the construction of the machine, I should not have made it. The inventors who live in provincial cities like Telz and Shavel are lost, for they toil like slaves for eight years and no one bothers to inform them of the facts known to everyone else in the rest of the country. Before beginning to work on a machine, I should have gone to a city like Riga, or Petersburg or Moscow, and made enquiries about it from the people who work in it. On the other hand, had I lived only in a large city, I would never have known about things needed in the provinces and which had not yet been made. To find something which does not yet exist, is an expensive matter. In those days, there was neither railway nor telegraph, so that every city was tightly enclosed, like Jericho.[340]

After this, I decided to make the four-sided pegs out of the hard, strong maple wood. Then I would be able to sell my products throughout the land for the same price as the broad-pointed ones. I looked around for partners in my invention. I was in the house of Ephraim Finkelstein, and Hartung was also there. He had been the source of all my hopes for the past two years. Having sympathy with me because of my poverty, he gave me fifteen roubles and said: "If you had come here twenty years ago, you would have found many customers for your invention. Today, however, hardly anyone will be interested." I then sat down and wrote, in Russian, a detailed account of the machine and the advantages that could be expected from it, and handed a copy to all those who were willing to seek clients for me in this big city. Finkelstein's oldest son, Zusman, also went looking on my behalf. He met the Graf Peter Kutuzov, a young man who had recently graduated in Law. He had inherited a large estate in the province of Tver, the district of Kasina, in the village of Shubina, which had vast forests of birch trees but not a single maple tree. The estate was poor, and the landowners were poverty-stricken and beset by creditors. The Graf thought he would set up the manufacture of the wooden pegs on his birch tree estate. Nearby, was the village of Kimri whose inhabitants were all cobblers. In this way, he hoped to improve the finances of the estate and pay off his creditors. He was willing to take me and my invention under his care. He had a close friend, a nobleman Ladizhinski, who had graduated at the same time as he. He described the machine to him, for the latter was familiar with technical matters. They sent for me, and I described the machine to them exactly as I had done to the Department. The nobleman reckoned that I had made an error in my calculations, and that the machine would produce one third more than I had calculated. This showed them that I was not a person to exaggerate or tell falsehoods. He also wished to take a share in the invention, with the Graf. They agreed on this.

Zusman Finkelstein, our middleman, told them that he was my relative, and that he had paid all the expenses for the production of this machine for the past eight years, and that we had agreed a long time ago to keep for ourselves forty per cent of the profits, twenty-five being for me and fifteen for him. Several days passed by. Each day they said: "Tomorrow we shall make an agreement." They went to the Department to ascertain whether a patent would be issued to me. One day Ladizhinski said to me that he had come across something new which would be very useful for my machine and would easily increase its productivity sevenfold.

He was not willing to inform me of his discovery because he wanted to obtain a patent for it for himself. He therefore wanted me to write a letter stating clearly that this discovery was not mine. He told me he would show me the invention after I had given him the letter disclaiming any entitlement to it. I gave him this reply: "Sir, a fortnight has elapsed since you agreed to become my partner. I am a poor man, and have a wife and six children. Yet you have not offered to help us even with so little as a penny. Now you make a strange request, but still you give me nothing. This is not right of you." My words embarrassed him, and he said: "If you will give me the document I want, I will give you fifty roubles." I replied: "Good. Now, write down your invention on paper, fold it and seal it. I shall make a written declaration on it, before witnesses, that whatever is written inside the letter does not belong to me, providing it has not been included in my application to the Department." "Very good," he agreed, and did as I proposed. We entered the shop inside the building, where he asked for witnesses to our agreement. However, the shopkeeper was afraid to put his signature to something he knew nothing about, and it was only after much persuasion that he and his assistant finally signed the letter. He gave me the fifty roubles, and I was greatly relieved. We then went to his room, where he showed me his notes. I saw that he had been mistaken in his basic concepts, like a man who knows the theory but not the practice. I pointed out his errors to him and, once he had understood what he had done, he threw the notes away in embarrassment. In the meantime, I found out that the nobelman Ladizhinski was in a worse financial position than the Graf. His inheritance had been administered by strangers until he had become of age, and now there was not a single tree left in his forests, and not a house on his estate. The two partners, he and the Graf, began to quarrel about the site of the factory, each wanting it in his own estate. I did not wish to be with Ladizhinski whom I distrusted, and perferred to be with the Graf who was an honest man — and that is how it turned out. We went to a notary and signed an agreement, giving 25% for me, 15% for Zusman and 60% for the Graf. I undertook to construct the machines for him at his expense. Afterwards, we went to the Department, where I submitted the patent in the names of all three of us. Then Finkelstein wanted to have control of the export and import side of the business as well as all the finances, with responsibility for making payments for everything and to everyone, including me. This did not seem right to me. I felt bound to inform the Graf of the true situation between Finkelstein and myself — that he was not a relative of mine, that he had not known anything about the machine before I had come to Petersburg, nor had he invested even one penny. The Graf was furious: "Why did you not tell me all this before we signed the agreement. Why have you delivered me into his hands?" I replied: "I was afraid to say anything before we had completed the agreement because, if you had known the truth, the man could have harmed me, and I should have lost you, too. You will surely appreciate that I cannot afford to lose a partner such as yourself." He was silent and, realising that I was being honest and sincere with him, he forgave me.

However, this brought upon me the wrath of the Finkelsteins, both father and son, so I left their house. The Graf loaned me a little money, and I rented a small room for myself. I wrote to my family, telling them to return to Vishevian, and to stay with their family there for the summer. After I had set up the machine, I would send for them and we would live on the Graf's estate. I brought over my oldest son, Judah Leib, to assist me.

Summer passed, and Autumn came, and the machine was completed. The Graf, on his part, had built a workshop on his estate, and also bought a steam engine for three hundred roubles. He sent for my wife and family, and Tsevi the carpenter who had helped me with my invention. I had promised Tsevi, at the time, to assist him with money so that he might divorce his barren wife, for whom he had lost all affection, and marry the girl Hinda, who lived with our family and with whom he had fallen in love when he was staying at my father-in-law's house. Now that the machine was finished, I fulfilled my promise to him and sent him money to divorce his wife. I also instructed my wife to bring the girl with her as well as our sons. They came, and we celebrated the wedding here in Petersburg, to the best of our means. We all went off together, including David the brother of Tsevi, to the village of Shubina on the Graf's estate. We arrived there after the festival of *Ḥanukkah*.

The place was situated in the heart of Russia, where no foot of Jew had ever trod before. Wherever we stopped on our journey, people came out to look at us. They were astonished to see that Jews did not have horns on their foreheads, or even have goat's feet. They said: ''Jews are human beings, too.''

Finally, we arrived at the Graf's estate. There were many broken-down houses there, and only the Graf's own house was still in good condition, standing inside a wooded park, with a locked gate. No one lived in it. There was a house nearby in which the estate manager lived. A house had been made ready for us; it was an old, broken-down building which had been repaired and made suitable for habitation. The workshop was also ready, with the saws for cutting the logs and the wooden mill-stones covered with leather bands for smoothing the pegs. We had bought our equipment in Petersburg, and now we set it out on wooden bases. Iron and copper had been brought from Tver and Kasina. In the village we found ironsmiths and carpenters. I supervised the workers and craftsmen. Although the cold was intense and lasted about two months, we had plenty of wood for heating. Our food was supplied by the estate manager at the Graf's expense. There was a German there who made Dutch cheeses, and gave us butter and milk, also at the Graf's expense for they were his cows. We baked our own bread. Kosher meat, however, could only be obtained from Tver. There was also the problem of a ritual bath for the women. We had built a pit in the new factory, with a deep channel leading to a pool which supplied water for the steam engine. We hoped to fill the well with hot water so that the women could use it as a legally fit ritual bath. Despite all our efforts to heat it with hot bricks and kettles of boiling water, hardly had the women disrobed than the water froze over again. It would have been fatal to immerse oneself even once. Tsevi's wife did not wish to bathe in the freezing water, as she had become pregnant.

Our days passed in peace and contentment until *Purim* came. Then the estate manager became hostile towards me, for he had expected that I would take him also as a partner in the business in return for all the favours he was affording us at the Graf's expense. I could not understand the reason for his antagonism, nor was I afraid of him. I wrote to the Graf explaining what was happening, and asked him to come down and confirm what I was doing. I was not aware that the Graf was in debt to his estate manager,[341] and therefore was not in a position to help me. I wanted to hire a good milch cow for our use, but the villagers were reluctant to hire their cows to Jews, knowing that we would not make the sign of the cross over it before milking it. One peasant, however, did pluck up the courage to hire his cow to us. We had everything, therefore, except money. The festival of Passover was approaching, when we would be unable to eat our normal food or even see it or keep it with us, since it was leavened.[342] To bring all the food and utensils required for the Passover from Tver would cost more money than we could afford. Moreover, the roads had become impassable, and no one could leave or enter. Even had we considered hiring a cart and two horses, it would have been beyond our means. We prepared to go hungry during the festival, and exist only on potatoes, milk and eggs. One morning, about a week before the festival, one of the farmers of Shubina came to us: he had brought us, on occasion, kosher meat from Tver. He was on his way to Tver, and asked us if we wanted any kosher meat. I told him: "This time we need not only a lot of meat, but also unleavened bread and fat and ritually slaughtered fowl. Unfortunately, I have not yet received any payment from the Graf, but if you will pay for all these out of your own pocket, you will earn your profit after you return." He agreed. I offered to give him a promissory note for the money. "I have no need of promissory notes," he declared. "But you must let me have the money back no later than one month after the festival, for at that time the payment for the lease on my land becomes due." He took Tsevi's wife on to his cart, and they left. They returned three days before the festival with everything except the meat — for a dispute which had arisen in Tver between the ritual slaughterer and the butcher had left the latter without meat. The butcher had promised, with many solemn oaths, to send meat to us in a day or two by special messenger. He had been a soldier in Nicholas' army,[343] and was a God-fearing man. He said: "How could I sin by permitting two families to celebrate the Passover without meat?" We believed him, and waited. The festival came and went, but there was no meat. We had goose-fat, unleavened bread, butter, cheese and milk. We began to feel the melancholy that comes over people who live in a foreign land. We were worried how we would celebrate the High Holy Days when they came. Where would we pray? If we went away for that period, it would need to be for two whole weeks, so whom could we trust to look after all our belongings?

And if, then, we were left with insufficient money, we would be lost indeed. . . .

Towards the close of the festival, I suffered discomfort from pains in my ribs, which I thought derived from the strange diet we had had to eat. Our despondency deepened. What were we to do in this awful wilderness, especially if the Graf would not, or could not, come to our aid and fulfil his promises? It was on the day after the festival, that I received a letter from the Graf saying that he had handed over the entire business to three partners and that from that day all affairs would be administered in the capital, Petersburg. Two of the partners were his relatives, Baron Kutuzov and Baron Karf. I would receive twenty-five roubles on the following day to pay for my journey to Petersburg in order to sign a new partnership agreement. After that, we would move with all our belongings to the capital. Heedless of the pain in my ribs, I climbed into the cart and left. For most of the journey, I was supporting myself with both hands in order to protect my aching ribs from the jolting of the cart. In Petersburg, I stayed in the Graf's residence for two weeks, during which time the two new partners dismissed Finkelstein whom they refused to have as their partner. They gave him one thousand roubles for his share. They said they would give me also one thousand roubles, for housing accommodation was more expensive in the capital than on the Graf's estate. However, I would be given the thousand roubles only after I had transported all the machines, at their expense, to Petersburg. The three of them signed a promissory note in my favour at the office of the Notary Ouspensky in Nevsky Street. It was there that we made an agreement concerning the new partnership, as well as the promissory note which was to be paid in a month's time. I had no desire to appear as a creditor to them, but I also knew that the first Graf was very poor, and therefore I was worried lest they give him all the money that was due to me before I returned from the village of Shubina. I therefore said to them: "Gentlemen, it is better that I do not take the note with me on my journey, in case it is lost. I shall therefore leave it here with the Notary." "Do as you wish." I set out on my journey hoping to return before Pentecost.

Summertime on the Graf's estate was a period of pleasure and peace. The fields were full of grain, and green vegetation flourished everywhere. Flowers and roses blossomed all around. There were ponds, both large and small, full of fish of every kind. With my pockets filled with provisions, I took my family out to the fields and woods for a stroll and to pick plants. We delighted in the pleasant peace brought by the gentle breeze that wafted over the hills. We went out every day. We noticed that one small lake had an abundance of fish in it, so we removed our clothes and waded into the water up to our chests, and caught the fish in little nets which we made out of our blouses. We spent our time so delightfully that I delayed my return to Petersburg until the day after the promissory note was due to be paid. I was sure that the Notary would not neglect to demand the thousand roubles. I loaded all the equipment on to carts, seated my wife and children together with Tsevi and his wife and brother in the wagons, and set off for Kortseva. There, we loaded everything on to a boat sailing along the Volga to Tver. From there, we took the train to Petersburg.

As soon as we arrived, I called upon the Baron, for he was the senior partner and managed all the affairs of the Company. He asked why I had tarried so long in coming. "You know, sir," I replied, "that I had to transport a thousand assorted pieces of equipment over a long and hard journey, in addition to all our personal belongings. I had to load them three times — from the wagons to the ship, and then on to the train." He was silent and then suddenly asked: "Have you been to see the Notary?" "No, sir, I have only just arrived." "Then you do not know about the thousand roubles?" "I know nothing at all. I have just finished the journey, and come immediately to you." The man was surprised, and said: "We have given the money to the Notary. You can get it from him." I said: "That is what I thought, for noblemen like yourselves would not deal falsely." He said: "Go now, and collect the money from the Notary." "I shall see him tomorrow." The following day, I went to the Notary who confirmed that he had the money. He ushered me into a room and said: "Wait here, and the money will be brought to you. You can then sign the receipt for it." I sat down feeling somewhat weak, for never before had anyone in my family possessed so large a fortune. One thousand roubles! It was enough to make me one of the wealthiest men in Telz!

There was a long table filling the width of the room. On both sides were crumpled, sloping covers embroidered with green braid. Over them was a short cover, smoothed straight. At the side of the table by the wall sat two clerks recording all the bills which had come into the office. On the other side, farther away from the wall, stood the people who had come to enquire about their accounts. I stood among them. One of the clerks called me by name, and said: "Here is your money. Count it and sign the receipt." I rose and began to count the money which had been piled into small denominations on the sloping part of the tablecloth. I counted the first bundle; it contained one hundred roubles — as did the second pile, and all the other bundles of notes. I then counted the number of bundles, and found only nine. My hands began to tremble. I thought I must have made a mistake, and that one bundle perhaps contained two hundred roubles instead of one. I began to count all over again from the beginning, very carefully so as not to err again: one, one and one, one and two.[344] The Notary Ouspensky was walking through the office from one room to another. He saw me standing and counting. He stopped and asked: "Well, is the money all there?" I replied: "I do not know yet." He went away without saying another word. I continued counting very carefully, and still found only the nine hundred roubles. One of the clerks looked up and, before I could say anything to him, said: "There is another bundle over here." I looked and saw another pile of notes, separated far from the other nine, not on the sloping side of the cloth but hidden by his hand, on top of the straight cloth. I put out my hand and drew the bundle toward me. I counted it and it contained a hundred roubles. I put all the notes into my wallet, signed the receipt and left. This is the sort of thing that happens. These people, Notaries included, are fully aware that a Jew fresh from the provinces, starving with hunger, his clothes threadbare and unable to speak the language, will not dare to lift his head or utter a syllable in the presence of the mighty noblemen in the Superior High Court in Nevsky Street. Therefore, though even pieces of wood should be counted in front of them as though they were a thousand roubles, they would be too overwhelmed to do otherwise than have confidence in the great lords, and would accept everything and sign their receipts. Once they had done that, even though they lamented loudly all day long, no one would heed them. The Notary, as he passed by me, had also been familiar with this stratagem — for they all know the same tricks — and had thought I would panic when he asked me about the money so that I would be too frightened to continue counting. Such is the behaviour of people who claim to be trustworthy, for a Notary is entirely dependent upon the trust and confidence of the people. There is an old saying which is very true: "Where there is a lamb, there will be many wolves."[345]

We rented half a factory on Vassily Island for smelting the metals and constructing the machines and for housing the 5-horse power steam engine. The landlord undertook to provide a partitioning wall for our half of the building and also a beam which revolved with all its wheels as the manufacture of our pegs required. We installed all our equipment in the building, and then hired smiths to work with Tsevi and his brother, whilst I supervised the completion of the parts of the machine which had not been finished in Shubina. Maple wood was delivered ready for cutting into pegs. By early autumn, the work was finished, the cutting machine was ready, and we began to make the pegs. Alas, an evil time came upon us! Trouble came from all directions. Firstly, the hard maple wood could not be split as straight as the soft birch wood, so that the pieces emerged sometimes thin and sometimes thick. The thick pieces, which were drawn along between two rollers before being cut into pegs, forced the upper roller to rise and thus caused the thin pegs either to come to a stop or to slow down to such an extent as to interfere with the cutting of the pegs. The machine which I had seen at Vishevian had permitted only two pieces of wood at a time to pass between the rollers, and if one roller rose out of position, the other remained in its place, so the wood continued to be carried along in the normal manner. However, this did not work in an operation involving twelve pieces at one time. I decided, therefore, to remove the upper roller and instead to depress each piece of wood down firmly with a strong, smooth spring, and to fix sharp studs in the lower roller to grip the pieces of wood and push them onwards. Then a further problem arose. The maple wood we kept in stock had come from old tree trunks and had been cut up a long time ago. The logs had been left lying in their barks. They had changed from a white to a reddish colour; the inside of the bark had rotted, and they were unsuitable for use. Even the white wood that was still in good condition turned as black as charcoal after it had been cut into pegs and laid aside to dry, so that it was unsuitable for sale.

My partners observed all these misadventures, and became despondent. I was greatly distressed. I told them we must make an earthenware stove which could be fired from below, and upon it we should place an iron cover which would be heated to a high temperature. On this cover, we would place a barrel-shaped container made of iron netting which would revolve continuously on its own axis. The damp pegs would be put into this immediately they emerged from the machine, and would then be rolled and spun round by the revolving net so that they would be thoroughly dried before they could become blackened by the acidity of the atmosphere. I had already proved this by experiment with some damp, white pegs which I had placed on an iron tray over a fire: they had dried quickly and turned as white as snow. My partners would not listen to me, for they had lost confidence in me. They did, however, hire a stove-maker to set up a large stove in the factory. They then spread out the pegs for drying along wall-shelves fixed in three tiers. I protested at this: "Gentlemen, I shall not prevent you from doing what you wish to do, but you ought to know that you are wasting both your time and your money, and you will eventually have to change your mind about this. If you do as I suggest, everything will be all right." They finally deferred to my wishes. I explained to the stove-maker the way I wanted him to fit the stove. I cast and moulded a thick iron cover which I placed upon the stove. Over this, I placed the network barrel-sieve which was kept revolving by a leather band attached to the steam engine.

During this time, whilst the manufacture of the pegs had come to a stop, I began to make broad-pointed pegs. I placed small boxes under the machine to collect the split pieces of wood. The machine cut the pieces into broad-pointed pegs. I found that I could produce many times more pegs of this kind than the four-sided ones, for to every twelve produced of the square-pointed pegs in one operation I could now get one hundred and twenty broad ones in a single operation — and they were the kind of products merchants would buy. The cobblers and merchants, from their experience with the broad-pointed pegs, would not doubt the quality of my products, seeing that they were white and made from maple wood, and therefore they would buy them without question. However, they would be doubtful about the four-sided ones and query whether they were made from maple wood and who made them — for they had not seen their like before. My noble associates knew nothing of what was going on, so when they observed that I was making broad pegs I simply told them that I was carrying out some tests. After I had produced a number of these broad pegs, I stopped, for I found it quite easy to produce as many as I wished in quantity: they were quickly placed, whilst still damp, into the heated barrel to keep their whiteness, and thence passed between wooden millstones which cleaned and smoothed their surfaces, so that they emerged like dry bones, white, smooth and hard. They were very good merchandise. I then made a net-sieve for winnowing the pegs. This consisted of three nets, one above the other, all rocking like a cradle and held over a large box. The uppermost net had wide spaces which retained only the thickest unserviceable pegs; the middle sieve retained those which were thinner but were not of the correct thickness; the third sieve winnowed out the very thin pegs and the badly cut ones which were unsuitable for any purpose. After I had prepared many sacks of pegs of different sizes, suitable for the market, my partners came and were delighted. They sent for a prominent merchant who dealt in these goods abroad. He examined my work, saw that the goods were excellent, and offered to buy all our produce at a price of five roubles per *pud* on condition that we sold everything we made solely to him. However, since we did not know the price of the wood, which we had bought only in small quantity, or the cost of its transport over any distance, whether by train or by boat in summer, or how many dry pegs could be manufactured, weight for weight, from the damp wood which we would have to purchase, or even the cost of the labour involved, therefore we could not come to an agreement with the merchant, for we were unable to decide on a price.

Then the Baron tried to interest certain army officers in our pegs: these officers worked in the Quartermaster's department responsible for the supply of trousers to the army. It so happened that a supply of pegs had just arrived at their stores from peg-factories in Berlin and Moscow. Three tests were carried out, on the same day. It was decided that the best product came from our factory, the second from Berlin and the last from Moscow. The lease agreement with the factory on Vassily Island now came to an end, so my partners decided to rent a larger factory and install in it a steam engine, which the Graf had bought and was capable of giving eight horse-power, together with all its equipment, and also steam-pipes for heating the building during the winter. We rented a three-storey building: the top floor was occupied by myself and my family, and the manager they were thinking of appointing; the second floor contained the peg-making machines; and the bottom floor the steam engine and machines for cutting logs and for drying. We moved into the new building. Meanwhile, my partners' money had so dwindled away that they could hardly pay for my family's expenses. They appointed my son Judah Leib as my assistant, with authority over the employees, and I was able to add his wages to my own, although even this was not sufficient for our needs. I therefore began to sell the pegs which had already been manufactured, and keep the proceeds for myself, but I gave my partners an account of all the sales, and they were satisfied.

The manager appointed by the Baron arrived. He was a Russian, in every sense of the word. I transferred to him the keys of the warehouse where we kept the sacks of pegs and the wood. From that day, I noticed a decrease in the allocation of funds for my expenses. Furthermore, my son Leib was dismissed on unfounded pretexts. I then realised that the noblemen had begun to consider me redundant, since the factory was fully prepared for production, and there was no need for any further inventions to perfect the operation. They considered various stratagems to remove me and to replace me with the carpenter Tsevi, my assistant. They were not satisfied with the contract of agreement we had made, so they decided to stop giving me my living expenses, which had not been included in the contract, and thus to compel me to leave them. I said to them: ''Gentlemen, you still have a long way to go before you will be able to produce saleable pegs without me, for I have many ideas for improving the process of manufacture of the product. Not all the pegs come out equal in dimension and thickness, as the cutting machine suffers from constant friction. I therefore made spiral frames in which to set the stand holding the cutter in its place according to the required width. The peasant who operates the machine cannot possible tell, by simply looking at the pegs as they are manufactured, whether they are a hair's breadth thicker than they should be. It therefore becomes a matter of conjecture as to whether the pegs are suitable or not. I have, however, made a circular gauge with a hundred numbered divisions on it: you will find it in your manager's locker. You will see that this provides us with an accurate measurement, and can be easily used by the peasant working the cutting machine to measure the dimension of any peg which he may remove, from time to time, from the machine. The long pointer from the centre to an arc on the circumference will show the thickness of the peg to half a hair's breadth — and other things which I cannot go into at this moment. You can prove this for yourselves.'' They, however, did not understand what I was telling them, for they laughed when I mentioned the name of the gauge, Micrometer, a fine-divider. They continued to ignore me, so I said: ''If you are going to treat me in this manner, and refuse to give me money for living expenses, I shall abandon the entire project, and shall return to clock-making for my livelihood, in this city. I must warn you, gentleman, that you are bound to fail, and the production of the pegs will cease.'' They paid no attention to me, but declared they would revoke the conditions of the contract.

Intending to take no further part in the affairs of the factory, I left and rented a room with a display-window in Vozhiesenski Street. I arranged for my son Simon Aaron to stay there to accept any clocks that were brought in for repair. Each morning I left my lodgings and spent the whole day with him until the evening. Some days later, they approached me concerning the contract of agreement. I told them: ''Gentlemen, if you will not adhere to the terms of the agreement, I shall leave the Company, for I see that you wish to do me harm. Therefore, pay me twenty-five thousand roubles for my twenty-five shares.'' About a month later, the Baron saw me in the street and stopped to ask me when I would alter the terms of the agreement. I told him I would do so on the day I received the twenty-five thousand roubles. He said: ''Indeed? So, in the beginning, we must make you a wealthy man, and then afterwards . . . ?'' I replied: ''Did the Baron intend, from the outset, to make me a poor man? The agreement itself states that you are to make me wealthy out of your own pockets.'' He remained silent.

At that time, I began to consider inventing a machine for making papiros-papers.[346] In fact, during the time when I and my family had stayed at the Graf's house in Petersburg, before we had left for his estate, I had been considering two inventions at the same time. One was a typewriter,[347] and the other a machine for making wrappers for tobacco strands. I decided to work on the latter idea: I had actually carried out some experiments on this whilst in Shubina, with the help of my son Leib. I was now without employment, for Tsevi had been given my post with an assistant, a Russian metalworker, who had previously been my assistant for about a year. I realized that the peg business had come to an end, for even if they were to change their minds, it would be too late. I asked myself: "Why lose the ship for a ha'porth of tar?" Let them agree to pay me one thousand roubles, and I shall leave the Company. However, in order to expedite the matter, I shall tell them that, even after I have left, I shall still be willing to work for them for a monthly salary. They know I am honest, and will trust me. Furthermore, if they do not have a thousand roubles to pay me that same day, I shall accept a promissory note signed by all three of them for the money to be paid over a period of four months; they will pay me fifty roubles every month until the amount has been paid in full.[348] With the thousand roubles, I would set up a small clockmaker's business and workshop, and also prepare the tobacco-strand machine. I therefore wrote to the noblemen outlining my proposals. On the morrow, I received instructions to see them and conclude the deal. When we were all together, they asked whether, in fact, I would be willing to remain in their employ. "Yes, indeed." "At what salary?" "We can discuss that later." They handed me a note for the thousand roubles to be paid over four months, and a second note for the payment of fifty roubles per month. I signed a cancellation of my agreement. So great was their joy that they played a new tune on the *Sheminit*,[349] a Psalm of Thanksgiving. I left unscathed.

At that time, I returned to my invention of a papiros-paper machine. I made an undertaking with Leib, my son, that if he would invest the remainder of his money, about thirty roubles, toward the cost of the machine, and would carry out all the work exactly as I showed him, then he would be entitled to one-third of the profits made from the machine. I rented a shop facing on to Yekateringev Street, and also lodgings for myself elsewhere. All three of us stayed in the shop all day long: Simon Aaron attended to his clock repairs, whilst my son, Leib, and I built the machine. As with all inventions, the work was very difficult. A process over which I may have toiled an entire month, I would discard in one day if I thought it unsatisfactory. We would then have to start again from a different approach. So it went on, without our knowing in advance what any particular process might produce. It is only after a job is completed that one learns, from experience, what errors lay in the original concept of the project. Such is the lot of all inventors everywhere, for experiment is of supreme importance in all matters involving technical construction; it is superior even to our intellect which first presents the idea to our imagination and inner vision. Once a device has passed the test of experiment and trial, people pay it scant regard. An inventor, however, will always note, with due care and consideration, the problems which accompany the gradual development and completion of a task — and will give little credence to the promptings of his own inner vision when it depicts a particular end-result before that result has been made manifest to human sight. There are, of course, exceptions. An ignorant peasant will see in his imagination the work he wishes to perform, and experience will prove him right. Therefore, should a Professor of Applied Physics in the Academy of Sciences in Paris declare that whatever is seen with the inner vision will always be manifested in practice, he will be speaking falsely — and he must surely be aware that there is no truth in his words from the outset, unless of course he is making a palpable error. If he refuses to believe you, then demonstrate by example so that he may see and be silent. Take, for instance, the spinning wheel, a simple machine which has been in every farmer's croft for a hundred years or more. Let him try to make a machine like it. Let him observe the farmer's wife turn the wheel by pressing her feet on the bar, whilst holding the spindle with her hands — and all the time the thread winds apparently endlessly round the bobbin. If he does not examine that machine minutely, then he will spend years trying to duplicate it, and without success. Therefore, any man who seeks to produce a completely new technical device, must be willing to exercise the greatest fortitude and suffer many tribulations before achieving his aim. I myself suffered innumerable tribulations for two continuous years before I achieved my goal and finally constructed a machine, not for the actual production of papiros-papers, but to prove experimentally that it could be built by a particular method. If proper machines were constructed according to the laws of mechanics, so that even the smallest process functioned correctly and dependably, then their performance would far surpass, in speed and precision, anything done by human agency.

Our money came to an end; even the thousand roubles vanished. I was reduced to poverty. I began to look for a new partner. I kept in mind the principle of the old saying: "Despise not your fellow man, nor dismiss any matter lightly."[350] There was a man who often came to my workshop: he was utterly useless, but I described my invention to him so that he might go and look for a partner for me. He had a friend who was more capable than he, and he brought him to see me. This friend brought along a friend of his, a Pole, who was blind in both eyes. He told me that he know certain distinguished people who would go into partnership with me, providing I could show them the machine in operation and producing good papers continuously, either in large or small quantity. Now, this was the first machine of its kind which had been built by me and my son Leib, who was not trained for this kind of work. It was excellent in concept but faulty in design and practice. I decided to improve it and strengthen it. Days passed, and the man came every other day to learn how the machine was developing. He had a friend, a Russian named Tutorski, whom brought to see me. This man had no profession: he had been formerly an officer in the Debtor's Prison, but had been removed from his post. The day after his visit, Tutorski came to see me alone, and said: "I am prepared to take a share in your invention. However, I have no desire to support this Pole so, if you are willing, let us make a partnership without his knowledge." I agreed, for I had given no undertakings to the Pole. The following day he brought along an expert technician to examine the machine and advise him whether he could build one properly according to the laws of mechanics that would work as well as I had promised, and how much he might charge. The technician declared that it was a good machine, and that if he were paid three hundred roubles for his services, he would construct a strong machine which would give long service. The man then said to me: "Look, I am not very wealthy. I can afford to invest about five thousand roubles but only in order to put the machine into good working order. After that, it will be possible to find any number of partners wealthier than I who will be willing to invest substantial funds to finance the production of the papers. Therefore, instead of your asking five hundred roubles for yourself plus one hundred roubles per month for the half share you will give me, I will give you two thousands roubles plus one hundred roubles per month for two-thirds of the entire business, or sixty-six and two-thirds per cent, leaving one third for yourself. Of my share, I shall give half — namely, one third of the whole — to the investor who is prepared to invest most in the business. Then I, with my small investment, shall have one third, and he will have one third in return for his substantial investment, and you will have the remaining third." I did not hesitate for one moment. We prepared the contract between us. Days passed, without the agreement being finalised. It contained a clause stating that, on the day the contract was signed before a Notary, he would hand me five hundred roubles for my salary for the first month. He would then instruct the technician to construct the machine and to prepare specifications for the Department in order to obtain a patent for ten years on both our names, for a fee of four hundred and fifty roubles. He would also purchase a long roll of papiros paper for converting into papiros-wrappers. When, finally, the technician had constructed the machine and it was working properly and *without fault*, he would pay me the balance outstanding of fifteen hundred roubles. I considered the words "without fault" to be most disturbing, for the man could use them as an excuse not to pay me even a single rouble if only one papiros-wrapper was faulty. Nevertheless, I said not a word, for I was exceedingly poor, and this business was a salvation to me, with the five hundred roubles in cash and the one hundred roubles per month for the whole year; and if the business prospered, then I would receive also one third of the profits. Therefore, I did not object to those two words, lest he think that I had no confidence in the efficiency of the machine. He, meanwhile, was bent on a scheme for not investing any money at all. He searched through the city from morning to evening for a partner who would be willing to invest money in advance for a third share, and also pay towards my monthly salary — for he was hoping to obtain his own third share through verbal investment alone. For this reason, he delayed the completion of our agreement, leaving it at the Notary's untouched. Every day he brought new people to the workshop to view the machine.

I was at a loss to understand what he wanted. One Friday, whilst his younger brother was with me in the workshop — he had told him to be there in order to watch over my actions — a finely dressed man arrived in his own horse and carriage to enquire about the machine. I told him that it was a new invention and I had not yet submitted an application for a patent to the Department, and therefore was unable to show it in detail to anyone who was unknown to me. However, I could show how the machine drew the paper inside it and produced correct and good papiros-papers. "This is all I wish to see," he said. I covered the machine as the man sat down beside it. I rotated the centre roll, and three papirosi-papers came out. The man picked them up, inspected them, cut them and squeezed them to see the inner glued portion. He said: "That is enough for me." He asked further: "Do you have a partner for your invention?" "Not yet." "Then what is the man Tutorski to you?" "He is an imaginary partner." "What do you mean by an imaginary partner?" "Simply that so long as I have not signed the agreement that is lying on the Notary's table and have not received a penny from him, then he is no more to me than an imaginary partner, and is not a partner in fact." "In that case, you can take any partner you wish?" "That is true, Sir." "Then why did the man Tutorski tell me that he is your partner, and ask me to finance him too?" "I do not know." "Well, know this. I am Bogdanov, and I am head of the firm of papiros manufacturers Bogdanov *et Comp*.[351] Here is my address. Come to my factory tomorrow at noon, and we shall discuss this matter seriously." I took his address and promised to be there. He left. The young brother of Tutorski, who had witnessed all that had happened but had said nothing, also left after him. An hour later, he returned and said: "My brother is not well today, and cannot leave the house. He therefore told me to ask you whether you would go to the Notary today to sign the agreement, if you were requested to do so?" "Gladly." He ran off swiftly. A half-hour later he returned, and said: "My brother is ill and cannot go the Notary's to sign. Will you come with me instead and sign the agreement, and I will give you the promised six hundred roubles. My brother will sign his name tomorrow when he is able to get up." "I will certainly go with you. However, I wish to make one slight alteration to the wording of the agreement. I wish to replace the words 'without fault' with the words 'producing good and proper papers'." "But why do you have to alter the wording of the contract? It is written on expensive paper." "No, sir. If the two words are not changed, I shall not sign. This is my final decision." He departed in a hurry, and returned quickly. He showed me a roll of money which he drew from his pocket. We left together.

By the time we reached the Notary's evening had drawn on. He entered the Notary's office ahead of me, whilst I remained in the clerk's office. Suddenly the Notary came out, strode up to me and thundered at me haughtily for refusing to sign, since it was all the same whether the words "good and proper" or "without fault" were used. At first, I requested respectfully, and without raising my voice, that he carry out my wishes and alter the words. When, however, he continued to pour scorn and wrath upon me, I arose from my chair and said to Tutorski: "I have noticed that, further down the street, there is another Notary. Let us go to him, and he will write the agreement in the way that we want.'' The Notary then realised his mistake, that I was not a contemptible Jew who was ignorant of the Russian language, so he took the contract, erased two whole lines, and inserted what I had requested. I read it and found it to be what I wanted. I signed it, collected the six hundred roubles, and left.

There is one rule I have always stood by, whatever the circumstance, and that is: do not throw out dirty water until you have clean water.[352] The man Bogdanov was a hundred times more preferable as a partner than the impecunious Tutorski, who, as I had seen from the very beginning, was not only poor and had no more than five thousand roubles — which he himself admitted — and would doubtless even try to deceive me over that amount, but had also delayed signing the agreement because he was looking for a partner who would support both the business and himself. If Bogdanov had not come to see me, who knows how long he would have continued to delay the matter? Even with regard to the two words to which I objected, it seemed that he had tried to find ways of delaying the fulfilment of my request. Bogdanov, on the other hand, was not only very wealthy, but he also had a large factory for the manufacture of papirosi. For him, it would be no problem to improve the quality of my machine until it produced the finest results: he had expressed this desire when he had visited me and had seen my imperfect machine. Nevertheless, when Tutorski came carrying his dirty water but also the money which he was prepared to give me that same day, I closed my mind to all the wonderful visions presented by the possible partnership with Bogdanov, and instead went through with Tutorski's contract. I regretted it later. However, I abided by my rule — which I follow to this day.

I now left the clockmaker's shop in Simon Aaron's care. I prepared the tools in my lodgings. The draughtsman sent by Tutorski stayed all day preparing lists and diagrams for the Department, and also moulds for the smelter. I altered certain parts of the machine to improve and strengthen it, so that it would work satisfactor- ily for a long time by means of steam power. Afterwards, I went to see the technician every day to supervise the construction of the machine. He set a place aside specially for me and the craftsman mechanic where we could continue our work. Meanwhile, Tutorski went about the city looking for partners willing to accept the business in its entirety. There were men who were willing to give him twenty-five thousand roubles for half for his share of the business — namely, one third of the whole — but he was arrogant and demanded fifty thousand. He did not ask my advice for he considered he had purchased the entire business and therefore could conduct all the transactions by himself. He was not aware of the rule which I followed, and so his negotiations came to nothing. Some nine months passed by, during which I worked on perfecting the machine. I also took the mechanic away from the technician to help me finish the machine. Finally it produced many good quality papers.

Tutorski tried daily to bring partners to see the machine, but without success. He brought in an Englishman named Dobbie, a qualified engineer who had built iron carriages to replace wooden railway carriages. When he saw me turn the centre axle of the machine by hand and produce quickly good quality papers, he came and embraced me. I thought he must be mad, for I had no idea who he was. His words confirmed my impression that he had lost his senses after seeing the machine in operation. This Englishman then began to look around for partners in the machine. He found an Englishman, named Laughton, who introduced Baranov. Both of them took over Tutorski's share — namely one third of the business — and gave him back the five thousand which he had paid of his own pocket, according to his own calculation. They agreed to pay me three hundred roubles per month to enable me to invent a similar machine which would produce complete papirosi filled with tobacco and having paper mouthpieces. We agreed to set up a company to be called *Firma Izobrietatel, Inventor*.[353] Tutorski took his five thousand roubles and ran out of the Notary's office, and hid himself, for he did not wish to pay me the three hundred roubles he owed me. I went to his house and told him that he was behaving dishonestly and that he would be harming himself by making it seem that I was his enemy. He refused to listen to me. I considered the situation was not good, for the man had presented me to the new partners as a failure in everything except the invention of machines, whereas he was a diligent and smart businessman. For that reason he had been appointed treasurer in charge of all expenses for the construction of the machines. I even received my monthly salary through him. Some days later, I went to see Baranov, at the usual hour of the afternoon when he was at home. He was not, however, at home, so I pencilled a note for him in Russian: "Because you told me, at the outset, that any time that I needed to see you, I should call at one o'clock in the afternoon, I called today for the very first time, and have not found you in. Since my time is limited, kindly let me know when I should call again to see you." I left the note on his table. He sent word that I should call the next day. I went, and he asked: "Is this your handwriting? How could Tutorski deceive me by presenting you as an incompetent person, untutored and ignorant of the Russian language? I see now that he is the failure, as he was formerly no more than a servant, a policeman in the Petersburg police force.[354] I can no longer be partner to the agreement I made with him, by which he and I would be in full control of the whole business, and all transactions could be carried out only with our joint signatures." His words alarmed me, for I was deeply concerned lest Baranov turn against Tutorski and sever the bond that united us, since he alone was the pillar which supported the Company. He was a wealthy man, respected and honoured, honest and sincere. There was no one else beside him — for even the Englishman Laughton was a poor man who had had to borrow his share of the investment by devious means. Tutorski himself was impecunious. I therefore decided to speak in favour of Tutorski. I told him that Tutorski had originally entered the police force to serve as a policeman for a short period, for the Tsar had decreed that anyone who wished to attain senior rank in the police force must first serve a short period in the city police. Concerning his honesty, I knew that during the period that he and I were the only ones in the business, he had behaved honestly, except for the deceitfulness he had displayed in the Notary's office when he had received his five thousand roubles but had refused to pay me the three hundred he owed me, and had fled. Baranov then agreed to put the expenses funds under my authority, whilst I would sent him a written account every month. As for Tutorski, he would have no further dealings with him, for he hated him.

I engaged a second mechanic, a locksmith, and also bought a variety of good tools, and began to build a machine for making complete papirosi. I hired a qualified mechanic to construct, at Baranov's request, six machines for making papiros-papers. I knew this mechanic, Beilstein; he had studied at the Berlin Academy, and I had seen his work in optics and physics. He compiled lists and diagrams for the machines, and also wooden moulds, and melted the iron and copper for the six machines. A month passed by, and I noticed that he was building the machines without any proper idea of what to do, for he was not smoothing and straightening the surfaces of the smelted iron, which was the base of the entire machine. The surface was pitted with depressions and bulges, to which he was fixing the uprights and the posts by means of thin screws. I told him that this was not the way to do it, but he merely remarked that the financial budget for the machines was inadequate. I wanted to inform Baranov that he was ruining the machines, but it was at that particular time that Baranov informed me of his decision not to continue his partnership with Tutorski and that he was determined to sever all connection with him. He was annoyed, furthermore, with his other partner, Laughton, for not having redeemed his share of the investment. If, therefore, I went and reported to him the mechanic's bad workmanship, he would abandon the business altogether. My one good machine which had produced such remarkably good results with papiros-papers, had been taken from me by the mechanic and destroyed, for he had learned how to make one similar to it. Now, if Baranov should desert me, and I was left without a single machine to display to clients, who would come to my aid and help me to build another? I suppressed my anguish, bit my lips, and said nothing. I believed I could speed up the construction of the first of the six machines and find ways of making it operate satisfactorily, so that I should have something to show, whatever else might happen. I began to spend entire days at the factory with the technician, bending all my efforts to the speedy completion of the first machine. Some five months passed by, and the man Laughton had not yet paid in his share; also, Baranov began to pay me only half of my monthly salary, leaving the other hundred and fifty roubles outstanding. Baranov called a meeting of all the partners, including the man he had appointed to represent him in the management of the business: he was a man he had commissioned to investigate all our affairs and to submit a true accounting of our funds, for some four thousand roubles of his money had passed through my hands. He himself would never have been able to make a complete audit, for his time was taken up with his new business, the laying of tram-rails in the capital.[355] Now, the technician had admitted to this Director that the machines were not working properly, and had actually accused me of being responsible for it. I, however, knew nothing of all this. When, therefore, we had assembled, Laughton announced that there was no money left. The technician complained that the machines were unsuccessful. Tutorski kept silent. The hired manager submitted a false report. Then Baranov turned upon me angrily. I told him: "If you do not have the time, Sir, to look after the business, you would be better advised to abandon it. Money alone will not bring the business the success which diligent hands will." He replied: "You are a Jew, and you are familiar with the fundamental principle of your belief, that what is hateful to you, you shall not do to your fellow-man.[356] You have advised me to leave, but who is going to give me back my money?" We departed after the technician said that, in fact, the machine would work satisfactorily if a further hundred and fifty roubles per machine were added to the original fee promised him, which was little enough. It was then that Baranov saw that the blame did not lie on me.

The following day, I called upon Baranov and found him at home, alone. I said: "Sir, this time I have come to offer you my apologies and to confess to you all the wrongs and errors I have committed since the time that I began this business." He sat down in a chair, and listened silently. I laid the whole truth before him. He then said: "If what you say is true, then you obviously knew that the technician was ruining the machines, so why did you not inform me?" I replied: "You will recall what you told me some time ago, just after the technician had been engaged, that you no longer wished to be connected with the policeman Tutorski, and that you also detested Laughton. How could I add fuel to the fire? Had I informed you of the technician's bad workmanship, you would have thrown me and my invention into the street. Then what would I have been left with? Even the machine which gave such outstanding results was broken to pieces by the expert. That is why I was silent. I thought I would continue with my toil and labour until I completed the first machine. Then, if I should be cast out like an abhorred offshoot,[357] some other person would be able to see the machine in operation and would agree to support me." The man was silent. He realised that I had spoken honestly, and that my innocence was plain to see. He ordered that all the six machines be taken out of the hands of the technician and returned to me. He said he would continue to pay the wages of the workers as well as my monthly salary until I had finished all the machines. I went to the technician and took the machines from him: three were complete with all their parts, and the other three only half built. I set to work to get the first three fully operational. Baranov paid for all the expenses, although reluctantly, for he had made up his mind to abandon the entire business; it was only out of compassion for me that he paid for the construction of the four machines which I had promised to complete. I intended to open a workshop where I could operate the four machines by means of a flywheel, and produce a hundred-thousand papiros-papers per day. This would provide a living for my family and myself. I requested him to fulfil the conditions in the contract of agreement requiring him to deposit some seven thousand roubles towards his share. He did so. The machines were finally completed. All four were activated by a flywheel which could be operated by one man. The machines prepared the papiros-papers and piled them neatly into separate piles of one hundred each, ready for sale to the merchants. I hired workmen and girls to set up the piles of hundreds. I also gave an order to a lithographer to print labels for gluing on to each hundred: they were very pretty, in gilt, and bore the name of the firm. Work commenced. I had prepared about a hundred thousand when my funds ran out. Baranov had completed his payments, as I had requested, so I wrote him a receipt for his entire share of the investment as per the agreement. Laughton had already been dismissed from the Company. Now I could sell the hundred thousand papers I had made and with the proceeds produce more. Alas, I could find no customers! Shopkeepers do not welcome newcomers who want to manufacture their goods, for they always fear that an expansion of the industry could lead to a fall in prices and therefore of profits. In this case, they all claimed that the paper rolls bought by Tutorski, and which weighed 8 *puds,* were too thick and heavy, and would emit smoke trails like an incinerator and were completely unsuitable. Our work came to a stop. Baranov became elected as head of the new horse-drawn tramway company. Since there was a regulation stipulating that no man could be the head of two Companies at the same time, he sent for Tutorski and me and asked to be released from his agreement. I gave him something he had not requested — a promissory note for five thousand roubles which I had undertaken to pay him once the papiros-papers business was functioning successfully.

It came to my notice at that time that no instruments existed for use in distilleries which were able to register accurately the amount of alcoholic spirits, in litres, their degree of proof and the excise payable on them.[358] Spirits, namely *aqua vitae* in its original form is one hundred percent proof and has no water content at all. Gradually, however, it loses its strength and the volume of water increases in it until finally the spirits content reduces to nil, and it becomes completely water. This is the opposite end of the hundred degree proof. It is no easy matter to invent an instrument which will show the degree of proof strength of every litre which issues from the vats of a distillery and the amount of water it contains; there is no duty on water, only on spirits. I also discovered that learned chemists had declared that instruments for measuring the degree of proof of alcohol should not contain an iron spring and should not vary from the true reading by more than one degree in a hundred. Many people had tried to make measuring instruments to this standard, but to no avail. If, therefore, a man did invent an accurate instrument for this purpose, he would reap a rich reward from the Government. Theft and smuggling from distilleries were commonplace, for it was impossible to appoint permanent excise officers to inspect distilleries day and night, without relaxing vigilance even for a moment. The system in use at the time was that of Siemens and Halske:[359] it had been approved and authorised by the Government but did not satisfy all their requirements, for the instrument only showed the number of litres which flowed through the vats' pipes, whilst to determine the degree of proof of the alcohol recourse had to be made to the Tralles measure.[360] In the vat was a measured litre: when this became full, it emptied into another and larger vessel, and at the same time a small amount of it was spilled out into a small container. Gradually, this small container filled with small amounts from every litre of spirit produced by the distillery. Whenever the excise-officer, who had charge of the key to the small container and also the seal, came to open it, he would insert the Tralles measure and read the degree of proof. In this way, he was able to measure the amount of spirits in the small container and calculate the number of litres in the large container as well as the degree of proof. However, even this was not accurate, because the proof strength escaped constantly from the small container which had to be kept open in order to receive the small amount of liquid which flowed into it, thereby reducing the degree of proof. If then the Tralles reading of the small container showed a reduction of even a fraction of one degree, this reading would be shown as a considerable increase in the large containers, and thereby cause a loss of revenue to the Government. For this reason, new measuring instruments were constantly being sought.

For my purpose, I followed the basic principle in physics concerning the attraction that exists between atomic particles in liquids, where the strength of this attraction varies according to the density of the liquid: atomic particles of water are attracted to each other by a force of one hundred degrees, and those of alcohol by eighty degrees. It seemed to me that alcohol would be able to reject any substance clinging to its surface with only one fifth of the force that would be required were it clinging to the surface of water. I decided to prepare a small vessel for containing the liquid which flowed from the vat. As this vessel filled and brimmed over, the liquid in the small vessel would be constantly changed by the fresh liquid which flowed into it. A thin wooden rod, pierced with many holes or hollow tubes, would float on the surface of the liquid: the rod would be attached to one end of one arm of the crossbar of a pair of scales. If a light weight were suspended from the other arm of the scales, equivalent in weight to the force of attraction exerted by the atomic particles of the liquid in the hollow tubes upon the atomic particles on the surface of the water in the small vessel, then the crossbar of the scales would remain balanced, for the weight exerted upon one arm would be equivalent to force of attraction of the atomic particles on the other arm. If however the weight were increased a little, then the force of gravity would become greater than the force of attraction of the atomic particles, and the rod would rise up and the weight on the arm would lower. If the volume of water in the small receptacle increased over that of the alcohol in the liquid, the rod would rise only gradually; if the volume of alcohol increased over that of the water, it would rise quickly. When then another, smaller vessel containing only one sixtieth of a litre is placed under the vat of liquid, and balanced in such a manner that, when fresh liquid overflows its brim, it will lose its level balance and incline to one side, for the overflowing liquid will draw it sideways. Thus it will teeter from one side to the other whilst being filled up. Under the rim, a small, narrow hole will allow the liquid to flow through slowly, so that the vessel remains in an inclined position until the liquid spills over and it is pulled in the direction of the first incline: another narrow hole underneath it will keep it in that position until it is filled again by liquid and is again drawn to the other side. Thus it will move from side to side at equal intervals. If however it inclines over beyond the point of balance, it will rest against the arm of the crossbar of the scales and, with its weight added to the force of gravity, will repel the atomic particles adhering between the rod and the surface of the liquid on the other arm, and will raise it. If the liquid is water without any alcohol content, the rod will rise slowly, for the force of attraction of each particle is greater and therefore prevents the arm moving until more liquid is poured and flows over the brim, depressing the arm with the weights in opposition to the arm with the rod. If the volume of alcohol surpasses the volume of water, the force of attraction of the particles is reduced, and the rod rises quickly to the surface of the liquid. A peg attached to the fulcrum of the crossbar of the scales and the vessel at its side, activates toothed wheels which indicate on a graduated dial the number of movements and oscillations. The number registered by the movement of the scales indicate the number of times the rod has been raised over the surface of the liquid during the period that the vessel moved to one side and spilt out liquid to the quantity of one litre. The greater number of movements of the crossbar per litre, the higher the degree of alcohol proof; conversely, the fewer the movements of the crossbar, the greater the volume of water in the liquid. It could be possible to make brass keys locking the vessel of liquid when the crossbar and vessel are inclined to one side, and for opening them when inclined to the other. This, then, was my idea — though it was never put into practice.

Before I began to construct the proof-measuring instrument, I tried an experiment to test the strength of adhesion existing between the liquid particles as compared with that of the alcohol particles, and their reading in degrees Tralles. I made a very sensitive balance; suspended from one arm was a hollow brass rod, about two square inches, with hollow tubes along its length and breadth which contacted the surface of the water in the vessel. Into this water, I poured measured quantities of strong alcoholic liquid in accordance with the Tralles measure and to certain degrees of heat. To the end of the other arm I attached a thin, perforated wire of polished brass which was contained inside an open-ended, hollow tube. To the end of the wire, I attached a bar which projected from its right-hand side and pressed upon the crossbar of the other arm against the rod. When the end of the wire-thread was twisted round, it would turn the bar and depress the arm of the crossbar causing it to descend, whilst the other end, with the rod, will rise up above the surface of the water, and break up the adhering particles of water. In order to calculate the force that twined the brass thread according to a hundred degree scale, comparable to the Tralles, I attached to the end of the brass thread a pointer which indicated the numbers on a semi-circle divided into one hundred segments. Turning the pointer round the dial in increasing number, tightened the wire so that one end exerted greater pressure upon the crossbar. The numbered dial would show the degree of alcoholic proof in the water: when the proof of the liquid is low, the numbers on the table increase, the thread becomes entwined more tightly and lowers the arm of the scales, thereby raising the rod; when the proof is high, and the water less, then the pointer will indicate fewer numbers on the table, and the rod will rise. I then found that in order to raise the rod clear of the surface of the water, I had to turn the pointer to a high number, to 100 for example. However, to raise the rod above the surface of the liquid containing alcohol to one hundred degrees on the Tralles scale, the pointer needed to move only one degree, namely the first number, because of the weaker force of adhesion. With regard to the temperature of the liquid — for heat can also lessen the force of adhesion between particles — I considered attaching inside the proof-measure a thermometer made of two kinds of metals and curved like the arch of a horse's harness, which would expand under heat causing its ends to move apart, and contract under cold causing them to draw together; one end would be permanently upright, whilst the other end would rest on the bar of the scales, its pressure increasing or decreasing according to the degree of heat or cold registered by the particles of liquid. However, tests and experiments I conducted with this instrument gave no true relationship between the numbers registered by the force of attraction between the water particles, as, without any change having been made to the water, the pointer registered, on one occasion, twenty degrees, and on another occasion thirty, and even forty degrees, without indicating any clear cause for it. The water had been taken from one vessel, and the temperature had been the same on each occasion. I was unable to discover the reason for these variations, so it remained a mystery to me.

Some days later, I was honoured by a visit from the distinguished engineer Wolfson.[361] I recounted to him all my ideas and experiments, and also described the measuring instrument. He himself had carried out a number of experiments with water at the time when he had invented the submarine. He told me that the force of attraction between particles of water is a phenomenon whose cause is unknown, for it might possibly depend on the situation of the moon, the atmosphere, or the electricity in the wind. From that moment, this invention of mine, which is named Sinafioskop, [362] has been put aside and will remain forgotten until future knowledge can explain it.

When I had first entered into partnership with Baranov and Laughton, and had begun to construct the papirosi machine, I gave some of the money I had received to my son Leib, in accordance with my promise to him at the outset. He became arrogant, pretended to be ill, and refused to work any more. When, later, I began to receive a monthly salary of three hundred roubles, he begged me to have pity on him because of his illness. I gave him twenty five roubles every month to enable him to spend the summer in the suburban parks and woods in order to gain strength. I could not, however, find any symptom of illness in him, for he ate and drank, even the wine and beer that he liked, and he slept soundly. He appeared healthy, but was always sighing and complaining of the severity of his sickness. He spent all summer in the outer suburbs of the city, and in the autumn returned to me in the city. He was constantly depressed. He often spoke of visiting the baths abroad to find a cure. Then a Russian came to see me — the same Yeliseyev who had given three thousand roubles to Laughton to become a partner with Baranov: after we had dismissed Laughton from the Company, he had discovered that the three per cent of shares he had bought from Laughton were worthless, and so had lost his money. He then decided to buy three per cent from me, in the hope that these would not suffer the same fate so long as the business remained in operation — for so I had assured him, and he trusted me. He had paid me four hundred roubles for each share, making a total of one thousand and two hundred roubles for the three per cent. Now, I had also promised to give my son Leib three shares in the paper-wrapper machine. When he learned of the transaction I had made, he pleaded and begged that he be given the money in cash for his shares; he would then renounce his claim to any rights in the business. However , I understood my son only too well, and knew that the money would quickly disappear into thin air, for he was no good for anything. So I refused to give it to him, but counselled him to find a wife who had some money, one could diligently and shrewdly run a business in one of the provincial cities. Then I would give him his twelve hundred roubles. He refused. I continued: "Go, settle in Telz, the town we came from. Lend your money on interest for pawned pledges, and you will earn a living for yourself and become a man." He refused again. One day, I opened the book which I read constantly,[363] and found a letter from my son, in pleasing Hebrew phrases. In it, he lamented the hardness of his lot and complained of the severity of his ill-health, and declared his intention to put an end to his life, unless I gave him the money for which he had laboured so hard. I knew my son's condition, that he was not right in his mind, and I was greatly afraid lest he in fact put an end to his life. I thereupon gave him a lecture, and foretold what would happen to him in the future: instead of being, as now, rich and semi-ill, he would become destitute and chronically ill. I warned him: "You will assuredly lose all the money in some ill-fated venture. Do not imagine that you can then return to me, for your foot shall not cross my threshold unless you can afford to support yourself." I gave him the twelve hundred roubles, and sent him away.

After that, I rented a workshop with a display-window in the Street of Gardens,[364] and installed my son Simon Aaron there. I gave him money to carry on the business of clockmaking, and also silver and gold articles. The business did not prosper. He married Margelah, the sister of Leib and Jacob Ordman. They proposed that he attend the Leipzig market with them, and promised to help him to do business there. My son Leib also gave him about one thousand roubles of his own money. So he left, and lost half the money in business deals. His wife's brothers, however, did not help him at all. He delayed his return home a long time, without informing us of his whereabouts. When he finally returned, he told us what had happened to him at the frontier customs post. Most of his goods had been confiscated by the customs officers. When later, he had arrived in Telz to see his relatives, he had fallen ill. My son Leib went abroad to visit the spas, and travelled to the island of Heligoland. He urged his brother to send him money for his expenses, until eventually all the money had been spent. He had to abandon there all his clothes and belongings in pledge for his debts. On his return, we sent money to redeem his pledge for him. He was destitute. I did not allow him into my house, for I wanted to teach him the value of money, which was something he had never appreciated all his life. Later, he left and wandered from one place to another until he came to Kishinev, after which I lost contact with him. My son Simon Aaron had little success with his business, and I had to spend all my salary each month to support him, until Baranov stopped paying me. The workshop I had originally opened for clock-repairs, I handed into the care of my son Shraga, who was able to gain a living out of it for himself. Then Leib and Jacob, the brothers of Olga, moved to Revel, and Simon Aaron also wanted to go there, for he was unable to earn a living for his family. He handed over his shop to another man, and went to live in Revel.

I now began to consider building a machine for the production of complete papirosi by a different process from that performed by the machine I had built for Baranov. I thought of erecting a high platform over the paper-wrapper machine where the tobacco would be combed by roller-combs into broad strips of the required length for papirosi — in a similar operation to the machine which produces the cotton padding put into clothing. It was not successful, as tobacco fibres tear more easily than wool fibres. Baranov meanwhile had learned that an application, together with diagrams, had arrived at the Department from Paris for the patenting of a papiros machine invented by Graf Susini.[364a] He made enquiries and was able to obtain a copy of the plans and a detailed description of the invention. He brought them to me. I noticed that the tobacco was shredded by hand and placed in a wooden channel where it was pressed into the thickness of papirosi. A small piece, about a half-length in size, was cut off and fell into the trough of the iron vessel. It was covered by the other half-length above. It was again pressed, and emerged as a round cylinder of tobacco ready for insertion into the paper-wrapper. I liked the method, although not all of its operations. I therefore decided to make a machine on the same principle as the Parisian machine but according to my own ideas. I felt confident that it would be successful, and that I would not be accused of stealing from the Parisian design, and therefore would be able to obtain a patent. I already possessed many tools; there was also a large working area, as two smiths had been working in the house for the past year. However, I lacked workers. Then my sons Abraham and Mendel said: "We will do the work if you will show us what to do." "Very well. Let us see what we can do together." We began, although we had not a penny in our pockets. For a base, I used a thick plank of old weathered cedar-wood, which I reinforced with nails. On to it, I fixed all the parts of the papiros-paper machines which had been left over from the three disused machines, together with all the uprights and the centre bar and wheels, as well as parts for making the paper cylinders for the papiros mouth-pieces. I altered and remade them for the new machine. I was then left only with the task of modifying the part which prepares the tobacco. The boys were working industriously and tirelessly throughout the day and even after midnight. The four machines for making papiros paper-wrappers were standing ready, together with the flywheel, in the other room. Whenever anyone came to see them in operation, one of the boys would get up and turn the fly-wheel by hand, and perfect papiros papers would be tuned out by the machine. Now, Tutorski was the only remaining member of the Company after it had split up, and only his and my names were still on the patent. He often came to see me. He still went around the city looking for partners to start a new business, and even brought quite a few new people to see the machines in operation. However, no one was willing to take part in the business, even though an advance payment was no longer required, as it had been originally — for he had retrieved his initial investment. Now we were friends, but had no funds. I was not obliged to invest any money, for the original contract of agreement had expired when we had entered into partnership with Baranov and Laughton, and in that new agreement neither Tutorski nor I had undertaken to invest money. I said to him: "Justice and honesty will determine the course of our wretched Company — that is to say, if you find a man who will set up this project for us, then I shall have no complaint against you, and you may have two-thirds of the whole business including the first machine I made and also my present invention for making complete papirosi, on which I am now working just so long as you find enough money to ensure the completion of this invention. However, if you fail, and if I, despite my poverty, build this new machine without outside assistance, and I also find a man willing to undertake this business — in which you yourself have neither laboured nor invested — then you shall have as your share only the two-thirds of the first machine, plus only five per cent, of the new one." The man begged me to increase it to ten per cent, and I acceded. He himself was in straitened circumstances, for the money he had received from the Company had been spent, and now he was even hungrier than I. He had to resort to a devious stratagem to find money. He told me that his only concern all day long was to find support for me so that I could complete the machine. If he had the ten per cent which he could show to a credit loan company, that company would lend him eight hundred roubles on the surety of a promissory note for a thousand roubles made to him by another person. He therefore asked me to let him have a promissory note for six hundred roubles, on the strength of which he would be able to borrow five hundred. He would give me three hundred to continue my work, and keep two hundred for himself, whilst the remaining one hundred would have to be given as a bribe to certain men in the company willing to accept him and speak in his favour. The loan would be for a period of six months, during which we should be able to find someone to invest money in the business. He would then repay the loan out of his own share. I told him: "I agree, providing you give me a receipt against my promissory note. You must sign that I repaid you, at the expiration of the six months period of the loan, the six hundred roubles I borrowed from you on the particular date mentioned in my promissory note; that, furthermore, you solemnly promise to transfer the money to the company on that same date and to return to me my promissory note which the company is holding." He agreed, but told me not to write my Hebrew name on my note, for he would not be granted a loan on the strength of a note from a Jew. I therefore signed the note with my Russian name Mikhael, instead of Chaim. Later, he gave me one hundred and fifty roubles out of the amount he had borrowed, explaining that he had not been able to borrow all he had wanted. I, however, was glad to have found something, however little, with which to support my family.

One day, Derevitski came to see me, having been told about my machine. He said he would find reliable noblemen who would back me in my invention. I asked him: "What will you then be, Sir? A middleman or a partner?" He answered: "They are the same thing." The following day, he came with two noblemen — Strogovstsikov, a young man who had recently married a wealthy woman who possessed one million and a half roubles, and Yerakov, a very wealthy elderly man, who was an Imperial Counsellor, and whose son was a professor of Mechanics. Yerakov was a very kind-hearted person: he treated all people alike without distinction of religion. The machines were started; the papiros papers were produced in quantity, and piled neatly and ready for packing in boxes for sale. The noblemen were astonished. The man asked me about my personal and family circumstances, and felt a great sympathy for me. I told him that I had worked long and hard on the machine but had not yet applied for a patent to the Department and therefore could not yet disclose all its secrets. He then said: "Arenson,[365] believe me when I tell you that we have not come here to harm you, but only to help you, for we can see how you and your sons have toiled and laboured by the sweat of your brows to produce something which will be of service to all mankind. My heart feels for you." I then opened the door to the second room where I kept all my tools and the half-built new machine, with its diagrams hung up on the wall beside it, and explained to them all my ideas in detail. I was not aware of who these people were or that the younger Yerakov, who behaved so respectfully towards this man, was a teacher in the Institute of Technology. Whilst explaining the advantages of my invention, I told them that I always favoured the quickest method for constructing machines according to my purpose, and therefore suggested that any technical expert would be welcome to come and give his views on how to improve the machine. I was confident that no one would find fault with it. To produce these paper-wrappers by hand required no less than twenty-four separate movements, but in concentrating all these movements within one small machine, around a central shaft, most of the working parts became revealed. Therefore, I had arranged that only those parts would be visible which were required to be on top. The nobleman asked me: ''What would you need from anyone willing to finance your machine?'' I replied: ''Let them support me with a little money whilst I complete the machine. After that, they can build as many machines as they wish. We can share the profits by agreement. However, they must return to Baranov, my first partner, the five thousand roubles he spent on my behalf and which I promised to repay him once the business was operating successfully.'' They thanked me and left. The wealthy Strogovstsikov was a close friend of Baranov, so he went to see him immediately to ask him about me and Tutorski. Baranov answered him in all honesty: ''You can trust Arenson for he is honest and straight-forward, although rather lazy and needs to be stirred up. As for Tutorski, keep well away from him and have nothing to do with him.'' The following day, Derevitski came and asked me how much I needed to complete the new machine for making complete papirosi — for when, the previous day, Strogovstsikov had asked me to set up the four machines with steam power and prepare a factory in every detail for the paper-wrappers, I had to tell him: ''This is not so, Sir. Those machines were indeed built but not according to the rules of mechanics, so the technician who constructed them ruined them and they could not be used for the regular work that machines should give.'' The noblemen, therefore, had discussed only the new machine which I was in the process of building, although they thought that, later, they might take an interest also in the first machines which made the wrappers alone. I therefore told him: ''Let me have, for the time being, five hundred roubles to complete this machine, after which you can take it away to be examined. If you are satisfied with it, a partnership can be arranged. If you wish to have fifty per cent of the entire business, then give me five thousand roubles; if you wish seventy-five per cent, then give me an additional five thousand for the extra twenty-five per cent. I cannot give more than that to any one, for I must have twenty-five per cent for myself and my family.'' He returned the following day, and asked: ''What will happen if your clients are not satisfied with the machine and decline to invest in it?'' I replied: ''When I have completed my work, they are free to take the machine for two months for inspection. If, after that, they do not want it, let them return it to me, together with the patent, and I will give them back a note for half of the sum of the five hundred roubles. They will not, however, be able to claim for any expenses they may have incurred.'' The middleman then said: ''If I ask them to give you an advance of one thousand roubles, and they agree, will you give me the additional five hundred?'' ''All right. Whatever you ask for that is additional to my own requirements, is yours, even though it be ten times as much — and no one will know. I shall do as you say, and will pay you.'' He said: ''Come tomorrow, to the rich man's house. We will meet there. You can ask for your thousand roubles, and they will give it to you the same day. Once you have completed the machine, and they decide to have it, they will have sixty per cent and will pay you seven thousand roubles, whilst I will take fifteen per cent and will pay you three thousand roubles to make up the amount you requested for a seventy-five per cent share. In addition, they will pay you from this day forth, every month for a whole year, one hundred and fifty roubles for the maintenance of your family and yourself.'' We agreed. The following day, I went to the meeting, and we discussed the terms.

When I returned home, Tutorski came to see me. I told him about the new partnership and how they had not wanted him to join them. However, he would receive his share from me personally. The man agreed to receive one-third of the profits of the paper-wrapper machine in which he had a share according to the licence that had been made out at that time, whilst from the new machine which would be licensed on their name and mine alone, he would receive ten per cent out of my twenty-five per cent, leaving me with fifteen per cent. He was delighted, and raised his arms to heaven in gratitude. We went to the notary where I was given the expired agreement that we had made with Baranov. We arranged to meet on the following day to make out a new agreement concerning the one-third and the ten per cent we had discussed. On the following day, I went to the rich man's house with the expired, former agreement to show him that I had completed the Tutorski affair as they had requested, and that he would receive his share from me but would not be involved with them. Then said Strogovstsikov: ''When I was on my way home last night, I met the Agent of this house who enquired about the papiros-machine in which I had become a partner. He told me that Tutorski had full control over all Arenson's inventions and would not accept us as partners unless we paid him fourteen thousand roubles in addition to his share, for he had controlling rights over any papiros machines Arenson made.'' His words sent me into a panic. I said: ''I know nothing at all about this. He said nothing about it to me but, on the contrary, he was so delighted that he raised his hands to heaven in thanks. Last night, he even gave me, of his own free will, the expired agreement which was still in his possession. How can the man become my enemy over-night. Now I shall go and take him to a Notary and come to a proper agreement with him.'' I sent word for him to come to see me, but instead he sent me a letter which was as long as a book, in which he said: ''Tell me, Arenson, how could you be so presumptuous as to take on partners in the machine without my permission? You surely knew that, after Baranov left, I remained the only one with control over your invention. Know, therefore, that if you do this again, I shall take you to Court. Anything you have undertaken with your partners is invalid without my agreement.'' I realised that the man had indeed turned against me, and had moreover lost his senses, so I quickly wrote him a strongly-worded reply: ''If you seek to clash with me, you should know that your sword is blunt and your arrows shattered. Hear my final words, for I will not see you again if you refuse me this day. Tomorrow, I shall wait for you until the hour of eleven in the morning. If you come with me to the Notary, all will be well. If, however, you do not come at that hour, then you will receive not one penny from the machines. I advise, and warn you, that either I see you tomorrow at eleven, or I will never see you again.'' The morrow came. The clock struck twelve, the hour of noon. The middleman arrived. I told him: ''Let my lords find a man in whom they have absolute trust. I shall hand over to him, on his name, the new papirosi machine with all the diagrams and specifications, and he will be known as the sole inventor. He can then apply to the Department for a patent for ten years on his name and the names of the partners. My name must not be mentioned in it at all. However, I shall still be entitled to my share.'' The man went and informed them of my proposals. They sympathised with me, for they realised that Tutorski had been making trouble for me. They agreed to do as I suggested.

There was a retired Officer over Thousands, called Marishev, who assisted them in their affairs, for a fee. We all went together to a different Notary, in another part of the city, and completed an agreement naming Marishev as the inventor: he was given a small share, whilst I retained mine. They gave me one thousand roubles. On my return home, the middleman came for his five hundred roubles. I received one hundred and fifty roubles per month from that date. I then removed the rotting wooden board which I had been using as a base for the machine, and prepared a new one out of polished brass. My two sons and I set to work on the machine, for I had undertaken in the agreement to complete the work within four months. A draughtsman was hired to prepare all the diagrams, whilst I prepared explanatory specifications. The four months came to an end, and so did the work on the machine. The rich man had spent about four thousand roubles out of his own pocket, for Yerakov had given nothing and the rich man had not presumed to make demands upon him, like a creditor. He, too, therefore, stopped paying any more. He said to the middleman: ''Find some other interested partners. I am willing to relinquish my share, and shall not ask to be reimbursed for the money I have already spent. If, however, the partners wish to retain me in the Company, I shall take a ten per cent share.'' So Derevitski rented two nice, large rooms in the Street of the Blacksmiths,[366] and installed the two machines there for public display: one machine, which made paper-wrappers for papirosi, was worked by a flywheel, whilst the other which produced complete papirosi was worked by hand. He paid me for two months, namely, three hundred roubles. He then went around the capital, seeking partners. He brought many people to see the machines. Finally, he met Khorvat and Zhadovski who agreed to give me seven thousand roubles plus one hundred and fifty roubles per month for a whole year for my maintenance. We met at a Notary's, together with Mitkov, a wealthy man and well-known in the capital, who was a friend of Zhadovski. He also became a partner. The business was divided into two hundred shares. I was given eighty shares, whilst they shared out the other hundred and twenty between them: Zhadovski, twelve per cent; Khorvat, ten per cent; Strogovstsikov, ten; Yerakov, ten; Mitkov, six; Derevitski, twelve.[367] Each owner of a share of the two hundred shares would have to put into the Company's funds one thousand roubles in case at times to be specified by the Company's counsellors; each was also required to put down an advance payment of two hundred and fifty roubles. My eighty shares were to be entered separately in red as B shares. The two Treasurers of the Company, Zhadovski and Khorvat, would sign and stamp all my shares with the Company's seal to show that the thousand roubles had been paid up in full. The other one hundred and twenty shares would be registered in green as A shares. Yerakov then took the seven thousand roubles from the Treasurers and handed it to me. I was about to put them into my pocket when Yerakov stopped me: "Count them first, and only when you arc satisfied that the full amount is there, put it in your pocket. This is the way it is done all over the world." I had, in fact, seen Yerakov count the money when he had taken it from the Treasurers, but whether in bundles of tens or hundreds or thousands, I did not know. I was feeling faint, and was hesitant to count it. He grew angry with me, so I counted the money, and put it in my coat-pocket. Then I took a quill pen and signed my agreement to all their conditions in the Notary's book. When I had finished, Yerakov said to Mitkov: "My friend, as you know I have very little time to spare and I have many affairs to attend to, so that I have hardly a moment for myself. Oblige me by taking my ten shares off me. I shall always, of course, be willing to offer my advice for the good of this venture, whenever you may wish it." Mitkov agreed to take his share, and it was so recorded in the Notary's book. Then we all went home. Yerakov never came again: he had accomplished what he had set out to do when he had promised, out of the goodness of his heart, to help me until the business was set up, but without having any intention of engaging in the affair himself. Now that he had done as he had promised, he left clear of all involvement. Strogovstsikov remained, receiving ten shares for the money he had spent; nor did he refuse them, lest it appear that he was belittling me before them. This was completed on the 30 December, 1876.[368]

The middleman had asked me, at the outset, that I lend him one thousand roubles against his promissory note. I had refused, but had said: "I can give you one thousand roubles for the thirty shares I have to give you for the three thousand roubles. Accept one thousand roubles, for I cannot give you a single share." He refused, so I said: "I will lend you the thousand roubles against your thirty shares. If you sell one or more shares to anyone else, you must pay me a hundred roubles for each share of the three thousand roubles for thirty shares, plus another fifty roubles to be deducted from the thousand loan." He agreed. On my return home with the money in my coat pocket, my sons counted the money, each hundred by itself, and the seven thousands by themselves. They found one hundred roubles missing from Khorvat's three thousand five hundred. I immediately wrote to him requesting that he should check his money to see if he had a hundred roubles too much for I was short of this amount. I received a reply from him the next day saying: "I myself received the money in full from the person who sent it to me, and who is well-known to me. I did not count it, for the sender would have reliably sent me the full amount. I did not, therefore, know of this.'' This was my punishment for not counting the money carefully when I had received it, as Yerakov had told me to do. I paid the middleman his thousand, and paid out another thousand in debts I owed, and had five left over. I bought some first and second loan bonds, and also other companies' bonds.

The two Directors of the new Company were Khorvat and Zhadovski. Khorvat had been formerly an exceedingly wealthy man, who had studied at an Academy in his youth but had since forgotten everything and retained only a superficial knowledge of science; he was impetuous, boastful of his learning, a lover of falsehood, and utterly foolish. The other Director, Zhadovski, was an honest and trustworthy person, who had studied at the same Lyceum as Mitkov, and since then they had been close companions throughout their lives. He had complete faith in Khorvat and his knowledge of technical matters. They proposed that Khorvat should have full charge of the production side of the Company, whilst Zhadovski would be the Director-Treasurer with responsibility for all income and expenditure. Khorvat taught him a significant principle in connection with all inventions: the inventor must be removed as far as possible from his invention, for inventors are always trying to improve their inventions, and therefore they constantly dismantle and destroy what they had built the previous day, only to start over again on the next day — and so on, endlessly. Zhadovski believed him. They both hid from me their intention to find craftsmen metalworkers to whom they could transfer my machine and who would learn how to operate it from my descriptions, after which they would build a new machine with modifications of their own without seeking my advice or deferring to my knowledge. They would sit at a table, and whilst one of them was copying down all the specifications the other would describe the modifications that could be made. For this, they would receive a fee of five hundred roubles. The new specifications would then be handed to Kolosov, who had an iron and brass foundry on the other side of Petersburg, and he would prepare everything according to the diagrams and specifications, and cast all the iron and brass required for their first machine: he would be paid a fee of one thousand and five hundred roubles. After that, they would order a further forty machines from him, at a lower price. They went ahead with their plan, preparing specifications without seeking my advice. Whenever I approached them to see what they were doing, they repulsed me; when I enquired about the machine, they refused to offer any reply except to say that I was only interested in obstructing their work, and that since they had free access to my machine, they fully understood how it worked. Thus passed days and weeks and months. Each month, on the first of the month, the Directors paid me my salary of one hundred and fifty roubles. However, whenever I complained to them that the draughtsmen would not permit me to approach them, they answered in a gentle and pacifying manner that I should not provoke the men for they were experts in their jobs. Nevertheless, when

I observed that they were deviating from my technical instructions, I rebuked them openly, and demonstrated to them that they were bound to fail. They made no reply. I complained vehemently to the Directors, and they also made no reply. The draughtsmen disclosed to me that they were only behaving as instructed according to the Directors' instructions. Three months passed by. The contract of agreement promising me eighty shares in the Company plus one hundred and fifty roubles per month for the whole year, had not been completed. I began to fear lest they intended to deceive me, to prepare the specifications without me and then give me nothing at all, unless I took them to Court. They were, however, more powerful than I. My suspicions made me very uneasy. I complained angrily to the Directors that the agreement had not been completed as promised, for only then would I be able to carry out my obligations to the Company and I would know how best to serve its interests. They hesitated and delayed, saying each time that I should come to see them again the next day. This went on until April when they intended to deliver the machine to Kolosov, on the pretext that the specifications would be made there. Two more months passed by, and still nothing had been done. The machine was stored in a shed, completely covered over with a cloth so that no one could see it. Meanwhile, the completion of the specifications was further delayed. Finally, because I was now complaining every day, the Directors wrote out a contract with me stating that I was to supervise the drawing up of the specifications and the photographing of the diagrams, and that I would be given my eighty shares and monthly salary: they also added that I was not to construct even the paper-wrapper machines without their participation and permission in return for the eighty shares I held — though this was something I had not previously promised them, since they had never asked. However, since I feared further deception on their part, I agreed to this stipulation also. This contract showed me that it was not because of their honesty and goodwill that they were not deceiving me, but only through their respect for Mitkov who would never have permitted them to defraud me of my shares, for he was a just and honest man and upright in all his ways.

Because the Directors of the Company would not allow me to work on the papiros machine in their service, I was left without any occupation. I wanted to invent a new kind of table or wall clock which would show the hours without the need for an arrow-pointer, as the rotation of the earth upon its axis would show the hours of the day and night. I based my idea on the principle laid down by the French inventor, Foucault,[369] that the direction of swing of a pendulum does not change with the rotation of the earth upon its axis. If the pendulum be moved from north to south — not the north and south of the terrestrial globe but the heavens — so that it swings towards the star of the horizon, namely the Plough, or the Bear in the northern sky,[370] its movements will always be in the direction of that star without ever deviating into an east to west direction or towards any point in the skies other than the original star. Even when the globe turns on its axis together with the table and its pillars from which the pendulum is suspended, so that the pillar which initially faced towards the Bear on the horizon now moves away and faces between east and west, nevertheless the pendulum will maintain its original movement in the direction of the north unless impelled by the gibbet from which it hangs. When the pendulum is suspended by a thin wire which exerts an equal pull upon all its sides, and the pendulum is made from iron or brass wire to whose lower end a heavy sphere is attached, then the pendulum will swing of its own accord by virtue of its inner force of flight, namely the perpetual force of inertia *(Inertie)*. However, this force does not endure for long because of the many opposing forces, as is well known. Therefore, when Foucault wanted to demonstrate this phenomenon to the scientists of Paris,[371] he made a pendulum, the equivalent of thirty storeys in length, and suspended it from the parapet of a very tall building. To its end he attached a heavy sphere so that its perpetual force would overcome the opposing forces and enable it to swing for several hours. We know from experience that even a simple pendulum, such as the seconds-pendulum *(Sekundenpendel)*,[372] will be kept moving by its perpetual force for some three hours from the stimulus of the initial impulse. I thought, if I make a pendulum two cubits long which I can suspend by a thin silk thread, and a motor to provide it with impulses which will enable it to overcome the opposing forces, then that mechanism with all its wheels and parts will also rotate around the iron-wire pendulum and will alter direction against the direction of rotation of the globe on its axis, and will change the place of the impulses caused by the crutch as it moves the iron-wire in accordance with all the changes made by the pendulum in the plane of its movement between the pillars. The pendulum, then, will swing continuously day and night as in all clocks without deviating from the direction in which it first moved. There would be no need to make an exact correction for the slight deviation caused by the impulses of the mechanism upon the iron-wire pendulum from its plane of movement relative to the point in the heavens, for the iron-wire was very thin and the impulse acting upon it to keep it moving would be very light, so that with every movement forwards and backwards the striker would move away from the wire and not touch it at all. I therefore calculated that it would not deviate during a period of a day or a week. Furthermore, the wheel mechanism which operated upon the pendulum would have to be made in accordance with precise calculation of the movement of the pendulum in relation to its length, so that it would rotate equally with the earth's rotation. If the angle of deviation resulting from each impulse acting upon the iron-wire during a complete day be about ten degrees, that is if the circle described around the iron-wire be divided into three hundred and sixty parts, then during a period of twenty-four hours the impulse upon the pendulum wire will not be on one-tenth of its circumference — as it should for precise movement — but will deviate between ten to twenty degrees, namely an error of one thirty-sixth from the correct position. Since each circular movement of the wire equals that of the clock hand, with a variance of only one in thirty-six, which is practically nothing, I therefore concluded that the plane of movement of the balance would remain constant. The end of the wire-pendulum which projects below its bob-weight would give indications on a horizontal, concave numbered table in accordance with the circle described by the pendulum. The number of the hours would be registered on the dial around the circumference, the tip of the arrow indicating the hour of the day as it moved closer to it with each movement. The numbers of the hours on the dial would be inscribed according to the place on the terrestrial globe where the clock was to stand. Now, in Petersburg, the capital, it would take the numbered dial thirty-six hours to turn a full circle, for the pendulum would turn one full circle in every 36 hours and 12 seconds, since its northern latitude is 59°57'. During a period of 24 solar hours, the earth rotates on its axis only 23 hours 36 minutes and 4 seconds terrestrial time, making a loss of 3 minutes 56 seconds.[373] From this, 354 seconds should be deducted every 36 hours for Petersburg, and to this should then be added a further 12 seconds to compensate for the northern latitude. The numbered dial, (which is the part that actually rotates and moves with the earth) would, however, move backwards on this clock (which I named the *Rotatiometer)* for 342 seconds during 36 hours. In order to overcome this deficiency, I thought of making a mechanism consisting of toothed wheels intermeshing with other toothed wheels, so that as the mechanism moved one day and a half, namely 36 hours, they would move the numbered dial backwards 342 seconds during that period. By this means, the clock would show precisely the rotation of the earth's globe in relation to the hours of the day. I inscribed twelve hours on the concave numbered dial three times, so that the hours of the day could be seen in the normal manner. As for distinguishing between the hour of the day or night, this would be evident to any observer. The rotating clock with the pendulum and its mechanism would be encased in a tall, round, glass case fixed firmly to a solid iron base, so that not even the slightest draught of wind would affect it. The entire mechanism would be attached firmly and immovably to the floor and a solid wall. These, then, were my thoughts. I prepared a practical test to ascertain whether my calculations were correct. I thought: if my idea be correct, that the impulses upon the wire pendulum will not cause it to deviate from its plane of oscillation, seeing that the angle of deviation is so small as to be practically nil, then if the length of the pendulum be short in relation to the calculation of the number of teeth — which, in the normal clock, would speed up the time and thereby make the hours shorter than normal day-time hours; in such a case, the clock is said to be running very fast — nevertheless the timing of this rotating clock would not alter at all, for the pendulum will maintain its plane of oscillation and will slow down its movement over the hour dial in conformity with the rotation of the globe, at least for a short period such as two or three hours, so long as the angle of impulse remains less than the circumference of the pendulum. If this happened, then I would know by experiment that my calculations were correct. If, however, the pendulum were too short, thereby speeding up its movement round the hour dial, then I would know that I had erred. Whilst making all the parts, I also shortened the length of the pendulum according to the calculations for the ratios of the wheels. I found that, for every one-third by which the pendulum was shortened, the dial registered four hours for every three,[374] as it was running fast like any pendulum would in any clock. I thought the matter over and realised that I had been wrong in my calculations, as the force exerted upon the pendulum was stronger than the force keeping it in its plane of oscillation, thus causing it to deviate with every impulse; each time the wheels and the crutch turned, the crutch pulled the pendulum round. This time, my invention did not work out. I considered various means of correcting it but, becoming confused and finding my time limited, I finally abandoned it. It is possible that the crutch was not striking the pendulum constantly at regular moments, as happens in all clocks, but instead wound up a spring lightly for about five or ten minutes or more, then released the spring and struck the pendulum once to increase its movement and swiftly disengaged itself and began to re-wind the spring. During the whole period of the winding of the spring, the pendulum oscillated freely from the force of that single stroke, maintaining its plane of oscillation.[375]

In that year of 1877, war broke out with Turkey over the Bulgarians.[376] Kolosov, the Director of the foundry, obtained orders for the manufacture of a large amount of war materials, cannon-balls and bayonets. He purchased the necessary equipment, and worked day and night producing weapons for the army. He abandoned his work on our machine: we had no agreement with him to have the machine ready within a specified period. Tutorski heard that I had transferred my invention to other people, without falling on my knees for his approval, but he did not know who or what they were. He therefore went to the Department with the complaint that Arenson, his partner and the inventor of the paper-wrapper machine, had now altered the machine to such an extent that it was capable of producing complete papirosi filled with tobacco. He applied for a patent on his name alone. The Directors of the Company went to see the Director of the Department, who informed them that the specifications for the first machine were solely for wrappers, and that these together with the specifications for the second machine for papirosi had been sent to Lavzin, the teacher in charge of the engineering department of the Academy. If he declared it his opinion that the second machine was a new invention, then a patent would be granted; but if he considered it only a modification of the first, it would not be given.

When I realised that the entire winter had passed by and no progress had been made on the machine, I said to my partners that, if they could obtain metalworkers for me from Kolosov's factory, I would show then how to alter the parts and operations of the machine for producing paper-wrappers so that they would be like new inventions in comparison with the machines which Tutorski had. They agreed. I went with my sons to the workshop each day, and dismantled the parts I required, and found other means for operating them. I also applied to the Department to transfer full authority over my share of the patent for my invention to the Company, to whom I was handing over all my rights. I realised that Kolosov was too interested in producing war materials to bother with the new machine. Further-more, the year had almost ended, and the licence held by Tutorski and myself would expire in another year and a half. It had been granted in 1875, and the law was that, if a period of three years passed — that is, one quarter of the period of the patent — without the machine being used in a factory within the empire, the control of the patent reverted to the Department which could then re-issue it to anyone who undertook to use it without delay. If, therefore, I did not complete the first machine so that it worked properly, who else would? I said to my Directors: "The man Kolosov will not build the machine for us so long as there is war between us and Turkey. If the war continues one more year, then the patent held by Tutorski will lapse and will be withdrawn. Let us not, therefore, be hasty in the matter of the patent." My words upset them for, up to this moment, they had not believed me when I had told them that Kolosov was deceiving them and that he would not consider constructing the machine so long as the war was on. I had spoken openly against him, and he had slandered me falsely to them, but they had believed him, rather than me. Now, however, they could see for themselves that I was telling the truth. Zhadovski went to Kolosov and spoke urgently with him. He replied: "Let us dismantle the machine, then you can give it to someone else to construct." My honesty and sincerity became apparent to everyone, in everything I had ever said, and even in connection with the draughtsmen who had refused to let me see their work. They began to look for a craftsman metalworker who would undertake the work. They came across Peters, who had studied at an engineering institute and was now a senior instructor in metalwork, with a salary from the Government. They brought him to have a look at the machine. He advised them to set up a small factory for building only four machines at first; later, if they were successful, they could expand production to hundreds of machines. He said he was willing to set up this factory, to be powered by steam, and to smelt and produce the iron and brass required, and that he would supervise the entire operation. He would prepare the calculations and specifications at home. He would also attend the factory, which should be near the Institute where he taught, twice a day for a few hours whenever he was free from his duties. He would prepare the machine according to my instructions entirely. I thought highly of Peters because of his knowledge of mechanics, which I had ascertained when speaking with him, as well as his grasp of the whole operation of the machine. Therefore, I praised him highly, and was delighted with him. Even though this meant that my monthly salary for the year would come to an end, for my one hundred and fifty roubles per month would be given to him, nevertheless the business would at last flourish and produce results, and this was more important to me than the salary. I told them what I thought, and they were pleased. I then asked: "Why did the man propose that you set up a place for smelting the iron and brass? This will consume most of your funds unnecessar-ily. There are many foundries in the capital where all kinds of metals are smelted, and which produce good work at a low price." They then explained the man's intentions: ''The Institute where he works possesses smelting equipment for a variety of metals, and these produce better work than any private foundry. In fact, the Institute's works are considered to be the Government's own foundry, and many people apply there daily to have moulds made according to their own specifications: they are often refused, because the workers there are not interested in doing additional work and making a profit for the Government Treasury. If, on the other hand, we had a foundry for iron and brass, he would send to us all the customers who came to the Institute. The profit we gain from them would more than cover the expenses of making our own machines in the foundry.'' I hardly knew what to say in answer to them, or against the man's proposals. ''Nevertheless, it does not seem right to me that you should have to lose the fifteen thousand roubles that will be required just to set up the business, especially when we do not have even one machine producing papirosi. If you think it a good idea to set up a foundry, you can always do it later, after our first machine has successfully manufactured complete papirosi. You can then open a large factory and foundry for the construction of scores of papiros machines. But, with regard to our first machine, have the parts smelted in the city's foundries, which will do them very quickly; at the same time we can be preparing the parts that have to be done by hand. In this way we can have the entire work done simultaneously.'' They replied: ''Peters has told us that he cannot be responsible for any machine whose parts have not been made under his supervision and that in any case no machine built by others can succeed without him.'' Their words were like a thunderbolt to me. I exclaimed: ''Gentlemen! You know that I loved this man Peters with my whole heart the moment I saw him, and you saw how impressed I was with his expert technical knowledge. When, however, he declared that many people would come to give you their smelting orders, thus increasing your profits, I simply thought that he was in error and was deceiving himself. Now, he states that the parts made by others, not by himself, will not be suitable for the machine. I fear greatly that it is not himself he is now deceiving, but you, with statements which he must know to be false. Has such a thing ever been heard of before, since the time that large machines were first built, that any that were not built under his supervision in the Institute were bound to fail? Had he said that the parts of the machine which were working had been made by an untrained technician and not in accordance with the laws of mechanics, and that therefore they would not operate successfully, I would have believed him. It is true that the parts cast for large machines are not to be compared with those for watches: when they are cast by unskilled workers, they could be hard enough to blunt the tools used upon them, but when cast by a skilled worker they will be suitable for the machine. But is there an iron smelter who is so unskilled that he cannot make castings sufficiently soft for use with tools? Gentlemen, take my advice: beware of this man for I see that he is deceiving you. I do not understand his intentions, but this much I do know, that he must be just as much aware of the situation as I am, and for that reason he is guilty of deceiving you. By all means give him his salary, but at the same time give instructions to have the first machine fully prepared by other people, and also that he must urge his workers to produce the wooden moulds and metal parts under his supervision. As for the foundry, you should abandon it until the first machine has proved successful. After that you can build your own foundry." I cautioned and warned them that they would lose both their money and their time, and would see no profit from their labours. I then left.

The next day, Khorvat, who considered himself wise, derided my words. Zhadovski believed him, for Peters was a qualified technician, and was well able to conceal his errors, so his opinion would be preferred to that of an unqualified person. They hired a three-storeyed house surrounded by a wall on the other side of the moat.[377] Against the outer wall they built a fence to contain the smelting oven. They covered the walls and roof with iron, and dug another oven into the floor of the building for smelting brass alone. They also had bellows and pipes and earth for making moulds. They lost twenty-five thousand roubles on the foundry alone, in addition to a further eighteen thousand roubles for me and for the contract, of which three hundred copies had been printed, on both sides, by the process of light imprint on zinc — and also the money they had expended on tools: on Peters' recommendation they had recklessly purchased tools, such as files etc., at a cost of two thousand roubles. They had to delay for two years before beginning to construct the papiros-machine, for in that first year the Paris Exhibition opened[378] and Peters was sent by his Institute to exhibit its work there. Then, towards the end of summer, he had to return there to assemble all the exhibits and bring them back. Meanwhile, each month, Peters received his salary of one hundred and fifty roubles from our Company, although money was deducted regularly from his salary to pay for the four shares he had bought costing nine hundred roubles. Eventually, the foundry was opened. No customers came from the Institute, despite the promises that had been given. In fact, no one at all came until the Company published notices proclaiming the opening of the new foundry bearing Zhadovski's name, and boasting of the superior quality of the technical work. Then the renowned engineer Richter, of Petersburg, sent small wooden moulds for smelting in iron. Peters prepared them all himself. When Richter received them, he sent them back to Zhadovski saying that they were totally unsuitable: the smelted iron was too hard and would resist any tool, and furthermore they were faulty. This, then, was the fruit of their confidence in that man despite my advice. In the event, the foundry was used only for making the parts for the ten machines originally planned, after which there was no further work for it, and it was closed down.

Derevitski, the middle-man, went around the city every day looking for buyers for his shares. He sold them to several people who wanted to join our Company. He paid me, as he had promised, one hundred roubles for each share, and a further fifty to pay off his loan. He received five hundred roubles for each share he sold, and sometimes even six and eight hundred — for my shares were unable to add anything to the Company's funds. He made about eighteen thousand roubles out of his business deals over my invention. I myself made, through Derevitski, more than sixteen thousand roubles out of my invention. Khorvat bought one of my shares for four hundred roubles, and then sold it to Von Wiesin[379] for nine hundred. Zhadovski bought two shares from me during the period when Derevitski stopped taking the shares I held as surety: Zhadovski had urged me to sell him the two shares, which I did for three hundred roubles. Derevitski was very bitter about it when he heard of it. I told him that the two shares would come out of my entitlement, so that he would lose nothing by it. Mitkov also bought one share from me for five hundred roubles.

At this time, I began to suffer from a pain in my left hand, and I was unable to turn my hand sideways. For a long time, from the summer of the previous year, 1877, I had sought the advice of physicians but without finding any relief. The winter aggravated my condition, so that my right hand also began to pain me. I was unable to raise or turn both hands, and only when they were straight in front of me did the pain leave me. My son, Simon Aaron, was living in the city of Revel. He had become very poor. He came to Petersburg to learn the art of light-imprints, *Photographie*. He would then set up in Revel in both businesses in order to increase his possibilities for earning a livelihood. I paid fifty roubles for his tuition to the famous photographer Shapira. I also purchased for him all the apparatus he needed. He returned to Revel where he opened a workshop for clock-repairing and a photographic studio. Every month I sent him money for his subsistence, and the rent of twenty-five roubles. Success, however, did not come his way, and he became increasingly dejected. In the beginning of the summer of 1878, my physician advised me to undergo a course of treatment with hot baths heated to a temperature of 20 degrees Réaumur.[380] The kind of baths he recommended were available in Revel, where one could also stroll in the fine parks or bathe in the sea. I travelled to Revel with my wife, who also wanted to take the baths — I in the warm spa water, and she in the cold sea-water.

In that year, I turned to inventing a new calculating machine. I had learned that, when parcels were handed in to railway stations for onward despatch, the clerks always erred in their calculations: they had to calculate the distance in *verst* from the station of despatch to the station of destination, the charge in kopeks according to the rate per *verst*, and the weight of the parcel in *pud*. In trying to make these three calculations quickly, they often made mistakes. When this involved the Company in a loss, the sum was deducted from their wages: they were not, however, penalised when they overcharged and made a profit for the Company. The customers often complained, and often loudly and violently. It would be a good thing to invent a machine made entirely of iron and brass, and which would give an accurate reading. I thought of a new method. The machine would be small, and shaped like a round clock. It would have a diameter of eighteen inches, and its wheels would be turned by the force of a strong iron spring. There would be a round tablet on top of it, which would pivot on an axis in its centre. The circumference of the tablet would be marked into eight hundred narrow divisions — which is the total of *verst* of the longest railway line in the land.[381] The name of every station which accepted parcels for despatch would be inscribed on it with the distance in *verst* between neighbouring stations. A pointer would be stationary on the tablet. When the clerk was told the station of destination of the goods, he would turn the pointer to that station: (for example), in Petersburg, he might turn the pointer to Tver or Moscow, the stations of destination. On a small round tablet by his side, he would find seven numbers corresponding to seven types of merchandise and the rate in kopeks per *verst*. The pointer, which had not moved, would be turned to each class of merchandise, from first to second or third, up to the seventh. He would then indicate the amount of *pud* weight. On the opposite side he would find seven tables of numbers, in groups of ten, from 1 to 0. When the pointers came to rest, they would show the total charge for the despatch of the goods. Over these numbers, would be three tables divided into tens. Each table would have its own pointer to indicate the weight in *pud*. The despatch clerk would set the pointers at their proper numbers: if the number of *pud* were 765, he would put the first pointer on his right to 5, and the second to 6, and the third to 7, whilst the seven pointers on the tables would be moved to 0. The clerk would then press his finger on a button on the machine, and all the wheels inside would revolve noisily. The clerk would then be free to attend to another parcel for despatch. By the time he returned, the machine would have stopped and the noise subsided. He would then find that the large round tablet had turned from Tver to Petersburg, with a pointer showing the number of *verst* and the three weight pointers indicating the number of *pud*. The seven small pointers on the seven price-list tables are read from left to right to calculate the cost in thousands and hundreds and tens and single units of a kopek. For example, 7654.32 mean 7 thousand 6 hundred and 54 kopeks, or 76 roubles and 54 kopeks, plus three-tenths and two hundredths. All this I designed with great skill. It was a new and astonishing method. The machine required few parts; it afforded me a great deal of satisfaction. Unfortunately, it worked very slowly: it took ten minutes or more to perform its calculations. I realised, to my intense disappointment, that my work had been for nought. Not one of the railway Companies would ever bother to put it to the test. I therefore placed the machine in a box and hung it on a peg on the wall as an ever-present reminder to me — and to all inventors who come after me — that it is essential to take special account of the operational time of an invention.[382]

Because of the pain in my arms, I decided to spend the summer in Revel. My sons, Abraham and Mendel, told me they would continue to work on the machine, and if they came across any problems, they would contact me in Revel personally or write to me. So my wife and I came to Revel, to find Simon Aaron and his family in dire poverty, for he was unable to earn a living from his two professions. I examined the situation and found that he was more interested in keeping his place clean and beautiful, as though it was a residence of aristocracy, than in fitting up a workshop. The three windows in the large entrance room which looked out upon the street had been dressed in fine taste, but his clock-repairing workshop was in the small inner room, with the stove; this room had a window which overlooked the wall of the house opposite, with an area of refuse between. The tools were in disarray and covered in layers of dust. The clocks on the wall had stopped. Here he lived with his wife and young daughters. Any man who had a clock for repair would not care to give it to a man who lived in such disorder. There was no sign or plaque on the outside walls announcing that a craftsman clockmaker lived in this house. I was very angry with him: "I am sure that if any stranger asked your advice you would have the sense not to advise him to do what you are doing yourself — for you are being terribly foolish in curtailing your own livelihood for the sake of this insubstantial vainglorious display." He excused himself by laying the blame on his wife. I thereupon brought out the metal name-plaques which I had had for some time, and fixed them to the window-shutters in the street. I placed the table-clock upon a shelf in the window, and hung the smaller ones by a metal wire breadthwise across the window. That corner became a partitioned working area with its own window. The other three-quarters of the room with its two windows became the photographic studio for receiving clients. Then, people began to bring him their clocks for repair, and his income improved. He realised how foolish he had been.

I found a specialist physician who visited me twice a week. I paid daily visits to the baths in the Ekaterini Park for treatment with mud-baths and hot baths. I spent some of my time strolling through the park with my wife, or lying down in the grass — something I had always been fond of doing since I was a boy. At other times I sat at home disgruntled, for I was accustomed to working on creative inventions; idleness depressed me.

I recalled that, when I had lived in Telz, I had seen the invention of the Parisian Dagron.[383] In this, a picture was made on a piece of glass, one end of which was polished and convex like a magnifying glass whilst the other was flat, and it was on this that the picture was fixed. Dagron was able to take photographs of anything he wished — and they were mostly subjects of love and lust.[384] I thought that I could make pictures of men and women and their families, which they could carry with them, and which would be superior to those produced by light imprints which cannot be worn around the neck — for the paper they were made on deteriorated and the pictures lost their colour under the effects of light and the damp, acid atmosphere. However, these conditions would have no effect upon my miniature pictures, for they would be held between two pieces of glass and protected from wind and light. When I had been living in Telz, my circumstances had not permitted me to engage in any experiments on this; in any case, Dagron had kept his process a close secret. Here, in Revel, I had the time and the money to attend to it. My first experiment was to attempt, with the aid of a small light-imprint machine,[385] to take a picture at a distance from the sitters. I seated my son, Simon Aaron, some forty cubits from the dark box[386] — and obtained a picture on sensitized glass, about the size of a small nut. My son looked at it and said: "This is not the way, father. Dagron did not take pictures of the subject's face but of the whole body and from that the face was copied on to a glass the size of the sheet of paper. This was then taken a second time in the machine, with light rays passing through the glass plate and making the picture smaller. It was a reverse process, from white to black, and black to white. These are called transitional pictures, *Transparant*.[387] I saw many of them when I was training at Shapira's studio." "You are right," I said. "I shall try it that way." I removed the glass from the pictures which had been finished on paper, and put it in the place of the dark glass. In front of the point of focus, I set up a small box containing the sensitized glass. I took a picture, and obtained a very dark print. The picture was very small and reversed, the white appearing black. I then removed the two magnifying lenses from a pair of binoculars and inserted them into a cylinder of thick gummed paper, making a small machine like those used for light-imprints, which I placed inside the dark box, in its centre. On one side, I fixed the glass for the picture at the correct distance from the lens in the cylinder, whilst on the other side I placed the frame of the sensitized glass. I then tested it by retracting the shaft of the small machine away from the sensitized glass, and then drawing it closer to it, until I was able to ascertain the focal point and obtain a very small picture, which gave full detail. I had discovered the basis of Dagron's secrets.[388] It was now necessary to fix the small picture to the half lens of the magnifying glass and to focus the rays of light which would bring the small picture into view. There was no way of obtaining a magnifying lens small enough for the process. I bought a number of hemispherical glass buttons which had been polished brightly and were flat on one side. I broke the sides off one of the buttons, leaving only its centre. On to its flat side I fixed my small picture, and placed both inside a cylinder of thin paper I had specially prepared for the purpose. By looking in the direction of a window, or a lighted candle, I was able to see the picture almost as though it were alive, with all its details enlarged, and amazingly defined. When I placed a dark glass, which I had lightly smeared with a red tint, in front of the small cylinder and facing towards the light, the picture became astonishingly life-like. I showed this to my son and to all my family, and cried exultantly: "Here is a new invention which even the Parisian Dagron did not know about. The aristocracy of our land will pay gold for these pictures, so that they can carry their loved ones in miniature lockets around their necks and upon their hearts, and whenever they look at them they will seem to be alive."[389]

I began experimenting to produce a small, convex magnifying lens which could be inserted into the lockets and trinkets of gold and silver so that they could be used as viewing tubes for the fine pictures. With the aid of a clockmaker's plane,[389a] I polished and ground the surface of the small convex lens until it became as bright as a magnifying lens.[390] I remembered that I had a small German book, written more than a hundred years ago, [391] which gave instructions for preparing focus and magnifying lenses. I knew that the piece of glass was attached to a wooden or metal tube which was ground and revolved inside a copper or tin bowl whose concave interior was equal to about the small hemisphere of the focal point. The bowl also revolved swiftly. It contained a solution emery powder in water, which smoothed the surface down to the concave hemisphere of the bowl. As the diameter of the hemisphere increased, so did its focal distance. The picture thereby receded from the convex sphere and diminished in size before the eye of the viewer — and similarly *vice versa*. I continued with my experiments until the summer had ended.

The mud-baths did not afford a cure for my arms, whilst my stomach pains increased. Some two weeks before the spa's summer season came to a close, my fingers and feet felt like dead limbs which I had borrowed from another body. When the physician came and asked me how I felt, I told him that I could feel nothing with my hands and could not raise them even to my face, that my extremities felt lifeless, and that I had pains in my abdomen together with constant rumblings. The physician replied: "There is no need to be worried. The baths have done their work exceptionally well, for you will certainly get well." I found his words too wonderful to believe. I gave him his fee of fifteen roubles. About a week before the New Year, my wife and I returned to the capital. The physician's prognosis was correct, although it took a year and a half to come about. About a month after my return, I began to feel a release in my hands and was able to raise them a little in front of me to the extent of an inch. The improvement continued, a little each month, until I was able to raise my hands on to the top of my head. By the end of the year and a half, I was able to raise my hands straight above my head, and even to touch the opposite ear. This was a surprise, for I had done nothing to assist my healing and recovery since the time I had taken the baths. The action of the baths had been to provoke a reaction — and the physician had known of this at the time.

I taught my son Mendel how to make the miniature pictures — and we then began to plough that foreign field. We conducted various tests and astonishing experiments. I found a way of making a very small machine for light-imprints: its rear lens was taken from a pair of binoculars, and it was capable of retaining colours, *achromatisch*, as it was composed of three kinds of lenses. I placed this inside a brass tube of the same diameter in width, and into this I inserted a shorter, narrower, brass tube to hold the lens of a microscope — which is a glass lens as small as the lens of the eye — and brought them close up to each other according to their focal distances. I put them inside a dark box, in the usual way. I made a frame for the box containing the lens, and a brass frame for the sensitized glass which was three inches long and one inch wide. This rested on glass plates so that the silver solution[392] should not spoil the brass. Over this I put a brass cover to enclose it completely in darkness. It was possible to make as many as twelve miniatures by moving it lengthwise in twelve positions, each time closing up the part of the tube behind in order to exclude the light which permeated through the picture-glass plate. It was very difficult to ascertain the focal point, for the picture was so small that even a magnifier could not position it accurately. I therefore made a frame for the tube containing the focal lenses: the frame moved on a slide so that, by means of an iron screw[393] set in an iron socket, the tube could be moved forward or backward, towards or away from the sensitized glass. On the end of the screw which projected from the box, above the frame with the sensitized glass, I attached an arrow pointer for turning the screw in its socket so that the tube could be positioned within a hairsbreadth distance away from the sensitized glass. Experiments were made over varying distances, and pictures taken to determine the correct focal point. I noted the position of the pointer and the degrees shown on the dial on the box, in accordance with the size of the picture I wanted to take. It transpired that the focal points of the picture, in their various sizes, remained constant, as indicated by the pointer on the dial. I also noted the distance in inches of the picture on the plate from the tube.

The lighting had to come from clear skies, and not facing the sun. If the light was obscured by clouds, it would be ineffective; even sunlight reflected from a white wall was inadequate. Only the light of the clear skies from the north, penetrating through the glass plate of the picture and the tube on to the plate of sensitized glass was suitable for imprinting fixed pictures within a time-rate of only a few seconds. For this reason, many miniature pictures could be prepared on the plate of sensitized glass instead of merely the one that was required. From these, the best ones could be selected with a microscope and the poor ones erased.

I made an onyx stone capable of cutting glass discs finely and cleanly, like the glass covers used for clock faces. I then fashioned a means of raising the delicate pellicle carrying the image from the sensitized glass with an adhesive solution of tragacanth, and placing it upon the prepared glass disc. When it had dried, I placed over the picture another glass disc which had been smeared lightly with a little Canadian balsam,[394] so that the two would adhere to each other, with the picture between them. I then warmed them in a copper tray over a stove for a half-hour until they fused together. Before it was possible to insert the tube inside a trinket, its edges had to be ground with a hard stone, or a file, until it fitted. At one end of the tube was a narrow hole, through which the semi-convex magnifying lens was inserted. A thread of burnished copper wire was drawn over it and wound into a spiral. The picture-glass was above this and fixed firmly inside an open brass ring, and set at the correct focal distance. The opening of the tube was covered with darkened glass tinted red in contrast to the black of the photograph. The interior of the tube was smeared with strong adhesive to keep it in a fixed position and in a permanent focus. Anyone looking through the small telescope-like barrel would see his loved ones as though they were alive — to his utter astonishment.

One day, Mordecai, my wife's uncle, and brother of my father-in-law, came to visit us. He lived in Kovno. He knew nothing of the miniature pictures inside the viewers. I handed him a small viewer-tube and told him to look into it whilst facing the light of a candle. The picture inside it showed only head and shoulders. When he saw the magnified living picture before him, he turned his head to see who was the man he had been looking at, because he thought he had been looking at a reflection in a mirror. He could not believe that he was only looking at a photograph inside a small viewer-tube. It seemed to me that I ought to be able to make a fortune from my invention, for myself and my sons and my grandchildren. I called it *Microdiorama*, namely, miniature transparent pictures. The first ones I made were pictures of the faces of loved ones inside small golden ornaments, which could be carried on the chain of a pocket-watch. When the wearers showed them to their friends, they were amazed; they asked for my name so that they could order one for themselves, whatever the cost might be, so impressed were they by the pictures. It seemed that my hopes of making a fortune would be justified. I considered applying for a patent, but then I reflected that, so long as I kept the secret of the process to myself, it would be safe, for it would be difficult for anyone else to discover it. I decided to wait and see whether the invention would succeed to such an extent that it would grow too big for me and my sons alone to attend to it, in which case I would take on outside workers but without divulging my secret to anyone, and would then apply for a patent. I found a simple machine for preparing the semi-convex magnifying lenses small enough to fit into the opening of the tubes: it could be worked by a young lad with the aid of a flywheel. Within a matter of ten minutes it produced six lenses polished and burnished to the lustre required for a sharp focus. Everything was prepared to perfection. Our hopes rode high.

In those days, work recommenced on the construction of the papiros machines. I noticed that Peters was not following the instructions I had laid down, but was seeking new methods of his own. When I rebuked him and told him that his ideas were not practicable, he refused to listen to me; he was qualified in mechanical science and so could not err. I broached the matter to the Directors, but they preferred to believe him than me. I withdrew from participation in the machine, warning them that their time and money would be lost for nothing, that the machines would not operate satisfactorily, and it was doubtful whether they could be repaired once they had been constructed. It so happened that, when all the work had been finished, they attempted to make the papirosi, but without success. They then called a meeting at Zhadovski's house, and sent for me, too. Khorvat announced that he was prepared to withdraw from the Company, abandon the machines, and lose his share. Peters requested a further two months in which to repair the machine and have it working properly. The time was granted to him on condition that, if he was unsuccessful at the end of the period, the machine would be taken from him and handed back to me, to repair it as I thought fit. The period came to an end, without his efforts bringing success. He was dismissed. The machine was put into my care, and the workers were ordered to carry out all my instructions. Although Peters had been dismissed, he had not been treated harshly; he had been asked politely not to interfere with me, but was allowed to come every day to examine my work. I decided to change the iron roller on the central beam; this moved the shaft backwards and forwards along the deep, curved channel, and thrust the tobacco from the shaft into the wrapper, then swiftly returned empty. However, the speed of the return movement dragged some of the tobacco back-wards out of the wrapper. Peters saw this and became very angry. He told Zhadovski: "Arenson will destroy this machine so that you will never be able to use it again. He is altering the roller and causing a lot of work, and for no good reason." Zhadovski then called us both together to argue the matter out before him, so that he could decide which of us was in the right. Peters gave his argument as follows: "The roller performs one revolution per second in making a complete papiros. Now there is one part of the roller which expands in the channel to make the shaft stop for a moment, but it is only one part out of a total of twenty. How can this one part, by itself, in the space of the one second it stops, retard the speed of its return so as to prevent tobacco being drawn out on the return movement?" I gave my reply:"If a man throws a small stone with great velocity at a window-pane, the glass will shatter into splinters. The velocity with which the stone is thrown from the hand propels it through the thickness of the glass at a rate of one-fiftieth part of a second. Now, if the stone were shot by explosive from a rifle-barrel, it would pass through the thickness of the glass without shattering it, but it would make a hole in it the shape of the stone: the speed of the stone as it is ejected from the barrel and through the glass is one-hundredth part of a second. How is it then that the window-pane shatters when the stone is forced through by hand-velocity, whereas it allows the stone to pass through a hole when shot out of a barrel? Because hardly has the barrel completed its forward propulsion than it recoils. A similar action occurs with the tobacco shaft before it has filled up the paper, for the force of recoil pulls it backwards quickly. By making it possible for the shaft to stop briefly between the termination of the insertion movement and the commencement of the withdrawal movement, the tobacco is allowed to settle in the wrapper so that it is not drawn back." His only response was to give a polite smile, in his usual manner, and say nothing. After the roller had been altered as I had instructed, the tobacco was no longer pulled backwards. There were other corrections I had to make because of his errors, and these delayed me three months. The Director did not allow me to perform all the alterations that were needed, to avoid shaming Peters, and did not supply tobacco for use in testing. I stopped working on the machine. Zhadovski forbade prospective share purchasers to be shown the machine without his permission, and ordered me to give him the name and address of a possible client so that he could speak with him personally. I knew his reason for this was to tell the client not to purchase my shares "for they are worthless, but purchase from the Company thé shares left by Strogovstsikov." Earlier, Strogovstsikov had contracted, in partnership with Baranov, to supply bread to the army in Romania:

he had invested more than two million roubles, whilst Baranov had invested more than three millions. They had stored up a considerable amount of bread. Then had come along three partners, Hurvitz, Greger and Kahn, who had set up a bakery with large ovens inside Romania, not far from the battle area. The former were left with their bread stale and unsold, so they lost not only their own money but also that of many others. Strogovstsikov, therefore, did not wish to remain in our papiros Company for he would have had to pay for his shares. Instead, he returned all his shares, and left. I was so angry with Zhadovski, the sole remaining Director, that I too abandoned the machine and the business. This was what he and the technician had wanted. They moved the machine to the hallway of the building, saying that it was not working properly. Then they took the other three or four machines they had been in the process of building, and corrected them according to all the improvements I had made to the first machine: they said that the improvements were good, but that the first Arenson machine had not been good and had needed to be improved. Meanwhile, my term of contractual obligation to assist with the construction of the first machines now came to an end, so I abandoned these machines. I had a slight argument with the Director in which I reproached him for his deliberate ill-treatment of me, which had stemmed from his desire to display his superior authority before the noblemen; this foolishness had prevented him from realising how right I had been about Peters, whom he had favoured only because of his qualifications in technology. From the outset, I had strongly urged that they should not pay attention to the technician's suggestion concerning the foundry, and then later I had protested stoutly against their permitting him to construct the first machine according to his own ideas. It was obvious to him now that I had been right in every particular. They had not only lost a great deal of money to no purpose, but three years had passed by like a fleeting cloud and the members of the Company had lost heart and stopped investing further funds, for there seemed to be no end to the affair. Zhadovski knew that I was right, and therefore displayed no anger at my reproaches. On the other hand, he was happy to hear that I was leaving the Company. I waited to learn whether any useful results would emerge from the machines. I had forty-eight shares in it plus the ones remaining which I had not been able to sell. Another two years passed by, during which I ran out of money and was left with no more than three hundred roubles.

When I had been in Revel, some dealers had obtained a load of cotton-wool which had been salvaged from a sunken ship; the cargo had been insured, and the insurance had been paid to the shipowners, so the insurance company had sold all of the cargo, including the unspoilt part, to the highest bidder. Dealers, both big and small, from Petersburg and Moscow and the suburbs of Revel, met at times to buy cotton-wool, and often gained a profit more than double the amount they paid for the goods. I was not willing to entrust my money to strangers in return for a possible future profit, in which I had no faith. However, it was explained to me that my son, Aaron, would do the bidding, and that everything that was bought would be in his name, and that the merchandise would be stored in his name in Koch's warehouse. Furthermore, the key would be in my possession, so that when they wished to sell some of the cotton-wool, I would receive my investment plus the profit, and I would hand the cotton-wool to the buyer. I would pay them their share. I agreed. Simon Aaron went with them, and they bought cotton-wool at a cost of three thousand roubles. They were delighted with their purchase, for they had paid a fair price and the merchandise was in good condition. They calculated that they could sell it within a few days at a profit of five hundred roubles. I intended to give the profit to my son Simon Aaron to help him to improve his personal circumstances. Perhaps it was this calculating in advance which spoiled things for us, for if we have even the slightest faith in luck, whether good or bad, as human beings have had ever since earliest times, we will find that bad luck will dog us constantly and there will be no escape from it. I was extremely cautious in the matter of this business. One of our partners brought a guarantee for the goods to cover any reduction in price or damage in any part, up to a value of one hundred and fifty roubles. It never occurred to me that we could both suffer a combined loss of more than three hundred. I accepted the guarantee of one hundred roubles plus a percentage over two months of about thirty roubles; he promised to bring me a further fifty towards the guarantee, but did not do so. In the final event, there were no buyers for our cotton-wool — and only ours, because other dealers from Petersburg and Moscow who had bought large quantities of merchandise did sell theirs at a profit. Our goods remained stored in Koch's warehouse for about half a year: I paid for the storage. When my partner realised that the loss would be greater than the guarantee of the one hundred roubles he had given, he withdrew from the business. In the following summer, I moved the goods from Revel to Moscow in Simon Aaron's charge. The cost of the transport came to almost one hundred roubles. With the help of an accredited broker, he sold all the merchandise to a prominent Russian businessman, Bogomolov, who first took some away to be treated, and then agreed to pay nine roubles per *pud*. I had calculated to lose a little from my capital investment after deductions for expenses and the hundred roubles guarantee. However, when the man took the cotton-wool into his warehouse, which was immense and filled to capacity with cotton-wool, he quickly loosened the iron bands around the bags, and emptied the wool until it mixed with his own merchandise and became indistinguishable from it. When it came to paying the account, Bogomolov offered to pay only eight roubles per *pud*. Simon Aaron protested that this was sheer robbery. The merchant said to him: "Your merchandise was not good quality, for it was half sand." He took some cotton-wool from the warehouse and showed him how, by moving it around, a lot of sand fell out of it. Simon Aaron refused to accept his payment, and declared that he would call in the accredited broker. He came, and also spoke angrily: "Shut your mouth, you contemptible, evil Jew. Be silent, or I will stuff your mouth with the sand and grit that you put into the cotton-wool. In any case, you do not even have a licence to trade, according to law. Nor will you get even one rouble until the Guild merchant who sent you comes here.'' Simon Aaron realised that he was trapped. He wept bitterly, but thanked the Lord that the man was willing to pay him eight roubles per *pud* — for what could he do if he paid only seven, or even less? The Moscow merchants are daylight robbers, no better than the man who attacks another person in a forest and kills him. So Simon Aaron accepted the payment, and signed a declaration that he had received payment in full for the cotton-wool as agreed. He then returned home.

I suffered a loss of some six hundred roubles in this matter — in addition to all the expenses I had incurred over my illness in Revel, and the money I had spent on my son and his family. When I had begun to make the Microdiorama tubes, I had sent for my son and his family to join me, for he had been taught by the photographer Shapira how to make good and true copies from paper photographs. I hoped that my invention would support us all. I expanded my business with my invention and rented a photographic studio in the Street of Sand, that is Pesky,[395] which is not far from Nevsky Prospect. I applied for a licence from the Governor's office, and was referred to the officials in charge of printing, whose responsibility this was. The young clerk in charge of the printing office demanded twenty-five roubles for himself before he would agree to hasten my application. I gave him the money. Six weeks later, I received a licence to open a photographic studio. Then I had to wait for a second licence to make the miniature pictures. A fortnight passed. The clerk, who was a Pole, asked me for a further twenty-five roubles. I was very annoyed, and so refused. Simon Aaron went to the official in charge of the printing department and asked him about it. He replied that there was no reason for refusing the application. He told the Polish clerk to make out the document. The Pole recorded: Permission has been granted to Arenson to make miniature pictures in tubes in his photographic studio in the Street of Sand. He stamped it with the official seal, so it could not be revoked. I complained strongly to this Pole, saying that I prepared these miniatures in my own room at home by applying them from paper pictures by the light from the window, so why should I be confined to making them only in the studio in the Street of Sand? He answered: ''What I wanted to do to you, I did.'' He was referring to my refusal to give him his bribe. Thus do corrupt officials pervert justice!

Simon Aaron lived there about eight months until he could no longer pay for the rent. He moved out of the Sand and came to live with me. Later, I had to carry on my work without a licence, when this merchandise was prohibited by the wickedness and folly of the corrupt laws which ruled this perverse land — for whatever a man did to earn an honest and upright living for himself and his family, and even for the benefit of others, was forbidden by law. Permission to carry on with one's production could only be obtained after petitioning the officials, the guardians of the law and obtaining from them the freedom to do one's work — such as the manufacture of dynamite,[396] which destroys cities and their inhabitants. No one came to have a miniature photograph inside. Although everyone who saw the pictures praised and lauded them as superior to the pictures made by light-imprint, and promised faithfully to bring the photos of their loved ones and to order silver and gold tubes in all kinds of ornaments to wear over their hearts, no one of them fulfilled his promise. I was astonished that rich men, to whom money was like dust, and who had no need to be false and were not therefore in the habit of telling falsehoods, also did not carry out their promises. I thought of printing notices in the newspapers, and of displaying replicas of the tubes in the more important thoroughfares so that everyone should see them. However, I had no money left over for this, and the rent for my apartment, which had a large display-window, was very high.

One day the physician Jochelson, who had attended to me when I had been suffering with my hands, and had advised me to take a course of treatment at the baths, came to see me. He looked at the miniatures, and was also amazed. He said: "This invention must surely bring you a fortune, for nothing like it has ever been made before. The picture-tubes which come from Paris are so distorted and abominable that they embarrass everyone who looks in them — and even the unspoilt ones bear no comparison with these pictures, which are alive and give a true likeness of living people." He took a few picture-tubes to show to the wealthy people he often visited. The following day, he brought a splintered glass picture of a young woman and asked me to make eight picture-tubes from bone-ivory: the girl was dead, and apparently had left no other photograph of herself than this glass one which had been found only after a photographer's studio had been destroyed by fire. I made the tubes, to the satisfaction of the girl's brothers who paid me my fee of ten roubles. They promised to bring many more pictures, but never returned. The physician showed the miniatures to many wealthy people, who all expressed amazement and calculated how many pictures they would want and talked in terms of hundreds of roubles, and said they would attend to it on the morrow. Their promises were false, as the physician learnt later to his astonishment. He could not comprehend their behaviour, after having seen the enthusiasm they had displayed. No one had compelled them to make promises and, had they wished, they could have easily tested the matter by ordering only one in ivory for the price of three roubles. So he remained bewildered — and we ourselves are still surprised to this day, for every man and woman, high or low, wealthy or poor, master or servant, who looked at the picture-tubes was profoundly impressed and amazed, and declared how delightful it would be to wear a picture of their loved ones over their hearts, and promised to bring photographs of their loved ones to be made into miniatures to fit into whatever gold or silver ornaments they chose. Only one in a hundred of all those who promised fulfilled his word; the other ninety-nine neither came nor gave any orders.

Now, the brother-in-law of our physician-friend owned a tobacco and papiros factory, called *La Foire*, and also a retail shop in the Nevsky thoroughfare where he sold his products. This latter had two nice rooms with three large windows overlooking the street, as well as a glass door. He used to rent out one room which had a window, but at that time he had no tenants living in it. The physician told him about the papiros machines I had invented, and also showed him the Microdiorama. The man agreed to let me have the room with the window in his shop, so that I could display the miniatures in the outside window, and to let me put up a sign over my window display. He said he would not ask for any rent during the first few months but would wait to see whether my MDR[397] would be successful, when he would then stipulate a rent. I fitted out display shelves on which I arranged twelve ivory tubes, with beautiful pictures, in a circle. In the centre, I arranged a light to illuminate the display: this light would burn day and night to attract the attention of the passers-by. I covered the shelf with a large sheet of plain glass on which I placed a large notice I had written in Russian, in big letters, describing the nature and virtues of the pictures. At first, it seemed as though all the residents of the capital would throng to give me their orders — for, no sooner had I finished setting out my display, then a passer-by stopped to look at it, and then another, until very soon a large crowd had gathered, waiting their turn to view the pictures. So it went on, with a host of people standing around the display all day and evening and night. On the very first day I put up the display, a man came with two photographs, one of himself and the other of his loved one, with an order to make a copy with an MDR and enclose it in a gold case, for which he would pay sixteen roubles. It seemed to me that, at last, I had come upon a fortune. My hopes began to mount.

Alas! What are we, and what are all our thoughts! Even this wonderful, beautiful invention was a disappointment. All who saw it praised and lauded it; it was extolled throughout the city. Those who came to see it declared: ''You are bound to make a fortune, and will be able to purchase many houses for yourself in the capital. Everyone is impressed and amazed, for it is truly a most beautiful thing.'' Nevertheless, nothing ever came of it, for only one person in a hundred brought his pictures. However, my landlord did not demand any rent. I made nothing out of all my investment in the MDR. Only occasionally did customers come to have a picture or two made, and some of them paid as much as a hundred and two hundred roubles. Even after a lapse of a year and more, some customers returned with further orders. These, however, were few. My invention brought me no benefit.

I stayed in the shop in Nevsky five months. In order to pay the landlord, I made for him a small machine which he had requested. He had seen papirosi imported from America. They had a long, thin paper tip, which could be held between the smoker's lips. If the smoker wished, he could extend the end of the paper cylinder a distance of three inches away from his mouth, leaving the end of the tobacco two inches away; or if he wished, he could retract it. He wanted to make papirosi like these in order to expand his business, for neither his factory nor his shop was doing a good trade. These long, paper mouthpieces were now manufactured by hand. He wanted me to invent for him a small machine for the manufacture of these paper tips. I did as he wished, and constructed the machine for him. Nevertheless, he did not, in the event, manufacture this type of papirosi, for he realised it would not sell. I deducted it from three months' rental which I owed him, and paid him fifty roubles rent for two months. When I found that I was not earning even this fifty roubles, I decided to rent a workshop in which I could combine both clockmaking and photography. I found a house, the fifth from the Nevsky end, in Little Morskaya Street,[398] which was not a superior commercial thoroughfare, but rather a residential street for the upper classes. I rented it for sixty-three roubles per month. I and my son, Simon Aaron, and his family, lived in a dwelling in the courtyard. We moved in during the month of February, 1881.

In the following month, in March, on the first day of the month, wicked conspirators arose and took the life of the Tsar Alexander the Second with bombs of dynamite which they hurled at him. Had I set up my Microdiorama equipment properly from the beginning, I could have sold numerous pictures of the Tsar, both as he was alive and also in death, in gold and silver and ivory tubes, for I had copied these pictures with superlative skill. However, my removal to my new home had delayed me for more than a month after that terrible event, so I managed to sell only about one hundred MDR tubes. Had I been ready, I could have sold thousands, for paper photographs of the Tsar were then selling in their tens of thousands.

During my first year in Morskaya Street, I earned from my two businesses combined about two hundred and thirty roubles per month. And the same, in the second and third years. Then, income from the MDR began to decrease, whilst my income from clock-repairing rose slightly, so that my combined incomes showed a slight decrease to two hundred and twenty, in the fourth year. During the fifth year, it reduced to two hundred. My expenses were greater than my income, for we all had to live from it.

During 1882, I received letters from New York — from my wife's brother Nehemiah, who had fled from the rioters when they had attacked the Jewish districts of Kiev, and had left to settle in America. He was followed by his brother, Saul, my wife's brother. They took their wives and sons and daughters, and found a good living in the new land. They were followed by Israel, the son-in-law of my wife's brother, Moshe, and he also settled down comfortably. Then Simon Aaron also wanted to go, but he had neither money nor provisions for the journey.

In that same year, the Moscow Exhibition was opened. The Director of the papiros-machine company, and his friend Mitkov, brought the two machines to the city to exhibit them at the Exhibition. They installed steam power and set them operating. Their purpose was to display them in public in order to attract men of wealthy means to join them in forming a public company *(Aktiengesellschaft)*. My Company had invested some eighty thousand roubles and, over a period of five years, had succeeded in building four machines and also prepared the iron and brass parts for a further six. At that time, I still held forty-eight shares. From the very first day of the Exhibition, word spread around Moscow and its environs that there was no exhibit more wonderful than these machines, which could be seen in operation. The general opinion was that the machines were a beautiful crown of glory to the Exhibition. The Tsar's brother, Vladimir,[399] also visited it. He disconnected the steam power from the machine, and turned the roller with his own hands, and made for himself a papiros which he put inside his pocket as a souvenir. He was followed by the rest of the royal family, and by Ministers, all of whom were amazed. The Tsar's brother asked Zhadovski who was the inventor of the machine. I was not present there, for those were days when Russian Jews were treated contemptuously and despicably. Pogroms broke out every day, even with Government support which encouraged the rioters — the deprived masses of the Ukraine — to look upon the Jews as people outside the law. So they brutally assaulted them, looting and maiming and slaying, and raping women and girls. The Government claimed that these were the acts of enemies of the State. Zhadovski, therefore, found it distasteful and bitter to say that the inventor was a Jew from Zamot — especially since my names did not appear on the patent which was registered in the name of the Directors. The technician Peters was in constant attendance at the exhibit, and boasted that he was the inventor. There was no one there to contradict him. When the Tsar's brother enquired concerning the inventor, Zhadovski pointed to Peters, who was standing near the machine. I heard nothing of this at the time. One day, Mitkov stopped his carriage outside my workshop in Little Morskaya Street. He entered and said: "Listen, Arenson. I am willing to buy all your shares and will give you fifty roubles per share." I asked him to raise the price of his offer. He replied: "I cannot fortell the future, but at this particular moment I am willing to pay you two thousand and four hundred roubles. What will happen tomorrow, I do not know: they may be worth more, and it is also possible that I might not be willing to pay even five kopeks for them. However, I will add this much to the price: if, during a period of one year from this day, we are able to establish the machine successfully and set up a new Company, or we ourselves open a large factory for the production of machines in quantity, then I will give you back fifteen shares free of charge." I agreed. I called upon him on the following day, and negotiated the sale on these terms: that I kept three shares for myself in perpetuity, and sold him the remaining forty-five on condition that if, at the expiry of a whole year, I returned to him the two thousand and two hundred and fifty roubles I received from him, he would hand me back thirty of the purchased shares, keeping the remaining fifteen shares for himself without payment; if, however, I did not pay him the money I had received, he would then give me back fifteen shares without payment. He gave me a document, stamped with the great seal of the Mitkov family, whose founder had lived some eight hundred years ago. He also paid the transaction fee. I then handed to Simon Aaron five hundred roubles to pay the fare for him and his family to travel to New York, in America.

The Moscow Exhibition had been open about a month. My friend Shapira, the renowned photographer, came to me and said: "If you would like to exhibit your Microdiorama at the Moscow Exhibition, let me have charge of it, for I have plenty of space at my own display area, where I am showing my pictures of all the leading writers of the country. I can show your miniatures at the same time." I made a table and board, and wrote on it in large letters that the twelve miniatures displayed in front of the board could be made for anyone in gold or silver or ivory, from their own paper photographs, and that these would be made in Moscow during the whole of the summer that the Exhibition was open.[400] I thought that Simon Aaron would be able to stay in Moscow to make the miniatures, either at the Exhibition itself or in some other place. He would receive the clients' pictures at the Exhibition, and there give them the finished work they had ordered. If the business became too much for him to handle, then one of my other sons would go to assist him. Then, before the summer ended and whilst the Exhibition was still open, he could take his family for a holiday in Revel, and then go on to New York. I was entirely mistaken in my plans, for I did not know — and had I been informed in advance, I should not have believed it — how strong had grown the hatred against the Jews among the ignorant masses, and the nobles and Government Ministers. No Jew, whatever his craft or trade, was allowed to exhibit his work at the Exhibition unless he had permission to reside in the provinces of Holy Russia outside the areas of Jewish residence. On his arrival at the Exhibition, his exhibits would be taken from him and put on display, but he himself could not attend the Exhibition for it was forbidden for a Jew to live in Moscow.

Because I had entered late, my display had not yet been accepted, although space had been reserved for me by Shapira at his own stand. They could not, therefore, refuse outright, although they could, by devious means, delay acceptance. One of the officials of the Exhibition was the Russian writer Grigoriev,[401] who was also a teacher at the Petersburg Academy: he took fifty roubles, and the display was accepted from my son. Since Simon Aaron had a craftsman's licence issued by the Guild House in the capital, he would not be prevented from living in Moscow. He did need, however, to make application to the Governor's office and submit all the necessary documents and the licence for the MDR. His application was not acknowledged. He lived in the city, and attended the Exhibition every day until it closed. Just two weeks before it finished he received a permit. Even then, police would not accept it from him, but told him to return it to the City Governor's office who would do whatever they wanted with it. I lost about three hundred roubles because he had to waste the whole summer in Moscow waiting for a permit.

During his daily attendance at the Exhibition, Simon Aaron stood near the papiros machine, and heard people talking about the inventor of that wonderful machine. Everyone mentioned Peters as the inventor. He was extremely angry, and asked Zhadovski the reason for this. He replied: "Your father has already gone off to America. If we had waited for your father to finish the work, this whole generation would have passed away and the work would never have been finished.

It is Peters alone who completed it. Nevertheless, I have never actually said, in so many words, that Peters was the inventor. Nor do I know who it is who has written to the German journal *St. Petersburg Herald* stating that Peters was the inventor.'' This was the first I knew that the *Herald* had written of it, although I had already heard there was a rumour spreading through the city that the machine had not been invented by me but by some other person. I bought all the copies of the *Herald*, and found that the Tsar's brother, Vladimir, had visited the Exhibition and enquired about the inventor, and that Peters had been pointed out to him. This made me furious. I wrote to Zhadovski in strong terms, saying: ''If I were to sell you a pen, which I myself had made, on the condition that I would not sell any others like it to any one else, would I then have sold you my name, too? Would you have called that pen your own, or given it someone else's name? Would you not be caught out in your own lie, even if you paid seventy-seven times its value? The same applies in this case. You know that both you and your friend Khorvat promised that, in due course, my name would be restored to my invention. Were I to lodge a complaint against you with the Department, your name would be put to shame.'' My son took the letter to him. He read it, and said: ''If your father intends to do this, then there is nothing for me but the gun.'' His words were ambiguous: either he meant to shoot me or himself. From his words, it seemed that he might be regretful of what had happened. My son asked him if he would include in his display an announcement that the inventor was Arenson and that the construction had been done by Peters. However, hardly had he turned from him, to leave the Exhibition, than he changed his stubborn mind and called out: ''Let your father do what he likes. I will not write his name.'' Apparently, he had been advised by his friends not to fear me, for the contemptible Jew would find no ears willing to listen to him, even were he being murdered in the street. So he refused. I called upon the famous Leib Mandelstamm:[402] I did not know him personally, but I had heard that he loved his fellow-Jews. I asked his advice, and he said: ''Write to the Director Zhadovski, saying that he should insert into his notice just three words: 'According to the Arenson model'. Also threaten him that, if he continues to refuse, you will publicise his falsehood in the Moscow journals published by Katkov,[403] the only publisher the Tsar reads.'' I had heard that he had been one of Mandelstamm's students. I followed his advice, but the Director still refused. I then asked Mandelstamm to request Katkov to accept my notice. He demurred, saying that Katkov was a very cautious person and would not take the part of an individual Jew against his noble protagonist. Instead, he advised me to see one of the deputies of Minister Bunge[404] who was in charge of the Exhibition: the deputy would listen to my complaint and would pass it on to the Minister who, in due course, would rule in my favour. However, I would have to bribe the deputy with one hundred roubles for his expenses, and also promise to give him more after it was all over. I rejected his advice entirely. I assembled all the documents I had concerning Strogovstsikov and Yerakov and the Company, as well as the letters written by Zhadovski and Peters testifying that I was the inventor, and handed them to a Notary to be copied at a cost of sixteen roubles. I wrote an application to the Governor-General of Moscow, Dolgoruki,[405] who was known as a friend of the Jewish people, enclosing the pages of the ''Herald'' which showed the infamy of Zhadovski. I sent them by horse-post to Governor Dolgoruki, who was the Director of the whole Exhibition. I received no reply, but did hear that the Governor had visited the Exhibition and walked arm-in-arm with Zhadovski. Some two months after the Exhibition closed, I was summoned to the City Hall where I was told, on behalf of the Governor of Moscow, that Zhadovski had never actually said that Peters was the inventor, and that all my documents were being returned to me. So the dispute came to an end.

The Exhibition's organisers awarded Zhadovski a large, gold medallion of honour, on which was engraved: ''For successfully resolving the problem of the manufacture of papirosi by machines.'' Peters was given nothing. Moreover, he was persuaded to announce in the Herald that the notice announcing him as the inventor of the papiros machine had been published in error, and that, though he was sound of mind and limb,[406] he could never have invented this machine. His notice was satirical, and did not clearly state the name of the inventor. I went to see the *Herald's* publisher, intending to have my name published as the inventor. He refused to see me. When the Company's Director returned home from Moscow, he called a meeting of all the shareholders, including myself. When I entered, Zhadovski was so furious that he did not greet me. I sat down amongst them. He spoke as Director and head of the Company, giving an account of the Exhibition and the medallion of honour awarded to him and the Company. At the end, he said that he had other wonderful things to declare to the meeting, but since there was in their midst an enemy of the Company who wished to destroy it, he would not disclose his information at the moment but would reveal it to some of them another time. I looked directly at him, waiting for him to name this enemy aloud. I prepared myself to place before this meeting, amongst whom sat Mitkov, all the facts of the matter in order to vindicate myself. My name, however, was not mentioned. Nevertheless, all the members understood, though they said nothing. Then one of the members arose, and addressed the Director: he was clad in the uniform of an Officer of Hundreds in the cavalry. He was unknown to me. He was the son of Yeliseyev, who had purchased from me three shares in the papiros machine plus a further three hundred roubles on top of the twelve he had paid me for three shares in the wrapper-making machine. He said: ''Indeed, Sir, it would seem that your words must surely be directed at me as your target. You should know, Sir, that I have come here to represent my father, who is ill in bed and has sent me in his place. He owns three shares which he purchased with his own money, in accordance with the Company's regulations.'' He was not aware of the events that had occurred in Moscow, having only recently returned from military service; he thought, therefore, that the Director was referring to him alone. I had to smile a little, but kept silent. The Director answered him with the greatest respect:

"No, Sir. My words were not meant for you, as I know that you have come as your father's representative. They were meant for another." Still he had not dared to mention my name. I remained silent until the end of the meeting. Then all the members signed a declaration to give a special grant of three hundred roubles to Peters for his work at the Exhibition in connection with the machines. I also signed, having given my agreement to it. So we parted.

At that time, I experienced a strong desire to invent something which I had once thought about but which had made me laugh when I had heard that some people had accomplished it, and I had ridiculed them. Movement without end, that is *perpetuo mobile*.[407] Scientists all over the world had declared that it was an impossibility, a philosopher's stone. I knew, of course, that whoever claimed to have accomplished it would be quickly thrown into an asylum for the insane. Nevertheless, because I could not understand why it had not been done, despite my investigations, I constantly enquired about it. I searched, not for the proofs and rules which would bear out my own ideas, but for their opposites, those which refuted the rules I knew and which prevented me from turning my theories into practice. I came to the decision that it would be all right to carry out experiments and tests on this matter so long as I did not impoverish myself in doing so. Past researchers had actually beggared themselves, and become reduced to their last loaf of bread. I considered, however, that it was right to sacrifice a little of the bounty the Lord had given me in an attempt to reveal the hidden forces which conflict with our understanding. Moreover, such new innovations have appeared lately, in our own day, that if a man, living in earlier times, had publicly announced to the scholars of his age that he was working on one of them, he would have been bound and trussed like a madman and pilloried in the stocks. Everywhere there are inventions which the scientists and scholars of the world once declared to be impracticable — such as electric power, the phonograph,[408] railways and steamships, and many more. Today, any country peasant knows they are in daily use. Scholars have little faith.

I determined to construct perpetual motion on such a firm foundation that, even though scientists would see it for themselves and would not fully understand it, they would be able to perform it themselves and prove it worked. Because the principle of this motion was far beyond their comprehension, they had termed it *"Paradox, a matter of analogy"*. On the basis of this extraordinary principle, I set out to construct perpetual motion. My idea was this: if a hollow tube, with an elongated base, were filled with a liquid, either water or mercury, the pressure of the liquid upon the base of the tube would be equal to the weight of the liquid contained in a hollow tube whose lengthwise diameter is equal to the diameter of the width of the base. For example: if a hollow tube twenty inches long with a lengthwise diameter of one inch, which has a broad base giving it the shape of a funnel, were to have the diameter of its base increased ten inches, then the liquid will exert a pressure equal to a tube twenty inches long with a lengthwise diameter of ten inches — and this pressure will be ten times greater than the pressure of the liquid in the tube with the funnel.[409] In order to test this phenomenon, let the following be done. Attach a leather bag, measuring 10 inches by 10, below the base; since the bag is soft, it can be firmly pressed into the tube, and this will raise the level of the liquid slightly. Beneath the leather bag place the arm of the cross-bar of a pair of scales so that, when the liquid presses downwards upon the bag, the latter will press upon the arm of the scales. This pressure of the bag on the arm will be equal to the pressure of a column of liquid 20 inches tall and 10 in diameter, that is 200 cubic inches. If another weight be placed upon the other arm of the crossbar of the scales in order to balance it, its weight would also be 200 cubic inches *(Kubikzoll)*.[410] If the tube and the bag filled with liquid be placed on the arm of the scales it will show a pressure of 20 cubic inches. If the weight of all the liquid in the tube measuring 20 cubic inches be 20 *gerah*,[411] it will exert on the base of a bag 10 square inches wide a pressure of 200 *gerah*. This may be simply proven with an ordinary pair of scales and a leather bag or vesicle, with a round base, measuring 10 square inches. Affix a small wooden bar measuring about 10 square inches under the base, and attach the top opening of the bag to the lower end of the tube by means of a clamp, such as a wooden ring or anything similar which will serve the purpose. Let the tube then be fixed securely to a wooden support on the table. The pan of the scales should be suspended near it from another wooden support on the table. One pan should be placed under the bag, and the other pan weighted until both balance. It will be observed that, so long as the weight in the second pan is less than 200 *gerah*, the pan will not descend, as the second pan is unable to lift the weight pressing upon the base of the bag. Although this is quite remarkable, yet it is so, as I myself have tried and tested.

Because scientists are unable to understand this thing which they can see for themselves, they go into lengthy rationalisations in an attempt to explain the phenomenon. But it is to no avail for they cannot account for it by example from the laws of terrestrial gravity acting upon solids. They have therefore termed the phenomenon *Paradox*. I considered that if I could construct an instrument of this kind which I could secure at its centre on a revolving bar, it would remain balanced on the bar. If, for example, a tube 20 inches long that had, at one end, a heavy bag filled with liquid which was 10 inches in diameter, were held at a point 6 or 7 or 8 inches from the other end so that both ends balanced, then one bar would rest with both its terminal pivots in the two anvil-like depressions. Four tubes would be secured to the bar at the point of balance, each secured independently and all to each other. If, then, the bags be moved towards the ring at the end of the tube so that it will balance on the rotating bar — and also all the four tubes — all the tubes will revolve freely, like a flywheel. If one bag with its pole should drop and press the end of the tube downwards, because of the force of gravity upon the liquid within the bag — this being the force of gravity pressing upon the base of the bag of the bag will be 200 *gerah*, whereas the motive force will be only 10 *gerah*. If I were to gather all the forces of the 200 gerah within a potential force, such as exists in an iron spring, then when the motive force attained its maximum power the potential energy from the 200 *gerah* would be released with a force exceeding the motive power, and would also increase the power required for rotating on the bar with its pivots within the anvil-holes: it would in fact rotate perpetually. There would also be a large surplus of energy remaining for practical use — for the 200 *gerah* which had accumulated within the iron spring would expend 10 *gerah* counteracting the pressure of the liquids within the bag, and 10 would be counteracting the pressure of the liquids within the bag, and 10 would be dissipated within the spring itself, and a further 20 would be expended upon raising itself — making a total sum of 40. If, in addition, a further 60 were lost for any unaccountable reason, there would still remain 100 *gerah* which could be used for practical purposes.

I constructed this and observed that if, during the time that the wooden bars of the bags were moving freely downwards and away from the tubes, the bar rotated upon its pivots, the two upper wooden bars would remain above and the two lower bars beneath. For each tube, I made two bags with wooden bars for both ends, and on the bars I placed two tubes balanced at their centres. Upon releasing them, the two upper bags remained permanently on top and on both sides of the plummet which depended from the centre of the bar resting on its pivots in the anvils whilst the two lower bags remained underneath the bar, on each side of the plummet: the liquids flowed from the two upper bags into the lower ones at an equal rate, filling the bags equally and causing their wooden bars to move away from the tubes. Since the bags would become equal in weight, they would come to rest with the plummet line between them. If we calculated the force of gravity of the four bags under such conditions, we should find that the upper two would offer no resistance to rotation, for as one bag began to descent its force of gravity would become equal to the other which was rising, and neither would be greater than the other. The two lower bags, on the other hand, would differ from each other in regard to their force of gravity: when a bag descends and approaches closer to the plummet, it consistently loses its force of gravity, whereas the rising bag, moving further away from the plummet, gains constantly in force of gravity. The maximum gravity is achieved by the descending bag when it comes to rest on the horizontal line, when it then has ample energy to descend at the rate of the revolving bar. However, the more it descends, the more motive power it loses, until it reaches the lowest part of the plummet, namely the minimum point of the force which has caused it to descend and rotate. On the other hand, the other bag gains in power as it rises from the lowest point of the plummet — the minimum degree of the force resisting its rotation. The force of resistance will increase until it reaches the topmost point of the horizontal line, the maximum point of resistance. When the two bags come to rest, it will be with their central points between maximum and minimum, and there they will stop. It will be seen that the motive power is lacking for supporting the ascending bag from the central point between minimum and maximum up to the horizontal. Since the overall weight of the bag is 10 *gerah,* it may be deduced that the potential energy accumulated within the iron spring due to the pressure of the wooden bar as it descended, and from the force of 200 *gerah,* will be seven times greater than the weight of the ascending bag and will raise it upwards. Similarly with the second and the third and fourth, repeating constantly and moving perpetually, and even providing power for any desired work — such as pulling steam locomotives over railway lines, or a ship across the ocean.

The liquid should be quicksilver; the instruments and bags should be of a suitable size.

How pleasant was the vision! Would that it had turned out as I had envisaged it!

It has been said that heaven and earth were adjured never to allow perpetual motion in this world. Why this should be so, is not easy to comprehend. With a great deal of effort, I had assembled almost every part of the apparatus, and done everything I considered necessary. Next to the tubes filled with quicksilver and with bags secured to them, I had placed narrow iron rods with lead weights at their ends equal to the weight of the quicksilver in the bags. I placed the beam of the scales under the iron rods and silver tubes so that, as the wooden bar of the bag descended it would cause the arm of the scales to drop; then the other would rise, with its lead weight, and would move out of the circle described by the bags and move further away from them. Since the iron rod passes freely through the hole in the revolving bar with the pivots, and since the beam of the scales moves about its centre unequally to its arms — for when the first arm descends one inch under the wooden bar of the bag, the second arm rises 6 or 8 inches, its arm being longer than the first — then the lead weight will exert a pressure six or eight times greater upon the bag near it, and its weight during its descent will equal the weight of the rising bag. I also noticed the short path which the bag took when moving one inch from the circle of the tubes and rising upwards 45 degrees diametrically from the centre of the pivots to the end of the wooden bar, a distance of 20 inches. This 20 inches multiplied by the 10 *gerah* weight of the bag make 200 *gerah.* However, the force of 200 *gerah* pressing upon the base of the wooden bar was insufficient to raise it up. The phenomenon of this matter of analogy, this paradox, remained a mystery.

After I had set up my 'immobile' apparatus, I was reminded of the verses in the prophet Zechariah, which had always attracted me. There was a commentary which I liked which I had not found in any of the usual biblical commentaries: I was even surprised that Mendelssohn had not explained this prophecy, in his *Biur,* [412] in this simple and plain manner. "And he said to me, What do you see? A golden candelabrum with a bowl upon its top, and seven pipes to the lamps, etc." When he asked what these were, he replied: "It is what I have said: Not by might, nor by power, but by My spirit, says the Lord of hosts."[413] None of the commentators gives a reasonable explanation of this parable — for in what way are the lamp and the bowl and the pipes and the olive-trees to be related to the reply 'not by might nor by power but by My spirit'? The true explanation is this: the Angel had shown the prophet in a vision that all the preparations had been made to illuminate the

Temple, to kindle the seven perpetual lights, including the lamp and the lights and the bowl of oil on top of it which continuously supplied the seven lights with oil, and the olives whose oil flowed into the bowl. Everything was ready. Nothing was missing, but yet there was no light in the Temple. Everything had been prepared, except for one little spark to kindle the lights. All the preparations and all the equipment were like a corpse bereft of the spirit of life. That is why, not by might nor by power can it be done, but by My spirit, for when I send a spark of fire from My spirit it will quicken into life. A very pleasing idea. So, I had prepared everything, but the spirit, the reviving spark, was missing: it did not come to life.[414]

At the end of the summer, before the Exhibition had closed, Simon Aaron's wife, son and daughters were living in Revel. The daughters fell ill with a dangerous sickness, typhus. Later, his only son was also taken ill. His wife was alone with the children. I wrote to him in Moscow that he must return home immediately. The Exhibition had brought us no good. The officials of the Exhibition had decided to award me an 'Honourable Mention' for my invention for producing miniature pictures which can be viewed through a magnifying lens: this was the least recognition accorded by the Exhibition — despite all the promises of the experts who evaluated the importance of every new exhibit displayed there. The head of that department was the photographer Levitski,[415] who had told me I would be awarded a large, gold medallion for my precious invention. Unfortunately, he broke his leg, and could not attend the Exhibition during its final days. Nevertheless, he gave me a letter to his friend, expressing his opinion. However, I was a Jew and had no influence, so it was decided to offer me the lowest award, which would be published in their notices. There was, therefore, no need for my son to tarry any longer: this humble award would arrive eventually, however much it might be delayed. He left the Exhibition, and went home to Revel. The children improved, and by the end of the festival of Tabernacles they had completely recovered. Then came a season of storms on land and seas. Because of their still somewhat frail condition at the time, neither his wife nor his children were able to undertake a long sea journey. I told him that he should go to America alone, and I would look after his family. His wife would not agree, saying that if he were going to drown in the ocean, it would be better if they all drowned together. I then suggested that he go and live in Warsaw, and set up the two businesses there, for Warsaw was a large city and he would be able to find a living there. He agreed.

I took his wife and children into my home. He possessed about three hundred roubles: the illness of his children, on top of other expenses, had reduced his capital by half. He went to Warsaw where, first of all, he had to obtain a licence from the Government officials to make the miniatures. He submitted his application together with the Petersburg licence to show that his application was valid. Two months later, he received a reply from the officials, who were Poles, that they would write to Petersburg about him; if they received a favourable reply, he would be granted a licence. Since the city of Warsaw was on the border of the Jewish Pale, no one interfered with him. About thirty days later, I was questioned by the police of the capital concerning my son. They said: "He is looking for a position in the Government Offices in Warsaw, and that is the reason why they are asking whether he is an honest and reliable person." Obviously, they were not aware of the nature of the investigation, since they had retained the Petersburg licence. Some time later, he again applied for a licence, but this time it was refused. He had now been waiting six months, so he complained vehemently: "You told me, in the beginning, that you would enquire about me in Petersburg. You have received a favourable reply, and yet you refuse to let me have a licence." The official answered: "If we give you a permit to make your miniature pictures, you will also make pictures which are forbidden by law." My son replied: "The thief is punished only after he is caught — otherwise, how can he be given punishment? Now I have used up all my money because I had to remain here idle these past six months." He was given no reply.

The following day, he went to the Civic Hall at a time when he knew that the city Governor would also be there, and loudly cried out his protests. The Governor, an honest man, heard him and questioned him. He recounted his complaints to him. The Governor asked: "Why has this man been refused a licence? He has done nothing illegal." The official who had refused him said: "In this city, sir, there are already some thirty photographers, as well as fifty printing houses. It is my responsibility to tour the city daily, inspecting their workshops and ensuring they do not contravene the regulations. If we increase these with more workshops for miniature pictures, I shall be at my wits' end how to deal with them all." He did not blush with shame at saying such foolish and ridiculous things to his superior, although they both understood. Nevertheless, the Governor said quietly: "It is only right that he be granted the licence, for I can see no reason for refusing him." My son then paid five roubles, and received his licence. Evil is in the place of justice, and wickedness in the place of righteousness.[416] By now, his money was spent, so he rented a workshop in the worst quarter of the city where, unknown to him, were the brothels. He went to live there, and published notices in the papers, saying that the Microdiorama company of St. Petersburg was making miniature photographs at his address. He also displayed a few clocks in his room, and fixed a plaque with the address on the wall outside. By now, he had hardly a penny left. Many people came to see the pictures, and many made promises, but only few returned. He considered: I am all alone here; if I bring my wife and children here I shall be able to go and look for clients in the city, and improve my living. So I sent all his family to him in Warsaw, paying a further one hundred roubles plus provisions for the journey. They stayed there until just before the Passover — namely, one year and a half since he had left here. I helped him by paying the rent all the time he lived there, although I had little enough myself. Their poverty increased alarmingly. In addition, his wife became pregnant. Their cramped, filthy lodgings were bad for them, and they had no one to assist or help them. How would this delicate, sick woman be able to manage alone when her time came, and even afterwards when they would still be without income? At that time, I was coming to the end of my resources, so I had to tell him that I was no longer able to support him. They sold all they had, and returned to Petersburg, about three days before the Passover.

In that same year, I fell ill with severe bowel trouble. My chronic complaint, compassionately described as 'swellings and tumours', *Hemoroiden,* [417] had changed into constant flatulent rumblings which recurred all day and were accompanied by uncontrollable evacuations. Everything I ate turned into diarrhoeia which was expelled by the flatulence and dirtied my clothes and my bed during the night. I was treated by physicians but their remedies were of no avail. I grew weary of my life. I did not believe that I could live much longer under such conditions. Poverty and want knocked daily at my door. Furthermore, the time was approaching for my son Mendel to leave for New York, as his time for conscription for military service was approaching. I had no money for his fare; my creditors were pressing hard upon me; I was in despair and without hope. It was at that sore time that I was saddled with the added burden of Simon Aaron and his family. I could see no better future for him than to go to America, which is what he himself desired. However, his wife would not let him go, either by himself or with her: if he went alone, she would have to be supported by me, which was against her pride; nor would she agree to travel together with him. It seemed to me that, if I permitted them to stay with me at all, I would have to continue supporting them, and then he would never leave of his own accord. It grieved me sorely not to be able to permit my children, whom I loved so much, to lodge with me. Nevertheless, my quarters were too small for all of us to live together. When, in due course, she bore the child in my home, I would have the whole burden on my own shoulders — and I myself was ill, and my coffers empty, and the needs of my own family were many. I was therefore compelled to harden my heart towards them and refuse to let them stay with me. They went and rented a small room in another street.

After the festival was over, they looked for a workshop for clock-repairs, and found one in a poor district at a rental of thirty roubles per month. He had to abandon the business of the miniatures because there was no space for it. He earned a small living, just sufficient to pay the rent. He also received some little support from his wife's brother, Abraham, and from myself. His friends brought him a few clocks to repair, but his income was insufficient. When Mendel realised that his brother would not be leaving, he decided to go on his own. He packed up the photographic equipment and left for New York.

On the day he left, his friends went to see him off on the ship going to Riga. One of his friends came to see me to talk a while. He was employed in making paper packets in which papirosi were packed in twenties and twenty-fives. They were cut by hand with knives and scissors. He told me how the workers glued the sides and tops together by hand, and were paid at a daily rate per thousand packets. As I listened, I thought: why should these not be made by a machine — like the machine I had made for manufacturing papirosi, which had been formerly prepared by hand? The man said that no such machine existed.[418] He explained to me the entire process of manufacture, from beginning to end, as well as the type of knives and scissors that were used for this work. I decided to invent a machine for making papiros packets in quantities of twenty-five thousand per day. It should then be easier to find wealthy investors for this invention than for any of my other inventions. The success of my other machines for making papiros-wrappers and whole papirosi depended upon a large number of customers, each of whom could criticise them for good or ill. The paper-packets, however, would be judged only in the few factories where they would be made. Although, on the one hand, the workers making the packets would receive only minimal payment — for the peasant working all day with a knife and scissors would never make more than three hundred packets in a full day's work, for which he was paid one kopek for every three packets, which covered the cost of the paper and glue and coloured strips, all complete, and this would hardly be enough to buy dry bread and salt — nevertheless, a machine producing twenty-five thousand packets could bring its owners a clear profit of about fifteen roubles per day.[419] Now, I had to invent the machine. Alas! The smith who had done all my metalwork previously, with the assistance of his brother Abraham, was no longer available. Nor was Mendel available, as he had left for New York. Abraham was occupied with his business of clock-repairing and miniature photography entirely on his own. There was no one to make the machine for me. There was no way to turn. Whenever I had begun to work on an invention, I had hired a good metal-worker for a wage of about thirty to forty roubles per month, and shown him what to do. At this time, I had no money, and I had no hope of being able to pay a worker his wages. I looked around for someone who would help to pay the wages of an employee as well as the purchase of iron and copper, and who, after the machine had been completed, would also take a partnership in it and continue to pay according to the agreed amount of his liability. It seemed to me that, now people had seen the machine I had made and which had been operating during the entire summer at the Exhibition, they would believe that I could build a paper-packet machine, and they would come forward with offers of financial support. So I went out to seek investors, and found none.

I remembered the man Baranov, whom I had not seen for nine years, although I had heard that he had lost a lot of money when he had contracted to provide bread to the army during the war. Later, he had invested in the talking-wire, the *telefon,* which the Government had ordered for the capital: the Slavophiles were as numerous as locusts at that time, and they had urged the Government not to award Government contracts to foreigners who deprive the Russian people of their sustenance. The telephone Company was the American Bell Company.[420] There were no men of distinction among the Slavophiles who could be compared to the foreign inventors, and even inventions which had been brought out fifty years earlier, like steam power and the telegraph, were introduced into our land only much later by foreigners. The telephone had only recently been invented by foreigners in countries which did not require permits. Nor was there anyone among the Slavophiles, who carried permits at all times, who would dare to install these telephones in the capital. So the French came and, cunningly, in order to appease the Slavophiles, engaged a native-born Russian, with common-sense, to whom they arranged to sell the telephone equipment so that he could then contract with the Government to install telephones in the capital. Having acquired the contract, he would sell all his rights to the French — or the English — and receive his reward, whilst the foreigners would carry out the contract, to the great distress of the Slavophiles. The foreigners found the man Baranov to be a wise, sensible and honest man, so they transferred their telephone affairs into his hands; he then applied for a contract for installing telephones in Petersburg, which he would later hand over to them.

I told my sons to ascertain his address, so that if he were in the city I could write to him and ask him to become a partner in the packaging machine. They laughed at me, saying that Baranov would not bother to reply to me. However, when I had discovered his address and written to him, I received a reply on the very next day, saying that I should call upon him on a certain day and at a certain time, and we could then discuss the matter. I outlined to him the machine I wanted to build, and proposed that if he would finance me with five hundred roubles and pay all the expenses of the machine over a period of four months, he could then take a share of the business equivalent to the amount he had invested. He asked: "What would be the total amount required for setting up the first factory for producing the packets?" I said: "Initially, twenty-five thousand would suffice. Afterwards, once the machine is able to prove to everyone that it is showing a profit, then there will be more than enough investors to enable us to increase the business." He said: "I have faith in your inventions, so I shall agree to your request. However, I am leaving today for the Crimea, so you will have to wait until I return." I said: "Very well. How long will you be away?" He answered: "Not more than two months." "If you promise faithfully to finance me upon your return, I shall wait for you." "Rest assured that I shall be back at the end of two months. I shall then give you three hundred roubles. After you have completed the machine, I shall finance the building of many more. I shall also set up an electric-power machine, and then when people can see the machines in operation, many will come forward to join us in expanding the business. I myself am no longer the Baranov you knew ten years ago, for however much I may have made since then, I have lost even more." I said: "Very well, sir. If you will indeed return in two months' time and give me the three hundred roubles with which to begin putting my ideas into practice, I on my part shall also borrow money and begin my work tomorrow, for people will believe your promise to repay my creditors in two months' time.'' ''Very good. Get the money and begin on the machine. In two months' time I shall repay everything to you.'' Now, I believed that, when previously he had been a partner in the first business, he had repaid to Tutorski the five thousand roubles he had spent — and similarly with the second Company. I had also heard that this was a common practice: once an inventor was known to be trustworthy, he would be financed to complete his invention; a large sum of money would be put aside for the expansion of the project, the inventor would be allocated his share and if the matter prospered the inventor would be able to reap a vast profit. For this reason, I did not go into details concerning all the conditions of our agreement, receiving only his assurance to finance me from the outset; once we had achieved our desire, we could then make an agreement of partnership. He also asked no questions about the terms. We therefore shook hands and made a verbal agreement between us. He left, and I hired a metal-smith for thirty-five roubles per month, and purchased all the equipment I required. I made a base of cedar planks fixed together three-deep cross-wise. They had a thick iron covering on their upper surface and on some parts of their underneath surface for holding the nails which secured all the different parts. The main central shaft which turned the whole machine was made from pure, hard iron. It was my idea not to copy, like a monkey, all the others who made these packets, but to introduce a completely new method. The thick paper would be held in a press to make a frame whose top half would fit over the bottom half. The sides and tops of the packets would be made from the same paper. The machine would detach square pieces from the long strip of paper, and place the sides of the packets against the cover, and then raise the four walls and stand them upright against the cover — and thus the first half of the packet would be ready. A thin band of coloured paper would encircle it and adhere to the outside of the walls, and similarly with the top half of the packet. In order to fit the walls securely inside the cover to ensure that they would not fall out — as happened when paper was scored deeply by handworkers using knives — I made a small, toothed wheel out of hard iron which would pierce small holes close together along the entire length of a line on one side towards the corners of the cover. I saw that it was good. I then had to arrange all the movements of the various parts, and the joining together of the two halves of the packet. On to both covers I glued the paper printed for the papiros factory, and finally dried the packets as they were produced so that they would not lose their shape.

The two months passed by. I believed that Baranov would contact me when he had returned, in order to fulfill his promise. I waited two, three days, but he did not come. I went to the house of the Baroness, where he was living. She told me: ''He did return from the Crimea, and stayed here a couple of days, but he had to return to the Crimea, where he has a house. He will be back in another month's time.'' I told her of our discussions about the machine, and his promise to repay the money within two months. I complained to her: ''If this honest man, Baranov, has lost his money in some unprofitable investment, has he lost his honesty and integrity too? How can he behave so badly towards me?'' She said: "It must be simply that he has forgotten about the matter, for his business affairs cause him a lot of worries. However, I know his address in the Crimea, and if you will pay the telegraph charge for ten words, I shall ask him to reply to you straight away.'' I gave her two roubles and thirty kopeks, and she wrote off to him. On the same day, a reply came back from him, saying: "I shall return at the end of this month, and shall fulfill all I promised.'' I waited. Towards the end of the month, I wrote down on paper the terms of the agreement we should make, similar to those we had made with the papirosi machine: initially, I would receive five hundred roubles — as promised — then, after completion of the machine and if he accepted half of the partnership, namely fifty per cent, he would pay me five thousand roubles, but if he took up to seventy five per cent then he would pay me ten thousand. He would also pay the charges for the patent. The equipment for the manufacture of the packets would be installed by him and the Company. I thought that, if he wanted to alter any of the conditions, I should agree. On the day he was due back, I did not linger but went straight to see him, to make sure that he would not forget me again. He was alone. I said: "Let us talk later about the terms of our agreement. Firstly, however, you told me to borrow money to be repaid within two months, and this I did. I have hired a metal-worker who has been employed for the past three months and whose wages I have paid. I have also prepared all the equipment so that there should be no delay in our work. Now, please, let me have the three hundred roubles to pay off my creditors.'' He took three hundred roubles out of his wallet and placed them on the table in front of me. I continued: "I have made out an agreement with conditions I deem favourable, but have left half the page blank so that you can insert the conditions you prefer.'' I handed it to him, and he read it, and said: "Not so, my dear Arenson.[421] Things have changed a great deal during the past ten years. You will no longer find the kind of partners you want. I did tell you at the outset that I myself am not the man you once knew. I want only the two of us to work on this matter — you as the inventor, and I as the one who will put this business on its feet, for I am well-known and trusted among the wealthy and the men of commerce. So you and I together will build up this affair, and together reap the rewards it will give us. However, it did occur to me that I must give you a large amount of money before the machine is in operation. In any case, even if you search every day for the kind of partners you require, you will never find them.'' I became very upset, and said: "Sir, I know that when the time comes that I shall have my music box — which is a new instrument, for which everyone who sees and hears it will pay well, but for which few will bother to finance me during its construction — nevertheless, you, Sir, because you believe in my ideas will be willing support me to produce this new invention. Afterwards, I could find partners who would not only pay me but would also restore your money to you along with your share, and would see that the machine is successful.'' He said: "Very well. Take the three hundred, and give me a promissory note stating that you received it today. After the machine has been completed, I shall give you the balance of two hundred. For this money, you will give me twenty-five percent of the machine, free of any further charges on my shares, and then my shares shall be like yours, enjoying the interest without investing the capital.'' His words upset me even more, and I said: "It would seem, Sir, that you wish to devour me whole. For the three hundred you offer me, you want to take a quarter of the entire invention — because the two hundred you will give me, after the preliminary work on the machine has been completed, will not be of any use to me, for how will I be able to finish it? Indeed, if I had a machine complete in all its parts, I could find seventy-seven times that amount." He said: "Then I will take only twenty shares. But you record in your note that I am to have twenty-five. You will have to believe me that I will not change my promise not to take the other five." I then said: "You have made it very difficult for me, Sir. Had you told me all this in the beginning, I should not have begun to make the the machine or borrow money. Well, it is done now. My debts press heavily upon me, and that is why you can force me to do exactly as you wish, for I have no way out of this dilemma." He said: "Then do as I say." I gave him a note for twenty-five shares for his five hundred, and received the three hundred roubles. I then left.

Three days later, he came to see how the machine was progressing. I explained all my ideas to him, and he understood and was delighted. I thought to myself that, at the end of the month, I would go to him and beg and cry that all the money had been spent and there was none left to complete the machine, and therefore he should graciously oblige me with further support — for I understood his nature. Two months passed by. I went and pleaded with him, but he would not listen to me. The Baroness told me that he had no money, for he had just purchased some land in the Crimea, and therefore could not support me further: he had also told her that he had lost a fortune on my inventions in the past, and was regretting his willingness to enter into another new partnership with me. I became very despondent, unable to find a way out of my trouble. The machine was only a quarter built: it would take almost a whole year to finish it. My income was insufficient for our needs, nor could we find the wages for the workman. One-fifth of the machine had been sold for three hundred roubles. I was completely at a loss.

A letter arrived from the Baroness asking me to see her in connection with a venture which would be to my benefit. I went, and she told me that the Russian inventor Vradi, whom I knew, had brought out a machine for cutting corks out of reeds to fit any type of liquor-bottle. Hitherto, no such machine existed, and therefore the cork-bark brought from Spain,[422] India and France was cut up with knives by hand, and then rounded with a very thin, sharp knife until it was completely rolled together; the knife had to be re-sharpened during the making of each cork. An able workman could produce two thousand corks in one day. The Russian had invented a machine which could produce three hundred thousand per day. His partner, Graf Schivers, had financed the construction of his machine, purchased a large amount of cork, rented a workshop with steam power, and even paid to have another machine built in another technician's workshop at his request. Nevertheless, neither of the machines was successful, as the knives quickly became blunted and spoiled. When, therefore, they heard from Baranov that I was an inventor of incomparable ability, the Graf offered to pay me two thousand roubles to work on the machines until they were operating successfully. I knew nothing at all about the manufacture of these stoppers, nor had I ever seen the bark from which they were made. Had I been told before, I should not have believed that there was nothing better than cork being used to stop the mouths of liquor bottles, for this has been the method used since time immemorial — or that even today, at the close of the nineteenth century, these corks are still made with knives by hand, as they have been since earliest times. Now that I heard that this was the case, I was utterly astounded.

I said to her: "If they allow me to see the machines working, I might possibly find a way to make them operate successfully." She said: "It will be done tomorrow. The Director of the Graf's cork factory, Kahn, who is a young man whom I know well, will be calling on me tomorrow. I shall speak to him about you, and he will take you to see the machines." The following day, the man came and gave me a full account of Vradi's invention, including all its defects. We went together to the factory, and found everything ready for production in quantity. An iron bar, fixed to the ceiling beams, rotated in a roller activated by steam-power which was installed in the basement of the building. Leather bands stretched from the roller to one of the machines and turned the round, sharp-pointed knife until it was revolving very swiftly. The pieces of cork-bark were placed on a shelf in front, and were cut up into strips two inches wide, the combined width of two stoppers, which were then cut into individual stoppers. The long strips were carried along to another machine, the one invented by Vradi, which comprised four knives. These were in the form of a hollow, iron tube whose interior width equalled the thickness of the cork-stopper; the mouth of the tube was thin, round and sharp, and the other end was thick. It rested on a brass base fitted with teeth, so that when it was rotated by the rotary power of a large toothed wheel, all the wheels and knives turned at the same time. The machine drew the four strips of cork under the blades of the knives. As the knives revolved, they moved downwards, together with the metal bar on which they rested. The blades sheered with great force into the soft cork-bark, cutting out round pieces of wood as it entered the hollow tube of the bar. The knives then rose up again, whilst the four strips of bark moved on to be cut into more round plugs, the last ones forcing the ones in front through the hollow tube, so that they came out in an upwards and backwards movement. This process was repeated all the time. I considered the machine to be satisfactory, and I thought that the knife was Vradi's invention and was a wonderful idea.

I observed two workers cutting the bark with their knives. They described the quality of the wood, the rotary cutting operation and the way they used the hand-knives. I asked the Director to let me have one of the knives from the machine and a strip of cork. I intended to test it in my workshop by turning it so that it would cut into the wood and produce a round plug in one movement. I could then observe the factors preventing the successful operation of the machine, and thereby re-design it and correct it. He acceded to my wishes and gave me everything I wanted. I returned home, and set up the knife-shaft to rotate in the roller, and cut the plugs from the cork. I saw that great pressure and friction were brought upon the soft cork inside the hollow centre of the rotating knife, and that furthermore the strip of bark clung so tightly to the knife-shaft as it rotated with extreme force that the diagonal of its point was slightly less than the diagonal of its other end which rested within the brass base. As the knife turned swiftly upon its axis and began to descend into the wood, it became hot, and softened, and the sharp edge blunted so much that it could not longer cut. If the operation were slowed down, it would not manage to cut through the wood, nor would its daily output be any greater than that performed by hand-work. I thought that if I arranged a bowl of cold water in such a way that water would drip constantly upon the iron bar before it began to descend, this would cool it down. When I spilled a little water over it, the water boiled up and turned into steam which filled the entire room. The plug which had been cut turned half-blue, for the acidity of the atmosphere had heated the internal surface of the hollow iron bar and caused a light rust discolouration. I concluded that the knife would be good enough for cutting a few, small plugs, and could be rotated slowly without over-heating, so that some five or six thousand plugs could be cut each day. Nevertheless, the blade would have to be re-sharpened after every hundred plugs. This machine which Vradi had invented could not operate in the manner he wished.

When Kahn came, I informed him of my conclusion that the machine would be a failure and that I could find no way of correcting its faults, and that in my opinion the Graf would do well to abandon the project, even though he would lose his investment. He departed to inform the Graf of my answer. Now, this new knowledge that had come my way, that no machine existed for the manufacture of these plugs, aroused my whole interest, for it has always been my nature to look for something new and profitable to invent. I had no rest or sleep, neither by day nor by night. I sought and searched for some new method of making these corks. The Director, Kahn, who had been a whole year in the Graf's factory and knew every aspect of the matter, told me all about the work as well as about other machines which were being used in other countries and in our capital, and the reasons for their failure. He said that the hand-knives were used for peeling off the outer layer of the plug, like peeling an apple, in order to give it a smooth, straight finish. By the third day, I had conceived the idea of cutting the plugs with a very long strip of hard iron, which was joined at both ends, like those saws which are known as 'endless saws'. I took a long iron wire, like a clock spring, and tried to sharpen one end until it was capable of splicing easily through a piece of cork. I saw that it would work, and was delighted. I realised that I could make my invention without a great deal of trouble, and that it would be welcomed not only throughout our land but also everywhere else in the world. The one thing that did worry me was whether anyone had brought out an endless knife before this, as stoppers had been used since time of old, and endless knives described as saws had been used more than a hundred years ago. Was it possible that technologists throughout the generations had not considered applying an endless knife like this to the making of corks? I conducted a diligent search, but found no one who could tell me whether such knives had been used for this purpose. In truth, I was wary of divulging the secret of the endless knife, before I made my own application to the Patents Department. I also investigated all machines which incorporated knives. I was told that there was a thick knife, about a cubit long, which had a very swift forward and backward movement. There was also a thin, round knife which rotated upon its own axis — and there were a number of other knives, but no machine which had a knife like this. I therefore believed, although against all logic, that no other machine existed and that I was the first to invent it. I entertained hopes that I could build the machine I wanted without too much trouble, for I thought it would require few parts, which would be simple to operate. However, I did not appreciate how much labour was involved in cutting the plugs by hand, nor how much strength was required by the sinews of the fingers when holding the knife during the cutting process, in comparison with the force required to operate the knife and rotate the wood. I made a serious miscalculation in estimating the force of the hand at half a *pud* and the speed of cutting at five seconds for the completion of one plug. I had forgotten that the machine cuts exceedingly swiftly during the five seconds required for one complete plug, making one-fifth in one second. According to the general principle of mechanics, weight is relative to velocity, so that the weight of an object moving the plug and the knife is five times five, which is twenty-five times half a *pud*, which equals twelve *pud* with a small remainder. This would not be a simple matter. Before I had prepared the machine for operation, I had decided to test it over a period of three months at a cost of a few hundred roubles. When the Director, Kahn, came to ask about Vradi's machine, I told him of my new ideas, and my firm hope to build the machine in a short time, but that I would need money in advance. He spoke to Graf Schivers, who also had confidence in me. The Director came back and asked me to go to see the Graf in order to explain my ideas to him; he would then take a partnership in my machine, and abandon Vradi's. There was, however, another partner in Vradi's machine who had invested some four thousand roubles, and the Graf asked that he should not be told that I had found no way of correcting that machine and that it was of no practical use, for he wanted to find partners who would return his capital investment to him when taking over Vradi's machine. The partner he mentioned was a Polish Jew who had become converted to Christianity. I went to see the Graf, at a time when that partner was not with him, and described my invention, and suggested that he abandon his present project as it would never bring him any profit. Then, suddenly the door was opened, and the steps of the partner Ostoya could be heard approaching — and, in a moment, the whole scene changed. We were talking about correcting Vradi's machine, and the Graf was not willing to pay out two thousand roubles, feeling that it was far better to lose a little of his money in order to be free, and especially as he was not feeling well and intended to visit a spa abroad during the spring. Ostoya, on the other hand, had friends who were willing to continue to support Vradi's machine, because he told them that the great inventor Arenson had agreed to complete the construction for a fee. The following day, the Graf sent Kahn, his Director, to agree to terms with me concerning the new machine. I told him that they should read the agreement I had made over the papirosi machine, and that they should be willing to offer me exactly the same terms for my new invention. The Graf should, therefore, give me one thousand roubles to construct the machine, and when it was completed and able to produce eight stoppers in one operation — namely, about two hundred thousand per day[423] — then he should pay me seven thousand roubles, I would transfer the patent on to his name and he would have sixty per cent. Kahn, on his part, wanted fifteen per cent for his services, so I would be left with twenty-five per cent. The Graf refused my terms. Kahn, however, told me in confidence that he would certainly agree, for he had a friend who had often asked to go into partnership with him in the cork business: this man, a senior official in the Government Service, was the Minister of all Prisons in Russia, by name Davidov. He revealed a secret concerning the Graf, that he was not rich and was hoping to recover his money from Ostoya's friends, in order to be able to pay me. About twenty days went by, and the prospective partners came to inspect Vradi's machine. They brought an expert with them, who pronounced the machine unsuitable. They refused therefore to accept it. Now, before they had come to view the machine, Kahn had been keeping me informed of the day-by-day proceedings. He now urged me to press the Graf for a decision. I wrote advertisements for the newspapers, stating that I possessed a new invention for making corks, and was seeking partners. When I showed the Graf these notices, he became very worried, for he did not want Ostoya's friends to know that I was not going to correct the machine, and that in fact I had a new machine, for then they would not be willing to invest in his machine. On the following day he came to see me, and said: "It is true that I did not wish to pay you the money you asked for, because it was a large amount and I cannot afford to pay it. Necessity compels me to pay you. Come with me tomorrow to the house of Minister Davidov and we shall make an agreement whereby you will receive five hundred roubles to commence work on the machine, and another five hundred a month later. After the machine has been completed to our satisfaction, we shall give you seven thousand roubles as well as the forty per cent, plus one hundred and fifty roubles per month during the first year. If, however, we do not like the machine and we refuse to accept it, then we shall restore the patent and the machine to you, and you must give half back to us, namely five hundred out of the thousand, with a promissory note for a period of six months.'' He told me to prepare all the descriptions and specifications of the machine, as well as an application to the Department in both their names and mine. When I was alone with the Graf discussing the terms of the agreement, he changed his mind so much that we had to rewrite the agreement seven times. It seemed to me that he was acting deceitfully, and that whatever he promised today he would change tomorrow, on the pretext that he had not stated this in the agreement in accordance with Russian law and the rules of Russian grammar — implying thereby that I, being a Jew, was not sufficiently familiar with his language. In truth, as I later found out, he was simply seeking some way to bind me with the agreement so that he would have complete possession over me and the machine; then if he found the machine satisfactory, he could give me whatever he pleased. I, however, had made agreements before, more than just once or twice. All my partners had been native-born Russians, and some had been senior officials who knew their own language thoroughly. None of them had ever said that I had been unable to record their words correctly in an agreement, for they had been honest men who had acknowledged my rights. Now he was sending me to his friend, the great Minister Davidov who, I had heard, was an even more wicked person than he was.

I went to see him at the appointed time, but without taking the machine's specifications with me. I wanted to see, first, the teeth and claws of this new animal, after which I would know what to do. However, Davidov appeared a very kindly man, friendly towards Jews and a patron of inventors. On a large sheet of paper he wrote down all the terms of the agreement, saying that he would alter only the style in accordance with the laws of Russian grammar, without altering the actual contents themselves. When he had finished, he began to read it aloud. The Graf said, ''Arenson can read'', and handed it to me. I read it, and found it full of distortions and falsehoods which we had never mentioned or even considered. I made a note of all the places which needed to be amended. He argued with me saying that it mattered little whether it was written one way or another, and that he had re-written it only in accordance with grammatical rules, whereas my comments were not in accordance with the rules of grammar and logic. I became quite furious, and said: ''Truly, gentlemen, you are learned men of high estate, whereas I come from the humblest and most afflicted of nations. I have had to learn this matter of preparing contracts of agreement. Here are contracts concerning three of my inventions which I made with men of high degree, Grafs and Dukes, and which were written by three different Notaries in the capital, who certainly know the Russian language. Look at them, peruse them, and you will see that what I have written is true, and that I have not erred against the rules of the Russian language. On the contrary, you can see for yourselves how your own first words, written at the beginning of the agreement, contradict the laws of logic.'' Davidov's eyes flashed with contempt as he said: ''Be good enough to show us where we have transgressed the laws of logic.'' Humbly I begged their indulgence, saying that I would do this if they would permit me to do so. They indicated their agreement. I picked up the contract and read: ''We, the undersigned, partners in the Company for manufacturing corks with machines invented by Arenson, the illustrious Minister. . . . and the illustrious Minister. . . . have made out this day this contract of agreement according to the conditions enumerated below.'' I asked them: ''Gentlemen, how do you come to be, today, partners in a cork-manufacturing company which does not exist and never has, but will come into being only after you have made out the agreement and signed it. Only then can you call yourselves 'Partners in the Company . . .' You have not become partners all of a sudden, out of the blue. Logically, it should have been written in the same manner as these three Notaries: ''We, the undersigned . . . named . . ., and named . . . have made this day a contract of agreement'' — and only later, in the fifth section, when the terms begin to refer generally to all the partners, are they then referred to as partners in the cork-manufacturing company. But not at the beginning . . .'' They understood. Davidov said: ''Then how is it that you can be referred to in the agreement as the inventor, when you have not yet invented anything? You have not even begun to make the machine.'' I answered: ''You must know, Sir, that every new invention originates in the inventor's own mind, and once he has translated his thoughts into diagrams or written descriptions, his invention exists. Even though he may be unable to construct it himself, and though it be built by others many years later, he will still be recognised as its inventor. Such is not, however, the case where a contract of agreement is concerned. If I should make an agreement with a first-class violinist who, according to our terms, will undertake to teach me to play the violin extremely well, and if I should write at the beginning of the contract that I, Arenson, the violinist . . . such and such, shall I not be contravening the laws of logic?'' They were silent. Then they said: ''Take the contract home with you, and read it for yourself. When you come tomorrow evening, you will find it written out exactly as you want it, without any alteration. You can then sign it and receive your five hundred roubles.'' He opened the drawer in his table to show that he was rich and had a lot of money. I departed.

The following evening, I went to Davidov's house. I took the diagrams and specifications with me. I stood in the hall. No one was about. I placed the lists, which were folded inside a newspaper, on a window ledge at one side of the hall, but I put the descriptions inside my coat pocket. I was afraid that this criminal might steal my invention and send it to the Department in someone else's name, for my own name had not been registered on it. I believed that they would not be able to understand the diagrams alone without the specifications and descriptions. On the window ledge were sheets of paper which had been left by people who had concluded transactions in the house. I waited a few minutes, but no one came. The door to the other room was ajar and I could hear the footsteps of a man walking from the inner room towards this room. Suddenly, a huge dog, as massive as a bear, came out of a room and looked straight at me. Then, the other door opened and the Minister appeared. He came towards me. He was muttering into his moustache, "Where is the servant? Why does he not receive the guests?" He went up to the window, lifted up the pile of papers and looked inside them. When he saw that the diagrams were not folded inside them he threw them away. He then called for his servant and cursed him for not keeping the hall tidy and clean. He overlooked, however, the bundle of diagrams which I had placed at one side. He called to me, and I went to him. A few minutes later, the Graf also came in, as though he had been hiding in an inner room. We sat down in the same places as before. Davidov said: "I have made out a new contract of agreement according to your wishes, word for word. Sign it, and you can have the money." I kept silent. The Graf said: "Let him read it." He gave me the contract, and I stood up to read it because the light was too far away. The Minister then said: "Sit down at the other table, and read; there is light there." Hardly had I read a couple of sections when I realised that they were behaving even more perfidiously than yesterday. I was reluctant to read it through entirely. I said: "I am sorry, gentlemen, but I cannot sign this document." "Why not? What have you found in it? It has been made out according to your wishes." "No, Sirs. I will not sell my birthright for a pottage of lentils. I will not surrender my invention for five hundred roubles." They replied: "It seems very plain that you have no confidence in your invention yourself, otherwise you would not be afraid to sell it even at a low price. Remember that, in these days, there are numerous inventors producing new machines daily but investors are few. If you wish, come here tomorrow and I will introduce you to expert technicians who can design a better machine than yours." I decided to alarm the Graf by telling him about the notices I was going to publish. I said: "It is true that there are only few investors for new inventions. That is why tomorrow I shall insert notices in all the papers. I shall find someone." I did not know that Davidov was also aware of the Graf's fear of this. He became furious; his eyes reflected murder and violence. He said: "I shall show you how powerful I am, you despicable Jew. Tomorrow I shall see Orzhevski, and he will forbid all newspaper publishers to print your notices." I answered him: "I do not fear even your friend Orzhevski. Not even his Majesty, the Tsar of Russia, can steal the creation of my own mind from me." He rushed at me in great wrath as though about to murder me, and thundered at the top of his voice: "How dare your contemptible lips utter the name of the illustrious Orzhevski! Do you know who he is? He is the Chief of all the Police forces in the country." "It is true, Sir, that I did not know who he was. When you said that you could ask him anything, and he would do it for you, I naturally presumed that he was simply a close friend of yours." His wrath subsided. However, I was afraid to leave them under such stormy conditions — not from fear of Orzhevski, but of the huge hound I had seen in the hall. If he were to set it on me and it bit me, I might sue him to all eternity without avail, since there would be no witnesses against him. I sought a way to escape from my predicament, and said: "I did not really intend to publish these notices, nor have I informed anyone concerning the machine. It seems that I misunderstood the Graf's intentions, for he has delayed this matter of the partnership for several days, and that is why I thought I might alarm him with these notices. I see now that I ascribed the wrong reasons to the Graf's actions.'' Davidov asked: ''What is the real reason which you have discovered? Will you not tell us?'' I said: ''I cannot reveal my thoughts concerning the Graf in his presence.'' Then both of them said: ''You must not refrain from divulging all your thoughts, for you are an honest and straightforward person, as many people have declared. Let us have the whole truth now.'' I then said: ''I learned today, here in your house, Sir, that this gentleman has no money. That is the reason.''Davidov turned his back on both of us, and mumbled softly to himself. The Graf remained silent. I said: ''Gentlemen, in all sincerity I say to you that I will not publish any notices nor commence to work on the machine for a long time yet. First, I shall complete my cigarette-packet machine, and find partners to finance me in it. After that, I shall build the cork-machine.'' Davidov asked me to give him a signed document endorsing that promise. I said: ''I have already told you that I will not sell my birthright for a pottage of lentils. I will keep my word.'' They were satisfied, and began to discuss the cork-machine again. Finally, after we had become friendly once more, I bade them farewell, and went out into the hall. The terrible dog was not there. I arrived home safely. Two days later, I was told that they had met again on the following evening after our meeting, and had waited for me to come, believing that I would surely return and enter into partnership with them. So do these illustrious officials of our country presume to behave in so contemptuous a manner towards a Jew, even after they have learned that he is a man of honesty and integrity — for how can they believe even what they see and hear so long as they consider a Jew to be less than human? My hatred of them burned deep. Though they were to heap gold upon me and my machine, and fill my house with silver, I would not wish to meet them again.

I abandoned the cork-machine for a while, and returned to the papiros-packet machine. I was desperately short of capital, and had no means of paying the worker's wages or buying the metal parts I needed. Then the Director, Kahn, came and said I should take his advice to see Ostoya, who had been the Graf's partner in Vradi's machine. He had shown the machine to some people who had been interested in becoming partners with him and purchasing the Graf's shares. They had brought expert technicians with them, who had declared that it would never operate successfully. Kahn, therefore, had disclosed my invention to Ostoya who had believed him and expressed himself willing to make an agreement with me instead of with the Graf. However, since he could not afford to pay the thousand roubles I requested for preparing the machine, the two of them would combine and give me five hundred roubles, so that I could build the first machine and produce only half the quantity of corks I had estimated to make for the Graf's thousand roubles: the rest of the terms would remain the same as those I had agreed upon with the Graf. He was confident that, once the smaller machine was working successfully, even though it produced fewer stoppers, they would be able to find many partners of substance and wealth who would extend the activities of the enterprise. He said that there were men of wealth who would be willing, even today, to make an agreement with us but, unfortunately, we did not have even a small machine producing stoppers for liquor bottles. I said: "Very well. I will make an agreement with both of you. It will not worry me if you decide to change your minds about entering into partnership over an invention which demands so much finance, for I know full well that once the machine is in operation, money will come flying in from all sides. The five hundred you are advancing for the construction of the machine will suffice for the present. You, however, must undertake in the agreement to have the machine set up for operation under steam power, and to provide a quantity of cork-wood for testing purposes. Then, after the machine has been running successfully for thirty days, you will pay me seven thousand roubles, in return for which I will give you sixty per cent and also transfer the patent to the name of the Company which you will form at that time." We agreed on this. On the next day, they both came to see me and we wrote down the terms of our agreement. However, the man Ostoya was unable to register the contract in his own name, for a reason he could not reveal to us, and instead asked for it to be registered in his wife's name. I acceded to his request. Then Kahn said that he would like to divide the payments that were due to me in two parts, one for each of them: the first payment would come from Ostoya's wife who would give two hundred and fifty roubles, and in a month'a time he would bring his share, for he did not have sufficient money at the moment. Similarly, he wanted to split the payments of the seven thousand roubles, enabling him to bring his half one month after the first payment had been made. When I began to record this in writing, Ostoya said that in the event that Kahn could not fulfil his obligation, and did not bring his deposit in a month's time, then the contract should not be declared void, but should remain in force on his wife's name. I could find nothing in this contrary to my interests, so I copied it down stating that, if Kahn could not fulfil his obligations as mentioned in the contract, he would lose his rights in our agreement, and the contract would remain in full force with Ostoya's wife. They also stipulated a penalty of ten thousand roubles which I would have to pay if I entered into any agreement over my machine with any other person beside them; I would also lose all my shares in it. So we agreed.

I have generally been very cautious when making an agreement with anyone concerning Company contracts, but this time however I did not give my usual attention to every detail. When I had first arrived in Petersburg, and had been living with Finkelstein, I had known nothing about legal matters and Notaries — for there were none in the rural districts at that time. I used to listen carefully to the discussions held by the many people who came to the house to do business, and thus learned the different aspects of the law presented daily in the capital. All of them had told me that any contract of agreement made in a private house and not stamped with a Notary's seal, had the force of a promissory note but not of an agreement; therefore, in a case where partners brought a suit before a judge, only the damages had to be paid for, but not any penalty which had been written into the document. Furthermore, if one party had obligated himself to perform any physical service for the other, such as lifting a heavy weight or some other labour, if the contract had not been stamped with the seal of the Notary, then no judge would compel him to perform anything against his will. I had believed what they told me, for I had no reason to doubt them. Even today I find it astonishing that they actually told me such things: either they themselves erred, because they were not learned in legal matters, or they entered into a conspiracy to deceive me and lead me astray. However, I believed them, and therefore did not seek the advice of a qualified person. In this present instance, my trust proved a stumbling-block and hindrance to me. I paid scant attention to the conditions they set out, for I believed that whatever penalty was included in the contract would be invalid, since it had not been testified by a Notary. Ostoya's wife handed me the two hundred and fifty roubles, and I signed the contract, and expected to receive the same amount from Kahn in another thirty days' time. I then moved the papirosi-packet machine to a corner of my factory, and began to prepare everything for making the cork machine. My partners urged me to disclose to them the basic secret of my machine, which was the knife. I assured them that, after I had submitted all the specifications to the Department and obtained the patent, there would be no need for further secrecy. Then they urged me to hasten my work. Less than a month later, I submitted an application to the Department. Ostoya came and urged me to reveal the secret of the knife to him; after Kahn had paid his share, I could reveal it to him also. I showed him the diagrams and the specifications and the special qualities of the knife. He was both astonished and delighted. He went away, and revealed the secret to Kahn. Kahn told him that, in fact, a similar knife already existed in Petersburg, that it was not a new invention, and that a machine with a knife like this existed in the cork-factory owned by Miller. He came and told me that the Director of Miller's factory had shown him the diagrams some time ago, including its endless knife. Had he not added more to this, I might have believed him, but he went on to say that he had seen the diagrams himself: there were numerous holes along the entire length of the knife, whilst the wheels which turned it were studded with nails which engaged with the holes in order to maintain the knife's movement; the knife was about one-quarter of an inch wide. It was this final part of his description which proved he was spreading a false report, as the movement of endless saws is not affected even when operated with wheels which do not have holes and nails. I realised that no such knife actually existed. At the end of the month, he said he had no money, and gave me back my note for fifteen per cent, which was his share, and the contract. He was removed from our Company according to our terms of agreement. I was left with Ostoya's wife, for her husband had not succeeded in finding other partners to take Kahn's place — nor had he undertaken, in the contract, to find other partners in addition to himself. I now realised my mistake. How could I carry out my project without money? Even if I did manage to construct the machine, Ostoya's wife would be a partner with thirty per cent, and would have to pay me three thousand five hundred; but, if she did not have the money, then I, with my seventy per cent, would be obliged to chase her all over Russia in order to sue her, and would have to wait for ever before she paid me. On the other hand, without her consent I could not dare take on any other partners, for her husband had warned me that, according to the contract, I could not seek any other partners without her permission. I went for advice to the Legal Advisory Department in the District Courthouse. They said that I could do nothing without her. They pointed out my long-standing error: any contract or agreement that had been signed by hand and witnessed, even without a Notary, had the same force in law, in all respects, including penalties and fines, as that signed and sealed by a Notary. However, the Government tax that had not been paid when the agreement had been made out would have to be paid tenfold by each partner to the agreement. If, therefore, I found other partners without her permission, I would have to pay the penalty mentioned in the agreement, and could be brought to trial as a criminal. (After Kahn had left our Company, her husband had stopped seeing me, for he believed he would see me again only after I had finished the machine, when I would then have to humble myself before him and his wife, and they would be willing to speak to me again.) The legal advisors took pity on me, and said: ''According to the terms of the agreement, you did not commit yourself to making the machine, and only after you have made it can this person have control over it. Therefore, abandon all the work, and tell him that you will do no work at all until he complies with your request to find other partners.'' In truth, who would want to become a partner to this poor and unworthy woman who ruled the entire business? They would invest vast funds to expand the business, and she would have control over them. An alternative solution was suggested for me: according to the terms of our contract, I could sell the patent to other people even without the woman's permission, although I was not permitted to sell the parts of the machine or its products. I then determined to deprive them entirely of the cork-producing machine, so I placed the papirosi-packet machine in the centre of the room to give the impression that we were engaged on that and also on the parts that we would have to make in his presence, as though they belonged to the packet-machine; then, as soon as he left, we would revert to the making of the corks. Ostoya came to see me at work, and I told him that I was going to sell the whole patent to others without asking his consent. He displayed no alarm at my threat, nor did his wife give me permission to find other partners. He left, and I did not see him again for three or four months.

After this, I began to look for partners in the cork-making machine who would finance me during its construction. I wrote notices giving full descriptions of the benefits it would realise, and added that any one who so desired could act as a middle-man for me. One of my acquaintances, the physician Samuel Aronovitz, of Plonghien in the district of Telz, showed one of the notices to his friend Friedman, who read it and said he would be willing to enter into an agreement with me. We did not disclose to him the existence of the other agreement — nor does he know of it to this day. He was engaged in a liquor-exporting business with a wealthy merchant named Freman. His fellow-Director in the business was another German called Weidenbrück. Now, the German Freman was a native of Hamburg, where he had once had a business dealing in these stoppers; there was a great demand in Hamburg for the stoppers, and thousands of millions were used there every year. Freman knew that there was no machine existing in the whole world that would produce hundreds of thousands of corks per day, and therefore when Friedman told him of my invention, he said: "I am sure that all this story about the machine is just another one of those legendary fables without reality." Friedman replied: "That could be true, for I myself have not seen the machine, either. I have heard of it only from the physician Aronovitz. However, the place is not far from here, since it is actually located in the capital, in Little Morskaya Street. Let us go and see for ourselves what substance there is in the man's dreams." Both Freman and Weidenbrück answered: "Very well. If such a machine exists, and is capable of producing more than a hundred thousand corks per day, its value will be incalculable. The price of only ten thousand, which the inventor has asked, is very small. Let us all go together tomorrow, and have a look at it."

I was working with one technician, and had built the machine to cut eight corks in one operation. I had arranged the four arms, which guided the four square pieces of wood to the knife, in pairs on each side of the machine, on the right and the left. Each of the square pieces of cork was two inches long, which would make two stoppers for liquor bottles: they would be spliced into two by a different machine which, at the time, I had not yet begun to build — nor had I yet made, for that matter, more than one of the four arms to guide the cork towards the knife, and even that one was by no means complete, although anyone with any technical knowledge would have been able to confirm that it was satisfactory. The following day, the three men came with Aronovitz. I demonstrated to them the operation of the single arm, and how it moved the square piece of cork so that it could be cut into a round shape by the constantly rotating endless knife. I also described how another machine, which had not yet been built, would assist the principal machine in the splicing of the cork, and a third machine would cut them into halves, making two stoppers. I also impressed upon them that the machine could produce any kind of cork required — long, short, thick, thin and even conical. They could all be made quite easily, simply by altering the arrangement and certain parts of the machine. The men looked at each other in astonishment, for they had never expected to see anything like this, even though they understood very little of what I told them. Since they had no choice but to believe the evidence of their own eyes, they were therefore able to believe also what I disclosed to them concerning my projected plans for the future. They enquired about the patent. I said: "I have submitted an application to the Department, together with most of the diagrams and specifications, which will not be completed until I have ascertained all the parts which the machine will require after it has been tested in operation. In any case, I have already changed many of them, and altered some diagrams. However, since the essential part of the invention is the endless knife, I have informed the Department of it, and henceforth no other person will dare to construct machines like these." They believed me, and departed.

Later, we discussed the terms of the contract. They were willing to accept all the conditions I had published in my notices: they would give me one thousand roubles to complete the machine; after it was finished I would build for them, still at their expense, the first machine, and this would operate under steam power; the diagrams and the specifications and the patent would be in the names of all four of us, and they would pay the tax on the patent for a period of ten years; after the new machine had been operating successfully for one month, they would pay me nine thousand roubles for their share of seventy-five per cent, whilst I undertook not to sell fifteen per cent to anyone else without their permission; from the day I began to draw up the new specifications for the new machine, and for one year thereafter, they would pay me one hundred and fifty roubles per month; if, during the first month when the machine was under test, they found it unsatisfactory, they would have the right to transfer the new machine to me, together with all the equipment pertaining to it, and the patent would be registered in my name alone — and I would then repay to them their deposit of one thousand roubles over a period of six months.

Then the Jew, Friedman, began to utter complaints against me and the conditions of the contract, saying that I was devising some method of cheating them and depriving them of their investment so that I could build an even better machine and take out a new patent and find new partners who would offer me even more money. He therefore refused to agree to the condition that the machine revert to me along with the patent if they changed their minds about financing it. When I observed how distorted were the Jew's thoughts, I became concerned in case he refused to finance the machine after the test period, and instead order me to improve and modify it, and thus I would not receive my nine thousand roubles possibly for years, until they had gained a substantial profit on their investment — which, I now realised, had been his intention ever since we had started to discuss the agreement. We disputed the matter bitterly, the Germans supporting him since it was in their interest. Days went by. I refused to budge from my stand, maintaining at all times: "If you, gentlemen, give me the nine thousand roubles, you can have the right over the patent. If you do not have the money, then you must return it to me at the agreed time. I have no alternative in this matter, for I know that no one, however genuine he may be, will wish to give his money to a poor inventor to support him with food and clothing for a number of years, so long as his invention exists solely in his own mind and he has produced nothing practical by his own labours.'' The man Friedman had not studied much Gemara in his life, but from the little that he had learned in his youth he was always able to find a reason of some sort for whatever he wanted and even to justify any dishonesty. He had realised that I could undoubtedly make a machine which would operate successfully, but that I might then spike it with a knife or a nail so that they would think it was unsuccessful. They would then refuse to finance it, and would restore the machine and patent to me. I would then sell it to anyone willing to pay my price. The Germans, who knew nothing of the Gemara and its methods, were unwilling to suspect me without reason, and therefore asked me about this. The question was a difficult one to answer, for if a man should say to you that he is afraid to walk through a forest with you in case you slay him, what answer can you give to assure him so long as he has no faith in you? I had to find a suitable reply, so I said: ''If, Sirs, during the test period, you are dissatisfied with the machine, then you may call in technical experts from the Academy to inspect it. If they declare that I have been deceiving you, or that I have committed an error, then I will make the correction according to their instructions. Afterwards, you can come back and inspect it again. Furthermore, even if you still refuse to finance the machine and you return it and the patent to me, I shall not claim the right to sell it or to take on other partners without first notifying you so that you may have the opportunity to come and inspect the machine, even as long as a year or two years later. Only then, after you have tested the machine and rejected it, will I have the right to appoint new partners in your place.'' No one could find any argument against this, so the contract was made out in accordance with my final terms. They gave me five hundred roubles, and arranged for me to see them in three days' time to sign the agreement which they would prepare and to receive a further five hundred roubles.

I arrived on the third day to find them in the other room, whispering together. The Jew did most of the speaking. He took the book from them and laid it in front of me for my signature. I picked it up, went over to one side of the room and sat down to read it. Everything which the Jew had planned from the outset, he had written into the contract. I was very upset. How could a man, who must have known that I would study every little word in the document, imagine he could deceive or blind me with the five hundred roubles that had been placed before me, so that I would not pay attention to the words in the document? I said: ''Worthy gentlemen, you are well aware that I am an honest man, and more trustworthy than most men. I find this difficult to comprehend. If you do not write into the contract all the things we agreed upon the other day, I will not sign the agreement, come what may.'' I left them. The following day, Friedman sent someone to enquire about the five hundred roubles I had already received. I replied that I would return the money to them, to the last rouble. It seemed that, when I had left them, the Germans had said: ''Arenson is right in refusing to sign this, but we must decide now whether to carry on or to bring this machine affair to an end.'' This messenger, therefore, had been sent to offer new, though dishonest proposals for inclusion in the contract. Finally, when he had grown tired of talking, he requested, on behalf of the three men, that I go to see them on the morrow in order to finalise the agreement to our mutual satisfaction. I went. Friedman had found a man well-versed in the law, a Senator named Saphir. He was an honest and just man, and a friend of his. Whatever he would advise concerning the terms of the agreement would be accepted. I complied with this, but decided that, if this legal expert tried to deceive me, I would not accede to him. Nevertheless, I would go and, at least, hear what he had to say. We went to see Saphir. He was at the house of the Notary who managed all his affairs. When I had put all my terms to him, he realised how just my case was. He said: ''Come back tomorrow, and I shall have a contract ready for you.'' So it turned out. We made the agreement according to the conditions I had stipulated. I was given the thousand roubles. They urged me to complete the construction of the new machine as quickly as possible, and to prepare the lists for all its parts. I knew that, until I had actually put each operation of the first machine to practical test, I could not be certain what might happen later, as some of the new parts might have to be altered. I therefore told them: ''Wait a few more days, until I have made all four of the arms which guide the square pieces of wood towards the knife. Then I shall prepare the specifications.'' However, they did not understand me, but urged me to hurry lest we should not be ready by the commencement of Spring when the ocean waters shed their covering of ice. It was during that time that the ships came from Spain laden with cork-bark: these trees grew abundantly in the forests of Spain and shed their bark once every six or eight years. The Spaniards would gather them, clean them, and sort them according to their different grades, and the best ones would be separated and kept to one side. They would tie these into bundles with iron bands, and load them on to ships for transit to all the countries of Europe. The larger merchants would purchase entire ship loads of cork, from which the stoppers would be made during the whole year, thus keeping their costs to the minimum. They told me that, since they would not invest in the purchase of entire shiploads of cork until they had seen my machine working, if I were not ready by the beginning of Spring, they would miss the arrival of the ships and would be therefore delayed for another year. I said: ''Bring me a technician who can prepare specifications from the machine I am making at the moment and I will submit them to the Department. In this way, he will learn about the different parts of the machine and will then find it easy to prepare the specifications for the new machine.'' They sent me a student from the Institute of Technology, a Jew, who had an excellent knowledge of mathematics and mechanics — whereas my own was only superficial. Because of their persistent urging that I hasten the work, I took him in and showed him all the machine's operations, and explained my intention to ensure that all the parts worked according to the proper laws of mechanics. Then the two Germans suffered a brainstorm and became terrified in case the technician who was constructing the new machine should steal the secret of its operation and sell it to others. Despite all my assurances that, once the secret of the machine's operation had been submitted to the Department, there would be no cause for alarm, for no one could then copy it until the ten-year period of the patent had ended, they would not listen to me. They maintained: "If it is not copied in this country, it could be copied abroad where the patent does not exist." When I said: "Then take out a patent in every country in the world", they replied that it would cost them about nine thousand roubles, which they would not spend until they had seen the machine in operation. Therefore, they wanted to keep the machine a complete secret, and to hide the first one to be finished in a secret place so that no one should see it. With regard to the preparation of the new machine, they had decided to divide it up into ten sections, and compile specifications of the parts of each section on its own, which they would then send to ten technicians in different districts of the capital, each one unknown to the others, so that none of them would know more than the work he was to do.

The draughtsman they had appointed to list the specifications demanded a fee of five hundred roubles: they paid him, since they valued the invention highly, knowing that there was no other like it in the whole land. They also paid me my monthly allowance, and even added a further two hundred roubles toward the completion of the first machine. They purchased a machine for cutting the cork-bark into strips, such as can be seen in any factory for making corks by hand: it cost one hundred and twenty roubles.

Now the Jew Friedman still harboured his hatred of me for not trusting him and not allowing him to write into the agreement the terms he wanted so that he could gain full control over me. He was constantly complaining against me, and spreading false reports about me to his friends, the Germans, Now it has always been my nature to despise arrogance and hypocrisy, and never to tolerate them. He, being a short-tempered person, announced his intention to abandon my invention and retire from our Company. The Germans would not permit him to do so. Because of all this, they instituted enquiries into the matter. Then some people came and told them they had seen a similar machine with a similar endless knife, which was working successfully. They made further exhaustive enquiries, but were unable to find any machine of this kind. They continued their enquiries at the Department concerning all the patents that had been issued for the manufacture of corks. They learned that thirteen patents had been issued in Petersburg. Two of them were for a machine with an endless knife: the first one had been issued seven years earlier, whilst the second one had been issued with a patent for the machine alone, but not for the endless knife, about two years before mine. It was explicitly stated in the document given by the Department that the patent pertained to the whole machine with the exception of the endless knife — for once the original inventor of the knife had obtained his patent, the later inventor could not obtain any rights over an invention that did not belong to him. Their faces fell, for I myself had assured them strongly that the particular foundation of my machine was the knife I had made. Now that the foundation had caved in, the walls also came tumbling down, and brought down the ceiling, too. The Jew fanned the flames of the conflagration. He advised them to abandon the machine altogether, even though during their investigations in the city they had discovered that not one of the thirteen machines used in the production of corks was working satisfactorily, and that most of them had been discarded altogether. Despite this, they listened to the Jew, and refused to support my machine. I was unaware of all that was going on, except for a rumour that changes had been made in our Company, and that a conspiracy was forming against me. It was their intention to lauch a sudden attack upon me and drive me out, for they thought that I myself had not known about the knives that had been made before mine. Since I had always maintained to them that the basis of my invention was the knife, the specifications I had sent to the Department for a patent had been principally for the knife. One day, they sent me a written summons to appear before them at a certain time, and to bring all the descriptions and specifications I had sent to the Department. They examined them but did not find what they were looking for. In truth, I had never exaggerated anything I had said about the knife, for I knew that the officials of the Department would know more than I about new inventions. My description of the knife had been, therefore, brief and precise. They were grieved at this. They spread out, on the table before me, the two patents which they had copied from the Department, and read them aloud. I was greatly alarmed, for the first patent nullified the rights of my basic invention, the knife, whilst the second inventor had himself been refused a patent for his knife. In my distress, I kept silent. I re-read the second patent, and then realised that it bore no comparison to my machine, and that its entire production for one whole day, according to its inventor, was estimated at no more than thirty-five thousand corks. I asked the Germans: "Tell me, Sirs, where is this machine located, and in which factory is it in operation?" They answered: "In actual fact, there is not one in the whole city. We know, also, that the machine has not been finished and so cannot be used to manufacture stoppers, although there is some hope that it may be finished one day." My spirits rose, and I said: "What have I lost by the fact that the knife is not accredited to me? I still have the rights to the rest of the machine — as you may observe from the second patent, where the inventor lost his rights to the knife but not to the machine, since it is different from the other. Had you shown me only the first patent, and not the second, I would have been extremely worried for I would have thought that the knife, which is the basis of my invention, had become invalid and that all was lost. Now I see that the machine is valid despite the knife, so I am confident that my machine will also be granted a patent without the knife. What more do I need?" Freman said: "That is so. Nevertheless, the machine has lost its crown of glory, which I had planned to be my main point of publicity." The man had, indeed, considered travelling to Spain and buying up forests of the trees over the whole period of the patent, and had imagined himself building factories for the production of stoppers in every city in Europe. I said: "Forgive me, gentlemen, but what you originally sought you have in fact achieved. You wanted to buy from me a machine whose like does not exist elsewhere in our land and which will produce some two hundred thousand corks per day. You yourselves will have control over it, and you will have the sole rights, gentlemen, during the ten year period of the patent. You have what you want — a machine which produces the quantity you require per day, and the sole rights for ten years. What more can you wish? It was not the beautiful appearance of the machine which you purchased from me for ten thousand roubles, but its capacity for profitable production." Since they continued to object, I said: "Do not imagine, Sirs, that because I became partners with you, that I will never leave you. This not so. I know that if you desert me there will be others who will come to my aid — men who will want the machine for its utility and not its beauty. I have disclosed to you this day what is in my heart, so if you were to leave me, you would be doing only harm to yourself. Had I known at the outset, before I began work on my invention, that the knife had been invented earlier, I would have said to you: The machine itself is new, and there is no other like it, but the knife is not new. What would then have happened? You would have concurred with me, and not panicked over the loss of rights for the knife. Not all the parts of all inventions that have ever been conceived were new at the time. Look at the machine which came out only recently — the *swift printer*.[424] Its inventor obtained the usual patent, but what was new in it? The letters used for printing are very old, and as for the frame and the press and the colour, they were all invented by Gutenberg.[425] There are printing presses everywhere, in fact. What, then, is new about this printing press? Only the non-basic parts. The same applies to the sewing machine. Needles can be obtained by the myriad, yet new sewing machines are constantly being produced,[426] and all are granted patents, each inventor receiving a patent of his own. So it is with my knife and my machine." They had no reply for me, and kept silent, Only the Jew found something to say, repeating what he had said before, all of which I found distasteful and did not honour with a reply. I merely asked the Germans if they would not be prepared to wait until the morrow, so that they might have time to discuss it on their own and make their own decision. They said: "There is nothing for us to discuss, and no other decision for us than to refuse to support it." Then I said: "If you have indeed made up your minds to leave me, then according to the conditions of our agreement I can refuse to release you until you have paid me a further thousand roubles for the new machine; also, for the four months which it will take me to build it, you must pay me one hundred and fifty roubles per month. Only then will you be able to withdraw. I will take everything under my own control. The thousand I owe you, I will repay with a promissory note. However, it is not my desire to acquire other people's property for nothing, and therefore I shall repay you all the money you expended on me for the machine, to the last penny. After I have sold my invention to other people, and have received their money in place of yours, I shall give you a note for all the money I have received from you.'' They began to calculate, even adding the five hundred they had paid to the draughtsman who had only just begun his lists. "No, Sirs, do not include the money you lost because of your own ideas and which was not spent for my benefit or for the machine. The diagrams which were necessary for my invention cost one hundred roubles: most engineers who build machines have good draughtsmen and metal-workers who prepare all the lists and specifications of the machine; only those lists which have to be sent to the Department are prepared by draughtsmen specially hired for the purpose. I, on the other hand, prepared all my own lists, and my own sons wrote them down. I cannot accept your calculation.'' They made out their account, to a total of two thousand and thirty roubles. They retained the machine which they had brought from Riga for cutting the cork into strips, and said that, if I wished, I could buy it from them for one hundred and six roubles. They also refused to let me have the lists which they had just begun to compile, although there was no sense in their refusal, for what would they do with them? I was concerned lest the Jew, in pursuing his conspiracy against me, should complete the lists with the aid of the draughtsman whom I had taught and to whom I had explained the operations of the various parts of the machine, and then send them abroad where no one knew that they belonged to me. I went to see the Clerk to the senior judges, the *Prokuror*, [427] and told him what they were planning to do to me concerning my invention. He recorded it all in a book, so that it should be evidence on my behalf, testifying that I had warned the conspirators in advance against their attempting to harm me. I handed them the promissory note for the two thousand and thirty roubles to be repaid, after I had sold my invention to others, over a period of nine months from the 14th December 1885. If by that time I had not been able to fulfil my part, then they would have the right to appoint receivers of the business and to take it from me according to the conditions I had agreed to. Furthermore, at the end of the full year of twelve months, the debt would be cancelled and the patent would be returned to me on my name alone. The agreement would then be cancelled — and everything would be in order.

Many days passed by. We made enquiries for partners for the stopper-making machine, but found none.

At that time, there came to my mind an idea which I had never tested by experiment. It was something new and totally unknown, which might become extremely successful if it could be put to practical use. Unfortunately, I missed the opportunity of inventing it, for my third son, Saul, departed to live in the city of New York, in America, where lived his two brothers who had preceded him. The first to go had been Menahem Mendel in 1884, on Friday the 18th of *Tammuz*. [428] He was followed, in the next year, 1885, on Tuesday the 2nd of *Av*, [429] by Simon Aaron with his daughters, the oldest of whom was Peshe, the second Blume, his son Isaac Leib and the youngest girl Sarah, who was one year and a few months old. They were followed by my son Saul, in 1886, on Monday, the longest day, the

25th *Sivan.* [430] The last to go was my son Shraga, in 1887, on Sunday the 20th *Tevet,* the 4th January or the 16th abroad.

I was left with no one to help me in my work, for Abraham, who was the only one who remained with me, was busy with clock-repairing and making miniature pictures with the Microdiorama. I had to dismiss the workers who had been in my employ for the past two years — for, in that year, the Government intensified its persecution of all the Jews who lived under its protective rule. Since the Government could not wreak its full fury upon them in one single day, and in one instant repeal all the good regulations introduced by the Tsar's father, it therefore proceeded slowly, changing the laws one by one. It was decreed, for example, that Jews serving in the armed forces could not rise to the rank of Officers over Fifty — whereas, formerly, in the previous Tsar's reign, it had been possible for Jews to rise to the rank of even Officers over Hundreds — and there are officers of such rank living today. Other similar changes were brought in. A decree has recently been promulgated that Jewish lawyers cannot be appointed as Commissioners for Oaths. It seemed that all the fury was directed upon the capitals, Petersburg and Moscow. In Petersburg, the officials went beyond what was required whereas in Moscow they acted under compulsion. Action was taken against Jewish artisans: permission was granted them to live in the city and carry on their daily work, but not to own any private property. In the beginning of the year 1886, all craftsmen clock-makers were compelled to apply for trading licences, which cost thirty-four roubles. In the following month, after they had obtained their licences, the 'searchers' went round to their workshops and stole all the gold and silver and brass clocks they could find, together with all their tools. The pretext was that "the benevolent Tsar Alexander II only permitted you to perform your work." When, therefore, a case was brought before the District Court, and Christian clock-makers were asked for their opinion, they declared that, for his employment, the only requirements were a certain number of tools, a clock-dial for display in the window, and a wall-clock that kept accurate time. Then a dispute broke out between them as to whether one should also have keys for winding the spring, and a glass display counter, since all these could be bought separately whenever required. Even those Jewish soldiers who had served for twenty-five years under Tsar Nicholas — who had issued a decree permitting them to reside anywhere in the land of Russia — and most of whom had permits for living in Russia, Kronstadt, Gatsina and elsewhere were now driven out of the capitals. Moreover, the cities in which they had registered themselves as residents, no longer wished to acknowledge them, so they were driven from station to station like murderers and criminals until they eventually reached the towns where they had been born and which they no longer remembered, for most of them had been dragged from the bosoms of their families at a young age to serve in the army. If any 'Nikolai soldier' took his complaint to the Governor of the capital, and requested: "Read, if you please, the law that explicitly refers to us, in the Book of

Statutes, section. . . . '', then the Governor would reply to him: ''There are no laws for you, since you are not human.'' In that year, multitudes of people were driven out of all the cities of Russia, and most of all from the capital cities. [431]

At that time, my own livelihood became very precarious. I was afraid to display in my shop window a clock with chains and keys, or the gold and silver ornamental lockets for the miniature pictures, lest the 'searchers' come and steal them from me, and as added punishment drive me out of the capital. Nor had I been able to find partners for the cork machine, now that the original partners had withdrawn. Even to this day, people come to see the machine is very good, but no one will invest any money because of their fear of disaster. Times were changing; and the scent of war was constantly in the air. I waited daily for someone to come with an offer of finance, but no one came. I therefore dismissed the workers after they had finished all their work on the cork-machines, as well as on a small machine for making cigarettes, which are papirosi without the paper-tip: in England and America different cigarettes are smoked from ours, theirs being a paper-wrapper filled with tobacco. I had made a machine which would manufacture them in an entirely different operation so that I would be able to obtain a patent for it in place of the machine which I had sold the the Company on their name. I was now left alone. My hands were too weak to continue working with iron and brass, so I went idle all day long. Then I began to write this book. I also read the works of Hebrew and German writers which I had not looked at for almost thirty years, since they had not been of any use to me. However, not being accustomed to idleness, I read them.

I used to take a stroll every day during the summer in the park. My thoughts turned towards the invention of a new kind of clock detainer, an *échappement*. [432] I found it, and this is how it works. All clocks are based on the principle of the force of flight, *Schwung*. [433] There is no exception to this, for the force of the earliest principle, the pendulum, depends upon its flight. When a pendulum is moved from its vertical position of rest to one side, it will return to its original position by virtue of the earth's attraction exerting a downwards pull upon it. It would remain in that position for ever were it not for pressure upon its mass by the force of flight which it acquired during its return downwards from its high point of swing. As it descends it gains speed and its movement increases considerably, and by the time it arrives at a particular point at the requisite speed, the force of flight — which is also the force constant in all movements, *inertsie* [434] — then propels it on past its vertical position of rest with such force as to raise it to the same height on the next side as on the first. Then the earth exerts a return pull upon it. It commences its return with nil velocity, increasing in velocity as it descends towards the vertical position, from which the momentum it acquired in its descent propels it on to rise again to the point it reached during its initial movement. And so *ad infinitum*. Because of this constant quality it would be compelled to oscillate to and fro endlessly were it not for the fact that it loses something of its momentum through the density of the air as well as other resistances, which all clock mechanisms are designed to overcome. The same law applies to a clock-spring, or the hair-spring, whose force of flight transfers from that of the pendulum to that of the flywheel, for the pendulum is in fact one part of a flywheel.[435] The hair-spring operates under the force of gravity exerted upon the pendulum. Its movement, therefore, depends on its force of flight. It is the same with all forms of movements and resistances, *échappement, Hemmung,* [436] in existence in the world. It had been in my mind to invent a new escapement, not based on flight at all, but a dividing resistor whose principle lay in this: liquids which have a pressure exerted upon them sufficient to force them through a narrow hole or hollow tube will lose their rate of flow to some extent. I therefore prepared a jar filled with mercury, this jar having tapering walls. A small hole was cut into one of the walls, and into it was inserted a hollow tube containing a tap which blocked the hollow centre of the tube and which, by turning screws, *Shroibe,* [437] narrowed or enlarged the hollow of the tube to the thickness of a hairsbreadth. As the balance staff moves to and fro, in the normal manner of clocks, it presses the free wall closer to the other wall and pushes the quicksilver out through the narrow hole in the hollow tube and the tap. The balance will slow down until all the liquid has emerged through the narrow hole. If, then, another vessel, similar to the first, be placed at its other side, and the other end of the tube be fixed to one of its walls, then its free wall will also press forward from the other side and push the quicksilver back into the first vessel, pressing the free wall back away from the tube. The liquid will flow from the second vessel to the first through the narrow hole of the tap, its return flow slowing down in the same manner as its outwards flow. Each movement of the staff to and fro will press the walls of the two vessels to and fro at the same time, so that one will be in the process of emptying whilst the other is filling up, after which the full vessel will empty whilst the first is filling up, as there is only sufficient mercury to fill one vessel. So the process will continue. The tooth of the wheel which pushes the hook of the staff will be detained until the staff moves and draws the free wall closer to the tube and drives the quicksilver from the one vessel to the other. The same occurs on the return flow — and so on perpetually.

In order to regulate the movement of the pointer precisely in accordance with the minutes and hours, an arrow pointer, such as obtains in all watches, would be attached to the top of the tap blocking the hollow tube. Below it would be a numbered dial divided into fine degrees, and on these degrees symbols for advancing or retarding the movement of minutes and hours, such as the symbols R.A.,[438] like in all clocks — for the tap enlarges and diminishes the hole of the tube by moving the pointers forwards or backwards. Then there was the problem of temperature variations which affect the movement of all clocks by shortening or lengthening the pendulum or the flywheel and the hair-spring. This was a particular problem with my invention because liquids, when becoming heated, lose their density and therefore flow more swiftly through a narrow hole, whilst their rate of flow slows down as they cool. I should have to make a *Regulator* for the different degrees of heat and cold, which would be placed against the pointer of the blocking tap: it would be composed of two kinds of metals joined together into one strip bent in the shape of a hook, with one end attached to the numbered dial of the wall of the vessel and the other end to the blocking tap. As the quicksilver heated up, it would flow quickly through the hole in the tube and the tap, and warm up the regulator wire whose ends would then move apart, the free end attached to the tap moving towards its pointer and closing slightly, thereby reducing the size of the hole of the tube — and *vice versa*. All these things would be first performed by trial and experiment, which are man's best teachers, and from which I would learn the simplest way of making them. Now, both the vessels as well as the tube and blocking tap would have to be made from iron, to which quicksilver does not cling, nor does it melt in them and spoil them. The sides of the moving walls would have to be of thin goatskin which would fold easily as the walls drew together. It seemed to me that there would be need of fewer wheels in such a clock, for as the volume of the liquid increased in the vessels, so would the staff's oscillations slow down. However, it was essential that this be tested in trials and experiments. It was possible that only a light force would be required to enable the balance wheel to push the quicksilver through a narrow aperture from one vessel to the other, so that a cubic inch of quicksilver would delay one quarter of an hour, and this with its return flow would total one half-hour, by which time one tooth of the wheel of the hook would have moved on. If, therefore, the wheel had forty-eight teeth, then it would take one complete day for the wheel to perform one revolution — this wheel being the only one moved by the spring, or the bob. The quiet movement of this mechanism would be very pleasant to the ear. I saw, in my mind, that this was very good and would be a worthwhile thing to make.[439] However, there were no hands to make it. Nevertheless, I still entertain hopes of making it.

Who can tell whether I shall ever return to the activity of my former days and be able to put my thoughts into practical realisation? Or my sons and their sons — whether they will be able to read this ancient Hebrew language?

Sunday, 15th Kislev, 30th December, or the 12th abroad.[440]

Text Notes

◇◇◇◇◇

1. The Hebrew, *Toledot Ḥayyim*, suggests a pun on his name giving an implied meaning: "The History of Chaim".

2. 5,585 in the Jewish calendar.

3. Deut. xxxii. 7.

4. French novelist (1804 – 57). His *Mystères de Paris* (1843) was translated into Hebrew (1857 – 60) by Kalman Schulman (1819 – 99).

5. i.e. a tumbril. The Hebrew, *Mirkevet Yehoshafat*, is an example of the interesting play on words typical of Aronson's inventive approach to linguistic problems. The phrase is a complex combination of ideas derived from *Merkavah* (chariot) and King Jehoshaphat (I Kings xxii. 35) and the noun *Shafot* (scaffold: in Yiddish, *Shafot*; German, *Schafott*; Russian, эшафот =*Eshafot*) which together form the concept of a "scaffold-carriage". K. Schulman describes the "scaffold" as *Bamat Matbe'aḥ* (*Shaffot*) in his *Misterei Paris*, vol. 1, Part 1, p.158.

6. Esther vi. 9 – 11.

7. Cf. Ezekiel i. 20 – 21 and x. 17.

8. The saying is based on Exod. iv. 11 and Prov. xii. 4. The identity of this particular *Eshet He-Ḥayil* is not clear. The term was popularly used as an analogous description to the Yiddish *Berya*, the Jewish housewife supreme.

9. Numbers xii. 8.

10. Charles Bonnet (1720—93). Swiss naturalist and philosopher, famous for his works on parthenogenesis in aphids. His *Contemplation de la Nature* (1764 – 5) expounds his views on the hierarchy of all creatures. His *La Palingénésie philosophique* formed the basis of Johann Lavater's disputes with Moses Mendelssohn, in the late eighteenth century.

11. Amos ix. 6.

11a. *Avot* iv. 3.

12. The connection between Amianthus (a crystal of the Brucite group, also known as 'earth-flax') and Mountain Flax (*Linum Catharticum*) and Limestone would appear to be that the Amianthus is found in limestone and can be threaded like fibre and spun like flax.

13. Psalm xvi. 11.

14. The Hebrew, *Keren Alon Ha-Me'ofef* (The Horn of the Flying Oak), is the translation of the German — although correctly, this should be *Flugeichhörnchen*. An almost identical term, *Keren Ha-Aloni Hame'ofef*, occurs in the *Sefer Toledot Ha-Teva* (The History of Nature) by S.J. Abramowitz (Mendele Mokher Seforim), part one, Leipzig 1862, p. 289.

15. Ecclesiastes i. 2.

16. From the Russian средн (middle).

17. Possibly the river Sheshupa. The Nieman has four affluents: Dubisa, Sheshupa, Viliya and Nevyazhe.

18. Equivalent to 1.067 kms or 0.663 miles. See Appendix p. 337 below on transliteration.

19. The danger of floods was a perennial threat in the country regions: see Shmarya Levin, *Galut Va-Mered*, pp. 3 and 8.

19a. The Hebrew poet H.N. Bialik mentions a similar experience when, as a starving infant, he "used to eat the plaster off the wall and chew charcoal" (*Kol Kitvei*, *Safi'ah* p. 148).

20. i.e. "life". This custom is mentioned in the Talmud, *Rosh Ha-Shanah* 16b. The Yiddish equivalent name is *Alter* (i.e. long life). See A.S. Rappaport, *The Folklore of the Jews*, pp. 87 – 90.

21. The *Torah* given to Moses on Sinai, as distinct from the Oral Law of the Sages and Rabbinic scholars.

22. The Statute of Conscription and Military Service, passed in 1827, was intended to introduce universal military service for all men over the age of 18. Special clauses within the act lowered the age for Jews to include the conscription of boys from the age of 12 (although, in practice, children even as young as 8 years old were kidnapped from their families). These minors became known as "Cantonists", originally a Prussian term for a recruiting district, and used in Russia to denote children taken into military service and sent to cantonal or district schools far removed from contact with their families. The oppressive demands which this act made upon the Jewish community gave rise to infamous practices which included the press-ganging of small boys, the forcible delivery to the army of transient Jews who had no residential permit, and the deliberate substitution of poor children in place of the rich. These practices were brought to an end by Alexander II who repealed the act in 1856. See L. Greenberg, *The Jews in Russia*, vol. 1, pp. 10 – 11 and 48 – 52; S.W. Baron, *The Russian Jew under the Tsars and Soviets*, pp. 35 – 8; H.M. Sachar, *The Course of Modern Jewish History*, pp. 86 – 7; S. Dubnow, *History of the Jews*, vol. 5, pp. 153 – 161. For an account of Ḥasidic activity on behalf of the Cantonists, see Rabbi J.I. Schneersohn, *The 'Tzemach Tzedek' and the Haskala Movement*, tr. Z.I. Posner, p. 9 note 11, and also p. 27 note 31 on the "Society of the Resurrected", the name given to children rescued from military service by the Ḥasidim.

23. Lev. xix. 23.

24. A meaningless, though humorous, confusion of the words *Mish'an U'Mivtah* (the Support and Trust) occurring in the *Shemoneh Esreh* prayer ("Eighteen Benedictions", also known as the *Amidah*, Standing, prayer). The quoted passage actually occurs in the 13th Benediction, *Al Ha-Tsaddikim* (for the Righteous), and not, as Aronson says, in *Vela-Malshinim*, which is the 12th Benediction. See J.H. Hertz, *Daily Prayer Book*, p. 144.

25. Quinine (*Cinchona*) was introduced to Europe in 1640 by the Countess of Cinchon (after whom it was named), the wife of the Viceroy of Peru, and had been used in the treatment of malaria ever since.

26. In the Hebrew, *Ba'alei Ha-Shemot* (Masters of the Names): this title was used as early as the geonic period (i.e. 6th to 11th centuries) to signify masters of practical Kabbalah able to cure illnesses and exorcise devils by means of the divine names of God and the angels — "On the whole, such figures were clearly identified with white magic in the popular mind as opposed to sorcerers, witches and wizards" (G. Scholem, *Kabbalah*, p. 184). "The term *baal shem* was used in those centuries to denote a healer, quack doctor, miracle worker or charmer. These people treated their patients with folk remedies such as herbs, ointments and salves, as well as incantations, prayers or study, talismans and similar 'cures'. Some also 'expelled evil spirits' or served their clients with advice, predicted the future or performed miracles." (B.D. Weinryb, *The Jews of Poland*, p. 264). See also D. Margalith, "Wonderworkers and Folk Healers", in *Harofé Haivri*, 33rd year, vols. 1 and 2, pp. 218 – 22 (in English) and 150 – 60 (in Hebrew); and *The Autobiography of Solomon Maimon*, footnote p. 170.

27. "Some people recommend the person suffering from fever to write on the door of his house the words: 'N.N. is not at home'." (A.S. Rappaport, *The Folklore of the Jews*, p. 108). For similar methods of treatment to those mentioned in this account see J.G. Frazer, *The Golden Bough, The Scapegoat*, p. 49; J. Trachtenberg, *Jewish Magic and Superstition*, pp. 202 – 206.

28. Rabbi Solomon Ben Isaac (Yitshaki: 1040 – 1105), pre-eminent French Biblical exegete.

29. Early Jewish sources regarded the "evil eye" simply as a flaw of character in a man who could not bear to "see" the good fortune of others: cf. *Avot* ii. 14. Although it does not occur in the Bible in a magical or superstitious connotation, the Talmud and Kabbalah contain many references in this sense. See J. Trachtenberg, *Jewish Magic and Superstition*, pp. 54 – 6; A.S. Rappaport, *The Folklore of the Jews*, pp. 71 – 9; B.L. Gordon, *Eina Bisha*, in *Harofé Haivri*, Israel Annual edition, 34th year, vols. 1 – 2, pp. 77 – 91; S. Thompson, *Motif-Index of Folk-Literature*, vol. 2, pp. 364 – 5, entry D2071.

30. The fourteenth letter of the Hebrew alphabet.

31. Lev. xiii. 9.

32. Num. xxxii. 32.

33. The mythical "Sabbath river" of stones associated in legend with the lost Ten Tribes of Israel. See *Encyclopedia Judaica* vol. 2, pp. 479 – 480. Identified in the Targum of *Pseudo-Jonathan* to Exod. xxxiv. 10 with the River Gozan across which the tribes were led into exile. See also Josephus, *Wars of the Jews*, Book 7, v. 1; *Sanhedrin* 65b; and the travels of Eldad Ha-Dani (9th century). See also A. Neubauer, "Where Are The Ten Tribes?" in the *Jewish Quarterly Review*, in 4 parts, October 1888 and January, April and July 1889.

34. See 1 Chron. v. 26, 2 Kings xvii. 6 and xviii. 11.

35. "Introduction", the opening words to an Aramaic poem by Meir ben Isaac Nehorai (11th century), recited in the synagogue service on Pentecost. Aronson here relates a traditional legend according to which the author of the poem saved the Jewish community of Worms with the help of a miracle-working emissary from the Ten Tribes.

36. An ironical description, in fact: not only did she sell eggs at an exorbitant price, but she also did the customer a favour in doing so!

37. See Lev. v. 16 and 24, and Num. v. 7.

38. The "Book of Splendour", the central work in Kabbalistic literature, generally ascribed to Moses de Leon (14th century).

39. "As the streams in the dry land", Psalm cxxvi. 4.

40. The Hebrew reads: כשימות אלכסנדר פאוולאוויץ ימלוך קאנסטאנטין ימים מעטים בימי ניקולי גאולה באה

41. "Here, stay". B.D. Weinryb, *The Jews of Poland*, p. 18, dates the Jewish settlement of Poland to the time of the Spanish expulsion in 1492; see *Jahrbuch der Jüdisch-Literarischen Gesselschaft*, no. 5, 1907, p. 147; S.J. Agnon, *Kedumot*, in *Kol Sippurav*, section *Polin, Sippurei Aggadot*, vol. 3, pp. 165–6.

42. i.e. a Russian Tsar of the "Greek" Orthodox Church.

43. The persecutions of Jews during the Cossack revolt of 1648 against the Poles, under the leadership of Bogdan Chmielnicki, and of the Jews in France and the Rhineland during the first Crusade of 1096–9.

44. It was the Kabbalist Rabbi Samson of Ostropoli who was murdered in the pogroms of 1648. Aronson seems to have erred here.

45. Exod. xxxii. 34.

46. The institution of serfdom in Russia was a gradual development that was finally fixed by Tsar Alexei's Code of Laws, 1649. During the reign of Catherine II, the serfs were reduced to wretched conditions under the dominion of the gentry and landowners. They paid their debt to their lords either by labour service (*barschchina*) or with money (*obrok*). "Jews had long been forbidden to possess serfs, but evasions were frequent. Powers of attorney were given to Jews and others by estate owners, and by this means persons to whom the law forbade the ownership of serfs became in fact owners of them"; see J. Mavor, *An Economic History of Russia*, vol. 1, p. 325 — the two volumes of this work give an extensive discussion of the condition of the peasants and serfs. See also H. Seton Watson, *The Russian Empire 1801–1917*, pp. 21–6, 227–230; W.E. Mosse, *Alexander II and the Modernization of Russia*, pp. 12–19; *New Cambridge Modern History*, vol. X, p. 361.

47. See W.E. Mosse, *Alexander II and the Modernization of Russia*, p. 14; Prince P. Kropotkin, *Memoirs of a Revolutionist*, vol. 1, pp. 56–71, and his *Russian Literature*, pp. 94, 97, 224 *et. al.* The abuses of serfdom were extensively denounced by Russian writers; see A.N. Radishchev, *Journey From Petersburg to Moscow* (1790), which had a strong influence on the Decembrists of 1825; N.I. Novikov, a leading satirical journalist whose first journal, *The Drone*, was closed by imperial order (1770) whilst his later journals also had short lives; N.V. Gogol, whose *Dead Souls* (first part, 1842) was acclaimed by radical critics such as V.G. Belinsky; D.V. Grigorovich, *The Village* (1846); I.S. Turgenev, *A Sportsman's Sketches* (1852); and Count L.N. Tolstoy, whose *A Landowner's Morning* (1856) recounts his abortive attempt to improve the conditions of his serfs. See R. Hingley, *Russian Writers and Society, 1825–1904*, pp. 140–2; see also the chapter on "The Peasant Question in the Russian Literary Movement" in J. Mavor, *An Economic History of Russia*, vol. 1, pp. 352–9.

47a. Israel Ben Eliezer Ba'al Shem Tov (*Besht*: c. 1700–60). Charismatic founder of Ḥasidism in eastern Europe. Lived in Medzibezh from about 1740 until his death. Aronson's use of the phrase "began to call upon" is reminiscent of Rashi's commentary on the phrase in Gen. iv. 26 as referring to idolatry, although Aronson may not have intended the same meaning.

47b. See below note 87.

48. The "Order" of the home service during Passover.

49. Num. xxii. 32.

50. Genesis xxvii. 40.

51. Poet of liturgical hymns. It has not been possible to locate the origin of the quoted verse.

52. Joshua v. 13.

53. The Russian forces finally defeated the Circassians in the campaigns of 1862–4, when the whole of the Caucasus region and Transcaucasia passed into Russian possession.

54. Jews played a prominent part in the production and sale of alcoholic drinks from the 16th century

on, through the *arenda*(rental) system. They were an obvious target for discrimination and oppression, especially in the rural districts where they were often accused of exploiting and debasing the peasants. S. Maimon's *Autobiography* describes the tribulations suffered by his grandfather, a tavernkeeper (see pp. 15 – 18). See S.W. Baron, *The Russian Jews under Tsars and Soviets*, p. 91ff; *Yahadut Lita*, vol. 1, pp. 168, 171, 175 (table of distilleries); the abridged summary of the *Law on the Tax on Spirits*(1887) in *The Persecution of the Jews in Russia*, Appendix, p. 62; and Baron and A. Kahan, the chapter on "Wine and Liquor" in *Economic History of the Jews*, pp. 132 – 8.

55. i.e. study the Torah meticulously as it contains all knowledge: see *Avot* v. 25.

56. A common term for the Russians.

57. Lithuanian: *pilnas* (full), *kalnas*(mountain).

58. These were six-sided initial letters, decorated in a variety of colours, and popularly referred to as *Ot Meshisha*.

59. The reference is to the *Statute on the Jews*, passed on 13 April 1835. In the event, the new law did not exempt married men, so the "panic" (popularly referred to as the *Behola*) was to no purpose. See S. Dubnow, *History of the Jews in Russia and Poland*, vol. 2, p. 28, and his *History of the Jews*, vol. 5, p. 160; S.W. Baron, *The Russian Jews under Tsars and Soviets*, pp. 38 – 40. Also see, I. Halpern, *Yehudim Ve-Yahadut Be-Mizrah Eiropah*, chapter *Nissu' ei Behalah Be-Mizrah Eiropa*, pp. 289 – 309.

60. See Talmud *Sanhedrin* 22a and *Mo' ed Katan* 18b.

61. Although cats are not mentioned in the Bible (perhaps because of their association with Egyptian idolatry), the Talmud contains a number of references to them: see *Eruvin* 100b, *Bava Kamma* 80b, *et. al.* See also J. Gutfarstein, *Folklor Yehudei Lita* in *Yahadut Lita*, vol. 1, p. 605.

62. Cf. Deut. x. 16 and Jer. iv. 4.

63 See Mishnah *Berakhot* 54a and 59a; also J.H. Hertz, *Daily Prayer Book*, p. 990; and *Kitsur Shulhan Arukh*, chap. LX. 2,3.

64. See Exod. xx. 1 – 17 and Deut. v. 6 – 18.

65. First published Amsterdam 1701; author unknown.

66. Lev. xxvi. 36.

67. Cf. James G. Frazer, *Baldur the Beautiful*, vol. 2, p. 40: "The cat, which represented the devil, could never suffer enough"

68. See *Bava Batra* 8b.

69. "Book of the Righteous", an anonymous book on the Pentateuch, first published Constantinople c. 1520.

70. "Remnant of Israel", Lvov 1804.

71. Anonymous pseudo-epigraphic historical work, possibly composed in the 10th century in Italy.

72. Ethical treatise by Zvi Hirsch Kaidanover: first Hebrew publication, Frankfurt-on-the-Main, 1705; first Yiddish translation, Sulzbach 1724. The name *Kav* denotes its division into 102 chapters.

73. "Joy of the Soul" by Elhanan Hendel Kirchan published Frankfurt-on-the-Main in two parts, 1707 and 1727.

74. Possibly first published in Fürth, 1791. The "many-eyed Angel of Death" is discussed by A.S. Rappaport, *Myth & Legend in Ancient Israel*, pp. 66 – 9.

75. "Silence" — the Angel of Death. See J. Gutfarstein, "Folklore of Lithuanian Jewry" in *Yahadut Lita*, vol. 1, p. 607; J. Trachtenberg, *Jewish Magic and Supersitition,* p. 66. See also above, p. 46.

76. Probably the type of watch popular in France and Switzerland, mainly during the 18th century, which was 1½″ thick and known as *oignon* (onion). The old English colloquial term for it was the "turnip" watch.

77. The festival of "Lots" derived from the Biblical story of Esther, and celebrated in the Hebrew month of *Adar*, which generally coincides with February.

78. It is interesting to note that the renowned 18th century English clockmaker John Harrison also, in his youth, made clocks out of wood, using wooden wheels and teeth: see Donald de Carle, *Horology*, p. 46.

79. A "pudding" described in the original as *Levivot Ha-Kaddur*, i.e. a dumpling kind of dish.

80. *Neshamah Yeterah*, the "additional soul" attached to every Jew by virtue of the sanctity of the Sabbath. It is used as a euphemism for great contentment and delight: see Rashi on *Bezah* 16a.

81. i.e. the Second, or Assistant, Cantor. See I. Klausner, *Toledot Ha-Kehillah Ha-Ivrit Be-Vilna*, vol. 1, p. 137.

82. "Hear, O Israel", a central prayer declaring the Jewish belief in the Unity of God. Recited twice

daily, it is composed of passages from Deut. vi. 4 – 9, xi. 12 – 21, and Num. xv. 37 – 41. It became the final profession of faith by religious martyrs.

83. *Podushnaya podat'* introduced by Peter the Great in the ukase of 11 January 1722, after the census of 1718: the tax was imposed on all males, irrespective of age, in all classes except the nobility and certain privileged groups such as the clergy, government officials and the higher strata of urban residents. It was abolished by Alexander III in 1887. Aronson mentions that the Jews filled in their poll-tax forms in Hebrew and paid 6 Tympfs *per capita* (see below, p. 48 and note 120). See H. Seton-Watson, *The Russian Empire 1801 – 1917*, p.22; S.Dubnow, *History of the Jews in Russia and Poland*. vol. 1, pp. 307 – 9.

84. See above, note 22.

85. "Every man and woman in Russia must have an inland passport as a legal certificate of their identity. This passport is delivered to them by their respective townships and must be changed, generally, at some interval of not over 3 years. But there is no necessity to live in, or to visit, one's parish to obtain this document. It is very common for a man to be settled and carrying on business for years in some town, and to be registered in some small village at the other extremity of the country. With tradespeople like the Jews it is particularly frequent." (See article "The Jews in Russia" by S.S., in the monthly periodical *Free Russia*, no. 2, September 1890, London, p. 7). The authority to issue passports was first provided in 1776 primarily in order to facilitate the collection of taxes by the Kahals (S. Dubnow, *History of the Jews in Russia and Poland*, vol. 1, p. 309). The *Law on Passports* (1857) prescribed specific restrictions on the use of travel passports by Jews (see *The Persecution of the Jews in Russia*, pp. 54 – 5).

86. I. Klausner describes the Beadles (in Vilna) as performing "very important functions. They were not only the Beadles of the Great Synagogues but also acted as intermediaries on behalf of the community. They signed the community's documents, bills and enactments, and their signatures gave these documents official authority . . . They were also the Ushers in the Court of the Deputy-Governor who was the judge over Jewish lawsuits. In this, they performed similar functions to those of the Ushers of the civil Courts of Law . . . The Beadles also, at times, fulfilled the duties of official representatives of the community." (*Toledot Ha-Kehillah Ha-Ivrit Be Vilna*, pp. 134 5). See Z. Scharfstein, *Hayyei Ha-Yehudim Be-Mizrah Eiropah*, pp. 99 – 100.

87. The "opponents" of the Hasidic movement; so-called after a ban issued against the Hasidim by the Vilna Gaon in 1772. The main points of opposition were: the use of Sephardi liturgy by the Hasidim and their use of separate synagogues; belief in *Tsaddikim*; and their tendency to pantheism. During the later 19th century, the two groups combined in their campaign against Haskalah. See S.M. Dubnow, *Toledot Ha-Hasidut*, vol. 1, pp. 58, 99, 112; vol. 2, p. 233; vol. 3, pp. 352 – 4.

87a. 1 Russian *fut* = 0.305 metres.

87b. Isaiah iv-1.

88. The Statute of 1835 imposed on the leaders of Jewish communities the responsibility for raising the full quota of military recruits in their districts, and also gave them the power to deliver to the military authorities (with the aid of the police) any Jew considered harmful or dangerous to their community in general. This Statute, therefore, provided communal leaders with very grave powers which were often tragically abused. See the article *La Question Isráelite en Russie* by Prince San Donato Demidov in *Les Juifs de Russie*, Paris 1891, p. 294. See also above, note 22.

89. For the Scriptural penalty for blasphemy see Lev. xxiv. 16.

89a. Decorated pictures or notices hung on the "eastern" wall of a synagogue or house. To western Jews the east is holy since it faces towards Jerusalem.

90. The palm branch, with twigs of myrtle and willow bound to it, is waved during the reciting of the Psalms of Praise during the feast of Tabernacles: see Lev. xxiii. 40.

91. Psalm cxxi. 1.

92. Between Passover and the Feast of Weeks (*Shavuot*, or Pentecost), 49 days were counted: see Lev. xxiii. 15 – 16. This period is kept as a solemn period of semi-mourning, except for the 33rd day (the 18 *Iyyar*) known as the "Scholar's feast", which presumes to celebrate the ending of a plague among Rabbi Akiva's pupils during the war against the Romans. Traditionally, children are given a holiday on which they re-enact the battles of that time.

93. The fifth month of the Jewish year. According to Jewish tradition, both Temples were destroyed on the 9th *Av*.

94. The feast of "Dedication" of the Temple after the Hasmonean victory over Antiochus Epiphanes in 164 B.C.E.: See Books I and II Maccabees.

95. Haman, the archetype of anti-semites: see the Book of Esther.

96. The sixth letter of the Hebrew alphabet.

97. Artaxerxes Longimanus, son of Xerxes and King of Persia 465 – 425 B.C.E. See Ezra iv. 7.

98. A "Comprehensive" order of services with additions to the regular services on festivals.

99. "Minor Day of Atonement". The eve of a New Moon is kept as a minor fast day: see Ḥullin 60b; *Kitsur Shulḥan Arukh*, chapter xcvii. 1; and Rashi on Num. xxviii. 15.

100. The Great Confession of R. Nissim Gerondi (died c. 1380). The wording of the prayer is actually in the singular: "I can neither speak..."

101. "Accept", the 17th Benediction. See J.H. Hertz, *Daily Prayer Book*, p. 149, and also above, note 24.

102. The first railway line in Russia was built in 1837 – 8, between St. Petersburg and Tsarskoye Selo, a distance of only 27 kms. During 1847 – 51, the St. Petersburg-Moscow line was built: it was called the 'Nicholas Railway', after Nicholas I, and renamed the 'October Railway' after the Revolution. These were the only two lines in existence in Russia before the Crimean War. (Compare this with western European countries which had, by 1850, an approximate total of 15,000 miles of track, over which railways were providing serious competition to other forms of transportation.) The Russian railway system began to expand in the 1860's to serve the needs of the industrial and grain areas of the southern provinces, and later the export of oil products from the Caucusus. See *New Cambridge Modern History*, vol. X, pp. 30 – 35, 365, 381; V.G Korolenko, *The History of My Contemporary*, p. 140 note 4; M.E. Falkus, *The Industrialisation of Russia, 1700–1914*, pp. 54 – 5 (with Table of Railway Construction). Jewish financiers (like the Rothschild family, the Pereire brothers, Samuel Poliakoff) played an integral role in railroad development generally, and in Russia particularly where railroad construction "created employment for numbers of Jews who filled technical and administrative posts. The advent of the railroads brought many changes in Jewish economic and social life, described for instance in the poem *Shenei Yosef ben Shim'on* of J.L. Gordon". (S.H. Baron and A. Kahan, *Economic History of the Jews*, p. 184; also *Kitvei J.L. Gordon: Shirah*, 148 – 66).

103. Whereas, prior to the Crimean War, telegraphy was in extensive operation in Europe and the USA, its development in Russia was insignificant, and only isolated lines were in use. In 1832, a needle-telegraph circuit was installed between the Tsar's summer and winter palaces in St. Petersburg. In 1849, the Siemens and Halske's *Telegraph-Bauanstalt* received the contract for an underground line from St. Petersburg to Moscow; an overhead line was constructed in 1854. In 1853 – 5 during the Crimean War, the same company was contracted to erect long telegraph lines: the posts they used were supplied by Jewish timber merchants. (See: *Recollections of Werner von Siemens, Inventor and Entrepreneur*, pp. 96 – 7, 110). It was, in fact, during the Crimean War that the first use was made of telegraphy for military purposes (at Vorne, 1854), and a submarine cable was laid across the Black Sea (in 1855). One of the fateful results of the projected, but abortive, proposal in 1865 to lay a line from New York to Paris via Alaska and Siberia, was the subsequent purchase of Alaska by the USA from Russia in 1867.

104. i.e. Pentecost: see above, note 92.

105. See *Service of the Synagogue: Pentecost*, p. 201. The italicised phrases are quotations from the hymn, and are treated here in the manner of Biblical commentary.

106 See Lev. xxiii. 7 – 8, and *Kitsur Shulḥan Arukh*, chapter xcviii. 4.

107. See Rashi on Deut. xxv. 2 – 3, and *Siphre, Makkot*, 22b – 23a.

108. See *Kitsur Shulḥan Arukh*, chapter cxvii. 12.

109. See Numbers xv. 38.

110. See above, note 75.

111. Psalm xxi. 5.

112. Malachi ii. 3.

113. cf. Joshua i. 8.

114. The "Separation" service conducted at the termination of the Sabbath.

115. *Avot* i.15 and *Avot De-Rabbi Natan* xiii.2.

116. The Order which deals with Festivals.

117. "Sisters-in-law", in the *Seder Nashim* (Order relating to Women); deals particularly with laws concerning levirate marriages (Deut. xxv.5 ff.) and forbidden degrees of marriage (Lev. xviii).

118. i.e. "Peace": see above, note 20.

119. "Admonitions", see Lev. xxvi. 14 – 43 and Deut. xxviii. 15 – 68.

120. A small Polish coin named after the minter Andreas Tympf. First issued during the second half

of the seventeenth century, it was intended to be equivalent to 30 groschen but achieved a real value of no more than 13. For note on the poll-tax, see above, note 83.

121. In the MS, *Hak tebya v gorlo*, a mixture of Yiddish and Russian.

122. In fact, кадык is the 'Adam's apple'.

123. Deut. xi.26.

124. The *melammed*'s translation was slightly inaccurate. [The modern Russian version reads: *Vot'*, *ya predlagayoo vam' segodnya blagoslovenie i proklyatie* (Behold, I offer to you this day the blessing and the curse)].

125. Judges xiv.6.

126. Bears also provided a favourite sport. *"La chasse de l'ours est pour les Russes une véritable passion; ceux qui sont fait une habitude de cette chasse ne peuvent y renoncer"* (Bear-hunting is a veritable passion with the Russians; those to whom it becomes a habit, cannot give it up): Alexander Dumas, *Voyage en Russie 1858*, p. 175; some experiences of bear-hunters are recounted by him on pp. 174 – 82.

127. i.e. a canopy. In the Hebrew original *Mittat Ha-Raki'a*, a plain translation of the German *Betthimmel* (canopy).

128. Hebrew *Parsah*: a parasang or Persian mile, variously estimated at 4,000 yards (see Soncino *Talmud*, Glossary to *Bava Kamma*) or 4 miles (in various dictionaries). Aronson uses the term loosely as his estimates of distances are not consistent with any one definition of *parsah* and do not correspond with the actual distances: often he also gives journeys in terms of days. It is interesting to note that he also uses "miles": he speaks of Kovno being *Ke-sheshet mil* (about 6 miles away), see above, p. 54.

129. Yiddish paraphrase of the Pentateuch, written before 1620 and attributed to Jacob ben Isaac Ashkenazi (c. 1550 – 1626). The title derives from *Song of Songs* iii.11: "Go forth and see, ye daughters of Jerusalem". It gained great popularity among Jewish women.

130. Isaiah xxxiii.4. It has long been the practice to study Gemara in the *steigen un reden* (singing and talking) manner, i.e. chanting, with students exchanging opinions and engaging in disputations over points of interpretation. Study, therefore, was never silent, except for those who preferred to study alone. A. Z. Zupnik makes the whimsical point that this practice is due to the phonetic similarity of the Hebrew words *Shi'ur* (lesson) and *Shir* (song), and that the students learned the *Shir* better than the *Shi'ur* (see: *Ha-Shaḥar*, year 4 (1873), the *"Ḥadashot Be-Yisrael"* (News from the Communities) feature, pp. 187 – 8). A more idealised description is given by A. Kariv: "Storms raged abroad, heralding upheavals and revolts, but in the vast wastes of Lithuania could be heard, just as in days of old, the sad-sweet melody, 'The Sages taught. . . .'" (*Lita Mekhorati*, pp. 58 – 9.)

131. In the Hebrew, *Hakhnasat Orehim* (literally, "taking in guests", namely "hospitality"). The practice of offering hospitality to wayfarers attained the status of a commandment in Jewish social traditions. Based on the incident of Abraham and the three Angels (Genesis xviii. 1 – 8), it was acclaimed by Sages and scholars throughout the ages: see *Shabbat* 127a; *Avot De-Rabbi Natan*, vii; *Avot* i.5; *Pe'ah* i.1; and the commencement of the Passover *Seder* service. Jewish communities generally kept a special guest-house for travellers, which was supported out of communal funds and was known as *Hakhnasat Oreḥim*. There were also Societies which bore this name, and had the specific function of raising funds for travellers and transients.

132. The censorship of Kabbalistic books was introduced in 1836, and of rabbinic works in 1841, see S. Dubnow, *History of the Jews*, vol.5, pp. 165ff. It is worthwhile to note that the phrase "in those days" *(Ba-Yamim Hahem)*, used here and elsewhere, is a typical example of Aronson's frequent digressions from chronological sequence in his narrative. Although this paragraph deals with the year 1836, yet on p. 51 above he describes the time when he was "fourteen years old", namely 1839–40.

133. A dissident sect of Jewish "Literalists" which originated in Persia in the 8th century under the leadership of Anan Ben David, and broke away from the authority of the Babylonian gaonate. After the Russian annexation of Lithuania and Crimea in the 18th century, the Government extended to the Karaites privileges and rights denied to the Rabbinite majority.

134. This incident, so contrary to strict Karaite dietary practice, sounds like a fabrication conjured up by traditionalist Rabbinites against Karaites in general and this Rabbi-Censor in particular. The Karaites, being literalists, follow Pentateuchal regulations meticulously although according to their own interpretation and not the Rabbinic tradition. They considered, for example, that the injuction: "Thou shalt not seethe a kid in its mother's milk" (Exod. xxiii.19, xxxiv.26, and Deut. xiv.21) was meant to extend the term "kid" to include animal meat of all kinds but not fowl. Therefore, though they could eat chicken boiled in milk, they did not eat animal meat which had come into contact with milk.

135. i.e. "unfit" to be eaten. Derived from Exod.xxii.30: "You shall not eat any flesh that is torn

from beasts in the field'', the injunction was expanded to include the flesh of any animal that dies from any cause except ritual slaughtering. Because of this comprehensive interpretation, the term *treifa* became popularly applied to any food ritually unclean.

136. Proverbs xii.21.

137. i.e. 1836.

138. i.e. facing towards Jerusalem and the Temple site.

139. Town in Mohilev province, White Russia. It was the seat of the Ḥabad Rabbis from 1814, when Dov Ber (1773 – 1828), the son and successor of Schneur Zalman of Lyady (1747 – 1813), the founder of Ḥabad, settled there, until 1917. See below, notes 141 and 144.

140. *Shalom Al Yisrael* by Eliezer Zvi Zweifel, in 4 parts, published in Zhitomir and Vilna, 1868 – 73 — "a bold attempt to defend Ḥassidism in a time when it was the target of ridicule both to the orthodox *Mitnagdim* and to all Maskilim." (M. Waxman, *A History of Jewish Literature*, vol. 3, p. 317).

141. Aronson has erred here. The Rabbi of Lubavitch at the time was Menaḥem Mendel Schneersohn (1789 – 1866) who settled in Lubavitch with his father-in-law, Dov Ber, in 1814, and assumed the leadership after Dov Ber died in 1828: see above, note 139. Menaḥem Mendel was popularly called after the title of his famous work *Tsemaḥ Tsedek*.

142. The "ram's horn" prescribed for blowing on the New Year and the year of release (see Lev.xxv.9). Later, the custom arose to blow it on special fast days and religious and national occasions. The blowing of the *shofar* mentioned here is performed in the synagogue during the month of *Ellul*, inaugurating a solemn period of penitential devotions in preparation for the approaching New Year and Day of Atonement.

143. "Righteous man", the appellation given by Ḥasidim to their spiritual leader. In the Bible and Talmud, the *Tsaddik* is noted for his faith and piety (Hab.ii.4; Prov.xx.7; *Sanhedrin* 92a; *Sukkah* 45b). The Ḥasidim regarded the *Tsaddik* as the intermediary between them and God. The title became hereditary in Ḥasidic dynasties. See S. A. Horodezky, *Ha-Ḥasidut Ve-Toratah*, pp. 86 – 93; A. Wertheim, *Halakhot Va-Halikhot Ba-Ḥasidut*, pp. 154 – 170; M. Buber, *Tales of the Ḥasidim: The Early Masters*, p. 4ff; M. Waxman, *A History of Jewish Literature*, vol. 3, pp. 38 – 40, and vol. 5, p. 181.

144. The term *Ḥabad* is the abbreviated initials of *Ḥokhmah* (Wisdom), *Binah* (Understanding), *Da'at* (Knowledge), the first three of the ten divine emanations, *Sefirot*, according to Kabbalistic teachings. The movement was founded by Schneur Zalman of Lyady — see above, note 139 — who attempted to synthesize intellectual learning with simplicity of worship. His ideas are set out in his main work *Likkutei Amarim* (Selected Discourses: published in 1797) which became popularly known as the *Tanya*. The movement gained its greatest following in northern Russia.

145. "Psalms of Praise": Psalms 113 – 118 in the synagogue liturgy, recited on special occasions of the Jewish year. See above, note 90.

146. The palm branch, with the *hadasim* (myrtle), *aravot* (willow) and *etrog* (citron) form the Four Species used on the feast of Tabernacles: see above, notes 90 and 145.

147. The cholera plague was known to originate in India. It spread via Turkey to Russia and the European continent. There were several outbreaks of virulent epidemics during the 19th century, and perhaps the outbreak of 1826 – 37 is the one referred to here. See S. W. Baron, *The Russian Jew under the Tsars and Soviets*, p. 79.

147a. The *Ḥevra Kadisha* (Holy Society). Originally a title of honour for members of the community who performed charitable acts for altruistic motives, it later became specifically applied to burial rites. See Yom-Tov Lewinsky, *Entsiklopediyyah Shel Havai U-Masoret Be-Yahadut*, pp. 175 – 80; *Encyclopaedia Judaica*, vol. 8, pp. 442 – 6; and *Ozar Yisrael*, vol. 4, pp. 244 – 5.

147b. The festive nature of this special event became a byword among Jewish communities. The Burial Societies observed a private day of fasting once a year — either on 20 *Adar* or 15 *Kislev* — to atone for any acts of transgression or dishonour they may have committed against the dead. The termination of the fast was celebrated by a profligate banquet. See Yom-Tov Lewinsky, *Entsiklopediyyah Shel Havai U-Masoret Be-Yahadut*, pp. 177 – 8.

148. In the original, *agilim ma'afeh* (baked rings). A similar term was used by J. L. Levanda in his *Ir U-Behalot*, p. 80: *ma'afeh agul* (крендель) — namely, a "round cake (krendel')", which in Russian is a type of biscuit.

149. *Shalosh Se'udot*, the three special Sabbath meals; the third, mentioned here, is eaten before the termination of the Sabbath.

150. *Sefer Ha-Berit*, by Pinchas Elijah Horowitz, first published Brünn 1797, and in Vilna, in 1818.

The section dealing with the sun is in Part One. *Ma'amar* 4, *Shenei Ha-Me'orot* (The Two Lights), chap. 7, whilst *Ma'amar* 20, *Derekh Emunah* (The Way to Belief), chap. 31, exhorts belief in Moses' miracles.

151. Above, p. 61; he mentions "four hundred students".

152. i.e. the New Year and Day of Atonement.

153. The system of providing a free daily meal for poor yeshiva students at the home of a local member of the community was referred to in Yiddish as *Teg* ("days"). Some students were fortunate enough to sleep as well as to eat in the homes of their hosts, who considered their hospitality as an act of piety. Students without such hospitality, slept on benches in the yeshiva, and went hungry. "A life based on studying the Law was always difficult. The yeshiva students were mostly young sons of poor parents, and the community organisations had to assume responsibility for them. Widespread was the custom of 'eating days' (*esn teg*). Every day of the week the student would eat in a different house". (A. Menes, "Patterns of Jewish Scholarship in Eastern Europe", in *The Jews, Their History, Culture and Religion*, ed. L. Finkelstein, p. 401.)

154. Aronson's dating is too vague to be estimated accurately and does not conform with the known historical facts. The contrivance he mentions was a type of "Instantaneous Light" which became popular during the late 18th century and early 19th century. Early in 1800, a "Pocket Luminary" was introduced in London, consisting of a bottle coated internally with phosphorus and some wooden matches tipped with sulphur: when the matches were withdrawn from the bottle, contact with the air caused ignition. An "Instantaneous Light Box" introduced in 1810, became the most widely-used of these devices. The box held a small bottle of sulphuric acid and some tiny matches tipped with a chlorate of potash compound; dipping the match into the acid ignited it. Another popular early form of "Lighter" was the "Döbereiner Lamp" of 1823, which made use of the chemical reaction between hydrogen gas and platinum; the latter became incandescent and ignited the gas. The "Instantaneous Light" bottle and box devices became obsolete when the "Friction Match" was introduced in 1826 by John Walker, an English chemist, who sold them for one shilling per hundred. By 1832 "phosphoric matches" were in wide use under names such as *Lucifers* and *Congreves*: See the Bryant and May *Museum of Fire-Making Appliances, London*, for sections on Matches and Instantaneous Lights which give a "safety match" made by a Russsian, Lapshin of Zubov, near Novgorod, who was the largest Russian match manufacturer of his time (unfortunately, no date is given). See also, A. H. Dunhill, *The Gentle Art of Smoking*, pp. 118 – 120, and G. West, *A History of Smoking*, pp. 45 – 8.

155. "Zinc strikers", from Russian *barbin*, to strike.

156. "The Strong Hand". His *Mishneh Torah* (Repetition of the Law: completed in 1180) is composed of 14 books (the Hebrew *Yad* adds up to 14) each dealing with a specific category of law. The first five books alluded to by Aronson (and which he calls *Hameshet Ha-Yadot*, the Five Hands) are: *Madda* (Knowledge), *Ahavah* (Love), *Zemanim* (Seasons), *Nashim* (Women), *Kedushah* (Holiness).

157. Aronson's meaning has been given here in preference to a plain translation of the literal original, which is a strong expression taken from Proverbs xxvi.11: "I was unable to return to my vomit" (as does a dog, or like a fool who repeats his mistakes).

158. The *Kitab as-Siraj*, concluded in 1168.

159. Approximates to January.

160. The prohibition is given in the *Kitsur Shulhan Arukh*, x.8.

161. 1 Samuel ii.3.

162. See J.H. Hertz, *Daily Prayer Book*, pp.508.10.

163. An "abstinent", a married yeshiva student who "separated" himself from (namely, abandoned) his wife and family in order to pursue his Talmudic studies. See R.A. Braudes, *Ha-Dat Veha-Hayyim*, abridged edn. J. Frankl, *He'arot* p.165.

164. See his commentary to *Avodah Zarah* iv.7, and *Guide for the Perplexed*, Part 1, chaps. 61-3, and *Hilekhot Tefillin* V.4.

165. "Acts of Kindness", a comprehensive term embracing all forms of kindness and charity: see also "hospitality", note 131 above. A charitable *Gemilut Hasadim Society* existed in every community, principally to arrange interest-free loans for the needy. These societies also maintained yeshivot from their contributions (as did the trades societies). See also *Avot i.2;* and *Kitsur Shulhan Arukh*, chapter xxxiv on "Charity".

166. Named after Reb Meile, one of the early owners of the property, it was popularly called *Reb Meile's Hoyf* (Court) from which derived the name "Remeile's yeshiva". See H.V. Steinschneider, *Ir Vilna* (Vilna City), vol.1, p.119 footnote; also A. Menes, "Patterns of Jewish Scholarship in Eastern Europe" in *The Jews: Their History, Culture and Religion*, vol.1, ed. L. Finkelstein.

167. The importance of these two particular days in Jewish tradition probably dates back to Ezra and his inauguration of the Reading of the Law on these market days: see *Bava Kamma* 82a.

168. The use of nicknames was a common practice and was particularly widespread in provincial areas. They were generally associated with some disreputable characteristic attributed, justly or not, to a person or a locality or even an entire town. These names, in all their explicit shades of contempt, have passed into Jewish folklore. For an amusing account, see J. Gutfarstein, *Folklor Yehudei Lita* in *Yahadut Lita*, vol.1, pp. 606-10, which includes a list of towns and their nicknames. See also M.L. Lilienblum, *Sihat Hullin Shel Talmidei Hakhamim Tserikhah Limmud*, in *Ha-Shahar*, year 4 (1873), p.363; and M.E. Eisenstadt, *Yeshivat Volozhin*, in *He-Avar*, vol. 14, pp.165-6. See also p. 112, regarding derogatory nicknames in the Vilki community.

169. i.e. Dokeliai.

170. *Kovheva De-Shavit*, by H.Z. Slonimski, published in Vilna 1835, and with addenda in Warsaw 1857.

171. *Mif alot Elohim*, by Joel Baal-Shem Heilprin, published in Zholkva 1727. For the preparations required in a case of theft, see section 69, p.11b.

172. A crude Rabbinic formula for seeing demons, performed by R. Bebai b. Abbaye (c.340 A.D.), is mentioned in *Berakhot* 6a.

173. An ancient prayer of "consecration", hallowing and praising God and expressing belief in His divine providence. Composed of mixed Hebrew-Aramaic verses, it is recited, with variations, in public worship *(minyan)*. The prayer referred to here is the Mourner's *Kaddish*, which is read by male mourners during the first year of mourning, and thereafter on the memorial anniversary.

174. "Writing", the term applied to the Jewish marriage document. Written in Aramaic, it includes economic and moral clauses intended to act as a protection for the wife. The tractate *Ketubbot* deals with the preparation of the document and the money due to the wife in the event of divorce or widowhood.

175. Israel Klausner describes the Vilna Courts as follows: "There were twelve Rabbinic judges divided into two groups. One group, in which sat the old men — (i.e. the elder judges) — was called the Upper Court, whilst the other group comprising the young men — (i.e. the junior judges) — was known as the Lower Court. Both groups joined together to deal with important cases." (See *Toledot Ha-Kehillah Ha-Ivrit Be-Vilna*, vol.1, p.96). Max Lilienthal who was in Russia between 1840-4, also mentions that Vilna had two Rabbinic Courts of Law and twelve Rabbis (see D. Philipson, *Max Lilienthal, American Rabbi, His Life and Writings*, p. 268).

176. Elijah ben Solomon Zalman (1720-97). Distinguished Talmudist renowned for his piety and learning; led the opposition to the Hasidim in Lithuania.

177. Isaiah iii.14.

178. "Almighty God". The Hebrew letters mentioned are written שד׳.

179. Deut. viii.3.

180. Z. Scharfstein, quoting from an article in *Ha-Melits* 1898, number 159 (no page given) entitled *Mikhtavim Mi-Kovno* (Letters from Kovno: no author given), relates that starving yeshiva students as young as ten and twelve years of age went round in pairs, knocking on doors and begging for food and alms (see *Toledot Ha-Hinukh Be-Yisrael Ba-Dorot Ha-Aharonim*, vol.1, p.381). Compare Aronson's inability to beg at private houses with similar feelings expressed by M.L. Lilienblum when obliged to sell his *Kehal Refa'im (Kol Kitvei*, vol.2, pp.411 – 69) from door to door (see *Hattot Ne'urim, in Kol Kitvei*, vol.2, p.331). A humorous account of this practice is given by S.J. Abramowitz in his *Fishke Der Krumer*, in *Ale Verk Fun Mendele Mokher Seforim*, vol.xi, pp.154-7.

181. A suitably contemptuous Yiddish salutation to the idle yeshiva student.

182. i.e. the Zarzecze district, situated immediately south-east of the river Viliya which runs through Vilna: it was the Jewish quarter "across the river".

183. i.e. "only a few": cf. Jer.iii.14 and *Sanhedrin* 111a.

183a. Homiletically defined by the Sages as "Father in wisdom, young in years" (Gen. Rabbah 90.3). It occurs in Gen. xli.43 as a possible title of eminence.

184. The Dibbuk is guilt-laden soul which endeavours to escape from the demons pursuing it by lodging in the body of a living person and taking possession of it. The word derives from the Hebrew root *Davok*, to cling. Its first appearance in Jewish literature was in a story in the *Ma'aseh Bukh* (1602), although it was mentioned in a Safed protocol of 1571 (see J. Trachtenberg, *Jewish Magic and Superstition*, p. 50 and p. 282, note 11). It achieved universal fame in S. An-Ski's Yiddish play *The Dibbuk*, first performed by the Vilna troupe in 1920. See G. Scholem, *Kabbalah*, pp. 349 – 50; A.S. Rappaport, *The Folklore of the Jews*, p. 49.

185. P. Smolenskin relates a similar tale of a fraudulent wonder-worker and his assistant, in his story *Ha-To' eh Be-Darkei Ha-Ḥayyim,* Part One, chapter 3, *Ha-Shaḥar,* year 1 (1868-9), p.26.

186. Aronson vocalizes the term as *Ha-Ḥevrah Ha-Leveinah* (instead of *Ha-Levanah*). These youths, known in Yiddish as the *Veisse Ḥevreh,* were a dissolute group whom J.L. Levanda describes as being wild and provocative (see his *Ir U-Behalot,* p.8).

187. i.e. the Pohulanka district, immediately south of the Viliya river, and west of the Jewish Zarzecze district.

188. There are conflicting opinions regarding the Rabbi's identity. Due to the miraculous acts connected with worship at his tomb near Lake Kinneret, the custom arose to donate money for its maintenance. For this and other charitable purposes, collection boxes were kept in most Jewish homes from the 18th century onwards.

189. The silver kopek was first minted in Muscovy in the 16th century and the copper in the 17th with the same value. Both depreciated in value in the course of time.

190. Aronson's calculation is not clear. The silver rouble had been equivalent to 100 copper kopeks ever since 1704 when Peter the Great had revalued it. Since, according to his account, each silver rouble could provide clippings equal to one-fifth of its value (namely, 20 kopeks), then 1,000 roubles should give 200 roubles worth of clippings, not 100.

191. *Ḥokhmat Ha-Yad,* by Moses ben Elijah Galina, 15th century. Published originally under the title of *Toledot Adam* (Constantinople 1515), and later in Yiddish (Salonika 1841).

192. i.e. Eisishkes, near Vilna.

193. *Ḥanukkah,* the festival of Dedication, falls in December, whereas the Passover festival occurs in Springtime, generally in April.

194. In 1847, the Vilna and the Zhitomir Rabbinic seminaries were opened. The Vilna seminary was closed in 1873: the Zhitomir seminary was converted that same year to a Training College for Jewish teachers for Jewish schools, and finally closed in 1885.

195. See *Beẓah* 6b, *et. al.*

196. i.e. *Shishah Sedarim* (Six Orders) of the Mishna, a popular reference to the Talmud.

197. Israel Klausner describes this house as follows: "In 1759, the [Vilna Jewish] community sold a large part of the house to Leib ben Eliezer for 5,667 zloty. Here, Reb Leib Lezers set up a House of Study which is still known as 'Reb Leib Lezers *Kloyz'* [House of Study] . . . In 1784, there were 58 families, totalling 182 people, living in the house. It is said that they lived here in basements beneath basements without light or air. People still point out the basements which are popularly believed to be inhabited by 'spirits'" *(Toledot Ha-Kehillah Ha-Ivrit Be-Vilna,* vol.1, p.72).

198. See above, p.32 and note 72. The book gives a description of a haunted house in Poznan, in the 17th century, whose 'spirits' were exorcised by Rabbi Joel Baal-Shem: see Part 2, chapter 69, folio 26a.

199. See Gen. xxxviii.9. Cf. G. Scholem, *On the Kabalah and Its Symbolism,* p. 155, which discusses demons born from onanism. *Seder Mo' ed, Eruvin* 18b, relates that Adam begot ghosts and demons through accidental seminal emissions.

200. This was a common subterfuge amongst the young generation of yeshiva students. An illustrative incident centered around M.L. Lilienblum's autobiography *Ḥattot Ne' urim* (Sins of Youth: 1876) is described by S. An-Ski in ''I Enlighten a Shtetl'', quoted in L.S. Dawidowicz, *The Golden Tradition,* p.308. See also Z. Scharfstein, *Ḥayyei Ha- Yehudim Be-Mizraḥ Eiropah,* pp.129 and 131; and D. Patterson, *The Hebrew Novel in Czarist Russia,* Edinburgh 1964, p.183.

201. "Old-new" and "new-old" were generally used to describe a building which had been rebuilt after its destruction, often as a result of fire. The rebuilt yeshiva would be known as the "old-and-new", the older portion being the "old-new" and the new part the "new-old".

202. i.e. "And he said".

203. From the meagre information given, it has not been possible to trace this book in German or Polish bibliographies.

204. Aronson uses the popular terms for zloty amongst the Jews of the time. It is given here as the Hebrew *Zahuv* (gold: in Polish *zlot),* and elsewhere as *Adom* (red). For a description of coins, see I. Halpern *Pinkas Va' ad Arba Aratsot,* the Glossary section.

205. The cubit is equal to 28 inches, which is the length of the Russian *arshin.* Aronson, therefore, is using the Hebrew *ammah* (cubit) to represent the Russian *arshin.*

206. E.B. Lanin gives a depressing report (written as late as 1890) of the deplorable conditions in which Jews lived in Russia. It is worth quoting at length: "The late Minister of Finances, Reutern,

declared candidly in a memôir to the Emperor that 'the poverty in which the Jews live is extreme, and the extraordinary demoralisation of the Hebrew race in Russia is mainly the outcome of the extremely unfavourable conditions in which they are placed for gaining a livelihood'. (Footnote: Cf. Complete Collection of Laws, vol.xl., 42264). . . . It was shown by the census that whereas the average proportion of Christians to the total number of houses owned by Christians in the governments of the Pale, is between 410 and 510 persons to one house, the average number of Jews is 1,229. (Footnote: Shooravski Statist., *Description of the Government of Kieff*, vol.i, p.247). In most parts of the Pale they are cooped up like insects or animals rather than men. In Berditscheff, the official statistician tells us 'the Jews are huddled together more like salted herrings than human beings; tens of thousands of them are devoid of any constant means of subsistence, living from hand to mouth; several families are often crowded into one or two rooms of a dilapidated hut, so that at night there is absolutely no space whatever between the sleepers . . . The lodgers turn these rooms into workshops in the daytime, refining wax therein, making tallow candles, tanning leather, etc.; here whole families live, work, sleep and eat together, in that fetid atmosphere, with their tools and materials lying around on all sides'. (Footnote: *Ibid.).'' (The Jews in Russia,* p.504). A similar description of Grodno says: "Frequently one hut consisting of three or at most four rooms lodges as many as *twelve* families, whose lives are an unbroken series of privations and pains. Whole families sometimes live on three-quarters of a pound of bread, one salt herring and a few onions. (Footnote: *Description of the Government of Grodno,* vol.i,p.858 and fol.)'' *(Ibid.* p.505).

207. Psalm xix.8.

208. *Avot* iii.17.

209. Psalm lv.23.

210. ''Scroll'', in *Seder Mo'ed* (Order of Festivals), it deals with the interpretation of Book of Esther and its place in the liturgy.

211. On p.38 above he mentions that he was studying the Talmud at the age of 11. At this time, therefore, he would have been about 27. This would date the present period as probably 1852.

212. In the words of the *Sefer Ha-Ḥasidim:* ''Those who engage in adjuring angels or demons or in casting spells will come to a bad end . . . '' (p.76, entry 211).

213. The names of angels used in amulets were written in this ''angelic writing'', which H.L. Strack describes as *Engelschrift d.i. unlesbare* (Angelic writing, i.e. illegible): see his *Jüdisches Wörterbuch,* p.106. Aronson's example is indeed illegible, for the name is not clear, and nothing resembling it has been found in any book on angelology. G. Scholem says of this type of script: ''In Kabbalistic literature they are known as ''eye writing' *(ketav einayim)* because their letters are always composed of lines and small circles that resemble eyes . . . Such magical letters, which were mainly used in amulets, are the descendants of the magical characters that are found in theurgic Greek and Aramaic from the first centuries C.E.'' *(Kabbalah,* p.186). For other examples, see J.L. Peretz, *Ale Verk* vol.8, pp.267 – 8; A. Goldfaden, *Meshi'ahs Tseitn?!,* p.65; T. Schrire, *Hebrew Amulets,* p.46; J. Trachtenberg, *Jewish Magic and Superstition,* pp.139-43.

214. i.e. ''devils''. In the original Hebrew, *Ashkenazim:* this was a term applied to Jews considered heretical because they adopted German, namely western, manners and dress. In the course of usage, it became a general synonym for evildoers and devils.

215. Yiddish for ''I do not want to dream, I do not want, not want, not.''

216. Corresponds generally to June-July.

217. See the *Kitsur Shulḥan Arukh* chapters cxciv.12, cxcvi.9, cxcviii.3 and cc.10.

218. Job xiv.22.

219. See J. Trachtenberg, *Jewish Magic and Superstition,* pp.176 and 180.

220. Prov. xx.27.

221. Corresponding generally to July.

222. i.e. the year 1843. Another example of Aronson's change from chronological sequence.

223. The figures are as the original. His calculation is once again in error.

224. The month of Passover, generally April.

225. ''Lyric Poetry''. No trace of this anthology has been found.

226. ''Light on the Path'', by Juda Leib Germeisa, 2 vols., Vilna 1835. See above, p. 112.

227. The *Get* (Jewish divorce) is invalid when the ''day'' and the ''evening'' occur on different dates: see *Gittin* 17a.

228. The two titles mentioned here, *Stanovoi* and *Pristav,* appertain to police officers. In 1837, the rural regions of Russia were divided into large districts *(Uezd),* each of which comprised a number of

Stani. Each *Stan* was administered by a *Stanovoi Pristav,* roughly equivalent in status to a District Superintendent of Police, who was subordinate to the *Uezdni Ispravnik* (District Chief of Police). The *Pristav,* although a police official, performed various other judicial functions in addition.

229. Probably the *Slovnik Polsko-Rossyisko-Niemiecki* by Johann A.E. Schmidt, published Breslau 1834.

230. The "Scroll" of Esther is recited aloud in the synagogue service on the feast of Purim. See above, note 210.

231. For these, see above note 90. The prescribed order of waving during the recital of the *Hallel* (Psalms of Praise) is given in the *Kitsur Shulḥan Arukh,* chapter cxxxvii.

232. Aramaic, "The Day", i.e. *Yom Ha-Kippurim* (the Day of Atonement). The fifth tractate in *Seder Mo'ed,* it describes the Temple service of the High Priest on this day, and describes regulations concerning the fast and other observances.

233. Although there are minor differences between the wavings performed by the Reader and the congregation (see: *Shulḥan Arukh* cxxxvii.4), the observant worshipper would be normally aware of them and certainly a student of Aronson's background would be expected to know them. The fact that he did not is, therefore, somewhat surprising and is indicative of indifference towards ceremonial ritual.

234. "Wife of My Youth": for the title, see Isaiah liv.6 and Prov. v.18.

235. The Vilna Gaon, Elijah ben Solomon Zalman (1720-97). His book *Ayil Meshullash* (The Three-year-old Ram) was published in Vilna, in 1835; its title, taken from Gen. xv.9, is a pun on the Hebrew word for a "triangle" *(meshullash).*

236. No trace of this book has been found.

237. From the Russian for "Sabbath", суббота. There was a sect of Sabbatarians who had inclinations towards Judaism. Here, the term refers to a person who worked on the Sabbath: see his comment on this page (112). The first Jewish contractors to the Russian Army appeared in 1812, during the Napoleonic campaign (v. *Yahadut Lita,* p.169).

238. The service "separating" the termination of the Sabbath and the following weekday: see above, note 114.

239. i.e. "Good luck!"

240. A strikingly similar episode is recounted by Solomon Maimon in his *Autobiography,* p.54.

241. *Mesillat Ha-Limmud,* by Judah Leib Ben Ze'ev, Vienna 1802.

242. The "Sabbath of Comfort" immediately following 9 Av when the Scriptural passage from Isaiah xl. is read: "Comfort ye, comfort ye, My people."

243. Exod. xxxii.18.

244. The brackets are Aronson's.

245. See above, note 234.

246. *Ahavat Zion,* Vilna 1853. Mapu (1808 – 67) lived in Rasseyn from 1837 to 1844. See D. Patterson, *Abraham Mapu.*

247. Cf. the death of Samson, Judges xvi. 29 – 30. The source of the quoted lines has not been ascertained, despite Aronson's statement that it was "composed by a famous poet".

248. Probably the *Kritisch-erklärendes Handwörterbuch der deutschen Sprache,* by F.A. Weber, publishing Leipzig 1838.

249. There is a chronological difficulty here. By calculating from his marriage with Bathsheba, the daughter of Hillel the tanner, which took place in 1844, this should now be the year 1847 and Aronson should be 22 years old. However, the Tsar's decree was issued in 1851, and Aronson would be 26 years old. This is one of several problems which illustrate his often hazy recollection of the exact dates of events and his insertion of episodes out of chronological sequence. Regarding the Tsar's decree, Nicholas had a phobia about clothes: previously, in 1837, he had banned the wearing of dresscoats and grey hats by the general populace.

250. See *Kitsur Shulḥan Arukh,* chapter ii.

251. Prov. xvii. 12 and Hosea xiii.8.

252. He was Isaac's father-in-law; see above, p.126.

253. Actually, *Shabbat Shuvah* (The Sabbath of Return), which occurs between New Year and the Day of Atonement: its name derives from the Scriptural portion in Hosea xiv.2. Aronson here uses the popular misnomer for this Sabbath, which arose from the phonic similarity of the words *Shuvah* (Return) and *Teshuvah* (Repentance), which are both appropriate to this solemn season.

254. The standard commentary on Maimonides' *Mishneh Torah* by Joseph Caro (1488-1575); it was published in Venice, 1574-5.

255. Rabbi Obadiah ben Abraham Yare (c. 1450-1516): foremost Italian commentator of the Mishna.

256. *Avot* iii. 19. It is a basic Jewish tenet that God, although omniscient, nevertheless allows man to choose good or evil as he wishes.

257. The "physical" illustration put forward by the anonymous Rabbi is an argument for the existence of the Spirit but it has no relevance to the problem of Man's Free Will and Divine Providence. This involved dissertation on physics applied to metaphysics sounds more like Aronson's own speculation than that of an unnamed Rabbi of the time; especially suspect is the abrupt concluding statement that this was "the burden of Maimonides' reply". Maimonides' own ideas on Free Will are set out in his two major works. "We do not have the capacity to understand how the Holy One blessed be He knows all creatures and their deeds; but we do know for certain that man's actions are under his own control and the Holy One blessed be He does not influence him and does not ordain his behaviour." (*Mishneh Torah, Sefer Ha-Madda, Hilekhot Teshuvah,* chapter 5, paragraph 5: this is in fact an affirmation of *Avot* iii. 19 quoted above on pp. 123-4 and above, note 256). In his *Guide for the Perplexed,* he states the accepted Jewish view that "The theory of man's perfectly free will is one of the fundamental principles of the Law of our Teacher Moses, and of those who follow the Law. According to this principle man does what it is in his power to do, by his nature, his choice, and his will; and his action is not due to any faculty created for the purpose" — and he then declares that everything that happens to man is the result of divine justice and that "every person has his individual share of Divine Providence in proportion to his perfection." (Part 3, chapter xvii, Fifth Theory, p.285, and chapter xviii,p.290).

258. A "deserted wife". A woman who has been abandoned by her husband, whose whereabouts are not known, remains legally his wife until his fate has been ascertained. Should he be still alive, she cannot re-marry until he has given her a divorce. The incidence of abandoned wives was a distressingly common effect of the poverty and oppression suffered by Jews in the Pale of Settlement, when husbands left their families in order to evade military service or persecution or simply to find employment. It was one of the bitter platforms of the religious reformers of the last century. It is still a bone of legal contention today, despite the efforts made by rabbinic authorities to relax halakhic restrictions in favour of the *agunah* ever since Talmudic times (see *Gittin* 3a; Maimonides, *Mishneh Torah, Sefer Nashim, Hilekhot Gerushin,* chapter 13, paragraph 29; and *Shulḥan Arukh, Even Ha-Ezer, Hilekhot Ishut* 17).

259. As in the Hebrew MS.

260. As in the Hebrew MS.

261. *Kaddish De-Rabbanan* (Scholars' Consecration Prayer). Consisting of the whole *Kaddish* with certain variations, it is recited by mourners after communal study and in the synagogue. It was early connected with public aggadic discourses, but became related to actual synagogual liturgy in tractate *Soferim* (c. 6th C.E.): see *Encyclopaedia Judaica,* vol. 10, pp.660 – 1; also note 173 above.

262. A fine of 300 roubles was imposed on the family of any Jewish youth who failed to register for conscription: this sum was often increased for those seeking exemption.

263. "Shield of David", commentary to the *Shulḥan Arukh* by David ben Samuel Ha-Levi *(Taz),* 1586-1667.

264. See above, p. 118 and above, note 246.

265. "Guide to Knowledge", part 2 of the *Arba' ah Turim* (The Four Columns), the basic halakhic work compiled by Rabbi Ya'akov ben R. Asher ben Yeḥiel *(Ha-Rosh:* died c.1350), which formed the pattern for Caro's *Shulḥan Arukh* (Venice, 1564). The *Tur Yoreh De'ah* (the title derives from Isaiah xxviii.9) deals with foods ritually pure or impure, prohibitive regulations, vows, mourning, etc.. The other three *Turim* are: (1) *Oraḥ Ḥayyim* (Way of Life: daily affairs, Sabbath and festivals); (3) *Even Ha-Ezer* (The Stone of Help: personal and marital regulations); (4) *Ḥoshen Mishpat* (The Breastplate of Judgment: civil and criminal laws).

266. The tax on the use of Sabbath candles was instituted in the first decade of the 19th century as part of the general tax upon the Jews — the *Korobochni Shor* or, for short, *Korobka* ("basket tax"). As a separate tax, collected independently of other taxes, it first operated in Vilna in 1831. Because of the special hardships and corrupt practices it engendered, the Government removed taxes on religious articles (including Sabbath candles) in 1839. After the decision was taken by the Government to set up Crown schools for Jewish children, the Candle tax was re-introduced in 1844 to defray the expenses of these institutions: this was the same year that the *Kahal* system was abolished, so that the collection of this tax came entirely under the authority of the Ministry of Public Instruction. The definition of "Candles" was broadened to include any source of domestic light. In 1855, the tax was incorporated into the tax on *Kasher* meat (introduced in 1809 as an additional tax to the regular impost on meat

required by the Jewish community: it was abolished in 1863). In the course of time, the collection of this tax became combined with the general *Korobka* tax, from which the expense for maintaining Jewish schools were then taken, so that the Candle tax was finally abolished by the High Commission presided over by Count K.I. Pahlen (which functioned from 1883–8). See M. Berger, *Mas Nerot Ha-Shabbat Be-Russia*, in *He-Avar*, no. 19, 1972, pp.127 – 31; S. Dubnow, *The History of the Jews in Russia and Poland*, vol. 2, pp.61 – 2 (and also his comparison with the Candle tax in Austria, in his *History of the Jews*, vol. 5, pp.120 – 2); E.B. Lanin, *The Jews in Russia*, pp.488 – 90; The Russo-Jewish Committee, *The Persecution of the Jews in Russia*, Appendix of Laws Relating to the Jews in Russia, pp.45-6; J.D. Clarkson, *A History of Russia*, pp.387-90.

267. By the edict of November 13, 1844. "The granting of teaching certificates to *melamdim* for the old Jewish schools was to be thwarted in every possible way. Within 20 years, no one lacking a certificate from an 'authoritative' Rabbinical Academy is to be a teacher or a rabbi." (S.M. Dubnow, *History of the Jews*, vol. 5, pp.172-3).

268. See "Home Service Prior to the Funeral" in Hertz's *Daily Prayer Book*, p.1072.

269. See above, note 266.

270. See above, note 194.

271. See above, note 267.

272. The eight threads of the *Tsitsit* are bound in 5 knots according to a prescribed manner. The word *Tsitsit* equals 600 in *gematria* calculation, and this plus the 8 threads and 5 knots, totals 613, which is the number of the Commandments *(Taryag Mitsvot)* ordained upon Jews. See: *Kitsur Shulḥan Arukh*, chap. ix, paragraphs 1 and 5.

273. Probably the Русская Грамматика (Russian Grammar) by Alexander Vostokov, published in St. Petersburg, 1831.

274. See above, note 5.

275. *Sic*. Unfortunately, Aronson gives no explanation for this assumed name. For the use of nicknames in general, see note 168 above. See the article on Names and Surnames in *The Jewish Encyclopedia*, vol. ix, p. 156, London 1905.

276. See Babylonlian Talmud, tractate *Derekh Erets Rabba*, chap.5. Also R. Alcalay and M. Nurock, *Divrei Ḥakhamim*, entry 2099, *Kabbedeihu Ve-ḥashedeihu*, p. 220.

277. The "Last Gate" tractate of the Order *Nezikin* (Damages). Originally it formed one complete section together with *Bava Kamma* (First Gate) and *Bava Metsi'a* (Middle Gate).

278. The "additional" commentaries on the Talmud developed by the descendants and disciples of Rashi and the French and German exegetes of the 12th to 14th centuries.

279. It has not been possible to find any record of this "story". The Kingdom of Loango was a Bantu state on the western seaboard of Central Africa, and formed part of the Congo.

280. *Eruvin* 13b.

281. Eccles.x.1

282. The general regulation is that a mourner is forbidden to leave his house during the seven days of mourning. There are, however, exceptional circumstances which free him of this restriction — one of them being that "if the Governor has sent for him, or if he has to attend to some other essential business, he is permitted to leave". *(Kitsur Shulḥan Arukh*, chapter ccxiv, paragraph 1).

283. "Benedictions", the first tractate of the Order *Zera'im* (Seeds): it deals mainly with the liturgy.

284. The Jewish year is based on a lunar calculation. It consists of 12 months containing either 29 or 30 days each, and totalling 354 days. It is thus 11 days less than the solar year of 365 days. To ensure that the festivals are celebrated in their proper seasons — Passover in springtime, Tabernacles in the autumn, etc. — an additional month is inserted in the calendar seven times in every 19 years: these leap years occur in the 3rd, 6th, 8th, 11th, 14th, 17th, and 19th years of each nineteen-year cycle.

285. Equivalent to June.

286. Among oriental nations, the cock symbolised the Devil "and was looked upon as a divinity of the night" (A. S. Rappaport, *The Folklore of the Jews*, p. 47). It is interesting to note that a cockerel (preferably white) is still used by some Jews for the *Kapparot* (expiatory sacrifice) ceremony on the eve of the Day of Atonement: see *Kitsur Shulḥan Arukh*, chapter cxxxi, paragraph 1.

286a. So-spelt on her tombstone in New York where she died on 26 December 1903.

287. Thus, the people who would make out the notes would be the girl's father, Samuel Ḥayyim and Todi (who would give his note to Aronson).

288. See *Kitsur Shulḥan Arukh*, chapter cxlvi, paragraphs 1 and 2.

289. *Ibid*. paragraph 1.

290. i.e. the congratulatory greeting, "Good luck!"

291. A Yiddish saying, given here in Hebrew, denoting a refusal to offer hospitality for even a limited period.

292. In the original, *Yemei Ha-Simḥah Bet Ha-Sho'evah* (lit.: the days of the rejoicing, the fountain-head). During Temple times, the *Simḥat Bet Ha-Sho'evah* (the Ceremony of the Water Libation: literally, the Rejoicing at the Place of the Water-drawing) was celebrated from the second night of the festival and continued for six days. Each morning, a libation of water taken from the Pool of Siloam was poured into a silver bowl by the Altar (see, *Sukkah* v. 1 – 4). Nowadays, the ceremony is celebrated in a modified form, and the prayer for rain *(Tefillat Geshem)* — which the libation symbolised — is read on the eighth day, *Shemini Atseret* (the Day of Solemn Assembly). Aronson's phrasing is ambiguous and capable of two interpretations. He uses his own phrase *Yemei Ha-Simḥah* (the days of the rejoicing) instead of the usual term *Simḥat* (the rejoicing of), and follows it immediately with a description of the revelry with which the day of the Rejoicing of the Law — see following note, below — is celebrated. In this passage, therefore, he may have meant, quite simply, to refer to the eighth day, on which the prayer for rain is read and which is followed on the ninth day by the Rejoicing of the Law. The translator feels, however, that Aronson's choice of phrasing may have been deliberate, and that he was indulging his sense of irony to describe the "drawing" of alcoholic drinks in the tavern (the *Bet Ha-Sho'evah*, the "fountain-head"). For this reason, the Hebrew phrase has not been translated in the text.

293. *Simḥat Torah*, the ninth day of Tabernacles in the Diaspora, celebrating the annual completion and re-commencement of the reading of the Pentateuch in the synagogue. It is a happy occasion and is celebrated with ceremony and joy. In Israel, it is combined with *Shemini Atseret*, the Day of Solemn Assembly, the name given to the eighth day of the festival.

294. Jewish scholars have taken an interest in astronomy since earliest times, and many works have been written on it. Aronson refers to his book simply as *Sefer Ha-Tekhunah* (book of astronomy) without indicating whether this was its title or simply its subject. It is therefore unidentifiable. The most famous work bearing this title and having the antiquity suggested in the text, was written by Levi ben Gershon (Gersonides, *Ralbag*: 1288 – 1344) as an astronomical treatise incorporated in Book V of his *Milḥamot Adonai* (Wars of the Lord), published in Riva di Trento, 1560. (Ḥayyim Vital's *Sefer Ha-Tekhunah* was not published, apparently, until 1866 in Jerusalem).

295. *Kalba Di-Shemaya*, a synonym for the Angels of Destruction who, according to Kabbalistic mythology, descended to earth in the guise of animals, often dogs. Applied to a human being, it becomes an illustrative description.

296. See, however, Deut. xiv.8: "The swine, which parts the hoof but does not chew the cud, is unclean to you . . ."

296a. Conjecturably, Guiseppe Pinetti de Wildalle, born in Italy 1750, died Russia 1800. Conjuror who founded the classical school of magic. See *New Encyclopaedia Britannica, Micropaedia*, vol.7, p. 1016.

297 i.e. Easter.

298. *Tof Turki*, in the original. "Turkish drum" was the nickname popularly given to the Kettle-drum. Here, Aronson applies it, because of its shape, to the clock which he had assembled and fixed to a sieve: see above, pp.153-5.

299. Presumably, he is referring to his own "modern" system of teaching, in which he combined both traditional and secular instruction. It should be noted that the poet J. L. Gordon taught for six years (1866–72) in a "school for girls" there: see, *Kol Kitvei: Shirah*, poem *Betseti Mi-Telz* (On My Departure from Telz), p. 38. Also, the edict establishing modern schools for Jewish children was passed in 1844, before Aronson opened his school.

300. See above, note 295.

301. The popular appellation for Jews who had become "modernised" in their customs and dress. See above, note 214.

302. *Rav Mi-Ta'am Ha-Memshalah*, in the original. Also known as the *Kazioni*(Government) Rabbis, they were not generally held in the same esteem by the Jews as the traditional ecclesiastic Rabbis. Often, therefore, a division of function ensued: the Crown Rabbi attended mostly to official and civil affairs of the community whilst the traditional Rabbi attended to its spiritual and religious welfare. See J. S. Raisin, *The Haskalah Movement in Russia*, p. 295; S. W. Baron, *The Russian Jew Under Tsars and Soviets*, pp. 140– 1; S. M. Dubnow, *History of the Jews in Russia and Poland*, vol.2, p. 176.

303. This was a mechanical leech, used as a substitute for the animal itself. Many of them had a

clockwork arrangement which projected the toothed bars into the patient's flesh — and, for this reason, broken instruments of this kind were given to a clockmaker for repair.

304. i.e. a small amount each. *Ke-Zayit* was a Talmudic expression for a small measure, equivalent to half a *Betsah* (egg).

305. i.e. technically, "pinion leaves".

306. Equivalent to the month of April.

307. i.e. Rite.

308. This type of watch, with a cylinder escapement, has a complicated mechanism. To make the cylinder and its parts would have required a great deal of ingenuity. It is a measure of Aronson's natural ability that he succeeded in doing so purely by trial and error.

309. Apparently, much of the non-medical folk-healing that took place in the small towns and villages of Russia was performed by the Turks and Tartars who were believed to possess special powers.

310. The modern study of Hypnotism was initiated in 1780 by the Marquis de Puységur, a disciple of Mesmer (1734– 1815). A Committee set up by the Academy of Medicine of Paris in 1831 reported favourably on "magnetism" as a therapeutic agent. By the 1840's it was extensively practised throughout Europe, and notably by the surgeon James Esdaile, in Calcutta. In 1841, the Manchester physician, James Braid, coined the term "Hypnotism". Aronson's note here, therefore, that Hypnosis was a recent discovery, can only refer to its practice in Russia.

311. See above, p. 102, notes 214 and 215.

312. *Sic*. Aronson's dates are inexplicable. It is possible that he may have inadvertently written תק"מ and תקמ"ה (1780 and 1785) in error for תר"מ and תרמ"ה (1880 and 1885). See above, page 131, where he records that he is writing his notes "in this year 1886".

313. Isaiah i.8.

314. *Sic*.

315. i.e. Lavkov.

316. i.e. Zhagare.

317. The Statute known as "The Temporary Rules Concerning the Assortment of the Jews", proclaimed on 23 November 1851. See: S. M. Dubnow, *History of the Jews in Russia and Poland*, vol.2, pp. 142– 3, and his *History of the Jews*, vol.5, p. 316; also J. Klausner, *Matsav Ha-Yehudim Be-Russia Bi-Shenot 1820 – 1860* (The Condition of Jews in Russia during 1820– 60), in *Historiyyah Shel Ha-Sifrut Ha-Ivrit Ha-Hadashah*, vol.3, (1953), p. 12.

318. Jewish artisans organised themselves into Societies (or Guilds) similar to those of the Christian, both for mutual aid and as a defence against against Christian professional opposition. Their Societies followed procedures common to other Societies. To become a member, the artisan had to have undergone six years apprenticeship followed by two years' full-time practice in the trade. Societies were often governed by as many as four *Gabba' im* (Wardens) assisted by eight officers elected from the membership (e.g. accountant, secretary, etc.). Societies also bought or built their own synagogues and held separate services. (See I. Klausner, *Toledot Ha-Kehillah Ha-Ivrit Be-Vilna*, pp. 123– 5). Merchants of the First Guild were, of course, the wealthiest, and paid a subscription of 1,000 roubles per annum as well as higher government taxes. In 1859, Jewish merchants who had traded for not less than five years as members of a First Guild within the Pale of Settlement, were permitted to reside freely outside the Pale to pursue their trade: other trades were not afforded this freedom until 1865. See E. B. Lanin, *The Jews in Russia*, p. 487; J. Klausner, *Historiyyah Shel Ha-Sifrut Ha-Ivrit Ha-Hadashah*, vol.4, p. 106; the Russo-Jewish Committee, *The Persecution of the Jews in Russia*, Appendix, pp. 19, 59– 63. For a general account, see M. Wischnitzer, *A History of Jewish Crafts and Guilds*.

319. Possibly the Act Concerning Municipal Administration 1785: see S. M. Dubnow, *History of the Jews in Russia and Poland*, vol.1, p. 308 and p. 313; also J. D. Klier, "The Ambiguous Legal Status of Russian Jewry in the Reign of Catherine II", pp. 510—3, which discusses the Charter of the Towns, of 1785, and the concessions permitted to foreigners and Jews. The Statute of 1835, issued by Nicholas I, allowed limited Jewish representation on municipal councils, but this was never fully implemented in Lithuania. In 1839, the restrictions were widened to reduce Jewish participation in local civic affairs to a minimum. "Jewish elections were to held separately from the Christians. Jews could not be elected as City Mayors or as Senior Magistrates of city lawcourts. . . ." (*Yahadut Lita*, vol.1, p. 86): see also the Russo-Jewish Committee, *The Persecution of the Jews in Russia*, Appendix, pp. 65– 6, which cites the restrictions imposed on Jewish guildsmen by the Law on Industrial Professions, of 1887.

320. The Crimean War began with the Russian invasion of Moldavia on 2 July 1853 and ended with the ratification of the Treaty of Paris on 27 April 1856.

321. "The war was accompanied by a rapid increase in the volume of money in circulation. Government revenues from customs duties fell during the war and receipts from direct and excise taxes did not rise significantly. As expenditures rose the state issued more paper roubles and the stability achieved by Count Kankrin's financial reforms in the 1840's was destroyed. It should be noted that the increase in money supply took place in 1856 and 1857 and not during the actual war years." (W. McK. Pintner, *Inflation in Russia during the Crimean War Period*, p. 85). Paper roubles, known as *Assignatsi*, were issued in 1768 – 9 to finance increasing state expenses, but excessive printing led to their devaluation. In 1839, a ukase of Nicholas I officially recognised the paper rouble as a subsidiary medium of exchange to the silver rouble, which became the basic monetary unit: the value of the silver rouble was fixed at 3.6 paper roubles. In the 1840's, new paper money, called *Kreditni Bileti*, was issued, and this was exchangeable for silver roubles at par rate. During the Crimean War, however, the exchange of paper roubles for silver was stopped. In subsequent years, the value of the paper rouble fluctuated due to changing economic and political conditions, until Count Sergei Witte, Minister of Finance 1893 – 1903, introduced the gold standard in 1896 – 7. A similar account of currency shortage was given by N. M. Gelber, *The Diary of a Jewess during the Polish Uprising of 1863*, who described how merchants had to issue their own paper-notes (*Kleingelt Tsetlen*, bills of small denomination) because of the shortage of coins; when these were returned to them for redeeming into cash immediately after the cessation of the revolt, many merchants went bankrupt (see *Yivo Bleter*, vol.xlii, New York 1962, p. 213).

322. In the Hebrew, *Sar Ha-Elef*. The use of decimal units for Russian military ranks was a feature of army organisation during medieval times: it is unlikely that Aronson is here using the title as a specific military rank in his own time. Elsewhere, he mentions Officers over Fifty, over a Hundred, over a Thousand and over Thousands. The same terms are also found amongst contemporary Hebrew writers. Abraham Mapu wrote of a *Sar Ha-Me'ah Asher Sar Ha-Elef Nish'an Alav, Ha-Adyutant* (the Officer over a Hundred who was the Adjutant to the Officer over a Thousand): see, Benzion Dinur, *Mikhtevei Avraham Mapu*, p. 214. M. D. Brandstetter, in *Tsorer Ha-Yehudim Be-Ir Griliv*, mentions a *Sar Asarah Be-Hel Ha-Parashim* (Officer over Ten in the Cavalry). Doubtless Hebrew writers were influenced by the identical Biblical terms for military ranks: "Officers of thousands, hundreds, fifties and tens" (Exod. xviii. 21). From Y. Yadin's *The Art of Warfare in Biblical Lands*, it would appear that 10 men constituted a section, 50 a platoon, 200 – 250 a company, 800 – 1250 a battalion and 5,000 men a brigade or division. See also Yadin's article "Warfare in the Second Millenium B. C. E." in *The World History of the Jewish People*, edited B. Mazar, vol.2, pp. 138 – 9.

323. The St. Petersburg winter palace was destroyed by fire in 1837. It was rebuilt in 1838 – 9 by Count Peter A. Kleinmichel (1793 – 1869), the Minister for Communications and Public Works under Nicholas I. "A conflagration, which is supposed to have originated in some defect in the stoves, consumed the whole interior of the building in December, 1837, notwithstanding every effort made to save it. It soon, however, rose again from its embers. In 1839 the Winter Palace was entirely restored" (J. Murray, *Handbook for Travellers in Russia, Poland and Finland*, p. 63).

324. Jews were forbidden to live within a distance of 50 *verst* (about 53 kms) — not 40 *verst*, as Aronson says — from the frontier. The prohibition to live near the frontier was first proclaimed in 1809, re-enacted in 1825 when the 50 *verst* limit was stipulated, and re-inforced in 1843. Although Alexander II relaxed some restrictions of this law in 1858, it was re-imposed with greater severity by Alexander III. The act was repealed in 1904. See I. Maor, *Tehum Ha-Moshav Ha-Yehudi*, in *He-Avar*, vol.19, pp.44f.; also Prince San Donato Demidov, *La Question Israélite en Russie*, p. 297; the Russo-Jewish Committee, *The Persecution of the Jews in Russia*, Appendix, pp. 48 – 9; and H. H. Ben-Sasson, *A History of the Jewish People*, map on p. 816.

325. It is known that wooden pegs were used for heels in the 16th century when heels were invented; they were also used on the soles of heavy footwear worn in bad weather conditions. Beside this, the view generally accepted is that pegged footwear became a common method of manufacture in the USA about 1815 and spread to Europe in the 1830's. Development was slow because the pegs had to be cut by hand and driven in by hand, after the hole had been made with a peg-awl. Pegs were preferred for use in wet conditions as they had longer wear than the more common waxed threads. The pegs were normally made of maple or birch. The first patent for a pegging machine (i.e. for driving pegs) was registered in the USA in 1829, and for cutting pegs in 1848: this would antedate Aronson's own machine by ten years or more.

326. In the original, *Beroshim (Berze)*. The Hebrew *Berosh* actually means cypress, not birch, and is equivalent to the Russian Кипарис *(Kiparis*: cypress). No doubt Aronson uses *Berosh* because of its phonetic similarity to *Berze* — which, itself, is a corrupt rendering, probably dialectical, of the Russian

берёза *(Berëza*: Birch). There is an Old Prussian term *Berze*, meaning birch, which was possibly used in the Lithuanian-Prussian border areas where Aronson lived. The birch *(Betula papyrifera)* is a whitish tree, as Aronson mentions, and is common throughout Russia (whereas the cypress tree in not native to northern Russia, Lithuania, Poland or the Baltic states). It was used for "toothpicks and shoe pegs" (H. P. Brown, *Textbook of Wood Technology*, vol.1, pp. 527).

327. The combination of these two particular professions was unusual, certainly in western Europe where each was considered sufficent to itself. In nineteenth-century England, many clockmakers sold a variety of goods, which included hardware and cutlery: see, E. J. Tyler, *The Craft of the Clockmaker*, p. 69. Aronson's willingness to pursue a multi-professional business demonstrates his sense of enterprise and capacity for industry. (It is interesting to note that Russian law did not accord photography the same professional status as the officially recognised trades, and subjected photographers to various disabilities: see, the Russo-Jewish Committee, *The Persecution of the Jews in Russia*, p. 63). By the late 1850's when Aronson opened his studio, the photographic art had been well-established in Europe. Nicéphore Niepce (1765 - 1833) produced the world's first camera photograph of nature, in 1829. His partner Louis Daguerre (1787 - 1851) introduced his daguerreotype, the first practicable photographic process, in 1839. The world's first photographic salon had opened in Paris in 1844. There had also been significant developments in microphotography, so that by 1859 microphotographs were popular in England and western Europe. Aronson's choice of photography shows him to have been in tune with the spirit of the century's developing technology. He was certainly one of the first Jewish professional photographers in the world. "The first photographer known to be of Jewish birth was the American, Solomon Nunes Carvalho, who in 1853 - 4 served as artist-photographer with John C. Frémont's expedition to the Far West. However, the 19th century did not produce many photographers with Jewish backgrounds." (Article on "Photography" in *Encyclopaedia Judaica*, vol.13, p. 438). Carvalho was engaged on his expedition only four years or so before Aronson opened his photographic studio. See: H. Gernsheim, *The History of Photography*, Oxford 1955; and F. Luther, *Microfilm, A History 1839 - 1900*, Maryland 1959.

328. A professor of physics at St. Petersburg university, Moritz Hermann von Jacobi (1801 - 74), brought out a method of galvanoplastics in 1840. Werner von Siemens, in 1842, applied for a Prussian patent for galvanic gilding and silvering; the process was unknown in Prussia at the time (see: Werner von Siemens, *Lebenserinnerungen*, p. 86). Aronson, therefore, at this particular period of time, had undertaken a new process which would have been unfamiliar to most provincial towns, and perhaps this may have been a factor for its failure in Telz.

329. The hosiery industry, as such, began with the invention of the stocking-frame in 1589 by Rev. William Lee of Calverton, near Nottingham. This machine became the basic design underlying "the whole family of knitting and lace-making machines developed in the 18th and 19th centuries" (A.P. Usher, *A History of Mechanical Inventions*, p. 281.) An interesting comparison of the worldwide state of the textile industry in 1812 is shown by a census compiled, at the time, of looms in use in different countries: Great Britain and Ireland — 29,588; France — 6,855; Germany — 2,340; Spain and Portugal — 1,955; Italy — 985; Netherlands — 520; America (i.e. USA) — 260; *St. Petersburg* — 200; Copenhagen — 35; Stockholm — 30 (see: J. Blackner, *The History of Nottingham*, pp. 238 - 245). Power machines were not brought out until the nineteenth century. Towards the latter part of the 19th century, the construction of hosiery-machines became an important industry in Germany and the USA (see: F.A. Wells, "The Textile Industry: Hosiery and Lace", in *A History of Technology*, ed. by C. Singer *et al.*, vol. 5, pp. 595 - 604). On the whole, the hosiery industry was comparatively slow to adopt mechanisation for, "even by 1870, most hosiery was still made by hand or at least by hand-driven machines. Thereafter, mechanisation became increasingly common" (T.I. Williams, "Science and Technology", in *The New Cambridge Modern History*, vol. xi, p. 98). The Russian industry developed with the help of English technology and equipment. It was particularly encouraged by the import of cheap English yarn, and further stimulated after 1842 when England lifted its ban on the export of textile machinery (see: M.E. Falkus, *The Industrialisation of Russia*, pp. 37 - 9). In the early 1850's there was a flourishing textile industry based in Moscow which had been established by a serf-entrepreneur, Sava Morosov. It had "74 power looms, 456 hand-looms and an annual output valued at nearly 2 million roubles" (W.O. Henderson, *The Industrialization of Europe*, 1780 - 1914, p. 121).

330. In the original, Aronson uses an interesting phrasal substitute: *Atsei Aharon*, literally "the trees of Aaron". This is an ingenious Hebraization of the German *Ahornholz* (maple wood), the *Ahorn* being given a strongly Yiddish pronunciation so that it sounds like *Aron*, namely *Aharon*. The term *klon* added in parenthesis is the Russian клён (maple). The maple wood used, then and also today, for

footwear — amongst many other uses — is the hard variety known as the Sugar Maple (*Acer saccharum*) and Black Maple (*Acer nigrum*): see, H.P. Brown, *Textbook of Wood Technology*, vol. 1, pp. 583—5.

331. The Russian *pud* = 40 Russian pounds (*funti*) = 16.3 kgs, or 36.113 lbs. avoirdupois.

332. i.e. 1868: see above, p. 194 ("1868, the year of the famine").

333. To engage in guerilla fighting. The quotation marks are Aronson's. This Revolt actually broke out on 22 January 1863 and ended in May 1864, although it was preceded by popular demonstrations against Russian rule during 1861 – 2 (the dates given by Aronson). No large-scale battles took place, the Polish forces acting mainly as insurgent bands.

334. "From 1792 the State could banish political prisoners to Siberia... The main waves of political exiles were the Decembrists of 1825, the Polish insurgents in 1831 and 1863..." (M. Gilbert, *Russian History Atlas*, p. 54).

335. The Kingdom of Poland endured many changes of sovereignty in its history. There was a Polish kingdom in the 11th century. The heyday of Polish power flourished between the 14th to 16th centuries, although King Jan Sobieski maintained its prestige in the 17th century. Thereafter, it declined. During the next two centuries, Poland suffered several territorial partitions (1772, 1793, 1795, 1815) and also uprisings (1794, 1830, 1846, 1863). It became an independent Republic in 1918.

336. Count M.N. Muraviev (1796– 1866) was appointed Governor-General of Lithuania in May 1863. The severity with which he suppressed the Polish revolt in Lithuania earned him the popular soubriquet of "the Hangman".

337. i.e. Libau (Liepaja).

338. The stringent residential prohibitions imposed by Nicholas I were gradually relaxed for special categories of Jews during the liberal period of his successor, Alexander II. In 1859, Jewish merchants of the First Guild were permitted to reside outside the Pale; in 1861, university graduates; in 1865, Jewish artisans, and in 1867 Jewish soldiers who had served their full term in Nicholas I's army (see below, note 343).

339. Kalman Schulman describes the St. Petersburg commercial centre as encompassing "Nevsky Prospekt, the shopping street known as the *Passage*, the Great and Little Morskaya Streets, Meshtshanskoi Street, Garden Street and Gorokhovaya Street" (*Kiryat Melekh Rav*, p. 67). Most of these places are mentioned by Aronson.

340. cf. Joshua vi. 1.

341. In the original, this is expressed by a quotation from Proverbs xxii. 7: "The borrower is a servant to the lender."

342. See Exod. xiii. 7.

343. The "Nicholas soldiers" — in Russian, *Nikolayevski Soldati* — were Cantonists (see above, note 22) who had managed to survive the full twenty-five years' service. After discharge from the army, they were compelled to return to their original places of residence, where they had become in fact strangers, and were forbidden to live outside the Pale of Settlement. In 1867, however, Alexander II repealed this prohibition and allowed these soldiers and their families to reside outside the Pale.

344. For this method of counting, see *Yoma* 53b and the Service (*Avodah*) of the High Priest in the Prayer Book for the Day of Atonement.

345. Alexandre Dumas held a similar opinion of the corruption prevalent in Russian legal practice: "*La justice, en Russie, est comme Atalante: elle s'arrête quand on lui jette des pommes d'or*" (The law, in Russia, is like Atalanta; it stops to pick up the golden apples): see his *Voyage en Russie*, p. 194.

346. The Russians used the word *Papirosa* (plural, *Papirosi*) to denote any smoking product which was not consumed in a pipe or not wrapped in a tobacco leaf, like a cigar. It was also used to describe both the plain and filter-tip cigarettes used in western Europe. Paper-wrapped tubes of tobacco, known as *papeletes*, were introduced into Europe from the Spanish colonies of America during the 17th century. The smoking of cigarettes first became generally fashionable in the 1840's in France. During the Crimean War, British troops adopted the habit from their cigarette-smoking French and Turkish allies, and popularised it in Britain on their return home. No doubt, they also encountered captured Russian officers who smoked cigarettes, for a cigarette factory had already been established in St. Petersburg in 1850 by a German, Baron Huppman. According to Kalman Schulman, there were "more than forty tobacco and cigar factories" in St. Petersburg in 1863 (see his *Kiryat Melekh Rav*, p. 67). Jews had taken an active interest in the tobacco and snuff industry ever since its beginning. Tobacco was a regular commodity of the Jewish pedlar. "Of 110 tobacco factories in the Pale of Settlement in

1897, 83 were owned by Jews, and over 80 per cent of the workers were Jewish'' (S.W. Baron, *Economic History of the Jews*, p. 207). Automation came late in the tobacco industry. ''Before the introduction of cigarette-rolling machines, a hand roller of 'long cut' tobacco (shredded for cigarettes and with its paper wrapper held together with a paste of moistened flour) could, in a very long working day, turn out 2,500 to 3,500. By 1884, a machine, an improvement of that registered in 1880 (and patented 1881) by James Bonsack of Virginia, was alone creating 120,000 a day, which was as much as forty-eight or more handrollers could produce in an equal time'' (J.E. Brooks, *The Mighty Leaf*, p. 253). ''Apparently the earliest effort with a mechanism which would turn out a rolled, wrapped cigarette was that of Albert H. Hook, in 1872 (in the United States). This seems not to have been put to commercial use, although it was patented in 1876'' (*ibid*, p. 253 footnote). See also A.H. Dunhill, *The Gentle Art of Smoking*, p. 20f.; *The American Tobacco Story* published by the American Tobacco Company, p. 21; and G. West, *A History of Smoking*, pp. 37 – 9. Since Aronson was working on his machine in the mid-1870's, he was certainly in the vanguard of inventor-entrepreneurs in this industry: see p. 226 where he mentions ''30 December 1876''. For transliteration, see p. 337.

347. The modern typewriter owes its development to the work of Christopher Latham Scholes, an American printer, whose first practical type-bar machine using an inked ribbon appeared in 1867, and his ''Universal'' keyboard for quick typing in 1876. See, C. Singer *et. al.*, *A History of Technology*, vol. 5, pp. 689 – 90.

348. The calculation, once again, is unclear, although it is repeated a few lines later.

349. See Psalms vi and xii.

350. *Avot* iv. 3.

351. *Sic*.

352. An old saying of uncertain origin. Aronson's Hebrew closely follows the Yiddish version of the saying: *Gis nit aroys dos umreine vaser kol zeman due host nit dos reine* (see, I. Bernstein, *Jüdische Sprichwörter und Redensarten*, p. 85, entry 1247).

353. Russian изобретатель = inventor.

354. This clashes with the description of Tutorski as an officer in the Debtor's Prison: see p. 208. No doubt Aronson is influenced here by bitter memories.

355. In the original, *mesillat burzel susim* (iron horse-rails) and also *mesillat ha-susim* (horse-ways). His use of the popular Hebrew term for railways (*mesillat barzel*) to describe the *konka*, the Russian horse-drawn tram, compares with a similar double usage in England and Wales where the terms tramway lines and railway lines were interchangeable for both kinds of track (see: F.E. Wilson, *The British Tram*, p. 2). Horse-drawn trams were in widespread use in Europe and America from the 1830's, although the first English passenger service was not opened until 1860. During the period 1870 – 1890, the London publishers John Murray brought out two editions of their travel series *Handbook for Travellers in Russia, Poland and Finland*: the 3rd edition, 1875, makes no comment at all on tramways in St. Petersburg, but the 4th edition, 1888, states: ''*Tramways*: These intersect the city in all directions, and maintain communication with the principal suburbs'' (p. 97). Presumably, therefore, the *konka* began to make its appearance in St. Petersburg in the late 1870's and early 1880's. See also E.M. Almedingen, *I Remember St. Petersburg*, p. 66.

356. For this ''Golden Rule'' see *Shabbat* 31a.

357. Isaiah xiv. 19.

358. It should be noted that the von Siemens Company had already taken out a patent for their alcoholmeter in 1865, and that since then it had been in successful use in Russia and other European countries (see: W. von Siemens, *Recollections*, pp. 231 and 296). In 1872, the *Gebrüder Siemens* Company was founded specifically for the manufacture of their alcoholmeter (*ibid*. p. 281).

359. The partnership of Siemens and Halske began in 1847 and ended with Halske's retirement from the firm in 1867. The partners were Johann Georg Halske (1814 – 90), Johann Georg Siemens (1805 – 79) and his cousin Ernst Werner von Siemens (1816 – 92). See also note 358 above.

360. Johann Georg Tralles (1763 – 1822), Professor of Mathematics, Berlin University.

361. Prolonged search has not revealed the identity of this Jewish ''inventor'' of a submarine. (Aronson's presentation of him in this casual manner with no supporting information is frustratingly typical of his treatment of other characters in the MS). The first submarine to be used as an offensive weapon in naval warfare was built by an American, David Bushnell, and had a one-man crew: it was used during the American Revolution (1775 – 83). In 1855, the Russian Government purchased a submarine from Wilhelm Bauer, a Bavarian: named *Le Diable-Marin* (The Sea-Devil) it made 134 dives and was displayed during the coronation of Alexander II.

362. *Sic*. Probably better: Synapeoscope (from Greek *Synapsis*, "contact"), namely an instrument for observing the cohesion of substances.

363. There is no indication which book this might be. Possibly his memoirs? Or perhaps the Bible, whose style is mirrored in his own?

364. In the Hebrew, *Reḥov Ha-Gannim*: i.e. *Sadovaya Ulitsa*, an important St. Petersburg thoroughfare.

364a. It was exhibited at the Paris Exhibition of 1867: see M. Corina, *Trust in Tobacco*, p. 25.

365. *Sic*. This spelling of his name ("e" instead of "o") is maintained throughout the remainder of the MS, and occurs fifteen more times. Cf. also the spelling "Aranzon" with which he was registered in Lavkov (see p. 176).

366. In the Hebrew, *Reḥov Ha-Peḥami*, namely *Kuznietsi Ulitsa*.

367. Thus, Aronson received 40 per cent, and his partners 60 per cent.

368. Or 11 January 1877, new style.

369. Jean Bernard Léon Foucault (1819 – 68), French physicist. He experimented with a pendulum made of a heavy iron ball suspended by a steel wire 67 metres long to demonstrate that, as the earth rotates, the pendulum will swing in a vertical plane which changes at a rate and direction dependent on the geographical latitude of the pendulum.

370. The seven stars of the Great Bear (*Ursa Major*) suggest the shape of a Plough, by which they are known.

371. At the Panthéon, in 1851.

372. Also known as the Royal Pendulum: see, D. de Carle, *Horology*, p. 31.

373. *Sic*. No doubt an unintentional error, for it should obviously read '23 minutes'.

374. Shortening a pendulum increases the speed of its vibrations, and thereby causes the mechanism to run fast. Aronson's description, however, is not mathematically precise, as shortening a pendulum by one-third (as he states here) would not result in a proportional change in the timekeeping. He is giving a loose and generalised description, intended rather for his family and friends than for a professional horologist. For a discussion of the pendulum and the formula for the calculations of the time of its vibrations, see J.W. Player, *Britten's Watch and Clock Makers' Handbook*, pp. 536 – 7.

375. This idea is possibly based on the *remontoire* movement such as that in the more expensive clocks and watches imported into Russia from France and Germany, and which Aronson may have seen.

376. The decline of Ottoman power during the second half of the nineteenth century aroused demands for independence from the empire's subject peoples. In 1875, revolts broke out in Bosnia and Herzegovina, followed by a brutally suppressed Bulgarian uprising. In 1876, Serbia and Montenegro declared war on Turkey. Alexander II, unable to withstand the pressure of the rising Panslavic movement, declared war in April 1877. The war ended with the Treaty of San Stefano, in 1878, which gave Russia extensive territorial gains. Although Serbia, Montenegro and Rumania gained independence, Bosnia and Herzegovina were placed under Austrian supervision, whilst Bulgaria suffered division into two provinces and was deprived of access to the Aegean Sea.

377. i.e. the Fosse, the old moat which encircles the city.

378. In 1878.

379. So spelt in the Hebrew. It was a common practice for foreigners who settled in Russia to give their names a more acceptable spelling. In this case, it could have been Fonvizin, i.e. фонвизинъ. The *Russkii Biograficheskii Slovar* (Russian Biographical Dictionary), vol. 20, St. Petersburg 1912, gives three people of this name — although unfortunately, none of them is the one mentioned by Aronson.

380. In this thermometric scale — devised by René Antoine de Réaumur (1683 – 1757) — the freezing point of water equals 0° and boiling point 80°.

381. 800 *verst* are equivalent to 853.6 kms or 530.4 miles. It is not clear to which particular line Aronson is referring. By this date, the late 1870's, there was a network of interconnecting railway lines running north to south from St. Petersburg to Odessa, via Moscow on the south-east and Warsaw on the south-west. The distances of the two cities mentioned in this passage, Tver and Moscow, are much less that 800 *verst*: Moscow is 403 miles from St. Petersburg, whilst Tver is on the direct St. Petersburg-Moscow railway line. "By 1875, the railroad network outlined in the decree on the organization of the Chief Company of Russian Railroads was in the main completed" — namely, the interconnection by rail of principal cities and ports with the inland waterways and grain-producing regions (see, P.I. Lyaschchenko, *History of the National Economy of Russia*, pp. 501 – 2).

382. Though Aronson failed in this venture, two other Jewish inventors successfully brought out

calculating machines (though not specifically for railway parcels) before this period. Abraham Jacob Stern (1762 – 1842), a Polish *maskil* and mathematician, produced his calculating machine in 1812, which brought him the honour of being the only Jew admitted to membership of the Royal Society of the Friends of Science (where he demonstrated it); he was also granted an annual pension by Tsar Alexander I in 1815. His son-in-law, Ḥayyim Selig Slonimski (1810 – 1904), Hebrew publisher, astronomer, inventor, and science author, invented a calculating machine for which he was awarded a prize by the Russian Academy of Sciences in 1844.

383. René Prudent Patrice Dagron (1819 – 1900). French pioneer of microphotography, he was granted the first microfilm patent, in 1859. At the Paris International Exhibition of 1867 he exhibited a microphotograph which showed all the 450 members of the French Chamber of Deputies: see, H. and A. Gernsheim, *The History of Photography*, p. 250. He was awarded Honourable Mentions at both the London Worlds Fair in 1862, and the Paris Exhibition in 1867.

384. "Suggestive and indecent microphotographs, made by some of Dagron's competitors, were on the market at least by 1874; more than any other cause they, for a time, retarded the general acceptance of microphotography" (F. Luther, *Microfilm – A History, 1839–1900*, p. 34).

385. i.e. a camera.

386. i.e. the *camera obscura*.

387. This is the Russian form of the term.

388. It should be noted that Dagron had already put his microfilm camera on public sale in 1864, and had also published his *Traité de Photographie Microscopique* (Paris 1864) which gave a description of his photographic apparatus and its operating instructions. By the time Dagron received his microfilm patent in 1859, microphotography was already well-known in Europe. A British optical manufacturer, John Benjamin Dancer (1812 – 87), is recognised as the inventor of microphotography: he made the first-known microcopy of a document in 1839 (the same year that Louis Daguerre introduced his daguerreotype). Dancer's miniatures were set into a special lens by Sir David Brewster, the Scottish physicist and inventor of the kaleidoscope, and exhibited in Italy and France during his travels in 1857: the French photographers especially took up his suggestion that these microphotographs could be set into novelty jewellery: see, F. Luther, *Microfilm – A History, 1839 – 1900*, pp. 32 – 33. Furthermore, "One of the first published accounts of a workable method of making microprints was that of Georges Scamoni, photographer for the Russian Imperial Office in St. Petersburg. His process was described in his *Handbuch der Heliographie* which appeared in 1872 . . . The inventor envisaged his process as being applied to large-scale production of microscopic books and maps which could be concealed with the greatest of ease" *(Ibid.* p.88). Here, Aronson is writing of the year 1878 – 9. It is difficult, therefore, to understand why neither Dagron's book and camera nor Scamoni's publication seems to have been available to him. They would have spared him a great deal of time, labour and expense.

389. "All the developments in microfilm trace their ancestry directly back to the efforts of two men: John Benjamin Dancer who pioneered the field in experimentation and tentative moves towards commercialisation; and René Prudent Patrice Dagron who placed the medium on a firm commercial basis" (F. Luther, *Microfilm – a History, 1839 – 1900*, p. 97). Dagron called his novelties *microscope-bijoux (Ibid.* p. 34): in 1862, he published a 36-page booklet entitled *Cylindres photomicroscopiques montés et non-montés sur bijoux, brevetés en France et à l'étranger (Ibid.* p. 39). By 1862, in fact, he had established a flourishing business which was selling picture-mounted novelties of varying shapes and sizes for only "a few cents apiece" *(Ibid.* p. 35). Both Dancer's and Dagron's processes spread also across the Atlantic so that, by 1866, the first studio in America for producing novelty microfilms had been opened by John H. Morrow in New York *(Ibid.* p. 43, which also quotes Edward L. Wilson's editorial in the *Philadelphia Photographer* of September 1866).

389a. There is no "clockmaker's plane" as such. Probably the reference is to a *Lap*, which is a polishing tool used by clockmakers to obtain flat surfaces on lenses; it is also used by gemstone cutters.

390. The magnifying lens used commonly at the time in microphotography was the Stanhope lens, which also became known as the "Coddington magnifier" and the "Brewster magnifier". It was a plano-convex lens whose thickness ensured that the focus of the spherical curvature coincided with the flat surface of the lens. It was used extensively by Dagron, who states in his *Traité de Photographie Microscopique* — v. above, note 388 — that he sold Stanhopes "cut and finished" and "trimmed and rounded off" with an optician's grinding wheel or lathe. See F. Luther, *Microfilm – A History, 1839 – 1900*, pp. 27, 36 and 123. Also, H. and A. Gernsheim, *The History of Photography*, p. 250.

391. The only listing that has been found of a German work of that date ("more than a hundred years ago") dealing with the manufacture of lenses is a reference in G. S. Duncan, *Bibliography of Glass*,

which gives the following under entry 3062, pp. 93 – 4; "Denicke, C. L.: 'Vollständiges Lehrgebäude der ganzen Optik oder der Sehe-Spiegel und Strahlbrech-Kunst'. Altona. D. Iversen. 1757. [Gives instructions for making lenses and optical instruments including microscopes. Also describes the grinding and polishing of glass, etc.]."

392. A solution of silver nitrate was commonly used in photographic sensitizing and developing processes.

393. The camera used by Dagron had a screw whose function was to rack the lens and microscope in and out for correct focusing: "By turning the focusing screw one way or the other you will soon see the image form on the little glass plate . . . You may then remove the micrometer scale and put in its place the photographic plate" (Dagron, *Traité*, quoted in F. Luther, *Microfilm — A History, 1839 – 1900*, pp. 121 – 2).

394. Cf. Dagron's instructions in his *Traité*: "Coat the flat surface of the Stanhope or gem with a little Canada balsam; take the little square of glass with tweezers, and press it . . . against the coat of Canada balsam and let it stand" (*Ibid.* p. 122).

395. In the Hebrew, *Rehov Ha-Ḥol*: the Russian name is *Pisochni Ulitsa*.

396. Patented in 1866 by Alfred Nobel (1833 – 96), the Swedish chemist.

397. i.e. Microdiorama.

398. i.e. *Malaya Morskaya Ulitsa*.

399. Grand Duke Vladimir Alexandrovich (1847 – 1909).

400. The Moscow Exhibition closed on 13 October 1882.

401. There is no reference to a Grigoriev of this description and date in biographical reference works and histories of literature. Possibly, Aronson confused him with Dmitri V. Grigorovich (1822 – 99), a distinguished author of the mid-century and former classmate of Dostoevsky at the Engineering Institute (although there is nothing to indicate that he was connected with the 1882 Exhibition): See F. D. Reeve, *The Russian Novel*, p. 208.

402. Leon (Leib) Mandelstamm (1818 – 89), the first Jew to graduate from a Russian university (St. Petersburg, 1844). Appointed in charge of Jewish affairs at the Ministry of Education in 1846, in succession to Rabbi Max Lilienthal. Established a network of Government schools and educational institutions for Jewish children and students. He left Government service in 1857. His Russian translation of the Pentateuch, which he produced in Germany, was introduced in Russia in 1872.

403. Mikhail Nikiforovich Katkov (1818 – 87). The most influential journalist of his time. A former assistant professor of philosophy at Moscow university (1845 – 50), he became editor of *Moskovskie Vedomosti* (Moscow Gazette) in 1851, and of *Russki Vesnik* (Russian Herald) in 1856. He held liberal views until the Polish revolt of 1863, after which he became an extreme reactionary. "His power, indeed, was so great in the State that he earned for himself, and with the good cause, the *sobriquet* of *Le faiseur des Ministres*" (F. Chenevix Trench, "The Russian Journalistic Press" in *Edinburgh Monthly Magazine*, vol.cxlviii, July 1890, p. 123). See also M. Raeff, vol.11. no.3, July 1952, pp. 157 – 67. There seems to be no basis for the rumour mentioned by Aronson that Katkov had been "one of Mandelstamm's pupils".

404. Nicholas Bunge (1823 – 95). A liberal politician, he was the first Minister of Finance (1881 – 6) under Alexander III.

405. Grand Duke Vladimir Andreyevich Dolgorukov (1810–91). Appointed Governor-General of Moscow in 1856, and retired in 1891. This noble family was also known as Dolgoruki. See S. M. Dubnow, *History of the Jews in Russia and Poland*, vol.2, pp. 400f., (where Dubnow gives him the title of "Count", although he was in fact a князь which, in Tsarist times, signified a Grand Duke).

406. The phrase is based on Psalm lxxiii.4.

407. *Perpetuum mobile*, perpetual motion.

408. An experimental prototype of a phonograph was made by a Frenchman, Léon Scott, in 1857; he called it the "phonautograph". Generally, however, credit for the invention of the phonograph is given to the American inventor Thomas A. Edison, who brought out his machine in 1877.

409. It is worthwhile noting that the pressure of a liquid depends upon its depth, not the shape of the vessel containing it — i.e. pressure is proportional to height.

410. Cubic inch, in German.

411. The *gerah* is a Biblical weight, equal to 0.59 grams. In order to avoid mathematical approximations, the term is retained here without translation.

412. "Explanation", the German translation of the Pentateuch with a Hebrew commentary based on rationalist principles which Moses Mendelssohn (1729 – 86) and his circle began to publish in 1778.

413. Zechariah iv. 2 – 6.

414. Aronson's interest in perpetual motion is strangely reminiscent of Perets Smolenskin's story *Ha-Tenu' ah Ha-Temidit* (Perpetual Motion). His hero, a clockmaker, endeavours to invent a clock which will run only by perpetual motion, based on the movements of its own mechanism. Somolenskin, however, was pointing the moral that the real perpetual motion is achieved in this world by man when performing "the motions of work and labour with satisfaction and pleasure". See *Kol Sifrei Perets Smolenskin*, vol.5, *Sippurim U-Feletonim* (Stories and Feuilletons), pp. 49 – 59. Aronson's contraption using weights is reminiscent of the attempts by medieval scientists who sought to rotate a wheel on its axis indefinitely by means of falling weights.

415. There is an interesting notice in John Murray's *Handbook for Travellers in Russia, Poland and Finland,* which states that in St. Petersburg "the best photographers are Bergamasco (12 Nevski Prospect) and Levitski (30 Moika Canal)": see, 1875 edition, p.162. With no corroborative evidence available, one can only wonder whether this Levitski is the same person as Aronson's photographer or if the names are no more than coincidence?

416. Ecclesiastes iii. 16.

417. I Samuel vi. 4 and 17. Aronson's spelling of the proper German term *Hämorrhoïden* illustrates the mixed German-Yiddish vernacular pronunciation (the Yiddish term is *Hemoriden).*

418. "The father of the present slide-and-shell packet was James B. Duke, the American tobacco magnate . . . This idea he invented some time in the late eighties" (G. West, *A History of Smoking,* p.36). See also, *The American Tobacco Story,* p.21.

419. *Sic.* A profit of only fifteen roubles per day hardly constitutes an attractive proposition for wealthy investors. It would be reasonable to assume that Aronson has unintentionally erred in recording the actual profit.

420. Alexander Graham Bell (1847 – 1922), Edinburgh-born Professor of Vocal Physiology at Boston university, patented the first practicable telephone in 1876, and displayed his invention at the Philadelphia Centennial Exposition in the same year. The world's first commercial telephone exchange opened at New Haven, Connecticut, in 1878.

421. In the original, *Arenson ahuvi* (my beloved Arenson) — an endearment which doubtless would have made Aronson suspicious of what was to follow!

422. The Spanish cork-tree *(Quercus Suber)* is the classical, popular source of cork for Europe. The soft, compressible outer layer of bark is the part used: this is stripped every eight to ten years, during the summer months. Although the use of cork for wine-bottle stoppers was recorded by Horace (v.*Odes,* iii. 8), it was not popularly so used until late in the 17th century; bottles were not generally used for storing liquids until the 15th century. It is interesting to note Aronson's choice of a Hebrew equivalent term for "cork-tree", *Atsei Gome.* The Bible has no reference to cork, whilst the Talmudic term is *Sha'am.* Aronson, however, has preferred the Biblical *Gome* ("reed" in both Bible and Talmud), which has an alternative form *Gemi* or *G'mi.* Aronson's *Atsei Gome* would seem to be related to the German *Gummibaum* (gum — or rubber-tree), the phonetic similarity enabling him to follow his usual method of offering pictorial explanation by borrowing from a European language.

423. See also p. 282 where the same estimate is given.

424. In the Hebrew, *Memaheret Ha-Defus,* a term borrowed from the German *Schnellpressen-druck.* Possibly, Aronson may have had in mind the new rotary press which had come into general use by 1860.

425. Johannes Gensfleisch zur Laden (zum Gutenberg); born towards the close of the 14th century, and died c.1470.

426. The first practical sewing machine was invented by Barthélemy Thimonnier in 1830. Isaac Merritt Singer brought out his machine in 1851, and popularised the use of foot-power as against the earlier hand-powered machines.

427. Russian: Public Procurator.

428. i.e. 30 June (o.s.), 11 July (n.s.).

429. i.e. 2 July (o.s.), 14 July (n.s.).

430. i.e. 16 June (o.s.), 28 June (n.s.).

431. For accounts of the intensification of anti-Jewish legislation from 1883 onwards, see S.M. Dubnow, *History of the Jews,* vol. 5, pp.550 ff, and his *History of the Jews in Russia and Poland,* vol. 2, pp.336-357; L. Greenberg, *The Jews in Russia,* vol. 2, pp.40-1; and J. Frumkin (ed), *Russian Jewry (1860 – 1917),* pp.85-109.

432. i.e. an escapement mechanism. The escapement is the part of a clock's mechanism which allows the driving power to "escape", and in so doing records the time.

433. i.e. "swing", or centrifugal force.

434. *Sic*. Hebraized spelling of the Russian: *Inertsiya* (inertia).

435. The flywheel operates on inertia, the pendulum operates on gravity, and the spring on tension. These are different forces — and therefore it would seem that Aronson errs in his assumption that the same law applies to them all.

436. Aronson gives both the French and German terms for "escapement".

437. The Yiddish plural is used here instead of the German *Schrauben*.

438. Initials representing *Retarder* and *Avancer* which Aronson would probably have seen inscribed on French clocks.

439. It is possible that this was based on an idea derived from the mercurial compensation pendulum, which he must have seen in certain types of clocks, and also perhaps from other compensatory devices. A particular example of a temperature compensation pendulum is the mercurial pendulum devised by George Graham in 1721: see E. Bruton, *Clocks and Watches 1400 – 1900*, p.113; J.W. Player, *Britten's Watch and Clock Makers' Handbook*, pp.361 – 2; and D. de Carle, *Practical Clock Repairing*, pp.80 – 1.

440. i.e. 30 December (1887 : o.s.), 12 January (1888 : n.s.). Regrettably, these dates do not tally with comparative Jewish and General Calendar Tables. Furthermore, because Aronson omitted to state the year in which he concluded these memoirs, the calculation of the date becomes even more confused — since the possibility cannot be overlooked that he may have added this final date at some later time, even after leaving Russia and arriving in New York. There are three signposts to the calculation problem set by this dating: (1) when Shraga left Russia on 4 January, 1887 (o.s.), or 16 January (n.s.), Aronson remained in Russia with his son Abraham — see p. 284; (2) he took out a patent for a clock in New York in December 1888 (n.s.) — see Appendix; (3) he died in New York in April 1893 (n.s.) — see photograph. Unfortunately, these factors, used in conjunction with Aronson's dates and a comparison with the Calendar Tables, do not produce in any year a "15 Kislev = 30 December (o.s.) or 12 January (n.s.)" — or, for that matter, any other Hebrew month which might correspond with the general dates (and which might, therefore, explain Aronson's dating as due to a slip of the pen). Nevertheless, since Aronson left Russia after Shraga — i.e. after 16 January 1887 (n.s.) — and was in New York before December 1888, there can be little doubt that his date "12 January" (n.s.) refers to 1888. How this dating error occurred, can only be conjectured, but it does provide a final illustration of the inexact chronological dating to be found throughout the memoirs. This is fully understandable when it is remembered that Aronson did not intend his autobiography to be an academic treatise, but a personal document for his family.

Appendix

◇◇◇◇◇

A. The Narrative.

"Who is entitled to write his reminiscences?
Everyone . . .

In order to write one's reminiscences it is not at all necessary to be a great man, nor a notorious criminal, nor a celebrated artist, nor a statesman—it is quite enough to be simply a human being, to have something to tell, and not merely to desire to tell it but at least have some little ability to do so.

Every life is interesting; if not the personality, then the environment, the country are interesting, the life itself is interesting . . ."[1]

Alexander Herzen's words were echoed, some twenty years later, by the Hebrew writer Moshe Leib Lilienblum in his own autobiography.[2] Whereas biographies, he declared, are written about personalities, autobiographies are important for the events they describe; it is not the man but the deed that matters. "I am not a renowned scholar and certainly not a man of action. I am an ordinary man . . . My *person* is of no importance, but the events of my life may afford a lesson to those who are inexperienced in life."[3]

It is an interesting coincidence that Lilienblum wrote these words at the beginning of his autobiography in the autumn of the year 1872, whilst Chaim Aronson began to write his own memoirs, expressing similar sentiments, in the summer of the same year. "I know that I am not a person of distinction", he wrote. "I shall not be counted among the great, nor will the third generation after me raise up a monument to my name". Nevertheless, believing that every man's life can be "a memorial to future generations", he pleads for the recognition of the ordinary individual in society and history:

"If every man were to cast a stone upon his land, all the highways would be paved. If every man were to write the story of his life, including all its events and all his thoughts, then succeeding generations would find wisdom and counsel and salvation tenfold more than they draw from the accounts and biographies left by the distinguished few." (*ibid.*).

Aronson was forty-seven years old at that time. He had been married three times and was the father of six sons. He could look back upon a life full of incident, tempered by both success and failure. As a Jew privileged to reside in the capital, St. Petersburg, he had every reason to look forward to a good future. Four years earlier, he had left the city of Telz (Telsiai) in the Jewish Pale of Settlement, where he had officiated for twelve years as the Elder of his Guild of Metalworkers, and had come to live in the capital under the protection of his aristocratic Russian business partners. He had achieved a reputation as an industrial inventor. During the remaining fifteen years of his stay in St. Petersburg, he was to show that his interests ranged over a wide field of technological enterprises — and that, in fact, he lived and worked in the spirit of the inventor-enterpreneurs of his century.

Chaim was born in the year 1825 in the small Lithuanian town of Serednike, some twenty-five miles to the west of Kaunas and situated at the confluence of the Dubisa and Nieman rivers. His family had originally hailed from Poland, but had settled in Lithuania when Chaim's grandfather, Mendel — a pedlar and the proud owner of a horse and wagon — had moved to Serednike with his son Aaron, Chaim's father. Aaron followed his father's trade, peddling his wares in the villages of Lithuania and Prussia, until he finally abandoned it for the ill-rewarded calling of a *melammed*, a private teacher of religion and Scriptures. It is from this period that Chaim's memoirs begin.

The autobiography — a 493-page manuscript, closely hand-written in nineteenth-century Hebrew style — is composed of three parts: an introduction, the account of his life in the Pale of Settlement, and his life in St. Petersburg. The introduction is a flowery-worded thesis of metaphysical speculation, in which he seeks to relate himself — as a man — with Creation in general, and his own life with the cosmic stream of Life. "You, too, have a place in Creation",he says, addressing his Spirit, and finding therein a validation of his wish to record his memoirs.

Part One of the narrative is a flowing survey of Jewish life in the towns, villages and country districts of Lithuania. Its dramatic beginning sets the tone for the whole of the story. The account of the annual springtime flooding of the lower parts of the town, and the consequent sufferings inflicted upon the inhabitants who were left destitute, is depicted in realistic detail and with imaginative feeling. It is followed by a succession of events and vignettes which describe the structures of social and religious life in the Jewish communities, and which range from the terrible housing conditions in which the Jews lived and which they called "home" because they had no other, to the deprivations of the yeshiva system, and to the recurrent panic engendered by restrictive imperial edicts. Through it all, the people, the personalities of the narrative, emerge as heroes transcending the vicissitudes of their life, stoically accepting the frequent bad with the occasional good, and always seeking a way to survive. The exceptional Moshe ben David, the first Hasid in Serednike, stands out as a person above the vivid events of the Polish Revolt of 1831: the account of how he saved the Jews of the town is implicitly contrasted with the brutality of the Polish troops. The story of the heretical, outcast blacksmith who became the victim of the ruthless and all-powerful Beadle, Joseph, is a significant comment on the conflicts that beset the people within the confines of their provincial communities. The adventures of the fascinating young Kabbalist, Eliezer, might almost have come out of the pages of a Gothic novel. The memoirs, indeed, are populated by a teeming throng of characters whose delineation is a remarkable tribute to Aronson's retentive memory.

Part One, in dealing essentially with life in the Pale of Settlement, throws light upon many of the aspects of individual and communal activities and beliefs. His accounts of the barbarous practices of quack healers arouse both repulsion for their methods and sympathy for their victims. Whereas his recital of the remedies inflicted upon himself, to cure his bout of fever, is written with wry humour, his description of the inexplicable rites practised upon his infant brother evokes only horror and distaste. The traditional orthodox education system pervades the whole of this first Part of the autobiography, as would be expected. His natural opposition to its confined restrictions can be seen throughout his accounts of his experiences, from his early tuition under his father to his subsequent sufferings at the hands of a sucession of teachers, from the "leprous *melammed*" of Keidan (Keidany) to the bullying Jacob. His life in the talmudical colleges of Kovno (Kaunas), Keidan and Vilna (Vilnius) was both a disillusionment and a waste of time and effort.[4] His denunciation of the ignominious *teg* system which so debased the young students that they resorted to begging and subterfuge in order to stave off the pangs of their hunger, is parallelled in the writings of many of the Hebrew authors of the period.[5] Whatever learning he acquired in these talmudical colleges was of no practical service to him when he needed a source of livelihood, for he made no use of it in later life, neither when he had to earn his living from private teaching nor when he was taking his first steps into the world of craftsmanship and began to study the arts of clockmaking and photography. It would seem, indeed, that his success as a teacher derived as much from his own restless search for secular knowledge as from the formal religious learning he received from his own teachers. The German language which he studied from the Bibles published by the missionary societies and from bilingual Hebrew-German prayer books, he was able to teach to the daughters of his wealthy patrons. Similarly, he picked up Polish and Russian mainly from dictionaries. It is clear, however, that from an early age he chafed at the limitations imposed upon his spirit by the heavy yoke of traditionalism.

Although Chaim displayed, at an early age, a natural talent for practical construction — he was only eight when he attempted, with some limited success, to fashion the mechanism of a watch out of pieces of wood — he was thwarted by the opposition of his father, who saw in it both a form of heresy (since it diverted the child's mind from Torah) and an obstacle to his son's future career as a Rabbi among his people (which was the dream of every orthodox parent). Therefore, it was not until many years later, when Chaim married and began to make his own living, that he was able to fulfil his ambition to become a craftsman. It was natural that the first craft he learned was clockmaking and repairing — but this had to wait until after he had ended his first marriage and had been saved from a potential second disaster. Unfortunately, his first entry into apprenticeship also ended disastrously, for it had lasted no more than four days when he was advised that it was not proper for him to be in the company of his dissolute teacher, Yehiel. He had to wait until his third and final marriage before he was able to gain the freedom to cultivate his restrained longing for a practical profession. With the support of an indulgent father-in-law, he studied clockmaking, both at home by personal experiment and in Mitau (Mitava) with professional craftsmen, until he eventually achieved a reputation as a successful clockmaker and repairer.

Although this note of success draws Part One to a close, Chaim's family affairs deserve special mention. He was the eighth child to his parents, the previous seven having died in their childhood before he was born.[6] He was the son of his father's first marriage. After his mother died, the father married twice more — the second marriage was to a girl so much younger than himself that he divorced her after only two months of marriage; the third was to his niece, Leah, whose shrewishness drove Chaim out of the house.

Interestingly, Chaim also married three times. He was eighteen years old at the time of his first marriage — which was somewhat old for that period when youthful marriages were the common practice. His wife, Bathsheba, bore him his first son, Judah Leib, but shortly thereafter the marriage broke down as a result of her parents' interference and hostility.

Before his second marriage, he was almost trapped into a disastrous alliance with an immoral girl of the town of Vilki. The episode illustrates the fundamental artlessness of his nature. The unexpected arrival of revellers announcing his sudden betrothal to the girl is a scene that might have come out of the pages of Solomon Maimon's autobiography.[7] Like Maimon's father, Aronson succumbed, but only under the threat of physical persuasion. Later, when the girl's immorality should have become obvious to him, he preferred to believe she was innocent. The incident left him confused by conflicting emotions. On the one hand, he loved the girl and was inclined to give her the benefit of any doubt — especially since promiscuity was foreign to his own nature — and on the other hand, he knew he had to behave with circumspection since, at the time, this was the only home he had. He therefore allowed events to run their own course. Eventually, because of his frequent absences from home in pursuit of a living, the affair brought itself to a close.

It was then that Aronson entered into his second marriage — which ended tragically only a year later. It was a marriage full of love and devotion on both sides. It was a time of peace and contentment. It came to an end with the death of his wife after a miscarriage. Her passing evoked one of the saddest pieces of descriptive writing in the entire manuscript. Her memory must have lingered strongly in Aronson's mind, for he penned his poignant description of her death some thirty years later, when it might be expected that time would have mellowed his emotions.

His third marriage lasted until his own death in New York in 1893. Chinah, the daughter of Shemiah, an innkeeper of Vishevian, near Telz, bore him five sons. It was a happy union, although it started with some misunderstanding and misgivings. There is no doubt that the father-in-law played a prominent part in furthering the couple's fortunes and this understanding and support enabled Chaim to revive his ambition to learn a craft, so that eventually, despite some initial setbacks, he gained fame in his chosen profession of clockmaker.

Part Two takes the narrative on from that point. It is instructive that Aronson gives this section its own title: The Period of the Craftsman Technologist. As its name indicates, it is concerned almost entirely with his life in the commercial world of the Pale of Settlement and his growing interest in automation which led to his acceptance into the industrial circles of the capital. It is in this part of his life, while he was still in his middle twenties, that his natural technical abilities were able to flourish and his restlessly enquiring mind to roam over the many aspects of the developing Russian economy. His interests and talents brought him both success and award. Indeed, two of his machines were displayed at the Moscow Exhibition of 1882, and both were given awards: his special photographic camera and miniaturization process, which he called *Microdiorama*, won an Honourable Mention; his machine for the automated manufacture of complete papirosi gained a Gold Medal of Honour — which, however, due to the duplicity of Aronson's business partners, was not awarded to him but to a Russian engineer whom they falsely nominated as the inventor.

Part Two, then, begins with his business life in Telz which, initially, was not financially productive. Suddenly, however, his fortunes changed. The imperial ukaze of 1851 which arbitrarily divided the Jews into five classes, and sent a shockwave of panic through the Jewish communities, spurred the Jewish craftsmen to unite and form artisan guilds for their own protection. The Jewish clockmakers of Telz united with the goldsmiths, tinsmiths and metalworkers among their co-religionists to form the Society of Metalworkers. Unfortunately, their first Elder and his assistant embezzled the Society's funds and had to be ousted from their positions. Because of Aronson's special knowledge of the Russian language, he was elected to serve as the new Elder — a position he held for a total of twelve years. This linguistic qualification provided a further and greater opportunity to him. By the majority vote of all the craftsmen of Telz, Jewish and Christian, he was elected to the position of Mayor of the city, much to his astonishment and extreme reluctance. It is to be regretted that, because of his wife's opposition and his own apprehensions, he refused the office. Aronson was not normally faint of heart; indeed, his later dealings with his influential Russian business partners show him to have been a man of courage and principle. In this instance, however, he rejected outright a position which he might possibly have used to promote the interests of the Jewish community and to foster good relations with the Russians, both in local, communal affairs and in civic and national proceedings. The fact that the government officials of Telz were prepared to accept his election should have been of some encouragement to him. Nevertheless, his fear of officialdom overruled all other considerations. The occasion ended up as one of those lost opportunities which become a source of nagging reminiscence in later life. It can be inferred that Aronson regretted his decision later, for he ends the episode with the wry comment that the new Mayor was an illiterate cobbler (p. 183) which he may have meant literally, but which sounds much worse when transposed into equivalent vernacular Yiddish.

This episode is followed by a fascinating sidelight on the economic effects of the Crimean War. On a personal level, the rise and fall of the war profiteers is described with psychological insight, albeit with bitter sadness, too. On the national, commercial level, the chaos engendered by the war's aftermath is portrayed in all its confusion. Its effects upon the Government, the merchants and the populace are delineated in a brief, sparse narration of events which emphasizes the turmoil of the times.

It was just after this that Fate took a hand in Aronson's fortunes. He had finished a particularly ornate clock-dial which, he believed, would bring him considerable profit providing he could sell copies of it in sufficient quantity. For this, he needed a mould from which to cast the copies. Since he was unable to make the mould himself, he sought the services of a tinsmith. He called upon the smith, but the man was not at home. However, "there was a cobbler in the house, sitting on a three-legged stool" (p. 186), repairing shoes with the wooden pegs in common use at the time. Aronson stopped, questioned the cobbler about the techniques of his craft — and then took the step which was to alter the whole course of his future career. He abandoned the clock-dial project and, instead, turned his inventive genius towards the construction of an automated machine for the manufacture of the wooden pegs.

The incident raises some points of minor speculation. What turn would Aronson's professional career have taken had he not stopped to talk to the cobbler but carried on with his clock-dial enterprise? Would he have remained in Telz for the rest of his life, a clockmaker-photographer? Why, indeed, had Aronson not considered the peg project earlier? He had already been living in Telz for several years, had achieved a reputation as a craftsman and was an influential official of his guild. Since, furthermore, there were a number of shoe-repairers in Telz,[8] both Jewish and Christian, with whom he must have had, at least, a fairly close contact, why had the idea of automation not occured to him before? Although he does not dwell upon these points himself, he does give some indication of a possible answer. He had always enjoyed his father-in-law's financial and moral support, so he spent his first years in Telz perfecting his knowledge of his craft and indulging his interest in technological issues — which included a digression into perpetual motion—"without looking for material gain" (p. 186). It was only when his family increased, and his responsibilities became more demanding, that he began to think in terms of obtaining financial reward from his technical expertise. It was at this point in his new outlook, when he realised the need to become independent of his father-in-law's support, that he met the cobbler. His technical interest in the shoemaker's craft developed into an interest in industrial techniques in general and his emergence as an industrial inventor. Aronson calls the meeting a "chance accident" (p. 187), but elsewhere he comments: "How wondrous is Divine providence. . . . " (p. 181).

After an initial setback — he was cheated out of his money by two Russians whom he had paid to assist him — Aronson laid his peg-machine project aside, albeit temporarily, and turned instead to photography which he studied under the tuition of a photographer in Memel (Klaipeda). He then added this new skill to his clockmaking craft in the hope of gaining a second source of income. Despite the fact that he was now nearing thirty, was married with a family, and was well-established in his profession and community, he willingly undertook the additional labour, and the burden of new experience, which this entailed. It is a tribute to his appreciation and awareness of the developing trends in nineteenth-century technology that he chose to wed the new art of photography to the old craft of horology. Although photographers did not generally combine any other profession with their art — a successful salon provided income enough — there were some who did make it an adjunct to some other form of business. Certainly, it was unusual to find it allied to another recognised craft, as Aronson had done.[9] On the other hand, it should be borne in mind that the Jewish craftsmen of Russia — who learned to live under the intolerable pressures of the hazardous and unstable economic competitiveness of the Pale of Settlement — were not loath to undertake other forms of labour whenever necessity required it. There were times when conditions were so desperate that they either found some other, more menial means of livelihood, or they starved.[10] When, therefore, Aronson shouldered the yoke of additional labour, he was acting in the manner of any craftman who sought economic security for his family. By choosing photography, however, he was behaving in harmony with his own technological inclinations.

His return to the construction of an automated peg machine met with both success and disappointment. He was to learn from temporary failure the fundamental lesson that an inventor must assure himself in advance that there is indeed a need for his product, and that the technical specifications of his product will be acceptable in the regions where it is to be marketed. It was a point which his own experience emphasized.

An improved prototype machine brought him into partnership with Russian investors in St. Petersburg. He was sent to establish a factory for producing the pegs on an estate owned by one of his partners near the village of Shubina in Tver province: there was a neighbouring village, Kimri, whose "inhabitants were all cobblers" (p. 197). It was in Shubina that he experienced the strange, uncomfortable feeling of being the first Jew to penetrate this part of the Russian hinterland. The village peasants were astonished to see that Jews were no more than ordinary human beings, without "horns on their foreheads or even goat's feet" (p. 199). It was there that he and his family, and the Jewish assistants he brought from Telz, spent some eight isolated months, during which they endured a distressing Passover festival, until they were recalled to St. Petersburg to conduct their activities from the capital.

Unfortunately, the automated peg machine ended as an ill-fated venture for Aronson. His aristocratic partners gradually reduced his authority in the factory until they finally ousted him from the project. He agreed to accept one thousand roubles, and then left the enterprise. It was his first experience of business life in the capital. Although he suffered from the defects of being both a provincial and a Jew, he was shrewd enough to look after his own interests, brave enough to confront his superiors and demand his rights, and realistic enough to write off his losses in the most advantageous way available to him. The episode ended probably in the year 1872 — the year he began to record his memoirs.

It was whilst he was with the peg-machine company that he came to appreciate the helplessness of the provincial Jew who arrived in the capital without a knowledge of the Russian language. His own experience at the hands of the notary Ouspensky, when he was almost robbed of a hundred roubles, served to illustrate to him the wretched subordination of the untutored Jew when he came from the Pale of Settlement, "starving with hunger, his clothes threadbare and unable to speak the language" (p. 203): he was like a lamb surrounded by a pack of wolves.

Aronson was not daunted by these initial experiences. Even before he had left the company, his fertile mind had conceived an idea for another machine — an automatic machine for producing cigarette-papers. In fact, Aronson's interest in tobacco widened until it embraced all the various aspects of cigarette-making and packaging. His first machine, for making cigarette-papers, again brought him into contact with Russian nobility, and further duplicity and disappointments. The machine was sufficiently promising for his partners to pay him a monthly salary and form a company. The four machines which Aronson constructed operated successfully, producing well-made papers and piling them into neat bundles ready for packing. Unfortunately, the partners could find no customers for their wares — so the enterprise slowly ground to a halt.

This led Aronson to proceed to another machine for manufacturing complete papirosi. With the support of new partners, a patent was taken out — not in Aronson's name — and a company formed on 30 December 1876 (old style). Aronson received forty per cent of the shares in the form of red B shares, a cash payment of seven thousand roubles, and a monthly salary of one hundred and fifty roubles.

It was after this that Aronson found history beginning to repeat itself. On the specious assumption that inventors should not be allowed to tinker with a machine once it had been finished, he was gradually made to withdraw from the factory in favour of other technicians who were brought in to look after the construction of the machines. This led to an open breach between Aronson and the company's Directors. When the machine was exhibited at the Moscow Exhibition of 1882, it received general approval and praise, and was awarded a Gold Medal. The invention, however, was ascribed to a technician, Peters, against all Aronson's protests. Aronson, helpless in the face of the growing anti-semitism of the period, retired from the company — comforting himself perhaps with the knowledge that he had produced a machine of great merit, and had also earned himself a total of some sixteen thousand roubles.

His third cigarette machine, for making cigarette-packets, was abandoned after it had been built (in 1884) because of a lack of financial support. His last tobacco machine, for the manufacture of cigarettes without the usual Russian type of mouthpiece, but modelled on the shape of American and English cigarettes, also failed because Aronson was unable to find financial backers for it. It should also be mentioned that, as a special favour for his landlord, who owned a tobacco shop, he constructed a small machine which could make telescopic filter tips. He gave it as a present to the landlord who, however, made little use of it.

This saga of Aronson's ventures in the developing tobacco industry is a truly remarkable story of technical ingenuity and technological prescience. Automation was a late-comer to this industry. At the same time as Aronson was perfecting the cigarette machine which earned the Gold Medal, technicians of the western hemisphere were producing similar automatic machines by their own independent investigations.[11] When it is remembered that western inventors could avail themselves of all the benefits of a free and modern society and the facilities of a sophisticated industrial technology, whereas Aronson had to labour within the stifling confines of an oppressive, anti-semitic regime which kept its citizens under ruthless subjection, then Aronson's achievements become a source of profound wonder.

Aronson was rarely satisfied to work on only one invention at a time. When, for example, he was busily engaged on his cigarette-manufacturing machines, he was also developing his microphotographic process, which he termed *Microdiorama*. Although microphotography was already well-established in western Europe, it had not been accepted by the Russian populace. Aronson's venture into this field, therefore, places him among the early entrepreneurs of microphotography in Russia: he was certainly one of the pioneer Jewish photographers in Russia, and indeed in the world.[12]

He first studied the art of photography during the late 1850's when he was living in Telz. The Polish Revolt of 1863 brought him a good income, but by 1868 — when he was preparing to leave for the capital — his photographic business in Telz had almost come to a standstill.

He did not consider photography again until 1878, when he was taking a health cure in Revel. He remembered that, when he had been living in Telz, he had seen a photograph taken by the French photographer René Dagron. When Aronson returned home to St. Petersburg, he began to build his own camera and develop his special miniaturization process. These miniature photographs he was adept enough to fix into novelty trinkets of various kinds.[13] Although his Microdiorama did not bring him the financial rewards he anticipated, it did gain an Honourable Mention at the 1882 Moscow Exhibition.[14]

Aronson appears to dismiss Dagron somewhat lightly, even though he does acknowledge that he was indebted to him for the idea of miniaturization (p. 237). There is, indeed, a strong similarity between parts of Aronson's process and the method detailed by Dagron in his *Traité de Photographie Microscopique*.[15] It is interesting to note that Aronson makes the point that, when he had first seen Dagron's pictures in Telz — i.e. about 1858 — "Dagron had kept his process a close secret" (p. 237). However, by 1859 Dagron had obtained his microfilm patent, by 1862 he had published his booklet *Cylindres Photomicroscopiques*, and by 1864 his *Traité* had appeared in print and his microfilm camera was on public sale. By 1878, therefore, when Aronson began to make his own miniatures, Dagron's processes were no longer secret. It seems that Aronson's son, Simon Aaron, was also familiar with Dagron's method, and possibly saw examples of it when he was apprenticed to the photographer, Shapira (p. 238). The question, therefore, must be asked: had Aronson in fact seen a copy of the *Traité*, and possibly also a Dagron camera? In the absence of any corroborative evidence, this can only remain a matter of conjecture. His narrative states, however, that he worked on his Microdiorama in isolation, without external help of any kind. His unflagging industry and technical expertise must, therefore, put him on equal level with western photographic innovators — if his account is completely true — even though they preceded him by a number of years. Certainly, Russian photographic history should be indebted to him. The fact that his novelty miniatures attracted large crowds when he displayed them in his shop-windows, arousing the astonishment of all who viewed them, and also indeed gained an award at the Exhibition, shows that these microphotograph bijoux were new to Russia, at least. For this act of commercial enterprise, he merited, and gained, recognition and honour. It is difficult to understand why his business was not the financial success in Russia that it already was in western Europe and America. Perhaps Aronson himself gave part of the answer when, in connection with an earlier invention of his, he remarked that the Russian people were generally apathetic about new inventions: "We were behind the times, both Russia and I" (p. 187). In saying this, he was by no means being just or fair towards himself.

Throughout all his business ventures, Aronson always held on to his clockmaking profession as his constant source of livelihood, supplemented by his studio photographic business. Whenever he was too occupied with constructing automated machines, he left these businesses in the hands of his sons — for, as a good father and also as a former provincial Jew who had learned the necessity for a practical profession, he ensured that his sons were trained in his own crafts so that they could be independent and self-supporting. In 1877, whilst still connected with the cigarette-machine company, he built a complicated clock mechanism based on the pendulum experiments conducted by the French physicist Jean Bernard Foucault.[16] His idea was to build a clock which would indicate "the rotation of the earth's globe in relation to the hours of the day" (p. 230). It was not, however, successful—for which he blames his own faulty calculations. Even the last entry in his autobiography is concerned with a theoretical description of a type of mercurial temperature compensation pendulum. This however remained a vision in his mind, for the constant deterioration in the condition of Russian Jewry under Alexander III had deprived many Jews of their livelihood and forced many to emigrate.

By this time, the year 1887, most of Aronson's family had settled in New York. Governmental oppression intensified. The Jewish artisans who remained in the capital found themselves being progressively restricted in their work. Aronson's "livelihood became very precarious" (p. 285). Eventually, he was left without business or work, his hopes resting solely on his sons in the United States.

The manuscript ends unfinished. It makes no mention of his emigration from Russia to America or of his life in New York until his death there in 1893. It is known, however, that he continued his horological interests in his new country, for he obtained a patent in 1888 from the New York Patents Office for a *grande sonnerie* set of chimes.[17]

Before closing this chapter on Aronson's inventive enterprises, it would be illustrative of his wide interests to give a list of the projects he undertook. Horology and photography, shoemakers' pegs and cigarette-machines, have already been discussed. There were also machines whose construction he was able to complete satisfactorily but which he was unable, for some specific reason, to put on the market. In 1878, he built a calculating machine for use in the parcels despatch offices of railway stations: by setting arrow-pointers to positions on a dial, and then pressing a button, the machine automatically indicated distances and prices — thus saving the despatch clerk's time and labour, and eliminating error in calculation. Unfortunately, the operation was cumbersome and took too long, and proved to be unacceptable. A machine for the automated manufacture of bottle-corks (c. 1885) was successfully built, but owing to the duplicity of his partners, Aronson was forced to withdraw from the company. He conducted experiments to make an alcoholmeter for use in government distilleries: he called the instrument, which was finished c. 1876, a Sinapeoscope. It turned out, however, to be unstable due to the chemical qualities of its liquid components. He mentions that he took particular interest in the automation of hosiery manufacture (c. 1860), but his efforts to build a machine ended in failure; that he made a music-box (c. 1884), but unfortunately he gives no information about it; that he considered building a typewriter (1868) but did not pursue the idea. Finally, in common with many scientists throughout history, he was drawn into experimenting with Perpetual Motion. It must have constituted a source of special fascination for him, because he made two attempts at it, in 1851 and 1883, which were unsuccessful.

B. The Problems of Translation.

There is an Italian saying *traduttori, traditori* (translators, traitors), which sums up in a very succinct fashion the basic problem which besets every translator. How closely must he keep to the original, and how far may he deviate from it? David Patterson comments that, in the case of translation from Hebrew to English, "the process becomes more of a transmutation than a translation, in which such fixatives as exist can only be the elusive qualities of the style and spirit of the original. Such elements as vocabulary, idiom and sentence structure must be poured wholesale into the crucible, melted down and then re-cast into an entirely different mould . . . All translation is commentary to some extent".[18] This translator has endeavoured to keep to a middle road in the hope of avoiding both betrayal and undue transmutation, whilst surrendering to the need to "reproduce the full sense of the original.[19] The requirement to be honest to the original composition is fundamental to every translation. This was the very point which aroused Lilienblum's ire against Schulman's Hebrew translation of Graetz's *History of the Jews:* "Who gave him permission to leave out the things he does not like?" he asks. "He is a translator. Who gave him the authority to falsify his translation?"[20]

The initial problem presented by Aronson's manuscript is the fact that it is hand-written in fine cursive script. Although the handwriting shows a generally admirable clarity of penmanship, it has its share of idiosyncratic flourishes and letter combinations. Once these have been deciphered, and the careless deviations which are to be expected from this hurried type of composition are noted, the script reads fluently and freely.

Aronson's punctuation is arbitrary and capricious, as is his use of paragraphs. Commas and stops etc. occur wherever and whenever he feels like inserting them; often, entire passages are left bare of any punctuation, the context being the only guide to the sense of the passage. This is a common characteristic of nineteenth-century Hebrew writing, and Aronson was a child of his times in this matter. Paragraphs are sometimes indicated merely by a dash at the end of a sentence, or, at times, are actually begun on a new line. For the sake of consistency and clarity, this translation makes use of the full punctuation which the passages — narrative, dialogue and descriptive — require. Similarly, paragraphs have been inserted in the translation wherever the sense and sequence indicated. Mention should also be made here of the convention he uses to italicize words by placing dots over the heads of the individual letters.

As is to be expected, Aronson wrote in the Biblical style commonly used by nineteenth-century Hebrew writers. Having received a traditionally orthodox education in childhood and youth, and earned his living for a number of years from teaching Hebrew, it was only natural for him to adopt the style of the Bible, and to fill his manuscript with scriptural (and also Talmudic) quotations, and to compose his sentences according to the rules of Biblical syntax and grammar. Every page abounds with the Vav Consecutive, as well as the Infinitive Construct combined with prefixes and suffixes. Like other Hebrew writers, he pays little attention to the rules for gender and number — and often also for spelling: it should be mentioned that he interchanges the *sin* and *samekh* arbitrarily, in the fashion of the times. Despite the restricted vocabulary and stilted style of the Bible, his narrative reads fluently and swiftly, as though it had been written by a practised Hebrew speaker.

It is interesting to observe how the language registers change to fit the subject matter. The descriptive passages are written in a different register from the theoretical, technical dissertations; the tragic incidents are recalled in sorrow, and the happy moments in remembered joy. His description, for instance, of summertime in Shubina village is almost idyllic (p. 201), whilst his account of the capture of his hometown by Polish troops during the Passover festival is highly dramatic (pp. 19–22). Particularly impressive is his description of the "plain of logs" (pp. 25-26), where the people went nightly to hew the wood, working in swift silence, pausing only when a passing coach trundled by on the highway.

His descriptions of people, individually and in groups, show him to be a keen observer of life. The manuscript is filled with a multitude of people, more so in Part One than Part Two, where the emphasis is on commerce and industry rather than social conditions. Perhaps the most fascinating character was the young kabbalist, Eliezer, whose adventures in practical Kabbalah and dishonest mendicity form a memorable section of the memoirs (pp. 77 ff.). The affairs of Joseph the Beadle and the victimized blacksmith (pp. 35-7), of Zalman the yeshiva student who was innocent of wrong but was called "Angel of Death" and hounded out of town (pp. 44-7), of Hirsch the Cantor and his hostility towards Aronson (pp. 66-8), are typical of the many human accounts given here. Although Aronson was not especially religious — certainly less so in the second Part than in the first — he took particular notice of the Ḥasidim who were then forming a growing movement in Lithuania (though they never achieved the influence there which they gained in other regions of Russia and Poland). Moshe the Ḥasid is a distinguished figure. He saved the Jews from the Polish troops (pp. 19-20), and was the Head of the local Ḥasidic community: his cavortings during the synagogue services (p.57) are reminiscent of similar comments made by Solomon Maimon.[21] The absentminded Abraham the Ḥasid is cleverly brought to life in a simple, seven-line sketch (p. 57). Particularly memorable is the account of the Ḥasidic crowds thronging in and around their Rebbe's home on the festival of Tabernacles (pp. 58-60). The public worship is effectively satirized as a military parade. Aronson's two-fold description of the Ḥasidim as a troupe of actors assembling in a "vast theatre" and then being herded, like animals, into "sheep-pens", recalls to mind Brandstetter's satiric comparison of Ḥasidim with satyr-goats.[22] It is noteworthy, however, that none of Aronson's descriptions of Ḥasidim contains the slightest trace of hostility: there is wonder, and also irony, but couched in restrained manner that enables

Aronson to act as observer rather than critic — and there is praise, too, for those individual Ḥasidim who, like Moshe and others, evoke Aronson's admiration.

On the other hand, some of his dealings with the religiously orthodox aroused mixed emotions. The corruption of the Vilna Ecclesiastical Court is strongly denounced (pp. 76-7), whereas his relation of the trial of the squatter-ghosts (pp. 93-4) is laced with implicit humour. Aronson's accounts of his religious education, in the *heder* and privately and in the yeshivot, form a document which pillories the rigorous and often heartless system of the times. The strange affair of the ruthless Berke, the "bear" of Shadova (pp. 121-2), is intermingled with the loyal friendship which developed between Aronson and Ḥayyim Ḥaikil.

In this delineation of examples of Aronson's descriptive powers, mention should also be made of his accounts of the many non-Jewish people and events in the memoirs. Of special interest are the episodes concerning bear-baiting and the house-trained bears which Polish noblemen kept both as pets and for sport (pp. 50-1). The account of the superstitious peasants of Shubina village who regarded Jews as devils incarnate (p. 199) and refused to hire milch cows to them because they would not make the sign of the cross over the cows (p. 200), depicts the depths of primitive ignorance in which provincial peasants were sunk. The wanton massacres perpetrated by the Polish troop leader Girkon (pp. 26-7) are typical of the centuries-old persecutions suffered by the Jews at the hands of the Poles: the description of Girkon himself is, incidentally, a good example of Aronson's tendency to portray in grotesque caricature the people he detests.

These passages, taken at random from the memoirs' numerous episodes and personalities, serve to exemplify Aronson's command of the Hebrew language and his literary talents. His ability as an author to tell a story is apparent throughout the text. It is in the selection of appropriate vocabulary that his principal problems lie. This is not only the case with modern theoretical concepts but indeed with all the simple and innumerable objects which form the background to everyday life and which are not included in the vocabulary of classical Hebrew literature. "Since I did not know the technical terms for the different parts of the machine, I had to provide names according to my own judgment" (p. 192). He could just as well have extended this admission to cover other aspects of human affairs beside technical terminology.

In this respect, Aronson suffered the same situation as all Hebrew writers of the time. It was a period in which the Jewish people — like other European nations — was moving towards emancipation, albeit more slowly than they and with greater difficulty. It was a period in which Hebrew writers sought to emancipate the Hebrew language, to bring it out of the confines of classical and religious limitations, and make it an instrument for contemporary communication. "The deficiencies of the language confronted the writers with terminological problems which they could resolve only by means of literary devices. Circumlocutory descriptions and hybrid terms are frequent in the literature of the period"[23]. Furthermore, the advocacy of a return to the ancestral language of the Bible, with

all its lexical limitations, in preference to the cramped Rabbinical style which had
been in general favour, led Hebrew writers to assume the florid, hyperbolic and
artificial style with came to be known as *Melitsah* (rhetoric). D. Patterson, in
discussing the Hebrew novelists of the nineteenth century, comments: "Only too
often the forcible injection of literary material into unsuitable linguistic patterns
seriously distorts the harmony between the form and content of their stories, with
the matter bulging and sagging pathetically through a patchwork covering of
biblical phrases. The enforced resort to clumsy circumlocutions and crude approximations even for the expression of common objects and ideas frequently resulted,
as will be seen, in a cumbersome terminology which sometimes borders on the
grotesque"[24]. Aronson's style is certainly replete with Biblical quotations, but
they are mostly woven into the fabric so that they form part of the general pattern
and design.

The style of Aronson's general descriptions is usually clear and straightforward.
When, however, he enters into philosophic speculation or technical and scientific
descriptions, he is much less clear and, in places, his theorising digressions tend
towards ambiguity and obscurity. In attempting to clarify his explanations, he
makes frequent use of terms borrowed from foreign languages, principally German and Russian, which he inserts into the text alongside either a Hebrew
translation or approximation, sometimes in parentheses. They include both general vocabulary and specialised technical terminology.

Particularly noteworthy are his linguistic inventions. These are presented quite
suddenly and without any indication of their nature, but apparently with the
puckish whim to present the reader with a riddle. They have been explained in
detail in the Text Notes, and therefore need only to be listed here: מרכבת יהושפט[25];
עצי נומא[28]; עצי אהרן (קלאן)[27]; ברושים (בערזע)[26]; both these two latter contain also
an element of folk-etymology.

Akin in nature to these original coinages are his straightforward Hebrew transla-
tions of foreign terms. Although Aronson accompanies some of these with the
original word in parentheses — in the accepted and popular fashion of the Hebrew
writers of the period — he uses this literary device very sparingly: there are, in fact,
hardly more than a dozen examples in the entire book. Mostly, these foreign words
fall naturally into place in the Hebrew text, either alone or following the translation
and in Hebrew transliteration. Some examples of these are: אבן השרפה (עלעקטראן)[29];
פילנאקאלניס, הר ממולא[31]; קרן אלון המעופף (פליענענדע אייכהארן) בערכשטיין[30];
מכלכל[35]; מכסה הרקיע[34] מטת הרקיע[33] which he also refers to as שכר (מעטה)[32];
תופשי היהודים[37]; סוחר קבלן, פאזריאציק; מזון עם מחנה הרוסים, מארקיטאָנד[36];
ארגז המנגן[41]; חסר, מינימום[40]; יתר, מאקסימום[39]; דבק גומי, מאַסטיקס (יודענהאַשער)[38];
ממהרת הדפוס[42] which he also refers to as מכונת מהיר הדפוס[43].

Aronson's use of Hebrew approximations includes attempts at an explanation of
terms and sometimes the insertion of a phrasal definition without commentary.
Aronson also makes use of the paronomastic expressions in current use at this
time — such as: דלנ רב[44] and פורט פייענה[45]. Examples of his Hebrew ex-

[48]יודע נגן; [47]לביבות הכדור (קוגעל); [46]מתבשלים בטרם עתם (פרייהצייטיג) :pressions are
[51]חוט המדבר; [50]בקבוקי תבערה, צינקס בארַאבינקס; [49]עגילים מאפה (באסיסט) [55]חיל
צבא[54]; קבלן הבי דואר להכפרים[53]; מכונת הקזת דם [52]; כלי שיר תיבה קטנה (הטעלעפאן)
[56]מעשה ציפוי המתכות נאַלוואַנאַפּלאַסטיק; רוכבים נוסרים; together with the form
[59]; מכונת כתיבה[58]; שרד מיקראַמעטער, מחלק דק [57]; כלי הנאַלוואַני in modern use
[62]; אנית הצוללים השטה תחת פני המים[61]; מסלת הסוסים and also [60]מסלת ברזל סוסים
[65]שתי הזכוכית המגדלת מן השתי עינים בינַאקל and also [64]; מכונת המספר[63]; שער המצבה
[68]; חברת השטרות[67]; קנה המגדלת, מיקראסקאפ; [66]כלי המביט הכפול, בינַאקל
[70].בית העצה ליודעי דת ודין; [69]מענה כבוד; אקציענגעזעללששאפט

Foreign words are used freely and in abundance throughout the manuscript —
some of which have already been referred to above[71]. Mention should first be made
of the interesting glimpse Aronson gives of the method of teaching the Bible in
Russian[72] which, he says, was a recent innovation in Jewish pedagogics. Just
before that episode, he discusses his mother's misuse of Russian terms[73], and
wonders at the corruption of Russian expressions when spoken by the Jews.

Many of Aronson's foreign terms are left on their own, without translation or
explanation. Indeed, the manuscript opens with four Yiddish words: מאַראל,[74]
[75]עטימאַלאַגיע; Other Yiddish examples are: היסטאַריע, ביאגראַפהיע; כראַנאַלאַגיע
[79]דעפּאַרטאַמענט; מיסיאַנער[78]; מַדֶה[77]; צענזאר[76].

Russian words and phrases are interspersed throughout the pages of the manuscript, although not so widely as might have been expected. Generally, Aronson
uses them either because he had no equivalent Hebrew, Yiddish or German
expression or because they fitted naturally into the context. His portrayal of the
melammed teaching the Hebrew Bible in Russian translation is a fascinating
anecdote in its own right[80]. Of particular interest, however, is the fact that
Aronson, the born educator, wrote the Russian version in Russian Cyrillic script,
and not in transliterated Hebrew characters, as was his usual custom. In doing so,
he was able to highlight Jewish ignorance of the Russian language. In the same
paragraph, he pursued this purpose further by recording in Hebrew letters his
mother's incorrect usage of Russian words — קאַדיק[82], גאַרלא[81].

Some other instances of Russian terms which occur without translation though
in Hebrew letters are: פריסטאַוו [87], סטאַנאַוואי [86], פּראַקוראַר [85], שקאַזקע [84], קאַטאַרנא [83],
אינטעלעַדאַנט [88], נאַטאַריוס [89]. and אַסטרַוו [90]. When discussing his cigarette machines, Aronson generally uses the Russian term *papiros*, but he also make use of a
somewhat inelegant combination of *papiros* with the Hebrew suffix *-im*, resulting
in a hybrid term *papirosim*[91].

A number of the German words have already been mentioned above[92], but to
them should be added also דיספּוט[93], בלעכַארבייטער[94], and פּראַפּעסַאר המעכאַניק[95].

His technical terms provide particular interest. Because Horology was his
principal profession, it might be most useful to begin with that. For a clock, מורה
[97]מורה שעות he uses a variety of words: [96]מורה שעות קטנה מהבצלים הישנות שעות
[100], מורה שעות במשקלים על הכותל [99], מורה שעות הסבוב [98], מורה שעות לקיר , לשולחן
[103].מורה שעות השנה [101]לו מורה שעות בצלחתו [102]מורה שעות לנשים אשר בצלחתה . The

different parts of a clock are: תכנית[104] and מכונה; נוצת השערה and העממונג[107]; עשאפפעעמאנט, מניעת עצר[106]; אופן המתנועע[105]; השערה השבלולית; מסגרת[112] and כדור משקלו[111]: סעקונדענפענדל[109], משקלת[110], and מטוטלת[108], צילינדער[117] and מחט[114]; אופנים וגלגלים[115]; קרס[116], לוח מספרי השעות[113], and שבלולים, שרויבע[118]. His כח המעוף[119] שוואונג, may be compared with other forces mentioned in other technical contexts.[120] To describe a clock striking the hour he uses the phrase הכה בפעמון (to strike the bell): מורה השעות הכה[121] בפעמון שתים עשרה חצות היום (the clock struck twelve noon).

His other profession, Photography, provides further terms. A photographer is known as רושם אור[122]; photography itself as מלאכת רשימת האור, פֿאָטאָגראַפֿיע[123]; and a photographic studio as בית מלאכת רשימת אור[124]. A camera is described as מכונה[125], תיבה חשכה and תיבת אפל[126]. The word זכוכית (glass) is used with עדשה זכוכית קטנה מאד[130] and זכוכית המגדלת[129] זכוכית השרפה[128], זכוכית מרגשת[127]. In his Microdiorama process, Aronson used תמונות קטנות עוברי אור[131] which are also referred to as תמונות המעבר, טראנספאראנט[132]. His camera was fitted with a variable נקודת שרפה[133]. The miniatures were viewed through a קנה שפופרת[134] or קנה ההבטה[135].

Other technical and scientific terms include: אופן מעופף[136]; אניות קטור[137] and עגלות הקיטור[138]; עצי תבערה also termed עצי גפרית and עץ המאור[139]. כפיסי Measurements are a mixture of Russian, Hebrew and Yiddish: אמה[140]; אצבע (finger) is used for one inch, מיל[144] ווערסט[143]; גרה[142]; אצבע מרובעי כפולים, קוביקצאלל[141] and פרסה[145] are interchangeable; מינוט and רגע[146] are also equivalent; פוד[147]; פונט[148]; and רגל[149].

Engineering terms occur frequently, and are based on the Biblical words חרש and חשב[150]. A technical institute is described as בית מדרש לחרושת המעשה,[151] טעבֿנאלאגיע. An instructor in engineering in a college is מורה מדרש החכמות[152] איש חרש[153]. A blacksmith is אשר על חרושת כל ברזל ונחושת ומלאכת חרש וחושב פחמי[154], and also simply ברזל עושה מלאכתו במפוח יד, whilst a craftsman smith is חכם חרשים מלא[156] אמן חרש ברזל וחושב[155]. An expert technician is בית מלאכת[158] בית יציקת הממשלה[157], whilst the government foundry is בינת מחשבת. הזכוכית is a glassworks.

Other establishments which take the word בית are בית מדרש החכמה[159], and בית חינוך[160].The names for religious establishments occur frequently: בית תפלה[161], בית מדרש[163] בית כנסת[162], and בית דין[164]. In transport, there occurs the term בית האוסר בעלי החובות[166] בית הדוהר[165], whilst stands for the debtors' prison. There are also בית מחזה[167], and בתי ירים[168], בתי עינים[169], and בתי רגלים[170] which is also found as מכנסים[171].

Before bringing this list to a close, certain Hebrew terms are worthy of final mention. Aronson uses the Hebrew reflexive conjugation when speaking of Jews who have partly or fully assimilated into a non-Jewish culture: מתרוסס[172], מתאשכנז[173] and מתנצר[174]. The word חרט is given a number of different uses: as a pen or skilful writing, חרט אנוש[175]; a scarf or shawl, חרט משי[176]; a hand-towel,

חרט יד[177]; and often simply as a piece of cloth.[178] Incidentally, the term for handcuffs is חריטי ידים[179].

The above list is not intended to be a word-by-word break-down of Aronson's vocabulary. It does, however, seek to show the manner in which he attemped to overcome the limitations of the Hebrew vocabulary of his day. Because Aronson gave no indication of the sources of the terms he used — nor is there any reason why he should have done — or the origins of his own lexical coinages, his vocabulary and phrasal structures have presented several translation problems. The Bibliography of Reference Works, especially the section on Dictionaries, affords an indication of the particular consideration which had to be given to them. The translator, in searching for the meaning of a word as Aronson would have understood it (remembering his religious educational upbringing) often found it necessary to compare the nineteenth century word with its possible original scriptural or Talmudic origin. This was then contrasted with modern twentieth-century terminology, in order to determine what further nuances of meaning, if any, had been added to it, and thus to obtain the fullest understanding of the term. Aronson's style was also compared with writings of other nineteenth-century Hebrew writers to ascertain how he fitted into the mainstream of contemporary Hebrew writing and to what extent he might have borrowed from their vocabulary: some of these writers have been mentioned in the notes, and their works are listed in the general bibliography; to them must be added the Hebrew periodicals, such as *Ha-Shaḥar* and *Ha-Maggid,* which were also read for information and background. The search for terminological origins was sometimes exasperating, sometimes exciting, and always fascinating — particularly so in connection with his linguistic inventions and adaptations (like *Atsei Aharon* appendix note 27), which involved research into social and historical conditions (for example, the horse-tramways, appendix note 60). With regard to the sources of scriptural and Talmudic quotations, these are so numerous and mostly so well woven into the fabric of the narrative, that it was not considered either practical or necessary to pinpoint every source. Only those which seemed to require a reference, either in order to give added point to the context or to explain the occasional jarring note caused by the artificial inclusion of a quotation, have been noted.

Names, whether of places or of books or of people, have been traced as far as it has been possible to do so. Places have been checked with gazetteers and atlases and maps; people have been sought in biographies and encyclopaedias; and titles of books in literary bibliographies. The Bibliography of Reference Works gives a list of the books consulted. Place-names have been left in their Yiddish form in the text, and a note appended giving their modern form. People's names have been given the accepted spelling according to their appearance in a work of reference; those names which it has not been possible to trace have been spelt as closely as possible to the pronunciation indicated by Aronson's spelling. On this point, the translator wishes to state that he has spelt Aronson's own name as *Chaim,* and not in the grammatically more acceptable form of Ḥayyim, because this is the spelling that is inscribed on his tombstone — a photograph of which is included in the Appendix — and which he himself must have used in America.

During the process of translation, additional notes were inserted which will be familiar to scholars in this field and may appear superfluous — in particular, the explanations of the dates of Hebrew months. Such notes are meant, not for the scholar, but for the general reader — for it is felt that an autobiography of this nature should be made generally available.

C. *Problems of Content.*

The memoirs constitute two separate books which differ from each other in both subject-matter and viewpoint. It is perhaps for this reason that the author gave Part Two a title: The Period of Craftsman-Technologist (p.175). This title constitutes a definition of his approach to this Part.

Part One takes a broader view of Jewish affairs in general. When Aronson began to record his memoirs, he commenced with his earliest recollections and then proceeded to build a series of events centred around himself, the Jewish communities in which he lived, and the Russian environment in which they all moved. His story is both self-centred and outward-looking. It is as though his own life was the medium for introducing the lives of others, almost as though he were playing the role of an Elizabethan Chorus discussing the personae of the drama. They are shown interacting not only with the author but also with each other, their lives are often dealt with as separate stories subordinate to the main narrative. The dominant theme of this Part is communal Jewish life, its internal affairs and its reactions to external pressures, and the place which the author assumed in that life.

The theme of Part Two is defined in its opening paragraph: the author's liberation from the bondage of his early years, from the restriction and poverty of the life of a *melammed,* and his search for independence as a skilled craftsman. This adumbrates the overall approach and attitude. Although the Jewish setting is still evident in the early pages, it gradually recedes into the background, and its place is taken by the busy whirl of commercial life in the capital. Thereafter, it is the technologist who speaks, although the reader is not allowed to forget that this is, after all, the story of a Jew in St. Petersburg. His Russian partners, influential and wealthy though they were, are rarely given a personal background, and whatever descriptions are included of some of them are given briefly and in a general manner. External events are allowed to intrude only in so far as they affected the author—with the memorable exception of his discussion of the Crimean War and its economic effects (pp. 183-4). Even the assassination of Alexander II is given only a passing mention (p. 248), without any indication of Jewish communal reaction to it.[180] It is only later when the new Tsar began to impose rigorous prohibitions upon the Jews (p. 284) that Jewish affairs return to prominence.

Every autobiographer has, of course, the right to include or omit whatever seems right to him. On the other hand, the reader has the privilege of comment on those inclusions and omissions. Although Aronson made it clear from the outset that the second Part of the memoirs would deal principally with his business affairs, the lack of a clearly-defined Jewish setting in this Part leaves a significant gap in the overall presentation. Certain general political events, as well as specific Jewish matters, do gain a mention, it is true, but they are meant to act mainly as pegs on which to hang the passing events of his life. The fact that Part One is so replete with Jewish people and affairs, and Part Two almost bare of both, presents a riddle to the reader who wishes to know more about his Jewish environment.

Aronson has nothing to say about the Jewish community of the capital, which is known to have been a thriving community and the hub of Jewish affairs in the country. It was the home of great Jewish bankers and industrialists, such as the Günzburg family and the Poliakov brothers; of renowned literary figures such as the poet Judah Leib Gordon, who settled there in 1872 as the Secretary of the Society for the Promotion of Enlightenment[181], and scientific writer and publisher Zevi Ha-Cohen Rabinowitz (1832– 1889) whose works popularised science and enriched Hebrew scientific terminology and who spent the last decade of his life in the capital; and of Jewish journals such as the Hebrew-language *Ha-Melits*[182] and the Russian-language *Raszvet*[183]. It was the scene of incidents significant to the Jewish community of the capital and of Russian Jewry in general: Sir Moses Montefiore, the English philanthropist, visited St. Petersburg in 1872; the sensational trial of the writer Abraham Uri Kovner for embezzlement of funds from the bank of Abraham Zak, for whom he worked, was held there in 1875; Perets Smolenskin, the publisher of *Ha-Shahar*, visited there in 1881 and was accorded an enthusiastic welcome by the Jewish students who formed, later that year, the Zionist Society called *Aḥvat Zion* (The Brotherhood of Zion); the Jewish community held a special day of fasting and mourning on 18 January 1882 in memory of the assassination of Alexander II (see appendix note 180); and, during the 1870's and 1880's several national conferences were held there, attended by religious and lay leaders of Russian Jewry, to discuss the situation of the Jewish people in Russia. On the broader political level, the capital was also the setting for the rise of the Russian anarchist movements, the ''Land of Freedom'' and the ''People's Will'' societies, whose revolutionary activities developed from dynamiting the Imperial train (near Moscow) in 1879 and the Winter Palace in 1880, to the various attempts upon the Tsar's life which culminated in his assassination in March 1881. This random, and by no means complete, list of events and personalities illustrates some of the activities and incidents which must have affected Aronson and in which he must have had some interest. His silence, therefore, is perplexing[184].

In matters of the Russian economy, it would seem that Aronson takes for granted the reader's familiarity with the subject. During the latter part of the century, the traditional rivalry between the two capital cities, St. Petersburg and Moscow, was heightened by the accelerating modernisation of the Russian economy — a particular consequence of the Emancipation of the Serfs in 1861. The growth of industry and commerce, the attempts by the Government to encourage the economy by financial regulations and tariff controls, receive no mention from Aronson. He makes no attempt to offer a perspective look at his own commerical activities in the general picture of the period. Although, for example, he was deeply involved in the formation of stock companies, he does not compare these with the expansion of trading companies in general — for the overall economic activity was highlighted by the rise in the number of joint-stock companies during his period[184a]. As an inventor, he saw the need for automation solely in financial terms, with little reference to the existing working conditions and forms of production. He gives no detailed description of the conditions of Jewish or Russian craftsmen, even in his own fields of horology and photography, beyond an account of the establishment of the Jewish Guilds in Telz (pp. 181f.), and the occasional comment on the lack of master craftsmen and the difficulty of finding adequate tools for his trades. Although he mentions eight clockmakers by name, he gives no description of their background, apprenticeship or standing in the profession[185]. Finally, it is noteworthy that he does not say whether he ever approached the Jewish bankers for finance for his inventions.

These problems of omission, however unsatisfactory they may be, can only be resolved by the solution which Aronson himself offers: that, in Part Two, he was recording his adult life as a man of business affairs in a capital city, a Jewish industrialist emancipated from the shackles of ghetto existence. It should be added, too, that his memoirs were recorded for the benefit of his own family and descendants, so that they should know how their forebear accepted the challenge of his times and bore the changing fortunes of his life. The book was meant to be a personal document, not a historical or social treatise.

There is, however, also a problem of *commission* which Aronson neither mentions nor explains. The photograph of his tombstone shows an epitaph in the form of a poem which bears the name of the poet Judah Leib Gordon. The epitaph translates as follows:

> To a craftsman, skilful and masterly,
> Who sought to be a man
> In a place devoid of men,[186]
> Commending, like Hillel, humble and high alike.
> Judah Leib Gordon.

The quatrain does not occur in any of Gordon's poems, nor in his collections of tombstone inscriptions. Aronson does not refer at all to Gordon in his autobiography — although they must surely have met either in Telz, where Gordon lived from 1865–72 and Aronson from about 1852 to 1867, and/or in St. Petersburg where Gordon lived from 1872 until his death in 1892, and Aronson from 1868–88. It would be macabre indeed to consider that Aronson com missioned the poem as his epitaph before emigrating to New York in 1888, where he died in 1893 (the year after Gordon's death in St. Petersburg)! There may be, however, a possible explanation which is offered here with due hesitancy, for want of any supporting evidence. Gordon's collected poems were published in St. Petersburg in 1884. It was a not uncommon custom at the time for readers who purchased a special publication to request the author to write a dedication for them in the book. Possibly, Aronson may have followed the custom, and bought a copy of Gordon's poems and asked for a dedication. If that was the case, then no doubt his wife and sons knew about it and, in due course, copied the verse from the book to serve as his epitaph. It is known that a number of books were left among his possessions after he died, but unfortunately they were stolen during a robbery and have not been recovered. The epitaph, for lack of any internal textual or external corroborative evidence, adds one more puzzle to those already mentioned.

D. Conclusion.

This review of Chaim Aronson should not close without a word about him in the context of his family life. As a child, he followed the traditional Jewish education provided by his father and his religion teachers until he was old enough to leave home and make his own way in life. He was a dutiful son, ready to assist his parents when they were in need. The fact that he was the only son to survive out of ten children—one of them, an infant, the victim of superstitious quackery (p. 14)—must have had an effect upon him that was stronger than he admits. During his mother's lingering terminal illness, he suffered the brunt of her shrewishness with hardly a word of complaint (p.48), whilst his description of her as a woman and a mother is loving and respectful (p.48). After his father died—"I was now an orphan and alone" (p.127), he says—he dutifully observed the prescribed year of mourning. The manner in which he relates this—as well as his mother's death (pp.103-4)—is restrained and succinct, almost matter-of-fact. It is a style that conceals more than it reveals, for the tragedy of the coincident deaths of his father and his brother, Shalom (p.127), must have been a shock to him.

As a husband, he was loyal and devoted. Even though his first marriage — to Bathsheba, the daughter of Hillel the tanner of Vilki — was a loveless union of convenience, he could honestly declare: "She is my first wife and I want to remain with her for ever" (p. 109). Although the marriage ended unhappily in divorce, it gave him his first-born son, Judah Leib. The same loyalty is shown in his two subsequent marriages, which were felicitous and blessed with love.

As a father, he was protective and attentive. Besides bringing Judah Leib into his own household (p. 181), he taught him a practical trade, enlisted his aid in the construction of the papirosi-papers machine (p. 207), and supported him until he left home. True to his belief in the necessity for a practical profession, he encouraged his sons either to take up his own crafts of horology and photography or to assist him with his inventions. When conditions deteriorated in Russia, he helped his sons financially to emigrate to New York, even though he stayed on in St. Petersburg till the last moment with his wife and son, Abraham.

In the matter of religious beliefs, there can be no doubt that Aronson maintained an honest attitude, for he did not hide his modernistic outlook and studies either from his parents or his own families. His modernism was a product of the spirit of the times. The emancipatory movements that swept across Europe during the late eighteenth and the nineteeth centuries highlighted the wretched conditions suffered by Jews in many lands, and instigated a corresponding movement of emancipation amongst European Jewry, which came to be known as the *Ḥaskalah* (Enlightenment) movement. Aronson was a child of this new spirit — a *maskil*, a traditional Jew who sought a modern and freer way of life outside the confines of the ghetto walls, whether real or imaginary. The movement towards modernity led many Jews to the extreme of assimilation and conversion. There were many more, however, like Aronson, who kept to the middle path, and effected a compromise between their religious upbringing and their desire to live in a wider world.

When he was studying at the Vilna yeshiva, he described his three ambitions for his future: to enter a Gymnasium and acquire a modern education; or, if that were not possible, to complete his yeshiva studies and qualify as a Rabbi; or, alternatively, to learn a craft (p. 91). In the event, circumstances and his own natural talents led him into an industrial career. The fact that he maintained a Jewish way of life in his family is evidenced by the hardships they willingly endured in the village of Shubina, where they tried to build a ritual bath for the women and endured a Passover bereft of the usual festive foods (pp. 199–200). Life in the village would have been easier for non-observant Jews. The argument can be made, of course, that an orthodox Jew would not agree to live away from a Jewish community — but this only proves Aronson's willingness to compromise, to endeavour to live in the world whilst remaining as loyal as possible to his Jewish traditions. It was not in his nature to be an extremist in anything, so he was neither a religious fanatic nor an avowed heretic: he was, simply, a "modern" Jew.

It is of interest that neither Aronson nor his sons manifested any interest in, or identification with, the rising Zionist movement. When their turn came to emigrate, they went as a matter-of-course to America — without engaging for a moment in the contemporary controversy between a national home in Palestine or a refuge elsewhere.

In his assessment of himself and his life, he concludes that, though he earned a reputation as "an honest and upright man" (p.4), yet his deeds were too insignificant to place him amongst the great personages of this world. "I know that I am not a person of distinction. I shall not be counted among the great, nor will the third generation after me raise up a monument to my name" (p.3). The fact that he did not rise to greatness was not his fault: the blame lies in the backward, antisemitic conditions of Tsarist society. His instinct to adopt the technological and scientific skills which were developing during his lifetime and to place them at the service of industry and commerce, would have earned him renown in a freer and more progressive environment. Had he been born a thousand miles or so to the west, his name would have found its rightful place beside those of the inventor-entrepreneurs of the age.

There is a fascinating story related by A. B. Granville of a poor, illiterate, self-taught mechanical genius named Kouliben who lived in the time of Catherine the Great. "The first work by which he attracted notice was a curious piece of clock-work. This was presented to Catherine, who rescued the author from his obscure condition and placed him in a situation in which his talents could be matured and become serviceable to the state."[187] Aronson, for his part, would have been content with less than royal patronage. He would have been satisfied had his aristocratic partners dealt honestly with him and thereby given him the freedom of mind and opportunity to concentrate his energies on perfecting new industrial techniques — which is what he really wanted — rather than expend them on the constant struggle to survive.

As for the "monument to my name" — there can be little doubt that the willing and determined effort made by his grandchildren and great-grandchildren to understand the record of his life, which he wrote in "this ancient Hebrew langauge" (p. 287), is the memorial which would have pleased him most.

(E) Transliteration

All the foreign words appearing in the MS are written in the Hebrew alphabet according to the Hebrew or Yiddish spelling which Aronson gave them. His method is basically phonetic, and therefore presented the problem of the choice of an appropriate transliteration system, particularly for Hebrew and Russian. It was decided that, in both cases, the criteria should be simplicity and clarity. This would enable the English reader to follow the narrative with the minimum of confusion, whilst the scholar would require no assistance in identifying the relevant variant spellings.

For the Russian transliteration, recourse was had to the several systems in use both in this country and the U.S.A. Although these are taken to provide a general guideline, preference has been given to Aronson's own phonetic spelling. Thus, for example, various Russian terminal — i forms (—ий, —ий, —ый) have been reduced to a simple — i to conform with his Hebrew-Yiddish terminal ׳—, except where a term or proper name has a familiar English spelling (e.g. Nevsky, Ouspensky). The initial and medial Hebrew *yod* have been transliterated as Y (e.g. Yeliseyev, Yerakov), and the initial Yiddish — ײ as ye-. However, titles of reference works appearing in the Notes or the Bibliographies have been transliterated according to the spelling of the particular title. A further factor in the decision to adhere to Aronson's Yiddish orthography has been the desire to avoid the grammatical variations in the structure of Russian nouns in declension. This is particularly so in connection with numerals which are followed by plural and genitive terminals, and therefore measurements such as *verst* have been left in their Yiddish form (in preference to their Russian forms *verstá, vërsti and vërst)*. Similarly, *papiros* has been left in its Yiddish form although, in the places where the plural form has been required on its own, the Russian plural *papirosi* had been used in preference to the awkward Yiddish *papirosen* and the incomplete *papiros*: for example, "cigarettes which are papirosi without the paper-tip" (p. 285). In the text, *papiros* has not been italicized, although it is found in Yiddish dictionaries, because of its various combinations — papiros-papers, papiros-wrappers, etc. — which would make italicizing clumsy; and therefore *papirosi* has been left without underlining.

The Hebrew transliteration method is based on that given in the *Encyclopaedia Judaica* (Index volume, p. 90) with one or two minor changes. The צ is represented by 'ts' rather than 'z', and the place of the א and the ע is indicated by an apostrophe. Proper names are given according to their accepted spelling — although the grammatically correct Ḥayyim has been preferred to the popular Chaim, except in the case of Aronson's own name (as explained above, pp. 331-2).

Appendix Notes

◇◇◇◇◇

1. A. Herzen, *The Pole Star*, 1855, quoted in *My Past and Thoughts: The Memoirs of Alexander Herzen*, page v.
2. *Ḥattot Ne'urim* (Sins of Youth), Vienna 1876, and *Kol Kitvei* (Collected Works) vol.2, Cracow 1912, pp. 201 – 410. A detailed review is given by N. Marsden in his *M. S. Lilienblum: His Life and Work* (to be published).
3. *Ḥattot Ne'urim*, p. 214.
4. For an account of Lithuanian talmudical colleges see A. Menes, "Yeshivahs in Russia" in J. Frumkin *et. al.*, *Russian Jewry* (1860 – 1917), pp. 382 – 407.
5. See D. Patterson, *The Hebrew Novel in Czarist Russia*, pp. 175 – 9.
6. For a discussion on child mortality, see A. Ruppin, *The Jews in the Modern World*, pp. 85 ff.; U. Z. Engelman, "Sources of Jewish Statistics" in L. Finkelstein, *The Jews, Their History, Culture & Religion*, vol. 4, pp. 1182 – 7; and S. W. Baron, *The Russian Jew under the Tsars and Soviets*, pp. 78 – 80.
7. See *The Autobiography of Solomon Maimon*, pp. 54 – 5. For a detailed account of Jewish marriage beliefs and ceremonies in the *shtetl* see M. Zborowski and E. Herzog, *Life is with People*, pp. 269 – 90; and Z. Scharfstein, *Ḥayyei Ha-Yehudim Be-Mizraḥ Eiropah Ba-Dorot Ha-Aḥaronim*, pp. 179 – 89.
8. Between 1841 and 1864 (some six years after the incident with the cobbler) the number of Jewish residents in Telz rose from 3,585 to 4,204. Cobblers and tailors composed the majority of Jewish craftsmen throughout Lithuania. For tables of statistics on Jewish artisans in Russia, see *Yahadut Lita*, vol. 1, pp. 169 – 79; and *The Jewish Encyclopedia*, vol. X, pp. 534 – 8. For a general account of Jewish craftsmen in the *shtetl*, see M. Zborowski and E. Herzog, *Life is with People*, pp. 239 – 65; and Z. Scharfstein, *Ḥayyei Ha-Yehudim Be-Mizraḥ Eiropah Ba-Dorot Ha-Aḥaronim*, pp. 52 – 64 (in which he also includes a description of two distinguished cobblers).
9. See text note 327.
10. For an account of their conditions see *Yahadut Lita*, vol. 1, pp. 172 – 3.
11. See text note 346, and text note 418.
12. See text note 327, and text notes 383 – 9.
13. See Appendix for photocopies of both Aronson's and Dagron's novelty miniatures.
14. See Appendix for photocopy.
15. See text note 388. For some points of similarity, see text notes 390, 393 – 4.
16. See text note 369.
17. See Appendix for photocopies of this patent.
18. D. Patterson, *Hebrew Literature, The Art of the Translator*, p.9.
19. I.F. Finlay, *Translating*, p.2.
20. M.L. Lilienblum, *Al Devar Ha' atakat Graetz* (On Translating Graetz), in *Ha-Tsefirah*, 1877, and *Kol Kitvei*, vol. 2, Cracow 1912, p.118.
21. See *The Autobiography of Solomon Maimon*, p. 172.
22. M.D. Brandstetter, *Ha-Kadosh Mi-Galizien* (The Galician Saint), *Ha-Shaḥar*, year 1 (1869), pp. 105-8.

23. N. Marsden, *M.L. Lilienblum: His Life and Work*, chapter on "Literature and Style" (to be published).
24. D. Patterson, "Some Linguistic Aspects of the Nineteenth-Century Hebrew Novel" in *Journal of Semitic Studies*, vol. 7, no. 2, Autumn 1962, p. 311. See also his *The Hebrew Novel in Czarist Russia*, pp. 98-101.
25. Tumbril: MS* p. 4, and text note 5.
26. Birch: MS. p. 326, and text note 326.
27. Maple: MS. p. 331, and text note 330.
28. Cork: MS. p. 473, and text note 422.
29. Amber: MS. p. 9.
30. Flying squirrel: MS. p. 12, and text note 14.
31. Stuffed mountain: MS. p. 45, and text note 57.
32. Mead, from Yiddish מעד: MS. p. 67.
33. Canopy: MS. p. 90, and text note 127.
34. MS. p. 90.
35. Sutler, from Russian маркита́нт: MS. p. 200.
36. Contractor, from Russian подря́дуик and Yiddish פּאָדראַטשיק: MS. p. 244.
37. "Jew-snatchers", from German *Juden Häscher:* MS. p. 283. Strictly, the noun *Häscher* means a "guard" or "constable", whilst it is the verb *haschen* which means "to snatch". It is interesting to see Aronson's use of א (instead of the normal ע) to denote the German umlaut *ä*.
38. Gum or mastic, from German *Mastix:* MS. p. 419.
39. Maximum: MS. p. 444.
40. Minimum: MS. p. 445.
41. Either a music box, from German *Spieldose,* or a barrel-organ, from Yiddish שפּיעל־קאָסטען: MS p. 457.
42. Printing-press: MS. p. 488, and text note 424.
43. MS. p. 488. Cf. also מכבש הדפוס, MS. pp. 35 and 488.
44. Telegraph: MS. p. 76 *et. al.*
45. Pianoforte: MS. p. 288.
46. Early maturity: MS. p. 53.
47. "Dumplings": MS. p. 57.
48. Musician, Bass: MS. p. 59, and text note 81.
49. "Baigels": MS. p. 107, and text note 148.
50. Kindling bottles: MS. p. 112, and text note 155.
51. Telephone: MS. p. 453.
52. Music box: MS. p. 289.
53. Mechanical leech: MS. p. 290, and text note 303.
54. Rural postal contractor: MS. p. 295.
55. Hussars: MS. p. 323.
56. Galvanoplastic: MS. p. 328.
57. Galvanic: *ibid.*
58. Micrometer: MS. p. 359.
59. Typewriter: MS. p. 360.
60. Horse-tramway lines: MS. p. 373, and text note 355.
61. MS. p. 375.
62. Submarine: MS. p. 381.
63. Exhibition: MS. p. 408. Probably derived from German *Ausstellung* (exhibition).
64. Calculating machine: MS. p. 410, and text note 381.
65. Two lenses from a pair of binoculars: MS. p. 415.
66. MS. p. 417.
67. Microscope: MS. p. 417. Cf. with זכוכית המגדלת, magnifying lens: MS. pp. 76 and 416.
68. Joint-stock company: MS. p. 433. It is interesting to see his unconscious use of a double ל in the Hebrew spelling of the German term.
69. "Honourable Mention": MS. p. 447.
70. Legal advisory office: MS. p. 476.

*In these Notes, MS refers to the Hebrew manuscript.

71. See appendix notes 26, 27, 29, 30, 31, 32, 35, 36, 37, 38, 39, 40, 46, 47, 48, 50, 51, 55, 56, 58, 65, 66, 67, 68.
72. See above p. 49, text note 124, and MS. p. 85. Cf. this with the Courland student who learnt the Talmud in German: see above p. 71, MS. p. 125
73. See above pp. 47-8, text notes 121-2, and MS pp. 84-5.
74. Chronology, history, biography, moral: MS. p. 3.
75. Etymology: MS. p. 70.
76. Censor: MS. p. 98.
77. Fashion: MS. p. 115. His spelling is idosyncratic; the Yiddish word is מאָדע.
78. Missionary: MS. p. 168.
79. Department: MS. p. 336.
80. MS. p. 85 and appendix note 72.
81. гóрло, throat. MS. p. 84 and text note 124.
82. кады́к, Adam's apple. MS. p. 85 and text note 122.
83. кáторга, convict, i.e. penal servitude. MS. p. 338.
84. скáзка, tale. MS. p. 217.
85. прокурóр, Public Prosecutor. MS. p. 490 and text note 427.
86. станово́й, District police officer. MS. p. 195 and text note 228.
87. при́став, Police officer. MS. p. 195 and text note 228.
88. интендáнт, Commissary. MS. p. 358.
89. нотáриус, Notary. MS. p. 346, 370. Aronson also uses the German term *Notar,* MS. pp. 352 ff.
90. óстров, island. MS. 354.
91. פּאַפּירוסים. MS. pp. 366, 370. See also text note 346, and p. 337 for the transliteration of *papiros.*
92. See appendix notes 27, 28, 30, 33, 37, 38, 41, 42, 46, 48, 68.
93. *Disput* (debate): MS. p. 293.
94. *Blecharbeiter* (metalworkers): MS. p. 317.
95. *Professor ha-Mechanik* (instructor in mechanics): MS. p. 387. Note the Hebrew Definite Article.
96. The *oignon* watch: MS. p. 55, and text note 76. Aronson makes the distinction between a clock, מורה שעות, and a watch מורה שעות קטנה. M.A. Günzburg used the German *Uhr* in term for a clock, מורה השעות (אוהר): see his *Aviezer,* p. 143.
97. Table-clock: MS. p. 288.
98. Wall-clock: MS. p. 284.
99. Rotating clock: MS. p. 401. This was a special clock which he called a ראָטאַטיאָמעטר, Rotationmeter: see MS. p.400 and above p. 230.
100. Wall-clock with weights: MS. p. 280.
101. Annual clock: MS. p. 283. He called this his תוף הטורקי (Turkish drum): see MS. p. 280, and text note 298.
102. Man's pocket-watch: MS. p. 298.
103. Woman's watch, for either the handbag or the pocket: MS. p. 299. The ambiguity is due to the use of צלחת as sometimes a man's wallet, bag or pocket: e. g. Grand Duke Vladimir placed a cigarette in his צלחת (MS. p. 433); Aronson carried a bundle of money in "the צלחת of my coat" (MS. p. 394). Kalman Schulman uses it in the sense of a "pocket" in his *Misterei Paris* (vol. 1, pt. 1, pp. 162 and 164).
104. Mechanism: MS. pp. 401 and 271.
105. Hair-spring: MS. pp. 274 and 494.
106. Balance-wheel: MS. p. 496.
107. Escapement: MS. pp. 496, 492 and 494. For the French and German terms see text note 436. Note the double פפ and מם.
108. Pendulum: MS. p. 398.
109. Second's pendulum: MS. p. 399.
110. Weight (on a pendulum): MS. p. 496.
111. Bob: MS. p. 400.
112. Case: MS. p. 60.
113. Dial: MS. p. 325.
114. Hand: MS. p. 400.
115. Wheels and pinions (used interchangeably): MS. p. 271.
116. Crutch: MS. p. 495.

117. Cylinder: MS. p. 299
118. Screws: MS. p. 494, and text note 437.
119. "Force of flight, swing": MS. p. 493, and text note 433.
120. For example: gravity, כח הכובד הוא המושך אל מרכז הארץ (MS. p. 378); force of adhesion, כח המחזיק אשר להתדבקות (אדהעזיאן) (MS p. 380); inertia, אינערציע, כח המתמיד (MS. p. 398).
121. MS. p. 392: also pp. 272 and 273. This construction compares favourably with K. Schulman's "sound the hour": השעה התשיעית בבקר מורה השעות השמיע את השעה (the clock sounded the ninth hour in the morning), see *Misterei Paris,* vol. 2, pt. 3, p. 9.
122. Lit. "light imprinter": MS. p. 340.
123. "Light imprinting, photography": MS. p. 409.
124. "Light imprint workshop": MS. p. 338.
125. "Machine": MS. p. 414.
126. Camera obscura: MS. pp. 414 and 417.
127. Sensitized glass: MS. p. 414.
128. Lens: MS. p. 416. From the German, *Brennglas.*
129. Magnifying lens: MS. p. 415.
130. Very small,glass lens: MS. p. 417.
131. Transparent miniature pictures: MS. p. 420.
132. Transparencies: MS. p. 414.
133. Focal Point: MS. p. 414. From the German, *Brennpunkt.*
134. Telescope tube: MS. p. 419.
135. Viewing tube: MS. p. 416.
136. Flywheel: MS. p. 374.
137. Steamships: MS. p. 441.
138. Steam locomotives: MS. p. 445.
139. Matches: MS. pp. 110, 113 and 56.
140. Cubit, used for Russian *arshin*= 28″: MS. p. 172, and text note 205.
141. Cubic inch: MS. p. 442, and text note 410.
142. *Gerah:* MS. p. 442, and text note 411.
143. *Verst:* MS. p. 15, and text note 18, and above, p. 337.
144. Mile: MS. p. 95, and text note 128. Cf. Russian миля (mile).
145. Parasang: MS. p. 93, and text note 128.
146. Minute: MS. p. 129.
147. *Pud:* MS. p. 336, and text note 331.
148. *Funt:* MS. p. 325, and text note 331.
149. *Fut:* MS. p. 60, and text note 87a.
150. Exod. xxxv. 31-35.
151. MS. pp. 483-4.
152. MS. p. 403.
153. MS. p. 58.
154. MS. p. 250.
155. MS. p. 404.
156. MS. p. 406
157. MS. p. 405.
158. MS. p. 142.
159. Academy: MS. p. 371. For the same meaning, see J.A. Tretsek, *Ha-Me' assef* dictionary, under entry אקאדעמיע (Akademie).
160. College: MS. p. 405.
161. House of Prayer: MS. p. 32. *et. al.*
162. Synagogue: MS. p. 121.
163. House of Study: MS. p. 32.
164. Ecclesiastical Court: MS. p. 134.
165. Post house: MS. p. 213.
166. MS. p. 364.
167. Theatre: MS. p. 103.
168. Sleeves: MS. p. 62.
169. Spectacles: MS. p. 128.

170. Trousers: MS. p. 90
171. MS. p. 111.
172. Russianized: MS. p. 85. These constructions are based on the Book of Esther viii.17.
173. Germanized: MS. p. 292.
174. Baptised a Christian: MS. p. 464.
175. MS. p. 50.
176. Silk scarf: MS. p. 240.
177. MS. p. 94.
178. MS. pp. 23 (the incident of the quack healer who held a piece of cloth in his mouth), 48 ("he bound his hand in a cloth"), 111 ("to polish with a cloth"), and 397 ("the machine was covered with a cloth").
179. MS. p. 79.
180. It is known that Russian Jewry was generally deeply affected by the assassination. The poet, J.L. Gordon, mentions that he wrote an epitaph for the wreath presented by the St. Petersburg Jewish community: see *Kitvei Yehuda Leib Gordon: Shirah,* p. 312.
181. Founded in 1863 in St. Petersburg by prominent Jewish philanthropists with the object of disseminating modern culture and knowlege among the Jews. One of its most important achievements was the Russian translation of the Old Testament, published in 1875, on which both Gordon and Levanda collaborated.
182. "The Herald": published by Alexander Zeberbaum in St. Petersburg, 1871 – 3, and 1878 – 93.
183. "The Dawn": the first Jewish Russian-language journal, and platform for the Zionist movement. Published by Zederbaum, 1879 – 83.
184. An interesting account of the St. Petersburg Jewish community is given by S. M. Ginsburg, *Amolike Peterburg*, New York 1944, in Yiddish.
184a. "Between 1861 and 1865, 44 such companies were established with a total nominal capital of 99 million roubles. In the years 1869 – 73, however, no fewer than 281 were established with a capital of 697 million roubles." (M. E. Falkus, *The Industrialisation of Russia 1700 – 1914*, London 1972, p. 53).
185. Nor do they — or Aronson himself — appear in V. L. Chenakal's *Watchmakers and Clockmakers in Russia 1400 – 1850,* trans. W. F. Ryan, London 1972.
186. *Avot* ii.6. For the photograph, see Appendix.
187. A. B. Granville, *St. Petersburgh, A Journal of Travels to and from that Capital*, vol. 1, p. 415.

Bibliography
i. General

◇◇◇◇◇

Abramowitz, S.J. *Fishke der Krumer* (Fishke the Lame), in *Ale Verk Fun Mendele Mokher Seforim* (Complete Works, in Yiddish), Warsaw 1911-3.
———. *Kol Kitvei Mendele Mokher Sefarim* (Complete Works), Tel-Aviv 1947.
———. *Sefer Toledot Ha-Teva* (The History of Nature), Leipzig 1862, in three parts.
Agnon, S.J. *Kol Sippurav* (Complete Stories), Berlin 1934.
Alcalay, R. and Nurock, M. *Divrei Ḥakhamim* (Words of the Wise), Jerusalem 1970.
Almedingen, E.M. *I Remember St. Petersburg,* London 1969.
American Tobacco Company. *The American Tobacco Story,* New York 1964.
An-Ski, S. (Rappaport, S.Z.) *The Dibbuk,* Vilna 1920.
Baron, S.W. *et al., Economic History of the Jews,* Jerusalem 1975.
———. *The Russian Jew Under Tsars and Soviets,* New York 1964.
Ben-Sasson, H.H. (ed.) *A History of the Jewish People,* London 1976.
Berger, M. *Mas Nerot Ha-Shabbat Be-Russia* (The Candle Tax in Russia), in *He-Avar,* no. 19, Tel Aviv 1972.
Bialik, C.N. *Kol Kitvei* (Collected Works), 9th edn., Tel-Aviv 1947.
Blackner, J. *The History of Nottingham,* Nottingham 1815.
Brandstetter, M.D. *Ha-Kadosh Mi-Galizien* (The Galician Saint), *Ha-Shaḥar,* year 1 (1869), xi-xii.
———. *Tsorer Ha-Yehudim Be-Ir Griliv* (The Oppressor of the Jews in Grylev), in *Ha-Shaḥar,* year 4 (1873), pp.441-71.
Braudes, R.A. *Ha-Dat Veha-Ḥayyim* (Religion and Life), Lvov 1876-7, Warsaw 1878-9; abridged edn. J. Frankl, Jerusalem 1946.
Brooks, J.E. *The Mighty Leaf, Tobacco Through The Centuries,* London 1953.
Brown, H.P. *et al., Textbook of Wood Technology,* 2 vols., New York 1949 and 1952.
Bruton, E. *Clocks and Watches, 1400-1900,* London 1967.
Buber, M. *Tales of The Hasidim: The Early Masters,* New York 1970.
Clarkson, J.D. *A History of Russia,* London 1962.
Corina, M. *Trust in Tobacco,* London 1975.
Dawidowicz, L.S. *The Golden Tradition,* New York 1967.
de Carle, D. *Horology,* London 1965.
———. *Practical Clock Repairing,* London 1968.
Demidov, Prince San Donato. *La Question Isráelite en Russie,* in *Les Juifs de Russie,* Paris 1891.
Dinur, B. *Mikhtevei Avraham Mapu* (The Letters of Abraham Mapu), Jerusalem 1970.
Dubnow, S.M. *History of the Jews,* trans. M. Spiegel, vol. 5, 4th definitive revised edn., New York 1973.

————. *History of the Jews in Russia and Poland*, trans. I. Friedlaender, 3 vols., Philadelphia, vol. 1, 2nd edn. 1946 (first pub. 1916); vol. 2, 2nd edn. 1946 (first pub. 1918); vol. 3, 1920.

————. *Toledot Ha-Ḥasidut* (History of Hasidism), 3 vols. in one, Tel-Aviv 1930-1.

Dumas, A. *Voyage en Russie 1858*, Paris 1960.

Duncan, G.S. *Bibliography of Glass*, London 1960.

Dunhill, A.H. *The Gentle Art of Smoking*, London 1969.

Eisenstadt, M.E. *Yeshivat Volozhin* (The Yeshiva of Volozhin), in *He-Avar*, vol. 14, Tel-Aviv 1967, pp.159-172.

Falkus, M.E. *The Industrialisation of Russia 1700-1914*, London 1972.

Felkin, W. *A History of the Machine-Wrought Hosiery and Lace Manufacturers*, London 1867.

Finlay, I.F. *Translating*, 2nd edn. (first pub. 1971), London 1974.

Finkelstein, L. (ed.). *The Jews: Their History, Culture and Religion*, 2 vols., first British edn. London 1961.

Frazer, J.G. *The Golden Bough: Baldur the Beautiful*, 1st edn. reprint, London 1930.

Frazer, J.G. *The Golden Bough: The Scapegoat*, 3rd edn. reprint, London 1933.

Frumkin, J. *et. al.*, (ed.). *Russian Jewry (1860-1917)*, New York 1966.

Ganzfried, S. *Kitsur Shulḥan Arukh* (Abbreviated Codes of Jewish Laws), Jerusalem 1955.

Gelber, N.M. *Zikhronos fun a Yidisher Froi vegn Poilishn Oifshtand fun 1863* (The Diary of a Jewess during the Polish Uprising of 1863), in *Yivo Bleter*, vol. xlii, New York 1962, pp.206-23.

Gernsheim, H. and A. *The History of Photography*, Oxford 1955.

Gilbert, M. *Russian History Atlas*, London 1972.

Ginsburg, S.M. *Amolike Peterburg*, New York 1944.

————. *Jewish Martyrdom in Tsarist Russia*, New York 1938.

Goldfaden, A. *Meshi'aḥs Tseitn?!* (Messianic Times?!), Cracow 1900.

Gordon, B.L. *Eina Bisha* (The Evil Eye), in *Harofé Haivri* (The Hebrew Medical Journal), Israel Annual edn., 34th year, vols. 1-2, New York 1961.

Gordon, J.L. *Kitvei: Shirah* (Works: Poetry), Tel-Aviv 1956.

————. *Kol Shirei* (Complete Poems), 2 vols., Warsaw 1905.

Granville, A.B. *St. Petersburgh. A Journal of Travels to and from that Capital*, 2 vols., London 1829.

Greenberg, L. *The Jews in Russia*, 2 vols. in one (vol. 1, 4th printing, first pub. 1944; vol. 2, 2nd printing, first pub. 1951), Yale 1965.

Günzburg, M.A. (RaMAG). *Aviezer*, Vilna 1863.

Gutfarstein, J. *Folklor Yehudei Lita* (Folklore of Lithuanian Jewry), in *Yahadut Lita* (Lithuanian Jewry), Tel-Aviv 1959.

Halpern, I. *Pinkas Va'ad Arba Aratsot* (Minutes — Book of the Council of the Four Lands), Jerusalem 1945.

————. *Yehudim Ve-Yahadut Be-Mizraḥ Eiropah* (Jews and Judaism in Eastern Europe), Jerusalem 1969.

Heilprin, J. (Baal-Shem). *Mif'alot Elohim* (Works of God), Zholkva 1727.

Henderson, W.O. *The Industrialization of Europe, 1780-1914*, 2nd edn., London 1970.

Hertz, J.H. *The Daily Prayer Book*, London 1959, revised edn., first pub. 1946.

Herzen, A. *My Past and Thoughts: The Memoirs of Alexander Herzen*, trans. G. Garnett, revised and abridged edn., London 1974.

Hingley, R. *Russian Writers and Society 1825-1904*, London 1967.

Horodezky, S.A. *Leaders of Hassidism*, trans. M. Horodezky-Magasanik, London 1928.

————. *Ha-Ḥasidut Ve-Toratah* (Hasidism and its Teachings).

Horowitz, P.E. *Sefer Ha-Berit* (The Book of the Covenant), Brünn 1797.

Josephus, Flavius. *Wars of the Jews,* Book vii, London 1957.

Kaidanover, Z.H. *Kav Ha-Yashar,* Frankfurt-on-Main 1705.

Kariv, A. *Lita Mekhorati* (My Homeland, Lithuania), bilingual Hebrew = Yiddish Yiddish edn., Tel-Aviv 1962.

Klausner, I. *Toledot Ha-Kehillah Ha-Ivrit Be-Vilna* (History of the Jewish Community of Vilna), Vilna 1938.

Klausner, J. *Historiyyah Shel Ha-Sifrut Ha-Ivrit Ha-Ḥadashah* (History of Modern Hebrew Literature), 6 vols., Jerusalem 1952-8.

Klier, J.D. "The Ambiguous Legal Status of Russian Jewry in the Reign of Catherine II", in *Slavic Review,* vol. 35, no. 3, New York, Septemer 1976, pp.504-17.

Korolenko, V.G. *The History of My Contemporary,* (tr. N. Parsons), Oxford 1972.

Kropotkin, Prince P. *Memoirs of a Revolutionist,* 2 vols., London 1899.

————. *Russian Literature,* New York 1905.

Lanin, E.B. *The Jews in Russia,* in the *Fortnightly Review,* London October 1890.

————. *Les Juifs de Russie,* Paris 1891.

Levanda, J.L. *Ir U-Behalot* (Terror and Alarms), trans. into Hebrew by S. Friedberg, Warsaw 1903.

Levin, S. *Galut Va-Mered* (Exile and Revolt), Hebrew trans. Z. Woyslawski, Tel-Aviv 1967 (abridged from original Hebrew publication in 4 vols. entitled *Mizikhronot Ḥayyai,* Tel-Aviv 1935-42).

Lilienblum, M.L. *Kol Kitvei* (Complete Works), 4 vols., Cracow 1910 and 1912, Odessa 1912 and 1913.

————. *Siḥat Ḥullin Shel Talmidei Ḥakhamim Tserikha Limmud* (The Secular Discussions of Scholars Require Inquiry), in *Ha-Shaḥar,* year 4 (1873), no. 6, Vienna.

Lite (Lithuania). 2 vols. (vol. 1, New York 1951, vol. 2, Tel-Aviv 1965).

Livni (Weisbord), D. *Yerushalayim De-Lita* (The Jerusalem of Lithuania), Tel-Aviv 1930.

Luther, F. *Microfilm — A History, 1839-1900,* Maryland 1959.

Lyashchenko, P.I. *History of the National Economy of Russia,* New York 1949.

Maimon, S. *Autobiography,* trans. J. Clark Murray, London 1954.

Maimonides (Rambam), M. *Mishneh Torah* (Code of Laws), Book 1, *Sefer Ha-Madda* (Book of Knowledge), Tel-Aviv 1946.

————. *Moreh Nevukhim* (Guide for the Perplexed), New York 1942.

Maor, I. *Teḥum Ha-Moshav Ha-Yehudi* (The Pale of Jewish Settlement), in *He-Avar,* vol. 19, Tel-Aviv 1972.

Margalith, D. "Wonderworkers and Folk Healers", in *Harofé Haivri* (Hebrew Medical Journal), Annual Israel edn., 33rd year, vols. 1-2, New York 1960.

Marsden, N. *M.L. Lilienblum: His Life and Work* (to be published).

Mavor, J. *An Economic History of Russia,* 2 vols. London 1925.

Menes, M. "Patterns of Jewish Scholarship in Eastern Europe", in L. Finkelstein (ed.), *The Jews: Their History, Culture and Religion,* vol. 1, first British edn., London 1961, pp. 376-426.

Mosse, W.E. *Alexander II and the Modernization of Russia,* London 1970.

Murray, J. *Handbook for Travellers in Russia, Poland and Finland,* 5 edns., London 1865-93.

Neubauer, A. "Where Are The Ten Tribes?" in *Jewish Quarterly Review,* October 1888 and Jan, April and July, 1889.

New Cambridge Modern History. Vol. x (first published 1960), Cambridge 1971 and vol. xi (first published 1962)Cambridge 1970.

Patterson, D. *Abraham Mapu,* London 1964.

————. *Hebrew Literature, The Art of the Translator,* London 1958.

————. *The Hebrew Novel in Czarist Russia,* Edinburgh 1964.

————. "Some Linguistic Aspects of the Nineteenth-Century Hebrew Novel", in *Journal of Semitic Studies*, vol. 7, no. 2, Autumn 1962.

Peretz, J.L. *Ale Verk* (Complete Works), New York 1947.

Philipson, D. *Max Lilienthal, American Rabbi, Life and Writings*, New York 1915.

Pintner, W. McK. "Inflation in Russia during the Crimean War Period", in *The American, Slavic and East European Review*, vol. xviii, no. 1, February 1959.

Player, J.W. *Britten's Watch & Clock Maker's Handbook*, (revised edn.) London 1955.

Rabinowicz, H.M. *The World of Hasidism*, London 1970.

Raeff, M. "A Reactionary Liberal: M.N. Katkov", in *The Russian Review*, vol. 11, no. 3. New York, July 1952.

Raisin, J.S. *The Haskalah Movement in Russia*, Philadelphia 1913.

Rappaport, A.S. *The Folklore of the Jews*, London 1937.

————. *Myth and Legend of Ancient Israel*, 3 vols, New York 1966.

Reeve, F.D. *The Russian Novel*, London 1967.

Ruppin, A. *The Jews in the Modern World*, London 1934.

Russo-Jewish Committee *The Persecution of the Jews in Russia*, London 1890.

Sachar, H.M. *The Course of Modern Jewish History*, Cleveland 1958.

Scharfstein, Z. *Ḥayyei Ha-Yehudim Be-Mizraḥ Eiropah Ba-Dorot Ha-Aḥaronim* (Jewish Life in Eastern Europe in Modern Times), Tel-Aviv 1973.

————. *Toledot Ha-Ḥinukh Be-Yisrael Ba-Dorot Ha-Aḥaronim* (History of Jewish Education in Modern Times), 2 vols. Jerusalem 1960.

Schneersohn, J.I. *The 'Tzemach Tzedek' and the Haskala Movement*, trans. Z.I. Posner, New York 1969.

Scholem, G. *Kabbalah*, Jerusalem 1974.

————. *On the Kabbalah and Its Symbolism*, London 1965.

Schrire, T. *Hebrew Amulets*, London 1966.

Schulman, K. *Kiryat Melekh Rav* (A Great Capital City) Vilna 1869.

————. *Misterei Paris* (Mysteries of Paris), Vilna 1857-60.

Seton-Watson, H. *The Russian Empire 1801-1917*, Oxford 1967.

Shochak, A. *Mosad 'Ha-Rabbanut Mi-Ta'am' Be-Russia* (The Office of 'Government Rabbi' in Russia), Haifa 1975.

Siemens, W. von. *Lebenserinnerungen* (Berlin 1892), first translated by W.C. Coupland under the title *Inventor and Entrepreneur: Recollections of Werner von Siemens*, London 1893; 2nd English edition, London 1966.

Singer, C., *et al. A History of Technology*, vol. 5 (1850-1900), Oxford 1958.

Smolenskin, P. *Ha-Tenu'ah Ha-Temidit* (Perpetual Motion), in *Kol Sifrei* (Complete Works), vol. 5, Warsaw 1910.

————. *Ha-To'eh Be-Darkei Ha-Ḥayyim* (Wanderer in the Paths of Life), in *Ha-Shaḥar*, years 1 (1868-9) and 2 (1870-1).

S.S. "The Jews in Russia", in *Free Russia*, no. 2, September, London 1890.

Steinschneider, H.N. *Ir Vilna* (Vilna City), Vilna 1900.

Strack, H.L. *Jüdisches Wörterbuch*, Leipzig 1916.

Thompson, S. *Motif-Index of Folk-Literature*, 6 vols., Indiana 1955-8.

Trachtenberg, J. *Jewish Magic and Superstition*, Philadelphia 1961.

Trench, F. Chenevix. "The Russian Journalistic Press", in the *Edinburgh Monthly Magazine*, vol. cxlviii, July 1890, pp.115-126.

Tyler, E.J. *The Craft of the Clockmaker*, London 1973.

Usher, A.P. *A History of Mechanical Inventions*, Harvard 1954.

Waxman, M. *A History of Jewish Literature*, 5 vols., New York 1960.

Weinryb, B.D. *The Jews of Poland*, Philadelphia 1973.

Wells, F.A. "The Textile Industry: Hosiery and Lace", in *A History of Technology*, ed. C. Singer *et al.*, vol. 5 (1850-1900), Oxford 1958.

Bibliography
ii. Reference

◇◇◇◇◇

Note: These lists give source works of a solely referential nature. Those marked with * have also been included in the General Bibliography.

Bible, Talmud, Religion:

H. Freedman & M. Simon. *The Midrash*, (English edn.), 10 vols., London 1939.
*S. Ganzfried. *Kitsur Shulḥan Arukh*, Jerusalem 1955.
H. E. Goldin. *Code of Jewish Law*, New York 1927.
*J. H. Hertz. *The Authorised Daily Prayer Book*, revised edn., first published 1946, London 1959.
Soncino. *Babylonian Talmud*, English edn., 36 vols., London 1935 – 71.
————. Set of *Books on the Bible*, 14 vols., London.
A. I. Sperling. *Sefer Ta'amei Ha-Minhagim*, Jerusalem 1957.
*J. Wistinetzki (ed.). *Sefer Ha-Ḥasidim (Das Buch der Frommen)* Frankfurt-on-Main 1924.

Bibliographies, Biographies, Encyclopaedias:

ENGLISH
F. L. Cross and E. A. Livingstone. *The Oxford Dictionary of the Christian Church*, Oxford 1974.
Encyclopaedia Judaica. 16 vols., Jerusalem 1971 – 2.
M. T. Florinsky. *McGraw-Hill Encyclopedia of Russia and the Soviet Union*, New York 1961.
*Funk and Wagnells. *The Jewish Encyclopaedia*, 12 vols. New York 1901 – 5.
H. and M. Garland. *The Oxford Companion to German Literature*, Oxford 1976.
J. Hastings. *Dictionary of the Bible*, 5 vols., Edinburgh 1903 – 05.
C. G. Herbermann *et. al. The Catholic Encyclopaedia*, 15 vols., London 1907 – 12.
I. Landman. *The Universal Jewish Encyclopedia*, 10 vols., New York 1939 – 45.
D. D. McGarry and S. H. White. *Historical Fiction Guide*, New York 1963.
McGraw-Hill's *New Catholic Encyclopedia*, 15 vols., Washington 1967.
New Encyclopaedia Britannica, 30 vols., New York 1974.
J. S. G. Simmons. *Russian Bibliography, Libraries & Archives*, Oxford 1973.

349

W. Smith and S. Cheetham. *A Dictionary of Christian Antiquities*, 2 vols., London 1875 and 1880.
S. V. Utechin. *Everyman's Concise Encyclopedia of Russia*, London 1961.
R. J. Z. Werblowsky and G. Wigoder. *Encyclopaedia of the Jewish Religion*, Jerusalem 1966.

FRENCH

M. F. Bourquelot and M. A. Maury. *La Littérature Française Contemporaire 1827 – 1849*, vol. 5, Paris 1854.
G. Vapereau. *Dictionnaire Universel des Contemporains*, Paris 1870 and 1880.
G. Vapereau. *Dictionnaire Universel des Littératures*, Paris 1876.

GERMAN

J. Baer. *Der Romanführer*, 8 vols., Stuttgart 1956 – 7.
K. Böttcher und G. Albrecht. *Romanführer, A-Z*, 3 vols., Berlin 1972 – 4.
J. Fürst. *Bibliotheca Judaica*, 3 vols., Leipzig 1849 – 63.
W. Heinsius. *Allgemeine Bücher Lexikon 1700 – 1810*, Leipzig 1812.
M. Holzmann und H. Bohatta. *Deutsches Anonymen Lexikon*, vol.3 (1500 – 1850), Weimar 1905.
H. Kindler. *Literatur Lexikon*, 7 vols., Zurich 1965 – 72.
W. Olbrich. *Der Romanführer*, 8 vols., Stuttgart 1951 – 7.
J. C. Poggendorff. *Biographisch-Literarisches Handwörterbuch zur Geschichte der Exakten Wissenschaften*, vols. 1 & 2, Leipzig 1865; vol. 3, Leipzig 1898.
W. von Maltzahn. *Deutscher Bücherschatz*, Jena 1875.

HEBREW

I. Ben-Jacob. *Otsar Ha-Sefarim*, Vilna 1880.
C. B. Friedberg. *Bet-Eked Sepharim*, 4 vols., Tel-Aviv 1951 – 6.
Ha-Entsiklopediyyah Ha-Ivrit, vol. 21, Jerusalem 1969.
Yom-Tov Lewinsky. *Entsiklopediyyah Shel Havai U-Masoret Be-Yahadut*, (Encyclopedia of Folklore, Customs and Tradition in Judaism), Tel-Aviv 1975.
M. Margalioth. *Entsiklopediyyah Le-Toledot Gedolei Yisrael*, 4 vols., Tel-Aviv (undated).

RUSSIAN

F. A. Brockhaus and E. A. Efron. *Entsiklopedicheskii Slovar*, 40 vols., St. Petersburg 1890 – 1906.
I. Granat. *Entsiklopedicheskii Slovar*, 58 vols. Moscow 1910 – 48.
A. Polovtsova. *Russkii Biograficheskii Slovar*, 25 vols., St. Petersburg 1896 – 1913.

Concordances:

C. J. Kasovsky. *Otsar Leshon Ha-Mishnah*, 4 vols., Jerusalem 1956 – 60.

C. J. Kasovsky. *Otsar Leshon Ha-Talmud*, 35 vols., Jerusalem 1954 – 75.
B. Kosovsky. *Otsar Leshon Ha-Tanna'im*, 4 vols., Jerusalem 1967 – 9.
S. E. Loewenstamm and J. Blau. *Otsar Leshon Ha-Mikra*, 5 vols., Jerusalem 1959.
S. Mandelkern. *Concordance on the Bible*, 2 vols. (revised), New York 1955.

Dictionaries, Lexicons:
HEBREW
R. Alcalay. *Leksikon Lo'azi-Ivri Ḥadash*, Ramat Gan 1967.
R. Alcalay. *Millon Ivri-Angli Shalem*, 4 vols., Jerusalem 1964 – 5.
E. Ben-Yehuda. *Millon Ha-Lashon Ha-Ivrit*, 16 vols., Jerusalem 1959.
F. Brown, S.R. Driver and C.A. Briggs. *A Hebrew and English Lexicon of the Old Testament*, Oxford 1955.
I. Efros. *Philosophical Terms in the Moreh Nebukhim*, New York 1924.
A. Even-Shoshan. *Ha-Millon He-Ḥadash*, 7 vols., 1974.
W. Gesenius. *Hebräisches und Aramäisches Handwörterbuch über das Alte Testament*, Leipzig 1921.
M. Jastrow. *A Dictionary of the Targumim, Talmud Babli and Yerushalmi, and Midrashic Literature*, 2 vols., New York 1950.
J. Klatzkin. *Otsar Ha-Munaḥim Ha-Pilosofiyyim*, 4 vols., Berlin 1928 – 33.
L. Koehler and W. Baumgartner. *Lexicon in Veteris Testamenti Libros*, Leiden 1953.
A. Kohut. *Natan ben Yehiel: Sefer Arukh Ha-Shalem*, 5 vols., Vienna 1878 – 92.
M. Letteris. *Y.L. Ben-Ze'ev: Otsar Ha-Shorashim*, Lemberg 1879.
B. Natanson. *Sefer Ha-Millim*, Warsaw 1880.
I.B. Schönhak. *Sefer Ha-Millu'im O Mashbir He-Ḥadash (Aramäisch-rabinisch-deutsches Wörterbuch)*, Warsaw 1869.
M. Schulbaum. *Otsar Ha-Millim Ha-Kelali (Neuhebräisch-Deutsches Wörterbuch)*, Lemberg 1880.
J. Steinberg. *Mishpat Ha-Urim (Neues Hebräisch-Deutsch-Russisches Lexicon)*, Vilna 1897.
J.A. Tretsek. *Me'assef*, Warsaw 1880.
YIDDISH
I. Bernstein. *Jüdische Sprichwörter und Redensarten*, Warsaw 1908.
A. Harkavy. *Yiddish-English Hebrew Dictionary*, New York 1928.
M. Schechter-Ḥakham. *Millon Ivri-Yiddish*, Tel-Aviv 1963.
*H.L. Strack. *Jüdisches Wörterbuch*, Leipzig 1916.
U. Weinreich. *Modern English-Yiddish, Yiddish-English Dictionary*, New York 1968.
RUSSIAN
M. Dror. *Millon Ivri-Russi*, Tel-Aviv 1975.
V.K. Müller. *English-Russian Dictionary*, Moscow 1969.
S.G. Pushkarev. *Dictionary of Russian Historical Terms from the Eleventh Century to 1917*, Yale 1970.
F.L. Shapiro. *Ivrit-Russkii Slovar*, 2 vols., Moscow 1963.
A.I. Smirnitsky *et al. Russian-English Dictionary*, Moscow 1969.
J. Steinberg. *Russko-Evreiskii Slovar (Millon Russi-Ivri)*, Vilna 1879.
M. Wheeler. *The Oxford Russian-English Dictionary*, Oxford 1972.
GERMAN
C.F. Grieb and A. Schröer. *Dictionary of the English and German Language*, 2 vols., Berlin 1907.
Muret-Sanders. *Encyclopaedic English-German, German-English Dictionary*, 2 vols., Berlin 1900.

M. Schulbaum. *Deutsch-Hebräisches Handwörterbuch*, Lemberg 1904.

FRENCH
A. Hatzfeld, A. Darmesteter and A. Thomas. *Dictionnaire Général de la Langue Francaise*, 2 vols., Paris 1895—1900.

LITHUANIAN
I. Karsavinaitě and D. Šlapoberskis. *Lietuviu-Anglu Kalbu Žodynas* (Lithuanian-English Dictionary), Vilnius 1960.

POLISH
K. Bulas and F.J. Whitfield. *English-Polish, Polish-English Dictionary*, 2 vols., The Hague 1959.

Folklore:
*S. Thompson. *Motif-Index of Folk-Literature*, 6 vols., Indiana 1955—8.

History and Travel:
M. Gilbert. *Jewish History Atlas*, London 1969.
M. Gilbert. *The Jews of Russia*, London 1976.
*M. Gilbert. *Russian History Atlas*, London 1972.
McGraw-Hill *International Atlas*. New York 1963.
*J. Murray. *Handbook for Travellers in Russia, Poland and Finland*, 5 edns., London 1865—93.
The Times Atlas of the World. vol. II (South-West Asia and Russia), London 1959.
U.S.S.R. Official Standard Names. Gazetteer no. 42, 7 vols., Washington 1970.

Technical:
V.L. Chenakal. *Watchmakers and Clockmakers in Russia, 1400—1850*, trans. W.F. Ryan, London 1972.
*G.S. Duncan. *Bibliography of Glass*, London 1960.
F.T. Jane. *The Imperial Russian Navy*, London 1904.